JOSEPH CONRAD

GARLAND REFERENCE LIBRARY
OF THE HUMANITIES
(VOL. 868)

Joseph Conrad was originally part of the
Northern Illinois University Press Series:

AN ANNOTATED
SECONDARY BIBLIOGRAPHY SERIES
OF ENGLISH LITERATURE
IN TRANSITION
1880–1920

W. EUGENE DAVIS
GENERAL EDITOR

JOSEPH CONRAD
An Annotated Bibliography

Bruce Teets

GARLAND PUBLISHING, INC. • NEW YORK & LONDON
1990

Bruce Teets is Emeritus Professor of English,
Central Washington University, Ellensburg

Library of Congress Cataloging-in-Publication Data

Teets, Bruce E., 1914–
  Joseph Conrad : an annotated bibliography.

  (Garland reference library of the humanities ;
vol. 868)
  Bibliography: p.
  Includes indexes.
  1. Conrad, Joseph, 1857–1924—Bibliography. I. Title.
II. Series.
Z8189.7.T38 1990 [PR6005.04] 016.823'912 88-24312
ISBN 0–8240–7037–2

Printed on acid-free, 250-year-life paper
Manufactured in the United States of America

THE CONTRIBUTORS

Werner Bies
Universität Trier

Mario Curreli
University of Pisa

Neill R. Joy
Colgate University

Harold F. Mosher, Jr.
Northern Illinois University

Donald Rude
Texas Tech University

Eugene Steele
University of Jos (Nigeria)

Michael Stewart
Tomball, Texas

Bruce Teets
Baltimore, Maryland

Jeffrey Treder
Ellensburg, Washington

Larry Uffelman
Mansfield University

Victor Vitanza
University of Texas at
Arlington

David Welsh
(Deceased)

CONTENTS

PREFACE

With the coeditor of *Joseph Conrad: An Annotated Bibliography of Writings About Him* (DeKalb: Northern Illinois University Press, 1971), edited by Bruce E. Teets and Helmut E. Gerber, the present editor, Bruce Teets, repeats that without omitting any accessible important work, he has attempted to compile a bibliography as broadly representative of the writings on Joseph Conrad and his works as possible. He also reminds the users of the present book that *Conrad I* was considered an exploratory volume on this subject. This second work has, then, been thought of from the beginning as *Conrad II*.

Various unforeseen changes have, however, caused the second volume to be very different from the one projected. The editor now wonders whether *Conrad II* can possibly receive the kind of attention which *Conrad I* was fortunate enough to have. It was a selection of The Scholars' Library of the Modern Language Association, an honor which came as a surprise to both the editors and the publisher.

Conrad I, ranging from the year 1895 to 1966, contains 1,976 entries. *Conrad II* contains 762 items for these years and 1,389 for those of 1967 to 1975, making a total for this volume of 2,151 listings. The grand total for the two volumes is 4,127. The entries through 1966 supplement the earlier volume published by Northern Illinois University Press (1971) and have been assigned numbers keyed to those in that volume. Entries from 1966 on update the preceding volume and have been assigned numbers which follow sequentially the last entry number for that year.

Conrad I contains abstracts from some fourteen languages, and *Conrad II* includes material from some fourteen languages also, if not the same ones. The editor deplores his inability to obtain materials from such sources as Dutch, Japanese, Hungarian, Finnish, and certain African languages.

Another difficult problem, a new one since *Conrad I* was published, has made this manner of obtaining abstracts very difficult. This was caused by the general economic condition of the nation, which was suffering from the effects of a declining economy that followed an unparalleled period of expansion and inflation. As a result, several universities require more time than usual for their faculty members for instructional and institutional duties so that several willing abstracters were unable to continue their work with this project. Economic restrictions also made it necessary to include only shorter abstracts than usual, frequently so short as to make major material impossible to treat with justice. Some physical changes in the book also required much revising and rewriting. And one unavoidable delay in publishing the volume was caused by the untimely death of Professor Gerber, who was guiding the series of bibliographies in its progress to completion.

This is perhaps the proper place to say that I am relieved to have brought much effort on the part of many people, over a period of several years, to this conclusion.

Acknowledgments

Those persons who have contributed most fully to this annotated bibliography during the years it has been in progress, the contributors, are named earlier. Their patience in the face of difficulties and much uncertainty as to whether all the effort they had invested would, indeed, ever result in a book, warrants more than the minimal reward I am able to bestow. These contributors have been colleagues in the better and larger sense of the term, and most of them have been friends for most of this period of time. Only their sustained interest, often in times of stress of which they were unaware, has saved this project from collapse.

In addition, during all the years this bibliography has been in the making, I have benefited from the assistance at critical moments of nearly a small army of busy people who allowed me to enlist their talents for more limited but nonetheless important tasks. First among these, I want to recognize one of the very greatest, the late Professor Helmut E. Gerber, my coeditor for *Conrad I*, whose untimely death in 1981 left the series of Annotated Bibliographies of English Literature in Transition, 1880–1920, almost completely at a standstill. "Hal" Gerber was not only known for his founding of the annotated bibliography series but also for his founding of the periodical, *English Literature in Transition, 1880–1920*, as well as the writer of much critical material and several books. He was, indeed, in the best sense of the term, a friend of every worthy student or scholar who needed his assistance. He was all that a fellow worker in the vineyard of research in English can be—a dear and loyal friend and helper. Fortunately the series of annotated bibliographies was rescued by Garland Publishing, Inc., which was able to continue on a direct course with the will to keep the series going in the preparation and publication of other volumes. And Professor W. Eugene Davis, of Purdue University, was willing and able to follow creditably in the footsteps of his mighty predecessor, Hal Gerber, as general editor of the annotated bibliography series.

Several graduate students helped to maintain card files, check and correct bibliographical data, and generally lent their able support to me when it was needed. For typing I am indebted to Nancy Brumfield and Jennie Patten, Central Washington University. Many librarians, such as Jennifer Jacques and Robert Novak of Central Washington University Library, and those of the University of Washington, the University of Oregon, Oregon State University, and the University of British Columbia, were very kind and helpful.

This book was partially supported by the Faculty Research Funds of Central Washington University, in Research Grants made in 1972 and 1975, for which I am grateful.

And now, with the poet, I dedicate this work to the one who was with me "in our first world."

This book is the latest volume in the Annotated Secondary Bibliography Series on English Literature in Transition, 1880–1920, that was published by Northern Illinois University Press, with W. Eugene Davis as general editor. Other volumes in this series were books on W. Somerset Maugham, Joseph Conrad, Thomas Hardy, E.M. Forster, John Galsworthy, George Gissing, D.H. Lawrence, and H.G. Wells.

A Checklist
of the Works of Joseph Conrad
Cited in This Bibliography

I. FICTION

A. Separate Works

Almayer's Folly. Lond. and New York, 1895.

An Outcast of the Islands. Lond. and New York, 1896.

The Nigger of the Narcissus. New York (as *Children of the Sea, A Tale of the Forecastle*) and Lond., 1897.

Tales of Unrest. Lond. and New York, 1898. Contents: "The Idiots," 1896; "Karain," 1897; "The Lagoon," 1897; "An Outpost of Progress," 1897; "The Return," 1898.

Lord Jim, A Tale. Edinburgh and Lond., New York, and Toronto, 1900.

The Inheritors, An Extravagant Story. (With Ford Madox Hueffer) New York and Lond., 1901.

Youth, A Narrative, and Two Other Stories. Edinburgh and Lond., 1902; New York, 1903. Contents: "Youth," 1898; "Heart of Darkness," 1899, "The End of the Tether," 1902.

Typhoon. New York and Lond., 1902.

Typhoon, and Other Stories. Lond., 1903; New York, 1923. Contents: "Amy Foster," 1901; "Typhoon," 1902; "To-morrow," 1902; "Falk," 1903.

Romance, A Novel. (With Ford Madox Hueffer) Lond., 1903; New York, 1904.

Nostromo, A Tale of the Seaboard. Lond. and New York, 1904.

The Secret Agent, A Simple Tale. Lond. and New York, 1907.

A Set of Six. Lond., 1908; New York, 1915. Contents: "An Anarchist," 1906; "The Brute," 1906; "Gaspar Ruiz," 1906; "The Informer," 1906; "The Duel," 1908; "Il Conde," 1908.

Under Western Eyes, A Novel. Lond. and New York, 1911.

'Twixt Land and Sea, Tales. Lond. and New York, 1912. Contents: "The Secret Sharer," 1910; "A Smile of Fortune," 1911; "Freya of the Seven Isles," 1912.

Chance, A Tale in Two Parts. Lond. and New York, 1913.

Victory, An Island Tale. New York and Lond., 1915.

Within the Tides, Tales. Lond. and Toronto, 1915; New York, 1916. Contents: "The Partner," 1911; "The Inn of the Two Witches," 1913; "Because of the Dollars," 1914; "The Planter of Malata," 1914.

The Shadow-Line, A Confession. Lond. and Toronto, and New York, 1917.

The Arrow of Gold, A Story Between Two Notes. New York and Lond., 1919.

The Rescue, A Romance of the Shallows. New York, and Lond. and Toronto, 1920.

The Rover. New York and Lond.,1923.

The Nature of a Crime. (With Ford Madox Hueffer) Lond. and New York, 1924.

Suspense, A Napoleonic Novel. New York, and Lond. and Toronto, 1925.

Tales of Hearsay. Lond. and New York, 1925. Contents: "The Black Mate," 1908; "Prince Roman," 1911; "The Tale," 1917; "The Warrior's Soul," 1917.

The Sisters. New York, 1928.

B. Collected Editions and Article

The Works of Joseph Conrad. Lond., 1921-1927. 20 vols.

The Works of Joseph Conrad. The Uniform Edition. Lond. and Toronto, 1923-1928. 22 vols.

Collected Works of Joseph Conrad. The Memorial Edition. New York 1926. 21 vols. (Several additional sets—Concord, Kent, Canterbury, etc.—are substantially the same.)

Collected Edition of the Works of Joseph Conrad. Lond., 1946-1955. (Reprinted from the Uniform Edition, without the dramas.) 21 vols.

"The Silence of the Sea," *Daily Mail* (18 September 1909).

II. ESSAYS AND MEMOIRS (INCLUDED IN THE COLLECTED EDITIONS)

The Mirror of the Sea, Memories and Impressions. Lond. and New York, 1906.

A Personal Record. (Under title, *Some Reminiscences*, New York, 1908, to secure American copyright, probably only six copies printed) Lond. (as *Some Reminiscences*) and New York, 1912.

Notes on Life and Letters. Lond. and Toronto, and New York, 1921. Contents: "Books," 1905; "Henry James," 1905; "Alphonse Daudet," 1898; "Guy de Maupassant," 1914; "Anatole France–I. Crainquebille," 1904; "Anatole France–II. L'Ile des pingouins," 1908; "Turgenev," 1917; "Stephen Crane, A Note Without Dates," 1919; "Tales of the Sea," 1898; "An Observer in Malay," 1898; "A Happy Wanderer," 1910; "The Life Beyond," 1910; "The Ascending Effort," 1910; "The Censor of Plays," 1907; "Autocracy and War," 1905; "The Crime of Partition," 1919; "A Note on the Polish Problem," 1921; "The Shock of War," 1915; "To Poland in War-time," 1915; "The North Sea on the Eve of the War," 1915; "My Return to Cracow," 1915; "Poland Revisited," 1916; "First News," 1918; "Well Done!" 1918; "Tradition," 1918; "Confidence," 1919;

"Flight," 1917; "Some Reflections on the Loss of the *Titanic*," 1912; "Certain Aspects of the Admirable Inquiry into the Loss of the *Titanic*," 1912; "Protection of Ocean Liners," 1914; "A Friendly Place," 1912.

Last Essays. Lond. and Toronto, and New York, 1926. Contents: "Geography and Some Explorers," 1924; "The 'Torrens,' A Personal Tribute," 1923; "Christmas Day at Sea," 1923; "Ocean Travels," 1923; "Outside Literature," 1922; "Legends," 1924; "The Unlighted Coast," 1925; "The Dover Patrol," 1921; "Memorandum on the Scheme for Fitting Out a Ship," 1926; "The Loss of the 'Dalgonar,'" 1921; "Travel," 1923; "Stephen Crane," 1923; "His War Book," 1925; "John Galsworthy," 1906; "A Glance at Two Books," 1925; "Preface to 'The Shorter Tales of Joseph Conrad,'" 1924; "Cookery," 1923; "The Future of Constantinople," 1912; "The Congo Diary," 1925.

III. DRAMA

A. Separate Works

One Day More, A Play in One Act. (Adaption of "To-morrow") Lond., *English Review*, 1913.

The Secret Agent, Drama in Four Acts. (Adaption of the novel) Canterbury, 1921.

Laughing Anne, A Play. (Adaption of "Because of the Dollars") Lond., 1923.

B. Collected Edition

Three Plays: Laughing Anne; One Day More; and The Secret Agent. Lond., 1934.

IV. LETTERS: MAJOR COLLECTIONS

Five Letters by Joseph Conrad Written to Edward Noble in 1895. Foreword by Edward Noble. Lond., 1925.

Joseph Conrad's Letters to His Wife. Lond., 1927.

Joseph Conrad, Life and Letters. G. Jean-Aubry. 2 vols. New York and Lond., 1927.

Conrad to a Friend, 150 Selected Letters from Joseph Conrad to Richard Curle, ed. by Richard Curle. New York and Lond., 1928.

Letters from Joseph Conrad, 1895-1924, ed. by Edward Garnett. Indianapolis, 1928.

Lettres françaises, ed. by G. Jean-Aubry. Paris, 1930.

Letters of Joseph Conrad to Marguerite Poradowska, 1890-1920, ed. by John A. Gee and Paul J. Sturm. New Haven and Lond., 1940.

Joseph Conrad: Letters to William Blackwood and David S. Meldrum, ed. by William Blackburn. Durham, N.C., 1958.

Conrad's Polish Background: Letters to and from Polish Friends, ed. by Zdzislaw Najder. Lond., New York, Toronto, 1964.

Acronyms of Selected Books and Periodicals

B   *BOOKMAN* (NY).

BJPC   *BOOKMAN'S JOURNAL AND PRINT COLLECTOR.*

CCH   *CONRAD, THE CRITICAL HERITAGE*, ed by Norman Sherry (Lond and Bost: Routledge and Kegan Paul [The Critical Heritage Series], 1973).

CEA   *CEA CRITIC.*

COKS   *CONRAD W OCZACH KRYTYKI SWIATOWEJ* (Conrad Seen by World Criticism), ed by Barbara Kocòwna (Warsaw: Panstwowy Instytut Wydawniczy, 1963).

CON   *CONRADIANA.*

CSAC   *CONRAD, THE SECRET AGENT: A CASEBOOK*, ed by Ian Watt (Lond: Macmillan, 1973).

DLOP   *DIZIONARIO LETTERARIO DELLE OPERE E DEI PERSONAGGI.*

DN   *DAILY NEWS* (Lond).

DT   *DAILY TELEGRAPH* (Lond).

EIC   *ESSAYS IN CRITICISM* (Oxford).

ELT   *ENGLISH LITERATURE IN TRANSITION, 1880-1920.*

JC   *JOSEPH CONRAD: A COMMEMORATION*, ed by Norman Sherry (NY : Barnes & Noble, 1976).

JCCC   *JOSEPH CONRAD: A COLLECTION OF CRITICISM*, ed by Frederick R. Karl (NY: McGraw-Hill [Contemporary Studies in Literature], 1975).

JCCE   *JOSEPH CONRAD: COMMEMORATIVE ESSAYS* (Selected Proceedings of the International Conference of Conrad Scholars, University of California, San Diego, August 29-September 5, 1975), ed by Adam Gillon and Ludwik Krzyzanowski (NY: Astra Books, 1975).

JCCEP   *JOSEPH CONRAD: CENTENNIAL ESSAYS*, ed by Ludwik Kryzyzanowski (NY: Polish Institute of Arts and Sciences in America, 1960).

JCCP   *JOSEPH CONRAD COLLOQUY IN POLAND: 5-12 SEPTEMBER 1972: CONTRIBUTIONS*, ed by Roza Jablkowska (Wroclaw, Warsaw, Krakow, Gdansk: Polish Academy of Sciences, Neophilological Committee, 1975).

JCHD   *JOSEPH CONRAD, "HEART OF DARKNESS," AN AUTHORITATIVE TEXT, BACKGROUNDS AND SOURCES, CRITICISM*, ed by Robert Kimbrough (NY: Norton [A Norton Critical Edition], 1968).

JCHD&SS   *JOSEPH CONRAD, "HEART OF DARKNESS" AND "THE SECRET SHARER,"* ed by Franklin Walker (NY: Bantam, 1969).

JCLJ   *JOSEPH CONRAD, LORD JIM: AN AUTHORITATIVE TEXT, BACKGROUNDS, SOURCES* (ed by Norman Sherry), *ESSAYS IN CRITICISM*, ed by Thomas C. Moser (NY: Norton [A Norton Critical Edition], 1968).

JCSN	*JOSEPH CONRAD SOCIETY (U.K.) NEWSLETTER.*
JCT	*JOSEPH CONRAD TODAY: THE NEWSLETTER OF THE JOSEPH CONRAD SOCIETY OF AMERICA.*
JCTWF	*JOSEPH CONRAD: THEORY AND WORLD FICTION* (Proceedings of the Comparative Literature Symposium, Vol. VII, January 23, 24, and 25, 1974), ed by Wolomyr T. Zyla and Wendell M. Aycock (Lubbock: Interdepartmental Committee on Comparative Literature, Texas Tech University, 1974).
JJCS	*JOURNAL OF THE JOSEPH CONRAD SOCIETY* (U.K.).
JML	*JOURNAL OF MODERN LITERATURE.*
KN	*KWARTALNIK NEOFILOGNICZNY* (Warsaw).
LC	*L'EPOQUE CONRADIENNE* (Amiens).
LCS	*L'ITALIA CHE SCRIVE.*
MFS	*MODERN FICTION STUDIES.*
MG	*MANCHESTER GUARDIAN.*
MP	*MORNING POST.*
N	*NATION* (Lond).
N&Q	*NOTES AND QUERIES.*
NC	*NAD CONRADEM* (On Conrad) (Warsaw: Panstwowy Instytut Wydawniczy, 1965).
NCF	*NINETEENTH-CENTURY FICTION.*
NOVEL	*NOVEL: A FORUUM ON FICTION.*
NYTBR	*NEW YORK TIMES BOOK REVIEW.*
NYTSBR	*NEW YORK TIMES SATURDAY REVIEW OF BOOKS.*
PCK	*THE PORTABLE CONRAD,* rvd by Frederick R. Karl (NY: Viking P, 1969).
PCTE	*PENNSYLVANIA COUNCIL OF TEACHERS OF ENGLISH, BULLETIN.*
PCZ	*THE PORTABLE CONRAD,* ed by Morton Dauwen Zabel (NY: Viking P, 1947).
PMLA	*PUBLICATIONS OF THE MODERN LANGUAGE ASSOCIATION OF AMERICA.*
PolR	*POLISH REVIEW.*
RES	*REVIEW OF ENGLISH STUDIES.*
SJC	*STUDIES IN JOSEPH CONRAD,* ed by Claude Thomas (Montpellier: Université Paul Valéry [Cahiers d'Etudes et Recherches Victoriennes et Edouardiennes, No. 27], 1969).
SNNTS	*STUDIES IN SHORT FICTION.*
SOC	*SZKICE O CONRADZIE* (Sketches on Conrad).
SR	*SATURDAY REVIEW* (Lond).
SRL	*SATURDAY REVIEW OF LITERATURE.*
SSF	*STUDIES IN SHORT FICTION.*
TCLJ	*TWENTIETH CENTURY INTERPRETATIONS OF LORD JIM: A COLLECTION OF CRITICAL ESSAYS,* ed by Robert E. Kuehn (Englewood Cliffs, NJ: Prentice-Hall [A Spectrum Book], 1969).
TCNN	*TWENTIETH CENTURY INTERPRETATIONS OF THE "NIGGER OF THE NARCISSUS": A COLLECTION OF*

	CRITICAL ESSAYS, ed by John A. Palmer (Englewood Cliffs, NJ: Prentice-Hall [A Spectrum Book], 1969).
TLS	*TIMES LITERARY SUPPLEMENT* (Lond).
Tw	*TWORCZOSC* (Creativity) (Warsaw).
TSLL	*TEXAS STUDIES IN LITERATURE AND LANGUAGE.*
WSOC	*WSPOMNIENIA I STUDIA O CONRADZIE* (Recollections and Studies of Conrad), ed by Barbara Kocówna (Warsaw: Panstwowy Instytut Wydawniczy, 1963).
YR	*YALE REVIEW.*

INTRODUCTION

Although much criticism of Joseph Conrad and his works was available for use in the preparation of *Conrad I*, which included items for the years 1895 to 1966, much more became available for these years in *Conrad II*. A particularly useful book for preparing this purpose was *Conrad, the Critical Heritage* (1973), edited by Norman Sherry, which supplied a large number of hitherto uncollected book reviews contemporary with the publication of Conrad's works from *Almayer's Folly* (1895) to *Suspense* (1925).

Sherry's collection reveals that, on the whole, Conrad fared "extremely well" at the hands of contemporary commentators but that from the beginning of his career certain characteristics were recognized which would prevent him from becoming a "popular" writer until his late renown with the general reader came with the appearance of *Chance* in 1913. At that time, according to general agreement, his greatest work lay in the past. Less important and more curious aspects of his reputation lay in the uncertainty of reviewers as to how to "place" him, with the result that he was consigned to the island of Borneo as his proper domain and to a series of contemporary writers (Balzac, Turgenev, Kipling, and Stevenson) as his kind of achievement, both of which conclusions, understandably, irked him. Sherry's invaluable introduction to his collection of reviews consists of a generous survey of the critics' comments as they were published, with a glance at what is still needed, and provides a wealth of information which does not need to be repeated here.

The introduction to *Conrad I* contains a tentative plan for an account of the secondary material on Conrad, 1895 through 1966, divided somewhat arbitrarily into three convenient periods. Since the years 1967 to 1975 make up too brief a period of time to comprise one period of Conrad criticism, I include here a short account of the major publications of these years.

The late nineteen sixties and the early nineteen seventies saw a spate of published work on Conrad, much of which appeared in periodicals. I concentrate here on some of the most helpful books and a few specialized journals. One of the best books of this kind is Bruce Johnson's *Conrad's Models of Mind* (1971), which is an illuminating study of the fundamental models which allow a writer to organize and come to grips with the ultimately mysterious phenomenon of mind. Johnson follows these metaphors of mind through Conrad's works, observing him move steadily away from deductive psychology and involving "faculties" or entities such as will, passion, ego, or sympathy, toward a flexible new psychology that has implications for his entire development as writer. These models are simply Conrad's beliefs. In *Conrad: The Psychologist as Artist* (1968), Paul Kirschner studies Conrad's psychology to find that an inner tension in his life caused his novels to show some degree of decline in the later works. In *Joseph Conrad's Fiction: A Study in*

Literary Growth (1968), John A. Palmer strove valiantly if not with entire success to strengthen the reputation of Conrad's later works. And Lawrence Graver in *Conrad's Short Fiction* (1969) produced the best book to date on this subject.

In reevaluating Conrad's works in 1969, Douglas Hewitt, in *Conrad: A Reassessment*, published his second edition of this book, in which he saw Conrad as a "modern classic" and a part of the "academic critical industry." In *Conrad: "Nostromo"* (1969), Juliet McLauchlan provided hard information with perceptive readings of the novel. Maurice Beebe, a highly respected critic, wrote a small *Critical Study Guide to Joseph Conrad's "Lord Jim"* (1968), in which he turned out, not the usual very poor study guide for students which is too readily available, but a masterpiece of factual knowledge, suggestive topics, and basic interpretation of a novel in his completely reliable guide. In his book on 1967, Avrom Fleishman supplied one of the very best works on his subject, *Conrad's Politics: Community and Anarchy in the Fiction of Joseph Conrad.*

During these years, several books with "authoritative texts" of some of Conrad's works appeared, with varying kinds of accompanying materials called critical editions, casebooks, or collections of critical writings on the Conrad text. One of the best known was edited by Thomas C. Moser, *Joseph Conrad, "Lord Jim": An Authoritative Text, Backgrounds, Sources* (edited by Norman Sherry), *Essays in Criticism*, of 1968. Another was edited by John A. Palmer, *Twentieth Century Interpretations of the "Nigger of the Narcissus": A Collection of Critical Essays* (1969). Frederick R. Karl followed this with his *Joseph Conrad: A Collection of Critical Essays* of 1975. In 1973 Ian Watt edited his *Conrad: "The Secret Agent": A Casebook*. Robert Kimbrough edited a similar book, *Joseph Conrad's "Heart of Darkness": An Authoritative Text, Backgrounds and Sources, Criticism*, revised in 1971, attesting to the popularity of his first edition. Some of these works with so-called "authoritative" texts have, however, been found by more recent Conrad scholars to be unacceptable as authoritative editions. The time for a large number of reliable authoritative editions had not arrived.

In 1973, Olivia Renato and Alessandro Portelli edited *Conrad: L'Imperialismo Imperfetto* (Conrad: The Imperfect Imperialism) in Italy. The year 1974 saw the appearance of two such books: Wolodymyr T. Zyla and Wendell M. Aycock, editors, *Joseph Conrad: Theory and World Fiction*, containing the papers given in January 1974, of the symposium commemorating the fiftieth anniversary of Conrad's death, and Zdzislaw Najder, editor, *Conrad W Oczach Kryryki Swiatowej* (Conrad Seen by World Criticism), published this collection in Warsaw. In 1975, Claude Thomas edited *Studies in Joseph Conrad* for publication in France. In this year also, Adam Gillon and Ludwik Krzyzanowski edited *Joseph Conrad: Commemorative Essays*, the selected proceedings of the International Conference of Conrad Scholars at the University of California, San Diego.

Somewhat similar to these collections of essays on Conrad were the journals of various Joseph Conrad societies of different countries. There are *Joseph Conrad Today: Conrad Society of America*, edited by Adam Gillon; *The Conradian: Journal of the Joseph Conrad Society* (UK), edited by Owen Knowles in Hull, England; *L'Epoque Conradienne: Bulletin Annuel de la Société Conradienne*, edited by François Lombard in Limoges, France; *Joseph Conrad in Italy*, edited by Mario Curreli in Pisa, Italy; and *The Conrad News Polish Conradian Club Society of Friends of the Maritime Museum in Gdansk, Poland*, edited by the Editorial Board: Andrzej Braun, Joanna Konopacka, Stefan Zabierowski, Andrzej Zgorzelski. And for several years the journal *Conradiana*, edited by David Leon Higdon, has been known as the major periodical devoted only to Conrad studies.

In the years 1967-1975 there appeared only one biography of Joseph Conrad, *Joseph Conrad: A Psychoanalytic Biography*, by Bernard C. Meyer, M.D. (1967), which is an interesting work even if one might not care for the psychoanalytic approach to Conrad. Two bibliographies of Conrad appeared. The earlier one, *A Bibliography of Joseph Conrad* by Theodore G. Ehrsam (1969), is a good work to let one see what is actually needed for a completely satisfactory bibliography. The second one, *Joseph Conrad: An Annotated Bibliography of Writings About Him*, compiled and edited by Bruce E. Teets and Helmut E. Gerber (1971), does not pretend to take the place of Ehrsam's work.

One special book of criticism, written in Polish and published in Gdansk, Poland, in 1971, is that of Stefan Zabierowski, *Conrad W Polsce: Wybrane Problemy Recepji Kryryeznej w Latach 1896-1969* (Conrad in Poland: Selected Problems of Critical Reception in the Years 1896-1969). This is a much needed analysis of the critical reception of Conrad's work in Poland.

In books and journals alone, then, these years produced a large number of very valuable works on Conrad and his works.

The Bibliography

1895

0.9 "*Almayer's Folly*, a Dreary Record," *World* (London), 15 May 1895, p. 31 [not seen in this form]; rpt. as "Unsigned Review" in CCH, p. 51.

Almayer's Folly, a "dreary record" of a "still more dreary existence," is "as dull as it well could be."

1.1 [Almayer's Tragedy], *Speaker* (London) 29 June 1895, pp. 722–23 [not seen in this form]; rpt. as "Unsigned Review" in CCH, pp. 55–56.

Almayer's Folly is somber but "distinctly powerful" and original. Almayer's deterioration of character caused by his life of "semi-barbarism," exiled among "an inferior race," is forcefully presented. The unforgettable tragedy is told with "reticence and self-restraint."

1.2 [Conrad and Kipling], *Spectator* (London), 19 October 1895, p. 530 [not seen in this form]; rpt. "Unsigned Review" in CCH, p. 61.

Almayer's Folly, "extremely powerful all through though the plot is not as compact as it might have been," contains well drawn characters and some "admirably graphic" passages. It seems that JC may become the "Kipling of the Malay Archipelago."

1.3 "Fiction: *Almayer's Folly*," *Literary World* (Boston), XXVI (18 May 1895), 155.

In *Almayer's Folly*, JC tells "a rather dull and dreary story," but the book contains one strong scene in which Almayer's Malay wife advises her daughter "on how to manage her Malay rajah." This scene shows "remarkable insight into the point of view of the Eastern woman." As a whole, "the book is crude and repulsive, but the local color is vivid." [Interesting as one of the very early reactions to JC's first novel.]

1.4 MacArthur, James. "New Books: Romance in Malaya," B, II (August-September 1895), 39–41.

"Destined to excite the wonder of many a reader," *Almayer's Folly* surpasses *Malay Sketches* by F. A. Sweetenham in its "superior force of imagination," in its characterization, and in its "descriptive power." Built around an original idea, the development of motive is splendidly executed and the characters of Almayer and Nina are masterly. "In the novelty of its local colour, in the daring originality of its dramatic force, in the fresh disclosure of new scenes and characters, in the noble and imaginative handling of life's greatness and littleness," this novel has no place in "the prevalent fiction of the hour, which . . . sweeps past us into oblivion. It leaps at once to a place of its own—a place which ought to rank its author high among novelists worthy of the name."

2.1 [On *Almayer's Folly*], *DN*, 25 April 1895, p. 6 [not seen in this form]; rpt. as "Unsigned Review" in CCH, p. 47.

JC, a "new writer," is about to annex the island of Borneo in *Almayer's Folly*. His story is praised by persons who have seen it in manuscript. The physical setting is "as picturesque as the world offers," and the reassertion of an old savage instinct in the ex-pirate's daughter is one of the chief incidents of the tale.

2.2 [Original *Almayer's Folly*], *B*, II (1895), 39–41 [not seen in this form]; rpt. in *Literary News* (London), XVI (September 1895), 268–69; rpt. as "Unsigned Review" in CCH, pp. 59–60.

Almayer's Folly is original in showing the unequal contest in Almayer's mind, in illustrating what may happen to the Malay in contact with Europeans, in its local color, in the originality of its dramatic force, and in the "noble and imaginative handling of life's greatness and littleness." It is a book to "read and reread."

2.3 [Review of *Almayer's Folly*], *Guardian* (London), 3 July 1895, p. 1001 [not seen in this form]; rpt. as "Unsigned Review" in CCH, p. 57.

Almayer's Folly is "a charming" romance "in all senses of the word," including the "freshness and loveliness of theme, of expression, of grouping."

2.4 [Review of *Almayer's Folly*], *Scotsman*, 29 April 1895. p. 3 [not seen in this form]; rpt. as "Unsigned Review" in CCH, p. 48.

"Dr. Joseph Conrad's story" [sic, apparently the only occasion on which JC was referred to as "Dr."], *Almayer's Folly*, is "powerfully imagined," done with a "fine unity of effect," but it is "depressing in its sombreness."

2.5 [Setting of *Almayer's Folly*], *Nation* (New York), LXI (17 October 1895), 278 [not seen in this form]; rpt. as "Unsigned Review" in CCH, p. 60.

Even if Almayer, in *Almayer's Folly*, seems pathetic in the setting, Borneo is "a fine field for the study of monkeys, not men."

2.6 Waugh, Arthur. [Review of *Almayer's Folly*], *Critic* (London), XXVI (11 May 1895), 349 [not seen in this form]; rpt. as "Notice" in CCH, pp. 50–51.

In *Almayer's Folly*, JC demonstrates that he understands both the scenery and the inhabitants of Borneo, a new country for the novelist. Not far from being a master of his art, JC has a "strong motive" and "knows something" of human nature.

2.7 [Wearisome *Almayer's Folly*], *Bookman* (London), September 1895, p. 176 [not seen in this form]; rpt. as "Unsigned Review" in CCH, p. 58

Although *Almayer's Folly* is "beautiful, delicate, and sympathetic," when dealing with the outdoor world, as a whole it is "wearisome," hard to follow, and dragging in action.

2.8 Wells, H. G. [A Gloomy Tale], *SR*, 15 June 1895, p. 797 [not seen in this form]; rpt. as "Unsigned Review" in CCH, p. 53.

Almayer's Folly is a "very powerful story," with effects that "will capture the imagination and haunt the memory of the reader." A "gloomy tale," its gloom is relieved by the "rare beauty" of the love story and by "flashes of humour." It is so "exceedingly well imagined and well written" that it will place JC high among contemporary storytellers.

2.9 "White Men and Brown," *Daily Chronicle* (London), 11 May 1895, p. 3; [not seen in this form]; rpt. in CCH as "Unsigned Review," pp. 49–50.

In *Almayer's Folly*, JC is content with an idea rather than a plot, the idea of a white man with the "nervous" tensions of the West condemned to live in a native settlement on a river in Borneo. JC shows the "emasculating and despair-breeding" effect of the "scheming" East on a weak, "neurotic" Western organization, but he also creates a "poetic, romantic" atmosphere.

1896

2.10 [Characterization in *An Outcast of the Islands*], *DN*, 4 April 1896, p. 6 [not seen in this form]; rpt. as "Unsigned Review" in CCH, p. 68.

JC, in *An Outcast of the Islands*, tended to go beyond approved limits in his characterization.

2.11 "Chronicle and Comment," *B*, III (July 1896), 396–97.

JC's stories of wild nature and strange humanity reflect his adventurous life, and their unfamiliar, vaguely illusive tone might be explained by his non-English origins. [Includes some biographical notes and praises *Almayer's Folly* and *An Outcast of the Islands*.]

2.12 [Conrad as a Genius], *Spectator* (London), 30 May 1896, p. 778 [not seen in this form]; rpt. as "Unsigned Review" in CCH, pp. 78–79.

An Outcast of the Islands suggests the view of the well known hymn that in the tropics it is as usual for man to be vile as for "Nature" to be beautiful. The one "grand" character in the book is the old seaman, Tom Lingard. Much of the novel displays genius. [In this review, JC is called a genius, it seems, for the second time.]

2.13 [Conrad's "Weird" Story], *Scotsman*, 16 March 1896 [not seen in this form]; rpt. as "Unsigned Review" in CCH, p. 65.

Especially notable in *An Outcast of the Islands* are the setting and JC's skill in describing his "western [sic] river." A "weird" story of a "strange and unnatural life," the novel contains enough human nature to make it convincing.

5.1 "Novel Notes: *An Outcast of the Islands*," B, IV (September 1896), 166.

Displaying the same power as *Almayer's Folly, An Outcast of the Islands* is "terrible in its analysis of man's moral progress to damnation." It causes the reader to feel the "thirst and intensity of the tropics, their gloom, their alluring beauty, their poison for the northern nature" as JC depicts the tragedy of two civilizations—East and West. JC's chief power is "psychological," and "his psychological moments" exercise a "relentless hold on the memory and make a narrative of terror from which the imagination shrinks" in a work that may be "too intense, too prolonged, too unmitigated for artistic harmony or truth to life."

6.1 [*An Outcast of the Islands*], *Glasgow Herald*, 19 March 1896 [not seen in this form]; rpt. as "Unsigned Review" in CCH, p. 65.

An Outcast of the Islands is a book of "singular and indefinable power, . . . always beautiful in its style, rich alike in passion and in pathos."

6.2 [*An Outcast of the Islands*], *MG*, 19 May 1896, P. 5 [not seen in this form]; rpt. as "Unsigned Review" in CCH, p. 77.

An Outcast of the Islands contains an "extraordinary vitality and virility" as "the bitter struggle that goes on endlessly between the white race and the yellow [sic] is described with force and insight."

This "genuinely remarkable book" has only one real fault, a tendency towards "affectation and mannerism" in the writing.

6.3 [*An Outcast of the Islands*], *National Observer* (London), 18 April 1896, p. 680 [not seen in this form]; rpt. as "Unsigned Review" in CCH, pp. 69–70.

An Outcast of the Islands is diffuse, the characters are not very effective, and the novel is "undeniably dull."

6.4 [*An Outcast of the Islands*], *Sketch* (London), 6 May 1896, p. 62 [not seen in this form]; rpt. as "Unsigned Review" in CCH, pp. 70–71.

In *An Outcast of the Islands*, JC is only a "star in the making," not a nebula, a lack of proportion and of concentration being the chief fault. But his "overluxurience" is the promise of youth.

6.5 Payn, James. [A Disjointed Story], *Illustrated London, News*, 4 April 1896, p. 418 [not seen in this form]; rpt. as "Review" in CCH, pp. 66–67.

The story of *An Outcast of the Islands* is somewhat "disjointed," but the characters and descriptions are "admirable." JC makes the reader feel at home in the Indian Archipelago. As for the outcast himself, "never did so mean a skunk figure as the hero of a novel." JC is the only disciple of Victor Hugo.

6.6 [A Romance of the Far East], *Daily Chronicle* (London), 16 March 1896, p. 3 [not seen in this form]; rpt. as "Unsigned Review" in CCH, pp. 63–64.

An Outcast of the Islands is a "work of extraordinary force and charm," but in it JC tends toward superfluity. This review seems to be the first occasion on which JC is compared favorably with Herman Melville and R. L. Stevenson.

6.7 Wells, H.G. [Conrad's Wordiness], *SR*, 16 May 1896, pp. 509–10 [not seen in this form]; rpt. as "Unsigned Review" in CCH, pp. 73–76.

An Outcast of the Islands, "a remarkably fine romance indeed," has one glaring fault—wordiness; JC has still to learn "the great half of his art, the art of leaving things unwritten." But otherwise this "real romance" is certainly authentic, even if the author writes "despicably." "Only greatness," though, "could make books of which the detailed workmanship was so copiously bad, so well worth reading" as *Folly* and *Outcast*.

1897

6.8 Bennett, Arnold. [Arnold Bennett on Conrad and Kipling], *The Letters of Arnold Bennett*, ed by James Hepburn (London: Oxford UP, 1968), II, 94; rpt. as "Arnold Bennett on Conrad and Kipling" in CCH, p. 82, extracted from a letter to H. G. Wells, 8 December 1897.

Both JC's style and attitude in *The Nigger of the Narcissus* are "affecting." JC is "so consciously an artist," whereas Kipling is "a great writer but not an artist." [Kipling and JC had been compared both favorably and unfavorably.]

6.9 "The Book of the Week: *The Nigger of the Narcissus*," *Books and News Gazette*, 11 December 1897.

JC's work will be more enduring than Clark Russell's or Captain Marryat's. In *The Nigger of the Narcissus*, JC, with "scanty material, has produced "not only an artisitc book, but one that is full of interest from beginning to end," a book which gives "the most artistic and natural picture of sea-life that has yet been produced in literature."

6.10 "The Book Table," *Detroit Free Press*, 28 March 1897, p. 7.

A new novel by " a strong and original writer who has already made an impression on the public" is all the more welcome when it is a work of such quality as *Children of the Sea*, which as *The Nigger of the Narcissus* won recognition as a candidate for *The Academy's* best book of 1897 and drew praise from H. G. Wells, A. T. Quiller-Couch, and Stephen Crane, who has lavishly praised the author's descriptive powers. Crane's commendation is merited, for JC's novel is "unique, fascinating, thrilling." Capturing the vividness and mystery of the ocean, it has "an exotic quality" that sets it apart from all other sea tales, strongly suggesting that the author was an "eye witness" to the events he records. No doubt, the secret of the "dramatic" quality of the book lies in JC's association with "the life of which he writes," for his own life has taken him from the Congo to the Archipelago, and "his genius" allows him to "crystallize" his experiences in his books, which, though unusual, ring true because of his "familiarity with wild life and strange humanity." Like *Almayer's Folly* and *An Outcast of the Islands, Children of the Sea* is "decidedly out of the ordinary." [Rev of *Children of the Sea* (with portrait).]

6.11 "A Book to Buy," *Glasgow Evening News*, 16 December 1897, p. 2

Although there is some similarity between *The Nigger of the Narcissus* and Kipling's *Captains Courageous, Nigger* is superior to that sea tale and to those of Marryat, Cooper, Scott, Melville, and Russell, none of which contains JC's poetry. JC is "essentially an impressionist and a stylist." [The review is interesting in that it reprints the preface to *Nigger* and derives its illustrations of JC's prose from the serial edition of the text appearing in *The New Review*.]

6.12 Courtney, W. L. [*The Nigger of the Narcissus*], *DT*, 8 December 1897, p. 4 [not seen in this form]; rpt. as "Review" in CCH, pp. 85–88.

JC, an "unflinching realist," makes the seamen in *The Nigger of the Narcissus* "very real, picturesque, and living personages." He works like an artist, but the reader is left with "only the vaguest idea" of what the story is about: the plot is merely an episode. JC has done for the sea what Stephen Crane has done for war and warriors in *The Red Badge of Courage*. When JC builds up his scenes piece by piece, he resembles Crane; when he turns from man to nature, he resembles Pierre Loti. The characters of the book are "vivid and lifelike," and "very human," so that we part from them with regret.

7.1 [A Disappointment], *Daily Mail* (London), 7 December 1897, p. 3 [not seen in this form]; rpt. as "Unsigned Notice" in CCH, pp. 83–84.

The Nigger of the Narcissus is disappointing because there is no story in it, only men performing their "commonplace" duties. Apart from a storm and a death and a burial, there is no incident. The best quality of the book is the characterization of old Singleton and the other sailors.

7.2 [The Effect of Foreign Travel], *Nation* (New York), 15 April 1897, p. 287 [not seen in this form]; rpt. as "Unsigned Review" in CCH, pp. 80–81.

The effect of foreign travel seems harmful in JC's novels: the climate and the vegetation of the East Indies and the disreputable black and white society of this area are opposed to all possible "edification." The moral of *An Outcast of the Islands*, for example, seems to be that "white Christians can be much worse than the black pagans, and generally are."

7.3 "Mr. Conrad's New Book," *Pall Mall Gazette* 20 December 1897, p. 11.

JC's unique style appears in *The Nigger of the Narcissus*, as well as his vivid descriptive writing and his capacity to create "a queer ship's company" that is "drawn from life with convincing skill."

7.4 "The Newest Fiction: A Guide for Novel Readers," *Academy, Fiction Supplement*, LII (4 December 1897), 117.

The Nigger of the Narcissus is "a book for men" which describes the events of a ship's voyage "ruthlessly and vigorously."

7.5 "*The Nigger of the Narcissus*, A Tale of the Sea," *Irish Independent*, 18 December 1897.

Without love interest and depending on shipboard routine as a source of action, *The Nigger of the Narcissus* is distinguished by its powerful and vivid style and its "admirable" characterizations. Only the protrait of Wait is "overdrawn."

7.6 [The Old Sea Salt], *Daily Chronicle* (London), 22 December 1897, p. 3 [not seen in this form]; rpt. as "Unsigned Review" in CCH, pp. 89–91.

The Nigger of the Narcissus is "simply an account of an ordinary voyage made by an ordinary ship" sailing from Bombay to the Thames. "Nothing particular happens"; there is a "big storm," some dissatisfaction among the crew, and the death and burial of "the least admirable" of the men. But it is "far above" the ordinary level of sea tales, because the author has "irony, humor, a sense of words, a power of choice, and also a steady sympathy" with mankind. The value of the book is in the telling, not in the contents.

7.7 Payn, James, [Review of *The Nigger of the Narcissus*], *London Illustrated News, CXII* (5 February 1897), 112.

With no hero or heroine (nor, indeed, any women characters at all), *The Nigger of the Narcissus* is more hard-hearted and truthful than works of earlier sea novelists, but readers "not content with

[JC's] ships and his ships' crews . . . may land and leave him." JC almost equals Zola in his realism, for he succeeds in interesting the reader in "worthless personages" despite the slight plot. His treatment of seamen resembles Kipling's treatment of the British soldier.

7.8 [Plain Realism], *Glasgow Herald*, 9 December 1897, p. 10 [not seen in this form]; rpt. as "Unsigned Review" in CCH, pp. 88–89.

In *the Nigger of the Narcissus*, JC describes simply a voyage from Bombay to England, using a "plain, unvarnished realism" which only "the hand of a master" could make attractive. The reader seems to know the characters well, if not to love them. In spite of JC's occasional fondness for unusual words, his book is a "distinguished contribution to modern literature."

7.9 "Rambles in Bookland: Good Christmas Fare," *Morning Leader*, 3 December 1897, p. 9.

The Nigger of the Narcissus reflects JC's love of ships and seamen. Although there is little plot in the novel, the author overcomes its absence by the spirited description of life on board ship and the interesting characters.

8.1 [Review of *The Nigger of the Narcissus*], *Birmingham Gazette*, 27 December 1897, p. 8.

The Nigger of the Narcissus represents improvement over *An Outcast of the Islands*. JC's "sharp, incisive, and illuminative use of words" enables him to do with "a dozen words" what "a dozen pages of elaboration would not make more perfect."

8.2 [Review of *The Nigger of the Narcissus*], *Court Journal*, 11 December 1897, p. 2086.

In spite of the "contrast between the coarse brutality and depravity of some of his characters and the ideas to which they give rise in the mind of the author," *The Nigger of the Narcissus* pays for its realism by shocking the propriety of the reader.

8.3 [Review of *The Nigger of the Narcissus*], *Daily World*, 7 December 1897.

The Nigger of the Narcissus fails to fulfill expectations raised by *Almayer's Folly* and *An Outcast of the Islands*, but the "distinctness" of its characterizations is excellent.

8.4 [Review of *The Nigger of the Narcissus*], *The Glasgow Herald*, 9 December 1897, p. 10.

The Nigger of the Narcissus is welcome to critics for "no writer" is "more original" in his methods than JC. His marine pictures triumph in comparison to Clark Russell's. Lacking both romantic and adventurous elements, this novel offers "plain unvarnished realism . . . which only the hand of a master could make attractive." JC brings the crew to life, making us know them and "respect them." James Wait is like the Ancient Mariner, "a hindrance and a curse" to his companions, but he fascinates them and they are overcome by "an almost insane devotion to him, a hypnotic pathos" as they attempt to deal with his harassment. JC's description of the storm leaves the reader breathless. This author has made a distinguished contribution to modern literature, weakened only by his tendency to use "most unusual words," such as "inabordable."

8.5 [Review of *The Nigger of the Narcissus*], *Liverpool Daily Courier*, 9 December 1897, p. 6.

The Nigger of the Narcissus is "a memorably splendid narrative," distinguished by its character studies, its vivid descriptive passages, and its portrayal of "the rugged, picturesque life of the forecastle."

8.6 [Review of *The Nigger of the Narcissus*], *Manchester Courier*, 22 December 1897, p. 3.

Despite the total originality of *The Nigger of the Narcissus*, it contains no plot; the novel maintains our interest through its "admirable and vivid pictures of different sailor-types" and its "impressive and masterful" description of an ocean storm.

8.7 [Review of *The Nigger of the Narcissus*], *News Agent*, 11 December 1897, p. 544.

JC's book, *The Nigger of the Narcissus*, presents a "wonderful and startling picture" of the life of the forecastle that will especially please readers "who have seen something of life on board ship."

8.8 [Review of *The Nigger of the Narcissus*], *Publisher's Circular*, No. 1641, 11 December 1897, p. 690.

JC is a "thorough sailor" who, in *The Nigger of the Narcissus*, makes his reader feel "the magic of the sea." His "graphic and powerful tale" displays a style so "picturesque and vivid that we seem to see for ourselves the decks and the forecastle of the 'Narcissus' with its heterogeneous crew." The author's portrayal of the storm at sea is particularly powerful.

8.9 [Review of *The Nigger of the Narcissus*], *Scotsman*, 6 December 1897, p. 3.

The Nigger of the Narcissus is excellent for its "vigorous description" and for its "intimate knowledge both of the sea and of human nature." For "artistic finish," it can compare with anything of the kind in English fiction.

8.10 [Review of *The Nigger of the Narcissus*], *Standard* (London), 20 December 1897, p. 6.

Like the stories of Kipling and Bret Harte, *The Nigger of the Narcissus* begins with an introduction worthy of an epic but ends "in mere futility." The quality of the descriptive writing and the "excellently sketched" characters are admirable, but JC represents the tendency to write "'studies' without plot, and stories of adventure without character."

8.11 [Review of *The Nigger of the Narcissus*], *Star*, 16 December 1897, p. 1.

[*The Nigger of the Narcissus*] is one of the "most powerful books of the year." It reveals JC's ability for defining characters and interpreting a mood of nature, and displays his graphic descriptive ability.

8.12 [Review of *The Nigger of the Narcissus*], *Sunday Times* (London), 19 December 1897, p. 2.

The Nigger of the Narcissus is notable for its "hearty freshness of style and power of word-painting" and for its admirable characterizations and "splendid" descriptive passages.

1898

8.13 "The *Academy's* Awards to Authors," *Academy*, *LIII* (8 January 1898), 34.

In responding to the request of the editors of *The Academy* for nominations for prizes to be given to the most excellent books of 1897, I. Zangwill and H. G. Wells named *The Nigger of the Narcissus* among the works which merited consideration. Wells wrote of JC's book that it "is, to my mind, the most striking piece of imaginative work in prose this year has produced."

8.14 Alden, William L. "London Literary Letter," *New York Times Saturday Review of Books and Art,* 5 February 1898, pp. 90–91.

JC's "intimate knowledge of the sea" is shown in *The Nigger of the Narcissus.*

8.15 Alden, William L. "London Literary Letter," *New York Times Saturday Review of Books and Art,* 6 August 1898, p. 520.

JC could destroy Clark Russell's monopoly on sea fiction were he continue to write in the vein of *The Nigger of the Narcissus.* JC, possibly indebted to Melville's *Redburn,* may start a Melville revival.

8.16 Alden, William L. "London Literary Letter," *New York Times Saturday Review of Books and Art,* 21 March 1898, p. 197.

Sales of *The Nigger of the Narcissus* are increasing, and the book is becoming one of the most popular works of current fiction in London. It reveals JC's power as does nothing he has previously written.

8.17 "Book Notes," *Citizen,* IV (June 1898), 87.

JC is a budding genius who "has made it apparent that nothing of the commonplace is to be looked for from him," an artist whose work, like Velasquez's paintings, is unique, as *Tales of Unrest* indicates. A former sailor, JC eschews the romantic plots of the Clark Russell order to write of "strange barbaric people in far-off lands where life is unhampered by conventionalities and the background takes on unrivaled richness of warmth and colour. Nothing escapes its ardor of appreciation, which thrills as responsively to sensuous loveliness as to the drama of romance and passion. . . ." Written in "melodious English," his descriptions of nature illustrate his "singular charm" at its height. While "The Return" is not particularly new, "The Idiots," a story reminiscent of Maupassant, displays "haunting horror pure and simple," and "its equal will not be easy to find."

8.18 "The Book Table," *Detroit Free Press,* 4 April 1898, p. 7.

Tales of Unrest is one of a number of collections of short stories to come recently to the United States from abroad. These "strange, weird tales" are filled with "elemental passion" and "savage natures." They are told with the same descriptive power and "vividness and charm" which made *Children of the Sea* "notable." [Rev of *Tales of Unrest*. This seems to be one of the most knowledgeable and complimentary reviews of this book. It confirms one's belief that JC was far more widely recognized throughout the United States in 1898 than anyone has noted previously.]

8.19 "The Book World," *Cleveland Leader*, 15 May 1898, p. 17.

In *Tales of Unrest*, JC "adopts an air of mystery with reference to locality and characters and even to language itself, the reason for which is inexplicable." The opening paragraph of "Karain" illustrates this vagueness, and as the story continues "things get darker." [Rev of *Tales of Unrest*.]

8.20 "The Book World," *Cleveland Leader*, 23 May, 1898, p. 23.

As the title suggests *Children of the Sea* is a novel of the forecastle life, which is mostly concerned with "character drawing" and "graphic depiction of the crew." A great number of personages is drawn vividly in this "interesting study of human nature." [Rev of *Children of the Sea*.]

9.1 "Books and Authors," *Outlook*, LVIII (16 April 1898), p. 979.

Tales of Unrest confirms JC's power as a storyteller and skill as a writer. These tales are "introspective and psychologic to the point of morbidity" but possess a "virility of spirit, freshness of subject, and charm of style" which would make them not discreditable to Kipling.

9.2 "Books of the Week: A Novel of Nightmares," *Chicago Tribune*, (26 March 1989), p. 10.

Those who love literary novelty should seek out the "lowering" pages of *The Children of the Sea*, a book which raised some stir when published in England as *The Nigger of the Narcissus*. This "weird, garish, nightmarish description of sailor life" contains the same hint of "Kipling's bludgeon-like strength" that characterized JC's *Almayer's Folly* and *An Outcast of the Islands*. However, while JC succeeds in conveying the "murderous midnight mystery" of angry ocean and in vividly portraying his seamen, the narrative element is slight and "what there is of it is revolting." Undoubtedly the characters in the book have real prototypes, but JC's narration is diffuse and portrays a loosely connected sequence of "disagreeable and gloomy events" in such a way as to leave only an "impressionistic picture" of the entire crew and the ship, surrounded by the midnight sea.

10.1 Bouton, Emily S. "Emerson and Other Essays: Spring Literature," *Toledo Blade*, 14 May 1898, p. 13.

Children of the Sea is "notable" for its strength and for its unusual point of view. This "marvelous portrayal of forecastle life" has no hero and is "rather a study than a story," for the men aboard the *Narcissus* are the commonest individuals, and their experiences are at times "common," at times "extraordinary." JC draws a "striking picture," but it is "one without attractions"—except for his depiction of a storm at sea. He there creates "a tremendous impression of old ocean's midnight and stormy moods."

11.1 *"The Children of the Sea," Saturday Evening Gazette* (Boston), 16 April 1898, p. 6.

Despite the absence of a conventional maritime plot, *The Children of the Sea* (*The Nigger of the Narcissus*) is a "most absorbing and enthralling" book in which JC tells "a strong, masterful story of the life of sailors in trading vessels." The "real interest" of the novel lies not so much with "its accuracy of detail" as with the graphic manner of its telling. Each character possesses the "strongest individuality" and none is idealized. We feel the sea on the sailors' "grimy faces," recognize their near illiteracy, and sense that they are, nonetheless, "dignified and heroic because of their calling" and that the mystery of the sea permeates each face and each heart. The hero, James Wait, provides the book with grim humor through his pretending illness when, in fact, "death is slowly gnawing out his life." His shipmates alternately pity, suspect, and dislike the Negro, even as they show devotion to him, acting out their story against the backdrop of the "infinite ocean" which dominates the entire work. When the sea bursts into storm, "we hold our breath through the very power of it," for JC, the "master" of a dramatically powerful title, possesses a sense of humor and pathos as well. He has written "an unrivaled sea story." [This review is one more indication that *Nigger* was better received in America than in England.]

11.2 "Chronicle and Comment," *B*, VII (March 1898), 3.

JC is "delighted" with the title *Children of the Sea*, which gives a better picture of the nature of his book than *The Nigger of the Narcissus*. [Quotes favorable comments from reviews by Stephen Crane and L. F. Austin.]

11.3 "Chronicle and Comment," *B*, VIII (September 1898), 91.

[Summarizes a review in *Criterion* (not located) which compares *Children of the Sea* favorably with *Typee*.]

12.1 "Collections of Short Stories," *Literary World* (New York), 25 June 1898, p. 204.

JC's *Tales of Unrest* is a disagreeable book, emphasizing the seamy side of life and displaying a mania for treachery.

13.1 "Current Fiction: *The Children of the Sea* (*The Nigger of the Narcissus*)," *Literary World* (Boston), XXIX (14 May 1898), 187.

The Children of the Sea offers evidence of our superior refinement, "but under either name the odor of this rose" would be "acceptable." Distinguished by its characterizations and by its "unique" description of the storm at sea, it is a book "that repays reading."

13.2 "Current Literature," *Daily Inter-Ocean* (Chicago), 2 April 1898, Part II, p. 10.

The Children of the Sea is a striking book, "strong, and as an English admirer says, 'ferociously vivid.'" Its author knows sea life, and his work conveys the impression that he has been a "common seaman and taken down the extended conversations of the rough and uncouth seamen in shorthand; for we doubt whether memory or imagination would carry him through the wearying recitation of savage speech which his characters indulge in." The novel's "aggressive strength" makes it read like a story modeled after "the plan of Carlyle's histories," where "words are piled on words until the whole stands out before you like an overcoloured picture." No other writer has succeeded in putting so lifelike a "company . . . into a book," but its strength should have been tempered "with not to say grace, but less desire to 'make the most of it.'" While it succeeds as graphic realism, its "literary style is unpolished to a painful degree."

13.3 "Fiction: A Strong Sea Story," *New York Tribune Illustrated Supplement*, 3 April 1898, p. 17.

The Children of the Sea should have retained its English title, *The Nigger of the Narcissus*, because the "nigger" provides the "starting point for the psychological analysis" of life on board a merchant vessel which stands at the center of the novel side by side with brilliantly realized, completely accurate, descriptions of shipboard life and a storm at sea. These elements combine to make the book one of the "most diverting, readable" and promising works in recent years. *Tales of Unrest* comes as an anti-climax, for it contains self-consciously clever stories, which could have been produced by a number of other writers. It is a "minor book" by "a man who in one happy moment at least has demonstrated that he has a major gift."

13.4 "Fiction: *Children of the Sea (The Nigger of the Narcissus)*," *Literary News* (New York, XIX (May 1898), p. 152.

Lacking romantic interest, *Children of the Sea* consists of a "succession of episodes, humorous and tragical, which illustrate the human nature of the sailor man."

13.5 "Fiction, Poetry and the Lighter Note in the Season's Books," *American Monthly Review of Reviews*, XVIII (1898), p. 729.

Beyond a doubt, JC is among "the coming men" whose reputations as writers can "still safely be called minor." His admirably named *Tales of Unrest* is "enough to create a nightmare in their sheer bald horror." The volume develops two themes: the sea and fear, and JC "proves himself so masterful a writer that it is not easy to set any limit to what he may do." England's most conservative critics have praised his "pictures of the ocean" and even the most jaded reader will be pleased with the five stories in *Tales of Unrest*.

13.6 Fitch, G. H. "Reviews of Recent Book and Other Publications," *San Francisco Chronicle*, 1 May 1898, p. 4.

The charm of *Tales of Unrest* is difficult to describe, but it is akin to *An Outcast of the Islands*, which "laid hold on imagination of everyone who read it." Of particular interest are the two stories which mirror life in Malaysia for no author other than JC has succeeded in endowing Malaysian characters with "attributes of real life." All of the stories possess a grim power but, while "The Idiots" might have been produced by other masterful authors, "Karain" and "The Lagoon," which resemble some of Turgenev's tales, are unique.

13.7 Frederic, Harold. [Conrad and the Sea], *SR*, 12 February 1898, p. 211 [not seen in this form]; rpt as "Unsigned Review" in CCH, pp. 98–100.

Some of JC's tales contain a single theme: the degeneracy of the white man under the influence of the South Seas. There is always the Caucasian enslaved by the forces he came to conquer. In *The Nigger of the Narcissus*, however, JC presents the sea as no other writer of this generation has been able to render it; but the interest in the characters is but slight. JC has not yet realized the importance of what is called "human interest" in fiction.

14.1 Garnett, Edward. "Joseph Conrad," *Public Opinion*, 17 November 1898, pp. 628–29.

In an excerpt from a review in the London *Academy* for 15 October, JC is said to have "the poetic realism of the great Russian novels." His art is compared to great music because "the author's intense fidelity to the life he has observed seems to melt and fade away in the lyrical impulse," as seen in *The Nigger of the Narcissus*.

17.1 "New Books: *The Children of the Sea*," *Brooklyn Eagle*, 9 April 1898, p. 5.

A novel of "very unusual strength," *Children of the Sea* suggests that JC will surpass Clark Russell as the sea novelist par excellence with this narrative of "daily life" on board "a common trading vessel," told from the unique point of view of the "common sailor." If the book has a hero, it is the nigger, for the narrative focuses upon the manner in which the crew responds to him in "dumb sympathy." Through its descriptions of the sea and its depiction of the thoughts and feelings of the crewmen, the novel becomes "a masterpiece of realism," accomplishing for the sea what Stephen Crane accomplished for the battlefield, though JC achieves his effects in a simpler manner. His achievement is all the more remarkable because he avoids the usual romantic adventures of sea novels in favor of creating a "panorama of real life" that while devoid of plot is more "vividly picturesque than any romance."

17.2 "New Books, *The Children of the Sea*, " *Indianapolis News*, 13 April 1898, p. 5.

The success of *The Nigger of the Narcissus* in Great Britain was so great, its popularity "so instant," as to insure its publication in America, where it has appeared with a new title. The "brutality" of the English title was deemed a possible detriment to its success. The novel paints the most realistic picture of shipboard life since Dana's *Two Years Before the Mast*, recounting a daily record of the seaman's experience not from the point of view of a detached observer but from that of participant, who suffers with the crew, sympathizes with them, and conveys his sympathies to us. The characterizations of Donkin, James Wait, and Captain Allistoun are particularly effective.

17.3 "New Books," *St. Paul Pioneer Press* (Minnesota), (14 August 1898). p. 17.

Children of the Sea is the powerful story of a shipload of sailors, presumably of the "commonest type." Presented in a manner that is real to the eye and ear, they emerge as tragic figures. Developing all of the possibilities presented by a voyage from India to England, JC makes the central figure a Negro dying of tuberculosis who, "though uninteresting in himself and in some sense obnoxious to the entire crew, becomes the chief . . . interest of their common life." Although the story is not pleasant, JC endows it with "that strong biting flavor" pleasing "to the artistic palate, which modified and kept in place by other qualities made Stevenson's sea stories so satisfying."

17.4 "New Books," *St. Paul Pioneer Press* (Minnesota), 31 July 1898, p. 17.

Whereas *Tales of Unrest* contains stories of "remarkable power," its fatalism and pessimistic tone work against its success. The most successful story is "The Idiots," which paints a "striking" picture of despair; "The Return" is equally effective though more subtle.

17.5 "New Books: *Tales of Unrest, Indianapolis News,* 4 May 1898, p. 5.

Tales of Unrest resembles *The Nigger of the Narcissus* in its "vividness of detail and characterization." "Well worth reading," its five stories are "set in the waste places of the earth." While none of the work is dull, "An Outpost of Progress" is the most effective piece in the collection.

17.6 "New Publications," *Publisher's Weekly,* No. 1366, (2 April 1898), p. 605.

[Notes the publication of *Tales of Unrest* and *The Children of the Sea,* describing the plot of the latter work.]

17.7 "*The Nigger of the Narcissus,*" *NYTSRB,* 28 May 1898, p. 344.

[After decrying the change of the title of *The Nigger of the Narcissus* in America, the anonymous reviewer calls *Nigger* a great sea novel, but notes that it will not lure boys to the sea because it leaves one "with a new and profound impression of the tragic helplessness of the sailor's life."]

19.1 O'Brien, Desmond B. "Letters on Books," *Truth* (London), XLIII (19 May 1898), pp. 1262–63.

Tales of Unrest will sustain the sudden reputation which *An Outcast of the Islands* conferred upon JC. His "descriptions of Malayan scenes and scenery" remain vigorous and vivid, but his one excursion into London, "The Return," relies on overdone and ineffective psychology.

19.2 "Our Awards for 1897: The 'Crowned' Books," *Academy, LIII* (15 January 1898), p. 47.

Among the contenders for the *Academy's* prizes for the best books of 1897, *The Nigger of the Narcissus* seemed "slight and episodic" and was rejected, even though it is a remarkably imaginative book, expressing "striking literary power."

21.1 Quiller-Couch, A.T. [Review of *The Nigger of the Narcissus*], *Pall Mall Magazine*, XIV (March 1898), pp. 428–29.

The characters in *The Nigger of the Narcissus* are "the most plausibly life-like set of rascals that ever sailed through the pages of fiction." JC is like Crane and Browning in several ways, and his power to squeeze "emotion and colour" out of the situations he presents is very great.

27.1 [Review of *The Nigger of the Narcissus*], *Army and Navy Gazette*, 19 February 1898, p. 195.

The Nigger of the Narcissus is "a psychological study of great value and interest" which deserves high commendation for its description of the storm at sea. JC possesses "a knowledge of seamanship which is rather surprising in modern fiction" but which is "so technical that we should rather doubt whether the book can be properly appreciated by the landsman."

27.2 [Review of *The Nigger of the Narcissus*], *Christian World*, XLII (27 January 1898), p. 13.

The Nigger of the Narcissus is told from the point of view of a crewman with such skill that the reader is persuaded that JC "must have been one of the 'hands' of the old ship."

27.3 [Review of *The Nigger of the Narcissus*], *Country Life*, 1 January 1898, p. 544.

[Like *Captains Courageous* in some ways, the plot of *The Nigger of the Narcissus* is thinner than Kipling's, but the marvelous force of JC's scenes of seafaring life, his description of the storm, and his special capacity to compress "a vivid picture into a sentence" excel Kipling's writing.

27.4 [Review of *The Nigger of the Narcissus*], *Guardian* (London), 2 February 1898, p. 106.

The Nigger of the Narcissus is an original novel which is "in some ways exceedingly good." JC's depiction of the "unidealized" crew of the ship—particularly Donkin, Belfast, and Wait—is effective, but the book occasionally lags and the effect of James Wait on the crew seems both "exaggerated and improbable."

27.5 [Review of *The Nigger of the Narcissus*], *Literature*, 26 March 1898, p. 354.

The absence of plot, love interest, and conventional incidents of life aboard ship make *The Nigger of the Narcissus* "unique" among pieces of seaboard life in its portrayal of the "hard, bitter, strenuous, more or less unconsciously brave, and almost wholly unconsciously dignified . . . life of the seafaring man." The book is "an 'epical' fragment" whose "inarticulate and indispensable" characters possess a "tragic appeal" and whose power can be traced to the author's "vivid, dynamic, often almost too consciously acute and nervous style." Its one weakness lies in the fact that JC's passion for the "right word" leads him to "relapse into artifice."

27.6 [Review of *The Nigger of the Narcissus*], *Pearson's Weekly*, 15 January 1898, p. 2.

The "freshness of style" and the "revelation of unexpected reflection" contained in *The Nigger of the Narcissus* fascinate the reader against his own will by making him realize the "terrors of life on a sailing vessel . . . with a fresh sense of awfulness."

27.7 [Review of *The Nigger of the Narcissus*], *Speaker*, (London), 15 January 1898, pp. 83–84.

The Nigger of the Narcissus reflects the influence of Crane's *The Red Badge of Courage* in that both JC and Crane "aspire to make visible to us the inside of great scenes." The novel presents "a wonderful picture" which "*looks* like the truth," which is valuable for its "vivid colouring," and which "bites into the mind of the spectator."

27.8 [Review of *Tales of Unrest*], *Cosmopolis*, XI (August 1898), 412.

JC is the only living writer who approaches Kipling, sharing with that author "reticence, dramatic power, mastery over both ideas and language" and disregard for sentimentality. His work is notable for the poetic beauty of his descriptions and its brutal acceptance of the unpleasant facts of life and human character.

27.9 [Review of *Tales of Unrest*], *Saturday Evening Gazette* (Boston), 9 April 1898, p. 86.

Like a "skillful cook devoting all his talents to the serving up of putrid game," JC tells "unpleasant" tales, but tells them in a "most artistic manner." Concerned with "morbid psychology," stories such as "Karain" and "The Idiot" are told with great "vigor" and contain "descriptive portions . . . written with rare artistic taste." Nonetheless, despite JC's "strong, bold and vivid" storytelling, the works in the collection remain "unwholesome and ugly."

27.10 "Reviews: *Tales of Unrest,*" *Academy Supplement,* 16 April 1898, pp. 417–18.

In *Tales of Unrest,* JC reveals the fact that he has seen "strange things . . . and can describe what he has seen impersonally, incuriously, without sentimentality, and without wailing," presenting inevitable tragedy without attempting to suggest "why heaven remains sealed and unanswering" or "why illusions are better aid to living than the naked truth." A "writer's writer," he requires in his tales that the reader assimilate his background to comprehend the significance of those figures who appear in his "middle distance." He brings "the same restraint, the same artful choice of words and the same sincerity of expression" to "The Return," which treats a modern subject, as he brings to his stories set in more exotic locales.

27.11 "A Set of Six," *Outlook* (London), XXXI (22 August 1898), p. 296.

JC enjoys "a lonely eminence among modern novelists," being "unique in the union of a realistic intellect with an absolute imagination." The stories in *A Set of Six* reveal the "veneer of social humanity . . . cracking under the pressure of the instincts." The collection will delight JC's audience and bring him many new readers.

28.1 "Some New Novels," *DN,* 7 January 1898, p. 6.

One seldom encounters "a book so strong and original as *The Nigger of the Narcissus.*" Wait's position in the novel is clearly pivotal, every member of the crew is convincingly individualized, and the entire work is a finely realized portrait of the sea in a book that creates the impression of a work of art.

29.1 Symons, Arthur. "Arthur Symons on Kipling and Conrad," *SR,* 29 January 1898, pp. 145–46; rpt. as "Arthur Symons on Kipling and Conrad" in CCH, pp. 97–98.

Kipling's *Captains Courageous* is an admirable mystery of a "single bit of objective reality of the adventure of a trade"; JC's *The Nigger of the Narcissus* is an almost endless description of "a ship and its company during a storm," but the idea that such things as these "should be but servants" has been left out.

29.2 Symons, Arthur. "D'Annunzio in English," *SR,* LXXXV (29 January 1898), pp. 145–46.

English literature has produced no works comparable to D'Annunzio's. Two recent novels, *Captains Courageous* by Kipling and *The Nigger of the Narcissus* by JC, display "admirable mastery of a single bit of objective reality."

29.3 "A Tale of the Sea," *Literary World*, LVII (28 January 1898), pp. 78–79.

The Nigger of the Narcissus, "a wonderful and fascinating piece of workmanship," contains excellent description and characterization and reminds the reader of Crane: "There is the same virility, the same extraordinary force and fluency of phrasing. Blemishes there are and mostly they lie in the direction of a want of restraint and a too realistic rendering of forecastle dialogue."

29.4 "*Tales of Unrest*," *Academy*, LIII (16 April 1898), pp. 417–18.

JC, who has visited strange places and "seen strange things," describes what he has witnessed "impersonally, uncuriously, without sentimentality and without wailing" in *Tales of Unrest*, a volume of stories possessed of a sense of "tragic inevitability." His stories are remarkable for his vivid descriptive power, a power which he applies equally well in dealing with the Malay setting of three tales and the domestic tragedy, "The Return," which is set in contemporary London. With this volume and *The Nigger of the Narcissus*, JC, who is a "writer's writer," acquires a reputation "to be reckoned with."

30.1 "Talks About Books," *Chautauquan*, XXVII (July 1898), p. 428.

JC chose an appropriate title for *Tales of Unrest*, for the stories in the volume are "veritable pen pictures of mental agitations with very appropriate scenic surroundings in which the effect is suggested without any elaborations of detail."

30.2 [*Tales of Unrest*], *Daily Mail* (London), 12 April 1898, p. 3 [not seen in this form]; rpt. as "Unsigned Review" in CCH, p. 103.

The stories in *Tales of Unrest* show great "breadth of view," "much power," and "a conspicuous lack of literary training." JC's grammar is weak and his "general method" is "slipshod." "The Return," however, grips and holds "by sheer force" of the author's psychological insight and his unusual ability "to see common things in an uncommon way."

30.3 [*Tales of Unrest*], *DT*, 9 April 1898, p. 8 [not seen in this form]; rpt. as "Unsigned Review" in CCH, pp. 101–02.

Tales of Unrest is correctly named for the unrest that comes from "a constant struggle against a gloomy and burdensome fate." The finest story is "Karain, A Memory." JC's depiction of Malaya is real, "drawn to the life." The "sheer morbid horror" of "The Idiots" does not lie within the province of the novelist. Gloomy and "fantastically" morbid in "An Outpost of Progress," JC should choose more pleasant themes for future work.

30.4 Zangwill, I[srael]. "A Reviewer's Puzzle," *Academy* (London), 1 January 1898, pp. 1–2 [not seen in this form]; rpt. as "Unsigned Review" in CCH, pp. 94–96.

Although *The Nigger of the Narcissus* contains much good writing, it has weaknesses: the material is too slight for the length of the book, the tale has no plot, and it has no motif to lead the reader on. As a long story, it lacks organic unity and fails to exhibit character "under many lights"; it has only atmosphere. Gradations of light and shade are lost. Even if the author is clever, his "first duty . . . is to interest." [A serious attempt at criticism. This reviewer may have led JC to introduce Marlow in *Lord Jim* and "Heart of Darkness" as a narrator whose language is appropriate to his position as a sailor.]

1899

31.1 Lutoslawski, Wincenty. "Emigracja zdolnosci" (Emigration of Talents), *KRAJ* (St. Petersburg), No. 12 (1899); rpt. in WSOC.

Expressions of regret are often heard in Poland when anyone with unusual talents settles in a foreign country, seeking a wider arena for his activities. When JC was interviewed near London and was asked why he did not write in Polish, he replied, "I value our Polish literature too highly to introduce my incompetent piping. But my talents suffice for the English, and assure me my daily bread." The truth is that Polish literature is mostly of the gentry. The purpose of a literary work is the distribution of thoughts and feelings. The work of Poles executed abroad is not lost for the Polish nation; it is the fruit of the Polish spirit. [In Polish.]

1900

37.1 Courtney, W. L. [Difficulties in Reading *Lord Jim*], *DT*, 7 November 1900, p. 11 [not seen in this form]; rpt. as "Review" in CCH, pp. 114–15.

In *Lord Jim* , JC suffers from an "exuberance of ideas"—too many episodes and side issues. The reader has "to work, positively work, through some eighty or ninety pages" before arriving at any conception of the author's design. And JC has such unusual strength and power that his "faults of method" are especially regrettable. Even if the book contains "charming" character sketches, many fantastic or tender situations, "the appetite is wearied with an excess of good fare."

38.1 [Jim As a Romantic], *DN*, 14 December 1900, p. 6 [not seen in this form]; rpt. as "Unsigned Review" in CCH, pp. 124–25.

Aside from such "defects of style" as the useless "wandering" of the story in a "morass of wonderful language and incomprehensible events," *Lord Jim*, of epic proportions, is "powerfully enthralling." The central idea is Jim, around whom everything revolves. Although Jim is a sailor and a "visionary," he is no coward, as events later in the story prove. *Jim* is the "dramatic history of an uncomprehended and tortured soul—the soul of a dreamer" who rises, under affliction, to "even higher flights of altruism and self-sacrifice." The book is an "artistic success."

39.1 [*Lord Jim*], *MG*, 29 October 1900, p. 6 [not seen in this form]; rpt. as "Unsigned Review" in CCH, pp. 111–113.

Lord Jim displays "remarkable originality and merit." The curious "mechanism" of the story includes a long story, too long to be told in one night, but the "essential construction" of the work is "fine and right." This is a book to make the world "wider and deeper": it is moral because "morality is at the root of humanity, and it is profoundly true." An entire gallery of sketches and portraits other than that of Jim is "hardly less perfect of their kinds."

39.2 [*Lord Jim*], *Spectator* (London), 24 November 1900, p. 753 [not seen in this form]; rpt. as "Unsigned Review" in CCH, pp. 119–20.

JC writes, in *Lord Jim*, not of the "vagaries of fashion or of pseudo-culture," but of unfamiliar regions "amid outlandish surroundings." The "sombre fascination," however, arises from the "poignant interest" of his tale, the "restrained yet fervid eloquence" of the style, the "vividness of the portraiture," and the "subtlety of psychological analysis," all of which are united in this "remarkable" and "engrossing" novel.

39.3 "The Phantasmagoria of the East," *Pall Mall Gazette* (London), 5 December 1900, p. 4 [not seen in this form]; rpt. as "Unsigned Review" in CCH, pp. 122–24.

JC belongs to "a certain school" which finds its expression best in "very intense and subtle analysis," but the result is a "definite formlessness," a disproportion, as in *Lord Jim*. This novel is also a "very broken-backed" narrative, consisting of two separate episodes with only the character of Jim to provide unity. The book is "tedious, over-elaborated, and more than a little difficult to read." [The first occasion on which *Jim* was unfavorably criticized for being "broken-backed".]

39.4 [The Philosophical Romance], *Speaker* (London), 24 November 1900, pp. 215–16 [not seen in this form]; rpt. as "Unsigned Review" in CCH, pp. 120–22.

Lord Jim is a profound psychological study of the discovery by a romantic young sailor that he is not as brave as he thought himself to be. His experiences in Patusan almost give him complete confidence. Accident, however, removes the confidence of the savages, and he leaves a "living woman" to pursue a shadowy ideal of conduct. JC uses different points of view so effectively that he seems to have solved one of the major difficulties of the "philosophical romance."

39.5 [Review of *Lord Jim*], *Sketch* (London), 14 November 1900, p. 142 [not seen in this form]; rpt. as "Unsigned Notice" in CCH, p. 118.

Lord Jim is a "short character sketch, written and rewritten to infinity, dissected into shreds masticated into tastelessness"; but the little story there is "undeniably the work of a man of genius."

40.1 [Two Reviews of *Lord Jim*], *New York Tribune*, 3 November 1900, p. 10 [not seen in this form]; rpt. as "Two Early Reviews" in JCLJ, pp. 359–60.

The expansion of *Lord Jim* to a "full fledged" novel does not spoil the "simplicity and balance of the design." What JC says is absorbing, but even more so is the way he says it. As for the story, on a calm tropical night, the *Patna* "goes to the bottom like a shot" [sic], leaving Jim the choice of helping some of the sleeping pilgrims or of jumping from the ship. He jumps, and he pays for his "bodily salvation" by years of remorse. Marlow "muses like an oracle," making Jim's story a "record of little truths," like a mosaic. *Jim*, a difficult book to read, is a work of "great originality." [A perfect example of misreading a book.]

40.2 [Two Reviews of *Lord Jim*] *Spectator* (London), LXXXV (24 November 1900), 753 [not seen in this form]; rpt. as "Two Early Reviews in JCLJ, pp. 360–62.

JC's subject matter is too detached form "actuality" to please the "great and influential section of readers." His scenes are laid in

"unfamiliar regions, amid outlandish surroundings." But JC, beyond
all other writers, has identified himself with the standpoint of the
natives so as to interpret their aspirations and illuminate their
motives. In *Lord Jim,* the central figure finds at last, in Patusan,
"beyond the ken of civilization," the occasion of rehabilitating
himself in his own esteem. This "strange narrative" contains a
"poignant interest," a "restrained yet fervid eloquence of style," the
"vividness of portraiture," and the "subtlety of psychoanalysis" which
are reunited in JC's best work.

1901

40.3 Cooper, Frederic T. "The Sustained Effort and Some Recent
    Novels," *B,* XVIII (1901), pp. 309–14.

Traditional distinctions of length separating the short story and
the novel are blurred in the works of many modern writers, but JC
compresses "a world-wide theme into the limits of a few pages" while
"stretching out some transitory theme into the bulk of a portly
volume." "The Heart of Blackness" [sic] is an example of the former
practice; *The Nigger of the Narcissus,* an example of the latter.

46.1 P., J.B. [Conrad's "Psychologic" Story], *Critic* (New York), May
    1901, pp. 437–38 [not seen in this form]; rpt. as "Unsigned
    Review" in CCH, pp. 127–28.

The plot of *Lord Jim* is like a "marvellous" spider web, a "marvel"
of workmanship; it is the "psychologic" study of a romantic young
man who meets fear and is conquered. If a man without fear exists,
the story will be simply "the involved and somewhat tedious history
of a young man who yielded to an impulse of fear and then gave his
life to living down the sequences"; for a man who fears, this book will
have both "fascination" and "moral lesson."

46.2 [Too Much in *Lord Jim*], *Bookman* (London), February 1901; rpt.
    unchanged in B, April 1901 [not seen in this form]; rpt. as
    "Unsigned Review" in CCH, p. 126.

Lord Jim is very serious and depressing. "There is no bad work in
it, but there is far too much good—which amounts to the same thing."
The book is "all Jim"; nothing else counts. Jim is "a romanticist, a
sentimentalist, a sailor made of fine stuff"; speaking "brutally," he
"proved himself a coward"; speaking charitably, he "lost his
opportunity." But he knows show to expiate his "mistake." Judged as
a story, *Jim* may find adverse criticism; judged as a document, it
"must be acknowledged a masterpiece."

1902

48.1 "Mr. Conrad's New Book," *MG*, 10 December 1902, p. 3 [not seen in this form]; rpt. as "Unsigned Review" in CCH, pp. 134–35.

In *Youth: A Narrative and Two Other Stories*, "The End of the Tether" is admirable, but relaxed in tension in comparison with the other two stories. For JC, "Youth" is not the time of freedom and delight, but "the test, the trial of life." And "Heart of Darkness" is also a significant adventure of youth, but in *Youth* JC makes no "attack upon colonisation, expansion, even upon Imperialism." Justice, "cheap ideals," and "platitudes of civilisation" are "shrivelled up" in the heat of youth "in the toils."

1903

57.1 "Joseph Conrad," *Book News Monthly*, XXI (April 1903), p. 594.

[A brief but inaccurate life of JC which shows how the writer's life has "from the beginning been rich in change."]

58.1 "Mr. Conrad's Philosophy," *Glasgow Evening News*, 30 April 1903, p. 2 [not seen in this form]; rpt. as "Unsigned Review" in CCH, pp. 148–50.

Very deep in JC's philosophy of life is his "intensely individualistic regard" of the essential loneliness of the human soul "face to face with the universe." This problem in all his writings has been the revelation of the soul "wrestling with or sinking beneath its own weakness, thru [sic] elemental forces of nature, or the mysterious force of circumstances"—struggling, yielding, suffering—but "always solitary, individual, isolated." The four stories in *Typhoon, and Other Stories*, though, are of little importance.

61.1 "Recent Fiction: 'Falk,'" *Literary World* (Boston), XXXIV (November 1903), p. 308.

Though not up to the standard of "Youth" and *Lord Jim*, "Falk" is "one of the best books of the autumn." The characters in the story "breathe of the sea and the East as only Mr. Conrad can make his characters live and breathe" while "To-morrow" and "Amy Foster" are "permeated with the sea and made sad and pitiful by the tragedy of the ocean."

62.1 "The Sea Between Covers: Mr. Joseph Conrad's New Book," *Daily Mail* (London), 22 April 1903, p. 4 [not seen in this form]; rpt. as "Unsigned Review" in CCH, pp. 145–47.

In *Typhoon, and Other Stories*, JC is, more nearly than any other author, a "real and intimate" interpreter of the sea in literature. In "Amy Foster," as well as in the other stories, it is not so much the characters in the story who live as it is the "great neighboring sea" that lives in them. And JC is a master in his treatment of the primitive "passion of love."

64.1 [*Typhoon, and Other Stories*], *Speaker* (London), 6 June 1903, pp. 238–39 [not seen in this form]; rpt. as "Unsigned Review" in CCH, pp. 157–58.

The four stories in *Typhoon, and Other Stories* are "interesting exercises," all concerned with the sea, JC's "source of inspiration." "Amy Foster" is "one of the most perfect" short stories "we have ever read." JC is "in the line of our great writers of the romance of the sea." Smollett, Michael Scott, Marryat, and he have "introduced something new into our fiction, . . . the psychology of action."

64.2 [Universality in Conrad], *Academy* (London), 25 April 1903 [not seen in this form]; rpt. as "Unsigned Review" in CCH, P. 151.

JC is greater than either Kipling or Bret Harte in his combining a "largeness of literary purpose" and universality. [Quoted largely from the *New York American*, with disapproval of *Typhoon, and Other Stories*: finds JC the "New Great figure in Literature."]

1904

66.1 Barrie, C.D.O. [Review of *Nostromo*], *British Weekly* (London), 10 November 1904, p. 129, [not seen in this form]; rpt. as "Review" in CCH, pp. 169–70.

Nostromo is " a serious study of human characters," with such power that "the most insistent merit of the book is its life." It has also a "sense of movement" and vividness of description, but "judged as an ordinary study, . . . [it] is not well told": the plot is confused, and the story does not move smoothly from incident to incident. [A somewhat typical comment, but more perceptive than several other reviews of this time.]

73.1 Garnett, Edward. "Mr. Conrad's Art," *Speaker* (London), 12 November 1904, pp. 138–39 [not seen in this form]; rpt. as "Review" in CCH, pp. 174–77.

Nostromo is unorthodox in its structure, and its canvas, larger than usual for JC, gives more room to show the "working unity" and the "harmonious balance" of his "fascinating gifts." Except for the lengthy handling of the early history of the silver mine and the "abrupt and hurried" final chapters, scarcely a line in the book is not essential to the development of "this dramatic pageant of life in a South American State." JC's subject is the "great mirage" of the life and nature of the Costaguanan territory. In this work, JC's "special power" is his "poetic sense" for "*the psychology of scene*," out of which "the tiny atom of each man's individual life emerges into right."

73.2 "Joseph Conrad," *Book Review Monthly*, XXIII, September 1904, p. 23.

Although JC knew both Polish and French well and did not begin to learn English "until he was nineteen years old," at age thirty-eight he "suddenly was moved to write." He expressed his "literary creed" in the passage in *Nigger* containing his major "aim" of making the reader feel and see, and although this experience is "a bit pompous and upon first thought even seems bombastic," his achievement has justified this aim.

74.1 [*Nostromo*], *Black and White* (London), 5 November 1904, p. 668 [not seen in this form]; rpt. as "Unsigned Notice" in CCH, pp. 166–67.

In *Nostromo*, JC "has hidden what grain of romance or of realism was in him under a multitude of words and lowering paragraphs." What "truth of life" he intended cannot be understood.

74.2 [*Nostromo*] *Illustrated London News*, 26 November 1904, p. 774 [not seen in this form]; rpt. as "Unsigned Notice" in CCH, p. 180.

Nostromo is formless and makes too great a demand on the reader's concentration, but if not JC's most perfect piece of work, it is "incomparably the work which most clearly shows his extraordinary power."

75.1 [*Nostromo*], *Review of Reviews* (London), 1 November 1904, p. 539 [not seen in this form]; rpt. as "Unsigned Notice" in CCH, p. 166.

Nostromo is "hardly up to" JC's previous work.

77.1 [The Powerful World of *Nostromo*], *MG*, 2 November 1904, p. 5 [not seen in this form]; rpt. as "Unsigned Review" in CCH, pp. 171–73.

Again, in *Nostromo*, JC has imagined a "vast and solemn world full of passion and mystery," even if he seems sometimes to "lose sight of the end or to obscure the design." Eventually, though, the reader may "perceive something of a design that is independent of

formal construction," and the art of the narrative finally brings the
"strange array of characters and figures into significant relations." In
a corner of the world that is "hardly worthy of our perfunctory and
impatient regard," JC finds a "richness and variety of life that cannot
be matched in our careful civilizations." Against the "barbaric forces"
of this region are ranged "respectable patriots, vaporous
Parliamentarians, a general who had received a command out of
consideration for his creditors." Decoud is JC's "mouthpiece."
Nostromo is a curious but not quite convincing egotist. The entire
presentation of this "new and strange world" is, though, "very
powerful and very fascinating."

77.2 [Shapeless *Nostromo*], *TLS*, 21 October 1904, p. 320 [not seen in
this form]; rpt. as "Unsigned Review" in CCH, pp. 164–65.

In *Nostromo*, JC has made a novel of a short story, and the drama
is "overwhelmed by machinery." The narrative is largely "allegation
rather than proof." A "shapeless work," satisfying "only
occasionally," this book is "never undistinguished." As a whole,
though, it is disappointing.

77.3 [Weaknesses in *Nostromo*], *DT*, 9 November 1904, p. 4 [not seen
in this form]; rpt. as "Unsigned Review" in CCH, pp. 167–69.

In *Nostromo*, JC has "almost a touch of genius," but not enough
of "that divine spark to atone for the lack of artistic instinct which
always mars his work as a whole." Whereas parts of the novel have
an "absorbing interest," the work as a whole has "longeurs of a
wearisome nature," "vital situations" suffer while the author
"indulges in characteristic digressions, "detail absorbs the position
of outline"—"the spell is broken." The original conception, fine as it
is, fails because of the absence of the "faculty of construction." JC
shows "extraordinary power" in delineating his minor characters,
but he is less successful with the most conspicuous figures.

77.4 Weslawska, Emilia. "Przedmowa do *Lorda Jima* w przekladzie z
1904 t" (Preface to *Lord Jim* in the 1904 Translation), *Lorda Jima*,
(Warsaw: Silorski, 1904) [not seen in this form]; rpt. in *WSOC*, pp.
31–34.

We can only admire the linguistic talents of JC and the power of
his descriptive passages and atmosphere. His favorite theme is the
transformation of the ideas and instincts of civilized individuals in
barbaric surroundings and of the fatal power of sensual love. But his
stories have a marked monotony and his landscapes are uniformly
somber, though he has flashes of humor. He rarely goes straight to
the point and is indifferent if he bores or confuses his readers. In
some works he overestimates the interest in exotic adventures and

quarrels between Malaysian or Arab characters. *Lord Jim* has no love interest, but it is permeated by Romanticism; only a Slav could have written it. JC betrays too much "trembling of the spirit" to be regarded as foreign. [In Polish.]

1905

81.1 Gomulicki, Wiktor. "Polak czy Anglik?" (Pole or Englishman?), *Życie I Sztuka* (Warsaw), No. 1, 1905; rpt. in *COKS*, pp. 731–35.

The content of *Lord Jim*, recently translated into Polish, is entirely English and maritime. A Polish reader can only describe its form as "eccentric," which is a trait Poles find objectionable in the English. The English do not write simply; they produce a labyrinth in which a Polish reader finds his way only with an effort. JC does this to a high degree. In *Jim*, it is as though the printer had placed the middle at the end. This is not a reproach to JC. Perhaps it is all symbolic? But only JC can tell us that. [In Polish.]

81.2 Komornicka, M. "*Lord Jim,*" *Chimera* (Warsaw), IX (1905), pp. 333-34 [not seen in this form]; rpt. in *COKS*, pp. 739–40.]

Lord Jim is unusual in content and artistry and is a delight for the most fastidious reader. It is a drama of heroic imagination and idealized egoism by an author who is cultivated to a standard almost unattainable in Poland. He ranks with the greatest English masters of the novel. [In Polish.]

82.1 O[verland], M. U. "Joseph Conrad and Henry James," *NYTSRB*, 4 February 1905, p. 74.

The publication of a letter in the *New York Times Saturday Review of Books* (14 January 1905), largely laudatory of JC's *Nostromo*, throws "new light" on the "wordiness" of this novel. It appears that JC, like Henry James, having said by this time all he had to say that was worth saying, intends to enter upon the "same futile word play Henry James entered upon some ten or twelve years ago." The only trouble with James's later novels is that "from the point of view of all honest persons . . . there is too little, if anything, in the books at all worth understanding." One must suppose that for the last decade James has allowed the public to buy his "trash." [Unfair, of course, to both James and JC. But supports the theory of the latter's "achievement and decline," which was developed much later, especially by Thomas C. Moser in *Joseph Conrad: Achievement and Decline* (1957).]

82.2 O[verland], M. U. "Some Criticism of Joseph Conrad and His
Critics—Nostromo, the 'Vanishing Hero,'" *NYTSRB*, 21 January
1905, p. 42.

The elusiveness of construction and the hide-and-seek
confusion of characters are two important charms of *Nostromo*, and
they are at once evident to the veteran novel reader. But JC faults
himself by using words merely for the sake of using them—words
which say little or words which are meant only to sell. The reader's
interest, nevertheless, is continuously renewed, so that when the
reader gives up the man Nostromo for lost, he appears on stage again
with all his glitter until the reader is tantalized to know more of him.

84.1 Wright, Edward. "The Romance of the Outlands," *Quarterly
Review, CCIII* (July 1905), pp. 55–61.

JC has developed an elaborate romantic style which, while
occasionally burdened with too many epithets, is luxuriant and
picturesque. Since his attention, though, falls primarily on the
particular temperament of an individual, he tends to neglect action
and the effects of character interaction. His focus on the
temperament does not, however, lead him into an overly melancholic
point of view, but is saved from this by a romantic sense of life.

1906

[No entries for this year.]

1907

95.1 [Arnold Bennett on *The Secret Agent*], 25 September 1907, *The
Journals of Arnold Bennett*, ed by Newman Flower (1932), I. 256–
57 [not seen in this form]; rpt. in CCH, p. 190.

The Secret Agent is a "sort of sensationalism sternly treated on
the plane of realistic psychology. . . .Nothing but a single episode told
to the last drop." Coming after *Nostromo*, the novel gives a
"disappointing effect of slightness." [In 1912, Bennett was much
kinder to *Agent*.]

95.2 [An Attack on Conrad], *Country Life* (London), 21 September
1907, pp. 403–05 [not seen in this form]; rpt. as "Unsigned
Review" in CCH, pp. 186–89.

"A less amusing set of people never filled the imaginary world of
a novelist" than those in *The Secret Agent*. Verloc and his wife are

dull and the revolutionists are "stagey." JC is not convincing; the entire book is "indecent." [An imperceptive attack on *Agent*; its strengths are taken for weaknesses and its humor misconstrued.]

99.1 Galbraith. "Joseph Conrad Has Many Plans," *NYTSRB*, 16 November 1907, p. 726.

JC is now living in Bedfordshire, working on a novel called *Chance*, which will be completed by the end of the year. He says that his novel is a story of the sea, "a discursive sort of thing; by no means what the reviewers call 'a well-told story.'" He is also engaged in completing "The Duel: A Military Story," which he plans for *McClure's*, and an English serial. For the future, he plans a large novel with its setting in London and another novel which will be European in scale.

99.2 Garnett, Edward. [Some Insight into *The Secret Agent*], *N*, 28 September 1907 [not seen in this form]; rpt. a "Unsigned Review" in CCH, pp. 191–93.

By his "astonishing mastery" of English, JC makes clear to his English audience, in *The Secret Agent*, the secrets of Slav thought and feeling. The secret of his power is his possession of a philosophy "impartial in its scrutiny of the forces of human nature, and his "ironical insight" into the natural facts of life serves him well instead of his usual backgrounds of tropical skies and seas. He goes "down into the dim recesses of human motive," even to that of the "real heroine" of the story, Mr. Verloc's mother-in-law. [Even Garnett failed to understand this novel fully.]

99.3 "A Great Book," *Glasgow News*, 3 October 1907, p. 5 [not seen in this form]; rpt. as "Unsigned Review" in CCH, pp. 195–97.

JC's Polish birth has caused him to import a new mood and temperament into English literature: a "grave irony" or a "faint tinge of melancholy"—something "Slavonic." *The Secret Agent* is not only a "masterly revelation" of some unfamiliar aspects of London but also a "revelation of all human life itself." JC leaves here the impression of "absolute truth, of profound and comprehensive knowledge of human nature."

99.4 "Joseph Conrad—A Unique Writer of the Sea," *Current Literature*, XLII, No. 1 (January 1907), 58–59.

JC has made the mundane routine life at sea remarkably understandable as only a poet or a psychologist could do. Much of JC's current unpopularity results from the subjective quality of his work. It has an indirect and melancholy charm, but such charm does not appeal to the public. "Heart of Darkness" is a sinister narrative, and *The Mirror of the Sea* is frankly autobiographical. [Includes a brief biography and a long quotation from *Mirror*.]

100.1 MacCarthy, Desmond. "*The Secret Agent*," *Apollo Review* (London), II (1907), 229–34.

In *The Secret Agent*, JC is concerned with the portrayal of the "inner history" of the Greenwich Park outrage. While his plot has much in common with "sensational literature," his vivid description and keen psychological insight allow him to charge the "slow and furtive lives of his principal characters and their surroundings with Balzacian significance," and like Balzac, JC uses details that are "definite and real" but which "give the impression of having been imagined and then felt, rather than observed and recorded." While JC's earlier works have achieved their impact through their cumulative effect, *Agent* is far more concentrated and reveals the influence of Henry James upon his work.

100.2 Monkhouse, A. N. [*The Secret Agent*], *MG*, 12 September 1907 [not seen in this form]; rpt. as "Review" in CCH, PP. 181–84.

In *The Secret Agent*, JC "breaks fresh ground" in his "grim comedy of anarchism." "If it be straining the conception of comedy to find in it the idea of madness and despair attempting the renovation of the world, the story that enforces this idea is rich in comic types and details." Here "the obscure and terrible is revealed as comic." [This appears to be the first instance in which JC's "sordid" tale was considered for its comic elements.]

102.1 [Portraying a Real World], *Truth* (London), 2 October 1907, p. 817 [not seen in this form]; rpt. as "Unsigned Notice" in CCH, p. 194.

The Secret Agent is "notable" for its simplicity, for JC's freedom from his Jamesian "intricacies of style." This book displays the seamy side of "unfortunately too possibly real a world," but it does so with "humor and imagination."

102.2 [*The Secret Agent*], *Star* (London), 5 October 1907, p. 1 [not seen in this form]; rpt. as "Unsigned Notice" in CCH, P. 198.

The imaginative force of *The Secret Agent* is "terrible." JC "stirs and mixes" London "into his characters," nearly all alien anarchists; one feels "its fat, foul, heavy mysterious presence behind these strange dim folk who move like fish in a dingy aquarium." The "imaginative realism" of the murder of Verloc is "the fine art of murder in fiction."

1908

1.05.1 Courtney, W. L. [Conrad and Nature], *DT*, 12 August 1908, p. 4 [not seen in this form]; rpt. as "Review" in CCH, pp. 213–17.

Although JC is interested in his characters, his "puppets," he is much more interested in the forces of nature, the "obscure dominion of fate," and the "unyielding tyranny of circumstance." For him, the best and wisest man does the work at hand with "greatest amount of efficiency." "Gaspar Ruiz," "The Brute," and "An Anarchist" are "fine achievements," even if JC's philosophy is a dreary one. He belongs to the "modern" school of "psychological violence."

107.1 [From "On Ugliness in Fiction"], *Edinburgh Review*, April 1908 [not seen in this form]; rptd as "Unsigned Article" in CCH, pp. 201–02.

The reviewer selects *The Secret Agent* as an example of modern ugliness in fiction. After a synopsis of the plot, he concludes that "If any embellishment of art, or service to society, is done by the concoction of such a story, clever as it may be, we confess that we fail to detect either."

108.1 Garnett, Edward. "The Genius of Mr. Conrad," *N*, 22 August 1908, pp. 746, 748 [not seen in this form] ; rptd as "Unsigned Review" in CCH, pp. 221–23.

The "humor that plays about his [JC's] stories" is essentially Slav in its ironic acceptance of the pathetic futility of human nature, and quite "un-English" in its refinement of tender, critical malice. The stories in *A Set of Six* are "Continental in their literary affinities, Slav in their psychological insight, and Polish in their haunting and melancholy cadence." "An Anarchist" is a "gem" of JC's art, and "Gaspar Ruiz" is lacking in its "subtlety of atmosphere," but "The Duel" unites all the author's rare capabilities" to produce a "perfect whole."

111.1 Lynd, Robert. [Conrad and Turgenev], *DN*, 10 August 1908, p. 3 [not seen in this form]; rpt as "Review" in CCH, pp. 210–12.

JC, a Pole, should have written in Polish. His story in *A Set of Six*, "Gaspar Ruiz, " is much like Turgenev's "A Lear of the Steppes"; it alone would make the volume of stories memorable. But "The Brute" and "The Duel" especially are very good.

117.1 [*A Set of Six*], *Country Life* (London), 15 August 1908, pp. 234–35 [not seen in this form]; rptd as "Unsigned Review" in CCH, pp. 217–19.

A Set of Six is "no book in any real sense of the term." JC shows his best command of the ironic spirit in "The Duel," but he fails to use irony well. "Gaspar Ruiz," probably the best story in the volume, displays JC's "power of brutal realism," which is "not very great art." [As JC correctly assumed, this review was by Anderson Graham.]

118.1 Thomas, Edward. [*A Set of Six*], *Bookman* (London), October 1908, p. 39 [not seen in this form]; rptd as "Review" in CCH, pp. 225–26.

The stories in *A Set of Six* are "All perfect tales": the substance is "of precious material," the English that "of a master," and the content bearing "a heavy weight of experience, of observation and reflection."

1909

118.2 Magnus, Laurie. *English Literature in the Nineteenth Century* (New York: G. P. Putnam's Sons; London: Andrew Melrose, 1909), 248, 408.

JC does not evade the "remorseless conclusions" derived from the logic of facts. He belongs at the top of the list of writers whose subject is psychology and emotions.

1910

[No entries for this year.]

1911

118.3 "Betrayal," *Pall Mall Gazette* (London), 11 October 1911, p. 5 [not seen in this form]; rptd as "Unsigned Review" in CCH, pp. 227–28.

Under Western Eyes is a "psychologic study of remarkable penetration," one of JC's best. It startles one by its "amazing truth" and the "intimate knowledge of the human heart." Although JC still confuses tenses of verbs, his "nervous and polished" prose is as noteworthy as usual.

122.1 Curle, Richard. [*Under Western Eyes*], *MG*, 11 October 1911, p. 5 [not seen in this form]; rptd as "Review" in CCH, pp. 228–30.

In *Under Western Eyes*, we miss the atmosphere which gave us Jim, Mrs. Gould, and Winnie Verloc; we miss the "enthralling" power that brooded over the destinies of men in JC's earlier "romantic realism." *Eyes* is the work of a great writer for whom psychology is swallowing romance, for whom form is becoming more and more impersonal; something is now lacking so there is "less of original genius." Though not typical of JC's works, it is a "remarkable book," one with a "pitiful" description of tragedy at the end.

125.1 Ford, Ford Madox. *The Critical Attitude*. (London: Duckworth, 1911); rptd. (Freeport, New York: Books for Libraries P, 1967), 88–94.

JC and Henry James, for all their dissimilarity as artists, have in common an extreme literary conscientiousness. They share the defect of a too close engrossment in the matter in hand, leading to digressions. JC is less concerned with spiritual relationships (as is James) than with a sort of material fatalism: for him, every situation in a story must be rendered inevitable. Still, this quality gives his work its extraordinary sense of reality.

125.2 Garnett, Edward. [*Under Western Eyes*], *N*, 21 October 1911, pp. 140–42 [not seen in this form]; rptd as "Unsigned Review" in CCH, pp. 237–39.

The "anonymous chronicler" of *Under Western Eyes* is a "blank screen" on which JC projects a series of psychological analyses of his people's deeds, modes, and temperaments." The "types" of the revolutionary party in part III are etched bitterly, but placed against this "merciless picture" is the "admirable" figure of Sophia Antonovna. But the artistic intensity of the novel lies largely in the "atmospheric effect of the dark national background" and the "rare, precious figure" of Natalia Haldin. [Shortly before his death, Garnett wrote that Miss Haldin is "the weakness of the book."]

129.1 Placci, Carlo. "Joseph Conrad," *Il Marzocco*, *XVI*, 42 (15 October 1911), p. 2.

Although JC is considered the greatest living English novelist, his works show some inexplicable faults, especially in the writer's involuted narrative technique, in his use of timeshifts and multiple narrators [for JC's reply, see Angeleri (1957).] The hero of *Lord Jim* has the same magnetic qualities as those of the Rajah Brooke. *Nostromo* is grandiose canvas, and Decoud is its most memorable character. JC's epic imagination is at times surprising and enrapturing, occasionally tiresome, but he never falls into the vulgarities of the sensational novel nor into Marie Corelli's melodrama. [Review-article: gives summary of *Under Western Eyes*.] [In Italian.]

129.2 "The Riddle of Russia," *MP*, 12 October 1911, p. 3 [not seen in this form]; rptd as "Unsigned Review" in CCH, pp. 213–33.

Under Western Eyes contains JC's usual "intensity of vision," his "complete absorption in and by the subject," and his astonishing mastery of the subtleties of language," and it is constructed with greater ability" than his long stories usually display. JC does not solve the riddle of "Russian freedom"; all the professor can do, which is indeed very much, is to make it clear why he does not understand. It seems that the professor "must have been a Jew, holding the balance between the West and the East." But the racial problem is not the chief interest of the novel: rather *Eyes* is a study in remorse.

129.3 *[Under Western Eyes]*, *Westminster Gazette* (London), 14 October 1911, p. 2 [not seen in this form]; rptd as "Unsigned Review" in CCH, pp. 233–35.

JC bares the Russian soul in *Under Western Eyes*, which therefore becomes "an explanation of the works of Russian novelists"; it is a "brilliantly successful effort to make the Russian comprehensible to the Westerner." JC's characterization here is "some of the most vivid and convincing work" he has ever produced.

1912

130.1 Bennett, Arnold. "Arnold Bennett on *Nostromo*," [a letter of 22 November 1912], *Letters of Arnold Bennett*, ed by James Hepburn, 1968, II, 321–22 [not seen in this form]; rptd as "Arnold Bennett on *Nostromo*" in CCH, p. 161.

Higuerota seems to be the "principal personage" in *Nostromo*, the finest novel of this generation (bar none)."

133.1 Brzozski Stanislaw. "O Jozefie Conradzie" (On Joseph Conrad), *GLOSY WSROD NOCY* (Voices in the Night), (Lwow: Poloniecki, 1912), 369–77.

With Hardy, Kipling, and Wells, JC is one of the most distinguished figures in contemporary English writing. He represents that direction in the English novel most closely connected with the belief that the intellectual structure of a given society, in all its classes and individuals, constitutes its deepest reality. In *Lord Jim*, for example, the protagonist loses his self-respect, and from that moment the entire material world is lost to him. The problem is made more complex and modern because the material world is exotic and one in which our ethics and consciences are something relative and accidental. [Unfinished, published posthumously.] [In Polish.]

133.2 [Conrad and Russia], *Russkoe Bogatstvo*, (Russian Wealth), I (1912), 221; taken from a summary in Roderick Davis, "Under Eastern Eyes: Conrad and Russian Reviewers," CON, VI, No. 2 (1947), 127.

JC tries, with "conscientious attentiveness," to make Russian life easily understood, especially the political activities of such men as the models for the double agent Nikita and police chief Mikulin. But *Under Western Eyes* has no "artistic significance." JC himself observes that he does not have enough of the great gift of imagination and talent. He considers his great worth to be "an adequate knowledge of the Russian language" [thereby seriously confusing the narrator's voice with that of his author's]. Only with "everyday details" does JC "move away from well-known and studied events and facts." Basically, JC "translates the content of Russian political life 'under western eyes' fairly correctly." [In Russian.]

137.1 [Curle, Richard]. "'*Twixt Land and Sea*," *English Review, XII* (November 1912), 668–69.

Concerned with the tropics, the three stories in *'Twixt Land and Sea* are typical of JC's later period in "the finish and precision of the language," but possess "the opulent glow of his earlier, tropical tales." The most remarkable story is "A Smile of Fortune," because it contains two of JC's "most startlingly vivid figures." "The Secret Sharer" is impressive, and "Freya of the Seven Isles" is a "beautiful but very painful story" whose tragic episodes, set "amidst the poisonous luxuriance of the East," may be flawed by the melodramatic nature of the villain of the piece. [Curle claimed this unsigned review in his *A Handlist of the Various Books, Pamphlets, Prefaces, Notes, Articles, Reviews and Letters Written About Joseph Conrad* (Bookville, Pa: 1932).]

137.2 C[urle], R[ichard]. "'*Twixt Land and Sea*," *Everyman*, 24 December 1912, p. 338.

The three stories in JC's latest book, *'Twixt Land and Sea*, mark a reversion to his "earlier and richer" manner of narration, possessing the "rich fancy" and "exuberant touch" of the stories in *Youth*. The most impressive of the three tales is "Freya of the Seven Isles," a tragic love story that is perhaps the "most painful" work JC has produced because of the "extraordinary sense of fatality" hovering over the lives of the characters. Throughout, JC's style is distinguished by his subtle psychology and a controlled use of language that has been "toned down into a mellow but still musical

use of words." *Twixt Land and Sea* is "a book far beyond the capacity
of anyone but a man of genius."

138.1 "Extract from *Spectator*," *Spectator* (London), 16 November
1912, p. 815 [not seen in this form]; rptd as "Extract from
Spectator" in CCH, p. 258.

Although JC has recently been influenced unfavorably by Henry
James, In *'Twixt Land and Sea* he has shaken himself free, to be "as
triumphantly successful in it as he has ever been in the past."

145.1 Lynd, Robert. ['*Twixt Land and Sea*], *DN*, 14 October 1912, p. 8
[not seen in this form]; rptd as "Review" in CCH, pp. 251–53.

As usual in his works, JC creates a living atmosphere as he adds
"nervous sentence to a nervous sentence" in *'Twixt Land and Sea*. He
expresses his sense of life not so much through his human beings as
through his winds and seas and ships. Frequently, his characters
have something of the quality of victims, as in "Freya of the Seven
Isles." In "A Smile of Fortune," a spell is cast on the captain of the
ship; but in "The Secret Sharer," "surely a masterpiece," JC himself
casts a spell. The concluding scene provides "one of the great thrills
of modern literature."

145.2 Masefield, John. ['*Twixt Land and Sea*], *MG*, 16 October 1912, p
7 [not seen in this form] rptd as "Review" in CCH, pp. 254–56.

'Twixt Land and Sea contains three stories written in the "new
and handy" (about one third the length of the ordinary novel), all of
which display JC's complete mastery of his art. "A Smile of Fortune"
is another study in the manner of "Heart of Darkness"; "The Secret
Sharer" is a new "romance" of the sea, a second "Youth"; and "Freya of
the Seven Isles" seems to have its "movement rather clogged" and its
complications a little slow.

158.1 ['*Twixt Land and Sea*] *Standard* (London), 25 October 1912, p. 7
[not seen in this form] rptd as "Unsigned Review" in CCH, pp.
256–58.

In *'Twixt Land and Sea*, JC naming scarcely any theme at all, has
caused us to realize as never before the things he can do. His
achievement, evident in "A Smile of Fortune," is complete in "The
Secret Sharer," the "most perfect" of all of JC's stories. "Freya of the
Seven Isles" is less mysterious in its appeal, but Freya is "perhaps
the most poignant" of all JC's heroines.

159.1 Wells, H. G. "The Contemporary Novel," *Atlantic Monthly*,
CXIX (January 1912), 1–11.

Those novels which survive the test of time to reach "an assured position of recognized greatness" are novels which are "saturated in the personality of the author" and contain "quite unaffected personal outbreaks." While the first personal interventions in Thackeray are "profoundly vulgar," JC's intervention, as in *Lord Jim*, is "done without affectation" and gives his work "a sort of depth, a sort of subjective reality, that no such cold, almost affectedly ironical detachment" such as one finds in Galsworthy "can ever attain."

1913

160.1 "Chronicle and Comment: Joseph Conrad," *B*, XXXVII (August 1913), p. 594.

While JC has not previously received the financial success his work merits, the publication of new editions of *Youth* and "Point of Honour" may indicate that such success is now at hand. "A courageous publisher would have no cause to regret the launching of a uniform edition of Conrad's works."

160.2 "Contemporary Reviews: From *The Independent* (New York), March 6, 1913," *JCHD & SS*, p. 216.

In "The Secret Sharer," JC creates a situation of tension through character rather than incident.

171.1 [*Typhoon, and Other Stories*], *MP*, 22 April 1913, p. 3 [not seen in this form]; rptd as "Unsigned Review" in CCH, pp. 143–44.

Kipling is the only writer of short stories who can be compared with JC, as *Typhoon, and Other Stories* indicates. "Typhoon" contains the "terrible appalling beauty" of the sea, a description of "the elements at war with each other," and the "magnificent picture" of MacWhirr. "Falk," with "a strong dash of horror in it," "To-morrow" with "a touch of the grotesque," and "Amy Foster" give some glimpses of "the pain and terror which have been and must be." But these stories lack that "genial humor" which makes the terrible and the painful "less to be feared."

1914

171.2 Austin, Mary. "A Sermon in One Man," *Harper's Weekly*, LVIII (Part 11), (16 May 1914), 20.

At every port where JC's imagination "puts in, one feels a sense of the continuity of human experience running through" his works.

Chance portrays a ruined financier "as a man of a little cheap cunning" rather than as "the product of an iniquitous 'system.'" Indeed, in all his work, JC is more concerned with "the secret recesses of a man's soul" than with the sociological and moral theories that dominate other contemporary writers.

172.1 Bennett, Arnold. ["Arnold Bennett's Opinion"], (18 January 1914 and 24 January 1914), *The Journals of Arnold Bennett*, ed by Newman Flower (1932), II, 79, 80; rptd as "Arnold Bennett's Opinion" in CCH, p. 276.

Chance is a discouraging book for a writer, "because he damn well knows he can't write as well as this." On the whole, the indirect narrative is "successfully managed," even to "fourth hand narrative."

175.1 [*Chance*, A Work of Wizardry], *Punch* (London), 28 January 1914, p. 79 [not seen in this form]; rptd under "Some Opinions of *Chance*" in CCH, p. 282.

The very best clichés, such as "supersubtle analysis," "intimate psychology," "masterly handling," and "incomparable artistry" are insufficient to describe *Chance;* "the whole thing is much nearer wizardry than workmanship."

176.1 [*Chance*, One of Conrad's Best], *Spectator* (London), 17 January 1914, p. 101 [not seen in this form]; rptd under "Some Opinions of *Chance*" in CCH, p. 281.

It is a "red-letter day" to a reviewer when a new novel like *Chance* "falls to his lot." But it is another matter entirely when he attempts to fulfill his duties as a critic and render justice to "one of the most gifted and original writers of our time."

176.2 [*Chance* Well Planned], *Standard* (London), 16 January 1914, p. 10 [not seen in this form]; rptd under "Some Opinions of *Chance*" in CCH, p. 281.

JC, a "great architect of novels," has planned *Chance* "wonderfully and ingeniously."

176.3 "Chronicle and Comment: Notes on Conrad," *B*, XXXIX (1914), 352–55 (with photographs).

Summarizes the contents of Alfred A. Knopf's *Joseph Conrad: The Romance of His Life and Art* (Garden City: Doubleday, Page, 1914).]

177.1 Colvin, Sir Sidney. [*Chance*, a Work of Genius], *Observer* (London), 18 January 1914, p. 5 [not seen in this form]; rptd in CCH under "Some Opinions of *Chance*," pp. 281–82.

For the last eighteen years, JC has been contributing to our literature work which sets before the reader "the fruits of a remarkable experience" which is enriched greatly "in the ripening light and head of imagination." This work combines, as scarcely any other in our times combines, the "three fold powers of enthralling narrative": "magically vital" description, an "unflagging subtlety and sanity of analytic character study," and work "distinguished by so resourceful a mastery of English speech and style." *Chance* leaves the impression of "a work of genius in the full sense," the "work of a master from which we may all learn." Also, *Chance* should appeal to a wider public than JC's previous works have done. [A very perceptive review of *Chance* for the time, January 1914.]

179.1 Courtney, W. L. [Conrad, A Marvel of Our Literature], *DT*, 21 January 1914, p. 15 [not seen in this form]; rptd under "Some Opinions of *Chance*" in CCH, p. 282.

JC, "one of the marvels of our literature," is probably one of England's best writers. *Chance* is comparable with *Lord Jim* and *Nostromo;* the interest of the novel does not depend on plot. It arises partly from the literary style, partly from an "acute psychological analysis," and partly from the "peculiar technique and workmanship," which this book "in a superlative degree, exhibits."

179.2 Cross, Ethan A. "'Heart of Darkness' by Joseph Conrad," *The Short Story. A Technical and Literary Study* (Chicago: A. C. McClurg, 1914), pp. 406–10.

A very brief introduction to JC's life and works, with a synopsis of the first two sections of "Heart of Darkness" and the text of the third section.

185.1 Garnett, Edward. [*Chance*], *N*, 24 January 1914, pp. 720–22 [not seen in this form]; rptd as "Unsigned Review" in CCH, pp. 277–80.

Chance, though not one of JC's most powerful novels, is an "artistic web" made of ordinary material. As with all of JC's art, the importance of the book is in the "magical lighting of the whole human landscape." Very artful, too, is his method of telling his story, if a "trifle artificial"; but the tale is a "masterpiece of indirect narrative." The flaw is the "deliberate engineering" of the lovers' "sustained tragic misunderstanding" on their honeymoon voyage.

189.1 "Joseph Conrad, A Polish Leader of English Novelists," *Sun* (New York), 31 January 1914, p. 10.

Announces the forthcoming publication of *Chance* and provides a brief biography of the author.

189.2 Lynd, Robert. "Mr. Conrad's Fame," *New Statesman* (London), III (4 July 1914), 401–02.

The "chief novelty" of Richard Curle's book, *Joseph Conrad: A Study* (1914) is the assertion that *Nostromo* is JC's masterpiece, and its chief contribution is an explanation of JC's genius. JC is best as a writer of mystery stories that dramatize the demonic element in men's lives. His characterization of women and his psychological insight are overdone by Curle, and his novels lack unity and economy. His stories, therefore, will create his lasting fame.

189.3 Meldrum, D. S. [The Best of Conrad's Books], *Daily Chronicle* (London), 15 January 1914, p. 4 [not seen in this form]; rptd under "Some Opinions of *Chance*," in CCH, p. 281.

As one comes from the spell of *Chance*, he may "well declare" this one to be "the best of his [JC's] books.

190.1 Montague, C. E. [Review of *Chance*], *MG*, 15 January 1914, p. 6 [not seen in this form]; rptd as "Review" in CCH, pp. 273-76.

Chance is a great book, displaying JC's "unmistakable" method of telling a story. As a result of this method, one of the narrators in the novel may be said to have seen or heard whatever needs to be told to the reader on the word of an eyewitness, and characters who are narrated about are seen under "variously searching lights" of several observant temperaments. A "quickened sensitiveness" results from the reader's seeing each new point through the emotions of curiosity and sympathy raised in someone who is ostensibly not the author.

191.1 "New Books Seen Through Review and Comments: New Kind of Story from Joseph Conrad," *Sun* (New York), 21 March 1914, p. 10.

"A masterly piece of workmanship," *Chance* is all the more remarkable because it is "unlike Conrad's other books." JC's elaborate narrative machinery, which involves the use of a first-person narrator to report the conversations of others, gives "a marked tone of reality" to the story, which, though possessed of a "slight" theme, is achieved with "true literary art."

197.1 "Some of the 'Best' Books Found During the Past Year: Fiction and Serious Works Named by Prominent Citizens," *Sun* (New York), Spring Literary Supplement, 4 April 1914, p. 1.

The JC manuscript collector John Quinn was among the respondents to a survey. Citing *Chance* as the most important work of fiction published in 1914, Quinn called JC "a pure artist," whose genius Americans have failed to recognize.

197.2 [Weakness in *Chance*], *Glasgow News*, 5 February 1914, p. 10 [not seen in this form]; rptd as "Unsigned Review" in CCH, pp. 283–84.

Although *Chance*, as is usual with JC's works, contains a special preoccupation with psychology, an unusual trait in English storytelling, JC seems to sink deeper than usual in the "slough of introspection" and to "suggest" a "formidable scaffolding" with too little to be supported by it.

197.3 "When Joseph Conrad First Heard English," *Sun* (New York), 11 January 1914, Section 7, p. 12.

Notes the publication of a promotional pamphlet by Alfred A. Knopf and recounts an anecdote, deriving from Knopf, regarding JC's having first heard English spoken by a sea-captain in Marseilles when he was nineteen.

1915

198.1 Bliss, Reginald (ed). *Boon, The Mind of The Race, The Wild Asses of the Devil, and the Last Trump: Being A First Selection From the Literary Remains of George Boon, Appropriate to the Times*. With an introduction by H. G. Wells (New York: George H. Doran, 1915), pp. 136, 147.

George Boon could not endure JC's respectable success.

204.1 [Conflict in *Victory*], *N*, 2 October 1915, pp. 25–26 [not seen in this form]; rptd as "Unsigned Review" in CCH, pp. 295–97.

Victory is an excellent example of the "concrete" and "objective" values of first-rate narrative as opposed to the variations of the author's personality in the "realistic-cum-autobiographical" novel. The main "feature" of JC's work is the "equipoise" he preserves between action and psychology; the issue in *Victory*, the conflict between the forces of darkness and of light, is "as clear as in a mystery play."

208.1 De la Mare, Walter. [*Victory*], *Westminster Gazette*, 2 October 1915 [not seen in this form]; rptd as "Review" in CCH, pp 292–94.

Just as form and content in a work of art are inseparable, so the originality of a novelist consists only in the life that he has created, of which, "without his witness," we would be ignorant. JC alone could create his characters in *Victory*, just as he alone could "float before our eyes" Samburan and its archipelago in an unfamiliar world. Thus JC's genius is " a power of receptiveness so individual that its revelation in the form of art is the revelation of a new universe." JC's universe is "haunted"; his curtain, falling on an empty stage, leaves us with the quality we need so much "just now"—"Victory."

217.1 Gould, Gerald. [The Fineness of *Victory*], *New Statesman* (London), 2 October 1915, pp. 622–23 [not seen in this form]; rptd as "Review" in CCH, pp. 299–301.

Victory may be credited not so much with greatness as with fineness. Heyst is at once both the central and the most successful character in the novel; Lena fails to give the "smallest impression of reality." The "profoundest" things in the novel are "generalizations and descriptions." The work is "neither tragic nor melodramatic," and the philosophy which informs the whole "has the strength of terror but the quietness of depth."

221.1 Lyndm Robert, [*Victory*], *DN*, 24 September 1915, p. 6 [not seen in this form]; rptd as Review" in CCH, pp. 285–87.

JC's theme in *Victory* is the virtuous man "in conflict with demons," but the demons display some "fine touches of comedy." The ending seems "somewhat mechanical," but it is true to JC's philosophy, in which he sees no triumph of the fine over the foul except in the fact of its being fine. Compared with *Chance*, which is unambitious, *Victory* is likely to be one of JC's most popular stories.

230.1 [Two Kinds of Humanity], *Scotsman*, 27 September 1915, p. 2 [not seen in this form]; rptd as "Unsigned Review" in CCH, pp. 287–88.

In *Victory*, JC intermixes his two moods of envisaging humanity: the simple, elemental beings people are in their last analysis (Lena and Heyst) and creatures in a melodramatic world (the other characters). JC, however, seems to penetrate to an "essential and spiritual reality which underlies the ordinary world."

230.2 [*Victory*], *Glasgow Evening News*, 7 October 1915, p. 8 [not seen in this form]; rptd as "Unsigned Review" in CCH, pp. 301–02.

If the artist's symbolic intention becomes visible, the art fails. This fact is seen in *Victory* when the solution of the well created situation comes from without in the form of the two ruffians who are "stock types of villainy in the lower regions of literary and dramatic art": "If only Martin had been a little less like a jaguar and his master a little less reminiscent of the villain of the third-rate theater." Anyhow *Victory* is "a fine book by a great artist."

1916

232.1 Donlin, George B. The Art of Joseph Conrad," *Dial*, 21 September 1916, pp. 172-74.

JC stubbornly persists in ignoring the taste of the public for which he writes, producing a kind of personal prose that is "confessional" and regarded by many readers as egocentric. He is neither an ironist nor a rational philosopher, though he is often so regarded, but delights in portraying the manner in which "the wild places of the earth work upon and alter our conventional attitudes and judgements." His work is not influenced by modern philosophers such as Nietzsche nor does it reflect modern thought nor the problems of the modern world; in fact, he seems not to understand "the twisted and inexplicable structure of modern finance" in *Chance*. "His veracity and his love of beauty" deny him a "wide public," but his consummate mastery of style, his magnificent word pictures, and his ability to create a sense of atmosphere, both external and internal, make his work worth the effort, for "he is one of the few living writers of romance who can take readers out of themselves without taking them out of reality also."

1917

255.1 Fryer, Eugenie M. "New Books of the Month," *Book News Monthly*, XXXV (1917), 422.

JC is a master of mood, character analysis, and atmosphere, all of which abound in *The Shadow-Line*, a book which shares the "extraordinary psychological analysis" of *Lord Jim*.

256.1 Gould, Gerald. [*The Shadow-Line*], *New Statesman* (London), 31 March 1917, p. 618 [not seen in this form]; rptd as "Review" in CCH, pp. 310–12.

The Shadow-Line suggests a comparison to *The Rime of the Ancient Mariner*. J. C's psychological method here does not contain the "old magic" of his earlier works.

263.1 Phelps, William Lyon. "William Lyon Phelps on *Victory*," *The Advance of the English Novel* (1917), p. 217 [not seen in this form]; rptd as "William Lyon Phelps on *Victory*" in CCH, p. 303.

Victory "reads" as if it were intended for a "popular" audience. In spite of many "fine passages of description, it is poor stuff." It is, for JC, though, "one of those lapses of which nearly all great writers have shown themselves capable."

265.1 [*The Shadow-Line*], *N*, 24 March 1917 [not seen in this form]; rptd as "Unsigned Review" in CCH, pp. 304–08.

JC's romantic inheritance gives him something of his extraordinary power of narrative, with which he combines his unusual analysis of character. JC is the "greatest living psychologist writing in English," partly because of his method of revealing a personality "from every possible angle of words." His "elfin power" of mingling the natural with the supernatural is notable. If there were nothing in *The Shadow-Line* but Captain Giles, it "would be a masterpiece."

1918

280.1 Moore, Edward [pseud of Edwin Muir]. *We Moderns: Enigmas and Guesses* (London: George Allen & Unwin, 1918), p. 130.

JC will be remembered not for his representative qualities of the age, but for his exceptions to them.

1919

287.1 [*The Arrow of Gold*], *MP*, 6 August 1919, p. 3 [not seen in this form]; rptd as "Unsigned Review" in CCH, pp. 314–16.

The story of *The Arrow of Gold* is a very vague and "emotional adventure, if ever there was one." It is an "extraordinarily fascinating work," but it is also a testing of how far JC's method can be carried.

292.1 Courtney, W. L. "Mr. Joseph Conrad," *DT*, 29 August 1919, p. 4 [not seen in this form]; rptd as "W. L. Courtney on Conrad's Admirers and Detractors" in CCH, pp. 324–25.

The Arrow of Gold has aroused both JC's admirers and detractors; the latter claim that JC has never been able to tell a story, that in *Arrow* he has no particular story to tell, that his psychology is not altogether satisfactory, and that there is much in *Arrow* that is tedious.

293.1 [A Disappointing Novel], *New Statesman* (London), 16 August 1919, p. 497 [not seen in this form]; rptd as "Unsigned Review" in CCH, pp. 321–24.

The Arrow of Gold is disappointing: the story is unfortunate and the character of Doña Rita is not completely successful. The astonishing thing about the book is "the wealth of living, vivid and recognizable persons in it"; not a single character can "walk for a moment across his [JC's] pages without becoming a distinguished figure." Even if JC failed somewhat in the construction of his story, the result is only another proof of his ability to enrich any theme so that "it is delightful while the reader recognizes its defects."

300.1 Giovannetti, Eugenio. "Letterature Straniere—Joseph Conrad" (Foreign Literatures: Joseph Conrad), *Il Tempo*, 29 November 1919, p. 3.

JC, one of the most original European authors, has brought into the English novel the melancholic idea of an obscure, ironic, merciless, Shakespearean fatality. In the great night of the ocean in *The Nigger of the Narcissus*, the Nigger's ambiguity is frightening; "Youth" is a poetic exaltation of man's struggle against Fate. JC's spirit is, however, permeated with the warm humanity of a cosmopolitan ideal. [In Italian.]

300.2 "The Gossip Shop," *B*, XLIX (July 1919), 640.

The complete first sketch of the plot of *The Arrow of Gold* appears in "The Tremolino,'" one of the last sketches in *The Mirror of the Sea*.

300.3 "An Illusory Conrad," *N*, 6 September 1919, pp. 680–82 [not seen in this form]; rptd as "Unsigned Review" in CCH, pp. 325–27.

The reactions to *The Arrow of Gold* cannot be explained, but classified: (1) the springs of the action are in marked contrast to the suggestions it is intended to evoke, (2) Doña Rita as a goatherd and a fine lady in one demands much subtlety, but to make her foolish "flattens the illusion," and (3) the "notes" make a "very prickly hedge" between the reader and the remainder of the novel.

312.1 [*The Shadow-Line*], *MP*, 26 March 1919, p. 4 [not seen in this form]; rptd as "Extract from Unsigned Review" in CCH, pp. 308–09.

An anchorage to actual experiences steadies JC's stories against tendencies to "soar beyond the region of visibility," as *The Shadow-Line* demonstrates. Here, the young commander's story does not reach us directly but is seen as an oblique reflection of his experience in other men's minds.

1920

322.1 [Conrad as Realist], *N*, 17 July 1920, pp. 503-04 [not seen in this form]; rpt. as "Unsigned Review" in CCH, pp. 337–40.

JC is not an ordinary realist, obtaining pleasure, as Arnold Bennett does, simply from seeing a thing as it is; and he is an interpreter as well as a narrator. Life as seen in *The Rescue* is a "dark dream": the lovers, united by the "poetry of their passion," are separated by the "prose of daily existence." *Rescue* is remarkable in its study of atmosphere, both spiritual and physical, and it is rich in portraits of "grotesque figures in a tragedy."

330.1 Forster, E. M. "Joseph Conrad: A Note" [extract], *Abinger Harvest* (London: Edward Arnold, 1942), 134-37 [not seen in this form]; rpt. as "E. M. Forster's Criticism of Conrad" in CCH, pp. 345–48.

Notes on Life and Letters reveals a "profound and formidable" character, one who dreads intimacy and who constantly promises to make some general philosophical statement about the universe and then gruffly refrains; JC never "gives himself away." These essays are not philosophical; JC has no creed, only opinions. As the simple sailor, he is not difficult to understand, and it is this part of him that has given what is most solid to his books. His "central obscurity" appears because there are constant discrepancies between "his nearer and his further vision." Every line in these essays is important because the material differs from the "imperishable marble" that his readers know and may help to interpret the lines of that.

331.1 Hodgson, S. "Higher Prices for Conrad First Editions," *Publishers' Circular, cxiii* (16 Oct 1920), p. 476.

[Notes that first editions of JC's work have begun to bring high prices in book auctions and points out the sale of a copy of *Chance* containing a title page dated 1913.]

339.1 Newton, W. Douglas. [*The Rescue*], *Sketch* (London), 21 July 1920, p. 428. [not seen in this form]; rpt. as "Review" in CCH, pp. 341–42.

In reading *The Rescue*, one becomes "steeped in an atmosphere of tragic silences," but some of Lingard's conversations with Mrs. Travers seem to be partly the "stage-management" of JC.

341.1 [*The Rescue*], *London Mercury*, August 1920, pp. 497–98 [not seen in this form]; rpt. as "Unsigned Review" in CCH, pp. 342–45.

The Rescue, appearing when JC is universally recognized as one of the finest living and writing English novelists, is his "finest work." [The usual reasons are given to support this claim.]

341.2 [*The Rescue*], *MP*, 25 June 1920, p. 4 [not seen in this form]; rpt. as "Unsigned Review" in CCH, pp. 329–31.

Although JC "enriches our literature" in *The Rescue* with "still another romance," and although the complicated plot is perfectly managed and the setting is authentic, there is uncertainty as to whether the reader understands Lingard. And, too, Edith Travers may not be adequately drawn.

342.1 [*The Rescue*], *Punch* (London), 14 July 1920, p. 39 [not seen in this form]; rpt. as "Unsigned Review" in CCH, p. 336.

[A favorable review of *The Rescue*, which praises the author's style and the work's "profound and moving quality."]

354.1 Wise, Thomas J. "Conrad's First Editions," *BJPC*, III (31 December 1920), 160.

In the case of several of JC's books, it would be possible to manufacture "First Editions" by substituting spurious cancels. Collectors can protect themselves by buying books bound in original cloth and by checking to see that the title is an unsevered portion of the opening sheet. One may protect against frauds in purchasing rebound books by checking ink colors and paper. Several copies of genuine first editions have been made presentable by rebinding them in covers taken from later editions. [In this letter to the editor, Wise then requests a look at *A Set of Six*, mentioned by J. C. Thomson as having a cancel-title.]

1921

355.1 Birkhead, Edith. *The Tale of Terror: A Study of the Gothic Romance* (London: Constable, 1921), 194–95.

The experience of Byrne in "The Inn of the Two Witches" is a "masterpiece in the psychology of terror."

355.2 "Books and Authors," *NYTBR*, 2 Jan 1921, p. 25.

The "Preface" of *An Outcast of the Islands*, recently published in the Sun-Dial Edition by Doubleday, Page & Co., betrays a touch of sentimentality not usually associated with JC.

372.1 "Mr. Conrad's *Chance*," *BJPC*, IV (10 June 1921), 107.

A presentation copy of *Chance* given to Edward Thomas with JC's inscription in 1914 contains an inserted 1913 title-page, usually noted as a forgery. The book came straight from the publisher in 1914. A likely explanation is that when the publisher was issuing the book, cancelling the 1913 title-page and inserting the 1914 title-page, he erred. He probably reinserted the 1913 title-page by mistake.

373.1 "Mr. T. J. Wise's Bibliography of Conrad," *BJPC*, IV (3 June 1921), 91.

The second edition of the bibliography will be as welcome as the first. It has been brought up-to-date and thoroughly revised.

375.1 "New Discoveries in the Bibliography of *Chance*," *Bookman's Journal*, IV (December 1921), 81–82.

There exists one forged copy of the first edition of *Chance* whose cancel title pages were clearly not prepared by the publisher and a limited number of copyright editions published in America prior to the issue of the British edition of the book.

377.1 Pure, Simon [pseud. of Frank Swinnerton]. "The Londoner," *B*, *LIII* (1 March 1921), 65–66.

An announcement of three forthcoming books with JC's name on the title page: a Napoleonic novel, "Thoughts on Life and Letters," and his wife's cookbook.

378.1 "*A Set of Six*," *BJPC*, IV, (3 June 1921), 91.

In notes following his collation of *A Set of Six*, T. J. Wise observed that "the double-leaf carrying the half-title and title-page was bogus." Collectors could be spared difficulties if they would restrict their purchases to books bound in the original cloth and examine them sufficiently to guarantee against the substitution of any material leaves.

379.1 Wise, Thomas J. "More Frauds of the Book Forger," *BJPC*, III (7 January 1921), 177.

[About Thomas J. Wise's uncovering fraudulent first editions of *Chance* and *A Set of Six*, the detection of the latter forgery depending on Wise's examination of the paper and ink of the half-title and title pages, and Wise's revealing the discovery of two different issues of *A Set of Six*.]

1922

387.1 "The First U.S. Edition of *Chance*," *Bookman's Journal*, V (April 1922), 175.

Doubleday, Page & Co. issued a small American edition of *Chance* in 1913 to insure copyright of the book, whose publication in England was delayed by a binder's strike that resulted in delaying publication in book form on a regular basis in either country until 1914.

391.1 Pure Simon [pseud. of Frank Swimmerton]. "The Londoner," *B*, *LVI* (November 1922), 316.

Both the late W. H. Hudson and JC had little early recognition. The turn in reputation came first for JC, however, and his reward in popularity has been greater. The reason for writers suffering neglect during the years in which they create their best work may be due to a temperament which excludes them from the mainstream of contemporary literature.

1923

398.1 Aksenov, I. D. "Dzhozef Konrad. *Kapriz Ol'meira* (Petrograd, 1923); *Prilivy i otlivy* (Petrograd, 1923)," (Joseph Conrad. *Almayer's Folly*), (Petrograd, 1923); *Between the Tides* (Petrograd, 1923), *Pechat' i Revoliutsiia* (Moscow), No. 7 (1923), 268-71.

JC is now at the height of his fame in England, where his mastery of language, his art of narrative, and his psychological analysis are admired. Hitherto, JC's work has been entirely unknown in Russia, and the translations of *Almayer's Folly* and *Between the Tides* are the first attempt to make up this lamentable gap in Russia's translated literature. Russians have the right to be interested in his work, the more so because he was born within the frontiers of the country and undoubtedly his first literary impressions were strongly marked by the influence of contemporary Russian authors, especially of Dostoevski.

Not until the age of forty did JC leave the sea. His novels preserve the years of his youth with an undying feeling of rebellious protest, not against European civilization (as it might seem at first sight), but against contemporary Europeans, representatives of the ruling class. The voicing of this protest, concealed by the splendid imagery of *Folly*, becomes clearer with each succeeding work and reaches a tone of confession in *The Secret Agent*. JC is a pessimist—hence his anarchism. He depicts the guilt of educated Europeans who are masters of the world and parasites of the dark masses, instead of elevating them. Copious quotations can only give some idea of the variety of JC's style, which he uses to portray his own feelings and express his own thoughts. His narrative technique is no less rich. [Abstract added.] [In Russian.]

398.2 Albert, Edward. *A History of English Literature* (New York: Crowell, 1923), pp. 526–31.

JC is " the most un-English" English novelist. The strongest appeal of his novels is to the eye and the ear. His indirect narrative method "would probably be disastrous in hands less careful and adroit." He may be called the "novelist of doubt and hesitation, so skilled is he in the elaborate suggestion of such emotions." He demands a patient and wary reader who follows the course of the narrative carefully, because he has a "troublesome habit" of inserting important matter in the midst of less essential details.

398.3 "American Notes," *Bookman's Journal,* IX (December 1923), 105.

[Describes the JC collection of John Quinn, recently offered for sale, and that of T. J. Wise, and comments on the acquisition of JC manuscripts by the two collectors.]

403.1 "Books in the Sale Room," *BJPC,* 9 Jan 1923, pp. 145–46.

[Describes the items sold by Hodgson Co. on December 6, 1923. These include manuscripts of two JC works, "The Duel" and "Her Captivity" (a section of *The Mirror of the Sea*) from the library of Frederic Harrison.]

405.1 Butcher, Fanny. "The Bookman Advertiser," *B,* LVII (August 1923), [an unnumbered section of the journal].

[A travelogue which notes Naples as the scene of "Il Conde" and announces JC's "new" novel, *The Rover.*]

405.2 Butcher, Fanny. "Confessions," *Chicago Tribune*, 19 May 1923, p. 9.

When asked which book he would rather have written than his own *This Side of Paradise*, F. Scott Fitzgerald replied that his choice would have been *Nostromo*. It is the greatest novel since *Vanity Fair*, with the possible exception of *Madame Bovary*. Nostromo himself is intriguing, both as a character in the novel and as a constantly recurring character type in all fiction. Before JC created Nostromo, however, the character type was dismissed as superficial. But JC gave to this type an original and unique completeness. Hence *Nostromo* has always had a haunting and irresistible appeal.

412.1 "The Conrad MSS.," *BJPC* IX (December 1923), 144–45.

[Reports on the success of the John Quinn sale of JC manuscripts and synopsizes an article by Jessie Conrad appearing in the London *Daily Mail* (17 November 1923), quoting Mrs. Conrad's account of why she preserved the manuscripts that later went to Quinn.]

414.1 Curle, Richard. "Conrad in Extract," *TLS*, 1 March 1923, p. 138.

[Rev. of *Wisdom and Beauty from Conrad*, compiled by M. Harriet M. Capes (C, I, No. 202).] Whereas Miss Cape's selection "is excellent," her quotations "miss the real object of a novel, and thus . . . do a sort of injury to the novelist."

416.1 Curle, Richard. "The Story of *Lord Jim*," *TLS*, 13 September 1923, p. 604.

[Responds to Swettenham's letter stating that *Lord Jim* was based on historical incidents (C, I, No. 4460), noting that this view supports his assertion in "The History of Mr. Conrad's Books" that *Jim* derives its sense of finality from its basis in real life.]

416.2 Dabrowska, Maria. "J. Conrad. *Fantazja Almayera, Murzyn z zalogi Narcyza*" (J. Conrad. *Almayer's Folly, The Nigger of the Narcissus*), *Bluszcz* (Warsaw), No. 35 (1923), 310; rpt. in *Pisma Rozprozone* (Uncollected Writings), II (Cracow: Wydawnictwo Literackie, 1954), 443-47; rpt. in *Soc*, pp. 47-50.

JC's art is not "literary"; it is a stern, remorseless artistic account of a life experience. JC created his poetic world by unexpectedly fine metaphors, the revelation of psychic states, and the precise construction of sentences. None of the many details is superfluous. JC can summon up in his readers an emotional, almost passionate, attitude to all his concerns. We are deeply moved in reading *The Nigger of the Narcissus* and have a sense of identification with the

crowd of simple rebels. Almayer's return to the empty house gives us
the truth of isolation which JC can draw out of the secret depths of
every reader. [In Polish.]

418.1 Follett, Wilson. "Joseph Conrad; A Salutation," *New York
Herald Tribune Magazine*, 29 April 1923, pp. 19–20.

JC's approaching visit to the United States calls attention to the
distance which separates us from him and gives us the opportunity
to "realize the import of his haunting loneliness," whose recognition
is essential to our comprehension both of the man and of the artist.
JC, an exile from his homeland, has transformed his "great losses"
into "great gains" in works which express "unconquerable loneliness
of spirit" in the outcasts who populate their pages.

418.2 "The Gossip Shop," *B*, LVII (August 1923), 688.

Laura B. Everett quotes JC as saying in a preface to his wife's
cookbook that he is a product of her cookery. Facetiously, she
suggests that JC's and Carlyle's literary achievements are the results
of their wives' efforts in the kitchen. In reply, *Bookman* notes JC's
belief that although women are better cooks than men on the
average, men attain greater heights in the art. He suggests that this is
true in any pursuit which combines intellect and instinct.

418.3 Hammond, Percy. "Oddments and Remainders," *New York
Tribune*, 15 May 1923, p. 10.

Readers of JC's novels may have been surprised at newspaper
stories reporting the author as mousey and retiring. They may rest
assured that he is the "tranquil and dominant" person they had
thought. Surrounded by New Yorkers at a luncheon, he was at ease
and spoke at length on contemporary men of letters. It was at this
luncheon that JC and Paderewski met for the first time.

426.1 Lewis, Tracy Hammond. "News and Views: An Interview with
Joseph Conrad," *New York Morning Telegraph* (31 May 1923), 4;
rpt. in Dale B. J. Randall, "Conrad Interviews, No. 5: Tracy
Hammond Lewis," *CON*, III, No. 2 (1971-72), 67-73.

JC had lost the youth of which he wrote "with such poetic
longing," but he had gained fame instead. This was apparent on May
23, 1923, when, less than a week before boarding the *Majestic* for
home, he held a small group interview in the offices of the Country
Life Press in Garden City, New York. Seeming more "uptight" than in
previous interviews, JC revealed the fact that fame with her honor
had "exacted her pound of flesh." Shy and reserved, he looked for
assistance to Mr. Doubleday, his host, who calmly ignored him. He

claimed that New York City had "an amazing individuality" among cities; he spoke readily of the sea and of Mark Twain, whom he remembered with pleasure; and as for Paderewski, JC thought it absurd to believe he was ever in favor of the Jewish pogrom.

437.1 "Notes on Sales: Conrad Manuscripts," *TLS*, 22 November 1923, p. 796.

The collection of JC manuscripts recently sold by John Quinn in New York City brought remarkably high prices: $8,100 for *Victory*, $6,900 for *Under Western Eyes*, $5,300 for *Almayer's Folly*, and $4,500 for *The Nigger of the Narcissus*. While the high prices paid attest to JC's popularity with American readers and collectors, it is unfortunate that "it is the speculator who reaps the profit."

440.1 Phelps, William Lyon. *As I Like It* (New York: Charles Scribner's Sons 1923), pp. 207-08.

JC was willing to be judged on *The Nigger of the Narcissus* alone, although newcomers to his fiction might want to begin with the incomparable "Typhoon." JC's fame rests on his mastery of English prose.

440.2 "Port after Stormie Seas," *MG*, 3 December 1923, p. 5 [not seen in this form]; rpt. as "Unsigned Review" in *CCH*, pp. 349–50.

In *The Rover*, JC utilizes his usual direct methods of telling his story; then the end is fully illuminated and is told directly. It is "pure romance," from which JC has "scoured away all the superfluities on which the romanticist feeds."

442.1 Pure, Simon [pseud. of Frank Swinnerton]. "The Londoner," *B*, *LVI* (February 1923), 739–40.

In spite of the hostile criticism written about the dramatization of *The Secret Agent*, which ran for only a month, the play was moving and effective. The hostility of the critics' response is due to their belief that a novelist cannot write a play. However, *Agent* made the audience uncomfortable, and English audiences dislike being made uncomfortable or made to feel genuine emotion. Thus the real reason for the play's failure is that it made a pleasure-loving audience uncomfortable.

443.1 [*The Rover*], *Glasgow Evening News*, 6 December 1923 p.2 [not seen in this form]; rpt. as "Unsigned Review" in *CCH*, pp. 356–58.

In spite of JC's usual excellent characterization, his usual manner of telling a story, and the presence of his "basic philosophy,"

The Rover suffers from "lack of conviction" in the latter half; JC's gift of "sheer good writing" seems to have failed him.

445.1 Sherman, Thomas B. "Joseph Conrad and His Miraculous Career," *Journal* (Atlanta), 3 June 1923, p. 20; rpt. in Dale B. J. Randall, "Conrad Interviews, No. 3: Thomas B. Sherman, " *CON*, II, No. 3 (1969-70), pp. 122–27.

Thomas Sherman was one of the "chosen few" to meet JC at the home of F. N. Doubleday, JC's publisher, 7 May 1923, at JC's second "mass" interview. He thought—and so stated in his article on the interview—that "everything connected with the life of Joseph Conrad possesses somehow the flavor of the miraculous." During the session, JC appeared nervous, sensitive, and fragile, but "thoroughly good-humored." He denied having created any new technique and declared *Lord Jim* "a very defective book." He likewise denied having a philosophy. Of course, JC has a philosophy, though one must find it in "the overtones and the implications" of his writings.

445.2 S[horter], C[lement] K[ing]. "Literary Letter: Mr. Conrad's *The Rover*," *Sphere*, XCV (December 1923), pp. 364.

The rise in popularity of JC is "among my most interesting literary experiences." His popularity has resulted in the publication of two elaborate complete editions of his works as well as intense interest in his manuscripts and first editions. His newest work, *The Rover*, is, after *Victory*, "the best of all," revealing that JC is "a lord of language" possessed of "a beautiful style" which enchants the reader. Important glimpses of the retiring author's personality emerge in another recent work, *At Sea with Joseph Conrad* by J. G. Sutherland (London: Grant, Richards, 1923).

445.3 Smith, James Walter. "Joseph Conrad—Master Mariner and Novelist," *Evening Transcript* (New York), (12 May 1923); rpt. in Dale B. J. Randall, "Conrad Interviews, No. 2: James Walter Smith," *CON*, II, No. 2 (Winter 1969-70), 83–93.

On May 1923, Mrs. Florence Doubleday, the wife of JC's publisher, received nineteen reporters and JC at her Oyster Bay home, where JC was closely questioned about his friendship with Stephen Crane; about the techniques used in his novels, a subject he attempted to avoid; about his philosophy, to which he replied, "I have no philosophy. They have invented it for me"; about his style, to which he stated, "It's something I never bother about"; and about the "movies," which he considered "miraculous." This interview was the most "imposing" one of his life.

445.4 Spencer, Walter T. *Forty Years in My Bookshop* (London: Constable, 1923), pp. 276–77.

Thomas J. Wise's set of JC's works is "a series of gifts from the author, with a signed explanatory note on the blank fly-leaf" by JC himself. The information contained on these leaves concerns attempts to dramatize *Alamyer's Folly* and tries to change the title of *The Nigger of the Narcissus* for American consumption. It also deals with the phonetics of Donkin's speech, the serialization of *Nostromo*, and the popularity of *Under Western Eyes* in Russia. T. J. Wise published all these facts, along with others, in his JC bibliography.

448.1 Titus, Edward, K., Jr. "Write and Burn, Conrad advises Yale Aspirants," *World* (New York), (20 May 1923), "Second News Section," pp. 1, 3; rpt. in Dale B. J. Randall, "Conrad Interviews, No. 4: Edward K. Titus, Jr," *CON*, III, No. 1 (1970-71), 75-80.

One of JC's most pleasant interviews during his visit to the United States in 1923 was the one on May 16 with a college student, a junior at Yale, Edward K. Titus, Jr., in the home of William Lyon Phelps in New Haven. JC left a very favorable impression with Titus. During the interview, JC was unexpectedly affable, even affectionate; somewhat nervous at times, he was "always charming." His advice to college students was to "write and burn, although I never did it." He believed that college writers should aim first for self-perfection and only later, after they have lived through many experiences, for self-expression. He discussed literature and the sea. JC seemed "alive—breathing the spirit of adventure when he recounts his trips."

449.1 Van de Water, Frederick F. [A Simple, Powerful Story], *New York Tribune*, 4 December 1923, p. 16 [not seen in this form], rpt. as "Review" in *CCH*, pp. 351–53.

After many years of dragging oneself "inch by inch" through JC's works, the reader finds *The Rover* to be a "grand and powerful" story. In it there are no "disquistions" on ethics and psychology, and metaphysics are "conspicuously absent." The story is simple but "tremendous and Athenian" in power. The characters, "decidedly unordinary folk," live. The only possible fault is that the story is too long.

449.2 Weitzenkorn, Louis. "Conrad in Light and Shadow, Talks of Crane and Hardy and the Paleness of Words," *World* (New York), 3 June 1923, "Second News Section," pp. 1,3; rpt. in Dale B.J. Randall, "Conrad Interviews, No. 6: Louis Weitzenkorn," *CON*, IV, No. 1 (1972), 25–32.

Stephen Crane was the first person ever to call JC "Joseph." JC thought *The Red Badge of Courage* was "a notable book." He also considered Thomas Hardy the last of the Elizabethans as well as a Victorian. Writing was very difficult for JC: "It is impossible to reveal oneself," he said; "the words lose their meaning—pale." [Gives a biographical sketch of Weitzenkorn and reprints his article on JC. On May 30, 1923, F. N. Doubleday took him to see JC in Doubleday's apartment in New York.]

451.1 Wilson, Charles. "Three Master Novelists: I. Joseph Conrad," *New Rambles in Bookland* (Wellington: Whitcombe & Tombs, 1923), pp. 94–101.

JC is one of the most brilliant novelists in the English-speaking world. His background, his experience at sea, his rise to a master novelist, all make up a very romantic story. His first two novels, *Almayer's Folly* and *An Outcast of the Islands*, introduced him to the English reading public, but neither book became popular, probably because they were thought to be too dreamy and dreary. The same state of affairs applies to *The Nigger of the Narcissus* and *Lord Jim*. The stories in the volumes intitled *Youth* and *Typhoon*, and the novel *Romance*, however, helped to broaden JC's readership. He left off his romanticism in favor of realism in *Chance* and *Victory*. The more recent novels, though, *The Arrow of Gold* and *The Rescue*, have produced the original dislike of the psychological aspect in his work. *The Secret Agent* and *Under Western Eyes* are quite different from his other works, for neither the sea nor the Malayan background has anything to do with them. JC's best work is in the realm of his sea tales—such pieces as *Nigger*, *'Twixt Land and Sea*, and *Within the Tides*.

451.2 "Wonder What Mr. Conrad Says About It?" *New York Times*, 15 November 1923, p. 18.

Enormous prices were paid for JC manuscripts at this week's sale. Two views are possible: one is that the value placed on JC's work by collectors indicates their appreciation of his art; it is more likely, however, that collectors enjoy having something nobody else has. The other view is that the manuscripts are valuable because study of them shows JC at work and gives critics insight into the artistic process. To serve the latter purpose, the manuscripts should be housed in libraries or museums, not in the private collections of individuals. It would be interesting to know how the $120,461 "fetched" by the sale compares with JC's earnings in advances and royalties.

453.1 Young, Filson. "Conrad's New Book Appears in London," *NYTBR* 16 December 1923, p. 4.

The Rover marks JC's return to the style he followed a decade previously. Its characters exist " in a colorful tangle of psychology and adventure that is physically as well as spiritually thrilling." Like his early works, this novel puzzles and exasperates the reader even as it intrigues. At its conclusion, he realizes that "he has been in the presence of a great drama."

1924

454.1 Albert, Edward. "Joseph Conrad," *A History of English Literature* (New York: Crowell, 1924), pp. 526–31.

Almayer's Folly, JC's first novel, is immature because of its stumbling plot and faulty handling of character. It still retains, though, its power and originality, and it presents an entirely new style to fiction. The remainder of JC's novels are typical of *Folly*. *The Nigger of the Narcissus* is a story about the glory of the sea, and *Lord Jim* tells the tale of a bad sailor who makes good. "Youth" is probably JC's masterpiece. JC is, furthermore, the most un-English of English novelists, for he addresses himself to tropical lands and deep seas. But his strongest appeal is in his imagery. The pictures he paints of life connected with the sea portray a detail and beauty that only a sailor could know. And his narrative method is especially noteworthy; it is entirely his own: his way is to inform the reader indirectly through a narrator such as Marlow. Consequently, he demands that the reader be cautious, patient, and wary. [Includes a brief biographical summary.]

465.1 Baldwin, Charles C. "Bill Adams," *The Men Who Make Our Novels.* Rvd ed. (New York: Dodd, Mead, 1924), pp. 1–9.

Bill Adams, "whipped" by the sea, "aches" to be "back at his old adversary" and therefore cannot write of the charm of the waters; there is nothing mysterious about his sea. Unlike Adams, JC left the sea "with few illusions and no conceit," with resignation, so that his right to preempt the ocean goes unchallenged.

465.2 Binyon, Laurence. "The Rarest Lady of Her Time: Lady Colvin," *English Life,* III (September 1924), 219–22.

Lady Frances Colvin, wife of Sir Sidney Colvin, was a "beloved friend" of JC, as she was a "trusted" friend of other men as diverse as Browning, George Meredith, Henry James, Kipling, Masefield, and Hugh Walpole. She and JC "delighted in one another"; they were "lovers of everything human, creatures full of affection, charm, and character." [An appreciation of JC and Lady Colvin.]

467.1 "Books in the Sale Rooms," *BJPC*, 9 October 1923, p. 30.

[Reports the sale for eleven pounds of a first edition of *The Nigger of the Narcissus* at Sotheby's.]

470.1 "Bulletin," *Revue Anglo-Américaine*, II (October 1924), 95.

[Obit containing a brief survey of JC's life. Mentions his maritime experience in Marseilles, his acquiring the master's certificate, and his adopting the English language. Also includes a partial list of JC's works.] [In French.]

476.1 "A Collection of the Writings of Joseph Conrad (The Majority Inscribed or Annotated by the Author): The Property of the late James B. Pinker, Esq." *Catalogue of Valuable Printed Books* [to be sold December 15–17, 1924], (London: Sotheby Wilkinson and Hodge, 1924).

[Describes J. B. Pinker's collection of rare JC editions, proofs, etc. See items 620–77.]

476.2 "A Commentary: Joseph Conrad," *Criterion*, III (October 1924), p. 1; rpt. in *The Criterion, 1922-1939*, ed by T. S. Eliot (London: Faber and Faber; New York; Barnes and Noble, 1967), p. 1.

JC's reputation is as secure as that of any writer of his time. Critical analysis may "adjust, but it will not diminish."

482.1 Conrad, Jessie. "Why Lie?" *B*, LX (October 1924), 179–80.

When Mrs. Conrad was traveling to London by train on some forgotten occasion, she overheard two ladies who insisted that JC was unmarried but that as a foreigner he may have had a wife in his own country. One lady engaged in a "tissue of lies" about her own conquest of JC. Upon arriving at her destination, Mrs. Conrad had the pleasure of being greeted by name and informed that her husband was waiting for her and of seeing the discomfiture of the gossiping lady.

482.2 "Conrad MSS. to go Under the Hammer," *New York Times*, 4 November 1924, Section 2, p. 16.

An auction is to be held 12, 13, and 14 November in the Anderson Galleries in order to sell a part of the library of John Quinn, which includes many manuscripts and first editions of JC's works. Among them are *Almayer's Folly, An Outcast of the Islands, The Nigger of the*

Narcissus, "The Return," "Youth," and portions of the manuscripts of *Lord Jim*, "The End of the Tether," "Heart of Darkness," "Typhoon," "Amy Foster," "Falk," *Nostromo*, and *Victory*. The manuscript of *Almayer's Folly* is especially interesting because it is accompanied by a holograph history of the composition of the novel.

484.1 Crawshaw, William H. *The Making of English Literature*. Rvd. (Boston: D. C. Heath, 1924), pp. 435–37, 469, 482, 504, 506.

After a long journey across the desert of problems and their causes in several novels of the time, JC's "oasis of a true and fine artist" is refreshing. His romance is the "mystery of life, the romance of the human soul."

486.1 Czarnecki, Anthony. "An Evening with Conrad: The Famous Polish Writer at Home," *Chicago Daily News*, 14 August 1924, p. 8.

It was often reported that JC was difficult to meet and that it was even more difficult to get him to talk for publication, but he finally granted an interview and exhibited warm hospitality during the entire night. Immediately noteworthy was the brilliance of his eyes and the warm reflection in his face of a gentle soul which had suffered and fought. His responses in Polish were of the quality spoken in the universities of Poland. He conversed brilliantly and fluently, and hearing him was like reading his stories. It was obvious that he suffered mainly because of all the misunderstandings he experienced among Polish people. And contrary to what many Polish acquaintances have said, he was always very much interested in the Polish cause. He said that he was proud of his Polish blood and birth, and he explained how he always wanted to serve the cause in which his father had fought. But when in the early part of World War I the London chapter of the Polish relief committee asked him to join its ranks, he refused after learning that the Czar of Russia was a member. His refusal was misunderstood, though, because he was never able to explain it to anyone since he believed his reasons would offend the British allies. [Takes JC's statements literally, without allowing for the strong possibility that JC may have been posturing for the sake of his public image. But some quotations are interesting and valuable for the biographer.]

486.2 Dabrowska, Maria. "Nowe przeklady Conrada" (New Translations of Conrad), *Bluszcz* (Warsaw), 1924); rpt. in *Soc*, pp. 27–29.

JC never intrudes his personality onto the reader. His perfection of construction is not conventional, but a difficult necessity. We cannot imagine his telling us what he had to say by any other elements of artistic construction. [In Polish.]

487.1 De Lanux, Pierre. "Notes from France," *B*, LVIII (January 1924), 596.

JC's popularity in France is growing. André Gide, who translated "Typhoon," is directing the translation of a series of JC's novels.

490.1 Douglas, Norman. *D. H. Lawerence and Maurice Magnus: A Plea for Better Manners* (Pvtly ptd, 1924), pp. 37–38.

JC has been called a great psychologist, but in fact there is very little psychology displayed in his writings. His genius is the very opposite of psychology, for he drives his readers forward by sheer force. His characters are not motivated by psychology but by British morality. By rarely delving into the soul, he does not acquire any humor. [Largely a tribute to Maurice Magnus. Answered by Christopher Morley, "Bowling Green," *Saturday Review*, 14 March 1925, p. 597.]

490.2 Dyboski, Roman. "Samotny geniusz: Joseph Conrad (Solitary Genius: Joseph Conrad), [originally published in 1924, publisher not located]; rpt. in *Sto Lat Literatury Anglieskiej* (A Century of English Literature), (Warsaw: *Pax*. 1957) pp., 853–902.

JC's individual technique is to give the objective material of his narrative a subjective coloring, which sometimes changes during the course of a work. His aim was to demonstrate that human affairs are not simple, that motives are complicated and can never be expressed in a formula. In his later novels, the lack of clarity is deliberate and sometimes becomes a tedious mannerism. The atmosphere is tragic throughout his work. The emblem of tragic destinies is an exile outside the orbit of his native social, cultural, or national environment. JC as a Pole among English sailors was in this situation, and later, similarly, as a sailor among writers. [In Polish.]

492.1 Fairley, Barker. "The Modern Consciousness in English Literature," in *Essays and Studies by Members of the English Association*, Vol IX, ed by W. P. Ker (London: Oxford UP, 1924), p. 139.

JC stands with Hardy in the range of his consciousness and the setting of his figures against the universe. Like Hardy's, JC's figures are sometimes small, like Jim receding into the twilight; and they are sometimes large, like Lingard on the sandbank before sunrise. Hardy and JC are also the leading writers in the study of environment. *Tess of the D'Urbervilles* and *Nostromo* lie midway between the nature novel and the social novel.

493.1 Finger, Charles J. "A Giant Passes," *All's Well* IV (Fayetteville, Arkansas), (August 1924), 4–5.

If one wants to know the works of the late JC, he should read first *The Secret Agent* and then *Victory*, followed by *Nostromo*, *Chance*, and "Falk," by which time this author will be seen as "one of the great figures in the world of literature." JC has left "a rich and an artistic heritage." That he never wrote anything "to please the public is exactly what might have been expected of the great independent heart."

493.2 Finger, Charles J. "On Character Portrayal," *All's Well* IV (Fayetteville, Arkansas), (August 1924), pp. 5–6.

JC was successful in his writing because he "slashed his way out of the labyrinth of conventions," because he treated in simple and realistic manner that part of life of which he had personal experience, and because he, like all other writers of fiction who have gained success, had presented his fictional characters in such a way that "their prejudices, their motives and ambitions, their very thoughts were . . . evident to the reader." Given such characters, the action necessarily grew out of the "collision" of the characters just as action does in real life. JC set down his characters "exactly as they were in real life."

496.1 Friend, Julius Weis. "Joseph Conrad: An Appreciation," *Double Dealer*, VII (October 1924), pp. 3–5.

Critics are vulgar and ignorant when they focus on men of JC's magnitude. His work commands respect and immortality. JC wrote of the ideal which conquers everything but blind nature, and his work is entirely unrelated to modern readers who are too accustomed to sexual themes. But JC may be somewhat blind to sex. His women are mere shadows, although his work as a whole is an epic of fear and nobility, which recalls Don Quixote. He has earned his place among the immortals for his portrayal of men's eternal conflict and touch of divinity.

496.2 Furst, Henry. "L'arte di Joseph Conrad" (Joseph Conrad's Art), *L'Idea Nazionale*, 19 April 1924, p. 3.

JC has a preference for exotic backgrounds, but the object of his psychological art is always the mind of white men. Lord Jim is one of the finest creations of world literature [Gives first Italian translation of the final episode of *Lord Jim* to substantiate his affirmation that JC is one of the greatest living writers]. [In Italian.]

496.3 Furst, Henry. "Il poeta navigatore: Joseph Conrad" (Sailor-poet: Joseph Conrad), *L'Idea Nazionale*, 12 August 1924, p. 3.

JC was an incomparable, strong, sincere, and open man. Jessie, whom he married December 6, 1896 [sic], was the ideal, sensible, tactful simile. He never wanted to speak about his books unless he was forced to. Although JC did not have a philosophy of life, his greatest merit was that of rescuing narrative art from decadence. He injected new life into the tradition of sea novels. [In Italian.]

500.1 Gigli, Lorenzo. "Joseph Conrad," *Le Opere ei Giorni* (Genova), (September 1924), p. 45–49.

[An obituary note, with a brief survey of JC's life and works.] [In Italian.]

506.1 Guedalla, Philip. "Famous People: Mr. Guedalla's Gallery," *T. P. 's & Cassell's Weekly*, II (10 May 1924), 92.

In his early work, JC has a diffidence which suggests a slow but conscious beginner. He employs in nearly every work some casual narrator like Marlow who does the author's job of unfolding the story.

506.2 Guedalla, Philip. "Mr. Joseph Conrad," *A Gallery* (New York: Putnam's, 1924), pp. 77–84.

There is an "ingenious fascination" about "straining a thin trickle of narrative" through the minds of two or three intermediate narrators, as JC does in *Lord Jim*; but JC apparently invented Marlow and his "shadowy" successors because he feared to trust his knowledge of a strange language to direct description. JC is best when he is least exotic. Perhaps his best achievement is the "observant irony" of "The Duel." As queer as JC's gift is, it is actually "great."

523.1 Lann, Evgenii. "Dzhozef Konrad" (Joseph Conrad), *Izbrannye Proizvedenii* (Moscow: n.p., 1924); rpt. in *Przeglad Humanisryczny* (Humanistic Survey), (Warsaw), VI, No. 6 (1962), 53—69.

JC's first works opened his way into critical acceptance in England. His style became a model for English writers and motivated anyone who began writing tales or novels. By the time he reached England, he had behind him a knowledge of French, a language in which the academic canons were well established. As French critics were to point out, JC's tendency to imprecision and vagueness in the use of language was condemned by academicians. But he had fully thought out the theory of fiction. From his Slavic origins, JC brought into English literature a note of "refined psychologizing" bordering on the pathological, which the English had already seen in various poor translations of Russian fiction. He possessed an ability for psychological analysis which no Western writer yet had: it was a specialty of Russian writers. JC depicts situations in a Russian manner, with the help of some powerful strokes portraying not individuals, but passions. He was unlike English writers in being much more complex and subtle. His guide to the the the distant islands and archipelagoes of his fiction was his conscience, not leading articles in the *Times*. He saw into the hearts of all races, and did not differentiate between the colonizers and the colonized. Many of his heroes are defeated: passion and temptation force them to pass beyond the boundaries laid down for man. They bear the brand of crime, and know it, and cannot forget their fall and inevitable punishment. This attitude alarmed the West. JC shaped the artistic taste of his English contemporaries and taught them psychology which he learned from Polish sources. [In Polish.]

527.1 Lewis, Tracey Hammond. "News and Reviews: Conrad's Last Interview," *Morning Telegraph* (New York), 6 August 1924, p. 6; rpt. in part in Dale B. J. Randall, "Conrad's Interviews, No. 5: Tracy Hammond Lewis," *CON*, III, No. 2 (1971–72), 67–73.

During his meeting with a small group in the offices of the Country Life Press in Garden City, New York, JC looked and acted "painfully self-conscious and embarrassed." He displayed his lack of ease mainly in his "hurried speech and low-speaking voice." His foreign accent made him additionally difficult to understand.

529.1 Lucas, E. V. "Joseph Conrad," *English Life*, III (September 1924), pp. 247–48.

E.V. Lucas first met JC in 1893, when the Polish sea captain who had written a novel was very modest and "full of a charming self-depreciation" which he never lost. He spoke with a foreign accent in sentences "not too well constructed." John Galsworthy encouraged JC in writing *Almayer's Folly* and passed the manuscript on to Edward Garnett, who fostered genius in several writers. In later years, JC always seemed to be filled with melancholy, but he also enjoyed fun. For the most part, though, he was "smilingly inscrutable," "living his own life behing the mask." He was a "very great writer," an artist "through and through." [An appreciation of JC written because of the urging of the editor of *English Life*.]

1925

576.1 Adams, Elbridge L. *Joseph Conrad: The Man* (New York: W. E. Rudge, 1925); rpt. (Folcroft, Pa.: Folcroft P, 1969); rpt. (New York: Haskell House, 1972).

[Adams says little in this "nonbook" of some seventy slight pages, including J. S. Zelie's comments on JC in his "A Burial in Kent." Imperceptive, impressionistic comments on JC and his work contribute nothing of value, but of some importance are the responses JC made to questions asked of him by a book collector on each volume of a set of first editions.]

579.1 Block, Ralph. "*Suspense,*" *SR*, XI (12 September 1925), 130.

[Under the heading "Points of View," a letter to the editor points out similarities between Stendhal's *La Chartreuse de Parme* and JC's *Suspense*: the same historical setting; the importance of Napoleon; the presence of a Clelia; and roughly the same plot, though treated from different angles.]

582.1 "Books in the Sale Room," *Bookman's Journal*, XLVII (August 1925), 207.

[Reports the sale of a complete set of JC's privately printed pamphlets for £145 at Sotheby's.]

582.2 "Books in the Sale Room: The J. B. Pinker Collection of Conradiana," *BJPC*, XI (January 1925), 190–91.

[Describes the inscribed editions, corrected copies, and proof copies of JC's works sold by the J. B. Pinker estate, noting the prices paid for the items.]

582.3 Borowy, Waclaw. "Fredro i Conrad: z tajniko 'w sztuki pisarskiej" (Fredro and Conrad: Secrets of the Writer's Art), *Tygodnik Wilenski* (Wilno), No. 16, 1925; rpt. in *WSOC*, pp. 246–52.

Fredro's *Memoirs* (written about 1845, reprinted in 1917) are characterized by a deliberate absence of chronology and a use of digressions in the narrative, as in JC's *Some Reminiscences* (1912) and *A Personal Record* (1916), both written in the same fragmentary manner. Both writers disliked the literary conventions of autobiography, and choice of this method enabled them to depersonalize their works. [In Polish.]

585.1 Bromfield, Louis. "The New Yorker: Mrs. Conrad Drives in a Limousine," *B*, LXII (October 1925), 196.

When one visits the widow of JC at Canterbury, he is met with a limousine carrying two men on the box. JC, who wrote to please no one but himself, is "more alive today than he has ever been": he lives "with dignity, a beauty, and a fame" which will never come to people who "make spectacles of themselves on a platform raised above a two million circulation."

588.1 Collins, Joseph. "Littérateurs: Foreign Writers: Joseph Conrad," *The Doctor Looks at Biography: Psychological Studies of Life and Letters* (New York: George H. Doran, 1925), pp. 120–25.

Ford Madox Ford's *Joseph Conrad: A Personal Remembrance* is an informative, though not documented, personal book. JC hated the sea, writing, and English prose. Though Ford's picture of JC is interesting and touching, it neglects his art, which achieved realism through impressionism and conveyed character without the author's revealing his opinions.

593.1 "The Conrad Sale," *Publisher's Circular and Booksellers' Record* CXXII (21 March 1925), pp. 363–64.

[Reports the prices paid for JC books and manuscripts sold by Mrs. Jessie Conrad, noting that they compared favorably with the prices realized in the earlier John Quinn sale.]

595.1 "Crowding Conrad," *Literary Digest*, (New York), LXXXIV, (21 February 1925), 29.

Two writers currently threaten JC's preeminence: the American Bill Adams, author of *Senseless Meadows*, and the Englishman H. M. Tomlinson, author of *The Sea and The Jungle* and others.

596.1 Curle, Richard. "Introduction," *Suspense* (Garden City, New York: Doubleday, Page, 1925), pp. v–vi.

JC's last novel, the unfinished novel *Suspense* is a fragment "full of power and fire," one that will take "its place among the recognized masterpieces of this remarkable man."

597.1 Dabrowska, Maria. "Tragizm Conrada" (The Tragic in Conrad), *Wiadomosci Literackie* (Warsaw), No. 11, 1925, p. 2; rpt. in SOC, pp. 53–63.

Polish writers have the right to explain things which Western critics do not understand, such as JC's choice of English instead of French for his literary writing, though French was familiar to all cultured Poles from the eighteenth century to the time of JC's youth. But JC's attitude to the English language was that it was something to be conquered, whereas he loved French and Polish. A number of his characters resemble characters in the works of Mickiewicz and others—but not in Dostoevski. The feeling of responsibility is a basic element in JC's works, as in all great individuals. He called it "loyalty" and followed it as a principle in everything he undertook (not always with good fortune) in his life and writings. [In Polish.]

602.1 "Essays on *Suspense*," *SRL*, II (14 November 1925), 289–91, 315, 326.

Four writers speculate on the ending of *Suspense* in response to a contest sponsored by the *Saturday Review*: (1) Samuel C. Chew thinks that Napoleon would not have a "speaking" role. The plot would not cover a great amount of historical time. JC's interest was in the effect of great events on the group of fictional characters he had created. Napoleon's landing would bring to a climax the antagonism between the Marquis and the Count and enrage Clelia's jealousy of Cosmo's attachment for Adèle. But the ending would be a happy one for Cosmo. (2) David Lambuth believes that *Suspense* dramatizes the testing of fidelities. In the end, Adèle, despite Cosmo's love, would remain faithful to Montevesso. (3) J. De Lancy Ferguson considers JC's novels as both melodramatic and psychological. They dramatize the effect of underlying forces on man's will. These forces ultimately crush man, who attains a measure of victory only by holding close to his chosen way. The evil of Count Helion would destroy him but not the calm self-possession of Adèle. The indiscipline of Clelia would cause her downfall, but Cosmo would emerge master of himself. (4) Donald Davison thinks that JC's cherished human virtue is fidelity, which, however, causes his hero's downfall. Cosmo's interest in Napoleon would divert him from friendship and devotion while Adele would suffer for a misunderstood life of fidelity.

609.1 Fox. C, (ed). "Stories by Conrad and Others," "*Il Conde*" *by Joseph Conrad with Other Stories by Famous American Authors*, ed by C. Fox (New York: C. Reynard, 1925).

Included with a selection of other stories which first appeared in *Hampton's Magazine* in 1908 and 1909, JC's tale, "Il Conde," is a "fine colorful bit of character portrayal" with a dramatic conclusion that contains a note of "tragic pathos."

610.1 Galsworthy, John. "Joseph Conrad: Playwright," *New York Herald Tribune*, 3 May 1925, pp. 1–2.

The fact that JC's three plays are adaptations of works of fiction makes it difficult to determine whether the novelist might have become a great dramatist had he directed his energies toward writing for the stage. Whereas his short play, *One Day More*, succeeds,

Laughing Anne and *The Secret Agent* fail. The unproduced adaptation of *Because of the Dollars* centers on a "man without hands" whose presence onstage might have been unbearable in the theater and would require elaborate theatrical effects. The longest play, *The Secret Agent*, provides an "illustration not only of the difficulty of adaptation, but of the fundamental difference between novel and drama as a medium for presenting life. In adapting his work, JC failed "to balance his effects, . . . to economize his words," and he did not succeed in keeping his "line of action clear and inevitable." Prior to the production of *The Secret Agent*, JC expressed awareness of its dramaturgical shortcomings, but failed to realize that it could have been improved by the "elimination of longuers." Its failure underscores the view that it is fortunate he did not give more time to playwriting.

614.1 Garnett's Answer to Kennedy's Review," *Weekly Westminster*, 10 October 1925; rpt. as "Garnett's Answer to Kennedy's Review" in CCH, pp. 369–71.

Suspense, the "most mature" of all JC's works, is supreme in its "spiritual mastery"; JC has the ability of the "great composer" to carry out his theme so that "all the parts are in right relation to each other and to the whole." [Garnett's reply to the attack on *Suspense*– "*Suspense* does not come to life at all"–by P. C. Kennedy (C, I. No. 627).]

615.1 Gigli, Lorenzo. "Preface," *La Follia di Almayer* (*Almayer's Folly*), (Milan: Modernissima, 1925), pp. 9–20.

Into an exotic background, JC inserted, in *Almayer's Folly*, a psychological analysis conducted with a method that sounded new and revolutionary. [In Italian.]

620.1 Hopkins, Frederick M. "The World of Rare Books: Note and Comment," *SRL*, II (19 December 1925), 439.

The Yale Review has just published JC's diary account of a trip up the Congo in 1890 which fulfilled a wish he had expressed at the age of nine.

621.1 Hutchinson, Percy A. "Conrad Also Had a Play or Two in Him," *NYTBR*, 10 May 1925, p. 3.

In his plays, JC clings "too rigidly—to the originals in narrative form." *One Day More*, praised by Shaw in 1905, is the superior piece. *Laughing Anne* is weaker in that the elimination of the narrator forces the author to devote too much attention to the problem of exposition, and the action is therefore reserved to the last half of the play. It is further weakened by the "pathos" of the denouement, in which Davidson speaks to Anne's dead body. Neither play will enhance JC's reputation.

625.1 "Joseph Conrad's Library," *Publisher's Circular and Booksellers' Record*, CXXII (7 March 1925), p. 305.

[Identifies some of the manuscripts and inscribed editions from JC's library then being offered for sale by Jessie Conrad.]

627.1 Kolaczkowski, Stefan. "Jozef Conrad (Korzeniowski)," Przeglad Wspolczesny (Warsaw, 1925); rpt. in *WSOC*, (1963), pp. 185–246.

Chance, which plays a great part in JC's novels and tales, expresses his concept of life: unexpected things are a "vital truth." JC thought in concrete images. One of his most characteristic attitudes is humanitarian, the opposite of romanticism. He treated with contempt aristocrats, moralists, and others not in contact with life. This attitude reflects his sober, clear intellect, and his condemnation of dried-up feelings. [In Polish.]

629.1 Lanux, Pierre [Combret] de. "Notes from France," *B*, LXI (April 1925), 245–46.

La Nouvelle Revue Francaise devoted an entire number to JC. Among the contributors were André Gide, G. Jean-Aubry, Chevrillon, Larbaud, Jaloux, Ramon Fernandez, Joseph Kessel, John Galsworthy, and others. [Not seen.]

635.1 Loveman, Amy. "Every Man to His Taste," *SRL*, II (5 December 1925), 388.

Among adventure books recently published is JC's unfinished *Suspense*, which inspired writers of a recent essay contest sponsored by the *Saturday Review* to compose violent endings.

635.2 Loveman, Amy. "Unfinished Novels," *SRL*, I (27 June 1925), p. 849.

To speculate on the ending of Conrad's *Suspense* requires taking into account the author's other works and his complaint about the difficulty of treating Napoleon.

635.3 McFee, William. "In the Bookman's Mail," *B*, LXI (June 1925), 500.

Notwithstanding Mrs. Conrad's dislike of Ford Madox Ford and his book on JC, it is a good and revealing study of JC as a living man rather than a monument. Would that Ford's influence on JC, as seen in *Romance*, extended more fully to some of his other novels.

638.1 Morley, Christopher. "The Bowling Green," *SR*, 14 March 1925, p. 597.

A response to Norman Douglas, *D. H. Lawrence and Maurice Magnus: A Plea For Better Manners* (Privately Printed, 1924).] Douglas's comment on JC—that he "seldom explored the human heart" and lacked humor—is "renegade and absurd." Douglas wrongly assumes that others cannot feel as deeply as he does.

645.1 "Notes on Sales: Conrad Books and Manuscripts," *TLS*, 26 February 1925, p. 144.

[Describes the manuscripts, typescripts, proof sheets, and books from JC's library offered for sale by Jessie Conrad through Hodgson & Company on March 13, 1925.]

646.1 O'Flaherty, Liam. *Joseph Conrad: An Appreciation*, *Blue Moon Booklets*, No. 1, 1925; rpt. (New York: Haskell House, 1973).

JC creates in his work a sense of romance that enables the reader to identify with the characters and the events. The sense of dream or fairy tale that pervades JC's work produces "great horizons" in the imagination. Among great men, JC is superb because he writes of empires and imperial men. [This work is interesting for its exuberant style but of little value critically.] [Original *Blue Moon Booklets* unseen.]

654.1 [A Sale at Sotheby's], *SR*, 12 September 1925, p. 123.

[Records the sale at Sotheby's of twenty-six privately printed JC pamphlets.]

656.1 Squire, J. C. "Conrad's Last Book," *Observer* (London), 20 September 1925, pp. 270–79; rpt. in *Sunday Mornings* (London: Heinemann, 1930), p. 4.

Suspense is well narrated and it promised to be JC's most grandiose work, though unfinished in theme and plot. Very likely the love story would have predominated over the political, and the latter would not have been about Napoleon but rather about obscure events and a predestined victim.

659.1 [*Suspense*], *Spectator* (London), 10 October 1925, pp. 613–14 [not seen in this form]; rpt. as "Unsigned Review" in CCH, pp. 372–74.

Suspense contains little more than "the psychology of romantic love." The best part of the book is the last fifty pages. JC's greatest quality in his works is the "tasteful restraint which enables him to say as much, and only as much, as he wills." He had stories to tell, but he had nothing to say. His work as a whole lacks "some element of humanity, of wildness and disorder, lacks any continuity fo contact with the deepest instinct of his land of adoption. He wrote as an aristocrat, but as a Continental not a British aristocrat."

661.1 Tittle, Walter. "Mrs. Conrad Not Eclipsed by Her Husband," *NYTBR*, 17 May 1925, p. 2.

Unlike the wives of many other famous men, Jessie Conrad was not hidden by her husband's shadow. Rather, Mr. and Mrs. Conrad complemented one another admirably. Her sense of humour, preserved even when her injured left knee caused her continual pain, her "constant vigilance" in matters of the household, and her "tender solicitude" for JC made her the "ideal artist's wife." JC responded to these traits with displays of deep affection. [With a portrait of Jessie Conrad.]

667.1 Woolf, Virginia. "Joseph Conrad," *The Common Reader* (London: Hogarth P. 1925), pp. 282–91; rpt. in *Collected Essays* (London: Hogarth P, 1966 New York: Harcourt Brace & World, 1967), I, 302–08.

Before *Nostromo*, JC's novels portrayed characters who were "simple and heroic." They were mostly connected in some way with the sea, and their conflicts were mostly with nature, not with man. The character of Marlow is unique: fitted for retirement, he likes to speculate and to recollect, and he reveals a profound respect for his fellows. For several years, he dominated JC's works, and it was he who enabled JC "to shift his angle of vision" now and then.

668.1 Zeromski, Stephan. "Joseph Conrad—rodak" (Joseph Conrad—Fellow-Countryman), *Naokolo Swiata* (Warsaw), February 1935, n. p., rpt. in *Dziela (Pisma Literackie)*, (Warsaw: Czytelnik, 1960), pp. 151–70.

JC's life and work testify to unequalled power of will. JC's finest achievement is *Lord Jim*, which depicts the innermost soul. It is a symbolic confession in the form of a parable. JC's Polish origins remain a secret from the West and from himself; his works, except for a few journalistic articles, cast the shadow of oblivion over both the man and his writings. French and English critics cannot understand his aversion to "Muscovites." But our extraordinary indifference towards matters of culture means that we have not yet attempted to illuminate the Polish aspect of JC's spirit. We have, however, no intention of annexing him as belonging to Polish literature. [In Polish.]

1926

669.1 Angioletti, G[iovan] B[attista]. [Review of Two Novels], *La Fiera Letteraria*, II, No. 49 (5 December 1926), p. 8.

JC was a true artist who chose by chance the form of the adventure novel; his real end was psychological interpretation. [In Italian.]

680.1 "Books in the Sale Rooms," *Bookman's Journal*, XII (April 1926), pp. 30–32.

[Comments on the high prices realized by Jessie Conrad's sale of her husband's manuscripts, typescripts, and books from his library.]

686.1 [A Conrad Memorial], *SR*, 24 April 1926, p. 735.

[Comments on plans to construct a JC memorial in Bishopsbourne.]

693.1 Curle, Richard. "Conrad's Diary," *YR*, XV (January 1926), pp. 254–66.

The diary kept by JC in the Congo in 1890, or the part of it which has survived, is contained in two small black "penny notebooks" and is written in pencil. [This article reproduces the first of the notebooks, except for the lists of names, persons, books, stories, and the calculations that fill the last pages. Passages from "Heart of Darkness" serve to show how closely some of the earlier pages of "this masterpiece" are a recollection of JC's journey. The notebook helps to prove the contention that nearly all of JC's work is founded upon autobiographical resemblance. The second notebook is not printed here "simply because it has no personal or literary interest." JC's Congo diary is "a strange tantalizing fragment" and must eternally remain so.]

695.1 Dabrowska, Maria. "Na drodze uczynkow" (On the Path of Deeds), *WL*, Nos. 18–29 (1926), 1; rpt. in *Soc*, 2nd ed (Warsaw: Panstwowy Instytut Wydawniczy, 1974), pp. 79–83.

Lord Jim and *The Rover* are especially helpful in understanding the drama of JC's personal life. Despite great differences, Peyrol's life is a paraphrase of JC's own, though JC was not a patriot in the conventional sense of the word. [In Polish.]

695.2 Dabrowska, Maria. "O *Smudze cienia*" (On *The Shadow-Line*), *Glos Prawdy* (Warsaw), No. 94 (1926), p. 6; rpt. in *SOC*, 2nd ed (Warsaw: Cyztelnik, 1974), pp. 69–72.

The Shadow-Line is a variation of the theme of responsibility, depicted as a dangerous line warning youth of the boundaries of hope and the relentless burdens of life. Its construction is simple, and the vocabulary is heavy with the burden of content. It is curious that the best translators of JC into Polish have been women (Zagorska, Kornilowiczowa). [In Polish.]

699.1 Finger, Charles J. "The New Conrad," *All's Well* VI (Fayetteville, Arkansas), (January-February 1926), p. 12, back to 2

JC's works will endure largely because of his creation of memorable characters. Actions grows, not out of plot but, as in life, out of collision of character upon character or out of the battling of character against "evil chance, or fate, or destiny."

710.1 "Joseph Conrad, from the Oil Portrait Painted from Life by Walter Tittle," *World's Work in Literature*, LIII (November 1926), faces p. 3. Frontispiece.

[A full page black and white reproduction of the portrait Conrad sat for.]

725.1 Morley, Christopher. "The Bowling Green," *SRL*, III (30 October 1926), 255.

[Reprints some "memorable words" that Cunninghame Graham wrote just after JC's burial, which were included by Mrs. Conrad in "her little book about J. C."]

726.1 "Mrs. Joseph Conrad's 'Don'ts' for an Author's Wife," *Literary Digest*, XCI (30 October 1926), 50–52.

[Lists eight "don'ts" which, according to Mrs. Joseph Conrad, are useful for the woman who wants to succeed as the wife of a great man and quotes from Jessie Conrad's recently published book, *Joseph Conrad as I Knew Him* (1926).]

729.1 Pure, Simon [pseud. of Frank Swinnerton]. "The Londoner," *B*, 13, LXIV (December 1926), 485–91.

A monument to the late JC is being erected in the village in which he lived. Perhaps some more worthy method of commemoration could be found.

735.1 Shand, John. "Books of the Quarter," *Criterion*, IV (October 1926); rpt. in *Criterion*, 1922–39, ed by T. S. Eliot (London: Faber and Faber, 1967), pp. 782–85.

JC is not at his best in an essay; he is interesting, but not great. In *Last Essays*, his style has lost its individual quality; he seems to be writing as a matter of duty. Apparently the critic and the artist are not to be found in one person. JC's success is due to the fact that he is primarily a teller of tales. His essays lack information, interest, and amusement.

1927

747.1 Bidou, Henry. "La Vocation de Conrad" (Conrad's Vocation), *Journal Des Débats* (Paris), XXX (15 April 1927), 615.

JC's novels of adventure are popular in France. JC's life as well as his work is especially adventurous. [In French.]

756.1 Dabrowska, Marie. "Joseph Conrad and Poland: Lord Jim's Burnt Ship," *New Age*, 3 March 1927, pp. 208–09. [Trans from *Pologne Littéraire* by Ina Beasley. [Not seen.]

A full understanding of JC's works depends on a study of the facts of his early youth on his knowledge of Slavic literatures. JC showed a "kinship of soul" with the Polish Romantic movement, from which he developed an instinctive idea of responsibility. For him, the refusal to obey this instinct renders existence unendurable. But the fact that JC had abandoned his native land at the time of its greatest disasters, had burned his boats, as it were, contradicted his instinct for fidelity and loyalty; and like Lord Jim, he was always searching for a suitable opportunity to "settle accounts" or undergo his punishment, an opportunity which never arose. The story of *The Rover* seems a paraphrase of JC's life: if the desertion of his country was a fault, it has been redeemed by this novel of "sheer and inestimable value." [In Polish.]

757.1 Dyboski, Roman. "Z mlodosci Jozefa Conrada" (The Youth of Joseph Conrad), *Czas* (Warzaw, No. 296, 1927; rpt. in *WSOC*, pp. 35–42.

Jadwiga Kalusha was brought up in the neighborhood of the Korzeniowski family and knew JC in Lwow in 1867. He amazed everybody by repeating long passages from *Pan Tadeusz* by Mickiewicz (1834). JC met Kalusha again in 1873 when he was planning a career at sea, though not in the Austrian Naval Academy. [In Polish.]

757.2 Eliot, T.S. "Short Reviews" *Joseph Conrad as I Knew Him*, by Jessie Conrad, Heinemann, 6s, net, " *Criterion*, V (January 1927), 159; rpt. in *The Criterion*, 1922-1939, ed by T.S. Eliot (London; Faber and Faber, 1967), p. 159.

Jessie Conrad's book *Joseph Conrad as I Knew Him* is not skillfully written and it fails to reveal the wealth of information that would be both interesting and significant to the scholarly world.

760.1 Gissing, George. "George Gissing on Conrad," *Letters of George Gissing*, ed. by A. and E. Gissing (1927), p. 391 [not seen in this form]; rpt. as "George Gissing on Conrad" in CCH, p. 140.

Youth: A Narrative and Two Other Stories presents JC as the "strongest writer—in every sense of the word—at present publishing in England." It is a miracle that a foreigner should write like this.

762.1 Grabowski, Zbigniew. "'Romantyzm' Conrada" (Conrad's Romanticism), *Ze Studiow Nad Josephem Conradem* (Poznan: [no publisher given], 1927); rpt. in *WSOC*, pp. 253–69.

The words "Romantic" and "Romanticism" have a particular shade of meaning in Polish which differs from the meanings in English. In Polish, the words express a tendency for an individual to form his own reality and become the center of creative energy, a desire for changes and a new order, leading to disillusionment, revolt, isolation, and contempt. These characteristics occur in *Victory*, and disillusionment sounds throughout JC's works. [In Polish.]

763.1 Hopkins, Frederick M. "Choosing a Title," *SRL*, IV (8 October 1927), 187.

JC avers that he can offer no explanation as to how he chose a title for *The Arrow of Gold*. [Quotes JC's unpublished letter to his publisher, Doubleday, Page & Co, but gives no date.]

763.2 Hopkins, Frederick M. "Conrad Collection," *SRL*, 23 April 1927, p. 775.

[Announces the forthcoming sale on 28 April 1927 of Richard Curle's collection of first and other rare editions of JC's works, at the American Art Galleries.]

764.1 Hopkins, Frederick M. "High Conrad Prices," *SRL*, 14 May 1927, p. 835.

The collection of first and rare editions of JC's writings formed by his friend Richard Curle was sold at the American Art Galleries on April 28, 1927, bringing extraordinarily high prices for an author whose full recognition is so recent.

766.1 Korzeniowska, Jessie Conrad. "The Romance of First Editions," *Poland*, VIII (November 1927), 662–65.

The sale of Richard Curle's collection of first editions and typescripts of JC's works might well have pleased the author, who played an important part in the compilation of the collection. JC often gave away his last remaining copies of early editions, even those inscribed to his wife, but some of the rarest items were saved from the bonfire by Mrs. Conrad. [The memoir reprints two letters written to JC when he commanded the *Otago*.]

769.1 Morley, Christopher. "The Folder," *SRL*, 10 December 1927, p. 429.

Ben Gun reports that he knew JC well and sailed with him. Apparently, Gun says, JC always wanted to be a "black-and-white artist" and always carried ink and paper with him. Interestingly, too, although he loved the sea, he hated passengers; yet in this way he was typical of many officers. JC was a good officer, even if he tended to dream too much. Nevertheless, his fellow seamen always held him in the highest respect.

769.2 Morley, Christopher. "The Folder," *SRL*, III (21 May 1927), 845.

[Quotes three autograph letters of JC: 18 February 1923, to the Vice Chancellor of Oxford University, 15 March 1923, to the Vice Chancellor of Cambridge University, and 27 May 1924, to The Right Honourable Ramsay Mac Donald, M.P.]

770.1 [Notes for a Conrad Library], SR, 15 January 1927, p. 521.

[Notes plans for the JC Library at the Seamen's Church Institute, New York.]

771.1 Pavolini, Corrado. "*Lord Jim,*" LCS, X, 8 (August 1927), 183.

The tragic, picturesque, pathetic, cruel, totally true and untrue story of Jim in *Lord Jim* is presented to readers in a translation not in the least up to the splendor of the original. [Review of Italian translation of *Lord Jim* (Milan: Corticelli, 1927).] [In Italian.]

771.2 [Review of Jessie Conrad, *Joseph Conrad as I Knew Him*], *Criterion*, V (January 1927), 159 rpt. in *The Criterion*, 1922-1939, ed by T. S. Eliot (London: Faber and Faber; New York: Barnes & Noble, 1967), p. 159.

Mrs. Conrad wrote her reminiscences of JC as she knew him. She "must have buried in her mind much that would be interesting and important in the world of letters" which an experienced biographer "might have made really vital."

771.3 Romano, Alberto. "Esoticism" (Exoticism), *Il Popolo Di Roma* (23 August 1927); rpt. in *Scrittori Letterari* (Literary Writers), (Napoli: Guida, 1930), 121–24.

It is wrong to see in JC's work a direct derivation from the adventure story tradition or to look for exoticism as a mere pretext, as in Stevenson. [In Italian.]

778.1 Vines, Sherard. *Movements in Modern English Poetry and Prose* (Tokyo: Humphrey Milford, Oxford UP, The Onkayama Publishing Co., 1927), pp. 247–48.

[A very brief comment on JC, on the nonexistence of a JC "school," and on JC's part in calling novelists' attention to style.]

1928

781.1 American Art Association. *Important First Editions: Manuscripts and Letters of Jane Austen, J. M. Barrie, William Blake, Robert Burns, Lord Byron, Joseph Conrad, . . . Et. Al. To be Sold on Wednesday Evening February 1 1928 (New York, 1928).*

[Describes thirty-four pieces of Conradiana for sale and quotes from JC's letters to Mark Twain and Henry Devray as well as from letters written to JC by Cunninghame Graham and Ford Madox Hueffer. Some interesting quotations are from letters which are apparently unpublished.]

786.1 "The Book Mart," *B*, LXVII (June 1928), xxvii–xxx.

The book auction season in the United States brought the sale of a series of letters from JC which extended over a period of twenty years, only a few of which are included in Jean-Aubry's work. Sold also was the Edward Garnett collection of books and autographed letters of JC. An unpublished JC autobiography in the third person, about 400 words written in 1900, brought $650. The original typescript of *Under Western Eyes* was sold for $2,200, but the "gem of the sale" was one of seven copies of *The Nigger of the Narcissus* printed by Heinemann in 1897 for copyright purposes, which was sold for $4,900.

786.2 "The Book Mart," *B*, LXVII (July 1928), xxvii.

[A report on the sale of 100 letters written by JC and of one copy of "The Personality of Joseph Conrad." Includes some historical background on the early publication of JC's letters.]

787.1 Brown, W. Sorley. *The Life and Genius of T. W. H. Crosland* (London, Cecil Palmer, 1928), pp. 69, 217, 452, 479.

T. W. H. Crosland was responsible for the literary part of *The Outlook*, which JC contributed to, and he also published *The Academy*, with "long, detailed and scholarly critical appreciations" of JC's works, among others. Crosland's last poem was a sonnet on the death of JC, printed in *The First Edition* for December, 1924. [Not seen.]

793.1 Curle, Richard. "Joseph Conrad as a Letter-Writer," *New York Herald Tribune: Books*, 30 September 1928, pp. 1, 6.

While the mere bulk of JC's letters, perhaps as many as 6,000, is surprising, the "uniform quality" of his correspondence is "really astonishing," for his briefest notes express his personality as well as do his longer essays. Never losing an intimate tone, his letters provide an index to his moods and individuality. Indeed, his finest correspondence ranks beside the novels that made him famous.

794.1 Dabrowska, Maria. "Zwyciestwo J. Conrada" (J. Conrad's *Victory*), *Swiat Ksiazik* (Warsaw), 1928, n. p.; rpt. in *SOC*, 1959, pp. 47–51.

In *Victory*, JC depicts unusual events but extracts from them something general and human. Although the characters are unusual, they are full of human, ordinary passions. [In Polish.]

795.1 Dent, Joseph Mallaby. *The Memoirs of J. M. Dent, 1849-1926* (London: Dent, 1928), pp. 227–28.

J. M. Dent's friendship with JC started as a business connection and soon ripened into a strong personal admiration. [Issued also in a revised edition in 1938 as *The House of Dent, 1888-1938.*]

799.1 "The First Issue of *Chance*," *Bookman's Journal*, Third Series, XVI, No. 6 (1928), 352–53.

Recent sales at the Hodgson galleries in London affirm the continued interest in JC on the part of book collectors. An inscribed copy of the first issue of *Chance*, dated 1913, realized 420 pounds while an inscribed copy of *'Twixt Land and Sea* with the error in the "Freya" lettering realized 71 pounds.

816.1 Kocienski, Leonardo. "*Sotto gli occhi dell'Occidente*" (Under Western Eyes), *LCS*, XI, 12 (December 1928), 320.

In this story of an almost unconscious betrayal, *Under Western Eyes*, there are some very beautiful pages, full of interesting studies of the Russian psyche. [Review of *Under Western Eyes: Sotto gli occhi dell'Occidente* (Milan: Corticelli, 1928).] [In Italian.]

828.1 Nitchie, Elizabeth. *The Criticism of Literature* (New York: Macmillan, 1928), pp. 188, 231, 244, 247, 362, 363.

JC is a great writer who, like Horace, Virgil, Keats, Thackeray, and Flaubert, strives on paper to construct perfect sentences. A sense of style is as natural to him as is his willingness to work for perfection. His characters are mainly interesting because of the new and strange adventures they experience; and as for setting, he is unlike Dickens, who employs the same backgrounds, but he is more like Austen in choosing a specific type of setting—for him the sea. [In the appendix, Nitchie includes exercises for students. One exercise cites a passage from *A Personal Record* and requests an identification or description of descriptive words. Another exercise, citing another passage from *Record*, requests an identification of suggestive word and phrases.]

828.2 Orvis, Mary B. *Short Story Writing* (New York: Ronald P, 1928), pp. 74–75, 130–32.

"The End of the Tether" illustrates the principle of implication, the highest technique a fiction writer can have. JC never says, for example, that Captain Whalley is blind but rather merely hints at this fact along the way. It is only through Whalley's own action that the reader discerns the blindness.

837.1 Swinnerton, Frank. *A London Bookman* (London: Martin Secker, 1928), pp. 6–7.

JC's *Notes on Life and Letters* is not an intimate revelation of the author, but it is the serious expression of "sage artistic reflections."

837.2 T., G. M. "The Compleat Collector," *SRL*, V (22 December 1928), 546.

G. A. Parker, 247 Park Avenue, now has in his possession, the original typed letter by JC, the letter which Thomas J. Wise had spoken of too freely.

837.3 [T. J. Wise Condemns]. *SR*, 20 October 1928, p. 285.

[Quotes T. J. Wise's condemnation of the pamphlet *To My Brethren of the Pen.*]

838.1 Wise, Thomas J. "The Bibliography of Joseph Conrad," *Bookman's Journal*, Third Series, XVI, No. 6 (1928), 226–27.

[Thomas J. Wise responds to Mackay's claim that his figures on the number of copies of the first edition of *Almayer's Folly* and *An Outcast of the Islands* were erroneous, noting that the figures derive from the actual records of T. Fisher Unwin.]

838.2 Zeromski, Stefan. *"Pisma wybrane Joseph Conrada"* (Collected Works of Joseph Conrad), *Elegie* (Warsaw), (1928), n. p.; rpt. in *WSOC*, pp. 163–84.

The Mirror of the Sea is the best conspectus of all of JC's works which are concerned with the sea. Every impression is based on years of experience. JC was able to render the speech of engines and their sounds long before the time of the Italian Futurists. His comments are not those of an observer, who might be mistaken, but facts acquired by means of the unconscious knowledge and feeling of a sailor in active service, not seeking impressions and generalizations, but learning how best to get a ship off a sunken reef. His are recollections drawn from the mind's depths, as are the places and characters JC absorbed and later recreated. But this is not all: in *Lord Jim* we are faced with the problem of heroism and cowardice; in *Nostromo*, we see the history of revolution in general. In 1914, it seemed that the musicality of the Polish language remained in JC's ears, especially the Polish method of linking periods and admiring strange things. [In Polish.]

1929

843.1 Benet, William Rose [The Phoenician]. "The Phoenix Nest," *SR*, V (22 June 1929), 1136.

Earle F. Walbridge, librarian of the Harvard Club, writes that an amusing confusion of characters on page 78 of Jessie Conrad's *Joseph Conrad as I Knew Him* proves, at least to the writer, that Mrs. Conrad read *Peason's Magazine* "as thoroughly as Conrad's manuscripts."

853.1 Dabrowska, Maria. "Prawdziwa rzeczwistosc Conrada: poza krytwriami formalnymi" (Conrad's True Reality; Beyond Formal Criteria), [wr. 1929]; rpt. in *SOC*, 1959; rpt. in *WSOC*, (1963) pp. 27–89.

JC's works consist either of accounts of events experienced, seen, or heard, or deliberately composed artistic works on a theme which pervades the writer's works. The latter works usually have more complex construction, as in *Nostromo*, which must be read at least twice with notetaking. By artistic criteria, its construction is not good, but its virtues include the language, descriptive passages, wealth of thoughts, feelings, associations, and moral ideas, which are outside formal criteria. [In Polish.]

877.1 Kridl, Manfred. "*Lord Jim* Conrada" (Conrad's *Lord Jim*), *Przeglad Wspolczesny* (Warsaw), Nos. 81–82 (1929); rpt. in *WSOC* pp. 290–328.

There is no clear analogy between Jim's act in *Lord Jim* and JC's so-called "desertion" of Poland. Jim's temporary weakness and later fate are common to all men and require investigation of JC's personal experiences. The "personal" element lies in Jim's character and experience, e.g., his longing for a romantic life, loyalty to tasks set him, feelings of foreignness and home-sickness. A Polish reader feels close to Jim, with his exuberant individuality, exaggerated point of honor, noble temperament, impulsiveness, and improvidence. [In Polish.]

894.1 Staniewski, Maurycy. "Angielskosc' Conrada: Anglia w powiesciach Conrada" (Conrad's Englishness: England in Conrad's Novels), *Wiadomosci Literackie* (Warsaw), No. 14, 1929 ; rpt. in *WSOC*, pp. 48–60.

JC's England is a ceremonial, dreamed-up place. Contemporary England did not impress JC: his typically English characters are treated ironically, and his tragic English figures are in subtle conflict with official England, its morality and customs. [In Polish.]

899.1 West, Rebecca. "Why H. M. Tomlinson Was Called an Imitator of Conrad," *B*, LXIX (July 1929), 520.

When H. M. Tomlinson first began publishing his stories of the sea, JC was just rising to popularity. Because of this similarity of time and subject, Tomlinson has fallen under the label of an imitator of JC, but this judgment is unjustified. Tomlinson's writing is precise, and he exhibits a deep concern for realism. JC, however, is at best a very inexact writer of English; his tangled language weakens his images, and he can strengthen them only by juxtaposing hazy phrases with more hazy phrases. Essentially, the very differences in Tomlinson's and JC's characters necessitated a difference in their method.

1930

903.1 Conrad, Jessie. "A Personal Tribute to the Late Percival Gibbon and Edward Thomas," *Bookman* (London), LXXVIII (September 1930), 323–24.

[Contains only passing references to JC.]

908.1 Heydrick, Benjamin A. "Joseph Conrad," *Familiar Essays of To-Day* (New York: Scribner's, 1930), p. 68.

[Brief sketch of JC's life introducing "My First Book" as a familiar essay.]

909.1 Hicks, Granville. "Ford Madox Ford—A Neglected Contemporary," *B*, LXXII (December 1930), 365.

Early in his career (1897) JC, conscious of inadequacies in his English style, sought out Ford Madox Ford as a literary collaborator. Ford recorded the details in his *Joseph Conrad* and in an appendix to *The Nature of a Crime*. The difference in the two men's temperaments made collaboration unprofitable, except that JC learned a good deal about English style from Ford.

914.1 Mumby, Frank Arthur. *Publishing and Bookselling* (London: Jonathan Cape, 1930), pp. 346–47, 377.

In 1894, just after he had finished *Almayer's Folly* and while still in ignorance about book publishing, JC thought this, his first novel, would be perfect for Fisher Unwin's The Pseudonym Library. Three months after submitting his manuscript, he received the acceptance letter, which he records as the very first typewritten letter he had ever received. This acceptance was largely due to the efforts of Edward Garnett, then reader for Unwin. Moreover, it was Garnett who also saw in JC the potential for a great writer and accordingly persuaded him to write a second novel.

916.1 Riovallan, A. "L'Alchimie de Conrad" (Conrad's Alchemy), *Bulletin de France Grande Bretagne*, XCVI (May 1930), 5–10.

To verify the verisimilitude of JC's fiction set in foreign lands, an examination of "The Idiots" from *Tales of Unrest*, set in Brittany, provides a control. First, JC changes place-names of some locales while preserving those of others, thus allowing himself some freedom for his imagination as well as providing the reader with guideposts. He is less successful with his adaptation of family names, which are quite unrealistic. Furthermore, except for his characterization of Mme. Levaille, the characters are unconvincing psychologically; they seem more allegorical figures than real ones. On the other hand, some of the action seems true to life, but on the whole, his attempt to bring together Mme. Levaille with the idiots seems arbitrary and melodramatic. [In French.]

916.2 Segur, Nicolas. "La Vie Littéraire" (The Literary Life), *Revue Mondiale (Ancienne Revue des Revues)*, CXCIV (1 March 1930), 88.

The Shadow-Line marks the transition from the careless period of JC's youth to the period of maturity characterized by darkness and shadows. This story, typically autobiographical, is remarkable for its depiction of the sea, the eternal center of JC's novels. [In French.]

1931

918.1 Bement, Douglas. *Weaving the Short Story* (New York: Farrar & Rinehart, 1931); rpt. (New York: Ray Long & Richard R. Smith, 1932), pp. 120, 123, 124n, 129, 146, 171–72, 173, 202–03, 213.

The author-participant "angle of narration" in "Youth" adds realism to the story by making the narrator seem a real person. This angle is subjective in this story: the narrator, while not the chief character, reflects the entire mood of the work. JC often shifted his angle so frequently that the reader is left in some confusion.

924.1 Cruse, Amy. "Joseph Conrad," *The Golden Road in English Literature* (New York: Crowell, [1931]), pp. 630–39, 642, 643.

JC wanted to become a sailor because he desired to be free from the Russians. [An unimportant sketch of JC's life.]

929.1 Korbut, Gabrjel. *Literatura Polska Od Poczaykow Do Wojny Swiatowej*, IV (Polish Literature from the Beginnings to the World War), (Warsaw: Kasa im. Mianowskiego, 1931), pp. 313–16.

[Bibliography, including articles 1899–1931 (selected).] [In Polish.]

935.1 Penton, Brian. "Note on Form in the Novel," *Scrutinies*, II [by various authors, Collected by Edgell Rickword], (London: Wishart, 1931), pp. 243–44.

JC loses control of form in *The Arrow of Gold* after he had mastered it completely in *The Nigger of the Narcissus*, "Typhoon," and "Youth."

938.1 Tobin, A. I., and Elmer Gertz. *Frank Harris: A Study in Black and White* (Chicago: Madelaine Mendelsohn, 1931) ; rpt. (New York: Haskell House, 1970), pp. 22, 136.

As editor of the *Saturday Review*, Frank Harris helped "discover" JC. H. G. Wells's review of *Almayer's Folly* made JC's reputation. Yet, strangely enough, JC was unsuccessful when he sought employment on the staff of the *Review;* in spite of Cunninghame Graham's good offices, it seemed that Harris would not heed JC's overtures.

939.1 Ward, Alfred C. *Foundations of English Prose* (London: G. Bell & Sons, 1931), pp. 32, 79, 80, 123, 125, 181, 243, 244.

In *Victory*, JC tells of Axel Heyst, whose carefully constructed philosophy of nonparticipation in life is shattered. He is trapped in a tragic situation which destroys him and others. He is surprised, as people often are, by doing something he never expected to do. JC was not only a psychological novelist, but an adventure novelist also, and it is possible to read much of his work for enjoyment. Of his shorter works, "Youth" and "Typhoon" may be considered condensed novels, whereas "The Secret Sharer" is a short story: it concerns itself with one piece of action or one situation. In four pages of *A Christmas Garland* (1912) by Max Beerbohm, JC's style and ironic outlook are parodied.

1932

947.1 Caprile, Enrico. [Review of *Il Reietto della isole* (*An Outcast of the Islands*), trans. G. D'Arese (Turin: Slavia, 1932]; *LCS*, XVI (1 January 1933), 22.

[Wrongly states that all of JC's works have appeared in Italian.] [In Italian.]

947.2 Chwalewik, Witold. "Jozef Conrad w Kardyfie" (Joseph Conrad in Cardiff), *Ruch Literacki* (Warsaw), No. 8, 1932 ; rpt. in *WSOC*, pp. 61–69.

The first published comment on JC's links with Poland was in *The Western Mail* (Cardiff, 1 January 1897), when Arthur Mee published "A New Writer on Dickens" (JC's opinions). When JC made the acquaintance of the Kliszczewski family in Cardiff in 1885, they were surprised by his poor spoken English. During JC's third visit (December 1896), Jozef Kliszczewski asked JC to write in praise of Poland, but JC protested that he would lose his public if he did so. [In Polish.]

951.1 Dabrowska, Maria. "Spoleczne i religijne pierwiastki u Conrada" (Social and Religious Elements in Conrad), *Wiadomosci Literackie* (Warsaw), 1932, n.p. [not seen in this form]; rpt. in *SOC*, pp. 78–101.

Time has almost no role in JC's work as a factor in construction. The elements are situations which JC uses without considering whether they occur in the past, present, or future. JC does not adopt a moral attitude, nor does he draw conclusions. He depicts the factual influence of life on board trading-ships and in international commerce, in which he had taken part and knew well. Not until he quit seafaring did he see the dark side of that existence, but he did not then hesitate to depict it. The capitalist, militaristic European expeditions into the wilderness were condemned according to JC's own attitude, not on general ethical principles. When JC's heroines struggle for honor, it is struggle to preserve their connections with the ideal elements of existence, since only this connection gives value and honor to human life. [In Polish.]

966.1 Weeks, Edward. "Method in Their Madness," *B*, LXXV (June-July 1932), 225–32.

JC began the writing of *Almayer's Folly* without a single note of any kind, but this method allows many valuable details to be lost.

967.1 West, Herbert F. *A Modern Conquistador: Robert Bontine Cunninghame Graham, His Life and Work* (London: Cranley & Day, 1932), pp. 22, 99, 107–15, 119, 123, 149–50, 158, 163, 165, 180, 186, 191, 193, 214, 217, 220, 221, 235, 236–37, 242, 278, 279–80.

JC knew W.H. Hudson only slightly, though he had dined with him in London in 1902. Nonetheless, he always appreciated Hudson's writings and once wrote that Hudson was a "privileged being." JC first met Cunninghame Graham in 1896, when Cunninghame Graham became enthralled with JC's story, "An Outpost of Progress." JC later affectionately call Cunninghame Graham "Prince Errant," and by the time JC died, he and Cunninghame Graham had become intimate friends.

1933

973.1 "England Buys Tittle's Portrait of Conrad," *Art Digest* (1 January 1933), 5.

Walter Tittle's portrait of JC, painted a few months before JC died in 1924, has been acquired by the "British nation" for the

National Portrait Gallery in London. It is the only portrait for which JC ever posed.

985.1 Stevens, Alfred A. *The Recollections of a Bookman* (London: H. F. & G. Witherby, 1933), p. 81.

JC, a "wizard of the sea," "cast a very real spell" over the British, who loved the sea. Understanding the "mental and moral make-up " of Britons, he presented his findings "as in a mirror."

986.1 Walpole, Hugh. "Tendencies in the Modern Novel—I. England," *Fortnightly Review*, CXXXIV (October 1933), 407–15.

JC was a true novelist because he created characters "beyond [his] own autobiographical experience and engaged in some kind of narrative."

986.2 Wolter, Karl Kurt. "Joseph Conrad: Herz der Finsternis "(Joseph Conrad: "Heart of Darkness", *Jugend* (Munich), XXXVIII (1933), 519.

[A review of "Heart of Darkness" as translated into German by E. W. Freissler (Berlin: S Fischer, 1933). JC's novel is an adventure story told with appalling apathy.] [In German.]

986.3 "W. Somerset Maugham on Conrad's Bornean Novels," [an extract from Maugham's story, "Neil MacAdam"], 1933 [not seen in this form]; rpt. as "W. Somerset Maugham on Conrad's Bornean Novels" in *CCH*, pp. 377–78.

Although JC did not know Borneo as we know it today, he succeeded in creating a country, "a dark, sinister, romantic and heroic country of the soul." [Although fictional, this point of view may be taken to represent Maugham's own.]

1934

986.4 Camerino, Aldo. "Joseph Conrad: 'Three Plays,'" 1934, (unlocated); rpt. in *Scrittoti di Lingua Inglese* (English Writers), (Milan & Napoli: Ricciardi, 1968), pp. 179–85.

JC's plays seem to accentuate his worst faults when he adheres too much to reality, when he removes the screen that veiled his creations in a magic atmosphere. *Laughing Anne* does not contribute to his fame. *One Day More* is less alive than *Tomorrow*. The play *The Secret Agent* has no resemblance to the novel: in common they have only a mysterious touch. [In Italian.]

989.1 Duncan, Robert F. "Conrad's Art of Characterization," *Creighton Quarterly,* XXV (June 1934), 337–44.

JC's "forte" as a novelist lies in his art of characterization: he usually portrays an individual, not a type; each of his protagonists is haunted by a powerful motivating principle; his use of action as a means of portraying character is constant because the actions are those of human beings; his protagonists speak with a purpose, for dialogue must further action and reveal character; and other characters express their opinions of another person in the story. JC's use of characterization is seen well in *The Nigger of the Narcissus, Victory,* and *Lord Jim.* [An early but representative and limited attempt to assess JC as a writer, revealing some real perception and some serious errors. The author, for example, consistenly misspells "Marlow," and he makes the wild statement that with James and JC, the "psychological novel" reached hitherto unknown heights, but "in the hands of such new men as Joyce and Lawrence, . . . it has fallen into excess and worse."]

990.1 Krzyzanowski, Julian. "O tragedii na Samburanie" (On the Tragedy on Samburan), *Pion* (Warsaw), No. 50, 1934 ; rpt. in *WSOC,* pp. 333–37.

Most attempts to investigate JC's "Polishness" are futile. As the Polishness is a biographical and psychological problem, it should be studied in terms of the psychic trauma cause by Orzeskowa's attack. Of equal importance is JC's position as "defender of Poland" in English journalism, which in turn is a psychological and literary problem not yet investigated adequately by Polish critics. The conclusion of *Victory* is a parallel to that of Mickiewicz's narrative poem *Grazyna,* but probably unconsciously so. [In Polish.]

993.1 Morley, Christopher. "The Folder," *SRL,* XI (22 December 1934), 387.

Bruce Rogers, the printer, has been carving a head of JC out of a block of weathered pine. This will be placed as a figurehead on A. J. Villier's full-rigged ship, the *Joseph Conrad.*

993.2 [The *Otago*], *SR,* 24 November 1934, p. 310.

[On the "recent" scuttling of the *Otago.*]

994.1 Stewart, Powell, and Michael Bradshaw. *A Goodly Company: A Guide to Parallel Reading* (New York: American Book Co., 1934), pp. 5–7, 46–48, 184–85, 273–74.

[Contains useful synopses of *Lord Jim, The Nigger of the Narcissus, The Mirror of the Sea, The Rover, Victory, Tales of Unrest,* and *Youth and Other Tales*, which increase one's interest and perception for a profitable reading.]

998.1 Wells, H. G. *Experiment in Autobiography: Discoveries and Conclusions of a Very Ordinary Brain (Since 1866)*, London: 1934; rpt. (Philadelphia and New York: J. B. Lippincott, 1967), pp. 525–35.

At first, Wells was impressed by JC as "the strangest of creatures" because of his unusual head and face, his gestures, and his strange manner of speaking English. Yet his English prose was "extraordinarily rich," with a "foreign" flavor. The "deepest theme" of his work is the simple terror of strange places such as the jungle, night, and the "incalculable" sea. Another "primary topic" of his is the feeling of being incurably "foreign." He pursued a "phantom 'honor,'" (in *Lord Jim*, for example); he had little humor and tenderness and "no trace of experienced love or affection." He and Wells "never really 'got on' together." One day on the Sandgate beach, when JC asked Wells how he would describe a boat out on the water, he replied that he would just let the boat "be there in the commonest phrases possible." But it was against JC's "over-sensitized receptivity" that a boat could ever be just a boat. He wanted to see it with a "definite vividness of his own"; he was a "vivid impressionist." JC owed much to the early association with Ford Madox Ford, who helped greatly to "English" him and make him acquainted with the English literary world. Much of JC's work is oppressive; only in some of his short stories is he on a level with the "naked vigour" of Stephen Crane. [Contains Well's amusing first impressions of JC, emphasizes JC's insistence upon "seeing" beneath the surface of things, and explains how Wells moved away from Ford and JC's interest in finding the perfect expression to follow his own—journalism.]

999.1 Wingfield-Stratford, Esmé. *The Victorian Aftermath* (New York: William Morrow, 1934), pp. 151–52.

JC is an intense psycological novelist using the sea story to depict adventures of the spirit.

1935

1005.1 Collette, Elizabeth. "Conrad, Chronicler of the Sea," *Highroad to English Literature* (Boston: Ginn, 1935), pp. 500-05; 395, 492, 493, 494, 498, 509, 512, 517, 519, 524, 527, 546, 554.

JC is read largely for his description of the sea "in all her moods." Many of his plots are based on facts. We can understand his characters as he searches for motives back of passions and actions; we understand his creations because they are "pieces of Life with a capital L." [Somewhat typical of the many imperceptible comments about JC which are intended for teachers.]

1011.1 Fryde, Ludwik. "Conrad i kryzys powiesci psychologiczenj" (Conrad and the Crisis of the Psychological Novel), *Tygodnik Ilustrowany* (Warsaw), No. 30, 1935 ; rpt. in *COKS*, pp. 385–94.

Lord Jim is the first great psychological problem in JC's work. Despite his basic dislike of analysis, JC penetrates deeply into this character, but the deeper he goes the less real Jim becomes, whereas his flight becomes more comprehensible. In *Lord Jim*, JC comes into conflict with determinism and realism, apparently accepting psychological determinism. *Jim* is the evidence of failure of psychologism in his work. A scrupulous analysis of JC's act proves pointless, as JC can neither justify nor explain Jim's irrational impulse. JC's weakness in consistent psychological analysis is evident also in *Nostromo*, despite the dazzling visions of the first part. But the novel confirms the fact that the motives of human behavior were an impenetrable system to JC. *Victory*, however, is a resolute break with the schematic psychological novel. JC's depiction of Heyst proves that he had overcome psychological determinism. It is facts which create, then shatter, Heyst, not the other way around, including love, which overcomes him from outside. But JC's novels are too different to treat them as a series of transitory steps leading to a peak. Yet there is clear evolution from *Jim* to *The Rover* in JC's attitude towards the psychological novel. [In Polish.]

1011.2 Fryde, Ludwik. "Realizm w tworczos'ci Conrada" (Realism in Conrad's Work), *Pion* (Warsaw), No. 52, 1935 ; rpt. in *WSOC*, pp. 368–78.

The chaotic compositon of *Nostromo* and many other works by JC is explained by his artistic attitude. As a visionary, JC was not concerned with a logical and consistent course of narrative, but placed all emphasis on individual scenes and moments, which had to be seized and rendered permanent. JC used chronological disorder to enfold his readers in an aura of the weird and the strange. The turning-points are unmotivated and improbable in the ordinary course of events, but they gain an inner, artistic truth, that of visions, which are usually colorless, though illuminated by lights and shadows. Indirectness (the narrator as witness) provided JC with his essential and unavoidable mask. [In Polish.]

1018.1 Linn, James Weber, and Houghton Wells Taylor. *A Foreword to Fiction* (New York: Appleton-Century, 1935), pp. 30, 36, 49, 51–52, 57–58, 61, 66, 89, 113–15, 120, 144, 192, 193.

The styles of both Fielding and Hemingway are "classic" in that they have "lucidity, ease, and directness"; opposed to them are the styles of Henry James and JC, which, not easy, direct, or lucid, illustrate the evolution of a style out of the particular temperament of the writer. JC's is extremely complex and individual. [Includes JC's works only as illustrations of such fictional techniques as point of view, character, and style.]

1021.1 Maurois, André. "Joseph Conrad," Prophets and Poets (New York: Harper, 1935) [not seen in this form]; rpt. in *Points of View: From Kipling to Graham Greene* (New York: Frederick Ungar, 1968), pp. 177–211.

JC, a foreigner, has been even more exactly than Kipling, the interpreter of "what is best in the English soul" : man standing alone facing the universe. Basically, he is a novelist of certain moral themes. To JC, the battle between the man of action and the "blind forces" seemed not always hopeless, but always unequal. The crowd, the people, are like the ocean or the jungle—foes for the hero; JC pessimistically believed in the essential "badness" of man in the mass. Even the born leader, the man of honor, can sometimes fall before the powers of darkness, as does Jim in the finest of JC's novels. But JC is not simply a pessimist and fatalist; he is an optimist as regards the qualities engendered by action: although men often wage a desperate battle and victory is always inperfect and not worth all the trouble, unavailing struggles cause sentiments excellent in themselves—devotion to a leader or a group, loyalty, honor. Man is thus the only treasure.

JC liked England well mainly because he found there a setting favorable to the cultivation of the loyalties he appreciated most: Captain MacWhirr, without too much intelligence or imagination, represents JC's ideal Englishman, one who takes facts as they come, turns them to the best account, and performs his duty. In action only does human destiny, a poor thing in relation to the universe, recover its own nobility. For JC, the artist must seek only the truth and be the best possible craftsman.

1024.1 Morley, Christopher. "Granules from an Hour-Glass," *SRL*, XII (6 July 1935), 16.

The Lookout, a monthly bulletin published by the Seamen's Church Institute of New York City, reports that JC's "old command," the barque *Otago*, of which JC was master 1888-89, is rotting away, moored "up the river Derwent," near Hobart, Tasmania. *The Shadow-Line* "immortalizes" this ship.

1027.1 Ujejski, Jozef. "Conrad i swiat" (Conrad and the World), *Skamander* (Warsaw), *PWN*, IX (1935), 596–613; rpt. in *Romantycy* (The Romantics), (Warsaw: *PWN*, 1963), pp. 311–32.

JC's attitude toward spiritualism was ambiguous, and basically he was unable to come to terms with it, as witness "The Black Mate" (1886) and his essay in *The Daily Mail* on Jasper Hunt's *Existence After Death (1910)*. His national hopes for Poland's independence were colored by Polish Romantic traditions and Christianity. His most extreme pessimism and revolt occurred between 1890 and 1900, though during this period his vitality enabled him to work out an inner *modus vivendi*, as his letters, prefaces, and memoirs show. [Contains copious quotations.] [In Polish.]

1027.2 Ujejski, Jozef. "Konrad i sztuka" (Conrad and Art), *Pion* (Warsaw), III: 52 (1935); rpt. in *Romantycy* (The Romantics), (Warsaw: *PWN*, 1963), 332–85.

JC's intuitive method, rather than intellectual, is illustrated in his letters and prefaces. The writer used, of course, intellectual control in his choice of themes and incidents and in ensuring the plausibility of characters and incidents. His intense dislike of Russian novelists (Dostoevski, Tolstoy, Gorky) is attested, as is his attitude towards Polish, French, and English writers. [In Polish.]

1027.3 Walbridge, Earle. "Footnotes to Romans à Clef, " *SRL*, XII (22 June 1935), 12.

Robert H. Davis wrote in the *New York Sun*, 4 April 1933, that Jim Lingard, "one of the Lingard brothers," was the model for JC's protagonist in *Lord Jim*.

1936

1032.1 Blüth, Rafal Marcelli. "O tragicznej decyzji krakowskiej Konrada Korzeniowskiego: pare uwag w zwiazku z ksiazka professora Ujejskiego *O Konradzie Korzeniowskim*" (On the Tragic Decision in Cracow of Konrad Korzeniowski: Comments on Professor Ujejski's Book *On Konrad Korzeniowski*), *Verbum* (Warsaw), No. 2, 1936; rpt in *WSOC*, pp. 379–405.

The unconscious played an important part in JC's life and work as evidenced in constant psychic tension and sudden changes of mood apparent in his method of creativity and his psychological and social isolation. The death of his father was a deep psychological shock to the young JC, especially since Tadeusz Bobrowski, who adopted him as a "homo duplex," was like JC himself—sensitive, with a cult of "family." At the same time, Bobrowski was an extreme intellectual rationalist, proud and ambitious, but afraid of failure, who withdrew from life. He was also a snob, impressed by titles and family crests, who despised his environment (as witness his *Memoirs*). He hated the 1863 Insurrection. His wife, his sister, and his brother all died early. [In Polish.]

1035.1 Dyboski, Roman. "Tragizm zycia i bohaterstwo czlowieka w twòrzosci Jozefa Conrada" (The Tragedy of Life and Heroism of Man in Joseph Conrad's Works), *Miledzy Literatura A Zyciem* (Between Literature and Life), (Warsaw: "Roj," 1936), pp. 73–80.

JC's most frequently used and his main theme is man's struggle with the elements, reflecting his own isolation as an emigré and sailor. The elements are the sea, or the society of other races and civilizations, or the dark side of man's own nature. The conclusion is always failure. In works of his second period (from *Nostromo*), the heroes tend to become saviors and victors, at least spiritually, and the elements are embodied in wicked individuals. [In Polish.]

1038.1 Mais. S. P. B. *A Chronicle of English Literature* (London: Heinemann, 1936), pp. 322–24.

JC's method of writing was that of the romantic realist. His characters are "shadowy enough to be universal." The outstanding feature of his work is his artistic integrity.

1044.1 Sibley, Carrol. "Mrs. Joseph Conrad," *Barrie and His Contemporaries: Cameo Portraits of Ten Living Authors* (Webster Grove, MO.: The International Mark Twain Society, 1936), pp. 48–51; rpt. in *CON*, II, No. 2 (Winter 1969–70), 95–96.

A visit to Mrs. Joseph Conrad revealed her to be jovial and very humorous in her conversation. She lived in a beautiful home "Torrens," in Canterbury, in remembrance of JC's last ship. Mrs. Conrad said that she had had literary ambitions but that "Conrad," as she called him, had always put her "stuff" aside so she could not see it again. She related how she had sold her late husband's private papers for two thousand pounds, to learn later that they had been sold to an American collector for more than ten times that amount.

1045.1 Ujejski, Jozef. *O Konradzie Korzeniowskim* (About Konrad Korzeniowski), (Warsaw: Dom Ksiazki Polskiej, 1936).

Ujejski's book is large in scope and cognizant of romanticism and some permanent values created by the movement. A fascination with JC, both as man and writer, caused him to discern a "spiritual kinship" between JC and himself.] [Review, "Ujejski and Conrad," *Conradiana,* VIII, No. 1 (1976), 88–89.]

1048.1 Wyatt, Alfred J., and Henry Clay. "Joseph Conrad, 1857-1924," *Modern English Literature, 1798-1935* (London: University Tutorial P, 1936), pp. 213–16.

JC's works frequently demonstrate the theme of man struggling against the sea. Although this theme leads him into the ostensible adventure tale, he does not employ the romance of the adventure but emphasizes realism with only a touch of romanticism. Hence his descriptive passages produce clear visual images and verbal melody.

As a psychologist, JC is entirely original. He does more than simply explain the effects on his characters; he exhibits "life in the round." Moreover, his subtlety of analysis entails his narrative method and loose form with a vagueness of outline.

In his outlook, he is a pessimist. An apostle of Nihilism, he yet emphasizes the goodness of struggling and enduring. In addition, as is characteristic of Slavs, he reveals in much of his work a religious mysticism. [Includes a brief biography and an incomplete list of JC's writings.]

1937

1050.1 Buchan, John. "Joseph Conrad," *A Shorter History of English Literature* (New York: Thomas Nelson, 1937), pp. 439–40.

[Presents a concise biography of JC with some critical reasons for his "high place among the great writers of our time." Shows how he was influenced by Henry James and the Russian writers.]

1050.2 Chwalewik, Witold. "Literatura angielska i anglo-amerykanska" (British and British-American Literature), *Rocznik Literacki Za Rok 1936* (Literary Annual for 1936), (Warsaw, 1937), pp. 112–13.

An Outcast of the Islands (third Polish version translated by Aniela Zagorska, 1936) is one of JC's works in which appear stylistic reminiscences of Polish Romanticism. For instance, the phrase, "But why lament the past and speak of the dead? There is one man—living—great—not far off," is a rendering of lines from Mickiewicz' *Konrad Wallenrod* (1828). In *The Sisters,* JC refers to "blacklands," i.e., Ukranian *czernoziemie*. *Outcast* is an unsuccessful attempt to find a style. [In Polish.]

1051.1 Crosbie, Mary. "Conrad Explains. His Debt to Garnett: The Collected Prefaces," *John O'London's Weekly*, (10 September 1937), 849.

Since the late Edward Garnett was the "discoverer" of JC, it is fitting that he should introduce *Conrad's Prefaces to His Works*. It is curious that English readers were brought to accept the "exotic" JC in the time of such publicly acclaimed writers as Mrs. Humphrey Ward. Although a "continental influence in grace and style" had been reflected in the work of Henry James, and Kipling by a very different method had "broadened" the horizon of English readers, JC's early works through *Youth* of 1902 "threw a bridge between the British public and the British sailors abroad" as well as placing "*a bridge between the British and the Continental spirit.*" The force of these words can be felt by the reader of JC's prefaces even if he lacks knowledge of the books themselves.

1051.2 Ellis, Amanda M. *The Literature of England* (Boston: Little, Brown, 1937), pp. 419–23.

The pictures JC paints in his works are unforgettable. While his women are usually "weak, pale, silent, easily hurt, misunderstood, or deserted," his men are "vivid, usually strong." He suggests a wide range of emotions. He sees men isolated by their personalities; if his pessimism is too dark, the cause is his own experience in the world; his aim is to show life as he found it.

1052.1 Gerould, Gordon H. *How to Read Fiction* (Princeton, New Jersey: Princeton UP, 1937), p. 47.

As a writer, JC is mainly interested in the mental and spiritual reactions of men to the crises they have to face in life.

1053.1 Kremer, Helen. "Conrad's Definition of Fiction," *SRL*, XVI, (18 September 1937), 9.

JC includes the necessity of the author to make the reader feel a sense of the truth in the events he describes in his definition of fiction when he states the necessity of making the reader hear, feel, and see, including "perhaps also that *glimpse of truth* for which you have forgotten to ask."

1055.1 Praz, Mario. "Joseph Conrad," *Storia Della Letteratura Inglese* (History of English Literature), (Firenze: Sansoni, 1937), pp. 36–63; rpt. in *La Letteratura Inglese Dai Romantici Al*

Novocento (English Literature from the Romantics to the Nineteenth Century), (Firenze-Milan: Sansoni-Accademia, 1968), II, 207–12.

JC wrote with admirable style a quantity of works of sea life in tropical settings, but even if he belongs to the tradition of the adventure story writers in the interior aspects of his novels, he is distinguished from it by the peculiar quality of his art and by his technique. He should be associated instead with introspective writers like Dostoevski, James, and Proust. [In Italian.]

1056.1 Shiller, Frants. "Dzhozef Konrad" (Joseph Conrad), *Istoria Zapadno-Evropeiisokoi Literatury Novogo Vremeni* (History of Modern West European Literature), III (Moscow: "Khudozhestvennaia literatura," 1937), pp. 92–94.

JC continued to develop the psychological novel of adventure from the "neoromanticism" of R. L. Stevenson, but with more emphasis on the psychological. His basic characters have lost contact with ordinary life and suffer from deep spiritual disorders. This isolation of his heroes is important in composition, and JC sees all their activities as being in romantic opposition to boring everyday existence. Working on Henry James's theory of "oblique narrative," JC uses various persons to narrate his tales in an impressionistic manner. *Almayer's Folly* is the most characteristic of his novels in regards to composition. *Lord Jim* and *Nostromo* also reveal his impressionistic technique in settings and the relativity of his philosophy. [In Russian.]

1938

1058.1 Blyton, W. J. "Trophies of Truth," *We Are Observed: A Mirror To English Character* (London: John Murray, 1938), pp. 254–64.

Stevie in *The Secret Agent* is a measure of JC's "profound social vision and large heart." JC's portraits of English seamen in *The Nigger of the Narcissus* have not been matched in the author's "precision of touch, and urbane irony." And Captain MacWhirr, Jim, and Kurtz are major creations. [Slight.]

1064.1 Las Vergnas, Raymond. *Joseph Conrad* (Paris: Didier [Les Grands Écrivains Étrangers], [1938]).

Critics have noticed faults in JC's English usage and his style, with its verbalisms, redundancies, and lack of economy, his excessive use of imagery, his careless constructions, and the influence of French methods in his later works. JC hoped the reader would evoke a coherent personality behind his works. His themes include illusions in the nature of the man regarding youth, money, love, fidelity, loyalty, solitude, exile, the theme of secrets and pursuit, and the question, "What is reality?" Being certain of his own aims, JC chose an artistic method perfectly adapted to his purpose, which was to reflect reality faithfully by means of special techniques such as avoidance of the omniscient author point of view, creation of effects of dislocation, and even incoherence in chronology.

JC's male characters represent either a simple Stoic ideal unsuited to analysis or one exaggeratedly complex and subtle. His women are either exaggeratedly simple and silent or highly complex: they are ideas dressed up. In general, however, he avoids abnormality, psychoanalysis, and sexuality. JC's belief that man's only solution to the problem of the human condition is loyalty, even though to a lost cause; it is reflected in his art, where man is depicted as seeing a soul similar to his own in the cosmos. His work draws its finest effects from stressing the reality of the human spirit. [In French.]

1069.1 "Notes on Rare Books," *NYTBR*, 24 July 1938, p. 19.

Summarizes J. A. Gee's "The Conrad Memorial Library of Mr. George T. Keating" (C, I, NO. 1061) and describes the content of an exhibition of rare items from that collection then on display at Yale University.]

1069.2 Quercus, P. E. G. [pseud. of Christopher Morley]. "Trade Winds," *SRL*, XVIII (6 August 1938), 24.

JC's letter of June 2, 1923 "to the sailing ship *Tusitala* has been given by her owner James A. Farrell to the Seamen's Church Institute of New York." The ship was recently sold to the Marine Liquidating Corporation of Fall River, Massachusetts, to be broken up. This manuscript letter will be placed in the Conrad Memorial Library at the Seamen's Institute.

1069.3 Quercus, P. E. G. [pseud. of Christopher Morley]. "Trade Winds," *SRL*, XVII (8 January 1938), 24.

JC, who received an offer of knighthood in an official envelope marked *On H. M. Service,* thinking it from the "Income Tax," delayed opening it until the Prime Minister had to send a discreet messenger to inquire about the response.

1069.4 Quercus, P. E. G. [pseud. of Christopher Morley]. "Trade Winds," *SRL*, XVIII (19 February 1938), 21.

In Robert Housley's little portrait studio opposite the Heinz Pier is a drawing, a very good likeness, of JC. Mr. Housley said he keeps it there to see how many of his customers identify it. "Most people think it's the former Kaiser," he remarked.

1069.5 Sitwell, Osbert. "The Modern Novel: Its Cause and Cure," *Trio: Dissertations on Some Aspects of National Genius*, by Osbert, Edith, and Sacheverell Sitwell (London: MacMillan, 1938), p. 58.

A novel like *Under Western Eyes* is better than JC's sea tales whose heroes are unbelievable. JC's English is perfect but artificial.

1069.6 Slater, John Rothwell. *Recent Literature and Religion* (New York: Harper, 1938), pp. 57–60.

Irony and pity pervade many of JC's best works, but neither quality figures into an awareness of Christ. In this respect, JC is modern, for much modern fiction does not concern itself with religion. The virtues of modern fiction are no longer faith and love, but courage, honesty, and sympathy.

1072.1 Villiers, Allan John. *The Making of a Sailor: The Photographic Story of Schoolships Under Sail* (New York: William Morrow, 1938).

[Contains photographs of the Bruce Rogers figurehead-bust of JC on a ship named *Joseph Conrad*.]

1939

1075.1 Chase, Roy. "When Joseph Conrad Came to Sydney," *Australian National Review* (Canberra), V (May 1939), 64–66.

The journeys JC made to Australia had an important influence on both his life and his work. On his first visit, in 1879, he acquired his impressions of Sydney, which he recorded in *The Mirror of the Sea*. He left no record of his second visit, in 1880, but he wrote amply of his third journey, for which he left England in 1887 and during which he became master of the *Otago*. In 1892–93, as chief mate of the *Torrens*, he made his last visit to the country. On this trip he met John Galsworthy and also, years later, recreated in "Because of the Dollars" an armless French sailor who sold matches and tobacco on the street in Sydney.

1078.1 Elwin, Malcolm. "Galsworthy and the Forsytes," *Old Gods Falling* (New York: Macmillan, 1939), pp. 363–90.

Romantic critics have subjected John Galsworthy to unfair abuse, simply because his successful life in the world contradicts their conception of the requisite sufferings of a man of genius. Unlike his close friend, JC, Galsworthy was immensely successful with both the sophisticated and the popular literary audiences. The literary relationship between these two men dates from the early 1890s. Galsworthy met JC while he was sailing in the Pacific on a ship aboard with JC was first mate. They cultivated their friendship upon their return to England and spent a great deal of time together in the late 1890s. JC encouraged the development of Galsworthy's literary career by introducing him to Ford Madox Ford and Edward Garnett and by arranging for the publication of Galsworthy's first stories with his own publisher, T. Fisher Unwin.

1081.1 Lucas, Audrey. *E. V. Lucas: A Portrait* (London: Methuen, 1939); rpt. (New York: Kennikat P, 1969), p. 69.

JC was greatly amused, about 1904, over an "immature *affaire de coeur*" between Audrey Lucas and his elder son Borys.

1082.1 Phelps, William Lyon. *Autobiography with Letters* (New York: Oxford UP, 1939), pp. 38, 430, 494, 570, 752–54, 822.

In JC's visit to Phelps' home in New Haven, JC and Rufus, Phelps's dog, accepted each other readily: "that was an unforgettable scene when the old seadog conversed so intimately with the dog of the fields." J. M. Barrie told Phelps that one evening during the war JC, along with Thomas Hardy, Shaw, Galsworthy, and Bennett were present in his flat when a bomb exploded nearby. If the bomb had dropped closer, "It would have been a sad and sensational loss to English literature." Phelps first met JC (10 May 1923) at Mr. and Mrs. Arthur Curtiss James' home in New York, where JC read from *Victory*, but with "frequent mistakes in the pronunciation of words." JC did not "easily understand English conversation." Later, on 15 May 1923, JC stayed at Phelps' home in New Haven; JC was suffering from gout, but he did not complain.

1082.2 Stauffer, Ruth Matilda, and William H. Cunningham. "*The Rover* by Joseph Conrad (1857-1924)," *Adventures in Modern Literature* (New York: Harcourt, Brace, 1939), pp. 952–55.

The style of JC's books makes them memorable. JC is certainly one of the masters of the English language. His books are generally romantic tales of strange experiences in foreign places, yet they are also revealing examinations of the soul in conflict. "Youth" and "Typhoon" are good works with which to begin a study of this author. *Lord Jim*, a more difficult work, concerns man who struggles to regain self-respect. *Nostromo* concerns a South American country and a silver mine. *Victory* has been made into a movie, and *The Rover* is about Napoleon. [Somewhat typical of early comments about JC's works. Includes a biographical sketch and a few paragraphs on the historical background of *The Rover*.]

1940

1093.1 Evans, B. Ifor. *A Short History of English Literature*, (1940; rpt.1 Harmondsworth, Middlesex, England, 1943), p. 131.

JC's fiction is written in an elaborate and rhythmical prose; and while its base rests upon the adventure story of violence and danger, the center of interest is found in psychological character studies. "It is as if the work of R. L. Stevenson had been re-written by Henry James." Like the Impressionist painters, JC seeks to capture moods; like the Russian novelists, to develop the mysterious consciousness of those moods. And as with Flaubert, JC strives for perfection, whose self-conscious artistry at times intrudes on his work.

1098.1 Halle, Louis J., Jr. "Nihilism, Literature, and Democracy," *SRL,* XXIII (14 December 1940), pp. 3–4, 16–17.

Since we learn about life from literature, JC is an excellent illustration of the serious writer who becomes familiar with many aspects of life. What impressed him most was the heroic quality of the life men led at sea. When he came to portray the life he knew, it was this aspect of it that he singled out for special emphasis, and by his emphasis on the heroic he gave that life in particular and all life in general an aspect of heroism that it could not otherwise have had. He gave his readers a heroic model for their emulation. Unlike Hans Otto Storm in *Made in U.S.A.,* JC exhibited both the desirable and the undesirable sides of human character while emphasizing the heroic, "that aspiration of man's highest aspiration," thus opposing the nihilistic trend of modern literature for many years now. [Followed by Louise Davies, "N. L. &. D.," *Saturday Review of Literature* (4 January 1941) and Harrison L. Reinke, "N. L. & D." *Saturday Review of Literature* (18 January 1941).]

1099.1 Kowalska, Aniela. "Czlowiek i morze w tworczosci Conrada" (Man and the Sea in Conrad's Works), *Prace Polonistyczne* (Polish Studies), (Lodz), Seria IV (1940–46), 117–37.

JC's tragedy, as a man and a writer, was that the raw material which made him famous (the sea and the English language), deprived him of the right to his homeland, which he never ceased to love. Both the language and the sea betrayed him, for their apparent importance overshadowed his psychological insights. His art is rooted in the Stoic ethics of Marcus Aurelius, with the latter's profound respect for man and work, and skeptical attitude towards the world. Jan Kott's attack on JC is that of a doctrinaire commentator demanding black or white types, either socially useful or harmful, and he fails to recognize moral qualities which do not submit to any mechanical laws or schemes, but are unique. [In Polish.]

1941

1101.1 Bates, H. E. *The Modern Short Story: A Critical Survey* (London: Thomas Nelson, 1941), pp. 35, 66, 105, 119, 141–42, 182–83.

JC is not a part of the "main lineage" of the short story; he lacked the art of compression vital to expression in a very brief space. His stories differ little from his novels. He stands outside the main English short story somewhat as he stands, the only important writer of sea stories, outside the main stream of the English novel. His characters are shaped less by conscious and rational forces than by the vaguer, larger forces of atmosphere and destiny.

1102.1 Cannon, Carl Leslie. "John Quinn," *American Book Collectors and Collecting* (New York: Wilson, 1941), pp. 228–30.

[Describes Quinn's JC holdings and gives the prices they realized when the lawyer sold his library in 1923.]

1103.1 Davies, Louise. "N. L. & D.," *SRL*, XXIII (4 January 1941), 9.

Unfortunately, the days of JC's sailors are gone and the days of Hans Otto Storm are "very much with us." If one is looking for a "philosophy of souls," he may read either Lloyd Douglas or he may go back to JC himself, who "really had something to say and was enough of an artist to be able to say it." [Preceded by Louis J. Halle, Jr., "Nihilism, Literature, and Democracy," *Saturday Review of Literature* (14 December 1940) and followed by Harrison L. Reinke, "N. L. & D.," *Saturday Review of Literature* (18 January 1941).]

1108.1 Reinke, Harrison L. "N. L. & D.," *SRL*, XXIII (18 January 1941), 9

Evil and sordidness were no less prevalent in JC's time, or in any other time, than they are in ours. Our attitudes have been conditioned by our reading such works as Hemingway's *For Whom the Bell Tolls*, in which Robert Jordan is "merely a sensitive, courageous, admirable animal." [Preceded by Louis J. Halle, Jr., "Nihilism, Literature, and Democracy," *Saturday Review of Literature* (14 December 1940) and Louise Davies, "N. L. & D.," *"Saturday Review of Literature* (4 January 1941).]

1110.1 Young, Karl. "The Uses of Rare Books and Manuscripts," *Yale University Library Gazette*, XVI (October 1941), 36–37.

The JC Memorial Library of George T. Keating is incomparable in its magnitude. It contains, besides all printed JC works, a considerable number of early letters that reveal much about JC's methods of writing.

1942

[No entries this year.]

1943

1131.1 Evans, B. Ifor. *A Short History of English Literature*, 1940; rpt. Harmondsworth, Middlesex, England, 1943, p. 131. (See entry 1093.1).

1944

[No entries this year.]

1945

1145.1 Kott, Jan. "O laickim tragizmie: tragizmi maski tragizmu" (On Secular Tragedy: Tragedy and the Masks of Tragedy), *TW*, I, No. 2 (1945), pp. 137–60; rpt. in *Mitologia I Realizm* (Mythology and Realism), 2nd ed. (Warsaw: Panstwowy Instytut Wydawniczy, 1956) pp., 159–231.

JC's world is a real one in which man must bear entire responsibility for good and evil, taking responsibility for life and showing man's greatness in his conscious choice in the struggle with blind passions and elements. During World War II, Poles read JC as the last bourgeois moralist who sought ultimate values to justify human life. This was secular tragedy—the impossibility of expressing full agreement with reality and accepting the world as it is. The tragic form which human affairs take in JC's works separated him from his contemporaries, but the works themselves–like those of all the great writers of his generation–grew out of the breakdown in those values in which the nineteenth century believed. The great secret of JC's artistry is his skill in almost imperceptible transitions from realism of details and the precise construction of facts to the creation of a spectacle where a world of good and evil powers revolves around the heroes. JC allows us to gaze at the darkness in the depths of the soul, but mentions it briefly and rarely gazes into the depths, to withdraw immediately. The impossibility of finding any justification for moral values in the meaningless course of human concerns is what distinguishes JC's attitude from the optimistic attitudes of the nineteenth century. [In Polish.]

1946

1148.1 Alliney, Giulio. *"L'agente segrete"* (The Secret Agent), *DLOP*, 1946; rpt I (1963), 42.

[Brief summary of *The Secret Agent*, with brief notes.] [In Italian.]

1148.2 Alliney, Giulio. *"Caso"* (Chance), *DLOP*, 1946; rpt. II (1963), 157.

[Brief summary of *Chance* with critical notes.] [In Italian.]

1148.3 Alliney, Giulio. *"Nostromo,"* *DLOP*, 1946; rpt. V (1963), 82.

[Brief summary of *Nostromo* with some critical notes.] [In Italian.]

1150.1 G[adda] C[onti], P[iero]. *"Il negro del 'Narcisso"* (The Nigger of the Narcissus), *DLOP*, 1946; V (1963), 36–37.

[Brief summary of *The Nigger of the Narcissus*, with critical notes.] [In Italian.]

1150.2 G[adda] C[onti], P[iero]. *"Tifone"* (Typhoon), *DLOP*, 1946; rpt. VII (1963), 418.

[Brief summary of "Typhoon," with some comments.] [In Italian.]

1150.3 Grant Watson, Elliot Lovegood. *But To What Purpose: The Autobiography of a Contemporary* (London: Cresset P. 1946), pp. 148–51.

In 1913, E. L. Grant Watson, somewhat presumptuously as he thought, asked JC to read his first novel. JC and a qualified friend advised rewriting the novel as a long short story, but Grant Watson, eager to venture into further writing, left it essentially as it was. From this experience, though, he learned that literature, the work of the artist, is of first importance.

1152.1 Jahier, Piero. "Introduzione" (Introduction), *Racconti di mare e di costa* (Twixt Land and Sea), (Torino: Einaudi, 1946), pp. ix-xv; rpt. in *Racconti di mare e di costa* (Milan: Mondadori, 1971), pp. 3–8.

[Brief biographical and critical notes, with extracts from JC's letters. Badly proofread.] [In Italian.]

1153.1 Leavis, Frank Raymond. "Revaluations (XV): George Eliot," *Scrutiny: A Quarterly Journal*, XIII (Autumn-Winter 1946); rpt. (Cambridge UP, 1963), 173–75.

In a comparison of George Eliot and JC, both may be understood as writing moral fables; *Nostromo* may, in fact, be more justly termed a "moralized fable," James's term, than any work of Eliot's excepting her minor work, *Silas Marner*. Both writers are highly intelligent, and that intelligence is imparted to their own works. But JC is more wholly the artist, as his intelligence, personality, and need are more completely subordinated to, and transmuted into, the impersonalized, created work.

1155.1 Pioli, Giovanni. "Gioventù" (Youth). *DLOP*, 1946; rpt. III (1963), 644.

[Brief summary of "Youth" with critical comments.] [In Italian.]

1155.2 P[rospero] M[archesini], A[da]. "Cuore de tenebra" (Heart of Darkness), *DLOP*, 1946; rpt. II (1963), 539–40.

[Brief summary of "Heart of Darkness" with some comments; states that the story was published in 1906.] [In Italian.]

1155.3 P[rospero] M[archesini], A[da]. "*Il reietto delle isole*" (An Outcast of the Islands), *DLOP*, 1946; rpt. VI (1963), 162.

[Brief summary of *An Outcast of the Islands*, with some critical observations.] [In Italian.]

1155.4 P[rospero] M[archesini], A[da]. "*Lord Jim*, " *DLOP*, 1946; rpt. IV (1963), 441.

[Short summary of *Lord Jim* with some critical notes.] [In Italian.]

1157.1 Zanco, Aurelio. "Joseph Conrad," *Storia Della Letteratura Inglese* (History of English Literature), (Torino: Chiantore, 1946–47), II, 770–72; rpt. (Turin: Loescher, 1964).

JC loved the tropical countries but without the imperialistic fervor of Kipling or the impressionistic imagination of Stevenson. He showed a typical Slavic impulse (stimulated by the study of French naturalists) to develop the story of the souls and lives of humble people whose torments he seeks to reveal without reaching the final solution of the problem, which he offers us full of mystery.
[Brief biographical survey and general critical comments.] [In Italian.]

1947

1162.1 C[olombo], A[chille]. "*La linea d'ombra*" (The Shadow-Line), *Letture* (Milan), II, No. 7 (1947), 246.

[Brief review, mainly a plot summary, of the Italian translation of *The Shadow-Line* (Turin: Einaudi, 1947).] [In Italian.]

1163.1 Czarnomski, F. B. "Conrad Collected," *TLS*, 13 December 1947, pp. 614, 645.

The Secret Agent and *Under Western Eyes* should have been excluded from collected editions of JC's works because a comparison of them with "other available evidence" indicates that they are too truthful to the world of the anarchists and revolutionaries. These novels even occasionally appear to have been written by some member of the revolutionary community. *Nostromo* and *The Arrow of Gold* reveal JC's "continual scepticism" toward governmental machinery and official corruption. Indeed, the main theme of *Nostromo* is misrule. *Arrow* presents JC's mature style, and it contains autobiographical elements of his connection with the Carlist war. [Contains much on JC's life. Critical comments are often strained and pointless.]

1169.1 Karl, Frederick R. (ed). *The Portable Conrad*, ed by Morton Dauwen Zabel (New York: Viking P, 1947), (C. I. No. 1186); rvd by Frederick R. Karl (New York: Viking P, 1969).

[Contents, abstracted under Karl (1969): "Addendum, 1968"; "Bibliographical Note, Revised 1968, by Frederick R. Karl." Karl's revision of this book contains the same works by JC except for the addition of JC's letter, "To My Readers in America" [not abstracted], which adds two pages to the text as Zabel arranged it. Karl also adds two identical notes at the bottom of pages 51 and 113, both reading,

"See Addendum, p. 47.—F.R.K."; and he adds another note at the bottom of page 293, reading: "See pp. 705–710, where the Preface appears as 'The Condition of Art.'—F.R.K." Altogether, Karl adds two pages, JC's letter, to Zabel's book; but he uses blank spaces for them in order to retain the same total number of pages Zabel's work has. His contribution thus consists of the addition of one letter by JC, his very brief "Addendum," and a revised "Bibliographical Note." These slight changes scarcely justify a revised edition; they could easily have been made in another printing of Zabel's book.]

1172.1 Philip, Alexander J. *Fifty Glorious Years of English Romantic Literature,* 1870–1920 (Philip-Lodgewood-Gravesend: Mariner P. 1947), pp. 54–55.

Because of the inflation in England after World War I and the great need of publishers to issue more and more books at small individual profits, many well known writers were quickly forgotten, so that the best books had little chance of success. This condition affected JC's reputation: a few years after the publication of *The Rover* in 1923, he was almost forgotten and his books seldom read, and if read, scarcely understood and rated "dull."

1173.1 Rascoe, Burton. "Joseph Conrad Comes to Town," *We Were Interrupted* (Garden City, New York: Doubleday, 1947), pp. 291–95.

Upon his arrival in New York aboard the *Tuscania* in May, 1924, JC appeared sensitive and shy but is really complex, determined, and severe, though gentle and kind. As a writer, he is pessimistic, believing man to be a victim of his own codes and ideals. He reports to his feeling complimented by being called "Captain" aboard ship and claims to know little about the literary scene. He is "not a literary man."

1177.1 T., C. B. "Gabriel Wells," *Yale University Library Gazette,* XXI (April 1947), 53–54.

The late Gabriel Wells bequeathed, among other items, the complete autograph manuscript of JC's *Under Western Eyes* together with ten letters to Ford Madox Ford to the Yale University Library.

1183.1 Zabel, Morton Dauwen. "Note and Acknowledgement," *The Portable Conrad,* ed by Morton Dauwen Zabel (New York: Viking P, 1947), pp. 48–49; rvd Frederick R. Karl (New York: Viking P, 1969), pp. 48–49 (C., No. 1186).

The present collection of JC's works attempts to show the range of the novelist's art "early and late." Altogether, tales and passages from twenty-three of JC's books are printed here. Hopefully, they reveal JC to the reader "on his largest scale and in his fullest powers."

1948

1189.1 Evans, Henry Herman. *A Guide to Rare Books* (San Francisco: Porpoise Bookshop, 1948), p. 20.

[Includes the copyright issue of *The Nigger of the Narcissus* and the first impression of the first British edition of *Chance* as examples of rare JC publications.]

1189.2 Gaige, Crosby. *Footlights and Highlights*. (New York: Dutton, 1948), p. 209.

Richard Curle sold Crosby Gaige the original letters and the right to publish his correspondence from JC. The letters were "very frank," as if from one close friend to another. After they were in type, Curle spent more than a thousand dollars of his own money in making deletions and corrections of passages that might have offended some of JC's contemporaries.

1192.1 James, Henry. "The New Novel," *The Art of Fiction and Other Essays* (New York: Oxford UP, 1948), pp. 181–214.

JC's *Chance* is an "extraordinary exhibition of method by the fact the method is, we venture to say, without a precedent in any like work. JC posits a "reciter" possessed of infinite sources of reference, who immediately sets up another, thus requiring an effective fusing between "what we are to know and that prodigy of our knowing which is ever half the very beauty of the atmosphere of authenticity." This volume sets in motion a drama in which his own system and his combined "eccentricities of recital" represent the protagonist confronted by powers leagued against it. This is "*our* spectacle, our suspense and our thrill," with the one flaw the fact that the predicament was not the effect of a challenge from without but that of a "mystic impulse" from within. But the fusion takes place, by means of a "wandering, circling, yearning imaginative *faculty*, " by which new things have apparently been seen and understood by the common reader.

1196.1 Pellizzi, Camillo. "I Russi di Conrad" (Conrad's Russians), *La Fiera Letteraria*, III, 28–29 (10 October 1948), 4.

JC's desperate view of the Russian soul stems from the Tzarist persecution of his family. Thanks to his personal experience, in *Under Western Eyes* JC illustrated the tragedy of Russia better than in any historical essay written by himself or others. [In Italian.]

1196.2 Pioli, Giovanni. "*Sotto gli occhi dell' Occidente*" (Under Western Eyes), *DLOP*, VI, 879.

[Brief summary of *Under Western Eyes*, with some comments.] [In Italian.]

1949

1198.1 Bigongiari, Piero. "Presentazione di Conrad" (Introducing Conrad), *La Rassegna d'Italia*, IV (1949), 1053–57.

[Brief introduction by the general editor of the first Italian collected edition of JC's works in 24 volumes (Milan: Bompiani, 1949-66).] [In Italian.]

1199.1 Colombi Guidotti, Mario. "*Gioventu ed altri due racconti*" (Youth and Two Other Tales), *La Rassegna d'Italia*, IV (July-August 1949), 840–42.

[An appreciative review of the Italian translation of "Youth," "Heart of Darkness," and "The End of the Tether" (Milan: Bompiani, 1949).] The sentimentalism of "The End of the Tether" prefigures the psychological background of later major novels. [In Italian.]

1199.2 Colombo, Achille. *Gioventù e altri due racconti*" (Youth and Two Other Tales), *Letture* (Milan: Bompiani, 1949). IV, 5, 166–67.

[Brief review of the Italian translation of "Youth," "Heart of Darkness," and "The End of the Tether" (Milan: Bompiani, 1949).] [In Italian.]

1201.1 G[adda] C[onti], P[iero]. "*Vittoria, romanzo isolano*" (Victory: An Island Tale), *DLOP*, VII (1949), 867.

[Brief plot summary.] *Victory*, one of JC's best exercises in technique, shows that violence reigns on this earth and that noble, irresolute souls are exiles on it. [In Italian.]

1203.1 Jahier, Piero. "Note del traduttore" (Translator's Note), *Gioventu e altri due racconti* (Youth and Two Other Tales), (Milan: Bompiani, 1949), 11–24.

[Biographical and historical backgrounds derived mainly from Jean-Aubry.] [In Italian.]

1205.1 Pellizzi, Camilo. "L'avventuriero' di Conrad" (Conrad's *The Rover*), *La Fiera Letteraria*, IV, 20 (15 May 1949), 3–4.

The Rover is the epitome of JC's spiritual and earthly adventure, and the rover himself is a Dominic Cervoni brought back for almost a century. In this moral drama, JC contemplates his two adoptive countries, France and England. [Pellizzi developed the same ideas in his translator's note appended to *L'avventuriero* (The Rover), (Milan: Bompiani, 1950).] [In Italian.]

1205.2 Rossani, Wolfango. "Il magistero dell'arte di Conrad" (The Lesson of Conrad's Art), *La Fiera Letteraria*, IV,42 (16 October 1949), 5; rpt. as Part I of "La lezione di Conrad" (Conrad's Lesson), *Scrittori Stranieri; Saggi E Note Critiche* (Foreign Writers: Essays and Critical Notes) Pisa: Nistri-Lischi, 1963); Part I (1949), pp. 175–80; Part II (1951) [unlocated]), pp. 180–84.

In Italy, JC's work was first regarded as that of an adventure story writer. Emilio Cecchi in 1924 was the first critic to indicate that JC was interested in the everyday tragic aspects of life, in its moral reflections, and in the analysis of the inner self. [The rest of the article is a review of the Italian translation of "Youth," "Heart of Darkness," and "The End of the Tether": *Gioventu a altri due racconti* (Milan: Bompiani, 1950) and of *L'avventuriero* (The Rover): (Milan: Bompiani, 1950).] [In Italian.]

1205.3 Sackville-West, Edward. "The Moment of Silence," *Inclinations* (London: Secker and Warburg, 1949); rpt. (New York: Scribner's, 1950); rpt. (Port Washington, New York: Kennikat P, 1967), pp. 72–77.

By the nature of his temperament and imagination, JC was admirably placed to grasp the significance of the nineteenth-century English gentleman, a type which reaches back to the ideals of fifteenth-century Spain. In the widest acceptance of the two words "love" and "duty" are contained the conflict and resolution within a view of life which needs nothing else for its fulfillment. Essentially, this belief is Stoic, and in this vein JC is the last of the great nineteenth-century novelists. He is fond of the "silence of suspense" in scenes of high dramatic tension, as in *The Rover* where the lovers, Arlette and Réal, are spied upon by Scevola, and in the moment in *Nostromo* when the hero, after his long disappearance from the scene, comes back like a shadow into the presence of the reader. An acute sense of the human mystery, which has caused despair and contempt of life for many novelists of today, led JC to a high opinion

of men and women. In a way, courage is JC's theme, concealed in
many variations but most searchingly explored in *Lord Jim*. To
dramatize the frailties that great men successfully overcome, JC
found the moment of silence useful. In using this device, he advanced
to the greater ease and fluency of *The Shadow-Line*. *Suspense*, as an
important work, deserves much more recognition than it has
received.

1208.1 Webster, M. T. "Conrad's Changes in Narrative Conception in
the Manuscripts of *Typhoon and Other Stories* and *Victory*,"
PMLA, LXIV (December 1949), 953–62.

The typescript of "Typhoon" is "a mass of very thoroughly blotted
out sentences." The cuttings are largely responsible for the "rapid,
vigorous narrative pace" of this tale; JC was by this time sacrificing
things good in themselves for a unity of total effect. The "Falk"
holograph shows much the same general problem of revision as does
"Typhoon." The holographs of the two shorter stories in the *Typhoon*
volume, "Amy Foster" and "To-morrow," confirm one's impression of
the general direction of JC's revisions during this time without
materially altering his work. The MS of *Victory* reveals that JC's
pairing of the earlier text makes the published version of the story
much shorter than the MS, and the revisions are nearly all deletions,
although the published story contains reserves of meaning which
were explicit in the MS. Heyst and Lena show a greater objective
awareness of their emotional evolution in the MS than in the novel.
The published version is an admirable illustration of JC at his best.
Every word counts, and the reader must note each word for a clear
understanding of "this fine example of condensed narrative art."

1950

1212.1 Arcangeli, Francesco. "Per un racconto di Conrad" (On a Tale
by Conrad), *Paragone* (April 1950), 3–12; rpt. as introduction to
La linea d'ombra —Entro le maree (The Shadow-Line—Within the
Tides), (Milan: Bompiani, 1963), pp. 7–29.

[A perceptive article on *The Shadow-Line* and general critical
comments: JC is frequently quoted for supportive evidence.] [In
Italian.]

1214.1 Borowy, Waclaw. "Conrad krytykiem polskeigo przekladu swojej noweli 'Il Conde'" (Conrad as Critic of a Polish Translation of his Tale "Il Conde"), *Zeszyty Wroclawskie* (Wroclaw), 3–4, 1950, 36–47; rpt. in *Studa I Rozprawy* II (Studies and Essays II), (Wroclaw: Ossolineum, 1962) pp., 61–72.

Aniela Zagorska sent JC a copy of "Il Conde" translated into Polish by L. Piwinski (*Przeglad Warsawski, 1922*, no. 14), in which JC corrected errors in the translation of idioms into Polish and proposed altering the "d" to "t" in the title. JC concluded that the errors were "minor details" (*drobiazgi*). His corrections and suggestions for emended readings demonstrate, however, his mastery of English and Polish vocabulary and word-order. But Piwinski's translation was faulty, and JC missed a number of errors. [In Polish.]

1214.2 Camerino, Aldo. "'L'avventuriero' di Conrad," (Conrad's *The Rover*), (1950, unlocated); rpt. in *Scrittoti Di Lingua Inglese* (English Writers), (Milan & Napoli: Ricciardi, 1968), pp. 186–88.

The Rover has no vibrations; it is the work of a tired writer. The action, which flows slowly, enables the writer to analyze better, from a psychological point of view, a scene, a mood. [A review of *L'avventuriero* (Milan: Bompiani, 1950).] [In Italian.]

1215.1 Ellis, Havelock. "Joseph Conrad," *From Marlowe to Shaw: The Studies, 1876-1936, In English Literature of Havelock Ellis*, ed with a foreword by John Gawsworth (London: Williams and Norgate, 1950), pp. 303–13.

The sea has made JC a great artist, and his Polish background has made him imaginative, high strung, and excitable. The clash between his experience as an English sailor and his background as a Pole has made him the great artist he is. The essence of his genius lies in "the quality of his vision" and "the extraordinary and precise memory accompanying it." His vision is most evident in his methods of narration, in which he usually begins his stories in the middle. Also significant to his vision is his belief in the necessity of fidelity, which was his creed as a sailor but also his guiding principle as an artist.

1216.1 Guerard, Albert J. "Introduction," *"Heart of Darkness" and "The Secret Sharer"* (New York: Signet [New American Library], 1950), pp. 7–15.

JC is one of the greatest of English novelists and a fine prose stylist. Most of his tales are more experimental and modern than are his novels. Of these tales, "Heart of Darkness" and "The Secret

Sharer" are his best. The former contains a narrator who, after seeing Kurtz," can look on our original and savage nature in its nakedness"; the latter is a "double" story about a young captain who, by meeting Leggatt, is able to descend into the depths of his own unconscious. Both stories work on the mythical themes of initiation.

1219.1 Jahier, Piero. "Note del traduttore" (Translator's Notes), *Appunti di Vita e di Letteratura* (Notes on Life and Letters), (Milan: Bompiani, 1950), pp. 349–63.

[Brief bio-bibliographical and critical notes on *Notes on Life and Letters*.] [In Italian.]

1224.1 Routh, Harold Victor. *English Literature and Ideas in the Twentieth Century: An Inquiry into Present Difficulties and Future Prospects* (London: Methuen; New York: Longmans, Green, 1950), pp. 19–24, 43, 45, 69, 91, 147.

When JC was in the mood to write, he "acted on a hint from outside and then descended into the depths of himself. . . . What he found there he refashioned, and transposed into these figures [his characters], originally viewed at a distance." He made his externalizations seem real to his reader by surrounding them with the scenery to which they belonged, "on a background of the same tone and colour, in tune with their behaviorism." The "*psychology of scene*" (Edward Garnett) put a heavy strain on the author's powers of description. Since JC did not succeed in rendering his characters wholly, he achieved everything except his artistic ideal. His inspiration sometimes outruns his technique. But to admire him is to live up to his standard; therefore "his place is assured."

1224.2 Savino, Alberto. "L'errore di Conrad" (Conrad's Mistake), *Corriere Della Sera*, 15 September 1950, p. 3

JC is nearer to Plato or Brahms than to Stevenson. [Anecdotal review of Italian edition of *Notes on Life and Letters: Appunti di vita e di letterature* (Milan: Bompiani, 1950).] [In Italian.]

1225.1 Schorer, Mark. "Comment" [on "Amy Foster"], *The Story: A Critical Anthology* (Englewood Cliffs, N.J.: Prentice-Hall, 1950; second ed., 1967), pp. 243–46.

The plot, the setting, the style, and the structure together produce the "full, reverberative meaning" of "Amy Foster." Since the characters are inarticulate, the story must be given to Dr. Kennedy; then, in order to obtain still further distance, another narrator retells Kennedy's account. Also, the plot is objectified in unusual detail, as are the emotions of the characters in action so that the mystery of the story is at last not in Amy's behavior but in human life. The entire story has thus become a symbol.

1226.1 "Shapers of the Modern Novel: A Catalogue of an Exhibition," *Princeton University Library Chronicle*, XI (Spring 1950), 134–41.

[The Friends of the Princeton University Library arranged an exhibit called "Shapers of the Modern Novel," which was on view from March 1 to April 30, 1950. The "Shapers" were JC, Ernest Hemingway, Thomas Mann, James Joyce, Henry James, Sinclair Lewis, Marcel Proust, William Faulkner, and André Gide, as well as Karl Marx and Sigmund Freud. Listed in the catalogue are fourteen books, letters, and manuscripts by JC.]

1234.1 Woolf, Virginia. "Mr. Conrad: A Conversation," *The Captain's Death Bed and Other Essays* (London: Hogarth P, 1950), pp. 74–78; rpt. in *Collected Essays*, I (New York: Harcourt, Brace & World, 1967), pp. 309–13.

Penelope Otway and her old friend, David Lowe, discuss JC and his works. They find him a puzzling figure, but he is, of course, a romantic. "No one objects to that. But it entails a terrible penalty—death at the age of forty—death or disillusionment. . . . [JC] must make his music out of contrasts." His singing the old songs "shows a crack in the flawless strain of his youth." JC is not a simple person: he is a double, composed of two people who have nothing whatever in common: he is the sea captain, "simple, faithful, obscure,: and he is also Marlow, "subtle, psychological, loquacious." In the early books, the Captain dominates; in the later ones, " it is Marlow at least who does all the talking." But his books are "fine" in the grand manner; they are full of "moments of vision." JC's "peculiar beauty" is the product of the two together. He is very unlike an Englishman. *Chance* is a great book. [Contains several invaluable statements about JC. Written in 1923.]

1951

1237.1 Brewster, Dorothy, and John Angus Burrell. "Joseph Conrad: Effects of Seagoing Life upon Men and Women," *Modern World Fiction* (Ames, Iowa: Littlefield, Adams, 1951), pp. 45, 50–51, 148, 167, 184.

JC was not a novelist of the sea; he simply wrote about men who went to sea and women who were left behind. In *Nostromo*, he attacks the problem of imperialistic exploitation chiefly to observe the effect of exploitation on human character. He finds no easy answers to the ethical and moral questions he raises, but he enriches readers by his "wise and compassionate outlook." His "illusion" is the "beauty of the written word," and he seems to believe that where there is beauty there is truth also. [Interesting as an example of an outline intended as a guide for college students at midcentury.]

1237.2 Churchill, Reginald C. *English Literature of the Nineteenth Century* (London: University Tutorial P, 1951); rpt. (Freeport, New York: Books for Libraries P, 1970), pp: 105, 182, 234–35, 247.

Captain Frederick Marryat's novels were "one of the reasons why a romantic young Pole, Teodor Josef Konrad Korzeniowski . . . joined the British merchant service in 1878." [Somewhat doubtful.] The epigraph which JC placed at the beginning of *Youth —a Narrative: And Two Other Stories*, from *Grimm's Tales* is a "good illustration of his philosophy": ". . . but the Dwarf answered: 'No, something human is dearer to me than the wealth of the world.'"

1237.3 Connell, John. "Unpublished Letters," *National and English Review*, CXXXVI (January 1951), 29–32.

The author gives an account of his receiving, among a large number of unpublished letters, one of ten pages from JC which states the writer's "whole literary philosophy." He makes no further comment on this intriguing matter.

1237.4 De Robertis, Domenico. "Conrad," *Paragone*, February 1951, p. 78–80.

A favorable review of *Appunti di vita e letteratura* (Notes on Life and Letters), (Milan: Bompiani, 1950).] [In Italian.]

1238.1 Dupee, F. W. *Henry James* (New York: William Sloane, 1951), pp. 214, 256, 281.

In Henry James's later years, a period in which his solitude, his unavoidable sadness of old age, and his anomalous position as a writer caused him to be morose, few of his acquaintances, not even JC, saw in him any deep pathos. But when the reviews of *The Wings of the Dove* (1902) and of *The Ambassadors* (1903) were barely respectful, JC deafened him in "perceptive" essays. And JC, James's "greatest disciple," wrote that he sat for a long time with the closed volume, *The American*, in his hands after reading James's preface in the New York Edition, "thinking—that is how it began, that's how it was done."

1238.2 Frigerio, Mario. "*La freccia d'oro*" (The Arrow of Gold), *Letture*, VI, No. 6 (1951), 209.

[Short review of the Italian translation of *The Arrow of Gold* (Turin: Einaudi, 1951).] [In Italian.]

1246.1 Patterson, Beck. "Conrad Incident," *Sea Breezes, N.S., XL* (April 1951), 317.

JC reported that the *James Westoll* was rigged with three masts in 1874 while he was in Marseilles. This ship, however, was not built until 1884 and it had only two masts.

1952

Bardin, John Franklin. "Action vs. Idea in Conrad," *New Leader*, 7 April 1952, pp. 23–24.

While they contain isolated moments of brilliance, *Nostromo* and *Under Western Eyes* are disappointing in their overall artistic effect. The problem with them is that they stem from JC's inability to portray effectively the relationship of his characters' ideals. He attributes individual ambiguities to his characters in their application of general ideals to particular actions but, since he cannot always define the essence of the individual character's ideal in terms of action, he cannot always explain the active ideal to the reader. The turgid pace of *Nostromo* reflects JC's refusal to allow the straightforward development of characters along the lines of the ideals he has associated with them. In *Eyes*, Razumov's confusion over his motivation for betraying Haldin reflects JC's confusion in his characterization of Razumov. But JC's inarticulateness serves the artistic end of this novel; the reader perceives, in the struggles for articulation of JC and Razumov, the dangers of "the wasteland of intellect in which the monsters of hypertrophied idea thrive."

1259.1 Entwistle, William J., and Eric Gillett. *The Literature of England, A. D. 500-1950* (London, New York, Toronto: Longmans, Green, 1952), pp. 224-25. Third ed. [First ed, 1943, not seen.]

Consists of generalizations on JC's tragic plots and romantic settings, and claims JC's mastery to be revealed in the long stories, "Youth," "Typhoon," and *The Nigger of the Narcissus*, with *Nostromo* considered as his best novel.

1259.2 Ferrari, Carola. [Review of *Vittoria* (Victory)], *LCS*, XXXV, No. 10 (October 1952), 179.

The subtlest appeal of *Victory* lies in the ambiguity of its characters and in the narrative technique which renders the complexity of the characters and at the same time shows different aspects of reality. [In Italian.]

1259.3 Forti, Marco. "Per un secondo tempo di Conrad" (Conrad's second period), *IDEA*, Part I in IV, No. 52, (28 December 1952) and Part II in V. No. 1 (4 January 1953), 6.

JC's early works were mainly autobiographical. In *Under Western Eyes* (which, with *Lord Jim* and *Victory* is one of his greatest novels) the sense of guilt becomes a universal theme, the obscure appeal at work on the conscience of the protagonist. Natalia is one of his best female characters. [A review-article on Italian translation of *Eyes* (Sotti gli occhi dell'Occidente), (Milan. Bompiani, 1952), trans by Camillo Pellizzi.] [In Italian.]

1265.1 Herrig, Ludwig and Max Förster. *English Authors, With Biographical Notices* (Braunschweig: Georg Westermann Verlag, 1952), pp. 305–09.

[Contains a brief biography of JC and a selection, "The Nan-Shan in a Typhoon," from "Typhoon."]

1269.1 Ludwig, Richard M., and Marvin B. Perry, Jr. (eds). "Joseph Conrad," *Nine Short Stories* (Boston: Heath, 1952), pp. xxxvii–xlii.

"Heart of Darkness" is a tale in which JC relates the truth of human experience. Generally, though, it defies easy analysis. Its major concerns are exposing the greed, hypocrisy, and stupidity of the ivory trade in the Congo. It also deals with the effects of a tropical environment on an extraordinary man. The three parts of the story contain three major settings: the Thames, the Congo, and Brussels. They also point to the final stage of Marlow's experience: the first part establishes the mood of the story, the second prepares the way for Kurtz, and the third climaxes the moral issues of the entire tale. The theme is the "tragedy of moral desolation and defeated egoism." [Contains the text of "Heart of Darkness."]

1270.1 Najder, Zdzislaw. "Nad Conradem" (On Conrad), *Tygodnik Powszechny* (Cracow), No. 18 1952; rpt. in *TW*, No. 10(1955); rpt. in *NC*, pp. 11–45.

JC was closely connected to Polish literature in his handling of moral conflicts and the psychology of heroes, and with French literature in matters of style and his objectivism. When the heroes of Polish Romantic literature utter judgments on the world, their statements are, unlike English judgments, of a general nature and represent a social group or entire nation. They are solitary embodiments of many, and all have a deep sense of responsibility. In Poland, the question of the responsibility of individuals was the result of the nation's fate, which often resembled that of a besieged city. JC also inherited the flowery style of his early works from Polish in, for instance, the loose structure which reflects Polish syntax. His technique of a tale within a tale is sometimes likened to "genteel ancedotery" of Polish narrative tradition, but this practice has been taken too far. JC learned his art from Henry James, Flaubert, and Maupassant. [In Polish.]

1271.1 Noferi, Adelia. "Una 'testimonianza perpetua'" (A "Perpetual Testimony"), in *Un Reitto delle Isole* (An Outcast of the Islands), (Milan: Bompiani, 1952), pp. 5–24.

[An introductory note made up of cleverly assembled quotations from JC's writings to show his ideas about life and art.] [In Italian.]

1272.1 Pellizzi, Camillo. "Nota del traduttore" (Translator's Note), *Sotto Gli Occhi dell'Occidente)*, (Under Western Eyes), (Milan, Bompiani, 1952), pp. 489–95.

[In a note dated May, 1949, Pellizzi develops some ideas already expressed in his article, "I Russi di Conrad," of 1948.] [In Italian]

1272.2 Persone, Luigi M. "Conrad," *L'Eco di Bergamo*, LXXIII, 156 (2 July 1952), 3.

Both JC, an orphan at seventeen [sic], and Proust looked back to the appeal of the past, to the emotions that shaped them. In his own past and in his travels from continent to continent, JC found or discovered man, and in his various experiences he found the inspiration for his works, in which one finds not only an adventurous side but also a deep psychological analysis. [In Italian.]

1953

1286.1 Jahier, Piero. "L'uomo Conrad" (Conrad the Man), *Paragone* (October 1953), 16–25; rpt. "L'uomo Conrad" as an introductory essay in JC's *Lo specchio del mare* (The Mirror of the Sea), (Milan: Bompiani, 1954), pp. 5–15 (translator's notes, pp. 719–36).

In JC's artistic achievement, there is an echo of Henry James's poetics (the impassible observer, the pure, almost narcissistic artist). But JC is basically unlike the "historian of fine consciences":

his sympathy is for the obscure drama of mankind. [Brief biographical and critical survey.] [In Italian.]

1286.2 Kass, Robert. *"Face to Face," Films In Review*, IV (February 1953), 91–92.

Huntington Hartford produced and Aeneas Mackenzie adapted "The Secret Sharer," which is one half of the film entitled *Face to Face*, the other half being James Agee's adaptation of Stephen Crane's "The Bride Comes to Yellow Sky." Most other JC film adaptations have failed because the director tried to translate the essential psychological conflict by physical violence, but Mackenzie has succeeded by adhering to JC's text and the spirit of the novice captain who is in conflict with himself. By accepting the responsibility of judging his double, the captain gains self-knowledge necessary to command his ship. Some defects of the film are the amateurish hiding of the double's presence from the crew and the miscasting of Michael Pate as Leggatt.

1286.3 "Konrad, Dzhozef" (Joseph Conrad), *Bolshaia Sovetskaia Entsyklopediia* (Great Soviet Encyclopedia), Second ed (Moscow: Bol'shaia sovetskaia entsyklopediia, 1953), XXII, p. 399.

Most of JC's works are descriptions of distant seas and islands, depicting the romantic adventures and experiences of solitary outcasts of bourgeois society. [In Russian.]

1286.4 Levi, Abramo. *"L'agente segreto"* (The Secret Agent), *Letture* (Milan), VIII, Nos. 9–10 (1953), 331–32.

[Brief plot summary of the Italian translation of *The Secret Agent*, with the warning, "This is a novel for mature readers only."] [In Italian.]

1289.1 Schorer, Mark. "Women in Love and Death," *Hudson Review*, VI (Spring 1953); published as "Donne, Amore e Morte," *Inventario*, V (Autumn 1953); rpt. as "Women in Love" in *The World We Imagine: Selected Essays* (New York: Farrar, Straus and Giroux, 1968), pp. 107–21.

Henry James's *The Portrait of a Lady* is among the first demonstrations in fiction of the belief in the freedom of the will and the responsibilities of that freedom, a belief that necessarily selects from the phrase "character is fate" a strong emphasis on "character." This concept is unlike JC's, as seen in *Chance* and, in all his novels by implication, where chance is accident, accident in which lies opportunity, "*that* kind of chance: determinism and free will, the will operating out from the ground that accident allows it." In Lawrence, the two terms become "equivalents." The structure of *Women In Love*, unlike that of JC's works, has its own kind of coherence, a highly and complexly organized structural presentation of theme.

1293.1 Wood, Margaret Mary. *Paths of Loneliness: The Individual Isolated in Modern Society* (New York: Columbia UP, 1953), p. 76.

Some passages of JC's "Typhoon" portray how two men grapple with a problem and attain an understanding of its hidden meaning. MacWhirr and Jukes struggle against the storm at sea, but Mac Whirr's successful fronting of the violence produces a sense of relief in Jukes.

1954

1304.1 Legouis, Émile, and Louis Cazamian. *A History of English Literature*, Rvd ed. (New York: Macmillan, 1954), pp. 1331–34.

Several influences helped to form JC's work: French naturalism, English realism, the novel of adventure, the psychology of Henry James, a background of Slav sensibility, the spirit of the Russian novelists, and symbolism. His art is thus a "most composite product," a "complex of influences" dominated by a temperament which turns it into a "brilliant, rich, and original alloy." For JC, art is self-sufficient; the artist's only object is to transmit fully the impression of reality, and the senses are the only way available to this expression. But to JC, the inner world is no less a reality: at times a "raw" realist, he is also a poet and thinker. Ever present is a sense of the mystery of fate and an "implicit, diffused, profound ethical element." The mood of his thought is pessimistic: in spite of the endeavors of the best of men, themselves fallible, "ineradicable selfishness turns man into a wolf to man." But a "pressing suggestion" of "union, pity, and solidarity" emanates from his work, an appeal which lends it a "flow of sympathy"; and its most contagious idealism lies in the "tragic or dreamy sense of the unfathomable unknown," which is common to men at all times. JC, though, is not actually "one of the great creative geniuses."

1306.1 Rosati, Salvatore. "Joseph Conrad," *Il Mondo* (27 July 1954), p. 9.

JC introduced into English a phraseologocial flavor that is a real contribution to the language. *Nostromo* and *Lord Jim* do not avoid a certain clumsiness, but this fact makes evident the way in which his narrative technique alters the time perspective not solely to conform to a procedure dear to Naturalism, but to work in function of a character's vision or problem, or of an event, and the substance of its human meaning. [Review of *Lo specchio del mare* (The Mirror of the Sea), (Milan: Bompiani, 1954).] [In Italian.]

1307.1 Tredrey. F. D. *The House of Blackwood, 1804-1954: The History of A Publishing Firm* (Edinburgh and London: William Blackwood and Sons, 1954), pp. 181, 186–94.

JC's letters to William Blackwood chronicle his difficulties in writing *Lord Jim* and his financial problems and discouragement shortly after 1900.

1955

1312.1 Blotner, Joseph L[eo]. "Joseph Conrad: Early Cloak and Dagger," *The Political Novel* (Garden City, New York: Doubleday, 1955), pp. 21–21.

In its structure, its delineation of personality, and its "masterful manipulation" of point of view, JC's political novel, *The Secret Agent*, is a classic. An example of the superiority of the European political novel, it is "one of the finest work of the entire genre." In *Under Western Eyes*, JC deals with a wider area, larger figures, and bigger stakes.

1312.2 Bone, David. "Joseph Conrad," *Landfall At Sunset: The Life of a Contented Sailor* (London: Gerald Duckworth, 1955), pp. 154–60.

David Bone, the Scottish sailor and writer, first met JC in 1919 at a dinner given in honor of the Merchants' Service in Liverpool. During the years, the two men kept in touch by means of correspondence. In 1923, JC sailed with Captain Bone to America on the *Tuscania*. During the voyage, JC displayed some displeasure because seamen had come to rely on mechanical power to do much that had been done by hand in his sea days. Captain Bone's brother, Muirhead Bone, who made the voyage also, was a good companion for JC; indeed, he made the first portrait drawing of JC at sea. Upon the arrival of the *Tuscania* in New York, the ship-news reporters ignored other well known vessels to welcome the one that bore JC, and dancers in national Polish colors danced on the pier in honor of the famous writer.

1320.1 Friedman, Melvin. *Stream of Consciousness: A Study in Literary Method* (New Haven: Yale UP, 1955), pp. vii, 32, 50–52, 54, 73, 75, 179–80, 81.

JC, "on the fringes of the stream of consciousness tradition," anticipated Gide and Huxley with an awareness of "musical" structure (contrapuntal plots) in his novels. Following James, JC employed an intelligent observer, Marlow, in many of his novels in order to give focus to events. *Nostromo* and *Victory* fail without Marlow and become "whirlpool[s] of confused impressions." *Lord Jim* and *Chance*, however, are triumphs of technique; Marlow "has a controlling and chastening effect on the impression." Stylistic control is not as obvious in the mature JC, who was more concerned to produce impressions. One can point up a Sterne-Meredith-James-Conrad lineage in the English stream of consciousness novel.

1321.1 Gorlier, Claudio. "Lo specchio di Conrad" (Conrad's Mirror), *Il Nuovo Corriere*, XI, *109* (8 May 1955), 3.

The failure of JC's characters is often due to the impossibility of their attaining an ideal of rationality. It is not by accident that female characters are considered intrinsically irrational and are therefore banished from JC's pages. [Review of Italian translation of *The Mirror of the Sea: Lo specchio del mare* (Milan: Bompiani, 1954).] [In Italian.]

1321.2 Gose, Elliott Bickley, Jr. "Passion and the Tradition: A Critical Appraisal of Ford Madox Ford," *DA*, XV (1955), 123. Unpublished dissertation, Cornell University, 1954.

1330.1 Najder, Zdzislaw. "Conrad," *TW*, XI, No. 10 (1955), 143–55.

Critics regard JC as a three-fold patriot: Polish by origin, temperament, intellectual traditions and attachment; French in his warm liking for France, the number of French motifs in his works; and English for the language of his work, citizenship and scrupulous loyalty. Most critics regard his work as a monolithic entity, and little attention has been paid to the development of his views and artistry.

1330.2 Najder, Zdzislaw. "Igraszki losu" (Playthings of Fate), *TW* No. 12, 1955; rpt. in *NC*, pp. 171–84.

The Polish rendering of *Chance* is inadequate; it should be titled "Playthings of Fate." The basic moral problem in this novel is how to be noble and at the same time avoid failure. The uncomplicated characters and the duality of the ethical system contrast with the complicated artistic machinery constructed by JC. Sometimes all the misunderstandings and complications seem artificial, and melodrama appears, rather than tragedy, under the surface. But melodrama is a fault only in the eyes of critics. [In Polish.]

1330.3 Raimondi, Giuseppi. "Il Conrad di Jahier" (Jahier's Conrad), *La Valigia delle Indie* (The Indian Case), (Firenze: Vellecchi, 1955), pp. 300–03.

[A note on Piero Jahier, one of JC's Italian translators.] [In Italian.]

1956

1339.1 Andrzejewski, Jerzy. "Trzykrotnie nad *Lordem Jimem*" (*Lord Jim* Thrice), *TW*, XII: 2 (1956), 147–59.

The effect of reading *Lord Jim* several times in a person's life varies, naturally, according to the reader's age. Critics before and after World War II, for example, sought dependence on the novels of Andrzejewski and of JC, and rightly so. This dependence was due to the fact that only JC's work had the generosity to provide a mirror, which was what Andrzejewski sought. In the 1930's, however, a new generation appeared, rent by contradictions and ideological differences. For them, *Jim* provided order in chaos, confirming the concept that man is always alone and that the only reason for his existence lies in the depths of his inner longings, which are incomprehensible to others. In 1943, another reading of *Jim* brought disappointment, as it was inappropriate to the ruins of Warsaw and seemed unreal by comparison. A third reading in 1955 suggested that the exaggerated emphasis placed by certain critics on JC's "Polishness" is a delusion. To be sure, Jim's problem can be read as the sublimation of JC's complex of national betrayal, but it is less concerned with reproaches of conscience as a natural longing. Marlow's words should be taken literally. The drama of Jim is not that of an isolated individual: on the contrary, it is the drama of a thoroughly socialized individual who can see himself and make evaluations only amidst specific activities and moral norms measured by absolute social values. Many misunderstandings have arisen because we fail to observe that Jim seeks to conciliate his conscience with the world. [In Polish.]

1339.2 Bigongiari, Piero. "Conrad nei mari del Sud" (Conrad in the South Seas), *Il Nuovo Corrierre—La Gazzetta*: Part I, 3 (15 July 1956); Part II, 3 (16 July 1956); Part III, 3 (17 July 1956); Part IV, 3 (18 July 1956).

JC's fiction is a *recherche du temps perdu*; at a certain point in his life he began to recover his past through his imagination. [Biographical accounts of JC's experiences on the *Judea*, the *Highland Forest*, the *Vidar*, and the *Otago* are accompanied by long quotations from "Youth," *Almayer's Folly, The Rescue, The Shadow-Line,* etc.] [In Italian.]

1339.3 Brown, Calvin S., et al. (eds). *The Reader's Companion To World Literature* (New York: Dryden Press [Mentor Book], 1956), p. 108.

JC's greatest skill lies in his ability to evoke an atmosphere, "whether of a typhoon at sea or of the sultry mystery of the jungle." This he does by utilizing methods of the realists. Presenting his material in momentary impressions, he creates a mood of the moment which reveals only one facet of the real truth. A persistent part of that truth is man's inescapable loneliness. All JC's characters suffer from a sense of isolation, and their greatest need is for fellowship. Ironically, "the understanding or opportunity comes too late."

1341.1 Coombes, H. *Edward Thomas* (London: Chatto and Windus, 1956); rpt. (New York: Barnes and Noble, 1973), pp. 11, 48, 75, 84–86, 94.

The particular experience of the otherness and strangeness of nature is persistent and immediate in JC, but it is even more so in Edward Thomas, being a central aspect of his entire consciousness. Thomas is very much like JC in his conception of a natural immensity absorbing both physical things and mental activities. JC especially verbalizes this conception. His utterance of it is most impressive when it is synthesized into his work and made into a comment on all of man's vanity, greed, lust, pride, mistaken idealism, loyalty, and courage. All such immensity of nature becomes an integral part of *Nostromo,* "Heart of Darkness," and "Typhoon." Yet a fundamental and important difference clearly separates them: JC can find human endeavor and through that matter for art which, while it has its dark side, is not pessimistic; Thomas also is not gloomy, but his art is not as broad because it is more personal.

1347.1 Izzo, Carlo. "La vie del mare" (Seafaring), *La Gazzetta del Popolo* (18 July 1956), [not seen in this form]; rpt. in *Civiltà Britannica* (British Civilization), (Rome: Edizioni di Storia e Letteratura, 1970), II, 165–68.

In JC's mature works, the question of form is still acutely felt, but narrative structure is often clumsy. In JC, exoticism is strictly bound to his love for a seafaring life. [In Italian.]

1349.1 Luzi, Mario. "Nota su Conrad" (A Note on Conrad), *Giornale del Mattino,* X *164* (15 July 1956), 3; rpt. in *Il Popolo di Milano,* III, No. 173 (24 July 1956), 3.

The appearance of James Wait at the beginning of *The Nigger of the Narcissus* is in itself the principal event. The mysterious shudder that runs through the crew at the sight of him or at the sound of his voice contains already the sense of what will occur, and what does actually occur under the nightmare of that image, of that presence, oppressive and repugnant, which reminds one of the occult fascination of Coleridge's albatross. [Review of the Italian translation of *Nigger* and *Typhoon: Il negro del narciso—Tifone* (Milan: Bompiani, 1955).] [In Italian.]

1351.1 Muller, Herbert J. *The Spirit of Tragedy* (New York: Knopf, 1956), pp. 95, 333.

In Sophocles, irony is a way of viewing life, a philosophical perception of "the irony of fate," a condition rather than an act. The irony of Sophocles was not as comprehensive as that of modern writers like Thomas Mann and JC. The tragic writer is able to realize most nearly the ideal mission of the artist stated by JC. The writer "speaks" to us of delight and wonder, of the sense of mystery in our lives, of our sense of pity, beauty, and pain; to the "conviction of solidarity" that joins the loneliness of many hearts; to all qualities that "bind together all humanity—the dead to the living and the living to the unborn."

1351.2 Najder, Zdzislaw. "Conrad i Bobrowski" (Conrad and Bobrowski), TW, No. 11 (1956), [not seen in this form]; rpt. in *Życie Literackie* (Cracow), No. 40, (1957); rpt. in *NC* (Warsaw: Panstwowy Instytut Wydawniczy, 1965), pp. 46–69.

JC's father, Apollon Korzeniowski, was the complete opposite of Tadeusz Bobrowski, who merely tolerated him. Korzeniowski was sensitive, impulsive, with great charm, a radical supporter of the Insurrection (1863). Bobrowski had no close friends and regarded Korzeniowski's political views as irresponsible fantasies, though he unconsciously envied him for the affection in which he was generally held. Bobrowski's remarks in his letters and the *Memoirs* are almost always critical and malicious. He also "improved" on facts by describing Korzeniowski on his return from exile (1868) as "broken," although Korzeniowski remained active in literature and politics for the rest of his life. Bobrowski did his utmost to prevent JC from understanding his father, by depicting him as an irresponsible dreamer (critics have noted the dislike of fathers in JC's characters, e.g., in *Victory*). JC's recollections of his parents were associated with prison, exile, illness, and slow death, and he failed to understand the meaning of his parents' devotion which, Bobrowski said, was meaningless. Bobrowski taught JC to regard the 1863 Insurrection as unhappy madness. But his influence also taught JC the principles of honesty and responsibility. [In Polish.]

1352.1 Praz, Mario. "Giovinezza di Conrad (Conrad's Youth), *Il Tempo* IV, 17 April 1956 [not seen in this form]; rpt. in *Cronache Litterarie Anglo-Sassoni*, (Anglo-Saxon Literary Chronicles), (Roma, Edizioni di Storia e Letteratura, 1966), pp. 38–43.

JC's wish to become a seaman aboard an English vessel was reinforced by his encounter with an Englishman on the Furca Pass, he came to meet the *femme fatale* of *The Arrow of Gold* through an Englishman, and an English graduate of Cambridge was the first to read the MS of *Almayer's Folly*. It was the Englishman Galsworthy who discovered a new continent (JC) instead of an old one (Stevenson). This life of an "obscure Conrad," not as yet at maturity, engages the reader in the pages of Visiak. [A review-article on E. H. Visiak, *The Mirror of Conrad* (London: Laurie, 1955).] [In Italian.]

1353.1 Rosati, Salvatore. "Joseph Conrad," *Il Mondo*, VIII, 23 (5 June 1956), 8.

It is incorrect to link Stevenson and JC under the heading of exoticism. JC's novels home in on the individual existing in his own right, with his moral or psychological problems. This is the reason why they are set in those regions he knew so well, where white man was isolated and free of the constraints of civilization. [Review of Italian translation of *Almayer's Folly* and *Tales of Unrest: La follie di Almayer Racconti inquieti* (Milan: Bompiani, 1956).] [In Italian.]

1354.1 Sinko, Grzegorz. "Literatura angielska" (English Literature), *Rocznik Literacki Za 1955* (Literary Annual for 1955),(Warsaw), (1956), p. 427.

The first printing of *Chance* in Polish was sold out in a few weeks. The only previous translation, that of 1921, was good, except for the then unestablished Polish maritime terminology and the old-fashioned and diffuse language. The new translation by Teresa Tatarkiewiczowa is clear, a desirable achievement for JC, who is sometimes complicated and heavy. [In Polish.]

1957

1362.1 Angeleri, Carlo. "Joseph Conrad: Una lettera inedita a Carlo Placci (con una nota di Carlo Angeleri)" (Joseph Conrad: An Unpublished Letter to Carlo Placci, with a note by Carlo Angeleri), *Paragone*, VIII, 88 (1957), 55–58.

JC strove all his life to absorb the English language; his continuous efforts resulted in an exceptional wealth of his means of expression. Words are not a mechanical or objective device, but an instrument which must possess the value of the idea. Writing Placci a letter (26 October 1911) to thank him for sending a note ["Joseph Conrad," *Il Marzocco* (15 October 1911)], in which the Italian musicologist had expressed some reservations about the writer's narrative technique, JC said that "on the question of form there really is no defence to offer; . . . what I am looking for is the effect of the *living word* . . . it is in the living word que l'on saisit le mieux le forme du rêve." The effect of the living word should be charged with the idea; things should be described beyond material limitations: this is why in JC's work reality often dissolves in symbols and descriptive formulae lose their temporality to create an atmosphere of dream and the form of the dream is properly affirmed in the living word. Style must serve to reach the perfect matching of poetic inspiration and means of expression. [Facsimile of JC's letter is given between pp. 58 and 59.] [In Italian.]

1370.1 Camerino, Aldo. "Centenario di Conrad" (Conrad's Centennial), *Giornale Del Mattino*, 31 December 1957 [not seen in this form]; rpt. in *Scrittori di Lingua Inglese* (English Writers), (Milan & Napoli: Ricciardi, 1968), pp. 189–93.

JC will be remembered for his capacity of evocation of people and landscapes, for the misty atmosphere that envelops his characters, who incarnate honor and devotion or expiate betrayals, for the enchantment of solemn calms, of tempests and inner struggles. [In Italian.]

1370.2 Clark, Jeanne Gabriel. "London in English Literature, 1880-1955," *DA, XVII* (1957), 1761. Unpublished dissertation, Columbia University, 1957.

1370.3 Coleman, Marion Moore. "Folklore from Joseph Conrad (Korzeniowski)," *Polish Folklore* II (Alliance College), (June 1957), 33.

In "Prince Roman," the peasants working in the fields make the sign of the cross behind his back as if Prince Roman, walking about the fields in a trance after the loss of his beloved wife, were one of themselves. And in the same story, there appears the desire for news of a special wolf, a "wolf above all wolves."

1372.1 "Critical Approaches," *TLS*, 13 September 1957, p. 546.

It is impossible to consider the fiction of today without considering once again the inevitable names of Forster, Greene, Hemingway, Thomas Mann, and JC. Dickens, Hardy, Butler, and Henry James set forth the "terms of the appeal" from the nineteenth to the twentieth century, and the response appears in the works of Ford Madox Ford, Willa Cather, Lionel Trilling, Somerset Maugham, E. M. Forster, Graham Greene, and JC. JC and others join in agreement on the artist's necessity of ridding himself of his strictest standards of value. [Review of Morton Dauwen Zabel, *Craft and Character in Modern Fiction* (New York: Viking P. 1957).]

1381.1 Frye, Northrop. *Anatomy of Criticism: Four Essays* (Princeton: Princeton UP, 1957), pp. 39, 40, 100, 140, 155, 193, 247, 267, 306.

[Frye finds that JC observes and makes use of a number of conventions and techniques.] JC's Lord Jim is an *alazon*, or imposter, one who pretends to be something more than he is; he is a lineal descendant of the early *miles glorious*. If we desire to know how we come to know literature, we shall find that expanding images into conventional archetypes is a process that takes place in all our reading. A symbol like the sea cannot remain in JC only, for example: it must expand over many works into an archetypal symbol of literature as a whole. JC's use of irony simply continues the "romantic tradition of stylization." In secular quest-romances, obvious motives and rewards for the quest are common; the quest for buried treasure has been an actual theme from the Siegfried epic cycle to *Nostromo*. JC writes in such a manner that a narrator helps him to tell his story: here the genre of the written word is being assimilated to that of the spoken one. JC uses dislocation of the narrative to cause us to shift our attention from listening to the story to looking at the central situation. Also, an important theme in the bourgeois novel should be the parody of the romance and its ideals. The tradition established by *Don Quixote* continues in a kind of novel which looks at a romantic situation from its own point of view so that the convention of the two forms make up an ironic mixture instead of a sentimental mixture as in novels ranging from *Northanger Abbey* to *Madame Bovary* and *Lord Jim*.

1382.1 Garbaty, Thomas Jay. "*The Savoy*, 1896: A Re-edition of Representative Prose and Verse, with a Critical Introduction, and Biographical and Critical Notes," *DA*, XVIII (1957), 3014A-15A. Unpublished dissertation, University of Pennsylvania, 1957.

1391.1 Herling-Grudzinski, Gustaw. "W oczach Conrada," *Kultura* (Paris), No. 10 (October 1957), 16–32; trans into Italian (no

translator's name), with an Italianate name, Gustavo Herling;
"Sotto gli occhi di Conrad: Nel centenario della nascita dello
scrittore" (Under Conrad's Eyes: On the 100th anniversary of the
writer's birth), *Tempo Presente* (Rome), December 1957, pp. 939–
47. [An essay on *Under Western Eyes*.] [In Italian.]

1395.1 Isherwood, Christopher (ed). "Joseph Conrad: 'The Secret
Sharer,'" *Great English Short Stories* (New York: Dell [Laurel
Edition], 1957), pp. 13–14.

Although JC became an acknowledged master of English fiction
during his last twenty years, he remained essentially an alien, a fact
which gave him a critical distance from his subject matter and
enhanced his style by the "attractive strangeness" of his "foreign
accent." His characteristic tone is that of a man accustomed to
confront danger with "coolly observant detachment." The theme of
being alien is doubly woven into "The Secret Sharer": the young
captain is a stranger to his crew, and beyond him, at a further remove
from human society, stands the outcast "Sharer," who seems to
embody the "fundamental loneliness" of every individual on earth.
This story conveys many of JC's personal qualities—his "admirably
independent" moral sense, his "stiff but charming" courtesy, his
devotion to his command (he did not marry until he left the sea for
good), and his awe and wonder when alone in the presence of Nature.

1395.2 Jablowska, Roza. "Conrad w oczach nowszej krytyki
anglielskiej" (Conrad as Seen by Recent English Criticism), *KN*,
IV: 1 (1947), 47–56.

Although English, Polish, and American criticism of JC is well
developed, it has not yet produced a full, entirely satisfactory
evaluation of JC's works. His Polish heritage and gaps in his
biography cause difficulties. English critics deal with impressionism,
artistry, use of language, and JC's pessimistic outlook. Between the
wars, criticism was biographical and dealt with influences.
Gradually, JC has become an entirely English writer. The present
tendency is to investigate his biography and the genesis of his works,
as Bradbrook did, and to place him in the "great tradition," as F. R.
Leavis did. [In Polish.]

1398.1 Kagarlitzkii, Julius. "Joseph Conrad: A Centennial
Appreciation," *Inostrannaya Literatura*, No. 12, 1957, pp. 205–10;
trans by Madeline Long in *CON*, I. No. 3 (Summer 1969), 81–87.

In Russia, JC has been fortunate with both critics and
translators. Although enemies and friends disagree about his
complicated creative principles, all agree that he was a romantic

who lived the life of a romantic. Towards the end of the nineteenth century, English literature began to move away from the specific traditional realism of Fielding, Smollett, and Dickens, to become more concerned with the psychological analysis associated with twentieth-century literature. JC was a part of this transition; most of his heroes are placed in positions which require decisive action: thus one of the most important achievements of twentieth-century realism, the psychological undercurrent, appears in his work. The theme of JC's romanticism, even if somewhat indirect, is always the failure of the illusions of a bourgeois society and the hope for something new and brighter. His romanticism triumphed over his pessimism and skepticism. According to him, man is alone in a materialistic world, but he became more and more deeply convinced of the usefulness of his ideals. *Victory*, for example, portrays the victory of Heyst the man over Heyst the thinker. The themes of JC's works, unlike the poetizing and sufferings of loneliness of decadent literature, became the search for a way out; JC's heroes do not revel in their solitude—they search for a way of escape. JC does not, though, clearly define his attitude towards his heroes: it is not really sympathy and compassion, but "exacting love." [In Polish.]

1412.1 Mazzotti, Giuliana. "Sul 'metodo inversivo' di Joseph Conrad" (Joseph Conrad's Oblique Method), *Rivista di Letterature Moderne e Comparate*, X, 2 (April-June 1957), 142–46.

In order to reproduce what in life appears as fragmentary and incoherent, JC uses in "Karain," *Lord Jim, Nostromo,* and *Victory* an oblique method, with frequent hesitations, retrogressions, and interpolations. Whole chapters are dedicated to detailed discussions of motivations and to analyses of several points of view. [In Italian.]

1412.2 Miles, T. A. "Conrad Centenary," *Bulletin* (Sydney), 4 December 1957, pp. 11, 65.

[A biographical sketch of JC's life at sea, with emphasis on his first command, the barque *Otago*, and the fact that now the hulk of the ship, which for twenty-five years or more has lain on the eastern bank of the River Derwent, seven miles above Hobart, has now been sold and is being converted into scrap, so that " with her goes the last visible maritime link with Conrad."]

1423.1 Najder, Zdzislaw. "*Lord Jim*," *Nowiny Literackie* (Warsaw), No. 18 (1957); rpt. in *NC*, (1965), pp. 99–111.

In *Lord Jim*, the main character's outward appearance is described in some detail, but his psyche remains unexplained to the end of the novel, at least for Marlow. The reader knows more than he does. The novel is not only a description of certain physical and psychological facts, but also an account of obtaining information about them written by a philosopher brought up on Romantic poetry. Jim is like a stick pushed into an ant hill: JC is interested in the stick, but he devotes more space to the behavior of the ants. We are far from Dostoevski's moral exhibitionism. Jim is not wholly comprehensible as a Pole. No nation can claim a monopoly of his kind of noble endurance, and JC made him not only symbolic but also typical ("one of us"), though what he meant by "us" is not clear. [In Polish.]

1423.2 Najder, Zdzislaw. "'Malajska trylogia' Conrada" (Conrad's "Malayan Trilogy"), *Morze* (Danzig), No. 12, (1957) [not seen in this form]; rpt. with additions in *NC* (1965), pp. 70–88.

The general sense of *Almayer's Folly* is gloomy and hopeless, showing interpersonal relationships as unhealthy and deeply immoral. *An Outcast of the Islands*, the most complicated and uneven of JC's tales, represents a new stage in his development and is a rehearsal for *Lord Jim*. *The Rescue*, in which the action is replaced by a spider's web of allusions, is characteristic in dealing with a typically Conradian moral problem, but it is one of his weakest tales. [In Polish.]

1425.1 Osborne, H. J. "At Sea with Conrad," *Sea Breezes*, N.S. XXIII (January 1957), 22–25.

[Osborne prints a letter, dated 20 July 1917, which he received from JC, concerning JC's memory of sailing with Osborne aboard the *Ready* in 1916.]

1431.1 Retinger, Jozef R. "Z notatek o Conradzie" (From Notes on Conrad), *Kultura* (Paris) 1957, pp. 7–8, 117, 175–87.

JC said (1909) that he rarely spoke Polish. He paid much attention to an English style of living, but was more interested than the average Englishman in the private lives of those he met during visits to Poland. His reaction to Russia was very Polish. He regarded America as a sort of British colony, though his visit there changed this attitude. [In Polish.]

1450.1 Wimsatt, William K., Jr., and Cleanth Brooks. *Literary Criticism: A Short History* (New York: Knopf, 1957), pp. 682–85, 693.

According to Henry James, the novel was, or ought to be, a work of art. Flaubert was, for James, "the novelist's novelist," and Flaubert became, especially for Ford Madox Ford and JC, a "fountainhead." Ford and JC wanted to make the reader forget the writer entirely so that the story would seem to tell itself and develop its own life. The desire to *render* what happened instead of telling it caused photographic fidelity in writing called Impressionism. Also, the device of juxtaposition became the "Time-shift" developed by Ford and JC.

1450.2 Wright, Walter. "Maggie Verver: Neither Saint nor Witch, (1957)," *Henry James*, ed by Tony Tanner (London: Macmillan [Modern Judgments], 1968), pp. 316–26.

In James's novel, *The Golden Bowl*, Maggie Verver is saved by her adherence to the "forms" which come to her reserve to help her in the midst of her mental bewilderment; her "habitual concern for decorum" carries her through. In "Typhoon," JC stresses Captain MacWhirr's insistence upon proper order and when, during the typhoon, MacWhirr finds things in their proper places, he is steadied by the familiar experience. Maggie, likewise, is steadied by the outer, familiar forms. She does the things which a woman of her position and pretensions must do; the world of art in which she shapes her own life and judges Charlotte and Amerigo as if they were works of art is a world in which tensions are held in control so that the surface remains tranquil.

1958

1460.1 "Conrad, Joseph," *Das Kleine Lexikon Der Weltliteratur* (The Little Encyclopedia of World Literature), ed by Hermann Pongs (Stuttgart: Union, 1958), 3rd rev ed, cols. 339–41.

In JC's novels, the sailor represents the archetypal dimensions of man's life. [A survey of JC's life and works.] [In German.]

1470.1 Guerard, Albert J. "Two Versions of Anarchy: *Under Western Eyes*," *Conrad The Novelist, 1958* (C. I. No. 1470); rpt. in *JCCC* (1975), pp. 83–100.

In many ways, Razumov, in *Under Western Eyes*, is a tragic hero. A fatal decision diverts him from his own plans into a "wilderness of problems" he cannot fully understand or control. Racked by inner guilt, he is at the same time threatened with death. The content of the work is perfectly suited to the ironic manner because irony is a way of concealing and revealing. The strength of the novel depends on Razumov, not on JC's views of the revolutionaries.

1472.1 Hamalian, Leo and Edmond L. Volpe (eds). "Now That You've Read Conrad's 'The [sic] Heart of Darkness," *Ten Modern Short Novels* (New York: Putnam's, 1958), pp. 190–96.

[Contains a sketch of JC's life and a few ordinary comments on "Heart of Darkness." Typical of weak introductions to stories by JC in textbooks.]

1472.2 Harkness, Bruce. "Bibliography and the Novelistic Fallacy," *Studies in Bibliography: Papers of the Bibliographical Society of the University of Virginia*, XIII (1958), 59–74.

[Notes the discrepancies setting the various editions of JC's works apart from one another and argues the need for a carefully prepared edition of JC's novels.]

1479.1 Katarskii, I. M. and Iu I. Kagarlitskii. "Konrad" (Conrad), *Istoriia Angliiskoi Literatury III* (Moscow), (1958), 76–80.

JC's novels and tales are formally close to Stevenson's novels of adventure but differ in character. JC shifts the center of gravity to psychology. His early works have decadent traits, but later he became an opponent of naturalism and of extreme subjectivity. Social problems are most clearly dealt with in *Nostromo*. *Victory* is also among his best works. JC did not recognize social revolution, even though old bourgeois ideals had been compromised, and he did not believe in new ideals which were in any case related to the old. He saw no solution in Socialism either. His weakest novels are those in which he analyzes "broken-down, amoral psyches," as in *Under Western Eyes*. He valued Dostoevski's novels highly, but would not admit any debt to him. [In Russian.]

1492.1 Matuska, Alexander. "Silueta Josepha Conrada" (A Silhouette of Joseph Conrad), *Slovenské Pohl'ady A Portrety* LXXIV (Bratislava), No. 74 (1958), 292–96; (Profiles and Portraits), rpt. in *Profily A Portrety*, (Bratislava: Slovensky spisovatel, 1972), pp. 399–404.

JC's characters live more intensely than those of Kipling or R. L. Stevenson and are independent of their author. At first sight, JC is a writer of sea stories, but it was well said that he was concerned not with the sea, but with seafarers. Galsworthy and others admired JC primarily as an artist. He has also been called a bourgeois writer, yet he is far from the imperialistic ideas of Kipling. [In Slovak.]

1496.1 Najder, Zdzislaw. "Conrad i teatr" (Conrad and the Theater), *Dialog* (Warsaw), No. 7, 1958; rpt. in *NC* (1965), pp. 204–12.

JC's letters show his dislike of the theater, and his own plays did not succeed. The stage version of "To-morrow," *One Day More*, is better than the tale, still worth study and production. JC collaborated with Macdonald Hastings in the stage version of *Victory*

(1916), which ran for three months at the Globe. But the sensational and banal plot of the novel was elevated by symbolism and allegory, and JC's use of technical devices was entirely lost in the dramatized version. He had no illusions about the dramatization of *The Secret Agent*, which was a fiasco, and he quit the theater angry and bitter, an act typical of his rather stiff theoretical attitude toward creativity. [In Polish.]

1497.1 Najder, Zdzislaw. "Literatura angieslska" (English Literature), *Rocznik Literacki Za 1957* (Warsaw), (Literary Annual for 1957), (1958), p. 324.

Aniela Zagorska was a good translator of JC, especially in descriptive passages, though she tended to be too literary and did not learn how to translate dialogue. The editors of the new Collected Edition, in Polish, have corrected many of her mistakes, but there are still others. [In Polish.]

1959

1523.1 Bannikov, N. "Dzhozef Konrad. *Izbrannoe v dvukh tomakh*" (Joseph Conrad. *Selected Works in Two Volumes*), (Moscow: Gosudarstvennoe Izdatelstvo Khudsovzhestvennoi Literatury, 1959), pp. 5–7.

JC emerged in English literature as a Romantic, a writer opposed to the bourgeois reality of his own heroes. As a Romantic, he endowed them with exceptionally tense feelings and experiences. In JC's work, the reader encounters unusually original, traditional maritime Romanticism and serious moral, ethical, and social investigations. The lives of the characters with whom JC sympathized are challenges to bourgeois-commercial institutions and the norms of the bourgeois world, its ethics and morality. On the ships he describes are depicted not only scenes of struggle with the forces of nature but also the hostile, dark powers of bourgeois society. He also finds deep protest on behalf of the enslaved native masses of the East under the yoke of white colonizers. He believed the time would come when these oppressed masses would reveal the wealth of their creative possibilities.

Although JC is an outstanding stylist with his own original and artistic characteristics, not everything he wrote is of artistic value. He reveals strong notes of fatalism and lack of faith in the future. But an attentive reader will feel that he rejects bourgeois civilization, which deforms the best qualities in human nature. [In Russian.]

1532.1 Doblier, Maurice. "A Porch on Fire Island, A Hill in Mysore," *New York Herald Tribune Book Review*, XXXV (1 February 1959), p. 2.

Under the heading of "Books and Authors," this general introduction to Eleuzar Lipsky and R. K. Narayan reports that some of the most popular Western writers in India are Sartre, Bennett, Twain, Hemingway, Thoreau, O'Henry, and JC.]

1532.2 Folejewski, Zbigniew. "Ze studiow nad technika nowelistyczna Conrada," *Roczniki Humanistyczne*, VI, No. 6 Lublin (1959), 127–35 (in Polish); developed into "Short Story or Novel: The Ambiguity of Structure in 'The End of the Tether,'" in *The Novel and its Changing Form*, ed by R. G. Collins (Winnipeg: University of Manitoba P [Mosaic Essay Series], 1972), pp. 73–82.

Typical of JC's creative process on the whole is an oscillation between the short story technique of eliminating, or limiting, the elements of "normal" chronological events and the novelistic technique of building the structure form foundations with all useful biographical and psychological documentation. "The End of the Tether" consists of four divisions: (1) chapter 1, in which a fully developed character faces a predetermined situation pointing toward a "speedy short-story catastrophe"; (2) chapters II-IV, a retardation in the form of a "leisurely preamble" suggesting the typical form of the novel; (3) chapters VII-IX, an oscillation between the short-story and the novel techniques; and (4) chapters XI-XII [chapter X is omitted with no reason given], in which the story returns to a more direct course and ends abruptly, with a catastrophe, typical of the short story. Thus the structure of the tale is ambiguous. The catastrophe occurs on two levels: it is both the end of a ship and the end of a man. Retrospectively, the reader notes that the relatively short-story concept undergoes a gradual transformation into a more artful and purposeful construction, that of a "long short-story." [In Polish.]

1533.1 Greenwood, Thomas. "Joseph Conrad: Un centenaire litteraire" (Joseph Conrad: A Literary Centenary), *Études Slaves et Est-Européenes* (Montréal), II, No. 4 (1959), pp. 195–200.

JC demonstrates a special kind of genius partly due to his Polish antecedents which color his novels and autobiographical writings, even if Poland as such is neither the subject nor the matter of his work. His prodigious output manifests a philosophy of life which includes not only his own experiences but also his Polish temperament and the wide reading which colored this temperament. Sometimes in his fiction, JC reveals traces of his strongly Catholic education, although his work is not specifically Christian. [In French.]

1538.1 "Joseph Conrad," *Dizionario Universale di Letteratura Contemporanea* (Universal Dictionary of Contemporary Literature), (Milan: Mondadori, 1959), I, pp. 857–60.

[Biographical and critical note.] [In Italian.]

1548.1 Lewis, R. W. B. *The Picaresque Saint: Representative Figures in Contemporary Fiction* (Philadelphia and New York: J. B. Lippincott, 1959), pp. 61, 75, 92, 199, 216, 225–26, 232–33.

The twentieth century was "ushered in" in English fiction by the suicidal protagonists of JC—Winnie Verloc in *The Secret Agent*, Heyst and Jones in *Victory*, and Decoud in *Nostromo;* and since JC's time, the novel in all languages has found in suicide "one of the most revealing gestures of the modern world and of modern man." JC left an influence upon Graham Greene: a taste for the exotic, for wandering in the "uncharted sections" of the earth; an alternation of skepticism and faith; the idea that pity is a disguised form of contempt and a dangerous human weakness; and the image of persons who, feeling themselves psychically nonexistent, "flirt with" death and horror in order to come alive.

1549.1 Lynskey, Winifred. "A Survey of Reprint Texts of Twentieth-Century British Novels" *College English,* XXL (December 1959), 183–89.

Introductions by Morton D. Zabel for editions of "Youth," "Heart of Darkness," "The End of the Tether" (Anchor), for *The Portable Conrad* (Viking), for *The Nigger of the Narcissus,* for *Lord Jim* (Houghton Mifflin), and for *Under Western Eyes* (New Directions) are excellent, as is R. B. Heilman's introduction for *Lord Jim* (Rinehart). On the other hand, Robert Penn Warren's introduction to *Nostromo* (Modern Library) misses the pattern of moral attitudes in Gould's idealism, Decoud's skepticism, and Nostromo's simple faith, and overvalues the doubtful improvement of society at the end of the novel. Albert J. Guerard's introduction to *"Heart of Darkness" and "The Secret Sharer"* (Signet), though short, is provocative.

1551.1 Monsarrat, Nicholas. "Introduction," *Lord Jim: A Tale* (New York: Limited Editions Club, 1959), pp. vii–xi.

The facts of JC's life "give little clue to the enigma that is Joseph Conrad." *Lord Jim* has faults: the chief difficulty is that the bulk of the novel is "set down in the form of an after-dinner story-marathon" by

one man. At the end of his life, Jim "gave in to the nemesis of the
story, convinced at last that cowardice can never be redeemed." The
novel is not melodramatic; the writing is "first-class, rich, evocative,
and compelling." [A typical imperceptive introduction intended for
readers more impressed by the format of the physical volume than
by its contents.]

1960

1567.1 Allen, Arthur B. "Joseph Conrad," *A Tale That is Told: A
Pageant of English Literature, 1900-1950* (London: Barrie and
Rockliff, 1960), pp. 60–61; 33, 163.

JC became the master of turning personal experience into
romance. Writing "according to conscience," he gained recognition
slowly. He captured the atmosphere of the sea and "recorded the
temperament of the elements." The dramatic quality of his work lay
in "the drama of . . . one man's soul battling against a peculiar and at
times a self-determined fate." [An example of the inadequacy of many
general treatments of JC.]

1569.1 Behrman, S[amuel] N. *Portrait of Max: An Intimate Memoir of
Sir Max Beerbohm* (New York: Random House, 1960), pp. 255,
262.

Beerbohm caricatured JC in "The Young Self and the Old Self" as
an established writer proud of his profound books. Edmund Wilson
remarked to Behrman that Beerbohm was very fond of Henry James
and JC and respected them deeply.

1569.2 Bojarski, Edumund A. "Conrad's First Polish Interview,"
Polish American Studies, XVII (July-December 1960), 65–71.

[A translation from Polish to English of JC's interview with
Marian Dabrowska; the interview originally appeared in *Tygodnik
Illustrowany*, XVI (18 April 1914). In the interview, JC discusses his
Polish background, but the interview contains no insights into his
attitudes not already well documented in the standard biographies.]

1569.3 Brown, Douglas. "Conrad," *Lexikon Der Weltliteratur Im 20.
Jahrhundert* (Encyclopedia of World Literature in the 20th
Century), (Freiburg im Breisgau: Herder, 1960–61), I (1960), cols.
371–79.

JC was influenced by Henry James, Gustave Flaubert, and Guy de
Maupassant. His novels are "deck-logs" of great voyages in the

unknown realms of the soul. [A survey of JC's life and works.] [In German.]

1571.1 Dabrowska, Maria. "Przypis do *Skicòw O Conradzie*" (Comments on *Sketches on Conrad)*, *Nowa Kultura* No. 1 (Warsaw, 1960), p. 3.

Irony and humor were essential elements in JC's work as well as artistic deformation, a means of expression he often used, even in scenes consisting of commonplace elements of reality. He also used techniques drawn from the cinema, e.g., slow motion and close-ups of details so that uncomplicated incidents take on the power of weird adventures. [In Polish.]

1578.1 Ellman, Richard. "Two Faces of Edward," *Edwardians and Late Victorians*, ed by Richard Ellman (New York: Columbia UP [English Institute Essays], 1959], 1960), pp. 188–210, 230–33; rpt. in Richard Ellman, *Golden Codgers: Biographical Speculations* (New York and London: Oxford UP, 1973), pp. 113–31; rpt. in *Literary Criticism: Idea and Act*, ed by W. K. Winsatt (Berkeley, Los Angeles, London: University of California P [*The English Institute, 1939–1972: Selected Essays]*, 1974), pp. 560–75.

Among the Edwardians, who were looking for ways to express their conviction that we can be religious about life itself without accepting Christianity, JC is exceptional in choosing "extraordinary incidents." The "central miracle" for the Edwardians is the sudden alteration of the self. Representative of this interest is the struggle for selfhood in the hero's quest in *Lord Jim*, a quest achieved only in death. In JC a victory " in the spirit" is usually accompanied by some defeat. Edwardian writings also usually contain a "thematic centre," often some kind of external event or object, on which they bear down very hard until, as JC noted, they squeeze the guts out of it. He himself does this with the silver in *Nostromo*. In their theories, the Edwardians emphasized the importance of unity; JC twists and turns time, for unity has little to do with chronology. The Edwardians were concerned with the artist as were the writers of the nineties: they were concerned only with art, as JC as their representative, says in his preface to *The Secret Agent*, "In the matter of all my books, I have attended to my business. I have attended it to it with complete self-surrender." The sense that these writers had of the importance of their art can give value to life.

1578.2 Gilkes, Lillian [Barnard]. *Cora Crane: A Biography of Mrs. Stephen Crane* (Bloomington: Indiana UP, 1960), pp. 77, 126–28, 133, 134, 137, 140, 150, 153, 158–64, 169, 178, 181, 196, 198, 199, 204, 222, 252–54, 300, 303, 343, 346, 354.

Stephen Crane and JC developed a "singularly undemonstrative" friendship, founded on their "common vision of the creature man as a lonely pigmy in a universe indifferent, when not actually hostile, to his humanity." JC envied Crane and in his later years retained, as he said, " an abiding affection for that energetic, slight, fragile, intensely living and transient figure." In 1898, when Crane was desperately in need of money, JC attempted to obtain an advance for him. In 1899, JC, now heavily in debt to his publishers, was forced to refuse an appeal from Cora Crane to help Stephen. In 1908, JC wrote a note to Cora thanking her for a memento of "poor Stephen."

1581.1 Gillon, Adam. "Joseph Conrad in Present-Day Poland," *Joseph Conrad: Centennial Essays*, ed by Ludwik Krzyzanowski (New York: Polish Institute of Arts and Sciences in America, 1960), pp. 145–60.

The interest in Poland in JC's personality dates from the end of the nineteenth century. Considered at first as a guilt-ridden expatriate in 1925, JC soon came to be thought of as a great English novelist, even if his Polish heritage was still considered important by most commentators. There is, indeed, a certain spiritual and moral "atmosphere" in JC's works which relates him closely withsome great Polish writers. An excellent example is *Lord Jim*, with Jim's sense of mission and the dream of "hero leadership." Another subject in common with Polish novelists is the destruction of romantically-inclined man by his passion. JC is close to Zeromski in several ways. Such Polish writers as Chwalewik, Zeromski, Roza Jablkowska, Zdzislaw Najder, and Maria Dabrowska are assisting with the current revival of interest in JC. The scope of Conradian research in Poland is, however, modest because the Nazi occupation and the labor camps of Siberia were not conducive to literary studies of the writer. [Prints a JC letter of 17/29 March 1890 in Polish and English.]

1591.1 Janta, Alexander. "Conrad Family Heirloom at Harvard," *JCCEP* (1960) pp. 85–109; rpt. in large part as ["Tuan Jim: A Sketch"], in *JCLJ* (1968), pp. 276–91.

In July, 1925, the Houghton Library at Harvard acquired a small brown leather album containing twenty-five pages of Polish poetry which had been copied by a Teofila Bobrowska. The album had belonged to JC, who wrote in the blank pages left by Teofila the first draft of *Lord Jim*, a few sentences of *The Rescue*, some tentative titles, and what seems to be the draft of a play. This album, which has not been studied by anyone, belonged, it seems, to JC's grandmother. The sketch for *Jim* is of great value for new light on the origin of the novel. [Includes a transcript of the writings in the Bobrowska album.]

1591.2 Janta, Alexander. "Conrad's Place and Rank in American Letters," *JCCEP* (1960), pp. 9–26.

In 1957, the year of the JC centennial, a cross section of opinions on JC's position in and possibly his influence on American literature derived from answers to a set of four questions sent to about ninety American writers, critics, and literary historians revealed a variety of opinions, most of which were favorable to JC and to his definite effect on American literature. Most of the responses disagreed with Virginia Woolf's opinion that his later novels would not survive, and most of them agreed with Richard Curle that his works then ranked with the great classics of the English novel. Ralph Ellison notes JC's influence on Hemingway and Faulkner and repeated Hemingway's comment on his willingness "to see [T.S.] Eliot ground to a fine powder if it would bring Conrad back to life." Albert J. Guerard agreed with Curle's opinion; James A. Michener favored Woolf's. Henry Miller thought JC's work to be "immortal"; Wright Morris emphasized his genius. [No attempt is made to summarize the results of the questionnaire.]

1591.3 "Joseph Conrad: A Master in the Great Tradition," *TLS*, 5 February 1960, pp. 73–74.

Because of the use to which JC put his memory, writing his biography is a difficult task. JC used his memory as an aid to creative imagination and therefore his works are frequently a confounding of personal experience, fiction, and sometimes (as in *Nostromo*) the actual experience of others. The biographer must not only separate fact from fiction in JC's work but also separate the work from the actuality when discussing it critically. Herein lies Baines's strength: he presents the life of the man uncolored by his work, and vice versa. Baines is, perhaps, more successful in his grasp of the "biographical whole" than he is in his practical criticism. It is, however, for the biographical aspects that Baines "must be judged." [Essentially a review of Jocelyn Baines', *Joseph Conrad: A Critical Biography* (London: Weidenfield and Nicholson, 1959).]

1597.1 Krieger, Murray, "The Varieties of Extremity: *Lord Jim,*" *The Tragic Vision: Variations on a Theme in Literary Interpretation* (New York: Holt, Rinehart and Winston, 1960), pp. 165–79; rpt. in "Essays in Criticism," ed by Thomas C. Moser, in *JCLJ* (1968), pp. 437–47.

In *Lord Jim*, the sea in Stein's metaphor of the "destructive element" appears to represent the dream rather than the reality. For the romantic (both Stein and Jim), however, the dream *is* the reality. Like the modern existentialist, man proves his humanity by the strength of his response to the meaninglessness of the challenge.

Jim revolves about what Stein calls the "romantic" attitude: the "nightmare reality" of "Heart of Darkness" has engulfed Jim, and only from a kind of stubbornness does he resist his complete destruction. For Jim, the *Patna* affair casts a "circle of moral ambiguities" which has no simple answer like the simple about-face Jim makes in Patusan. In his complex manipulation of point of view, JC attempts to indicate how unreachable Jim's problem is. But in accepting his death, Jim has a moment of vision in which his opportunity is finally revealed—his last, one of "profound courage," is no failure. Jim as romantic insists on extremity, not even to exclude one like Brown; as an extremist, Jim embraces the dream in a final, full awareness of its destructive quality. Stein's recognition thus becomes Jim's also: inaction is as deadly as all other actions—and leads only to the tragic.

1597.2 Krzyzanowski, Ludwik. "Joseph Conrad: A Bibliographical Note," in *JCCEP* (1960), pp. 161–74.

Published on the occasion of the JC centennial, 1857–1957, was the excellent work, *Joseph Conrad at Mid-Century: Editions and Studies,* 1855–1955, ed by Kenneth A. Lohf and Eugene P. Sheehy (1957). Even with some minor flaws, this bibliography is "a magnificent attempt" to assemble as complete and accurate material as possible. [Contains a lengthy additional bibliography of Polish items published about JC.]

1597.3 Krzyzanowski, Ludwik (ed). *Joseph Conrad: Centennial Essays* (New York: Polish Institute of Arts and Sciences in America, 1960).

Contents, abstracted separately under authors, in alphabetical order: Ludwik Krzyzanowski, "Introduction" [not abstracted]; Alexander Janta, "Conrad's Place and Rank in American Literature"; Ludwik Krzyzanowski, "Joseph Conrad's 'Prince Roman': Fact and Fiction,"; Przemyslaw Moroczkowski, "A Glance Back at the Romantic Conrad: 'The Lagoon'"; Alexander Janta, "A Conrad Family Heirloom at Harvard"; Ludwik Krzyzanowski, "Joseph Conrad: Some Polish Documents"; Adam Gillon, "Joseph Conrad in Present-Day Poland"; Ludwik Kryzyzanowski, "Joseph Conrad: A Bibliographical Note." These essays, with one exception, were first published in slightly different form, in *The Polish Review*. The underlying theme of the collection is the exploration of JC's Polish antecedents, connections, and interests.

1597.4 Krzyzanowski, Ludwik. "Joseph Conrad: Some Polish Documents," *JCCEP* (1960), pp. 111–43.

Behind the "world-famous" English writer, JC, there is another man, almost unrecognized, the Pole, Korzeniowski, whose Slavic culture is almost unknown among Western nations. A "son of Poland," JC wrote of his love for England and its language, but he always retained fidelity to his "special tradition." Ties to the land of his birth appear in many places in his writings, some of which remain unpublished. As a sailor, he showed great anxiety for Polish affairs. "He was a genuine son of the tragic generation of 1863. . . . A fund of memories and sentiments was laid up in the heart of the Polish child, which nothing could tear out of his innermost soul." [Contains many quotations to support and illustrate the author's claims, and adds an appendix containing the original Polish text of the documents which are quoted in English translation.]

1597.5 Krzyzanowski, Ludwik. "Joseph Conrad's 'Prince Roman': Fact and Fiction," *JCCEP* (1960), pp. 27–72.

The period in which "Prince Roman" is set is that of the Polish November Insurrection of 1830–31, which caused sympathetic comments for Poland and condemnations for Russia from many well known writers of Western Europe and the United States as well as from the "international field." JC's hero, Prince Roman Sanguszko, was an actual person, an outstanding figure in nineteenth-century Poland who, with countless other Polish patriots, paid severe penalties for their devotion to the cause of their country. The immediate source of JC's story appears in the *Memoirs* of Tadeusz Bobrowski, JC's maternal uncle and guardian; others are found in *Pan Tadeusz* by Mickiewcz and in the works of other writers. JC's addition to the story includes fictional events and the generally accepted opinion that Roman's marriage was a love match. Fictitious also is the description of the way in which Roman joined the Rising. The innkeeper Yankel is a fictional character. The circumstances of Prince Roman's capture do not correspond to reality. The parents' endeavor to obtain leniency for their son and the account of the trial are founded on fact. Thus out of national tradition, family recollections, oral and written accounts, and dreams of his "tragic childhood" JC created a "Plutarchian" life. In his story, he placed all the bitterness which over the years he had felt because of the fate of Poland.

1599.1 Lewis, R. W. B. "Golding's Original, Searching Novel," *New York Herald Tribune Book Review*, XXXVI (14 February 1960), 5.

The test of individual confrontation by which man's true character is formed links Golding's novel, *Free Fall*, in which this theme is found, with those of James, Faulkner, Camus, Graham Greene, and JC.

1599.2 Lombardo, Agostino. "L'avventura di Conrad" (Conrad's Adventure), *Il Mondo*, XII, 31 (1 August 1960), 8.

The true core and cause of JC's art is the ethical world, and JC is certainly much more than a teller of sea stories, a definition which, however, continues to impoverish or attenuate its consequences, as it did during the writer's lifetime, even though time and time again he reacted against it. [Review of Baines's critical biography.] [In Italian.]

1601.1 Mayoux, Jean-Jacques. "Joseph Conrad (I) L'homme et sa liberté, (II) L'enfer des consciences," (Joseph Conrad (I) The Man and his Freedom, (II) The Hell of Consciences), *Vivants Piliers* (Living Pillars), (Paris: Juillard, 1960), pp. 117–54.

Patna in *Lord Jim* must not be read as "Poland," but in JC we can observe the fundamentally guilty JC in all the guilty individuals in his works and a defensive attitude demonstrated by the ironic game of Fate with impulse. Conrad-Heyst and Conrad-Decoud are examples. JC's novels, like his life, are full of masochistic love for cold, cruel, and inaccessible women, or for unreal idols, with the noble, knightly attitude of a Pole.

One of JC's main themes is the loss of freedom and vain attempts to regain it, resulting in disaster, as with Lord Jim, Gould, and Razumov. JC underwent the temptation of Decoud; later, he experienced that of Heyst, but rejected it. Yet social duty persisted. James Wait is fear, the presence of death, coming from a primitive world. In JC's work, the opaque, obscure characters are the artist's subject: "reality" appears to JC only as a system of signs which fascinated him and which he sought to reduce to coherence. [In French.]

1602.1 Mroczkowski, Przwmyslaw. "A Glance Back at the Romantic Conrad: 'The Lagoon,'" A Study in the Technique of the Short Story," *JCCEP* (1960), pp. 73–83.

In "The Lagoon," we find ourselves already in the boat, being carried toward the proper setting. The present scene appears pregnant with something. And then we arrive at Arsat's dwelling, still waiting for the curtain to rise. We soon learn about the illness of the Malay's wife. Eventually, with apprehension of evil to come, we listen to Arsat's story, which is written with "rhetorical solemnity." The "vexed question" of JC's exoticism arises; perhaps without it JC would not have attempted a tale of love and betrayal, or it may have encouraged the renewed "glitter of phrases and pictures" which Arsat uses in his account. If we can resign ourselves to JC's inconsistencies behind his attractions, we may enjoy them. The running away of the bride with the two brothers is recounted with several ornaments which enable us to share the emotion. At last, the story, with its epic qualities, is over, and the entire pattern is clear. Even with certain imperfections, the whole tale provides a rich display of color and a uniform atmosphere of "sad pagan beauty and fatalism." In future work, JC will balance these elements more effectively.

1602.2 Najder, Zladislaw [sic], and Lord David Cecil. "Joseph Conrad—A Recorded Discussion," *Gemini: The Oxford and Cambridge Magazine,* (January 1960), pp. 3–9.

A major reason why some of JC's novels are popular is that the problems of heroes have been traditional in Polish literature and dealt with by Polish writers for at least two hundred years, having been related to critical situations of the nation. *Lord Jim* is a variation in prose of some themes or solutions known already in Polish romantic poetry. The kind of hero Jim is, caught between his "internal impulse" and his duty, or between his duty to society or the nation and his self-preservation, became most popular in early nineteenth century poetry. Jim does not think about what he did wrong, but tries to do something good to make his expiation. *The Secret Agent* could not be very popular in Poland because of the author's detachment toward the problem the novel pictures, an attitude which is alien to Poles. JC's most popular works will always be *Jim* and "Heart of Darkness." "The Secret Sharer" is one of the most revealing of his books, one that tells us "very much about [JC] himself." JC's philosophy may be seen in "Kantian categories," especially in terms of Kant's ethics. JC was, in fact, at heart a romantic, and Kant influenced romanticism very strongly. And ethics for Kant is the problem of will, as it is for JC. Kant stressed the importance of duty; the role of duty is ethics, and duty is the "pillar" of JC's ethics. Again, a romantic hero is a lone individual (a typical concept of Polish romantic poetry) because he is more responsible than others. Since 1955, JC's popularity in Poland has greatly increased, with *Jim* being the most widely read of his books.

1604.1 Payne, Robert. *The White Rajahs of Sarawak* (London: Robert Hale, 1960), p. 171.

[Contains a previously published letter dated 15 June 1920 from JC to the Dowager Ranee Margaret, widow of Rajah Charles Brooke of Sarawak, a country in northwest Borneo. JC thanks the Dowager Ranee for her praise of his work and especially for *Lord Jim*, which was greatly inspired, he says, by the exploits of the first Rajah, James Brooke.]

1605.1 Praz, Mario. "Conrad, un romantico" (Conrad, a Romantic), *Il Tempo,* IV, 14 April 1960; rpt. in *Cronache Letterarie*

Anglosassoni (Anglo-Saxon Literary Chronicles), Roma: Edizioni di Storia e Letteratura, 1966), pp. 44–50.

With the necessity of maintaining a family on his earnings as a writer, JC could not let up in his work; from this fact derived his constant complaints of creative powerlessness, his crises of desperation, his lateness in the turning over the manuscripts, and the necessity of writing for popular magazines. But under the imposition of certain directives that were not his own as an artist, in order to assure a steady output of commercial material he found it necessary to take a collaborator, Ford Madox Hueffer. JC's English wife, a plain woman of humble social origin and a good cook, exerted a moderating influence on her husband's disordered and neurotic existence. JC was not endowed with a sense of humor but did possess a strong taste for irony, and for tragic irony also. In his exasperated isolation, his conception of life as a dream, his pessimism, his sense of guilt and expiation, his ruminating on the mysteriousness of life, which at times was expressed through adjectives of resonance and emptiness, and especially in his sense of the dramatic (and often of the melodramatic), JC was a romantic. His fatalistic pessimism rendered him skeptical regarding man's future. [In Italian.]

1605.2 Priestley, John Boynton, and O. B. Davis (eds). *Four English Novels* (New York: Harcourt, Brace, 1960), pp. 781–87.

"The Secret Sharer," an excellent introduction to symbolism in literature, may well be called "The Case of the Captain's Hat." The hat on the water at the end of the story may be seen as serving various, somewhat ordinary, purposes, but on a deeper level, the fugitive Leggatt represents the "shadow side" of the captain, that part of himself which he does not know. In accepting and helping Leggatt, the captain is really accepting this other side of himself. The shared hat thus symbolizes the whole personality, and the story is a "parable of self-knowledge." [Followed by "Study Questions" for students.]

1608.1 Scott, Nathan A., Jr. "The Literary Imagination and the Victorian Crisis of Faith, the Example of Thomas Hardy," *Journal of Religion*, XL (October 1960), 267–81.

Hardy never achieved in his novels the "self-conscious expertise" that was JC's "pride."

1610.1 Stallman, R[obert] W[ooster], and Lillian Gilkes (eds), *Stephen Crane: Letters* (New York: New York UP, 1960), pp. 48n, 63n, 92, 110n, 143n, 148–49, 153n, 165–66, 168, 169n, 178–79, 187n, 200, 202, 207n, 243, 256, 259, 283–84, 294, 325, 327, 331.

Stephen Crane wrote to JC (1897) that *The Nigger of the Narcissus* "is simply great. The simple treatment of the death of Waite [sic] is too good, too terrible. . . . It caught me very hard." [Contains an account of the JC-Crane friendship and several of Crane's opinions of JC's works.]

1611.1 Stevenson, Lionel. *The English Novel: A Panorama* (Boston: Houghton Mifflin, 1960), pp. 431–33, 434, 437, 438–40, 441, 452–53, 466–69, 476, 491, 514, 530.

The Nigger of the Narcissus has virtually no plot or action; it is purely a psychological study of a voyage home from Bombay, during which a dying Negro tyrannizes his shipmates. The total effect of the novel becomes a "sort of allegory of death." JC's primary concern was examing the inner complexities of character. His analytical subtlety accounts for the slow growth of his reputation; only a small group of perceptive critics recognized him as a major artist. *Lord Jim* established JC's characteristic subject matter and method. The fragmentary evidence about Jim adds up to a convincing picture of a distraught man who wins our respect as he attains, at the end of the novel, self-mastery. *Nostromo* is a memorable fable of man's struggle to maintain his human identity against the blank indifference of nature. *Chance* is one of JC's "finest and most complex" novels; *Victory* is "another masterpiece." Old Peyrol of *The Rover* is a sort of older version of Nostromo. [A rather conventional account of JC's life and works.]

1961

1629.1 Fleischmann, Wolfgang B. "Conrad's *Chance* and Bergson's Laughter," *Renascence*, X (Winter 1961), 66–71.

The main characters of JC's *Chance* practice or are beset by inappropriate laughter; Marlow, the principal narrator, laughs in strange places and makes clear that inappropriate laughter in *Chance* is more than a random device. The decade immediately preceding the period 1906–1912, in which *Chance* was composed, saw the publication of some thirteen books and articles concerned with the analysis of laughter written in languages JC could read. Among them, only Bergson's essay, *Le Rire* (1899), makes a statement which parallels Marlow's ideas in JC's novel: we laugh not only at the faults of our fellow-men but also at times at their good qualities. Bergson's essay, with its system of the ludicrous that sees comedy in human rigidity on the one hand and in the play of characters at the mercy of a determining force on the other, supplies

a means of understanding *Chance*. Marlow, as narrator, unfolds to
the reader a world which, both in its makeup and in the point of view
from which it is seen, is inimical to the author's beliefs. *Chance* can
thus be seen as the exposition of an impossible world which can only
provoke the laughter of the characters in their laughter of despair at
the superior laughter of Marlow who understands and communicates
their actions to the reader by the vehicle of a Bergsonian figure.

1633.1 Greene, Graham. *In Search of A Character: Two African
Journals* (London: Bodley Head, 1961), pp. 48, 51, 56; (New York:
Viking P, 1962), pp. 31, 33, 37.

Graham Greene abandoned JC about 1932 because his influence
on him was "too great and too disastrous." In rereading the volume
Youth in 1959, he felt again the "heavy hypnotic style: and was aware
of the poverty of his own. His "Heart of Darkness" he found still a fine
story, even if its faults showed: the language is too inflated for the
situation, Kurtz does not really "come alive," and JC seems to have
taken an episode in his own life and tried to lend it, "for the sake of
'literature,'" a greater significance than it will hold.

1635.1 Heilbrun, Carolyn G. *The Garnett Family* (New York:
Macmillan; London: Ruskin House, George Allan & Unwin, 1961),
pp. 107–32.

[Recounts the friendship of JC and Edward Garnett. Contains
twenty-one letters, dating from May 1896 to December 1923, from
Garnett to JC. The content of the letters is primarily one of moral
support and advice on various business and literary matters.
Invaluable as a supplement to JC's letters to Garnett.]

1635.2 Heppenstall, Rayner. *The Fourfold Tradition* (London: Barrie
and Rockliff; Norfolk, Conn: New Directions, 1961), pp. 94, 103–
05, 108, 114, 130, 139.

Leavis's and Tillyard's preferences for complex novels like
Nostromo and *The Secret Agent* reflect a misunderstanding of JC's
essence. He is a simple "poet of marine nature" who displays his
talent best in works like *The Shadow-Line*, "Youth," and "Typhoon."

1638.1 Kerf, René. "'Typhoon' and *The Shadow-Line*: A
Reexamination," *Revue des Langues Vivantes* (Brussels), XXVII,
No. 6 (1961), 486–500.

JC is essentially interested in the relations between the world of
action and people's moral principles. In "Heart of Darkness" and
other major works, there is a double aspect of JC's "philosophy": the
coexistence of doubt and belief and a fundamental pessimism

corrected by the practical conviction that evil must be opposed. Too much imagination and sensibility are dangerous, and this danger (and the need to fight it) is illustrated by "Typhoon" and *The Shadow-Line*. In the former tale, the dominant factor is the resistance of MacWhirr, not the weakness of Jake. Most of JC's "Author's Notes" reveal a lack of insight into one of his essential concerns, the problem of evil; *Shadow-Line* is a good example of this lack of insight. In this story, the dead captain manifests the "semi-mystical bond with the dead," which the hero overcomes by loyalty to the responsibilities of command, made possible only by resisting the influence of sensitivity and doubt.

1638.2 Krieger, Murray. "Afterword," *Lord Jim* (New York: Signet [New American Library], 1961) [not seen in this form]; combined in "From 'Youth' to *Lord Jim*: The Formal-Thematic Use of Marlow," in *The Play and Place of Criticism* (Baltimore: Johns Hopkins P, 1967), pp. 91–104.

Despite JC's scorn for what he saw as the "formless" Russian novel, he combined the "underground awareness" of a Dostoevski with the "technical improvisations" of a James. In "Youth," for example, the narrator soberly changes from his romantic earlier days with their fond illusions and expectations and comes to dote "condescendingly" on his own reminiscences. The story introduces some of JC's later devices and themes. He also employs the frame to pursue, simultaneously, two occasions: the one we are being told and the one of the telling. In *Lord Jim*, JC achieves even more with multiple perspectives; a single action or problem becomes endlessly complex, as it should in JC's world. Thematic elements that are, for JC, too neatly contained in "Youth" appear "monumentarily" in other works, especially in *Jim*. The movement from "Youth" to *Jim* is a movement from a relatively shallow world to a profound one. In *Jim*, we come to the very edge of tragedy. Marlow's role recedes so that he is converted almost entirely into a narrator. In Marlow, as in JC, one can find no single dimension of meaning; there is always a qualification, a sense of irresolution. JC's art is not designed to give final answers. In *Jim*, JC brings his innovations in fictional technique to the "service of his profound existential probings."

1639.1 Lid, R. W. "Ford Madox Ford and His Community of Letters," *Prairie Schooner*, XXXV (Summer 1961), 132–36.

When Ford Madox Ford and JC met and began to collaborate, JC regarded the arrangement as largely financial. It was he who turned Ford into a serious novelist. But Ford was to learn much more from Henry James than from JC.

1639.2 Lombardo, Agostino. "Il narratore come eroe" (The Narrator as Hero), *Il Mondon*, XIII, *49* (5 December 1961), 9–10; rpt. in *Ritratto di Enobarbo: Saggi Sulle Letterature Inglese* (Portrait of Enobarbus: Essays on English Literature), (Pisa: Nistri-Lischi, 1971), pp. 274–86.

In *Chance*, the narrating characters constitute the main theme of the work, and they become protagonists though the art of narrating, and it is their intervention far from being mechanical and external that is rather the crucial moment of their existence. *Chance* is one of the most significant works in modern literature, which is to say of a literature that has created out of the artist its most authentic figure. [Review of *Destino* (Chance), (Milan: Bompiani, 1961).] [In Italian.]

1656.1 Wagar, W. Warren. *H. G. Wells and the World State* (New Haven and London: Yale UP, 1961), pp. 157–58.

H. G. Wells reported that in a debate with JC about how to describe a ship JC was concerned with finding *le mot juste* whereas Wells sought to link the ship with an expression of his philosophy.

1962

1661.1 Bassan, Alberto. "*Destino*" (*Chance*), *Letture* (Milan), XVII, No. 1 (1962), pp. 34–37.

A review (but mainly a long plot summary) of the Italian translation of *Chance* (Milan: Bompiani, 1961). [In Italian.]

1664.1 Bryden, Ronald. "Graham Greene, Alas," *Spectator*, No. 7005 (28 September 1962), pp. 441–42.

Many writers have influenced Graham Greene's form and style, but JC has had the strongest and longest influence of them all. Greene acknowledges his indebtedness to JC in his novel, *It's a Battlefield*, his version of *The Secret Agent*. Greene also indulges in a private joke by naming one of his characters after JC. Furthermore, JC is the originator of Greene's early hero: the type of man whose anger pursues him and eventually leads him to recognition.

1664.2 ["The Conscious Artist: Ford Madox Ford"], *TLS* (15 June 1962); rpt in *T.L.S. 1962: Essays and Reviews from the Times Literary Supplement* (London: Oxford University Press, 1963), pp. 57–58.

During the early years of the twentieth century, while Ford Madox Ford was living at Winchelsea, he associated with a circle of "foreigners" in the neighborhood—Henry James, Stephen Crane, and JC—who "had designs on the novel quite alien to the English tradition." They considered the novel as a work of art and the "craft of fiction" a "high calling." H. G. Wells, for a time their neighbor, regarded them all with suspicion. No doubt the influence of these foreigners led Ford to write "the best French novel in English," *The Good Soldier*. In 1898, when JC wrote to him, inviting him to collaborate with him, Ford began his relation to JC, at which time his serious literary career began. In Ford, JC saw "poetry and style," and no doubt from Ford's "man-of-letters manner" he obtained the impression of literary facility and sensitivity to popular taste. But in later years he suggested in letters that he regarded the arrangement as a necessary exploitation of a "useful, expendable young man."

1667.1 Fletzer, Giovanni. "Nota del traduttore" (Translator's Note), *Incertezza* (Suspense), (Milan: Bompiani, 1962), pp. 353–59.

The unfinished *Suspense*, in its imperfect form, shows JC's working method. At the end of his life, JC was still writing in the same way as when he had begun his literary career, facing the usual difficulties. Had he been able to complete the novel, he would have repeated the same mistakes and reached the same greatness as that of *Nostromo*. [In Italian.]

1672.1 Greene, Maxine. "Introduction," *The Nigger of the Narcissus* (New York: Collier Books [Classic Collier Books], 1962), pp. 7–13.

The Nigger of the Narcissus reveals beliefs and sentiments we scarcely know we possess, things hidden beneath the surface of everyday life. JC's "reality" was beautiful and mysterious, one which he symbolized in the most extreme and desperate kinds of situations, usually those involving people living in abandoned places of the earth. The keynote of his life was exile because of his own exile and his moving among men who had to cope with the primitive and the violent both in the outside world and in their own natures. Thus he chose for this novel the crew of the *Narcissus*, the kind of men he knew well. The chill and gloom that exude from James Wait, the sick man, can be combatted by duty and discipline; all the postures and attitudes required for running a good ship can become a defense against self-serving sickness, as can responsible team work. JC's lesson, unspoken as it is, is that of commitment and devotion to ideal standards, norms outmoded by the time of his death in 1924 but still urgently necessary in our own unpredictable world. JC's work suggests that we must find a way of confronting the certainties as well as the uncertainties of life; we dare not engage in the evil of denial and withdrawal.

1676.1 Higashida, Chiaki. "The Style and Structure of *Victory*," *Anglica*, IV (April 1962), pp. 92–102.

Style in writing is the expression of the author's literary spirit, which is shown in his manner of stating his ideas. *Victory*, one of JC's representative novels, reveals style as affected by point of view. In part I, for example, the narrator, who is not an actual observer of the events, can have no point of view; therefore JC's writing here is monotonous and ambiguous, even cheap in places. Some of the vagueness of part I may be, however, intended as a preparation for the remaining parts of the novel. This novel has a number of points of view, those of Heyst, Morrison, Schomberg, and an omniscient author in part II, where the style carries a meditative tone which slows the progress of the story. In part III, with Heyst and Lena on the island, the style remains slow, but part IV, with its shallow plot which is almost melodrama, presents some truth about human relationships by describing complicated conflicts. Gradually, as the plot deals with distorted human relationships, the words of the story become complicated and their meanings are deepened. Here, too, JC heightens his drama by employing symbolism. At the end of the novel, where Heyst apparently states his affirmation of life and love, his philosophy actually implies that life still ends in tragedy. His defeat is caused by his lack of vitality. Lena's victory, likewise, leads to nothing since it ends in her self-sacrifice. [The translators, Shizumi Stewart, assisted by Michael W. Stuart, detect several contradictions, inconsistencies, and errors.] [In Japanese.]

1681.1 Manchester, William. *H. L. Mencken: Disturber of the Peace* (New York: Collier Books; London: Collier-Macmillan, 1962), pp. 52, 59, 64, 66, 87, 108, 124, 191, 257, 345.

From about 1906 on, H. L. Mencken devoted his spare time to reading Ibsen, Huxley, and JC. Between 1908 and 1914, Mencken reviewed many books for *The Smart Set*, devoting half his department to new books by Dreiser and JC. And "old" James Gibbon Huneker sat in his "white, carking, and befeathered hat," "monologuing" on the lives and works of such notables as Berlioz, Nietzsche, Flaubert, Shaw, and JC. In 1915, despite the great attention given to him in the United States, JC sent nothing to *The Smart Set*. Mencken at last wrote to JC, directly mentioning the serious economic situation of his magazine and asking that a nominal price be set on contributions. When a letter finally arrived from a London literary agent, with the information that a JC story was available for six hundred dollars, Mencken "shot back" the cable, "For $600 you can have *The Smart Set*." After reading Mencken's reviews of JC's works, a "downy-cheeked youngster named Alfred Knopf" called on Mencken to talk about his reviews of JC. Later,

Stuart P. Sherman declared war on Mencken in a review of the latter's *A Book of Prefaces*, which included an essay on JC. In later years, Mencken wrote about the celebrated trial of John Thomas Scopes for violation of the state of Tennessee's anti-evolution law instead of about such men as Shaw, Dreiser, and JC. After World War I, Mencken, filled with nostalgia for past years, talked with George Jean Nathan about the time thirty-five years in the past, when they would "dissect" their elders and "enthuse" about Shaw, Ibsen, and JC.

1682.1 McCullough, Norman Verrle. *The Negro in English Literature: A Critical Introduction* (Ilfracombe, Devon: Arthur H. Stockwell, 1962), pp. 14, 118, 136–41.

One of the most important writers in English literature to dwell at some length on the Negro and Africa is JC, with James Waite [sic] in *The Nigger of the Narcissus* looming as great in literature as Nigger Jim in Mark Twain's *Huckleberry Finn*, Babo in Herman Melville's "Benito Cereno," and Othello in Shakespeare's play of the same name. JC explores vividly and almost horrifyingly the theme of the white man's burden in "The Heart of Darkness" [sic]. These two works seem to offset each other: in the former, Wait holds an entire ship of white men almost completely under his spell whereas Kurtz, a white man, holds a group of African natives completely under his domination. [Slight.]

1687.1 Phelps, Gilbert. *A Short History of English Literature* (London: Folio Society, 1962); rpt. and rev. as *A Survey of English Literature* (London: Pan Books, 1965), pp. 261, 272, 286, 305, 336–45, 346, 349, 352, 357.

JC is not particularly an "heir" to Henry James; rather, both men have much in common. In *Lord Jim* and "Heart of Darkness," Marlow, one of the *dramatis personae* himself, is changed by the course of events he is narrating; but in other examples of JC's best work, such as *Nostromo*, objectivity is obtained through a whole series of focal points. *Under Western Eyes* is the only really successful example of a "Dostoevskyan" novel in English. Turgenev was a major influence on JC, as seen in *Jim* and *Victory*. JC had no great interest in psychological analysis, nor had he any profound philosophy to offer. Above all, he was concerned with basic human values, with fidelity being central. Like Kipling, he believed profoundly in Britain's imperial mission, but also like Kipling he knew that "the ideals he assumed it to embody were in danger of betrayal." Both E. M. Forster and JC felt a sense of a void "lying below the urbane surfaces" of things, a similarity that became more marked as the century proceeded.

1687.2 Piatowski, Boleslaw Pomian. "Proba wiernosci shipmastera Conrada" (Trial of the Loyalty of Conrad the Shipmaster), *Nowa Kultura* (Warsaw), No. 37 (1962); rpt. *WSOC* (1963), pp. 76–82.

Almost all of JC's biographers pass in silence over the period in Fall, 1916, when the Germans announced "total" war at sea and the British took to the use of Q-boats to ensnare them. JC sailed in a Q-boat as second officer. The HMS *Ready* was renamed the *Freya* in his honor; he became ill and was taken to hospital in St. Andrew's. [In Polish.]

1688.1 Scotland. National Library, Edinburgh. *English Literature: An Exhibition of Manuscripts and First and Other Early Editions* (Edinburgh: National Library, 1962), p. 25.

Blackwood exhibited five autograph letters dated 4 September 1897, 31 December 1898, 12 February 1899, 27 October 1899, and 14 July 1900. One descriptive sentence following the dates states that these letters deal with the progress of the serializations of "Youth," "Heart of Darkness," and *Lord Jim*. The letters are not reprinted here.

1690.1 Solomon, Rebecca G. "Identity and Joseph Conrad," *Psychoanalytic Quarterly*, XXXI (1962), pp. 440–41.

In discussion, Dr. Irving Harrison suggested a difference between the daydreamer and the artist. The strength of JC's fictional worlds rests on his portrayal of primal, mysterious forces which impel, and ultimately dispose of, man. Dr. Bernard Meyer emphasized JC's presentation of "the destructive woman" and confusion concerning sexual differences, which suggests JC's hope for a blissful reunion with "the mother." Dr. Phyllis Greenacre proposed that JC's guilt over his parents' deaths may have limited him to autobiographical expression. [A summary of Edward D. Joseph's "Identity and Joseph Conrad," which was presented to the New York Psychoanalytic Society on February 28, 1962 and of subsequent discussion.]

1699.1 Yaseen, Mohammad. "Joseph Conrad's Theory of Fiction." Unpublished dissertation, Aligarh Muslim University, 1962; largely incorporated in *Joseph Conrad's Theory of Fiction* (Bombay: Asia Publishing House, 1967). [See for abstract.]

1963

1699.2 Astaldi, Maria Luisa. "Ritorno di Conrad" (Return to Conrad), *Il Poeta e la Regina* (The Poet and the Queen), (Firenze: Sansoni, 1963), pp. 137–40.

A review of the critical biography of Jocelyn Baines, whom the reviewer calls "a young lady critic." [In Italian.]

1699.3 Baldi, Sergio. "Un romanzo non finito" (An Unfinished Novel), *La Nazione* (16 March 1963), p. 3.

In their unfinished state the characters of *Suspense* acquire an illusion of reality which goes well beyond the intentions of the author. [Review of *Incartezza,* Italian translation of *Suspense* (Milan: Bompiani, 1962).] [In Italian.]

1703.1 Bigongiari, Piero. "Nota al testo" (Note to the Text), *La Linea d'Ombra: Entro le Maree* (The Shadow Line: Within the Tides), (Milan: Bompiani, 1963), pp. 371–74.

A short afterword, mainly about "The Planter of Malata," with a long quotation from an article by Albert Saugere (N.R.F., December 1924). [In Italian.]

1704.1 Borowy, Waclaw. "O *Lordzie Jimie*" (On *Lord Jim*), in *WSOC* (1963), pp. 329–32.

The character of Jim interests us greatly because he is depicted as a man with a fundamentally healthy nature, capable of drawing pleasure and an affirmation of life from work and love. His "romanticism" is wrongly interpreted according to contemporary literary definitions instead of the traditional one, viz. a cult of the past and its knightly ideals, as in Sir Walter Scott's works. [In Polish.]

1708.1 Chwalewik, Witold. "Conrad a tradycja literacka" (Conrad and Literary Tradition) in *WSOC* (1963), pp. 439–56.

Before he became a sailor, JC might have drawn from the Polish literary tradition of the sea, e.g., *Crimean Sonnets* by A. Mickiewicz, but he restrained himself from this impulse to romanticism because of the influence of Flaubert and Maupassant. Flaubert's discipline, however, did not appeal to JC in every way. [In Polish.]

1708.2 C[olombi] G[uidetti], M[ario]. "Joseph Conrad," *Dizionario Letterario degli Autori* (Milan: Bompiani, 1963), I, pp. 538–39.

Brief biographical sketch, with list of JC's works. [In Italian.]

1708.3 "Conrad, Joseph." *Wielka Encyclopedia Powszechna* (Great General Encyclopedia), (Warsaw: Panstwowy Instytut Wydawniczy, 1963), II, pp. 594–95.

JC's work was largely based on personal experience connected with his travels and is one of the finest achievements in world literature of the sea. The real significance of his productions lies, however, in ethical problems such as duty, honor, and loyalty. It concentrates upon the fates of typical JC heroes: seamen in conflict with the elements. According to JC, the only honorable behavior in the face of inevitable physical destruction is the rigorous observance of a heroic moral code, the defence of honor in the face of opposition and temptation in a life which is directed by blind and ruthless fate without any subordinate moral order, either human or divine. JC's artistically most mature works are those with a maritime theme. In the novels set in Malaysia, JC severely criticized colonialism and its white representatives, mostly criminal degenerates, contrasted with idealized natives. Another group depicts moral questions against contemporary backgrounds. The collection of tales and historical novels constitute still another group of his works. Artistically and formally, JC was influenced by Flaubert and Turgenev, with objective realism in the description of details and penetrating psychological analysis which he blended with a poetic and romantic vision and a feeling for problems of existentialist philosophy. He used so-called indirect narration and devices such as digressions, retrospective viewpoints, to create an atmosphere of tension, mystery, and suspense, and he introduced new and original stylistic properties into English literature by his masterly use of the English language. [In Polish.]

1713.1 Evans, Ifor. *A Short History of English Literature* (Baltimore: Penguin Books, second ed., 1963), pp. 204–205; London: MacGibbon & Kee, 1964), pp. 167–68.

JC often writes like some of the Impressionist painters: he "seeks to capture elusive moods, using a rich and coloured vocabulary, almost as if he employed words as pigments."

1722.1 Guerard, Albert J. "Conrad's 'The Lagoon,'" Byron Matlaw and Leonard Lief (eds.). *Story and Critic* (New York: Evanston; London: Harper & Row, 1963), pp. 271–73.

Whereas the unnamed white man in "The Lagoon" is nominally present to listen to Arsat's story, he is really present to cause the rendering of a "highly subjective landscape" in language which is "certainly bad writing." This fact suggests that JC was moving toward the narrator as technical device with the involved narrator as intimate author-projection.

1723.1 Hay, Eloise Knapp. "The Artist of the Whole Matter," from *The Political Novels of Joseph Conrad* (1963), (C, I, No. 1724); rpt. *JCCC* (1975), pp. 121–37.

Striking a balance among several of JC's contrary positions shows that the novelist was a royalist who detested kings and leaders, a clearly political man who shunned politics, a Polish liberal who was suspicious of liberalism, an exile from Russian tyranny who feared and hated democracy but saw no alternative to it. As a practical thinker, he dreamed of utopias; as a writer, he strove for perfection in an admittedly imperfect world. In England, he considered himself a Tory, but his fiction manifests a philosophical anarchism.

1728.1 Kalenkiewicz, Irena. "*Lord Jim* J. Conrada: proba opracowania szkolnego" (Conrad's *Lord Jim*: Attempted Use in School), *Polonistyka* (Warsaw), XVI, 2 (1963), pp. 30–37.

Lord Jim was studied in Polish by pupils of Class V for two hours, with a required essay on "My Evaluation of Jim's Conduct." The reading of JC by adolescents left a permanent imprint on them. [In Polish.]

1734.1 Kocowna, Barbara (ed.). *Wspomnienia i Studia o Conradzie* (Recollections and Studies of Conrad), (Warsaw: Panstwowy Instytut Wydawniczy, 1963), p. 503.

Contents, abstracted under date of first publication: "Emigracja zdolnosci" (Emigration of Talents), *Kraj* (St. Petersburg, 1899), pp. 11–15; Eliza Orzeszkowa, "Emigracja zdolnosci" (Emigration of Talents), *Kraj* (St. Petersburg, 1899), pp. 16–30; Emilia Weslawska, "Przedmowa do *Lorda Jima* (Preface to *Lord Jim*), (Warsaw, 1904), pp. 31–34; Roman Dyboski, "Z mlodosci Josefa Conrada" (Youth of Joseph Conrad), *Czas* (Warsaw, 1927), pp. 35–42; Piotr Grzegorczyk, "Z dziejów J. Conrada-Korzeniowskiego w Polsce" (History of J. Conrad-Korzeniowski in Poland), *Ruch Literacki* (Warsaw, 1927), pp. 43–47; Maurycy Staniewski, "Angielskosc Conrada" (The Englishness of Conrad), *Wiadomosci Literackie* (Warsaw, 1929), pp. 48–60; Witold Chwalewik, "Jozef Conrad w Kardyfie" (Joseph Conrad in Cardiff), *Ruch Literacki* (Warsaw, 1932), pp. 61–69; Witold Wirpsza, "Smuga cienia" (Shadow of Darkness), *Nowa Kultura* (Warsaw, 1957), pp. 70–75; Boleslaw Pomian Piatkowski, "Proba wiernosci shipmastera Conrada" (Shipmaster Conrad's Trial of Faith), *Nowa Kultura* (Warsaw, 1962), pp. 76–84; Stanislaw Czosnowski, "Conradiana," *Epoka* (1929), pp. 85–88; Aniela Zagorska, "Kilka wspomnien o Conradzie" (Some Recollections of Conrad), *Wiadomosci Literackie* (Warsaw, 1929), pp. 89–104; Roman Dyboski, "Spotkanie z Conradem" (Meeting with Conrad), *Czas* (Warsaw, 1932), pp. 103–109; Jan Perlowski, "O Conradzie i Kiplingu" (On Conrad and Kipling), *Przeglad Wspolczesny* (Warsaw, 1937), pp. 110–31; Roza Jablkowska, "W rodzinie Josepha Conrada" (In Joseph Conrad's Family), *Ziemia i Morze*, No. 22 (1957), pp. 132–48; Maria Rakowska, "Jozef Conrad (Konrad Korzeniowski)," *Biblioteka Warszawska*

(1908), pp. 149–62; Stefan Zeromski, "Pisma wybrane Josepha Conrada" (Joseph Conrad's Collected Works), *Elegie* (Warsaw, 1928), pp. 163–84; Stefan Kolaczkowski, "Jozef Conrad (Korzeniowski)," *Przeglad Wspolczesny* (Warsaw, 1925), pp. 185–245; Waclaw Borowy, "Fredro i Conrad" (Fredro and Conrad), *Tygodnik Wilenski* (Wilno), XVIII (1925), pp. 246–52; Zbigniew Grabowski, "Romantyzm Conrada" (Conrad's Romanticism), *Ze Studiow nad Josephem Conradem* (Poznan, 1927), pp. 253–69; Maria Dabrowska, "Prawdziwa rzeczywistosc Conrada: poza Kryteriami formalnymi" (Conrad's True Reality: Beyond Formal Criteria), *Szkice o Conradzie* (Warsaw, 1959), pp. 270–89; Manfred Kridl, "*Lord Jim* Conrada" (Conrad's *Lord Jim*), *Przeglad Wspolczesny* (Warsaw), LXXXI (1929), pp. 290–328; Waclaw Borowy, "O Lordzie Jimie" (On *Lord Jim*), (n.p. [sic], 1942), pp. 329–32; Julian Krzyzanowski, "O tragedii na Samburnie" (On Tragedy on Samburan), *Pion* (Warsaw), L (1934), pp. 333–37; Jozef Ujejski, "Conrad i swiat" (Conrad and the World), *Skamander* (Warsaw), LXV (1935), pp. 338–67; Ludwik Fryde, "Realizm w tworczosci Conrada" (Realism in Conrad's Works), *Pion* (Warsaw), LII (1935), pp. 368–78; Rafal Marceli Blüth, "O tragicznej decyzji krakowskiej Konrada Korzeniowskiego (Pare mysli i usag w zwiaku z ksiazka profesora Ujejskiego, *O Konradzie Korzeniowskim*)" (On Konrad Korzeniowski's Tragic Decision in Cracow [Some Thoughts and Comments on Professor Ujujski's Book, *On Konrad Korzeniowski*], *Verbum*, No. 2 (1936), pp. 379–405; Waclaw Borowy, "*Szalenstwo Almayera* (czy 'tragedia Malosci')" (*Almayer's Folly* [or "tragedy of Smallness?"]), *Tygodnik Powszechny* (Cracow), XCVIII (1947), pp. 406–13; Zdzislaw Najder, "Conrad w Marsylli" (Conrad in Marseilles), *Zycie Literackie* (Cracow), XL (1957), pp. 414–26; Witold Chwalewik, "O glownym motywie wczesnej tworczosci Conrada" (On the Main Theme in the Early Work of Conrad), *Sprawozdania z Prac Naukowych Wydzialu Nauk Spolecznych Pan* (Warsaw, 1959), pp. 427–38; Witold Chwalewik, "Conrad a tradycja literacka" (Conrad and Literary Tradition), (n.p. [sic], 1963), pp. 439–56; Przemyslaw, "O Conradowskiej gnomice" (On Conrad's Gnomics), *Kwartalnik Neofilologiczny* (Warsaw), III (1959), pp. 457–93. [In Polish.]

1734.2 Kowalska, Aniela. "Wsrod Bohaterow Conrada" (Among Conrad's Heroes), *Prace Polonistyczne* (Polish Studies), (Lodz), seria XIX (1963), pp. 185–210.

JC's heroes are those of whom he is a hidden or open, reliable ally (the majority) and the few to whom he refuses his confidence for their hypocrisy or brutal egoism. If he is interested at all in the latter, it is as specimens of degeneracy, and he regards them with scorn or irony. Irony also allows JC to formulate moral judgments without preaching. His objectivity and contempt for easiness provided him with this difficult form of artistic expression. His irony can be bitter, tolerant, or jocular, and he used it to present difficult and complex problems. [N.B. On title page of journal "seria XIX," though dated 1963 on title page; has date of publication also on title page as 1964.] [In Polish.]

1743.1 Millar, Jack. "Melbourne's Link with Polish Novelist," *Port of Melbourne Quarterly*, XIV (April–June 1963), pp. 45–47, 49.

JC served on many ships over all oceans. His first glimpse of Australia was early in 1897, when he arrived at Sydney as "an able seaman" aboard the *Duke of Sutherland*. He went to Australia again in 1880 on the *Loch Etive*, belonging to the famous Loch Line of Glasgow. Early in 1888, JC unexpectedly received his first command, the *Otago*, with which he sailed the unusual route through Torres Strait and on to Mauritius. Since JC was not very popular with his colleagues, he became known sarcastically as "the Russian Count." On this voyage, JC reached Mauritius, then returned to Melbourne. He resigned his command rather than agree to return to Mauritius. The *Otago* served until 1931 as a coal hulk in Hobart, Tasmania. The old ship was sold at last to the highest bidder for £1, then towed to her final resting place at Risdon, near Hobart. There she still remains, a mere shell which no one has been able to purchase, even for the benefit of shiplovers and tourists.

1745.1 Najder, Zdzislaw. "Conrad i Dostojewski" (Conrad and Dostoevski), *Zycie Literackie* (Cracow), No. 8 (1963); rpt. *NC* (1965), pp. 150–70.

JC's attitude toward Russia varied at different times. In 1881, Tadeusz Bobrowski warned him against yielding to Pan-Slavism, which was an important instrument of the international policy of the Tsarist imperialists. In 1885, JC expressed extremely strong anti-Russian views, but this attitude was political, not hostile to the Russian people and Russian culture. Angry protests against Tsarist policies occur in the letters, though JC admitted that he knew very little about Russia (an odd statement from the author of "Autocracy and War"). The creative interests of JC and Dostoevski were similar: both were concerned with problems of moral responsibility, guilt and punishment, isolation and the bonds among individuals. But the attitude of each was opposite to that of the other. Dostoevski's careless style and construction were the opposite of JC's concern with language and construction, discreetly showing characters in action as opposed to Dostoevski's exhibitionism, ritual Christianity, and religiosity. The Russian writer hated Poles, and JC regarded him as a sick person, knowing also that he was an epileptic (as JC was when a child). *Under Western Eyes* was a reply to Dostoevski's *The*

Possessed and *Crime and Punishment*, as critics have pointed out.
[In Polish.]

1747.1 Ordoñez, Elmer A[lindogan]. "The Early Joseph Conrad:
Revisions and Style," unpublished Ph.D dissertation, University
of Wisconsin, 1963; pub. in part as "The Literary Impressionist
as Critic: Conrad and Ford," *Diliman Review*, XII (January 1964),
pp. 101–15; in part as "*The Nigger of the Narcissus*: From
Manuscript to Print," *Philippine Social Sciences and Humanities
Review*, XXX (March 1965), pp. 34–39; and as "Notes on the
Revisions of *An Outcast of the Islands*," *N&Q*, XV (August 1968),
pp. 287–89; expanded in "The Early Joseph Conrad: Revisions
and Style," *Philippine Social Sciences and Humanities Review*,
XXXIII (March–June 1968), pp. 1–192; and reprinted as *The
Early Joseph Conrad: Revisions and Style* (Quezon City:
University of the Philippines, 1969).

The textual revisions of JC's early works (*Almayer's Folly, An
Outcast of the Islands, The Nigger of the Narcissus, Tales of Unrest,
Lord Jim, Youth and Two Other Stories*, and *Typhoon and Other
Stories*, 1895 to 1903) as revealed by comparing the original
manuscripts, where available, with the immediate subsequent form,
either serial or book, include both expansion and revision, with a
consequent tightening of material. In general, JC tended to make
more revisions when his works published serially were to be
published in book form: his extensive revisions, as in "Heart of
Darkness," involved more cutting than adding. Among the stories
which were serialized, *Jim* underwent the most thorough revision,
with the major pattern being that of elimination: the results were a
reduction in verbosity, digressions, expository comments, and
philosophical statements. Changes in other works were to improve
stylistic matters. Major aspects of JC's style include rhythm,
description, and rendered and reported speech. His standard
rhythmic devices seem to be the balance of phrases and clauses,
repetition, and the measured pace of stressed and unstressed
syllables. In several instances, the pattern of repetition assumes
structural and thematic significance. Another mode of repetition is
the recurring incident, like Jim's jump from the ship in *Jim*. In
preparing his works for publication and republication, JC revised
many descriptive passages in an attempt to sharpen the images
used in the portrayal of a character or scene or action. Visual
description is JC's "forte," but at times, he makes a passage
describing the interaction of light and shadow more sensuous by the
addition of sound and smell. He also achieves patterns of description
in his character portrayals, in group portraits, and in a large number
of figurative comparisons. JC also gave considerable attention to

developing and improving upon certain devices which relate in some way to the rendering and reporting of speech, such as the internal monologue, the use of "I" and third person narrators, and choric passages and digressions. As for internal monologue, JC began in *Folly* to experiment with a mode of introspection by indirect discourse, but he also used indirect comment and introduced, very importantly, a narrator to stand between himself and the reader, e.g., Marlow in "Youth," "Heart of Darkness," and *Jim*. [This study concentrates, with some success, on JC's early use of expressive devices from the level of sound to that of discourse and indicates the need for further consideration of this matter in all of JC's works.]

1748.1 "The Power of Language," *Practical English* (13 September 1963), p. 7.

JC's life aboard ship provided him with a theme often found in his fiction, the test resulting from man's struggle with the sea—and also with the rhythm often found in his prose.

1748.2 Reeves, Ruth, and Shirley Wiley. *Understanding the Novel: A Seminar Approach. Book II: Nine English Novels* (Garden City, New York: Doubleday, 1963), pp. 62–94.

Analyses of "Typhoon," "The Secret Sharer," and *The Shadow-Line* consisting of a selection from each tale, questions with multiple-choice answers "For Interpretation and Insight," "Guide Questions for Reading and Discussion," and sections of essay assignments for "Developing Writing Style," each excerpt preceded by an "Introductory Note."

1753.1 Rosenheim, Edward W., Jr. *Swift and the Satirist's Art* (Chicago and London: University of Chicago Press, 1963), pp. 207–10.

Jonathan Swift has a view of "true knowledge" as a goal rarely and painfully attained, "terrible and violent to contemplate," remote from usual standards of conduct or satisfaction, desirable because it is "uniquely real." For those who find true knowledge, there is only the prospect of spiritual alienation from their fellows. This seems to be the curious heroism seen in Kurtz in "Heart of Darkness," JC's tormented and corrupted, yet strongly triumphant figure. At the end of his search, at the heart of darkness, lies the "quintessence of darkness itself," moving him to savage sentiments and to the final devastating account of his vision: "The horror! The horror!" Marlow is incapable of fully sharing Kurtz's experience and his stature, though he can trace and in some measure understand Kurtz's journey into knowledge. Although Marlow refrains, at the moment of real challenge, from embracing and speaking the terrible truth to Kurtz's fiancée, he reveals, in his own terms, an insight into the strange, inhuman heroism which he senses in the other man. Experience with the "inner actuality" is superior to the surface appearance only on the ground that knowledge of any kind is superior to ignorance. JC's Kurtz is thus a hero in only one sense—he has learned what other men cannot and will not learn.

1754.1 Serpieri, Alessandro. "Il valore di *Youth* nella prima produzione di Conrad" (The Place of "Youth" in Conrad's Early Production), in *Youth*, ed. by Alessandro Serpieri (Firenze: Sansoni, 1963), pp. 51–58; rpt. Z. Najder, ed., *Conrad w Oczach Krytyki Swiatowej* (Conrad Seen by World Criticism), (Warsaw: PIW, 1974), pp. 439–51.

JC's stories have not only a symbolic dimension: the realistic level is more important than is usually thought, and it is upon it that symbols and ambiguities grow. The autobiographical element makes the coexistence of symbolic and realistic levels possible. "Youth," one of JC's most straightforward tales and one of his highest achievements, is structurally perfect and possesses the magic qualities of plain things. It is a paradigmatic rather than dramatic "exemplum"; it is elegiac more than tragic. Marlow is telling more than a story; he is telling the myth of youth, that has a heroic dimension, with the usual contrast between illusion and experience, enthusiasm and disenchantment. Captain Beard is another instance of heroic determination destined to failure. [In Italian.]

1760.1 Stocks, Mary. *Ernest Simon of Manchester* (Manchester: Manchester University Press, 1963), p. 46.

Ernest Simon, later Lord Simon of Wythenshawe, determined to write in his diary reviews of all the books he read on the return voyage from South America in 1914, and proved that he could do so. His longest review was of JC's *The Secret Agent*, which left him with a depressing view of the human race. [A choice bit of useless information about JC.]

1767.1 Wickes, George. "Joseph Conrad," *Masters of Modern British Fiction* (New York: Macmillan, 1963), pp. 7–9.

Unlike other Edwardians, e.g., Wells, Bennett, and Galsworthy, JC was, like James and Turgenev, an "international novelist who regarded novel writing as an art." His concerns were ethical: he wrote to "bring values out of chaos," creating tragedies at a time when they were unthinkable. JC probed deeply into the human condition, and the Preface to *The Nigger of the Narcissus* can stand as a preface to the fiction of the entire period.

JC seems a character himself rather than a writer of fiction; he was an "ancient mariner," like Marlow, although JC sometimes disagreed with Marlow in point of view. JC displays an ability to see all sides of a situation or a character without seeming to impose judgment. [Wickes seems to contradict himself at times.]

1964

1784.1 Camerino, Aldo. "Racconti di Conrad" (Tales by Conrad), *La Nazione*, CVI, 105 (5 May 1964), p. 3.

JC's characters are often among the most bizarre and surprising of modern literature. [Review of Italian translation of *A Set of Six: Un gruppo di sei* (Milan: Bompiani, 1964).] [In Italian.]

1786.1 Day, Martin Steele. *History and English Literature: 1837 to the Present* (Garden City, New York: Doubleday, 1964), pp. 375–80.

By experimenting with form and language, JC brought to the English novel a cosmopolitanism which exhibited no concern about the problem of the novel as such. His main theme was responsibility based on fidelity. *The Nigger of the Narcissus* portrays a world where only the cooperation among the crew members saves them from destruction by an impersonal nature. The theme of *Lord Jim* is that of guilt and atonement. "Youth" is a paean to youth, to man's endurance. "Heart of Darkness" vividly and realistically portrays the evil life of the Congo, but this story is not so much an indictment of imperialism as it is of a materialistic society. "The End of the Tether" reveals Captain Whalley trying to compromise with his conscience for trying to hide his blindness from men. This tale concludes JC's study of youth, maturity, and age. "Typhoon," which contains the best descriptive passages of a storm at sea, is a simple tale of man versus nature. JC's masterpiece is *Nostromo*, comparable to *War and Peace*. In *The Secret Agent*, JC attacks science and materialism, and in *Under Western Eyes*, he treats Russian psychology. *Chance* is the most complex of all his novels, and *Victory* presents his attack on Western man of pre-World War I for failing to exercise brotherly love. *The Shadow-Line* is pure allegory of victory against a bitter enemy.

1787.1 Fletzer, Giovanni. "Nota del traduttore" (Translator's Note), *Un gruppo di sei* (A Set of Six), (Milan: Bompiani, 1964), pp. 371–76.

These stories are mere pot-boilers, written for the popular journals because of practical necessity. The title for the volume clearly reflects the evident thematic disparity that must have embarrassed the author himself, acutely aware of his stylistic discontinuity. [In Italian.]

1789.1 Gordon, Ambrose, Jr. *The Invisible Tent: The War Novels of Ford Madox Ford* (Austin: University of Texas Press, 1964), pp. 19, 38–40, 43, 44, 46, 50, 67, 70.

The visual aims of Ford Madox Ford and JC were called by Ford, as early as 1913, "impressionism," a "slippery" term when applied to writing. Ford's impressionism is unlike Walter Pater's and even unlike JC's. The strongest influence came not from painting and music but from literary works in France. The chief foreign influence upon both Ford and JC was the tradition of the French realists extending through Maupassant and Flaubert back to Stendhal. During the years of their collaboration, what JC already knew about design Ford was still trying to learn.

1789.2 Gorlier, Claudio. "Introduzione" (Introduction), *Avventura Romantica* (Romance), (Milan: Bompiani, 1964), pp. 5–23.

A detailed case history of the JC–Ford collaboration. [In Italian.]

1795.1 Hay, Eloise Knapp. "Political Use and Abuse: Conrad's Letters to Cunninghame Graham," *Dartmouth College Library Bulletin*, N.S., VI (January 1964), pp. 1–9.

The mutual sympathies of Cunninghame Graham and JC were "grounded" in the ancient nobility of their families and on the hatred of despotism and love of chivalrous indivdualism which colored their views of European politics in the years of their association, 1897 to 1924. The first spark of friendship between them was struck by the horror of imperialism—Russian, Belgian, Dutch, British, and American. The Dartmouth College Library owns seventy-seven letters from JC to Graham, including some that did not appear in Jean-Aubry's *Joseph Conrad: Life and Letters* (1927). Only one letter, it seems, did not reach Dartmouth; instead, it recently turned up at Yale. A critical passage of 30 July 1898 was omitted by Jean-Aubry: "If one could set the States & Germany by the ears! That would be *real fine*. I am afraid however that the thieves shall agree in the Philippines. The pity of it!" Clearly, JC reveals the "dye of family convictions" against which he had rebelled in his youth. His remark about the agreement in the Philippines reminds us that in 1898 Germany, still holding her share of defeated Poland, was both Britain's greatest rival for power in South Africa and was also at that time building a rival navy and negotiating to buy the Philippines from Spain. This letter documents JC's changing attitudes toward the United States, which eventually culminated in *Nostromo* (1904) and was not exhausted until the last of his great political novels, *The Secret Agent* and *Under Western Eyes*, were written (1911). [Reprints both JC's letter and a typed copy of it.]

1801.1 Hudson, Derek. "Reading," *Edwardian England, 1904–1914*, ed. by Simon Nowell-Smith (London: Oxford University Press, 1964), pp. 308, 309, 310, 315.

In the Edwardian period in England, a relatively small number of connoisseurs were as much aware of Max Beerbohm, Saki, or Ernest Bramah as they were of JC and Henry James. More books were published and made available then than ever before in England; a notable work of the time was JC's *Nostromo*. One important classification of major novelists included, in order of importance, Balzac, Meredith, Henry James, JC, and Turgenev. JC's Edwardian novels, though, including some of his best work, sold "notoriously badly" when they first appeared.

1804.1 Kocmanova, Jessie. "R. B. Cunninghame Graham: A Little-Known Master of Realist Prose," *Philologica Pragensia*, VII, No. 1 (1964), pp. 14–30.

JC paid a tribute to Cunningham Graham's "personality and genius"; Graham, in turn, encouraged JC when he "was still making his way." JC became famous and Graham did not because only JC wrote novels. Both men were "anti-imperialist" writers, but JC "retained more of the 'aristocratic' attitude" toward the rest of mankind whereas Graham's sympathy with the downtrodden "extended almost to identification." In the two men's correspondence, JC writes of the famous knitting machine which he sees as the universe.

1804.2 Leslie, [William] Seymour. *The Jerome Connection* (London: John Murray, 1964), pp. 105, 147, 150.

Leslie attended a dinner where Paul Valéry, Maurice Ravel, and JC "argued about the tone and music-value of poetry divorced from its literary content." JC, "a man of grave charm," used broken English which sounded very odd, coming from such a master of English prose. He was full of complaint at his wretched earnings from *The Nigger of the Narcissus*. He told Leslie in the 1920s that he was "deeply hurt at his MSS" being sold with the rest of the John Quinn collection.

1808.1 Long, William J. "Joseph Conrad," *English Literature: Its History and Its Significance for the Life of the English-Speaking World*, enlarged ed. (Boston: Ginn, 1964), pp. 585–88.

Unlike the realist he has been purported to be, JC seldom kept his eye steadily on an external object; instead, he portrayed the effect of the object upon its observer. Thus be became a "master of impressionism," which is "poles apart from realism." Another outstanding quality of JC's fiction is the ideal of personal honor which runs through it. A profound moralist, JC lets a character speak for himself by his actions and allows him to save or lose his soul by loyalty or disloyalty to a moral ideal. [One of the better examples of comments on JC intended for students and teachers.]

1815.1 Meyer, Bernard C. "Psychoanalytic Studies on Joseph Conrad. I. The Family Romance," *Journal of the American Psychoanalytic Association*, XII (January 1964), pp. 32–58.

JC's reading in his early childhood helped to create in him a "family romance fantasy." Such a fantasy plays a significant role in his personal life and in his fiction, but his family romance fantasies gained greatest treatment in his autobiographical writings, especially in *The Arrow of Gold*. With this treatment, JC frequently employs the theme of the rescue. "Amy Foster" is JC's "Christ story"; it reveals, through Yanko Gooral, JC's position of a Catholic living in a strange land. JC did not repudiate his Catholic upbringing, nor did he reject his memory of his father. *The Rover* illustrates his dream of returning to Poland. [Much of this article is incorporated in Meyer's *Joseph Conrad: A Psychoanalytic Biography* (1967). The next three parts of his series of articles appear under the entries for 1964.]

1815.2 Meyer, Bernard C. "Psychoanalytic Studies on Joseph Conrad. II. Fetishism," *Journal of the American Psychoanalytic Association*, XII (April 1964), pp. 357–91.

Fetishism plays a significant role in JC's portrayal of his characters. He frequently gives considerable attention to descriptions of the hair of his fictional women—especially of the women figuring in *An Outcast of the Islands*, "Heart of Darkness," "Falk," *The Rescue, Chance, Suspense*, and *The Arrow of Gold*. Foot and shoe fetishism figures prominently in *Victory, The Arrow of Gold*, "The Planter of Malata," and "The Inn of the Two Witches," and occasionally the references to these fetishes point to a strong concern with the female genitalia. It is interesting to note, too, that the fetishists often engage in voyeurism. Several of the heroes tend to be voyeurs, while many of the heroines tend toward exhibitionism. Both of these tendencies lead toward JC's treatment of love. Many cases of love involve narcissism and enslavement: some of the characters love themselves through others, and some characters engage in a marked subservience to others. [Much of this article is incorporated in Meyer's *Joseph Conrad: A Psychoanalytic*

Biography (1967). The next two parts of his series of articles appear under the entries for 1964.]

1815.3 Meyer, Bernard C. "Psychoanalytic Studies on Joseph Conrad. III. Aspects of Orality," *Journal of the American Psychoanalytic Association,* XII (July 1964), pp. 562–86.

JC's orality involves a fascination with cannibalism. References to cannibalism appear in "Heart of Darkness" and "Falk." Elements of it appear in *The Rover* and *Suspense.* Other works, notably "Amy Foster," *The Secret Agent,* and *Victory,* contain elements of orality that involve allusions to violent eating. In addition, several of JC's female characters possess qualities that are generally associated with "fire-breathing dragons or devouring witches." Orality plays a significant role in JC's art and in his personal life in the form of interest in eating and drinking. [Some of this article is incorporated in Meyer's *Joseph Conrad: A Psychoanalytic Biography* (1967). The last part of his series of articles appears under the entries for 1964.]

1815.4 Meyer, Bernard C. "Psychoanalytic Studies on Joseph Conrad. IV. The Flow and Ebb of Artistry," *Journal of the American Psychoanalytic Association,* XII (October 1964), pp. 802–25.

JC's career as an artist had some definite fluctuations. A decline in the quality of his work began with *Chance* in 1913, and it continued until his death. Yet what makes most of his work successful is his choice of conveying his writings in English rather than in Polish or French, for the demands of English enabled him to keep his emotional conflicts out of his art. Occasionally, though, in periods of extreme nervousness, he created in his works a powerful emotional climate. [Extensive analysis of JC's psychology and considerable biographical material are later incorporated in Meyer's *Joseph Conrad: A Psychoanalytic Biography* (1967). The preceding articles of his series appear under the entries for 1964.]

1815.5 Mizener, Arthur. *The Sense of Life in the Modern Novel* (Boston: Houghton Mifflin, 1964), pp. 110, 114, 144–47, 158, 159.

H. G. Wells, who thought of the novel as primarily an instrument for setting forth social ideas, told JC that he would describe a boat on the water "in the commonest phrases possible" unless he wanted to make it important (in *Experiment in Autobiography,* 1934), but JC wanted to see a boat with his own special vividness [a kind of impressionism]. Wells wanted to see it in relation to something else— a story, a thesis. Perhaps JC sometimes indulged the fine shades of his awareness of particulars at the expense of the familiar whole. *Lord Jim,* for example, sometimes gets a long way from any "natural" sense of life. No doubt JC was sincerely convinced that the civilized world is preserved from chaos and savagery only by man's faith in the major power of "a fixed standard of conduct," even though his awareness of the relativity of this standard often led him into irony and sometimes drove him close to despair. But, often desperately, he clung to the belief that chaos would be held at bay, if at all, only by the white man's assumption of his burden of providing order and progress for the world. Eloquently, if indirectly, JC realized in his work his desperate remedy for humanity. No doubt his tortured uncertainty seemed nonsense to Wells—if Wells detected at all this aspect of JC's works. By 1925, however, when Wells was fading out, JC's influence was still strong in the novel.

1818.1 Mroczkowski, Przemyslaw. "Tajemnica *Lorda Jima*" (The Secret of *Lord Jim*), *KN*, XI, I (1964), pp. 31–49. English summary, pp. 48–49.

In *Lord Jim*, the terms of moral and philosophical reference are partly independent. The story of Jim's "fall," which alternates with the story of the narrator's doubts (expressed partly by his skeptical aphorisms), is subtle and profound, but its complexity is occasionally trying and its inconsistencies vulnerable. [In Polish.]

1822.1 Ordoñez, E[lmer] A[lindogan]. "The Literary Impressionist as Critic: Conrad and Ford," *Diliman Review*, XII (January 1964), pp. 101–15.

After Ford Madox Ford and JC had completed some of their writings, both men developed their critical theories. Their method, called impressionism, is a way of presenting a particular situation "through the lens" of a particular temperament such as Marlow in "Youth," "Heart of Darkness," *Lord Jim*, and *Chance*, and such as Dowell in *The Good Soldier*. Point of view shapes the materials of the story and presents them in accordance with the psychological effect on the narrator. The use of a narrator like Marlow or Dowell necessitates such impressionistic techniques as the timeshift, the *progression d'effet*, and the deliberate employment of prose cadence. In *Jim*, Marlow reconstructs the story of Jim from other reconstructions so that in the novel there are at least three skeins of narrative: one "spun" by the original narrator, another by Marlow, and a third by Jim, Brown, and other lesser characters. Ultimately one must focus his attention not on Jim but on Marlow and his own internal conflict, a quest for self-knowledge. The impressionist design of *Jim* prefigures the "great renderings" of *Chance*, *Nostromo*, *The Secret Agent*, and *Under Western Eyes*. [Contains also an analysis of *The Good Soldier*.]

1822.2 Ostrowski, Witold. *"Tajny agent J.* Conrada jako powiesc kryminalna" (J. Conrad's *The Secret Agent* as a Criminal Detective Thriller), *Prace Polonistyczne* (Polish Studies), (Lodz), seria XX (1964), pp. 208–19.

The word "criminal" is the key to a proper understanding of *The Secret Agent.* Leavis called the material that of a thriller. The novel is based on a central incident and central moral ideas about political and social life, to which the anarchists are secondary. It was written in 1906–1907, when there was much curiosity about anarchists, political and social changes, and criminal themes. JC's own statements bear witness to this fact, as do the title, the plot, the characters, and the background. JC retained the three fundamental questions of the criminal and detective novel: Who? How? Why? but reached more deeply than popular fiction of this kind to the roots of the social and political bases of crime. [N.B. On title page of journal, "seria XX," though dated 1964 on title page, has date of publication also on title page as 1965.] [In Polish.]

1822.3 Padovani, Paolo. *"Un gruppo di sef"* (A Set of Six), *LCS*, XLVII, 11–12 (November–December 1964), p. 199.

This collection of tales, among which "The Duel" and "The Informer" emerge, is a further instance of JC's genius. [Review of Italian edition of *A Set of Six: Un gruppo d sei* (Milan: Bompiani, 1964).] [In Italian.]

1823.1 Pilecki, G. A. "Conrad's *Victory,*" *Explicator*, XXIII (November 1964), Item 26.

In the shooting incident near the end of *Victory*, Heyst, standing erect, caused Mr. Jones to shoot Lena instead of Ricardo; Heyst is thus really responsible for the girl's death. Heyst has often boasted of his innocence, but he is guilty, as the Eden imagery discloses, of Adam's sin of trying to be like God; he enjoys a "Divine self-sufficiency" and even a kind of "divine innocence." The action of the novel is essentially concerned with making Heyst human once again by having him learn of his own inherent weakness. If to err is human, to be human is to err. Heyst is actually responsible not only for Lena's death but also for Morrison's. But only his responsibility for Lena's death affects him seriously enough for him to abandon his inhuman aloofness and destroy himself in recognizing the folly of his attempt to maintain innocence through detachment.

1825.1 Rubadiri, David. "Why African Literature?" *Transition: A Journal of the Arts, Culture and Society* (Uganda), IV, No. 15 (1964), pp. 39–42.

At present, Africa as a literary theme is moving away from politics to become in itself a creative theme. This change is good. Three novelists have successfully managed to portray characters belonging to cultural groups outside of their own: E. M. Forster with Dr. Aziz in *A Passage to India*, William Faulkner with Joe Christmas, and JC with Nina Almayer. These are memorable characters because they cannot be hewn and carved to fit into the framework of local politics; instead, they are endowed with observable dimensions. They have human characteristics which are permanent and which suffer and endure historical change. JC's greatness as an artist lies in his disinclination to recognize boundaries in human nature.

1830.1 Sherry, Norman. "*Lord Jim* and 'The Secret Sharer,'" *Review of English Studies*, N.S., XVI (November 1964), pp. 378–92.

Both "The Secret Sharer" and *Lord Jim* are related in theme, that of men who violate a code and consequently become guilty wanderers, and also in drawing on real events occurring on shipboard. JC's use of three sources, the *Jeddah* and the *Cutty Sark* cases and his own experience aboard the *Otago*, is a complex combination. One similarity is the killing of a seaman on the *Cutty Sark* and Leggatt's killing of a sailor in like circumstances on the *Sephora*. The suicide of the captain of the *Cutty Sark* is the origin of the suicide of Brierly in *Jim*, and Jim's guilty flight is derived from the first mate's fleeing the scene of the crime. The intimacy between the narrator and fugitive in *Jim* is a forecast of the relationship between the narrator and Leggatt in "The Secret Sharer." On the other hand, the same stormy weather prevails when the murder is committed in "The Secret Sharer" as when the *Jeddah* is abandoned. Leggatt and Smith take command in a crisis when their captains panic. "The Secret Sharer" also owes much to JC's experience on the *Otago*, accounts of which are given in *The Shadow-Line*, *The Mirror of the Sea*, "A Smile of Fortune," and "Falk." [Included in *Conrad's Eastern World* (1966).]

1838.1 Texas, University of. "Joseph Conrad," *A Creative Century: Selections from the Twentieth Century Collections at the University of Texas* (Austin: University of Texas, 1964), pp. 14–15.

[Lists a few items, with some illustrations, of contemporary literary materials at The University of Texas. Includes, by JC, *Victory*, autograph manuscript, 1915; *Lord Jim*, Edinburgh and London, first edition, 1900; and a typed letter to Hugh Walpole of 7 June 1918. Includes a photograph of *Victory*.]

1840.1 Ward, A[lfred] C[harles]. "Joseph Conrad," *Twentieth-Century English Literature, 1901–1960* (New York: Barnes & Noble, 1964), pp. 47–55.

JC had "clear advantages" over his English contemporaries in that as a "citizen of the world" he was not linked to outlook or sympathy by national or racial consciousness. The stature of his characters is "heroic" and therefore unlike the "common" stature; universality and foreignness are distinguishing features of his men and women. JC did not invent plots; instead, he used reality as his material, subjecting it to the "transmuting process" of a lively imagination. In his writing, he had a double purpose: to make his novels true works of art and to arouse the philosophical feeling of "unavoidable solidarity" which binds together men and men, and "all mankind" to the "visible world." Above all, he admired the keeping of faith between man and man.

1840.2 Warner, Oliver. "Joseph Conrad, 1857–1924," *English Literature: A Portrait Gallery* (London: Chatto & Windus, 1964), pp. 178–79.

[A brief biographical sketch and appreciation of JC and his works, mentioning some titles, with emphasis on longer stories. Reproduces Walter Tittle's portrait of JC.]

1848.1 Wyka, Kazimierz. "Wyspa na polskiej zatoce" (Island in a Polish Gulf), *Tw* (1964), pp. 90–102.

The Sisters belongs more to Polish than to English literature for its unconcealed and emotional autobiographical aspect, its apotheosis of immaterial values and Romantic undertones, as Tarnowski pointed out (though he overlooked "Prince Roman" and descriptions of the Ukraine). Such things can only be perceived by historians of Polish literature but even then they are often oblivious to them. Indirect and direct allusions to Mickiewicz's works, especially *Pan Tadeusz*, and to Zeromski's among JC's contemporaries are audible. [In Polish.]

1965

1852.1 Anderson, Quentin. "Willa Cather: Her Masquerade," *New Republic* (27 November 1965), pp. 28–31.

In Willa Cather there is an impulse to disguise, or "to undertake impersonations in many modes," one mode being JC's. [The reviewer does not otherwise mention JC, although Cather's use of the "second self" may serve him as an indirect reference to JC.]

1853.1 Anozie, Lunday O. "The Theme of Alienation and Commitment in Okara's *The Voice*," *Bulletin of the Association for African Literature in English* (Freetown, Sierra Leone), No. 3 (November 1965), pp. 54–67.

Okara's *The Voice* echoes JC's theme of alienation between individual and society, though Okara's hero does not commit himself, as Heyst does in *Victory*, to human solidarity and consequently does not achieve dignity or victory. Like Shakespeare, JC shows his heroes attaining tragic nobility as a result of their being caught between their limitations and their capacities.

1855.1 Bojarski, Edmund A., and Henry T. Bojarski. "Masters and Doctoral Dissertations on Joseph Conrad, 1917–1963," *Polish American Studies*, XXII (1965), pp. 30–46; rpt. "Three Hundred and Thirty-Six Unpublished Papers on Joseph Conrad: a Bibliography of Masters Theses and Doctoral Dissertations, 1917–1963," Bulletin of Bibliography and Magazine Notes, XXVI (July–September 1969), pp. 61–66, 79–83.

[Based "primarily on a postal survey made early in 1964" and including many graduate schools abroad, this checklist, conservatively regarded, "contains at least seventy-five percent of all the pertinent titles on a world-wide basis." The entries are not verified. The list is arranged alphabetically by author, cites the title, place and year, page count, and when available (with the exception of the readily available *Dissertation Abstracts*) refers the reader to the location of the abstract.]

1856.1 Bonsanti, Marcella. "Introduzione al teatro di Conrad" (Introduction to Conrad's Theater), *Teatro di Joseph Conrad* (Joseph Conrad's Theater), (Milan: Bompiani, 1965), pp. 5–19.

[General critical notes, quotes extensively from letters in which JC shows his dislike for theaters and actors.] *One Day More* is the only piece that stands a comparison with the tale from which it is adapted, preserving all the lyrical intensity of the original. *Laughing Anne* is quite rudimental. In *The Secret Agent*, the figure of Verloc retains a certain pathos in his obtuse squalor. [In Italian.]

1857.1 Carr, W. I. "'Gracious Silence'–A Selective Reading of *Coriolanus*," *English Studies*, XLVI (June 1965), pp. 221–34.

In JC's *Nostromo*, the author's treatment of politics is wholly ironic, too "annihilatingly comprehensive," for us to regard the novel as tragedy. "Classic" irony characterizes the book. The gangsters and the charlatans are there, but so are the Goulds, neither of whom is "foolish, selfish, or dominated by the urge to power." Their ironic catastrophe is caused by their control of the mine, the uses to which they separately think material resources can be put in an "inflammable" political situation, whose requirements irresistibly sap the vitality of their early idealism and subtly poison their relationship. Only two characters remain clear-sighted, Martin Decoud and Dr. Monygham. JC presents his characters with "disconcerting rigour"; they are completely convincing. But we see nothing of them which is not consistent with the dominant ironic view; all we know of them is adduced by way of verification of JC'c central perception: the ironic futility which is the consequence of politics, leaving the reader with the radically uncomfortable sensation of living with a larger version of oneself than he can possibly afford. In *Coriolanus*, Shakespeare creates "as completely, as wholly credible a political context as that we see in *Nostromo*."

1858.1 Church, Richard. "How a Novelist Works," *Essays by Divers Hands, Being the Transactions of the Royal Society of Literature*, XXXIII (1965), pp. 56–69.

JC reveals in his letters that he was always irritable about his writing. His habit resembled that of most novelists; he shut himself in his study and waited for his inspiration. JC's letters also reveal that he wasted time and rarely produced more than five hundred words a day.

1858.2 Corrington, John William. "An American Dreamer," *Chicago Review*, XVIII, No. 1 (1965), pp. 58–66.

An American Dream by Norman Mailer "precisely locates" in the tradition of Dostoevski and JC at their best. It has a "strong hint" of "Heart of Darkness": if Mailer is to be faulted for his "super-dramatic portrayal" of Deborah Rojack, what can we make of JC's "equally dramatic recollection of Kurtz," through Marlow, his narrator? In both works, Rojack and Marlow are remembering and characterizing the "recently dead, thoroughly-evil," and Mailer's prose is no less effective than JC's. *An American Dream* is a "flawed masterpiece"—as is JC's "Heart of Darkness" and as is Dostoevski's *The Brothers Karamazov*.

1861.1 De Tomasso, Vincenzo. "*Vittoria*" (Victory), *LCS*, XLVIII (4 April 1965), p. 270.

Victory is undoubtedly JC's masterpiece. It is clear that the events narrated are of no intrinsic interest to the author; what matters is the characters that set in motion or undergo the events. It is in this, moreover, that JC stands out from the common (one can say even, the vulgar) author of "adventure novels." [Review of *Vittoria* (Milan: Bompiani, 1964).] [In Italian.]

1867.1 Fowlie, Wallace. *André Gide: His Life and Art* (New York: Macmillan, 1965), pp. 100, 105, 197.

On his travels in the Congo in 1925, André Gide based his book, *Voyage au Congo* (1927), in which he protested against the cruelty of man's treatment of his fellowmen, on JC's "Heart of Darkness," and it is of significance that he dedicated the work to the memory of JC. In his interpretation to France of the culture of Europe, Gide was one of the first Frenchmen to speak of JC, whom he introduced along with Dostoevski, Whitman, and Melville.

1870.1 Gilbert, Eliot L. "To Whom Does Kipling Speak Today?" *Kipling Journal*, XXXII (December 1965), pp. 56–65.

Both Kipling and JC believed that man could respond to an absurd universe; but JC thought that some responses were more heroic and some failures more devastating than others, whereas Kipling's outlook was more democratic. Thus JC is more Victorian than modern.

1876.1 Hagopian, John V. "The Pathos of 'Il Conde,'" *SSF*, III (Fall 1965), pp. 31–38.

In "Il Conde," a nameless Marlovian narrator who tells the story of the Count serves as a filter through which a pathetic melodrama is transmuted into an ironic commentary on the decay of the aristocracy and the vulnerability of innocence. The Count seems unworthy of fullest respect, admiration, or sympathy; he represents the degenerate aristocracy of Europe at the turn of the century. He is reduced from a tragic to a pathetic figure.

1885.1 Jones, Howard Mumford. "Introduction," *The Nigger of the Narcissus* (Los Angeles: Limited Editions Club, 1965), pp. vii–xvi.

JC's *The Nigger of the Narcissus*, his "book autobiography," rises into "imaginative splendor." James Wait is a "symbol of the power of darkness, or of the unconscious, or some other metaphor precious to *avant-garde* interpreters of the imagination." JC wrote what he thought; he insisted that Wait is a lone Negro in a ship's complement of white men and that this is the "occasion, or theme, or point" of the tale, and he informed us that Wait is an "imposter of some character," meaning, perhaps, an imposter of genius, a "great" imposter. Alone and dying, he not only manipulates the white men in his own interest, but he also survives the storm, mastering the compassion of the crew by overdramatizing his illness. They both hate and admire him, and he is able to take advantage of this ambiguity, now by being a triumphant malingerer, now by pretending a heroism he does not possess. His presence makes the book a "profound and subtle study of group psychology." Opposed to the corrupt and corrupting Wait, who is a deliberate affront to discipline, is Singleton, who is ancient wisdom, that of the sea. Since the sea cares nothing for mankind, the only weapon man has been able to invent as protection against it is the discipline of the old sailor.

1887.1 Killham, John. "The Use of 'Concreteness' as an Evaluative Term in F. R. Leavis's *The Great Tradition*," *British Journal of Aesthetics*, V (January 1965), pp. 14–24.

In *The Great Tradition*, F. R. Leavis ambiguously assigns the term "concrete" to different qualities of novels. He finds, for example, that *Nostromo* is concrete in representing attitudes and motives of characters and yet later says that JC's novel is not concerned with illustrating psychology. Rather, *Nostromo* is concrete in its "moral pattern," as is *The Secret Agent*. "Concrete" in Leavis's aesthetic becomes simply a blanket term for what achieves realism, but such methods are various and may change with different readers.

1889.1 Kohler, Dayton. "Introduction," *Lord Jim* (New York: Harper & Row, 1965), pp. xii–xix.

Lord Jim is primarily a tale about the loss of nerve, but it is not at all a mere adventure story. The novel functions, moreover, as a guide to the world of the novelist, for its major themes are illusion and reality, isolation and solidarity, fidelity and betrayal, loss of self, and guilt and expiation. Central to the whole story is Jim's quest for identity and redemption; central to the structure of the whole novel is the *Patna* episode. From this episode, the events and the characters expand in complexity and significance. Yet the book is plagued by its two-part division. The presence of Marlow is, though, a strong point, for he acts as a mediator between the reader and the writer, and he provides the logical means for telling the story. Stein's advice concerning the destructive element is central to the story, for it demonstrates that man's only hope for salvation is his committing himself to a "hard-won self-knowledge." The end of the novel is, though, vague, largely because of the way Marlow reports it. [Includes plot summary.]

1889.2 Kowalska, Aniela. "Problem polskosci i realizm bohaterek Conrada" (Problem of Polishness and Realism of the Heroines of Conrad), *Prace Polonistyczne* (Lodz), XXXI (1965), pp. 103–25.

Those of JC's heroines who were modeled upon his mother were precisely those which English critics found incredible. Other heroines are dark, wild women; yet others have a saving strength of faith, as in *Nostromo*. Lena is not based on personal recollections, but is the projection of JC's fantasies. JC's heroines may usefully be

compared with those of Zeromski—fascinating women who arouse
love at first sight. Like many of Zeromski's, JC's heroines are the
objectivization of the dreams and longings of their creator. As
Zeromski said of JC: "to understand fully . . . Polish illumination is
necessary." [In Polish.]

1891.1 Ludwig, Richard M. (ed.). *Letters of Ford Madox Ford*
(Princeton: Princeton University Press, 1965), pp. 8, 10, 15, 16, 25,
26, 27, 50, 60, 72, 80, 95, 119, 120, 127–28, 152, 157, 166–67, 169,
170–72, 177–78, 181–82, 213, 237, 267, 286.

JC, being a Pole, is "Elizabethan." "He has done an immense deal
for the Nuvvle [sic] in England. . . . I learned [Ford declares] all I know
of Literature from Conrad—and England has learned all it knows of
Literature from me." [Contains much important information about
JC and his collaboration with Ford.]

1892.1 Mackaness, George. "Joseph Conrad and Australia,"
Bibliomania: An Australian Book Collector's Essays (Sydney:
Angus and Robertson, 1965), pp. 159–63.

JC is one of the few great British men of letters to visit Australia.
He made four visits there, each one in a different ship. In 1879, he
arrived in the clipper ship *Duke of Sutherland*, which led him to write
his impressions of Sydney in *The Mirror of the Sea*; and in 1880, he
was there as third officer of the wool-clipper *Loch Etive*, but left no
record of this visit. In 1887, as commander of the *Otago*, he
experienced sufficient interest to echo later in "The Secret Sharer,"
"The Planter of Malata," and elsewhere. In 1892, as chief officer of the
Torrens, his voyage to Australia was the occasion of his meeting
John Galsworthy for the first time and also gave him some time for
writing his first novel, *Almayer's Folly*.

1893.1 McGahan, E. C. "Three Examples of the Exotic Novel in
English," *Prace Historyczno literackie* (Cracow), VIII (1965), pp.
47–74.

Almayer's Folly, an apprentice work produced from the writer's
imagination, is representative of a certain type of exotic fiction in
which the main inspiration results from the strange sights the
author has witnessed. The plethora of adjectives with physical or
color connotations and the overrythmic prose produce a
melodramatic effect. The novel is more subtle than exotic as a study
of the effects of exile and alienation. Religious feelings are simplified,
Eastern religion is treated as superstition, and there is no deep
penetration into the background of speech or customs. JC also uses
clichés in his portrayal of his women.

1897.1 Mudrick, Marvin. "Conrad: The Reputation and the Work," *Lugano Review*, I, No. 2 (1965), pp. 73–83.

Though JC poses problems for critic and biographer, critics especially have been insensitive to the unevenness of his work. He has been seen as either a political or a psychological writer. He may be an intense observer in "Typhoon" and his own parodist in "The Lagoon." He is much indebted to Flaubert and Dostoevski. *Nostromo* is a novel of extraordinary craftsmanship and at the same time hollow in its conception of human nature. The best JC is the body of novellas written between 1897 and 1902.

1897.2 Mukherjee, Sujit K. "Conrad's *Lord Jim*," *Explicator*, XXIII (January 1965), Item 42.

While JC was in the British merchant marine, he may have heard the name *Patna* from an East Indian sailor; it is the name of a city in Bihar, located approximately three hundred miles from Calcutta.

1897.3 Najder, Zdzislaw. "Polityka w pismach Conrada" (Politics in Conrad's Writings), *NC* (1965), pp. 128–49.

JC's political writings are marked by a tone of dissatisfaction and skepticism, of anger and bitterness. He regarded events in Europe from a Polish point of view, though without mentioning the tragedies of the Insurrections. Though he continued to watch international events which might affect the fate of Poland (e.g., "Autocracy and War"), he lost hope in the political rebirth of Poland. The theme of hopeless loyalty occurs in his letters. After 1914, he believed it possible to regain independent statehood for Poland. English and American critics usually describe JC as a conservative, though he had nothing to conserve: his anti-revolutionary statements expressed a fear of chaos and destruction, and he held a negative attitude towards socialism. In the novels, extreme radicals are nihilists. *Nostromo* is a novel about the political function of money, of its destructive effects on the community and on individuals. *The Secret Agent* is uneven: here JC chose easy subjects for his irony and the nihilists are primitive caricatures. [In Polish.]

1901.1 Ordoñez, Elmer A[lindogan]. "*The Nigger of the Narcissus*: From Manuscript to Print," *Philippine Social Sciences and Humanities Review*, XXX (March 1965), pp. 34–39.

From the autograph manuscript of *The Nigger of the Narcissus* through the serial version to the book form, JC was concerned largely with the sounds of the individual characters' speaking lines, with expanding the text by adding more descriptive details or more direct comment by the author, and with adding, substituting, and eliminating adjectives. The changes from serial to book form are not major stylistic revisions.

1901.2 Orwell, George. *Collected Essays*, ed. by Sonia Orwell and Ian Angus (New York: Harcourt, Brace & World, 1965), III, pp. 387–89.

JC's "great period" was from 1902 to 1915. Of the tales reprinted in the Penguin edition only one, "Typhoon," shows JC at his best. "The Planter of Malata" is not worth the reprinting: it merely illustrates the "vulgar theatricality" which was the reverse side of JC's "feeling for *noblesse oblige.*" "The Partner," marred though it is by the "queer shyness or clumsiness" which caused difficulty for JC in telling a story "straightforwardly in the third person," is "a very fine story." The most memorable things in *The Nigger of the Narcissus* are "certain irrelevant paragraphs" in which the author goes out of his way to express his "reactionary political and social opinions." *The Shadow-Line* is a "goodish" story. Nearly all of JC's charm springs from the fact that he was a European, not an Englishman. This is most obvious in his style of writing, which "even at his best, and perhaps especially at his best, has the air of being a translation." He also has the outlook of a European aristocrat. Another advantage derived from his European background is a "considerable understanding of conspiratorial politics." [Review of *The Nigger of the Narcissus*, "Typhoon," *The Shadow-Line*, "Within the Tides," rpt. from *Observer* (24 June 1945).]

1903.1 Riley, Anthony W. "Notes on Thomas Mann and English and American Literature," *Comparative Literature*, XVII (Winter 1965), pp. 57–72.

Thomas Mann referred frequently to the "virile humor" of English writers: he wrote of JC's "Englishness" ("sein . . . männlisches Talent, sein Engländertum . . . sein fester, kühler und humoristischer Blick"). Aware of the "sad dearth" of humor in German writing, he insisted that he learned much from the typically English "sense of humor," and began to make use of it about 1924. His deep respect for JC as an artist is always coupled with his admiration for the Anglo-Polish writer's liberal ideas and hatred of antidemocratic forces which appeared in any shape. In his foreword to *The Secret Agent*, Mann lists what JC, the Slav, gained by becoming an English writer: "Mass, Vernunft, Skepsis, geistiger Freiheitssinn und ein Humor, dessen ausgesprachen angelsächische Männlichkeit ihn davor bewahrt, jemals ins Bürgerlich-Sentimentale umzuschlagen." This humor he finds throughout *Agent*. He attributes this humorous tone to the spirit of modern art in general. Also, Mann's deep interest in political matters causes him to praise JC's liberalism and humanistic ideals.

1903.2 Rivera, Ruben O. "The 'Silver of the Mine': Conrad's *Nostromo*," *Diliman Review*, XIII (April 1965), pp. 199–214.

The strong structural dislocation about two-thirds of the way through *Nostromo* suggests that there are two plots in the novel: the story of Charles Gould, "material interests," and political turmoil in Costaguana; and the story of Nostromo's involvement with "the silver of the mine." Each story "resonates" in the other and rounds out the other's full significance. The "silver of the mine" weaves together the active forces of *Nostromo* and also symbolizes all the "material interests" at stake in Sulaco. Charles Gould sees, above all, the silver as a token of his desperate stratagem to win ascendancy for justice, peace, and decency in the land; but his failure leaves the reader with the sense that the cycle of intrigue and treachery will begin again. JC makes it clear that any effort to build the spiritual on the merely material is doomed to failure. Just as Gould's personality shrivels up under his misconception, so does Nostromo's become ultimately crushed by his "ill-gotten lucre."

1912.1 Slack, Robert C. "A Comment on Recent Victorian Scholarship," *PCTE (Pennsylvania College of Teachers of English Bulletin)*, No. 12 (December 1965), pp. 19–30.

The annual bibliographies of recent Victorian scholarship which appeared in *Victorian Studies, 1960–1964*, reveal that twelve writers have attracted the most attention. Three of them, George Bernard Shaw, William Butler Yeats, and JC should not be considered because they are not "true" Victorians. [One wonders what a "true" Victorian is.]

1914.1 Spivack, Charlotte K. "The Journey to Hell: Satan, the Shadow, and the Self," *Centennial Review of Arts and Sciences*, IX (Fall 1965), pp. 420–37.

[Spivack treats JC in one paragraph only, offering virtually no critical reading and giving a simplistic plot outline of "Heart of Darkness."]

1917.1 Tanner, Tony. "Conrad's *Victory*: An Answer to Schopenhauer," *London Magazine*, V (July 1965), pp. 85–90.

The many parallels between *Victory* and Villiers de L'Isle Adam's *Axel* suggest a common interest in the pessimism of Schopenhauer. However, whereas this pessimism is sentimentally treated in the ending of *Axel*, it is exposed as inadequate in *Victory*. Heyst questions the reality of the world but is nevertheless drawn toward the world by Lena and must suffer the consequences. Heyst, however, is unfit to recognize and deal with evil and ends doubting even Lena's love. Yet without her he cannot exist. The only victory is perhaps Lena's triumph over evil and negation.

1918.1 Trilling, Lionel. "On the Teaching of Modern Literature," *Beyond Culture* (New York: Viking, 1965), pp. 19–21.

JC's "Heart of Darkness" follows the "line" of Blake and Nietzsche, whether JC read them or not. This "very great work," though never lacking "the admiration it deserves," has not been confronted "in an explicit way" as to its "strange and terrible message of ambivalence toward the life of civilization." Kurtz, for example, yields to the "devilish baseness" of the primitive life, and yet Marlow does not suppose that Kurtz is "anything but a hero of the spirit." We are not even certain what his cry, "The horror! The horror!" refers to—to the approach of death or to his "experiencing of savage life." Whichever it is, to Marlow the fact that Kurtz could utter this cry at the point of death, while Marlow himself can know it only as "weary grayness," marks the difference between the ordinary man and a hero of the spirit. This is the essence of the modern belief about the artist, "the man who goes down into that hell which is the historical beginning of the human soul, a beginning . . . preferring the reality of this hell to the bland lies of the civilization that has overlaid it."

1919.1 Wasserstrom, William (ed.). "Introduction," *The Modern Short Novel* (New York: Holt, Rinehart & Winston, 1965), pp. v–xi.

[This collection of stories includes *The Shadow-Line*, but the introduction mentions neither it nor JC.]

1924.1 Williams, George Walton. "Conrad's 'The Lagoon,'" *Explicator*, XXIII (March 1965), Item 51.

There is no apparent contradiction in the opening paragraph of "The Lagoon": the canoe moves upstream (inland and westward) against the river, which flows eastward. [A response to one of F. A. D.'s questions in "Conrad's 'The Lagoon,'" *Explicator*, IX (May 1951), Query 7.]

1924.2 Wirpsza, Witold. "*Smuga cienia*" (*The Shadow-Line*), *Gra Znaczen* (Play of Meanings), (Warsaw: Panstwowy Instytut Wydawniczy, 1965), pp. 16–23.

The narrative of *The Shadow-Line* causes questions of responsibility and authority and of whether JC's problem of authority is merely one element in a much greater metaphor, that of the "shadow-line," without which there is no conscious life. [In Polish.]

1924.3 Zabel, Morton Dauwen. "Joseph Conrad," *Lord Jim* (New York: Harper & Row, 1965), pp. v–xi.

[A biographical sketch and a list of JC's major writings. Of little value.]

1966

1924.4 Allen, Jerry. "Conrad's Facts," *New Statesman* (London), LXXII (23 September 1966), p. 432.

Jerry Allen argues that Denis Donoghue "makes serious errors of fact" when he writes that Norman Sherry in *Conrad's Eastern World* has cleared up all speculation concerning the facts of the "incidents, people and places" in JC's eastern fiction. Allen points out that these "facts" were available prior to Sherry's book and are to be found in both volumes of her JC biography *The Thunder and the Sunshine* (1958) and *The Sea Years of Joseph Conrad* (1965) and in her article, "Conrad's River," *Columbia University Forum*, V (Winter 1962), pp. 29–35. [In response to Denis Donoghue, "Conrad's Facts," *New Statesman* (London, 26 August 1966), p. 291 (C, I, No. 1934). A missing link in the history of Jerry Allen's war with other JC critics (C, I, No. 1977).]

1927.1 Armitage, C. M. "The Location of Lord Jim's Patusan," *N&Q*, XIII (November 1966), pp. 409–10.

While preserving the artistically appropriate air of mystery surrounding Jim in *Lord Jim*, JC actually provided at various places in the novel enough details to point conclusively to northwest Sumatra as the location of Patusan.

1927.2 Baldi, Sergio. "Lettere di Conrad" (Conrad's Letters), *L'Approdo Letterario*, 34, N.S. (1966), pp. 122–23.

It appears from JC's letters, most of which are complementary to the novels, that the novelist considered art as an instrument for a deeper understanding of reality, the only means for attaining truth. Action appears as a way of redemption, not so much of a specific guilt as of the human condition itself. Other letters, instead, are much more revealing of JC the man and his political ideas. The general portrait is that of a respectable, though pathetic, English gentleman. [Review of *Epistolario di Joseph Conrad*, ed. by Alessandro Serpieri (Milano: Bompiani, 1966).] [In Italian.]

1927.3 Benson, Donald R. "'Heart of Darkness' The Grounds of Civilization in an Alien Universe," *TSLL*, VII (Winter 1966), pp. 339–47.

In the light of Victorian preoccupation with the issues of naturalism, evolution, and colonial expansion, "Heart of Darkness" needs to be seen as centering as much on civilization in an alien universe as on the psychological journey within. JC is searching for the origins and essence of civilization, the distinctly human, in a dark, indifferent universe; he is searching for any possible reality in civilization. The story opens with the suggestion that civilization carries with it a corrupting force while being at the same time a necessary stay for the mass of men. Idealism and work, while partially maintaining the human, cannot answer the question of the real essence of civilization. "The most essential human capacity given a name in this story is 'restraint.'" Marlow is put in the midst of the jungle and the primeval while being separated from the outer defenses of civilization, but Kurtz is the real test case. He, the civilized man, has been exposed to the solitude of the jungle; he has lost restraint; but the crux of his final moral victory is that he has regained a vantage point from which to judge his lack of restraint and his indulgence. Although little humanity remains in him and his capacity for corruption is vast, "this residue is irreducible and in it Conrad finds the essence he has sought."

1928.1 Bojarski, Edmund A. "Conrad in Cardiff: Impressions 1885–1896," *Anglo-Welsh Review*, XV (Summer 1966), pp. 57–63.

JC made three visits to the home of Jozef Spiridion (Kliszczewski), in Cardiff. The connection was initiated by another Pole, Komorowski, who requested JC to repay a sum of one pound to Spiridion, who had aided Komorowski when a friendless youth in Cardiff. Spiridion's grandson, Hubert, recalls JC on that first visit in June, 1885, as a man whose poor English pronunciation, distinguished manners, and appearance seemed incompatible with his profession of seaman. "A few years later," JC stayed in the grandson's home, a guest of the father, Joseph Spiridion. At this time, his language had improved and his appearance was conformable to English custom. The third and last visit, in December, 1896, took place after JC had become a writer of fiction and was at work on *The Nigger of the Narcissus*. Joseph Spiridion, Jozef's son, who had earlier lent JC ten pounds, gave JC the use of a room in which to write. At the Polish Christmas Eve table, the host appealed to JC to write of matters Polish, but JC vehemently rejected doing this, claiming he would lose his public and his livelihood. JC left Cardiff at the end of December. The *Western Mail* for 1 January 1897 published a short interview [quoted here] which angered JC because it disclosed his Polish background.

1929.1 Bojarski, Edmund A. "One Man's Conrad," *ELT*, IX, No. 3 (1966), pp. 169–71.

Only a Pole, and one "thoroughly steeped in the language and culture" of JC's homeland can understand and help others to understand the "deeper reaches" of JC's works. Zdzislaw Najder, himself a Pole, has done well in this kind of undertaking in his collection of essays, *Nad Conradem* (On Conrad), Warsaw: Panstwowy Instytut Wydawniczy (State Publishing Institute), 1965. Najder's grasp of JC's "philosophy" or "outlook on life" consists of "the acceptance of the tragedy of life while at the same time rejecting pessimism." [Comments briefly on each of Najder's eleven essays.]

1929.2 Bolt, Sydney. *The Right Response: Notes on Teaching English in Further Education* (London: Hutchinson Educational, 1966), pp. 28, 58, 73–78.

Read as a parable, *The Shadow-Line* reveals for each stage in the narrator's ordeal a corresponding progress of every man who has gone so far. [Explains how one teacher taught this story to a class.]

1929.3 Boyles, John. "Joseph Conrad's *The Rover*," *Use of English*, XVIII (Winter 1966), pp. 124–28.

Although *The Rover* is the work of an old man in that the events are seen at a distance, it is concerned with some of JC's favorite tragic themes, particularly that of involvement or withdrawal. Peyrol, the elderly hero, is doomed as soon as he begins to take an interest in the unfortunate Arlette; for her sake he takes upon himself the dangerous mission proposed by her lover, and she is the main reason for his sacrifice at the end. There is, though, a secondary reason: Arlette and her progress to life are in some ways symbolic of France, Peyrol's country, to which he is highly patriotic. France, like Arlette, had lived through some very difficult times and had to come to terms with this experience and make a new start. *Rover* is not particularly complex; JC's method is to place attention on a character in a particular situation and then to shift to the past to offer part of the explanation and to move thus from one character to another.

1929.4 Brady, Charles A. "From Broceliande to the Forest Primeval: The New-World Quest of the Chevalier Chateaubriand," *Emerson Society Quarterly*, No. 42 (First Quarter, 1966), pp. 17–31.

JC, who was James Fenimore Cooper's "disciple," like him "viewed Nature as a giant facsimile of human nature; irrational, dangerous, unfathomable, splendid, 'a rude touchstone, which often reveals traits that would have lain buried and unsuspected in civilized life.'" This view of nature appears throughout JC's Malayan novels.

1931.1 Clemens, Cyril. "A Chat with Joseph Conrad," *Hobbies—The Magazine for Collectors* (January 1966), pp. 85, 88, 92; rpt. *CON*, II, No. 2 (Winter 1969–70), pp. 97–103.

During the early twenties, Hugh Walpole took Cyril Clemens to tea with JC and his wife at "Oswalds," their home in Kent. There, JC observed that he thought of *Lord Jim* as his favorite book; that he found it necessary to write each work "about six times"; that he was not a writer of sea stories since he insisted mainly on effect through his characters; that a writer's proficiency became more than mere skill: it became "almost an inspiration" which is art; that he admired Stephen Crane's *The Red Badge of Courage* and his *Whilomville Stories*; and that he liked especially Mark Twain's *Life on the Mississippi*.

1932.1 D'Avanzo, Mario. "Conrad's Motley as an Organizing Metaphor in 'Heart of Darkness,'" *College Language Association Bulletin*, IX (March 1966), pp. 289–91.

In addition to seeing the Russian in "Heart of Darkness" as the fool "who completes the 'court' of King Kurtz," one may see him, in the context of the novel, as linking the incongruous and absurd presence of the fool to the "equally checkered, disorganized and contrarious presences" of all the European countries in the geographical heart of darkness. In tailoring the Russian in the motley colors of the map of Africa, JC seemingly creates the figure of the "capitalistic everyman," a composite of "fragmented, idiotic Europeans"; the perversions of Europe's aims are dramatized in JC's motley fool.

1936.1 Fleishman, Avrom. "The Criticism of Quality: Notes for a Theory of Style," *University Review* (Kansas City), XXXIII (Autumn 1966), pp. 3–10.

It is possible to see elements of texture or style in JC's works as independent aesthetic values, as ends of the work of art, and not only as correlates of meaning, as evidenced in *The Secret Agent*. Sensory qualities often introduce a freedom and spontaneity unrelated to structure or meaning, many instances of which occur in this novel. The *red*-ness of the wheels of the butcher boy's cart are arresting because the "suchness" or "firstness" of the quality red indicates a pure freedom rather than a tie to a thematic freedom. Vital qualities often relate to a moment of human perception where man fleetingly discovers the "ultimate impenetrableness" of other human beings or modes of being. Such an incident is the Assistant Commissioner's glimpse of the girl in the Soho restaurant. Rhythmical qualities often exist for the mere luxuriance of their own potency, as with the repetition of the word "secret." Pattern qualities involving size and order can also be qualitative, as seen in the triangles of Verloc and the circles of Stevie. Physical qualities can create a presence and an evocation of feeling outside the limits of structure and moral or symbolic overtones, as in the "curious" atmosphere of fatness in *Agent.*

1936.2 Fleming, Thomas J. "The Novel of the Future," *America*, CXIV (7 May 1966), pp. 654–55, 658.

The novel of the eighteenth and nineteenth centuries deals with historical and sociological issues; but because recent nonfiction has "deprived" the novel of these two functions it must "deal not simply with ideas but with values, with a vision of life." There is a tradition from which the present-day writers may draw. It is composed of such writers as Hardy, Kafka, Mann, Camus, Gide, and most of all JC, who "achieved [the] greatest triumph" of this tradition in *Victory.*

1936.3 Fraser, G. S. "*Lord Jim*: The Romance of Irony," *Critical Quarterly*, VIII (Autumn 1966), pp. 231–41.

JC's heroes, unlike Kipling's, are united by a sense of common isolation, of "loneliness calling to loneliness." JC's world is therefore largely an interior world: all things happen, for example, to Lord Jim, but the real drama and excitement of the story is, for JC, what happens inside him. But the reader is never "inside" Jim; he sees him almost entirely through the eyes of his skeptical protector, Marlow, who is himself probing but is finally baffled with Jim's inner life, which is deeply concerned with "honour" and "romance." JC himself, like Jim, was "excessively romantic," and both he and Marlow know, like Stein, that there is no final cure for this condition but death. Since the inward pain Marlow and Stein always feel reaches out in sympathy to the inward pain in Jim, JC's novel is not an immature work but a masterpiece.

1936.4 Fricker, Robert. *Der Moderne Englische Roman* (The Modern English Novel), (Göttingen: Vandenhoeck & Ruprecht, 1966), 2nd rev. ed., pp. 54–75.

[An introduction to JC's life and works; the usual themes: JC and the sea, JC's early difficulties with the English language, JC as a novelist of the "strong situation," the "dark powers" and the "moral idea."] If JC's philosophy resembles Hardy's, his technique resembles Henry James's. [In German.]

1936.5 Friedman, Alan. "Joseph Conrad: 'the end, such as it is,'" *The Turn of the Novel* (New York: Oxford University Press, 1966), pp. 75–105.

During the latter part of the nineteenth century and the early part of the twentieth, the English novel moved gradually from a closed form of experience to an open form, the "open" pattern reflecting and conveying a new attitude toward the process and goals of experience in life. In *Almayer's Folly* (1895), JC wants to close off the expanding moral agony of his central character in the custom of traditional novels, but he cannot do so: he allows the two sources of Almayer's frustration, his failure to obtain money and the nonwhiteness of his half-caste daughter, to lead to his death. In *Nostromo*, the Capataz's unthinkable corruption dominates the novel and becomes emblematic, a pattern for the corrupted experience of other people and of the entire country. Nostromo, (*nostr'uomo* in Italian) and "Ourman," is the hero of the secular morality of the work. The novel leads toward "a vague connection of silver with love and corruption" and ends with the corruption of love. As Nostromo's balance goes, so goes the entire nation's: both decide to "grow rich slowly." And once dead, Nostromo's domination continues: the process which the novel depicts throughout, the corruption of the spirit by "material interests," is still continuing and expanding. The form of *Nostromo* is thus that of a malignancy and also an example of the slow turn of the novel.

1937.1 Geddes, Gary. "Clearing the Jungle: The Importance of Work in Conrad," *Queen's Quarterly*, LXXIII (Winter 1966), pp. 559–72.

The importance of work, regardless of the nature of that work, is a recurring theme in JC's fiction. As a writer, JC regarded work as a metaphor for art. Work provides the mass of men with a sense of common destiny, a devotion to right practice, a sense of honor, and an idealism that is realistically based. His work ethic is similar to that of Carlyle, who asserts its spiritual nature. For both Carlyle and JC, work provides a means by which thoughts may be structured and fellowship established in a demanding universe. Trouble begins when the proper work of a community is interrupted, as it is in *The Nigger of the Narcissus* when the vagabond Donkin interferes with the regular functioning of the crew. But work has personal as well as social implications: "An Outpost of Progress" and "Heart of Darkness" explore the fate of the common man deprived of work and purpose. The importance of work as fidelity to duty is portrayed in several pieces of fiction, notably in "Typhoon," in which MacWhirr is dominant. Like the characters portrayed in his fiction, JC devoted himself to his appointed task, art, which he believed capable of "clearing the jungle, which is the human heart."

1937.2 Gerber, H[elmut] E., and Philip Armato. "Bibliography, News, and Notes," *ELT*, IX, No. 4 (1966), pp. 212–31.

[Includes unabstracted references to "all pertinent articles and reviews we have published in Volume IX, No. 1–4, as well as abstracts of items published elsewhere on the authors we have been listing regularly." Bruce Teets (Perdue University, Indianapolis Campus) is "completing a thorough annotated bibliography of works about Joseph Conrad."]

1938.1 Gillon, Adam, and Ludwik Krzyzanowski (eds.). *Introduction to Modern Polish Literature: An Anthology of Fiction and Poetry* (New York: Twayne Publishers; London: Rapp & Whiting, 1966), pp. 17, 29.

JC pointed out that the Poles, unlike the Slavs, are "Western, with an absolute comprehension of all Western modes of thought." All important Western novels have been translated into Polish, among them JC's works, by Anela Zagorska.

1940.1 Gorlier, Claudio. "Introduzione" (Introduction), *Gli Eredi—La Natura di un delitto* (The Inheritors—The Nature of a Crime), (Milan: Bompiani, 1966), pp. 7–17.

The Inheritors is a political satire of contemporary events and people and an allegory of the exploitation of the Congo that JC was to develop with better results in "Heart of Darkness." *The Nature of a Crime*, written when the collaboration of JC and Ford was coming to an end, is an exercise in style and structure which should be read for its analytical qualities in relation to *The Good Soldier*. [In Italian.]

1940.2 Hamer, Douglas. "Conrad's *Chance*: A Location," *N&Q*, XIII (November 1966), pp. 411–12.

In *Nor They Understand* (Brisbane: Jacaranda Press, 1966), Dr. L. B. Winter identifies the riverside inn in *Chance*, Part I, chapter 1, as the old Tillbury Hotel, and the creek, Part II, chapter 1, up which Powell ran his cutter, as the Hanengore Creek, one of three linked creeks on the Essex coast at the mouth of the Thames, 4 m. NE, Shoeburyness.

1941.1 Hemmings, F. W. J. *Emile Zola* (Oxford: At the Clarendon Press, 1966), p. 203.

It "can scarcely be doubted" that JC modeled the Professor, the "obsessional" manufacturer of dynamite in *The Secret Agent*, on the militant socialist Souvarine in Zola's *Germinal* (1884–85). The concluding words of JC's novels are a recognizable echo of a passage in Zola's book, describing Souvarine's departure in the dusk after he has caused the inundation of the coal mine.

1941.2 Hepburn, James (ed.). *Letters of Arnold Bennett. Vol. I: Letters to J. B. Pinker* (London: Oxford University Press, 1966), pp. 3, 23–26, 28, 106, 118, 173, 192–93, 217, 284, 288, 289–90n, 303, 317, 406.

For many years, JC's affairs were managed by his close personal friend, J. B. Pinker, the well known literary agent who for a quarter of a century advanced considerable sums of money to JC. When Pinker died in 1922, JC wrote that he felt "quite overpowered by this blow of fate." Arnold Bennett believed that Frank Harris was a genius, "comparable to Conrad at his best," and he thought very highly of JC's play, *The Secret Agent*.

1946.1 Kerf, R[ené]. "Symbol Hunting in Conradian Land," *Revue des Languages Vivantes*, XXXII (1966), pp. 266–77.

In JC's fiction, many critics wrongly assign symbolic meaning without considering the context. Examples are W. B. Stein's articles on Buddha metaphors in "Heart of Darkness" and R. O. Evans's study of the mythical descent into the underworld analogue to the same story. Ted E. Boyle in *Symbol and Meaning in the Fiction of Joseph Conrad* overemphasizes the nails in *The Nigger of the Narcissus*, the butterfly in *Lord Jim*, Marlow's abandonment and gift of his shoes in "Heart of Darkness," and the erroneous justification of JC's unrealistic writing in *Under Western Eyes* on the grounds that caricature of the revolutionaries is symbolic.

1948.1 Larsen, Golden L. "The Contemporaneity of Joyce Cary: A Comparison with Joseph Conrad," *The Dark Descent: Social Change and Moral Responsibility in the Novels of Joyce Cary* (New York: Roy Publishers, 1966), pp. 1–21.

Casual remarks about Joyce Cary's treatment of the African scene as compared with JC's appear to place Cary as a follower of JC. There are, however, differences between the two writers, including diverging philosophical orientations, differences in their respective conceptions of the limits of knowledge—their conceptions of the real. Cary's novels differ in their ideas from those of JC, and this difference is a mark of his contemporaneity and perhaps of his significance. Henry James thought that JC in *Chance* left the impression of "a wandering, circling, yearning imaginative *faculty*"; E. M. Forster considered JC elusive in his general statements about the universe, and F. R. Leavis found serious lapses in JC's works into the vague and indefinite. Cary, however, was more clearly concerned with communicating his "idea" than in solving technical problems. In their use of symbols the two writers differ significantly also: in general, while JC's symbols are expressive and suggestive, Cary's symbols are delimiting and definitive. JC's attempt to solve the problem posed by naturalism resulted in a retreat into the self, an obliteration of time in order to partake of the eternal; JC is thus typical of many great novelists of the twentieth century. His closed system is superseded by the open system of Cary, who is, then, JC's follower.

1948.2 Lass, Abraham H. (ed.). "*Lord Jim*," *A Student's Guide to 50 British Novels* (New York: Washington Square Press, 1966; rpt. 1978), pp. 219–26.

Lord Jim is a tragedy of a man who, like Hamlet, is indecisive, although he does have the potential for noble action. As such a man, Jim can never face reality nor accept his own limitations. His poor judgment at the end brings on him his final catastrophe. [Contains a list of major characters, a plot summary, and a biographical sketch.]

1948.3 Lodge, David. *Language of Fiction: Essays in Criticism and Verbal Analysis of the English Novel* (London: Routledge and Kegan Paul; New York: Columbia University Press, 1966), pp. 20, 27–29, 82, 83, 85, 121, 243, 263n, 267, 270, 274.

JC demonstrated that a work of art cannot be successfully achieved if its medium is misused, and he exemplified in theory and practice that form and content are inseparable, that style is not a mere decoration of subject matter but the very medium in which the subject is turned into art. The intentional repetition of key-words in novels may affect the nature of the work and the reader's response to it, as seen in JC's use of *darkness* in "Heart of Darkness," *youth* in "Youth," and *silver* and *material interests* in *Nostromo*. The important "moderns" of English literature were, and still are, James, Joyce, Lawrence, Forster, Virginia Woolf, and JC.

1953.1 Markovic, Vida. "The Emerging Character," *Northwest Review*, VIII (Summer 1966), pp. 80–97.

According to JC, Jim suffers from "the acute consciousness of lost honour." And that is all; *Lord Jim* revolves around it. The entire book is the author's attempt to explain Jim, not as a special person but as "one of us." Jim has a more refined sensibility than others; he "carries on his back the burden of humanity." Because he has no courage to look into himself, there is a "profound gap in his life, a split in his being." His incomplete existence prevents his admitting the existence of a dark side to his own personality. He is immature in refusing to grow out of his youthful daydreams, but he is human in his refusal to accept anything less than a "complete, integral dream." He dies to prove that he is true to his ideal of behavior.

1953.2 Maud, Ralph. "The Plain Tale of 'Heart of Darkness,'" *Humanities Association Bulletin*, XVII (Autumn 1966), pp. 13–17.

Kurtz is motivated by the desire to be extraordinary and thus must bring out of Africa an exceptional cargo of ivory. He finds the civilizing charge of the International Society to be a hypocritical contradiction to the orders given to the trader. "Exterminate all the brutes!" is the logical and horrible outcome of such policies.

1953.3 McCann, Charles J., and Victor Comerchero. "Setting as a Key to the Structure and Meaning of *Nostromo*," *Research Studies*, XXXIV (June 1966), pp. 66–84.

Nostromo is the embodiment of the author's intention—to isolate the major forces to which men give their allegiance and also to give form to a "comprehensive, pessimistic view of the emerging modern world." By the use of setting—by linking Gould to the San Tome gorge, Viola to Higuerota, Decoud to the Gulf, and Nostromo to all of them— JC makes the individual conflicts of the characters representative of larger social, political, and economic forces. And by associating at one point or another all of the principal images with Nostromo, JC makes the capataz the common center of all the thematic concerns. *Nostromo* is organized on two principles: (1) a radial grouping of characters by association, an establishment of conceptual relationships for the group as a whole, and (2) cyclic repetition, a consideration of history as nothing more than a series of monotonous variations on a tragic theme. In the final sense, Nostromo is the key to the meaning of the book. Gradually he realizes what he calls his betrayal, and JC finds his men and women without exception guilty of the "highest vanity"—self-idealization. Remarkable is the brilliant way in which JC recreates the "great disaster" of the country while still suggesting the disaster of the private individual. The calamity that overtakes Nostromo together with the particularized calamities of the other characters symbolize man's fate: "Life is unremitting conflict, and ultimately, as dramatized by Nostromo's fate, defeat." But JC's pessimism is "magnificent" because he charges events with a "grand, fated, almost mythical quality," so that the characters achieve almost epic proportions.

1953.4 Miller, J. Hillis. "Some Implications of Form in Victorian Fiction," *Comparative Literature Studies*, III, No. 2 (1966), (Literature and Religion: Special Section II), pp. 109–18.

JC's importance stems from his nihilism, arising from two different types of nothingness: the emptiness of space created by Nietzsche's concept of the death of God and the emptiness of human consciousness. The final step in the development of this Victorian concept, JC's contribution was to reveal the emptiness that results when man kills God and creates the universe subject to man's thought.

1954.1 Moore, Doris Langley. *E. Nesbit: A Biography* (Philadelphia: Chilton Books, 1966), p. 221.

JC was a contributor to *The Neolith*, co-edited by E. Nesbit, whom JC visited on occasion.

1954.2 Morris, Arthur Robert. *Barron's Simplified Approach to Victory: Joseph Conrad* (Woodbury, New York: Barron's Educational Series, 1966).

[Contains "An Introduction to Joseph Conrad," describes his work as being symbolic, ambiguous, realistic, and profound, and maintains that JC both sympathizes with and criticizes unfavorably the characters who are failures in his stories. Explains some characteristics of *Victory* and contains an introduction "To the Reader," a "Chronological Chart," a list of "Characters of Special Significance," "Plot Synopses and Critical Commentaries," "Study Guide Questions," and "Selected Criticism," including short excerpts from such critics as Ramon Fernandez, Montgomery Belgion, M. C. Bradbrook, E. K. Brown, Morton D. Zabel, Richard Curle, Albert J. Guerard, Jocelyn Baines, and F. R. Leavis. Leaves much to be desired for a book in an "educational series."]

1957.1 O'Connor, William Van. *Joyce Cary* (New York: Columbia University Press [Columbia Essays in Modern Literature 16], 1966), pp. 12, 16–17, 19.

When Cary had published his first trilogy, he was said to belong in the company of Dickens, Hardy, and JC. One of his manuscripts, "Daventry," is clearly related to some of JC's African stories and perhaps to *Lord Jim*. Daventry's "trek" is somewhat like JC's journey into his own soul and consciousness. *Aissa Saved* contains the British philosophy of "Let's-get-on-with-the-job," or JC's conviction that simple virtues such as duty and self-respect "keep society going" and help "redress wrongs." *The African Witch* is Cary's attempt to depict a chaotic state like that in *Nostromo*.

1957.2 Ohmann, Richard. "Literature as Sentences," *College English,* XXVII (January 1966), pp. 261–67.

When literature is broken down into sentences, an added insight is gained. The final sentence of "The Secret Sharer" expanded into thirteen sentences adds to the semantic development of the story. The final sentence carries out a completion of the meaning suggested in the first few sentences of the story.

1958.1 Owen, Lewis G. "Joseph Conrad: Dreamer of the Eastern Seas," *Sea Breezes,* XL (January 1966), pp. 7–10.

JC's books are classic fiction. Although the novelist wrote extensively about the sea, he did so only because he knew it at first hand. What is immediately evident in his work is his exalted attitude toward duty. His emphasis on verisimilitude is also important, and his use of his own experience serves to create a powerful verisimilitude. It is probable, too, that he has a message for the modern world.

1960.1 Perniola, Mario. "Joseph Conrad," *Il Metaromanzo* (The Metanovel), (Milan: Silva, 1966), pp. 55–65.

JC's technical evolution goes from third person objective narration in *Almayer's Folly* and *An Outcast of the Islands* (and partially in *The Nigger of the Narcissus*) to first person memoir-like narration in *The Arrow of Gold* and *The Rover.* The pivot of this evolution is, however, to be found in *Lord Jim* and *Chance.* Reality vanishes in JC's novels: the gratuitous and "proteiform" quality of reality is one of the characteristics of metanovels, with the crumbling of the realistic conventions of the naturalistic novel. [In Italian.]

1961.1 Rapin, René (ed.). *Lettres de Joseph Conrad à Marguerite Poradowska* (Geneva: Librairie Droz, 1966).

Madame Poradowska (1848–1937) was a prolific Polish novelist at the turn of the century. She lost her husband at age forty-two, at which time she met JC, who called her his "aunt." [The collection of letters consists of 110 letters in French from JC to Madame Poradowska. They were previously published in English by John A. Gee and Paul J. Sturm (1940). This French edition includes fragments of two letters from Madame Poradowska to JC, dated 1890 and 1891, and a letter from JC's French translator, H. D. Davray, dated 1908. The first ninety-two letters cover the period 1890–1895, a crucial time in JC's life. The letters are as nearly as possible in the order in which they were written. Several are reproduced in facsimile. The appendices include a genealogical chart, an inventory of the Yale collection of JC's French letters, and a selected bibliography of Madame Poradowska's works. Rapin's study reveals that although JC seems to have spoken and written French idiomatically, his spelling and grammar were often in error, more than Jean-Aubry makes it appear in his *Hommage à Joseph Conrad* and in his edition of the *Lettres Francaises*, in which he corrects many of JC's errors. [A careful study of JC's French.] [In French.]

1963.1 Resink, G. J. "Samburan Encantada," *English Studies*, XLVII (February 1966), pp. 35–44.

A comparison of Melville's sketches published as *The Encantadas: Or Enchanted Islands* with JC's *Victory* reveals many similarities which suggest that JC had read Melville's *The Piazza Tales*. Axel Heyst and Morrison are "enchanted," and Heyst is called "Enchanted Heyst"; Lena, the only white woman in Samburan, resembles the only woman mentioned by name in *The Encantadas*; and Samburan and the "Round Rock" lie close to the equator. There is also evidence that JC had read Albert S. Bickmore [*Travels in the Indian Archipelago* (1868)], a widely read contemporary of Melville. *An Outcast of the Islands* also supplies evidence of JC's knowledge of Melville. JC clearly familiarized himself with the region he wrote about in addition to relying upon his personal experience.

1964.1 Sale, Richard B., Jr. "Conrad's Stein and the Categorical Imperative," *Conference of College Teachers of English of Texas*, XXXI (September 1966), p. 27.

Stein of *Lord Jim* has no flaw, and he is the main spokesman for JC. The best explication of Stein's advice about Jim is that of Robert Penn Warren in his well-known Preface to *Nostromo*.

1965.1 Scholes, Robert, and Robert Kellogg. *The Nature of Narrative* (New York: Oxford University Press, 1966), pp. 54, 203, 251, 260, 263–64, 266.

One of the major trends in characterization in twentieth-century novels is away from an attempt to penetrate the individual psyche and toward a focus on the apprehension of "impressions" which have no absolute validity as facts. This preponderant technique appears in such "narrator-dominated" works as *The Good Soldier*, *Remembrance of Things Past*, *Absalom, Absalom!*, the *Alexandria Quartet*, and JC's *Lord Jim*. JC, in *Victory*, uses point of view as Flaubert does in *Madame Bovary*. In *Jim*, JC uses also a variation of the basic device of the eye-witness narrator, that of the unreliable eye-witness. In *Nostromo*, he takes advantage of the *histor*, the narrator as inquirer, not a character in narrative, not exactly the author, but a persona, a projection of the author's empirical values.

1965.2 Schultheiss, Thomas. "Lord Hamlet and Lord Jim," *PolR*, XI (Autumn 1966), pp. 101–33.

In Stein, JC portrayed two qualities that Hamlet admires in Horatio: submission to fortune and the equilibrium between judgment and emotion. Like Thaddeus Bobrowski, Stein advises Jim both to follow a dream and to accept the destructive element of reality outside and inside himself. Man must recognize the existence of passion within himself and express it, not suppress it, as Jim and Hamlet unhealthily do. Many parallels of action, character, and wording suggest that JC wrote *Lord Jim* with a reading of *Hamlet* fresh in his mind.

1966.1 Serpieri, Alessandro. "Introduzione" (Introduction), *Epistolario di Joseph Conrad* (Conrad's Letters), (Milan: Bompiani, 1966), pp. 5–31.

Every aspect of JC is found in the *Epistolario di Joseph Conrad*, from the most insignificant idiosyncracy to the defense of JC's art and his narrative method, from "ironic half smiles to bitter discontent." There are in addition many seminal ideas to be developed in his narrative: anecdotes, political discussions, doubts, and vast shadowy areas. Living isolated deep in the country, he found letters to be his only means of communication. Apart from formal letters, JC wrote hastily, usually at night after a hard day's work. If he had not written the author's notes to his works, which repeat most of the information he had already imparted in his letters but which cannot be considered a diary even though they are more valuable than *A Personal Record*, we might consider the letters as the most important source of understandings of his writings. In the first period of his writing career, JC's most important letters were written to Garnett, his critical guarantor, and to Graham, his moral warrantor, to whom he opened himself as he did not do to any other person. His few letters to Ford reveal much, but only about artistic matters. In his later years, he wrote an increasing number of letters to such persons as Galsworthy, Clifford, Curle, and others. JC's letters enable us to retrace his spiritual development from his original romantic impulse to isolation, skepticism, and disillusionment. [A perceptive, closely reasoned article, with 737 bio-bibliographical critical notes appended, pp. 339–83.] [In Italian.]

1968.1 Smaridge, Noah. *Master Mariner: The Adventurous Life of Joseph Conrad* (New York: Hawthorn Books, 1966; Tadworth, Surrey: World's Work, 1967).

Little has been written about JC for young people, but the filmed version of *Lord Jim* has created an interest in the story of "his strange childhood, his adventurous youth, and the sea experiences which eventually turned him into a writer of classic sea stories." [This "Hawthorn Junior Biography" is inaccurate and should be avoided. Critical evaluations of JC's work may be represented by a comment on *The Nigger of the Narcissus*: "In the book, James Wait is of no great importance."]

1968.2 Smith, David R. "Conrad's Manifesto: Preface to a Career," *Conrad's Manifesto, Preface to a Career: The History of the Preface to The Nigger of the Narcissus with Facsimiles of the Manuscripts Edited with an Essay by David R. Smith* (Philadelphia: The Philip H. and A. S. W. Rosenbach Foundation, 1966), pp. 47–79.

With *The Nigger of the Narcissus*, JC finally became a writer; he repeated a number of times in later years that he would "stand or fall" by this work. The preface to *Nigger* justifies a career. In it, the author states the philosophical or intellectual aims of art and also insists upon the necessity of craftsmanship. These two aspects meet to become meaning: JC describes the entire process as a symbolic solidarity which links the dead to the living and the living to the unborn. Writing the preface was hard work: JC had to bring his initial rhetoric under control and to marshal and organize his arguments, as the holographic first draft reveals. Above all, he had to unite form and content, a difficult process for him. Many of his changes are caused by his comparatively new language, English. This holograph is very valuable as a revelation of JC's actual practice of writing. After the first appearance of the preface in 1897, JC had to wait more than sixteen years to see the novel published with its preface—with, in fact, two prefaces—the second being "To My Readers in America," which introduced both the novel and the original preface.

1968.3 Smith, David R. (ed). *Conrad's Manifesto, Preface to a Career: The History to the Preface to The Nigger of the Narcissus with Facsimiles of the Manuscripts Edited with an Essay by David R. Smith* (Philadelphia: The Philip H. and A. W. S. Rosenbach Foundation, 1966).

Contents, abstracted under date of first publication: "Foreword" (1966); "Conrad's Manifesto: Preface to a Career" (1966).

By JC and not abstracted: "Facsimiles of the Manuscripts: 'The Preface of the N of the N' and 'To My Readers in America'"; "Transcriptions of the Manuscripts: 'The Preface to the N of the N," "To My Readers in America," and "The 'Hythe' Preface" "as it appears in the pamphlet Conrad had printed in 1902 by J. Lovick, High Street, Hythe, and Cheriton." [A boxed, limited edition of this work, with a woodcut portrait of JC by Leonard Baskin "printed from the block."]

1968.4 Smith, David R. "Foreword," *Conrad's Manifesto, Preface to a Career: The History of the Preface to The Nigger of the Narcissus with Facsimiles of the Manuscripts Edited with an Essay by David R. Smith* (Philadelphia: The Philip H. and A. W. S. Rosenbach Foundation, 1966), pp. 9–14.

In August, 1897, when JC first saw *The Nigger of the Narcissus* in print, he began to write his famous preface to this work. In writing *Nigger*, he had ended the first stages of his literary apprenticeship to Flaubert and Maupassant, and he had liberated himself from his first literary advisor, Edward Garnett. His preface seems not only a preface to this one novel, but to the whole of his career, and even, "one might contend, to modern fiction in English." It is, though, "a manifesto of feeling and personal dedication." Of major importance in the collection of JC manuscripts at The Philip H. & A. S. W. Rosenbach Foundation Museum in Philadelphia is a cluster of holographs which "centers on" *Nigger* and includes the Preface "To My Readers in America," a second preface which explains the importance of the first. These prefaces were acquired by Dr. Rosenbach at the Quinn sale of 1923. [Lists in chronological order the various important stages, from manuscript to the accepted printed version, of the two prefaces.]

1970.1 Tolley, A. T. "Conrad's 'Favorite' Story," *SSF*, III (Spring 1966), pp. 314–20.

In 1906, JC stated in *The Grand Magazine* that his best story was "An Outpost of Progress," without including any convincing reason for his choice. This tale, though, one of his best pieces of the "long short story/short novel" length, adds some understanding to its companion story of the Congo, "Heart of Darkness." Both Kayerts and Carlier go to pieces under the impact of their situation, one which JC used in other works also to illustrate his view of the relation of the civilizing achievement of men to the forces within and around them on which civilization must be imposed. His familiar theme of fidelity serves as a defense against the inchoate in the central incident of the story, and the civilizing theme is developed beyond satire. The presentation of Makola is particularly good in its insidious effect on the two white men. JC's attempt at simplicity was also helpful to him. Inferior as it is to "Heart of Darkness," this story helps to show the sorts of feelings JC had about his experiences in the Congo and the idiom of "Heart of Darkness."

1974.1 Walcutt, Charles Child. *Man's Changing Mask: Modes and Methods of Characterization in Fiction* (Minneapolis: University of Minnesota P, 1966), pp. 93–103, 124, 228, 239, 265–66, 267–80, 281.

In Marlow's "choice of nightmares" in "Heart of Darkness," the moral insanity of Kurtz is somehow preferable to the moral imbecility of the manager of the Central Station. Marlow lies, of course, to the Intended, but he also lies by implication by refraining from publicizing Kurtz's evil. And this lie by Marlow is a judgment of the world: better unspeakable degradation with the intellectual victory, at the end, of insight and judgment than the imbecile rapacity of the traders who could say only that Kurtz had ruined the district for trade by his "unsound methods." Marlow's journey up the Congo is finally a journey not into darkness but into illumination. His adventure explores the phenomenon of idealism tainted by lust for power, the source of this excess, in a sequence of highly charged intellectual disgusts. Both Kurtz and Marlow explore the fascination of the abomination, Kurtz sensually, Marlow intellectually. These two men are halves of the single person who penetrates and understands ultimate evil. JC's position as a writer is midway between the older novelist who works within the ordered society, accepting its values and problems, and the contemporary novelist, who moves away from this world because he thinks it has lost its vitality. JC's hero has an idea of his nature, of his destiny, of his proper relation to society, and JC tests his hero in an action free of the problems that surround the center of "our social decay." Such heroes are Kurtz, Jim, and Charles Gould, but Heyst of *Victory*, finding no forgiveness for him, kills himself.

1976.1 Watts, C. T. "Stepniak and *Under Western Eyes*," *N&Q*, XIII (November 1966), pp. 410–11.

JC's Razumov in *Under Western Eyes* stands in ironic contrast to the anarchist Sergei Stepniak [pseudonym of S. M. Kravchinsky] and to Stepniak's semi-autobiographical hero Audrey in *The Career of a Nihilist* (1889). Numerous parallels suggest that the contrast is "not entirely fortuitous."

1976.2 Wilding, Michael. "The Politics of *Nostromo*," *EIC*, XVI (October 1966), pp. 441–56.

The static unexplanatory fable-like quality suggested by the structure of *Nostromo* is supported by the characterization, in which each individual represents a certain quality, not complexities of character, and each exists in near-isolation from the others. For a novel dealing with social and political complexities, Mrs. Gould's inadequacies are very noticeable and weaken her part in the work. Antonia and Decoud are comparably isolated from society. There is, then, no portrayal of man's alienation from society, no society from which to be alienated. The confusion over the silver is associated with the confusion over "material interests," a phrase which is unclear. In the political revolutions of Costaguana, economic and social conditions play no part. *Nostromo*, then, is more a moral fable than a modern analysis of politics and society, a moral fable dealing with the corruptibility of man. [Followed by Ivo Vidan and Juliet McLauchlan, "The Politics of *Nostromo*," *Essays in Criticism*, XVII (July 1967), pp. 392–406; Jonah Raskin, "*Nostromo*: The Argument from Revision," *Essays in Criticism*, XVIII (April 1968), pp. 183–92; and Michael Wilding, "The Politics of *Nostromo*," *Essays in Criticism*, XVIII (April 1968), pp. 234–36.]

1976.3 Winter, John L. "A Conrad Letter," *N&Q*, XIII (March 1966), p. 94.

A letter "attributed" to JC is to be found in E. D. Morel's *King Leopold's Rule in Africa* (London: Heinemann, 1904), p. 117. In the letter JC claims that he can find no reason to believe that there is any truth to "the alleged custom of cutting off hands among the natives."

1976.4 Winter, J. L. "Conrad's San Tomé," *N&Q*, XIII (November 1966), pp. 412–13.

J. E. Saveson ("Masterman as a Source of *Nostromo*," *Notes and Queries*, CCVIII [1963], pp. 368–70) argues that JC's source for the name San Tomé and for the description of the San Tomé mountain in *Nostromo* is Masterman's *Seven Eventful Years in Paraguay*. JC's source, however, is most likely the Portuguese slave island of San Tomé, situated off the West African coast. This possible source is supported by a parallel in names between the Isabels, the three islands off Sulaco in *Nostromo*, and Santa Isabel, the capital of Fernando Po, which is situated north of San Tomé; and by another parallel between the American millionaire Holroyd, the evangelical Protestant who controls and reaps the profits of the mine in *Nostromo*, and William Cadbury, the "renowned Quaker" and "cocoa-king" who profited the most from San Tomé island.

1976.5 Zerbini, Rosa. "Vita e arte in Conrad" (Life and Art in Conrad), *Acme* (1966), pp. 269–79.

Solitude, which frequently drives man to suicide, is man's distinctive condition in JC's works. In early novels, many elements of Decadence in descriptive passages contribute to building up a projection of human feelings. In *Nostromo*, the town of Sulaco is almost an emblem of isolation. Dream and unreachable ideals are the ambiguous characteristics of JC's romanticism. Only the observation of life, enriched by poetic feelings, can supply art its material. [In Italian.]

1967

1977 Allen, Jerry. "Introduction," *Great Short Works of Joseph Conrad* (New York: Harper & Row [Perennial Classics], 1967), pp. 1–9.

As an artist, JC is an "original," but also an ancestor of much modern fiction: of the psychological novel, the political novel, and the "intellectual mystery story," as we now know them. A gifted linguist, JC made his style a kind of poetry which has something in it "of the rise and fall, the cadence, of the sea." The "core" of his concern is with what he called "the ideal value of things, events, and people." One basic theme is the inner isolation, the "apartness" known by everyone; but JC sympathizes with the outsider who, wanting to join the group, to become "one of us," remains an individual. Aware that no single viewpoint affords the truth, he uses an "ambling" method in his storytelling, thereby approaching a human problem from various directions. His intricate art is either direct and simple, as in "An Outpost of Progress" and "Typhoon," or very complex, as in *The Nigger of the Narcissus* and "The Secret Sharer." [In considering the biographies of JC, Miss Allen includes her own books and omits those of Jocelyn Baines and Norman Sherry.]

1978 Allen, Vio. "Memories of Joseph Conrad," *Review of English Literature*, VIII (April 1967), pp. 77–90.

JC's accent, his haste in speaking, and his mixing French words into his English conversation made him difficult to understand. In 1920 in Corsica, he complained of fatigue and expressed a desire to write for the theatre. He claimed to have written *Lord Jim* to defy a critic who said that a novel must have a limited number of characters. He thought that *A Set of Six* was his most successful collection of stories although he liked *'Twixt Land and Sea* better. He also believed "The Secret Sharer" to be his best single piece of writing. Three months later, at Oswald's in Kent, JC read and laughed at early criticism of his novels. He talked about the originals of Captain Brierly and Jim and seemed interested in a suggestion to write a book about Marlow. Upon hearing the news of Stephen Crane's death in Germany, he ordered Jessie to see to arrangements for the return of Crane's dog. Jessie spoke of the muddle of Poland and the immorality of Poles during the Conrads' visit at the outbreak of World War I.

1979 Anderson, Warren D., and Thomas D. Clareson (eds.). *Victorian Essays: A Symposium* (Kent, Ohio: Kent State University Press, 1967), p. 12.

Marlow experiences an epiphany when he sends Jim off to Patusan in *Lord Jim.*

1980 Angoff, Charles. "The Mystique of *The Smart Set,*" *Literary Review,* XI (Autumn 1967), pp. 49–60.

The really distinguished period of the American periodical *The Smart Set* came in the two-year span beginning in January, 1913, of Willard Huntington Wright's editorship, when the periodical provided first American publication of such authors as D. H. Lawrence, Ezra Pound, William Butler Yeats, and JC.

1981 Bachrach, A. G. H. "Joseph Conrad and the Dutch," *Review of English Literature,* VIII (October 1967), pp. 9–30.

In 1886–87, JC passed his Master Mariner examination, became a British subject, wrote his first story, and met the Dutch model for Kaspar Almayer, Karel Olmeyer, in North Borneo, whose acquaintance was his most important impulse in becoming a writer. In Olmeyer, JC recognized certain traits that he shared with the Dutch trader, most of all in being an exile from his birthplace. Like Olmeyer, JC wished to buy himself into the West, but he did it by marriage and by adopting the language and culture of England. Many of his heroes must confront the failure of their choices, and the Dutch Olmeyer's life not only provided a model for such heroes but also may have brought about a recognition in JC about himself.

1982 [Beebe, Maurice]. "Modern Fiction Newsletter: British Fiction," *MFS,* XIII (Winter 1967–68), pp. 529–60.

[Rev. of Avrom Fleishman, *Conrad's Politics: Community and Anarchy in the Fiction of Joseph Conrad* (1967), and of Claire Rosenfield, *Paradise of Snakes: An Archetypal Analysis of Conrad's Political Novels* (1967). Here are two more of the many JC's: Fleishman's contention that the standard view of JC as a conservative is a "myth" that ignores JC's lifelong adherence to a "centuries-old democratic revolutionary" tradition, and Claire Rosenfield's seeing JC to be much more "mocking, ironic, and sceptical" than he is usually thought to be.]

1983 "Beginners' Conrad," *TLS* (30 March 1967), p. 264.

Eschewing a chronological approach to JC's works, Neville H. Newhouse clearly defines the "symbiotic relation" between JC's complex techniques and his involved subject matter and thereby provides a clear and useful, if not particularly subtle, sketch of JC's development and themes. [Rev. of Neville H. Newhouse, *Joseph Conrad* (1966).]

1984 Benson, Donald R. "Eliot's and Conrad's Hollow Men," *CEA*, XXIX (January 1967), p. 10.

The crux of the connection between "Heart of Darkness" and Eliot's "The Hollow Men" lies in the third stanza of section I. Kurtz, one of the "lost/Violent souls," is not conceived as a hollow man in either the story or the poem. Eliot must have recognized something of his own vision in JC's world with its dying sun and hollow men, and found in Kurtz's terrible and excruciatingly limited "victory" a powerfully ironic comment on the even more terrible despair of his own hollow men.

1985 Bernaciak, Joel J. "Microcosm Versus Macrocosm: A Study of Setting in the Fiction of Joseph Conrad," *DA*, XXVII (1967), 3034A. Unpublished dissertation, University of Michigan, 1966.

1986 Bittner, Gerhard. *Der Symbolgehalt der Werke Joseph Conrads* (The Symbolic Content of Joseph Conrad's Work). Unpublished dissertation, University of Freiburg (Germany), 1967; (pvtly. ptd., 1967).

[Bittner discusses JC's novels and a number of his stories and points out which symbols JC uses to express the irrationality of the universe and man's tragic isolation. He distinguishes between traditional (snake, light-darkness) and modern symbols (river as image of desire, man as a puppet to indicate his helplessness in the scheme of things). JC prefers symbols which express contradictory experiences (the jungle as image of death and teeming life, the island as refuge and place of deadly isolation, the sailor as portrait of human weakness and strength, the silver that destroys the civilization which it has helped to found). In his brief analyses of JC's works, Bittner often describes the structural importance of certain literary patterns.] [A too rapid and unoriginal survey of JC's use of symbols.] [In German.]

1987 Bojarski, Edmund A. "A Conversation with Kipling on Conrad," *Kipling Journal*, CLXII (June 1967), pp. 12–15.

In 1898, JC wrote a defense of Kipling's *Captains Courageous* in "Concerning a Certain Criticism," which was never published. In 1906, Kipling congratulated JC on *The Mirror of the Sea*. Kipling's assessment of JC was given in conversation with Jan Perlowski in Madrid in 1928. To Kipling, JC's style was not typically English, and his exoticism was the quality that attracted British readers. JC's humanitarian attitude to James Wait in *The Nigger of the Narcissus* is not typically English, nor is his allowance that men like Lord Jim need not always be held accountable for their actions. Kipling believed that since JC understood Jim's desertion of the *Patna* to be cowardly, the ship cannot be symbolic of Poland and the novel cannot be autobiographical.

1988 Bojarski, Edmund A. "A Stranger and Afraid: Joseph Conrad," *English Studies in Africa*, X (March 1967), pp. 94–100.

[An account of JC's leaving Poland, feeling like a stranger afraid in his own country, exemplified by his strained meeting in 1890 with Jan Perlowski, also a legal ward of JC's uncle Tadeusz Bobrowski.]

1989 Brashear, William R. "'To-morrow' and 'Tomorrow': Conrad and O'Neill," *Renascence*, XX (Autumn 1967), pp. 18–21, 55.

The influence of JC on Eugene O'Neill extends beyond several rather inconsequential particulars to the core of their vision of man: a vision of despair, tragic in the deepest Nietzschean sense. Yet JC always remained more detached from the human plight than did the intensely involved O'Neill, who lacked both JC's artistry and his inhibitions, as seen in JC's story and O'Neill's play of the same title.

1990 Buckley, Jerome H. "Symbols of Eternity: The Victorian Escape from Time," *Victorian Essays: A Symposium*, ed. by Warren D. Anderson and Thomas D. Clareson (Kent, Ohio: Kent State University Press, 1967), pp. 1–16.

The Joycean epiphany represents a modern artist's desire to find in the aesthetic perception of life an assurance of value otherwise denied to a secular age; it offers for the moment at least the possibility of a fixed and ultimate pattern, like the spot of time of many writers between Wordsworth and Joyce. Among them are Rossetti, Meredith, Browning, Pater, George Eliot, Virginia Woolf, and JC. The last has Marlow in *Lord Jim* send Jim off to Patusan and share with the young man, as he writes, "a moment of real and profound intimacy, unexpected and short-lived, like a glimpse of some everlasting, of some saving truth."

1991 Burgess, Anthony. *The Novel Now: A Student's Guide to Contemporary Fiction* (London: Faber & Faber; New York: W. W. Norton, 1967), pp. 35, 165.

Among the "giants of the modern age" of the novel, JC is "up there, hard and bright, a fixed star," but he seems to belong to an age "anterior to Henry James." Some of his technical innovations have been influential, but he belongs to a time "which resists the new psychology and philosophy . . . and his ornate prose is a final fruit rather than a new seed."

1992 Cagle, William R. "The Publication of Joseph Conrad's *Chance*," *Book Collector*, XVI (Autumn 1967), pp. 305–22.

[Traces in detail the complex publishing history of JC's *Chance* as far as it is available at present.]

1993 Canario, John W. "The Harlequin in 'Heart of Darkness,'" *SSF*, IV (Spring 1967), pp. 225–33.

Critics are wrong to see the Russian in "Heart of Darkness" as simply a clown. He is also a modern type of the European aborigine. Marlow's first impression of him as harlequin is modified to respect as the Russian exhibits loyalty and humaneness, devotion to duty, and adventurous courage. These qualities and an awe of intellectuals like Kurtz are mutual characteristics of the Russian and Marlow. Marlow discovers those similarities but also a difference between the Russian and himself caused by Marlow's discovery of the evil of brutal selfishness in the Europeans of Africa, an insight the innocent Russian does not share with Marlow and which makes him an aborigine. He thus represents uncorrupted innocence and inner strength which the other Europeans, and especially Kurtz, have lost in their uncontrolled greed.

1994 Chandler, Arnold E. "'A Tiny White Speck in a Darkened World': A Study of Four Conrad Heroes," *DA*, XXVIII (December 1967), 2238A–39A. Unpublished dissertation, University of Texas, 1967.

1995 Clark, Charles C. "The Brierly Suicide: A New Look at an Old Ambiguity," *Arlington Quarterly*, I (Winter 1967–68), pp. 259–65.

Perhaps Brierly in *Lord Jim* committed suicide, not because of the reasons usually suggested, but because of the possibility of actual guilt in his past. There is some evidence in the novel for this conclusion, and such a reading is consonant with what we have learned to expect of JC, the "great impressionist"—every stroke has a special purpose.

1996 Crews, Frederick. "The Power of Darkness," *Partisan Review*, XXXIV (Fall 1967), pp. 507–25.

Bernard C. Meyer's *Joseph Conrad: A Psychoanalytic Biography* (1967), provides information about JC's psychological problems that will require taking a new view of his work, in which unconscious desires are guardedly expressed. Meyer calls attention to the Oedipal complex in many of JC's heroes who avoid coming to grips with sexual inhibitions by adventure and discipline. Thus they are eunuchs while the heroines are awesome maternal figures. In the later inferior works like *Victory*, woman is both idolized and denigrated. Lena is a "mother-Magdalen" who is rescued from the father-seducer Schomberg and transformed into a protectress of the hero-son. The plot is resolved by destroying the latent Oedipal relation by fire. The debate is suppressed and the novel ends— incomplete. In the better works like "Heart of Darkness," the inhibitions are dramatically and symbolically recognized. Thus Kurtz is the father-sinner guilty of sexual rites with the mother. The voyage up the winding river is a voyeuristic and incestuous trip into the female body. The purity of the father-mother relation is maintained by substituting the savage woman for the mother, though the Intended is equated with horror in Marlow's life. Recognition of certain suppressed biographical facts can help the critic understand better JC's inner conflicts and how he dealt with them in his work.

1997 Curley, Daniel. "The Writer and His Use of Material: The Case of 'The Secret Sharer,'" *MFS*, XIII (Summer 1967–68), pp. 179–94.

"The Secret Sharer" is a combination of story, history, and autobiography. The geographical location, the circumstance of a young man's first command, and the problem of responsibility, the moral center of the story, are all drawn from JC's first voyage as a sea captain. The incidents surrounding the disastrous voyage of the *Cutty Sark* in 1880 and the trial that followed supplied JC with material for placing his young captain in an almost insoluble position: a position, however, in which the captain finally proves himself able to balance the dual risks of responsibility to self and responsibility to society. Leggatt, the captain's double, represents his higher nature, his ideal self. The captain must make moral choices in totally unexpected situations; whereas Leggatt must remain steady throughout the story as a result of the moral strength he has already won by the choice he has made on the *Sephora*, where he killed, not deliberately, but of necessity. The total pattern of changes JC made in adapting the *Cutty Sark* material removes the episode of the death from the demesne of ordinary legality. "The Secret Sharer" is an unusual work; it is the unreflecting story of "a young man's moment" unqualified by the wisdom of age and experience.

1998 Dillon, Martin. "The Meaning of Time in the Development of Conrad's Fiction," *DA*, XXVIII (August 1967), 673A. Unpublished dissertation, State University of New York at Buffalo, 1967.

1999 Dobrée. Bonamy. *Rudyard Kipling: Realist and Fabulist* (London: Oxford University Press, 1967), pp. 135–36.

Kipling's story, "Sea Constables," often considered a "brutal" story because Maddingham does not take the Neutral across from Ireland to England so he can see his doctor in town, is similar to JC's "The Tale." In the latter, the Commanding Office gives the stray ship sailing directions which will ensure its being wrecked with the loss of the entire crew, not knowing whether he had done "stern justice or murder." He is far more "brutal" than Maddingham, who was at least surprised at his having acted as he did, but then came to see how the pressure of events sometimes forces people to do what they would normally revolt against.

2000 Donoghue, Denis. "Edward W. Said: *Joseph Conrad and the Fiction of Autobiography*," *NCF*, XXII (September 1967), pp. 199–202.

Beneath the values officially posited in JC's tales—duty, work, comradeship, patriotism, Poland, Europe, tradition, and the like—lies a void, a void which appears in JC's letters as well as in his novels.

2001 Duncan-Jones, E. E. "Mrs. Gould and Fairy Blackstick," *N&Q*, XIV (July 1967), p. 245.

Mrs. Gould in *Nostromo* is linked with the Fairy Blackstick of Thackeray's *The Rose and the Ring*. Another connection exists between Mrs. Gould's reflections and extracts from Coleridge's notebooks.

2002 Dunn, Richard J. "Conrad's *Lord Jim*," *Explicator*, XXVI (December 1967), Item 30.

The misunderstanding that arises when Jim takes offense at Marlow's friend's remark, "Look at that wretched cur" (chapter 6), does more than merely supply the occasion for Jim and Marlow to meet. When Marlow retrospectively describes the incident and hypothesizes that hearing the word "cur" stripped Jim of his discretion, the incident clearly presents an index to Jim's moral sensitivity at the conclusion of the inquiry.

2003 Espey, John. "Notes and Reviews," *NCF*, XXII (December 1967), p. 311.

A "double strain" existed within JC's Polish inheritance itself, a strain "between the 'visionary . . . patriotism' of his father and the 'common-sense, practical . . . views of his uncle and guardian.'" "Karain," *Victory*, "Amy Foster," and "Prince Roman" are related to Polish romanticisim, as many parallels and sources suggest. JC's indebtedness to Polish literature is, therefore, natural. [Rev. of Andrzej Busza, *Conrad's Polish Literary Background and Some*

Illustrations of the Influence of Polish Literature on His Work and of
Robert R. Hodges, *The Dual Heritage of Joseph Conrad.*]

2004 Fleishman, Avrom. "Conrad's Early Political Attitudes," from
*Conrad's Politics: Community and Anarchy in the Fiction of
Joseph Conrad* (1967); rpt. *TCNN* (1969), pp. 100–103.

In *The Nigger of the Narcissus*, the seaman-narrator expresses
JC's ironic tone and political bias. His scorn of well-meaning
"liberals" and of "whining workers" alike generates the plot. The
basis of moral criticism both of mutiny and of revolution is a breach
of the work ethic, but some elements of the plot do not fit this
formula. Wait exonerates himself by means of a legitimate complaint:
he simply dies. Then JC must introduce new elements to sustain the
tension, with some detriment to the credibility of the tale. For
Donkin, though, who anticipates JC's anarchists, JC has only
sarcasm. The crew, nominally the collective hero, proceeds to
mutiny, mainly because of its personal attachment to Wait and
because of "childish grievances" aggravated by Donkin. But the
moral sentiments of the lower classes are being portrayed in an
ambiguous manner, we are not to approve the crew's pity for
Donkin's indigence. This ambivalence toward the working class
remains with JC throughout his career; his sympathy with the labors
and sufferings of the poor is mixed with a reserve that borders on
contempt—on a contempt, however, found in the hearts of
organicists, liberals, and conservatives alike.

2005 Fleishman, Avrom. *Conrad's Politics: Community and Anarchy
in the Fiction of Joseph Conrad* (Baltimore: The Johns Hopkins
Press, 1967).

JC's early writings reveal his antagonism toward capitalism, his
suspicion of technocracy, and his disbelief in the optimism of H. G.
Wells and G. B. Shaw. In "Autocracy and War," he rejects economic
and military imperialism and promotes organic nationalism which
seeks to express the will of the people and favors a confederation of
nations linked by a common culture. The Polish idea of a nation as a
cultural unity rather than a political one and the British "Burke
tradition" provide the sources for his political thought. The more
contemporary developers of organicism who influenced JC were the
neo-Hegelians, F. H. Bradley and Bernard Bosanquet. From them he
developed his "work ethic" connected to the goal or vocation which
provides direction.

JC's attitude toward colonization evolved somewhat during his
career. In the early novels, European imperialists are virtually
criminals, exploiting conquered lands without concern for their
peoples. Both Dutch nonintervention in native affairs and British

intrigue lead to disorder; this state of affairs exists especially in the late novel, *The Rescue*. The African tales show even more barbaric treatment of natives by whites like Almayer, Willems, and Lingard, as well as by Kurtz, who are destroyed along with the natives when society breaks down. One reason for white decadence in the tropics is that European order does not provide training in self-defense. These conquerors, products of Liberal theory, are different from the colonists, issue of the organicist tradition, who are committed to a role, to the people, and to the place they adopt. Jim is the best example of the colonist. Even the British colonists are condemned, however, in the later fiction as JC became more severe with imperialism.

The first major political novel, *Nostromo*, shows the title character destroyed by the conflict between his egotism and his devotion to a class, as is Decoud. *The Secret Agent* exhibits the way in which secrecy protects a people from forces that would destroy them and do so when they are discovered. And in *Under Western Eyes*, JC speaks through the narrator's condemnation of the emptiness of Swiss uninvolved democracy. In sum, JC recognizes the danger to personal life in a political system but promotes the satisfaction of self-realization in the individual's identity with a community. [A major book on JC and his achievement.]

2006 Folejewski, Zbigniew. *Maria Dobrowska* (New York: Twayne, 1967), pp. 19, 20, 29, 30, 37–38, 53, 54, 62–63, 68, 92–93, 96, 101, 107.

In objecting to the pessimistic concept of man's absolute isolation on the way toward death, Maria Dobrowska's attitude is close to JC's. In 1932, she wrote that in her countryman's work, notwithstanding his pessimism and his feeling of loneliness of man confronted by both life and death, there are elements of struggle against this feeling, that there is "longing for community of man with humanity and even more than humanity." Her work shares certain similarities to that of JC's, especially in the views of her heroes about life and about human destiny in the world. She displayed a deep interest in JC's works, which were at that time appearing in Polish translation, and she echoed JC's anti-materialistic attitude in *Nostromo*, which she reviewed. A "spiritual kinship," rather than any direct literary influence, appears to have existed between these two writers. Both, though, used the technique of the time shift; both, too, displayed an artful and carefully planned construction in their productions which often appeared to be spontaneous. In 1945, Dabrowska came to the defense of JC's ideals against the Marxist view promoted by Jan Kott: for her, as for JC, an individual is of greater importance than a collective group.

2007 Frances, Sister Marian, SNJM. "Corruption as Agent in the *Narcissus*," *English Journal*, LVI (May 1967), pp. 708–15.

In *The Nigger of the Narcissus*, the ship, the crew, and the major characters are corrupted. This corruption, expressed largely through black-white symbolism, pervades the novel. Though ship and men journey through an imperfect world, the hope of brotherhood springs from the fallen nature of man, since he is white as well as black, Christ as well as Satan.

2008 Geddes, Gary. "Conrad and the Fine Art of Understanding," *Dalhousie Review*, XLVII (Winter 1967–68), pp. 492–503.

JC's *A Personal Record* was intended to reopen the question of his own subjects and motives as a writer in order to foster a healthier reading of his fiction. It is easy to understand why he chose to speak of his initiation into the world of art in moral or religious rather than in purely psychological terms. The artist, he explains, must virtually cease to exist, in the active or objective sense, and at this level the artist's experience parallels that of the religious in that both partake of the paradox of self-discovery through self-denial. JC's letters of the time of his composition of this book contain many references to his "piety" before the spectacle of the universe. Reality, for him, included everything that can be felt. Sympathy and compassion are at the heart of JC's creative ethic; the aim of his art, like that of George Eliot, is to awaken sympathy, to express one's understanding in such a way as to foster understanding in the reader. As JC demonstrates in much of his fiction as well as in *A Personal Record*, he advocates the "informing principle" of his life and art, "cultivation of the fine art of understanding."

2009 Gerber, Helmut E. (ed.) *The English Short Story in Transition, 1880–1920* (New York: Pegasus, 1967), pp. xi–xv, 486–87, 512.

The period from 1880 to 1920 contained the rise of the modern short story "in all its variety" as the form is now generally understood. Such writers as Wells, Kipling, Hardy, Maugham, Henry James, D. H. Lawrence, Joyce, and JC produced major work in the genre. At the back of the artistic values of JC's stories appears the work of anthropologists in the Malayan Archipelagos, recent Polish history, and perhaps Jungian psychology. JC, like Henry James, represents the crest of a wave consisting of lesser writers. His talent lies in his "often remarkable combination of close realistic observation of detail, suggestive biblical and mythological allusion and intrinsic image patterns."

2010 Gilley, Leonard. "Conrad's 'The Secret Sharer,'" *Midwest Quarterly*, VIII (Summer 1967), pp. 319–30.

The theme of "The Secret Sharer" is to test the captain who measures himself in accordance with his ideal, Leggatt. The captain-narrator is, however, unreliable, and Leggatt is far from ideal. Leggatt has killed a man and, although the narrator justifies this act, it is not clear what JC's judgment is. The narrator uses various tricks to excuse Leggatt—such as portraying the *Sephora*'s captain as stupid and the crew as bestial. Actually, the captain's dangerous maneuvering of the ship to save Leggatt is a selfish act. The story depends on the tricks of cheap adventure fiction and fails to judge reprehensible the actions of the two chief characters.

2011 Gillespie, Gerald. "Novella, Nouvelle, Novella. Short Novel?—A Review of Terms (Concluded), II," *Neophilologus*, LI (July 1967), pp. 225–29.

Any "short novel" in the "upper ranges of length" with features of the Continental species of *nouvelle*, such as Hemingway's *The Old Man and the Sea*, can be placed next to JC's tale, "The Secret Sharer." JC's story has its setting in a reality that is clearly a stage for some mysterious drama; it is the fundamental "unheard-of happening" that yet occurs, and JC uses a central symbol, the shadow or double, derived from the Romantics, in a special reality that conveys something about the psyche. This tale "borders on" a character study. [JC's tale is placed in a study of the story of intermediate length, which begins in Gillespie's "Novella, Nouvelle, Novella, Short Novel?—A Review of Terms," ibid. (April 1967), pp. 117–27.]

2012 Goens, Mary B. "The 'Mysterious and Effective Star': The Mythic World-View in Conrad's *Victory*," *MFS*, XIII (Winter 1967–68), pp. 455–63.

JC's works often demand, not just invite, the mythic critical perspective—*Victory* in particular. The community unconscious pervades the novel. JC moved his characters from the prosaic plane of the story to the sphere of ritualistic action through the principles of magic discussed by Frazer. *Victory* explores but does not supply facile answers to the problems of man's entrapment between the practical and the mystical.

2013 Gorlier, Claudio. "I capolavori di Conrad" (Conrad's Masterpieces), *La Stampa* (14 June 1967), p. 11.

JC is not really popular in Italy, and Mursia's edition of his works is all the more needed. Kurtz is the romantic hero shattered to pieces, the grotesque instrument of evil and agony. [Review of JC's complete shorter novels and stories, *Tutti i Racconti e i Romanzi Brevi* (Milan: Mursia, 1967).] [In Italian.]

2014 Graver, Lawrence. "Norman Sherry: *Conrad's Eastern World*," *NCF*, XXI (March 1967), pp. 403–405.

In testing JC's claim that the story of the novelist's first command is told in *The Shadow-Line*, Norman Sherry discovered that although JC "could not invent a convincing lie, he certainly could embroider reality." Sherry's "meticulous research" seemingly "makes possible for the first time a critical study of Conrad's use of fact," but such a book remains to be written.

2015 Gross, Theodore, and Norman Kelvin (eds.). "Joseph Conrad: Introduction" [to "An Outpost of Progress"], *An Introduction to Literature: Fiction* (New York: Random House, 1967), pp. 141–50.

The initial fraternity between Kayerts and Carlier in "An Outpost of Progress" is a pathetic and ironic suggestion of how JC believed men ought to relate to each other. Fraternity, for them, is an illusion, because they lack the courage and independence necessary to survive the test of isolation and the effect of primitive surroundings and behavior on the "veneer" of their "received" European ideas and standards. The central act of the story, the selling of station men into slavery for the sake of material gain (ivory here) starkly conveys JC's indignation at the greed and exploitation he saw in the Congo. At the end, Kayerts is granted a small degree of self-revelation: not strong enough to live once he has seen the truth, he is strong enough to die.

2016 Guerard, Albert J. (ed.). "Concepts of the Double," *Stories of the Double* (Philadelphia and New York: J. B. Lippincott, 1967), pp. 1–14.

Captain Brierly sees himself in Lord Jim as Jim sees himself in Gentleman Brown, and the reactions are surprising. In "The Secret Sharer," although temporarily the experiences of both men in their self-evaluations are paralyzing, the outcome is productive: they both arrive at self-knowledge.

2017 Guerard, Albert J. "Joseph Conrad," *Major British Writers*, shorter ed. (New York: Harcourt, Brace & World, 1967), pp. 931–38.

JC was divided "between love of freedom and a respect for authority; sympathy for the outlaw and committment to law; dreaming and action." His fiction is marked by "high art," tragedy, adventure, meditation, and politics. He belongs to both the Impressionistic and the Realistic schools: "Heart of Darkness" illustrates both, as well as being symbolic. This story attacks imperialism through Kurtz, who embodies primitive energy and godlessness, or spiritual apathy.

2018 Guidi, Augusto. "L'opera narrativa di Joseph Conrad" (Joseph Conrad's Narrative Work), *LCS*, L, 12 (December 1967), pp. 195–96.

JC is more at ease with male characters, who are the protagonists, often heroic, of the novels, than with female characters. The latter remain as though veiled in the reader's memory. JC's women are rarely presented in depth and instead are idealized in nineteenth-century fashion, or feared, or hinted at, almost a mirage, almost on one side or the other beyond good or evil. [Review of *Tutti i Racconti e i Romanzi Brevi* (Milan: Mursia, 1967).] [In Italian.]

2019 Guidi, Augusto. "Struttura e linguaggio di *Nostromo*" (Language and Structure in *Nostromo*), *Convivium*, XXXV (1967), pp. 289–302.

There are some faults in the usage of language in *Nostromo*, such as an indiscriminate use of "great," wrong shades of meaning in words like "perplexity," "distinction," "pretend," and "news" taken as a plural. JC's sentences are too long and slow. His landscapes, drawn from memory, are transfigured by lights and shadows and by rich aurorean and twilight colors. There is a constant correspondence between characters and the circumambient countryside which is often anthropomorphic. *Nostromo*'s international world of men is better seen in an exotic background; dialogues are often artful and prolix. Nostromo the man, possesses the simple qualities of the people. Decoud is the interpreter of society and the natural antagonist of Nostromo. Mitchell is the living example of the energy and fearlessness of the English, which JC greatly admired. Antonia was inspired by JC's first love; the novel is filled with innumerable real characters who make it incredibly fascinating and adventurous. From a social point of view, *Nostromo* represents the crisis of nineteenth-century individualism which, degenerating, will eventually lead to the waning of the West, from which will derive world wars and dictatorships. The symbolism of silver is so secret and subtle that perhaps the author himself was not fully aware of its insistent presence. The close of the novel is a splendid, grandiose, lyrical melodrama of love and death, which is preluded by the entire structure of the work. [In Italian.]

2020 Gupta, N. Das. "Conrad," *Literature of the Twentieth Century* (Gwalior: Kitab Ghar, 1967), pp. 163–70.

JC's is a new voice in the English novel in the early twentieth century because, unlike Bennett, Galsworthy, and Wells, who responded to the external world, the outer life, he sought to unravel the human mind, the mind that has ultimately to depend on its spiritual resources. He is further distinguished by the fact that not an Englishman, he wrote brilliant and at times poetic English. "Heart of Darkness" is a "brilliant travelogue" which "puts a straight question . . . to the colonial expansionists": "Why the greed and stupidity, why this moral squalor?" It is also the story of JC's and Marlow's self-destiny. In this tale and *Lord Jim*, the solution to the problems raised are only implied. In *Nostromo*, broad human relationships are explored and a definite moral vision is presented. *The Secret Agent* is "a story well-told but of no deep significance." *Under Western Eyes* presents a character "after the manner of Dostoevsky." JC believes, above all, in the sincerity of human relationships. He tests the theme of loneliness in *Victory*, with Heyst and Lena conquering, through human solidarity, their isolation from others. JC uses the indirect method of narration and the impressionistic method of characterization. He lays the characters bare before the reader; his attempt is always "to bring the inside out." He is concerned with life, and he wants his readers "to *see* that life." And he is concerned with the "ideal" values of things, with their spiritual values. He does not ask his readers to have faith in God; he asks them to have faith in themselves and to have a vision beyond immediate and material gains.

2021 Halstead, Isabella. "Joseph Conrad's *Nostromo: Chapter Notes and Criticism*.," with Critical Biography by David Mason Greene. (New York: American R.D.M. Corp. [A Study-Master Publication], 1967).

[A sixty-four page study guide to *Nostromo* containing, in addition to Greene's "Critical Biography," an "Introduction," "Chapter-by-Chapter Notes," "Critical Appraisal," "Analysis of Characterization," "Suggested Study Topics," and a "Bibliography." Slight.]

2022 Hamer, Douglas. "Conrad: Two Biographical Episodes," *RES*, XVIII (February 1967), pp. 54–56.

Capt. A. Burroughs related some information about JC: on Burroughs's first voyage in 1885 to Singapore, as a sickly youth of fifteen, JC was very kind to him. Later, in the home of Burroughs's mother, JC met a young girl named Ida Knight for whom he felt "considerable affection," but the situation was made uncomfortable by the jealousy of Burroughs's youngest sister.

2023 Hart, Evalee. "Aboard the *Narcissus*," *English Journal*, XLVI (January 1967), pp. 45–48.

The Nigger of the Narcissus can be taught successfully to above-average high school English classes.

2024 Heimer, Jackson W. "Betrayal, Confession, Attempted Redemption, and Punishment in *Nostromo*," *TSLL*, VIII (Winter 1967), pp. 561–79.

Nostromo focuses on ethics based on the human bond, and also on betrayal by four key characters: Nostromo, Gould, Decoud, and Dr. Monygham. The acts of betrayal of these characters and their consequences make up two definite yet closely related patterns: "major or basic pattern—act, confession, attempted redemption and punishment—and the minor pattern—isolation, involvement, and isolation." The patterns have social and political significance and center on the failure of the character to measure up to the demands of the human bond.

2025 Heimer, Jackson W. "The Betrayer as Intellectual: Conrad's *Under Western Eyes*," *PolR*, XII (Autumn 1967), pp. 57–68.

Under Western Eyes is an "intensely psychological" novel that illuminates political, social, and moral issues. Razumov's betrayal of Haldin and the revolutionaries establishes two distinct patterns: the major pattern of action, confession, attempted redemption, and punishment and the minor pattern of isolation, involvement, and again isolation. Razumov is so preoccupied with his inner being that he is not prepared for the "rash intrusion" of the world in the form of Haldin. He is attracted to Haldin but rejects him as a personal and social threat. Rejecting Haldin, Razumov begins a nightmarish journey downward. His second act of betrayal, spying on the revolutionaries in Geneva, is a morally reprehensible act even worse than his betrayal of Haldin because he is fully aware of what he is doing. Razumov's betrayals result in an intellectual guilt of which he tries to purge himself in his confession to Natalia. He has a "Dostoevskian world sense of guilt"; he tends to assume guilt for all men's crimes. His inner confession, made in his journal, still retains the intellectual's "propensity for analysis and introspection." Only Natalia, an "unstained force of goodness," saves him. The punishment for his betrayals is severe; he discovers that man cannot live the ideal of isolation and that betrayal is a violation of the human bond.

2026 Heimer, Jackson W. "Patterns of Betrayal in the Novels of Joseph Conrad," *Ball State University Forum*, VIII (Summer 1967), pp. 30–39.

Betrayal is an important but seldom recognized theme in six of JC's major novels: *Lord Jim, Nostromo, The Secret Agent, Under Western Eyes, Chance,* and *Victory.* A basic pattern by the betrayer is "act, confession, attempted redemption, and punishment." Two types of betrayers may be identified: those who, like Cornelius or Jones in *Jim,* are unaware of their betrayal, and those, like Jim or Nostromo, who are aware of it. These latter idealistic heroes are weakened by isolation, idealistic self-conceptions, and overintellectualization. After failure and vain confession, these heroes try to reject isolation by involvement, which also fails. Punishment follows. Though betrayal points out JC's reluctance to impose a universal code of judgment by offering a model hero, certain characters do dramatize an underlying ethic based on human solidarity, "courage, discipline, tradition." Isolation, then, is a serious type of betrayal.

2027 Howe, Irving. *Thomas Hardy* (New York: Macmillan; London: Collier-Macmillan [Masters of World Literature Series], 1967), pp. 16, 24, 62.

Unlike writers like Henry James and JC, who shared a reverent attitude toward the novel, Thomas Hardy was entirely too ready to follow the advice of editors and trim his serials to Victorian taste. Hardy was closer to Wordsworth than to JC because as novelist and poet he attributed meaning to the universe. A post-Romantic, he, unlike JC, "remained enthralled" by Romanticism. Compared to some writers, Hardy seems crude and rough: the ethical dilemmas that absorb George Eliot, the nuances of conduct that trouble Henry James, the "abysses of nihilism" that haunt JC are largely beyond Hardy's reach.

2028 Izzo, Carlo. "Un'opera di genio" (A Work of Genius), (1967, unlocated; rpt. *Civilta Britannica* [British Civilization], Roma: Ediozioni di Storia e Letteratura, 1970), II, pp. 169–72.

[Mentions, with general comments, the publication of *Gli eredi* and *La natura di un delitto* (The Inheritors and The Nature of a Crime), which shows how Ford's influence limited the creativity of his collaborator.] [In Italian.]

2029 Kilroy, James F. "Conrad's 'Succes de Curiosité': The Dramatic Version of *The Secret Agent*," *ELT,* X, No. 2 (May 1967), pp. 81–88.

Most critics of *The Secret Agent* have overlooked JC's insistence that the main character is Winnie Verloc. In the evolution of *Agent* from serial form to novel, Winnie is not the main figure. But in 1920 when JC added an introductory note, and later when he rewrote the story as a play, he insisted it centered on Winnie, not her husband. Although the domestic plot in which she is featured is not as extended as the espionage of her husband, it is the focus to which all other plots are related. How all else affects her domestic situation, particularly her love of Stevie, is the main concern of novel and play alike. Each of the subplots parallels the plight of Winnie: not only the anarchists but the police and polite society are engaged in cruel exploitation. The final meeting between Adolph and Winnie is not anti-climactic but is the inevitable working out of Winnie's catastrophe. The play is worthy of study both for its own artistic merit and for the light it sheds on the novel.

2030 Kocowna, Barbara. *Polskosc Conrada* (Conrad's Polishness), (Warsaw: Lodowa Spoldzielnia Ludowa, 1967).

The suggestion that the inhabitants of the Malaysian archipelago might have reminded JC of the demographic structure of the Ukraine is to some extent justifiable. Although Bobrowski was startled by JC's choice of a profession, he did not oppose the decision to leave Cracow for Marseilles. Government schools in the Ukraine were of a low standard, and it was usual for parents to send their offspring to France, Switzerland, or Belgium for schooling. JC may himself have translated *An Outcast of the Islands* into Polish when it was serialized in Warsaw in 1897, although it seems more likely that the translation was made by Maria Gasiorowska. In 1901, JC sent a copy of *Lord Jim* to the editor of *Chimera* (Warsaw), but it was not reviewed until 1905, delayed probably on account of the Polish translation of 1904. It was favorably received in most places. JC's patriotism was of two kinds. The first represents Romantic literature and the traditions of Poland's insurrections; the second includes his own doubts about the social changes in Europe during the last half of the nineteenth century. JC read Amiel's *Journal in Time*, passages from which may be compared with *Victory*, suggesting that it provided valuable nourishment for this second kind of patriotism. Loyalty to traditions with which man is always linked appears throughout JC's works, and the idea that man belongs to the land from which he comes is evident everywhere. [In Polish.]

2031 Krugliak, M. T. "Dzhozef Konrad v sovetskoi kritike" (Joseph Conrad in Soviet Criticism), *Uchenye Zapiski Permskogo Gos. Universiteta* (Perm), CLVII (1967), pp. 246–53.

JC's *Almayer's Folly* was his first work to be translated into Russian (during the Soviet period), with an informative note by K. Chukovskii. Gorky referred favorably to JC in 1926. Reviews, essays, and prefaces in various Soviet publications appeared in the 1920s (E. Lann, K. Loks, A. Azov, and others). The first serious commentary on JC's works from a Marxist viewpoint was that by F. Shiller in 1937, though he did not analyze individual works and sometimes contradicted himself. When JC was mentioned in textbooks during the period of the "Cult of the Individual," his works were evaluated wrongly, and otherwise they were scarcely studied at all. In the *Great Soviet Encyclopedia* (2d. ed., 1953), reference was made to the "subjectivism which brought him close to bourgeois decadentism." Such vulgarizations were, unfortunately, characteristic of certain Soviet publications in the first half of the 1950s. In recent years, interest in JC's works has greatly increased in Russia, although as yet no substantial monograph has been published. Essays and forewords to translations have appeared since 1957 (Iu. Kagarlitskii, 1957, and D'iakonova's preface to *Lord Jim*, 1958). More recently, JC has been regarded as belonging to the stream of classical English literature and as being a great national writer. Serious study of JC's works from the point of view of Marx-Leninist literary criticism is required. [In Russian.]

2032 Kubal, David L. "*The Secret Agent* and the Mechanical Chaos," *Bucknell Review*, XV (December 1967), pp. 65–77.

The world of *The Secret Agent* is chaotic. What holds this chaotic world together is, generally, the machine, which ranges from Stevie's mechanical circles through clocks to the mechanical piano in the Silenus Restaurant. The basic organizational principle is the circle. Through the paradoxical images of mechanism and chaos JC achieves thematic and structural unity. He presents the characters, their ideas, and London as "formless matter directed by machines," and he also organizes his novel on this basis, as the sequence of chapters, most of which disregard chronological time, indicates. Some chapters suggest the banality and monotony of the characters' lives; others are designed in an insular and repetitious manner. A "metallic" imagery occurs often in the novel, suggesting the machine-like gloss of the city. This mechanization causes a process of dehumanization to take place. Thus the representatives of the respected ruling class (Sir Eldred, the lady patroness, and the two policemen) are no better than the anarchists: all are entrenched in themselves and their own private interests. Stevie is more human than any other character in the book, for he resorts to something beyond himself and can recognize that all is not going well. At last, neither the machine nor chaos triumphs: the Greenwich affair is just another "border war."

2033 Larrett, William. "Joseph Conrad," *The English Novel from Thomas Hardy to Graham Greene* (Frankfort/Main: Verlag Moritz Diesterweg, [Studien zur Sprach und Literatur Englands 2], 1967), pp. 46–69.

JC's desire to be demanding both of himself and of his medium results at best in works which do not reveal the effort and deliberation which have gone into their making and which display a high degree of detachment. This desire places him in the tradition of writers who have realized that to "wed Truth and Beauty" their first concern must be the form. The complex *Nostromo* best reveals JC's imaginative powers. [Largely routine analyses of major works.]

2034 Magnusson, Harrold M. "Anarchism in Conrad's *The Secret Agent*," *Wisconsin Studies in Literature*, VIII (1967), pp. 75–88.

The four active anarchists in *The Secret Agent* represent a range from extreme *evolutionary* anarchism to extreme *revolutionary* anarchism; Michaelis is an evolutionary, the Professor a revolutionary, and Comrade Ossipon and Karl Yundt fall somewhere in between, although they tend to be more revolutionary. The Professor, Ossipon, and Yundt were created from the popular image of the anarchist in 1907, an image conceived by Michael Bakunin. Though they appear as caricatures of real anarchists, their espousal of revolutionary anarchism is genuine.

The anti-anarchists, represented by Mr. Vladimir and Chief Inspector Heat, are ignorant of the subtleties of anarchism (they cannot distinguish between the Michaelises and the Professors), and as a result, they blunder in ways which seem to prove the anarchists' case against established institutions. Both the anarchists and the anti-anarchists constantly maneuver for control of the destinies of the Stevies and the Winnies of society. *Agent*, of course, is more than a story about anarchism, but anarchism does play an important role, and the reader must appreciate JC's "obvious intimacy of understanding" of the subject.

2035 Maini, Darshan Singh. "Conrad's Moral Drama," *Literary Criterion* (Mysore), VIII (Winter 1967), pp. 79–84.

JC used the sea as a backdrop for the "saga of human action and struggle," to fathom the dark recesses and depths of man's mind. The outer voyage is in some respects an inner voyage: in his novels the ship becomes a "replica of man's tortured world," as in *The Shadow-Line*. For JC, the "primeval, dark, satanic character of the sea" has also something in common with the "inexplicable nature of sin" in man's world. The jungle, too, lends "epic dignity and stature" to the struggle of man. JC's hero is almost always a trapped man. His novels are "dramas of will and conscience, of choice and commitment," with the outward battle a reflection of the battle within. The central problem in the works is that of illusion and faith, of man's need for "spiritual ballast." Razumov in *Under Western Eyes* best reveals the poverty of existence without faith.

2036 Martin, W. R. "Allegory in Conrad's *The Rover,*" *English Studies in Africa,* X (September 1967), pp. 186–94.

The Rover allegorically concerns France: Peyrol represents "the ancient, at first slumbering, but enduring finer spirit" of the country. He is like Prince Arthur in the canto of *The Faerie Queene* from which JC takes his epigraph. Peyrol, sprung from the soil of France, has been untouched by the frenzies of the Revolution, and so, though tempted (like Spenser's Redcross Knight) to find "ease after warre," can play his part in the regeneration of France. His opposite, Scevola, represents the temporary aberration of France and the madness of the Revolution. Arlette, the France that Scevola has taken illegal possession of, recovers in stages. And Réal, "royal, a genuine coin," is a fit mate for Arlette. Through his wide brotherhood of seamanship, Peyrol's bonds stretch across the national barriers between England and France. He revives the true greatness of France after the temporary obscurity of its Revolution. Although Napoleon gives the impulse that launches Peyrol's response to France, the rover's response is to France itself, in the person of Arlette. And so he finds a heroic "ease after warre, death after life," in the tartane at the bottom of the sea.

2037 McDowell, Frederick P. W. "Review Article: Two Books on Conrad," *Philological Quarterly,* XLVI (January 1967), pp. 109–24.

[Two recent books emphasize the relevance of JC's political thinking to his art. Zdzislaw Najder's *Conrad's Polish Background* (1964) is a collection of documents, mostly letters, to and from JC's Polish friends. These documents extend our knowledge of JC's Polish antecedents, his early years in Poland, his subsequent continuing affection for his Polish relatives and friends, his relationships with Polish critics, translators, and writers, and the irresistible appeal to him of the "lost cause" of Polish nationalism. Eloise Knapp Hay's *The Political Novels of Joseph Conrad: A Critical Study* (1963) presents JC's political views primarily as the novelist transmuted them into his art. Both books demonstrate that one reason for JC's profundity as a political intelligence lies in the wealth of influences that formed his vision, not the least of which was the heritage from Poland.]

2038 McLauchlan, Juliet. "The Politics of *Nostromo,*" *EIC,* XVIII (July 1967), pp. 398–406.

The quotation, "The love of money is the root of all evil" (I Timothy, vi, 10), has been taken out of context and made to apply to *Nostromo* with "love" dropped from the aphorism. Also, Costaguana has been mistakenly translated as "coast of gull droppings" instead of "palm coast." These examples are symptoms of more serious critical errors. Although *Nostromo* is not a document of permanent roots and interrelated social reality, one should not condemn the novel on these grounds, for its point is, specifically: gulfs do indeed exist, separating the native population from its leaders and from responsible decision and action even as that same population persists as a recessive but also stabilizing background. These gulfs extend, too, among the influential class, isolating them as individuals and from cultural roots, while at the same time they pursue different ends under varying impulses.

The reader's relationship with the characters, then, functions differently from his relationship with the characters of *Middlemarch*, who share a community of values in whose patterns they move. JC's characters are totally alone, ideals are not commonly possessed, and therefore the effort the reader makes is "to place jig-saw bits into a slowly developing whole." Irony and characterization proceed in terms of contrast, division, illusion, misconception—all induced by utter loneliness—and exemplified by the Gould marriage, Nostromo, Monygham, the Viola sisters, and others.

2039 Meyer, Bernard C., M.D. *Joseph Conrad: A Psychoanalytic Biography* (Princeton, New Jersey: Princeton University Press, 1967).

In JC's childhood are to be found the causes of the psychological and physical problems of his adulthood: sickness and hardships of exile and especially his parents' deaths, his reading in adventure literature, and a desire for immortality. In his early writings, he expresses his yearning for Poland and his sense of love for his dead mother. In his youth, the first evidence of the repeated pattern of action followed by passivity which continued through his life can be detected in his sea adventures in Marseilles, followed by his attempted suicide; later, the same pattern is found in the writing of a book, followed by collapse. The pattern reveals the paradox of a man eager for action but also ready to shun responsibility, a paradox dramatized in many of his heroes, especially in Jim. JC's fear of abandonment such as that he felt with the death of his mother is found in his disappointment in such women as Eugenie Renouf, to whom he proposed in Mauritius. His Congo adventure is another attempt to assert himself. In his attempt to escape from the child's and lover's submission to a powerful woman, JC soon turned to Jessie George, but the device did not work: "An Outcast of the Islands" and "Youth" reveal the writer's interest in exogamy and his need to escape from the problems of marriage. Eventually, Ford Madox Ford's friendship helps JC by enabling him to examine his inner self in such works as *Lord Jim*, "Heart of Darkness," "The Secret

Sharer," and *The Secret Agent. Under Western Eyes* reveals poignantly the author's feeling of loss and isolation. After JC's breakdown in 1910, the quality of his work declines. [A fascinating biography—to be read with care.]

2040 Meyer, Bernard C., M.D. "On the Psychogenesis of the *Nigger*," from *Joseph Conrad: A Psychoanalytic Biography* (1967); rpt. *TCNN* (1969), pp. 112–15.

JC's creation of *The Nigger of the Narcissus* during his early months of marriage, when he no doubt found, in composing a sea story, escape from "the oppressive embrace of physical intimacy," is notable in that at this time he wrote no other major work. James Wait is, among other things, the "outsider," one of JC's multiple self-portraits: Wait's helplessness and his malingering are, no doubt, attributes of JC's own personality. And Wait's dying of tuberculosis derives from the slow dying of JC's own mother and father.

2041 Meyer, Bernard C., M.D. "The Secret Sharer," from *Joseph Conrad: A Psychoanalytic Biography* (1967); rpt. *JCC* (1975), pp. 13–25.

Biography and artistic achievement are inseparable. Accordingly, JC's intense introspection during the period of his life from 1898, when he began *Lord Jim*, to 1909, when he wrote "The Secret Sharer," was a result of his close relationship with Ford Madox Ford. Although the collaboration of these two men produced three works, for JC the relationship went far beyond that kind of sharing; it enabled him to penetrate psychic levels deep within himself, to that world of divided selves that characterizes "Heart of Darkness," *Jim*, and "The Secret Sharer."

2042 Mizener, Arthur (comp.). "Introduction to Part I," *Modern Short Stories: The Uses of the Imagination*, rvd. ed. (New York: Norton, 1967), pp. 1–4.

Some stories reveal an attitude describable as "twentieth-century romanticism," in which the writers do not surrender their perception of the nature of things, but neither do they abandon their belief in the "alien autonomy of the world outside themselves." This sort of writing often results in a type akin to social history. JC thus presents in "Heart of Darkness" a portrayal so brilliant and precise as to be unsurpassed by historians. Still, the darkness which concerns JC is that within man, not so much that of the African interior. What JC finally presents is metaphorical.

2043 Moll, June Madison. *British Heritage: An Exhibition of Books, Manuscripts & Iconology from the Collections at the University of Texas at Austin* (Austin: University of Texas, 1967), pp. 46–47.

JC's stories are often set in the tropics or at sea, yet this writer was not simply a recounter of romance or adventure. Rather, he wrote about the conflicts of "damaged souls." [Indicates that the manuscript of *Victory* contains extensive revisions and corrections. Includes a portrait.]

2044 Mursia, Ugo. "Nota alle opere," *Tutti i Racconti e i Romanzi Brevi* (Milan: Mursia, 1967), pp. xxxi–xli.

[Bio-bibliographical and critical notes to the complete tales and shorter novels of JC. The third edition (1971) contains also "Le sorelle" (The Sisters).] [In Italian.]

2045 Novak, Maximillian. "Alan Friedman: The Turn of the Novel," *NCF*, XXI (March 1967), p. 406.

[This review of Alan Friedman's *The Turn of the Novel* denounces JC for writing a traditional ending to *Chance*.]

2046 O'Brien, Justin. "Camus and Conrad: An Hypothesis," *Romantic Review*, LXVIII (October 1967), pp. 196–99; rpt. *Contemporary French Literature: Essays by Justin O'Brien*, ed. by Leon S. Roudiez (New Brunswick, New Jersey: Rutgers University Press, 1971), pp. 210–14.

JC's story, "The Secret Sharer," is similar to *L'Étranger* by Albert Camus (who may not have read JC's story) in that the narrator, the main character in each, is estranged from the environment that would naturally be his. But, more importantly, JC's young captain has the haunted impression during the whispered conversation with Leggatt that he is watching, listening to, and talking to himself, and the identification of the two becomes complete when the captain of the *Sephora* sits opposite the narrator, who later realizes that his visitor had seen in him something that reminded him of the man he was seeking. This is also close to the situation in Camus's *La Chute*, when Jean-Baptiste Clamens [sic] says suddenly to his listener, "But at the same time the portrait I hold out to my contemporaries becomes a mirror"; again, the fugitive from justice and his legal-minded listener are the same. But "L'Hote," a story by Camus, is even more similar to JC's story: the heroes of both works are unwilling enforcers of law, both befriend murderers and offer escape to freedom because of some obscure feeling of brotherhood, and both are young and testing themselves in their first positions of command. What is important to the reader is what goes on inside the man who befriends the murderers. Camus *may* have read "The Secret Sharer" and have found in it both an outlook on life like his own and a germ of his two tales written almost simultaneously, *La Chute* and "L'Hôte."

2047 Ong, Walter J., S.J. *In the Human Grain: Further Explorations of Contemporary Culture* (New York: Macmillan, 1967), p. 138.

Modern man has been somewhat prepared by literature, art, and humanistic studies for the new situation in which he finds himself, that of encountering his own interior consciousness as never before in history. Among the preparatory artists have been proto-existentialists such as Henry James and JC.

2048 Pavlov, Grigor. "The Theme of Alienation and Some Aspects of Presentation in Joseph Conrad's *Nostromo*," *University of Sofia Annual*, LXI (Sofia: Godisnik na Sofijskija Universitet, Fakultet Po Zapadni Filologii, 1967), pp. 245–78.

The concept of alienation as a psychological phenomenon caused by an economic fact was first celebrated by Marx in his early *Economic and Philosophic Manuscripts* of 1844, and the bulk of nineteenth and twentieth century literature portrays human relationships determined by fragmentation and alienation. The artist, however, must also offer a counter-measure to "re-humanize" the "area" of men's relationships shredded by private ownership. JC lived and worked in two centuries, and he explored the highest and last stage of development of the bourgeois world—imperialism. In *Nostromo*, the major theme of material interests reveals the impact of capitalism on human beings and shows how it determines and changes the psyches of men. Technically, *Nostromo* is a "brilliant tour de force." Here JC dispenses with the narrator, manipulates the time element, and uses Captain Mitchell to reflect ironic comment. The "great wonder" of JC's achievement is that "for all the complexity of structure, for all the involved pattern of timeshifts and multiple narrators," *Nostromo* emerges as "a solid chunk of life which the reader has observed from close quarters." With *Nostromo* "Joseph Conrad honourably acquits himself of the artist's supreme mission— to enlarge and quicken our awareness and our experience of the world we live in." [Although interesting, this essay finally fails to explain what JC's solution to alienation is.]

2049 Peyre, Henri. *French Novelists of Today* (New York: Oxford University Press, 1967), pp. 3, 57, 67, 68, 375.

Jules Romains found it "easy and a little cheap" to multiply strange actions and unpredictable behavior in his characters, as do some Russians, many Americans, and even JC, and then to "gape at the profundity of their contradictory, hence unfathomable, creations." Claude Simon, a practitioner of the so-called French "new novel," has felt strongly the impact of foreign literature, especially that of Dostoevski, Joyce, Faulkner, and JC.

2050 Poli, Bernard J. *Ford Madox Ford and the Transatlantic Review* (Syracuse, New York: Syracuse University Press, 1967), pp. 112–14.

At the time of JC's death, Ford hurriedly assembled a "Conrad Supplement" for the *Transatlantic Review* by asking various writers to send him short articles appropriate to the occasion. He was perhaps ill advised in doing so, since JC was not held in high esteem by most of the younger writers. The most notorious response was from Hemingway, then but little known, whose article at least had the virtue of candor to offset its impudent and indecorous stabs at Ford and T. S. Eliot and its flippant, left-handed compliments to JC.

2051 Powell, Marian C. "An Approach to Teaching 'The Secret Sharer,'" *English Journal*, LVI (January 1967), pp. 49–53, 96.

[Describes a unit of study devoted to an analysis and interpretation of "The Secret Sharer" exclusively from "the narrator-captain-(and at times)-author point of view." Includes questions formulated by students as well as the instructor, and records students' comments, suggesting through documentation the success of this critical approach.]

2052 Purdy, Strother B. "On the Relevance of Conrad: Lord Jim Over Sverdlovsk," *Midwest Quarterly*, IX (Autumn 1967), pp. 43–51.

JC remains in vogue in our universities today mainly because of his psychology, his shifting points of view, and his old fashioned code of honor in *Lord Jim* especially, but also in *Nostromo*, *The Nigger of the Narcissus*, and "Heart of Darkness." In our own age, Lord Jim was reborn as Gary Powers, who failed even as Jim failed, but was rewarded and honored by his country upon his return in 1962. In thus finding Lord Jim over Sverdlovsk, we note a social conclusion that we have lost something that is a part of fanaticism, militarism, and heroism, and perhaps bettered our chances of social survival by losing it. We have also lost something of what makes life worth living in discovering that moral values are illusions. We find, too, a literary conclusion in that JC rises before us to haunt us with his "impossible message" in which he wrote about not the nineteenth century, but about man. Lord Jim and Nostromo could regain lost honor in death; Gary Powers failed, no doubt because he, like most of us, was not brought up to believe that *he*, not others, would have to die. The *Patna* did not sink for Jim: the way of death is the way of life.

We know now that values are illusions, but JC knew the stage of knowledge beyond that, that brings us back to the starting point of simple acceptance of values, of values that are the message of Homer and Socrates—and of JC too.

2053 Raine, Kathleen. *Defending Ancient Springs* (London: Oxford University Press, 1867), pp. 176, 182, 183, 187.

St. John Perse's "earliest master" was JC, whom as a young man he knew intimately. Perse's concern with the metaphysical suggests JC's statement in the preface to *The Shadow-Line*, "a man that is born falls into a dream"; and his leader, his "superior man," is like JC's heroes, who are also men of "high caste." For Perse, man is "but the crest of the wave of nature," a concept taken from JC's "In the destructive element, immerse" of Stein, who was quoting Goethe.

2054 Rajiva, Stanley F. "The Singular Person: An Essay on Conrad's Use of Marlow as Narrator," *Literary Criterion* (University of Mysore), VIII, No. 2 (1967), pp. 35–45.

Marlow, who is neither JC's "mask" nor his "mouthpiece," "tells" four of JC's stories. JC "invented" Marlow as the archetype of the spiritual explorer of reality; he is "the artist, missionary and seeker after truth and true being." In "Heart of Darkness," Marlow comes "as close as any character can to being protagonist and narrator in one person"; "he dares to tell his own story and dares to find a meaning in that story." Ultimately, Marlow's "involvement" in the story is as total as JC's own. Altogether, in JC's works there are three Marlows [the Marlow of "Youth" is omitted]: the Marlow of *Chance*, a narrator so far removed from his story that he cannot "tell" it convincingly, the Marlow of *Lord Jim*, a "receiver and sifter" of evidence from several sources, as JC characterizes him, and the Marlow of "Heart of Darkness," who, through the pattern of Kurtz's life, his own voyage to find Kurtz, and his tranquil "recollection" of the whole thing in its spiritual focus makes of the telling a spiritual journey to the heart of darkness. In all this and through his narrator, JC is objectifying his own experience and providing himself, as the artist, with the emotional distance which irony provides. In "Heart of Darkness," Marlow makes the theme, man's inhumanity to man, universal. But here, Marlow is no longer the biographer: he reveals how he slowly comes to know Kurtz and searches for the truth—to the point where "his search for Kurtz's self and *our* search" become one.

2055 Raskin, Jonah. "'Heart of Darkness': The Manuscript Revisions," *RES*, XVIII (February 1967), pp. 30–39.

JC made five major revisions in "Heart of Darkness." In the manuscript, Marlow indicates preference for undisguised empire-building and by allusion mocks the masked Belgian imperialism and philanthropic associations. One exclusion makes the tale less specific politically: the metaphor of darkness is extended to a description of the earth as a "pea" spinning in the midst of the universe "on the heart of an immense darkness." By rejecting this image, JC withholds the notion that evil is inherent or embodied in the physical nature of the universe. The manuscript description of the imperial establishment in the Congo contained "far-fetched and uncontrolled" images; those of the text are more powerful. Together, they demonstrate a complex and varied experience in the Congo. The changes in the description of Kurtz diminish his corruption and partially make his fall a function of his role as a colonist in a primitive society rather than that of a bloodthirsty, cunning man endowed with mental powers. The manuscript revisions also show how JC moved from a notion that civilized man is "firmly divided" from the primitive to the notion that modern man is linked to the savage.

2056 Raskin, Jonah. "Imperialism: Conrad's 'Heart of Darkness,'" *Journal of Contemporary History*, II, No. 2 (April 1967), pp. 113–31.

Critics of "Heart of Darkness" have not devoted enough attention to imperialism in this work. Personal, social, and political influences account for the genesis of the story. JC used a personal experience, his trip up the Congo River, to create a historically and culturally significant achievement. He chronicled some modern achievements by chronicling those he saw in the Belgian Congo. In his diary (13 June to 1 August 1890), we learn that the Congo of "Heart of Darkness" was a less "civilized" one than the one JC saw in 1890. This tale revealed the hypocrisy of many Europeans in Africa well before Roger Casement's and E. D. Morel's exposés. Letters written later than the diary reveal JC to be disenchanted and depressed by the discovery of exploitation, even inhumanity, that underlay the empire builders. In *Nostromo*, he came to see his task as a writer to be the unmasking of society. Although "Heart of Darkness" demands to be read for its images of Africa, its moral condemnation of a colonialism which was, in his own words, "the vilest scramble for loot that ever disfigured the history of human conscience and geographical exploration," demands more serious attention.

2057 Raskin, Jonah. "The Mythology of Imperialism: A Study of Joseph Conrad and Rudyard Kipling." Unpublished dissertation, Manchester University, 1967; developed into "Conrad's Contradictions," "Season in Hell," "*Lord Jim*: White Skins," and "The Darkness of the Gulf," *The Mythology of Imperialism:*

Rudyard Kipling, Joseph Conrad, E. M. Forster, D. H. Lawrence, and Joyce Cary (New York: Random House, 1971), pp. 126–48, 149–61, 162–69, 170–205, 14–36 passim.

JC, in effecting a revolution in the novel, was preoccupied with race, with cultural and national conflicts. He was two men, Korzeniowski the Pole and Conrad the Englishman. The contradictions in his inner being account for the unevenness of his work: the trash—*The Rescue, The Arrow of Gold*; the mediocre work—*The Secret Agent, The Nigger of the Narcissus*; and works of power—"Heart of Darkness" and *Nostromo*. "Heart of Darkness" is a voyage into the hell of colonialism. Here, JC aims to transform the consciousness of his listeners, to "freak them out." In telling about Marlow's education, JC assumes that the novelist dives below the surface to bring up the "fundamental truth" of life. This tale, an epiphany, takes us behind the words "civilization" and "empire" to reveal there the European barbarism—a vision of evil. Marlow discovers that European civilization rests on the exploitation of black people by white people. At the center of hell which in Africa is Kurtz, the force of evil which men worship and lust after. Kurtz is JC's hero because he judges, he chooses and acts and he rebels. Lord Jim fails in achieving his ambition of being a hero; he is appealing because he does not become a racist or an imperialist. Costaguana, in *Nostromo*, is Marx's universe; the characters "spout" Marx. But JC had not understood Marx; nothing is settled in Costaguana's future except the certainty of revolution. [Obviously slanted and poorly written.]

2058 Rosenbach Company. *The Collected Catalogues of Dr. A. S. W. Rosenbach, 1904–1951,* 10 vols. (New York: Arno, 1967), IV, Catalog 26.

[Lists of first editions of JC's works and MSS, with dollar values.]

2059 Rosenberg, John D. "I've Been Reading: A Sermon to Soldiers," *Columbia University Forum,* X (Spring 1967), pp. 42–43.

"Heart of Darkness" combats imperialism and ideology. Kurtz depicts the sincere idealist and "fanatical, self-righteous savior of society" who degenerates into the savagery he hates and would exterminate; he becomes like it, and worse. Marlow is obsessed with Kurtz because his darkness is representative of us all. Marlow's journey performs a reversal: civilized man confronts, rather than represses, his primitive origins in order to slay the "pre-rational, anarchic, blood-lusting self."

2060 Rosenfield, Claire. *Paradise of Snakes: An Archetypal Analysis of Conrad's Political Novels* (Chicago and London: University of Chicago Press, 1967).

In his works, JC dramatizes the loneliness which an emphasis upon the private world and the interior journey toward personal understanding can cause, and in doing so he uses the myth of the hero to universalize a particular vision of reality. Myth is intricately related to religion, social forces, symbolism, and the interior world of dreams and fantasy. Every race evolves a myth of creation, and the collective unconscious is the source of the archetypes. Myth may be a necessary step toward a literature, and politics anticipate a timelessness within history, a time of apparently permanent, fixed social and political structures. Myth is a major aid to writers who live in a profane world instead of the older sacred one. Such novelists as Mann, Faulkner, Gide, Joyce, Lawrence, Camus, Dostoevski, and JC possess an intense and frustrated quest for identity and an equally intense and frustrated desire for community understanding. JC's novel *Nostromo* is an "astonishing failure": authorial detachment provides irony, authorial sympathy and tragedy, but the two fail to "fuse" with the characters of the men who assume the symbolic quests. The characters in *The Secret Agent* are imprisoned in time, and having fallen from an ideal of heroic action in a golden age, they still cannot act in order to arise to a better state. And in *Under Western Eyes*, Razumov's "self-communion" moves from personal history to universal myth in which Victor Haldin is a romantic parody of the hero of myth. [This book explains well the relation of myth to literature, but it is less successful in placing JC and his works in this context.]

2061 Roussel, Royal. "The Metaphysics of Darkness: A Study in the Development of Conrad's Fiction," *DA*, XXVII (1967), 3469A. Unpublished dissertation, The Johns Hopkins University, 1966; developed into *The Metaphysics of Darkness: A Study in the Unity and Development of Conrad's Fiction* (Baltimore and London: The Johns Hopkins Press, 1971).

In JC's world, the ultimate reality is "inert matter," "the darkness." Since for JC consciousness must always turn outside itself to find the source of its existence in some ground which does not share its own nature, man has an "orphaned quality," and thus all JC's major characters are, "in a fundamental sense," orphans. JC is concerned with man's need to find a "social or intersubjective ground" for his self, but in his world this search always occurs within the context of the "fundamental alienation of consciousness from its metaphysical source." Consciousness is, for JC, an accidental property. For most of his characters, the experience of vulnerability marks the real beginning of their voyage toward destruction, as with Marlow in "Youth," Lord Jim, Razumov, and the narrator of *The Shadow-Line*. Two general alternatives are open to man: (1) perhaps mind can confront the darkness directly and master it, but JC is skeptical about any such attempt, and (2) perhaps man can escape destruction by accepting the fact that it does not invalidate existence, and in this manner one's life comes to possess a certain stability. From this initial encounter with the darkness, JC's characters may then either return to commit themselves to the world and the men who inhabit it, thus affirming at least the possibility that man, through his own will, can master the darkness and win for himself a "stable identity," or they can accept the darkness as final and thereby come to terms with the "ephemerality of their own selves." This polarity between "a commitment to the dream" and "an acceptance of the darkness" marks the limits of JC's fictional world.

Seen as a whole, the Malayan novels lead inevitably to a nihilistic vision. *The Nigger of the Narcissus* and later works are, on one level, "redactions" of this completed vision of the darkness; each work records the defeat of some figure who is symbolic and confirms the inability of men to create through an act of will the ground of their lives. [Roussel's critical approach, working with a controlling metaphor, weakens his work.]

2062 Russell, Bertrand. *The Autobiography of Bertrand Russell, 1872–1914* (Boston: Little, Brown, 1967), pp. 320–24, 347–48.

When Bertrand Russell first met JC in 1913, he found him to be an "aristocratic Polish gentleman to his fingertips," who spoke English with a strong foreign accent. JC's feelings for the sea, as for England, was one of "romantic love—love from a certain distance." Although the two men differed in most of their opinions, "in something fundamental" they were "extraordinarily at one." Even if the two saw each other very infrequently through the years, they shared "a certain outlook on human life and human destiny" which made a "bond of extreme strength." "Heart of Darkness" best expresses JC's philosophy of life. For JC, man becomes free not by means of Rousseau's dictum but rather by "subduing wayward impulses to a dominant purpose." What interested him most was the individual human soul faced with the indifference of nature and often the hostility of man, and subject to inner struggles with passions "both good and bad" that led towards destruction. Two things seemed especially to occupy JC's imagination, loneliness and fear of what is strange. His point of view was far from modern, opposed as it was to Rousseau's sweeping aside of discipline and a belief in totalitarianism. [Contains three of JC's letters to Russell, dated 4 September 1913, 13 September 1913, and 22 December 1913.]

2063 Ryf, Robert S. "James Guetti, *The Limits of Metaphor: A Study of Melville, Conrad, and Faulkner*," *NCF*, XXII (September 1967), pp. 202–204.

Marlow, in "Heart of Darkness," looking over the abyss at the fallen Kurtz, sees his own reflection, a lesser Kurtz, and perceives there both his danger and the saving recognition of it. To Marlow, Kurtz was hollow at the core, lacked restraint, "played God," and fell. And Marlow lies to Kurtz's Intended, thereby accepting his own mortality and manifesting that solidarity which to JC is the only meaningful defense against the darkness. To JC, meaningfulness lies in meaningful acts.

2064 Sandison, Alan. "Joseph Conrad: A Window on to Chaos," *The Wheel of Empire: A Study of the Imperial Idea in Some Late Nineteenth and Early Twentieth-Century Fiction* (London: Macmillan; New York: St. Martin's Press, 1967), pp. 120–48; also vii, 59, 60, 61, 73, 78, 82, 94, 100, 111–12, 114, 149, 152, 160, 171, 176, 195–96, 198, 199, 200.

In his fiction, JC explicitly relates the "expansionist behavior of self" to that of the state; the individual consciousness practices a "moral imperialism." When faced with the unfamiliar and the incomprehensible, the white man loses faith in his fellows and turns inward. The theme of "An Outcast of the Islands" is one of complete incomprehension, and "Heart of Darkness" emphasizes the enemy within the self. Like Heyst, one cannot run away from life and remain whole; the human community is a moral necessity, and belief in an ideal offers some protection against "chaotic nature." JC's is a "highly pragmatic" idealism. In the Romantic tradition, JC shows that man is at war with nature even though he yearns to believe otherwise. Nature is a hostile principle, but it must be engaged for one to realize self-consciousness—this is Stein's advice to Jim. For JC, man creates an essentially illusory world which is his means to survival. The only solidarity for JC, though, is that of isolated victims—the lonely, imperial aliens of his colonial novels. As the men in "An Outpost of Progress" come to realize, they can maintain identity with the help of a familiar environment, human and natural. In recommending the virtue of sacrificing to an ideal, JC did not have a God.

2065 Scholes, Robert. *The Fabulators* (New York: Oxford University Press, 1967), pp. 72–73.

In JC's view, as expressed especially in "Heart of Darkness," if a man does not face and acknowledge the darkness within him in order to struggle with it, he will become its victim.

2066 Schultheiss, Thomas. "Conrad on Stage Censorship," *American Notes & Queries*, V (April 1967), pp. 117–18.

JC expressed his objection to English censorship of plays in a letter, jointly with several other objectors, to the editor of the *Times* in October, 1907; in his article "The Censor of Plays" of 1907; and in the expression of his views through John Galsworthy in a report by forty-nine witnesses to the Joint Select Committee of Parliament in 1909.

2067 Secor, Robert. "Hawthorne, Conrad, and the Descent into Darkness," *Mad River Review*, II (Summer–Fall 1967), pp. 41–55.

The descent or journey into the heart of darkness is basic in works by both Hawthorne and JC. The former's characters such as Young Goodman Brown, Ethan Brand, Roger Malvin, and Donatello and Hilda in *The Marble Faun* are much like JC's Marlow in this respect. In going along with their characters, into the darkness, Hawthorne and JC not only look back past the travels of Bunyan's pilgrim to those of the mythical heroes but also look ahead to the findings of the psychologists who, like Jung and Freud, have told us that we too, in order to attain self-knowledge and health, must journey into the deepest recesses of ourselves. Like Hawthorne, JC knew about man's instinctive desire to suppress knowledge of himself, and both writers force their characters to recognize their hearts of darkness. JC's use of the fear of madness in such characters is an extension of Hawthorne's suggestion of madness when our moral world begins to crumble. For both, too, confession as a restorative of sanity is dependent upon the fact that it restores to the individual an identity. But the characters who do not feel the need for confession no longer find certainty in the moral order, but find order and certainty instead in immorality, as do Goodman Brown, Ethan Brand, and Kurtz.

2068 Sherrill, Rowland A. "Conrad's *Lord Jim*," *Explicator*, XXV (March 1967), Item 55.

Perhaps because it is too obvious, critics have too often ignored the conflict in *Lord Jim* between man (Jim) and nature (as destructive of life). The critics' analysis of the relationship between Jim and the human moral community is valid and important, but it should be supplemented by analysis of the man-nature conflict.

2069 Sherry, Norman. "The Greenwich Bomb Outrage and *The Secret Agent*," *RES*, N.S., XVIII (November 1967), pp. 412–28; expanded in Norman Sherry, *Conrad's Western World* (Cambridge: At the University Press, 1971), pp. 228–47; rpt.

Also in *Conrad, The Secret Agent: A Casebook*, ed. by Ian Watt (London: Macmillan, 1973), pp. 208–28.

Although JC claimed that his source for *The Secret Agent* was not the Greenwich Bomb Outrage of 1894, several facts argue to the contrary. JC's claim that he was out of the country during the incident and thus not immediately in touch with the bombing is inaccurate; it is easily documented that he was living in London at the time. Furthermore, there are numerous parallels between *Agent* and the published accounts of the Greenwich incident. The first newspaper reports of the incidents are as vague as the accounts in *Agent*. In the actual incident, Bourdin, the anarchist, is badly mutilated, and his condition is described in great detail in the London magazines. Stevie, who parallels Bourdin, is described in the same manner. The apparent cause of the fatal accident is also identical. Moreover, Stevie is accompanied by his brother-in-law, Verloc, and Bourdin, according to a newspaper interview, met with his brother-in-law, Samuels, who was also an anarchist. There is also the suggestion that the Greenwich incident was really a "police plot to bring the anarchists into disrepute in England," an interpretation of which JC could easily have been aware.

2070 Smith, Jack E. "The Unity of Joseph Conrad's Short Story Collections," *DA*, XXVIII (1967), 243A. Unpublished dissertation, University of Arkansas, 1967.

2071 Soloman, Eric. "Joseph Conrad, William Faulkner and the Nobel Prize Speech," *N&Q*, XIV [Vol. 212 of the continuous series], (July 1967), pp. 247–48.

Faulkner drew on the "rich rhetoric" of his Nobel Prize Acceptance Speech (1950) "for the 'Thursday Night' section" of *A Fable*. What is less well-known is that "much of the rhetoric and many of the key ideas" of the final paragraph of Faulkner's speech appear in JC's "Henry James: An Appreciation," published in 1905 in the *North American Review* and reprinted in *Notes on Life and Letters*. Both Faulkner and JC present fundamentally "hopeful views of man's chances in a doom-ridden world."

2072 "Speculations," *TLS* (26 October 1967), p. 1011.

The commonly accepted conclusion that JC's later work is inferior to his earlier does not seem to arise from his "dual heritage," i.e. his "volatile and revolutionary" father and his "sober and conservative" uncle. Even if novels explore the resources of language, they also—and no doubt more importantly—like "Heart of Darkness," are about human feelings. [Rev. of Robert A. Hodges, *The Dual*

Heritage of Joseph Conrad (1967) and James Guetti, *The Limits of Metaphor* (1967).]

2073 Standop, Ewald, and Edgar Mertner. *Englische Literaturgeschichte* (English Literary History), (Heidelberg: Quelle & Meyer, 1967), pp. 535, 560–65.

Though JC is in many ways an outsider, he continues the major tradition of the English novel writing by placing his characters in situations that demand them to make a moral choice. A good survey within the limits imposed by the aims of this history of English literature.] [In German.]

2074 Subramanyan, N. S. "Henry James (1845–1916) and Joseph Conrad (1857–1924): The Point of View on Reality and Projection of Situations," *Movements in Modern English Novel* [sic], (Gwalior: Kitab Ghar, 1967), pp. 79–95.

JC widened the scope of the novel in two ways: horizontally, over the "vast expanses of the world's oceans" and vertically, to include mental and moral values through variations of narrative technique. He contributed characters whose inner motives he could lay bare. In *Lord Jim* and "Heart of Darkness," Marlow is JC's alter ego, "an extension of his mind." When Marlow repeats details of incidents and characters, JC cleverly demonstrates that "reality is not separate from the impressions left by it on a perceiving and recording mind." Marlow as narrator, "with his own independent personality, particularly his love of symbolism and a sense of universal values," was the product of JC's "serious immersion in the waters of Art." To achieve "the perfect blending of form and substance," Marlow became the "mind" through which JC unobtrusively presented his view of reality. In *Nostromo*, JC's presentation of a political revolution in a fictitious South American country, the scenes are selected and arranged almost as a film is edited for *montage*. JC added depth to the novel through the "startling presentation" of such "symbolisms" as the corpse of the Jewish hide-merchant. Each character in the novel is "of balance, proportion and value."

1968

2098 Alter, Robert. *Fielding and the Nature of the Novel* (Cambridge, Massachusetts: Harvard University Press, 1968), pp. 12, 24, 57, 130.

Henry James and JC wrote so-called art novels, works which contain so intricate a "reflexive system" that one reading is inadequate. For JC, as for Fielding, Proust, Joyce, and Faulkner, style is not merely the means of conveying or framing events but, frequently, the event itself. And JC's themes, like those of Thomas Mann and unlike those of Fielding, appeal not to the intellect but primarily to the imagination.

2099 "Ark and Archetypes," *TLS* (4 April 1968), p. 335.

Two recently published books on JC indicate that at the present time "the critical industry seems self-perpetuating": critics of JC may be trapped in an "unwieldy academic machine" or may be swallowing "a set of canting clichés about the modern world." [Rev. of Donald C. Yelton, *Mimesis and Metaphor* (1967), and of Claire Rosenfield, *Paradise of Snakes* (1967).]

2100 "Article Note," *CON*, I, No. 2 (Fall 1968), p. 14.

The two aspects of *Lord Jim* that most seriously interest Polish critics are the moral themes and JC's urge to suggest in his work a sense of guilt, a guilt believed by some critics to have emanated from JC's fear that he had deserted Poland. Other interests are JC's indebtedness to Polish literature. [These conclusions are from Stefan Zabierowski, "*Lord Jim* w Polsce (1904–1939)," (*Lord Jim* and Poland [1904–1939]), *Zesyty Naukowe Uniwersytet Jagiellonskiego* (Scholarly Fascicles of the Jagiollonian University), No. 168, Prace Historycznoliterackie Zeszyt 14 (Works on the History of Literature, Fascicle 14), pp. 193–209.]

2101 Ashley, Leonard R. N., and Stuart L. Astor. "Joseph Conrad" [Introduction to "The Secret Sharer"], *British Short Stories: Classics and Criticism* (Englewood Cliffs, New Jersey: Prentice-Hall [Prentice-Hall English Literature Series], 1968), p. 100.

"The Secret Sharer" interweaves two situations, each "fraught with dramatic potential": a young captain's first "bout" with the responsibility of commanding a ship and its men is joined with the equally powerful story of an alleged murderer who throws himself on the captain's mercy. The critics who see in Leggatt the narrator's own "self-doubt and irresponsible behavior" are aiming at a "fruitful" interpretation of this complex tale, but the nature of that irresponsibility and of the guilt that threatens each of the major characters provides another dimension for this story.

2102 Baumbach, Jonathan, and Arthur Edelstein (eds.). "Joseph Conrad," *Moderns and Contemporaries: Nine Masters of the*

Short Story (New York: Random House, 1968), pp. 41–43.
See 2106.

2103 Beachcroft, T. O. *The Modest Art: A Survey of the Short Story in English* (London: Oxford University Press, 1968), pp. 51, 71, 150–52, 155, 160.

JC is at his best when he can extend the short story to accommodate scenery and natural settings that help display moral character, as in "Youth" and the "more satisfying work of art," "Typhoon." JC's world, like Kipling's, is a "man's world." The sea makes character; isolation disintegrates character. "The Idiots" is related to the "dark side of Maupassant"; "The Brute" is "an old salt's yarn." JC's preoccupation with the personality of his narrators is at times a source of difficulty, which is cumbersome in "Heart of Darkness," disingenuous in "Youth," and perhaps becomes a "dubious trick," unconvincing since no narrator like Marlow could employ "Conradian prose." The "narrator approach" also encourages the interruption of the story in order to indulge in discussions of "problems of authorship." JC's prefaces, sorting out truth from fiction and hearsay, betray the uneasiness he feels about this device.

2104 Beebe, Maurice. *A Critical Study Guide to Joseph Conrad's Lord Jim* (Totowa, New Jersey: Littlefield, Adams [Era Key Guides], 1968).

[An unusually useful "guide" to a major literary work, prepared by a major critic. Contains visual aids to *Lord Jim*, a brief biography of JC, background material, a "capsule summary" of the novel, a comprehensive chapter-by-chapter summary with integrated commentary, a critical analysis of the work, a guide to analysis of characters, study questions, research areas, a bibliography, and a glossary-index. An excellent "critical study guide" to *Jim*, written with thoroughness and insight.]

2105 Begnal, M. H. "*Lord Jim* and 'The Rhyme of the Ancient Mariner,'" *CON*, I, No. 2 (Fall 1968), p. 54.

JC parallels the degradation and horror of the *Patna* incident in *Lord Jim* in Marlow's talk with the "*delirium-tremens* ridden" chief engineer of the ship and in Marlow's later meeting with Chester and Captain Robinson with Coleridge's Wedding Guest who, like Marlow, is both repelled and attracted by the tale in which he is involved.

2106 Bender, Todd K. "Fictional Time and the Problem of Free Will," *Wisconsin Studies in Literature*, IX, No. 5 (1968), pp. 12–22.

Ford Madox Ford's and JC's early collaboration on *The Inheritors* produced a bizarre and "awkward" work which, however, can best be understood as a "clumsy" expression of certain ideas in Henri Bergson's *Time and Free Will*, and approached in this way *The Inheritors* "illuminates" JC's later work, "Heart of Darkness." The "central circumstance" of the novel is a clear statement of the relation of Europe to primitive people (in Greenland), the problem at the center of "Heart of Darkness." In the love story, the characterization of the girl is absurd, but Granger's visit to her is similar to Marlow's visit to Kurtz's Intended. Bergson's vocabulary in *Time and Free Will* helps to explain the import of significant parts of Ford's and JC's novel: in telling his story, the fictional narrator naturally creates his fictive time and rules over his fictional characters as he wills. But Ford and JC avoid a serious treatment of the issue of the British and European attitude toward exploitation of primitive people by transferring the problem to the unlikely scene of Greenland, and they distract the reader's attention from the political situation by an unbelievable "boy-meets-girl" story. In "Heart of Darkness," JC reformulates this material by taking his characters directly to the "heart" of Africa and transfers the drama from a trite love affair to the quality of the consciousness of the storyteller Marlow, thereby developing a form worthy of the seriousness of the moral and political issue.

2107 Bernard, Kenneth. "Mr. Kurtz and the Lady," *CEA*, XXXI (December 1968), p. 17; rpt. *CON*, I, No. 3 (Summer 1969), p. 61.

Marlow found the "*horrid truth*" in Kurtz and the native woman "prancing" on the shore: "Adam undid us all." Kurtz was "*drowned* in sin," just as "I feel close, /Horribly, horribly *close* to him now," with you, "my dear." [A poem.]

2108 Besdine, Matthew. "The Jocasta Complex, Mothering and Genius, Part II," *Psychoanalytic Review*, LV (Winter 1968–69), pp. 574–600.

A character structure which is the result of "Jocasta mothering" has as its salient features "an unresolved Oedipus complex, the fear of love, an underlying sense of guilt, strong masochistic tendencies, paranoid trends, a significant homosexual component, extraordinary egocentricity, exorbitant striving for recognition, and overall narcissism." Jocasta mothering is an important component of genius. The life of JC (and others) reveals an unresolved Oedipus complex based on Jocasta mothering, which leads one to conclude that Jocasta mothering is one ingredient of genius. [Part I of this article contains no mention of JC.]

2109 Bickerton, Derek. "James Joyce and the Development of Interior Monologue," *EIC*, XVIII (January 1968), pp. 32–46.

James Joyce developed the interior monologue from the stories in *Dubliners* to *Ulysses*, refining this technique throughout his career of experimentation. Both Lawrence and JC employed Joyce's poetic patterns of repetition and parallelism, as well as free indirect speech and indirect interior monologue.

2110 Bojarski, Edmund A. "Conrad at the Crossroads: From Navigator to Novelist with Some New Biographical Mysteries," *Texas Quarterly*, XI (Winter 1968), pp. 15–29.

There is little information on the period of JC's life between 17 January 1894, when he disembarked from the *Adowa*, terminating his life on the sea, and 4 July 1894, when he sent his first novel, *Almayer's Folly*, to the publisher. On 3 July 1894, JC testified at the Trade Board's investigation into the proper manning of ships as his last official act as a master mariner. [Includes an exact record of JC's testimony before the Board in which he implies that the *Adowa* was undermanned, but he specifically denies later suggesting a necessary increase in manpower.]

2111 Brady, Marion B. "The Collector-Motif in *Lord Jim*," *Bucknell Review*, XVI (May 1968), pp. 66–85.

One of the series of interlocking motifs that serves as a pattern of communication in *Lord Jim* is the collector motif. In the basic conflict of the novel, the collectors share a desire for peace and irresponsibility, an evasion of "how-to-be"; their collections are "vast rationalizations that protect them from self-knowledge, from understanding." Most of them have been stranded in the East, and most of them confidently judge Jim and prescribe his cure. Marlow is a collector whose plan for Jim is only a variation of Chester's plan to bury Jim on a guano island. Marlow takes his prize specimen to Stein, the most distinguished collector in the novel. Marlow's certainty about Stein blinds the reader, who assumes Marlow to be objective. Stein is inadequate, however, for his collection is a celebration of immobility and death. Later, Jewel, probably Stein's daughter, is also added to Stein's collection. Stein and Marlow assist Jim into jumping into the "everlasting hole" of Patusan, which designates the bottom of the universe and is not only a grave but also a specimen case, for Cornelius and Doramin, as well as Jim, are collectors' items. The collector motif leads to an epiphany in which Brown is seen as Jim's alter ego, the negative potential of his dreams of glory, a man also favored by a collector. The collectors destroy life by breaking it up into a multitude of separate entities. Only Marlow searches for synthesis and integration.

2112 Braun, Andrzej. "Indonezja Conradowska" (Conrad's Indonesia), Part I, "Spotkanie ze wschodem" (Meeting with the East), No. 11 (17 March 1968); Part II, "Zeluga na *Vidarze*" (Sailing on the *Vidar*), No. 12 (24 March 1968); Part III, "Proba wybobrazni" (Trial of the Imagination), No. 13 (31 March 1968); Part IV, "Patusan," No. 13 (7 April 1968); all pub. in *Swiat* (World), on dates given; rpt. *Sladami Conrada* (In Conrad's Steps), (Warsaw: Czytelnik, 1972).

[Braun spent six months in 1966 touring Indonesia, Borneo, etc., visiting places associated with JC. He relies on the work of Norman Sherry, Resink, etc., for his sources. No bibliography; indexes of personal and geographical names, maps, and illustrations.] [In Polish.]

2113 Bross, Addison W. "Joseph Conrad's Female Characters in Selected Fiction," *DA*, XXVII (1968), 2675A–76A. Unpublished dissertation, Louisiana State University, 1967.

2114 Chinol, Elio. "Introduction," *Romanzi della Malesia* (Malay Novels), (Milan: Mursia, 1968), pp. xiii–xxxix.

Both *Almayer's Folly* and *An Outcast of the Islands* show the same defects: excessive verbosity and an inclination towards melodrama. *The Rescue* is the most nearly an artifact, a romantic and sentimental novel of the Lingard trilogy. Lingard himself is a sort of knight-errant of the sea and has the superficial traits of the conventional hero of popular fiction. In *Lord Jim*, a psychological and moral drama presents both advantages (in the sense of mystery and suspense created by Marlow's narrative) and difficulties, in that, lacking a full perspective one misses the meaning of many details and symbols that are fully appreciated only after several readings of the novel. [In Italian.]

2115 Choudhury, A. F. "The Enemy Territory: A Study of Joseph Conrad, E. M. Forster and D. H. Lawrence in Relation to Their Portrayal of Evil." Unpublished dissertation, Leicester University, 1968.

2116 Conquest, Edwin P., Jr. "The Abyss of Unrest: Joseph Conrad's Early Tales," *DA*, XXVII (1968), 5047A. Unpublished dissertation, Princeton University, 1967.

2117 Cook, William J., Jr. "*Lord Jim* as Metaphor," *CON*, I, No. 2 (Fall 1968), pp. 45–53.

In *Lord Jim*, JC blends theme and imagery so perfectly that the novel may be seen as an extended metaphor, firstly representative of Jim's plight as a member of the human society and finally suggestive of the universal human predicament. Jim, portrayed as a "dual creature, capable of both good and evil," "treads the ashy path" between the two poles. Since Jim, aware of both but neither possessed by nor possessing either extreme, cannot confront reality, and since to accept failure would be to forfeit his "noble illusions," he therefore lives in the "mist" of an illusion of grandeur and success which removes him from reality, in a continual conflict between the two worlds of the dream and the surrounding reality. Although Jim's dream will not let him be satisfied with his accomplishment in Patusan, possibly Marlow's last view of him is an indication of his success, a "paradoxical success-in-failure."

2118 Craig, Robert. "Conrad and the *Riverside*," *TLS* (25 July 1968), p. 788.

Since JC was requested to give evidence to the Departmental Committee on the Manning of Merchant Ships at the hearing held on 3 July 1894, it seems improbable that any stain on his character survived as a consequence of his experiences on the *Riverside*. [A reply to Geoffrey Ursell, "Conrad and the *Riverside*," (1968).]

2119 Cross, David. "Conrad's 'The Duel,'" *TLS* (15 August 1968), p. 881.

The source of "The Duel" seems to be a story from E. Colombey's *Histoire Anecdotique du Duel* (Paris, 1861), as taken from *L'Audience*, perhaps a periodical. But since the Colombey story appears in an English translation in Andrew Steinmetz's *The Romance of Dueling*, Vol. 2, 1968, there is no way of knowing whether JC first saw the account in French or English.

2120 Daghlian, Philip B. "Teaching 'Heart of Darkness,'" *Teaching Literature in Grades Ten Through Twelve*, ed. by Edward B. Jenkinson and Philip B. Daghlian (Bloomington: Indiana University Press, 1968), pp. 306–16.

"Heart of Darkness" may be read as "rather fuzzy melodrama and travelogue," as an "impressionistic" account of the evils of exploitation in the Congo, as a study of the effect of the jungle on "a man of extraordinary potentialities for good and evil" (Kurtz), or as a meditation on the very thin margin that divides our so-called civilization from primeval savagery. Marlow, not an ordinary Englishman, is an active sailor affected by the East; his mind is enlarged at last by his meeting with Kurtz, and in the last part of the story his conflict is resolved. From this story we learn that the power of evil, always around us, is "neutralized" by the conventions of our world, that only an "acid test" of an isolation like Kurtz's calls one "to face up to surviving or succumbing to the power of evil." [Followed by questions for study.]

2121 Dahl, James C. "Kurtz, Marlow, Conrad and the Human Heart of Darkness," *Studies in the Literary Imagination*, I (October 1968), pp. 33–40.

What "Heart of Darkness" reveals of the introspective journey into the dark side of human personality is of great importance to our present age. In the story, Kurtz's degeneration occurs because Kurtz in Europe has no idea of his potential for savagery, but he represents the shallowness of the philosophical thought of his time. Away from the restraints of civilization, Kurtz is helpless against his inclination toward the abominable which he encounters in the natives, and he therefore degenerates into a "ruthless egomaniac." Marlow, going to Africa for adventure and the desire to fulfill a childhood dream, also discovers there his own potential for evil. He eventually remains loyal to Kurtz because he himself is fearful of hollowness, and only the gospel of work and his dissimilar circumstances protect him from the temptations to which Kurtz succumbs. His thoughts about human life, after his return to the "sick" city, include his belief in the impossibility of real communication among men and hence of no real affection there, his conviction of the failure of idealism (based on Kurtz's example), and a belief that the most one can hope for from an understanding of the nature of human life comes too late. Carl Jung believed deeply in the importance of religion to human happiness, especially in regard to the descent into self; perhaps the Western world today, with little religious belief, has good reason to feel ill at ease.

2122 Diolé, Phillipe. "Un Sauvage en liberté," *Nouvelles Litteraires* (2 May 1968), pp. 1, 13.

Jerry Allen's *The Sea Years of Joseph Conrad* attempts to clarify the "savage" part of JC's life before he took up writing. His love for the mistress of the pretender to the Spanish throne, his career as a smuggler, his voyages in the South Seas, and his trip in the Congo all served as materials for his novels. He was able to dramatize the moral problems created by man's struggle with man, with the elements, with evil and with death. [In French.]

2123 Donoghue, Denis. *The Ordinary Universe: Soundings in Modern Literature* (New York: Macmillan, 1968), pp. 53–58, 158, 182, 304.

JC's symbolism is weak. Often he attempts to enlarge the significance of an event by surrounding it with "breathless prose and ominous suggestion" without reasonable preparation. *Chance* is "grossly overwritten"; *The Secret Agent* has no force or value other than the contemptuous narrative voice. After freeing himself from his Polish roots, JC never again committed himself to facts. His greatness consists, therefore, in the "moral resonance of his fables," with its source in sequences of acts and events, in plot.

2124 Duffy, J. J. "Conrad and Pater: Suggestive Echoes," *CON*, I, No. 1 (Summer 1968), pp. 45–47.

JC drew upon Pater's "Sebastian van Storck" for some of the character and vision of Stein in *Lord Jim*, upon *Marius the Epicurean* and "The School of Giorgione" for his concern with music and fiction in the Preface to *The Nigger of the Narcissus*, and upon Pater's passage about the Mona Lisa for Flora de Barral in *Chance*.

2125 Earnshaw, H. G. "Joseph Conrad," *Modern Writers: A Guide to Twentieth-Century Literature in the English Language* (Edinburgh and London: W. & R. Chambers, 1968), pp. 44–50.

JC, a man apart from other men, wrote novels about men who are "set apart from their fellows." He says, in effect, in "Typhoon," that the man who will not swerve from his duty in the face of danger will overcome difficulties, hardships, and dangers that daunt other men. In *Lord Jim*, *Nostromo*, and *The Rescue*, the mood is pessimistic in general. In *Nostromo*, a good example of JC's methods as a novelist, the characters reveal themselves so that the work displays human nature in its great variety. JC also shows that false beliefs influence men's actions as strongly as the truth, as we see in Nostromo himself.

2126 Edelstein, Arthur. "Joseph Conrad," in *Moderns and Contemporaries: Nine Masters of the Short Story*, ed. by Jonathan Baumbach and Arthur Edelstein (New York: Random House, 1968), pp. 41–43.

Into JC's own experience was built the "great symbol that rolls through his works," the sea, lending them the depth and magnitude consistent with the moral dilemmas they explore. From this sea, with its mythic, psychological, and literal range, mysteriously rises Leggatt in "The Secret Sharer," to supply the ship with a controlling purpose and to render to the captain his own ship, his own life. This story is a metaphor of initiation into that "moral atmosphere which is the difference between life and living." "Youth" joins two planes, or seas, of vision, the "surging" plane of the young Marlow's "bright youth" and that of the older Marlow who sees a truth invisible to the youthful Marlow—the "fact of morality."

2127 Elwin, Malcolm. "Introduction," *A Set of Six*, ed. by Malcolm Elwin (Geneva: Heron Books, 1968), pp. vii–x.

Because JC in 1905 was suffering from a constant lack of money, from insomnia, and from dyspepsia, he could not begin another novel at that time. Consequently, he produced the stories included in *A Set of Six*. Because of its numerous rejections, JC considered "Gaspar Ruiz" unsatisfactory. "The Informer" is better because of the personality of the narrator, "The Anarchist" reflects some of the sentiment that JC expressed in *The Secret Agent*, and "The Brute" shows a narrative technique which is particularly well handled. "The Duel" concerns Napoleon, and JC especially admired this story though its lightness of tone is not really characteristic of his other works.

2128 Enright, D. J. "Mistah Conrad—He Dead," *Southern Review* (University of Adelaide, Australia), III, No. 1 (1968), pp. 180–84.

In *Joseph Conrad and the Fiction of Autobiography* (1966), Edward W. Said loses "all meaning" of JC's texts: his "remarkable" analysis of the "unreworkable" "The Return" "out-abstracts" JC's worst style and is "actually . . . painful to read." Sometimes Said's style is "almost endearingly sloppy, again like Conrad." The chapter on *The Shadow-Line* is "the best section for those who still want to try to understand what Mr. Said is getting at." Bernard C. Meyer's *Joseph Conrad: A Psychoanalytic Biography* (1967) relates JC's life to his fiction and then reduces the fiction to "a single theme of formula"; in the end, JC was "a hair-fetishest, a mysogynist, a castration-hypochondriac" who was "looking for a mother-substitute rather than a wife or lover." Like Said, Meyer "tends to create artificial problems instead of solving real ones." *Conrad: A Collection of Critical Essays*, ed. by Marvin Mudrick (1966) remains in the world of criticism, "where speculation doesn't run utterly riot." [Points out through a few critics some weaknesses of JC's writings.]

2129 Esslinger, Pat M. "A Theory and Three Experiments: The Failure of the Conrad-Ford Collaboration," *Western Humanities Review*, XXII (Winter 1968), pp. 59–67.

The major problem for Ford Madox Ford and JC during their collaboration was style, a style that was to make the work interesting, that used fresh unusual words from beginning to end, and that avoided fatiguing the reader with either startling or outmoded words. But the actual products of the collaboration were abortive. *The Inheritors* (1901), a combination of science fiction and political satire, has a protagonist with no personality to unfold, no purposeful action, and no effective dialogue. *Romance* (1903) has an improbable plot, more successful characters than those of *Inheritors*, and a gain of emotional intensity, but neglects themes of human experience in favor of a pet formula. *The Nature of a Crime* (1909) is merely "self-conscious experimentation." Causes of the failure of the collaboration are the writers' acquiescence to English public taste, probably in order to produce works that would sell, and the fact that the two writers did not observe their theories. Also, when JC was apparently forced to follow a contrived theory of how to write a novel, he failed to produce either financial successes or works of art.

2130 Evans, Oliver. *Anaïs Nin* (Carbondale and Edwardsville: Southern Illinois University Press, 1968), pp. 92, 141, 198.

JC's "Impressionistic" technique, when employed by a master, can produce masterpieces. But it involves a certain sacrifice: invisible authorship and point of view subsume a very narrow view of fiction. JC attempts to maintain a technical objectivity toward his characters and at least theoretically allows the reader to form his own opinion of them, but his method of scattering clues and innuendoes that influence the reader's opinions is a kind of hypocrisy.

2131 "Exploring the Shadow-Line," *TLS* (26 December 1968), p. 1450.

Even if the "Conradian magic" sometimes seems in danger of disappearing behind "a cloud of hocus-pocus" [critical commentary], we are still left with the JC we admire and don't want to lose, the books in which "the shadow-line between what is clear and what is 'mysterious' cannot be fixed, nor the dark area explored for us." [Rev. of Bernard C. Meyer, *Joseph Conrad: A Psychoanalytic Biography* (1967); Douglas Hewitt, *Conrad: A Reassessment* (1968); Paul Kirschner, *Conrad: The Psychologist as Artist* (1968); J. I. M. Stewart, *Joseph Conrad* (1968), and Edward W. Said, *Joseph Conrad and the Fiction of Autobiography* (1966).]

2132 Farrell, James T. "On Joseph Conrad," *CON*, I, No. 1 (Summer 1968), pp. i–ii.

JC's viewpoint in his works is that of a spectator, and his world, or worlds, is that of sight, although he also uses the other senses. JC is at his stylistic best in *Lord Jim*. Jim is "enigmatically human"; he is not a type but a "tragedy"; and Marlow is an appropriate "fictional device" for narrating Jim's story. This work is the "greatest of Conrad's novels." JC is a great writer "who will survive if great writing survives." [Sketchy.]

2133 Flamm, Dudley. "The Ambiguous Nazarene in *Lord Jim*," *ELT*, XI, No. 1 (1968), pp. 35–37.

Jim, in *Lord Jim*, as "one of us" (a phrase from Genesis 3:22) suggests Jim as a fellow human being caught in a classically human dilemma, his values being a part of the common Western heritage. In this context, Tamb' Itam's reference to Cornelius as the Nazarene separates the Christian cultural tradition from the Malay tradition and also ironically emphasizes the fact that the betraying Nazarene too is "one of us," thus confirming the "tragedy of the world in ethical, moral, and religious terms." In recognizing Brown as a "sinner" like himself, Jim responds to the "same sense of 'one of us'" which had in part caused Marlow to respond to Jim. And at the end of the novel, when Jim remains ambiguous and "under a cloud," the moral implications of what being "one of us" means escapes any simple explanation. [For additional interpretations of the meaning of the "Nazarene," see Thomas Schultheiss, "Lord Hamlet and Lord Jim," (1966), and "Cornelius the Nazarene: Ambi-ambiguity in *Lord Jim*," (1969).]

2134 Fradin, Joseph I. "Anarchist, Detective, and Saint: The Possibilities of Action in *The Secret Agent*," *PMLA*, LXXXIII (October 1968), pp. 1414–22.

In *The Secret Agent*, JC puts in doubt even those possibilities of moral action which he sustains in his other novels. Every human action reveals its ambiguity by being set in the context of the anarchy which JC exposes as the reality underlying the city-world; and no human action seems capable of stemming the inexorable movement of the community toward inertia and death. Verloc's inertia, itself a form of death, is central in the novel; but the full contours of action can be decisively traced in four other characters who exhibit a wide range of responses to the condition in which they find themselves: the Professor, the arch-anarchist who believes that destruction can hasten a new era of freedom; the Assistant Commissioner, who seems on the surface most admirably Conradian in his ability to get his job done; and the very contemporary saint figures, Stevie, whose frustrated will to act for justice drives him to rages, and Michaelis, the paroled apostle of revolution. The last irony of *Agent* may be that JC, who despises inertia and who creates a world in which the ego turned in upon itself is everywhere part of the pattern of death, is brought by the logic of the novel to a final paradox: that in a disintegrated world in which to act may be to kill, totally self-preoccupied inertia, where it does no willful destruction, may become the posture of a saint. [A perceptive, closely reasoned essay to which a summary can hardly do justice.]

2135 Fradin, Joseph I., and Jean W. Creighton. "The Language of *The Secret Agent*: The Art of Non-Life," *CON*, I, No. 2 (Fall 1968), pp. 23–35.

In *The Secret Agent*, JC uses language to make the reader see the process of the world's descent into degradation and anarchy. This use of language is evident in the novel's many puns; in the central metaphor: the world as a drained aquarium; in the black humor involving Stevie; in the language which, like the differences in the moral energy among men, contains within itself a potential for anarchy and in the way in which words, "yielding to the pressure of Conrad's irony," drift toward meaninglessness and anarchy. *Agent* contains an important contemporary impulse in language: the stripping from language of the insubstantial values and illusions inherent in words to make them into more accurate "reflectors" of a "morally neutral and incoherent universe." The art of this novel then becomes the "art of non-life," of creating puppet-like beings whose "most salient" characteristic is the hopeless emptiness of their existence.

2136 Geddes, Gary. "That Extra Longitude: Conrad and the Art of Fiction," *University of Windsor Review* (Ontario), III (Spring 1968), pp. 65–81.

JC's main objective was to avoid the too apparent shaping of the novel. He sought implicit, not explicit, means of conveying theme, of giving reality a meaning through his work, as does Robbe-Grillet. Thus JC relied on impressionism and the objective correlative: time-shift and symbolism. To him the *mot juste* was important. He structured his narratives so that the final incident would give a meaning to the whole. He aimed at the illusion of freedom by means of a controlled technique.

2137 Gerber, Helmut E. (ed.). *George Moore in Transition: Letters to T. Fisher Unwin and Lena Milman, 1894–1910* (Detroit: Wayne State University Press, 1968), pp. 26, 27, 28–30, 216.

The publisher, T. Fisher Unwin, discovered JC and published his early novels; he also acted as agent. One of JC's work habits might have exasperated any publisher: intensive revision on the manuscript, typescript, and proof sheets, as well as much revision for later editions.

2138 Gillon, Adam. "Joseph Conrad and Shakespeare: Part I," *CON*, I, No. 1 (Summer 1968), pp. 19–25.

Shakespeare's impact on JC is seen in the extent of JC's textual borrowings from the plays and his inclusion of several major

Shakespearean themes and images in his work. There is plenty of "Shakespearean talk" in *Lord Jim* and many other writings by JC, epigraphs from the plays are used for several novels, distinct Shakespearean overtones are found frequently, certain "theatrical" terms are useful to JC, the motif of betrayal is important because of JC's emigration from his country, and the theme of life being a dream appears often in JC's later works. *The Tempest* and *The Shadow-Line* "illumine the transformation from youth (and magic) to maturity (and responsibilty)." [Followed by "Joseph Conrad and Shakespeare, Part II," *Conradiana*, I, No. 2 (Fall 1968); "Joseph Conrad and Shakespeare, Part III," *Conradiana*, I, No. 3 (Summer 1969); "Joseph Conrad and Shakespeare, Part Four: A New Reading of *Victory*," *Conradiana*, VII, No. 3 (1975); and "Joseph Conrad and Shakespeare, Part Five: *King Lear* and 'Heart of Darkness,'" *Polish Review*, XX, Nos. 2–3 (Joseph Conrad Commemorative Essays: The Selected Proceedings of the International Conference of Conrad Scholars, University of California, San Diego, August 28–September 5, 1974, ed. by Adam Gillon and Ludwik Krzyzanowski, 1975), pp. 133–39; rpt. *Joseph Conrad: Commemorative Essays*, ed. by Adam Gillon and Ludwik Krzyzanowski (New York: Astra Books, 1975), pp. 133–39; all five articles collected in Adam Gillon, *Conrad and Shakespeare and Other Essays* (New York: Astra Books, 1976), pp. 41–141.]

2139 Gillon, Adam. "Joseph Conrad and Shakespeare: Part II," *CON*, I, No. 2 (Fall 1968), pp. 15–22.

The strong "Hamletian streak" in JC is seen clearly in "The End of the Tether," in which the Captain's predicament appears against the background of a savage strife, and JC depicts the image of an Inferno, the hell on the *Sofala*. In addition, the Captain, like Lear, ends in despair. Jim, too, must "pay the price" like Lear, and the keynote of *Lord Jim* is betrayal and the "Hamletian theme," a man of noble intentions failing the major tests posed for him by relentless destiny. Hamlet fights a duel and kills Laertes and Claudius, but Jim refuses to fight or to run away after Dain Waris's death. Jim romantically defies his fate, but a romanticism which leaves one "alone and without appreciation" scarcely deserves praise; Jim's is but a hollow victory. In the existential sense, the deaths of Hamlet and Jim are an ironic redemption at best. But for both Shakespeare and JC, life is not an object of despair; there is some affirmation in Shakespeare's tragedies as well as in Jim's failure. JC thus remains an "original": he does not imitate other writers; like Shakespeare, he emulates them. [Preceded by Gillon, "Joseph Conrad and Shakespeare: Part I," *Conradiana*, I, No. 1 (1968), and followed by "Joseph Conrad and Shakespeare, Part III," *Conradiana*, I, No. 3 (1969); "Joseph Conrad and Shakespeare, Part Four: A New Reading of *Victory,"* *Conradiana,* VII, No. 3 (1975); and "Joseph Conrad and Shakespeare, Part Five: *King Lear* and 'Heart of Darkness,'" *Polish Review,* XX, Nos. 2–3; rpt. in *Joseph Conrad: Commemorative Essays,* ed. by Adam Gillon and Ludwik Krzyzanowski (New York: Astra Books, 1975); all five articles collected in Adam Gillon, *Conrad and Shakespeare and Other Essays* (New York: Astra Books, 1976), pp. 41–141.]

2140 Goldknopf, David. "What's Wrong with Conrad: Conrad on Conrad," *Criticism,* X (Winter 1968), pp. 54–64; rpt. in *The Life of the Novel* (Chicago: University Press, 1972), pp. 79–99.

Even if JC appreciated the futility of attempting to unite yarn spinning and thinking, an attempt which he claims to make in a preface prepared for the first edition of *The Nigger of the Narcissus* and elsewhere, he still persisted in it. Thinking an eyewitness would produce "the effect of actuality," JC attempted to have the "I-narrator" perform this service for him. In "Heart of Darkness," where "the horror, the horror" is an idea rather than a conviction, he fails in this attempt, as he fails in *The Secret Agent* because he does not "internalize" Winnie's love for her brother, leaving it as an idea in his own mind. In *Under Western Eyes,* JC's heavy reliance on the optic process is inadequate because he had observed many men but few women. For JC, the artificial liar, who is able to move freely in the realms of the imagination because he is not the author, may be exploited, as Marlow is in "Heart of Darkness," and thereby have his integrity compromised, as here, by a lie. In JC himself, a central conflict of an order different from that of other novelists, a struggle between factualism and romanticism, led to the overemployment of the I-narrator, to overintellectualization, and to temporizing and theatricalism.

2141 Greenberg, Alvin. "*Lord Jim* and the Rock of Sisyphus," *Forum* (Houston, Texas), VI (Spring 1968), pp. 13–17.

Jim, of *Lord Jim,* is an early absurd hero like the Sisyphus of Camus, in his willingness to engage himself and to make that engagement consciously, that is, with the full knowledge of the futility of doing so. To see Jim as absurd hero is difficult because he is filtered through the consciousness of Marlow, whose position is antithetical to Jim's. But Jim must realize that he is one with the "world of flesh and bone"—the captain and the engineer of the *Patna,* that he is fatally involved with his own deed and therefore with humanity. This differentiates him from Marlow. Jim, like Camus' absurd man, recognizes the futility of his struggle as well as the meaninglessness of the world in which he struggles, but out of this romantic recognition (as opposed to Marlow and Stein) he becomes "stronger than his rock." He must live—and die—aware of the paradox that he cannot overcome his rock, but the consciousness of his inner self is tragic in Camus' sense. Such tragedy, though, offers an "ennobling crown" to man's inherent absurdity. Jim's efforts yield two major achievements: a victory over the unbearable, achieved in a death which is the willing sacrifice of a self once the crushing truth about it has been discovered and, more significantly, the recognition that here at last "his fate belongs to him."

2142 Hall, James. *The Lunatic Giant in the Drawing Room: The British and American Novel Since 1930* (Bloomington and London: Indiana University Press, 1968), pp. 157, 223.

JC, like Lawrence and Joyce, is far less limited than Elizabeth Bowen, Graham Greene, or Iris Murdoch.

2143 Harris, Wendell V. "English Short Fiction in the Nineteenth Century," *SSF*, VI (Fall 1968), pp. 82–83.

The history of the English short story during the nineteenth century ends with JC's publication of "Karain" in *Blackwood's Magazine* in 1897. This tale is the epitome of the kind of romantic story many writers were striving to create for *Blackwood's*. JC's standard themes—fidelity, duty, faith in an ideal—appear in the volume, *Tales of Unrest*, in which "Karain" is found. Although JC is not the only major writer of the short story, he serves to illustrate the important differences between nineteenth and twentieth-century techniques of short story writing.

2144 Harris, Wendell V. "Of Time and the Novel," *Bucknell Review* (March 1968), pp. 114–29.

The reader of *Nostromo* who is familiar with the tradition of the English novel is conscious of an unusual form of dislocation, basic to which is a "wrenching" of one's sense of time. The usual measure of time, the span of human life, is replaced in this novel by a sense of timelessness, even if the action of the book takes place during two weeks, between the morning when the deposed dictator Ribiera is aided to escape from Costaguana and the return of General Barrios and his troops. Although little allusion is made to the generations which preceded and are to follow the central figures in the brief series of events in the book, the reader knows that the past has been filled with turmoil, folly, and cruelty, and that the future will be the same. The major problem is that the subtlety of the pattern leads many readers to mistake parts of the pattern for the whole, in the overemphasis, for example, of the importance of Dr. Monygham or of Mrs. Gould. Many ironic contrasts reinforce the pattern: for instance, the silver of the mine brings, for a time, order and a preferred way of life even for the Indian miners. It also brings evil, however, and will in all probability precipitate new disorders in the future. JC's entire system of balances and ironies is made meaningful by the sense of timelessness which the structure of the novel creates.

2145 Heimer, Jackson W. "Betrayal, Guilt, and Attempted Redemption in *Lord Jim,*" *Ball State University Forum,* IX (Spring 1968), pp. 31–43.

In Jim's "betrayal act" in *Lord Jim,* the young sailor violates both the code of the sea and his own ideal conception of himself because his ideal conception is based on an illusory view of life. Like Don Quixote, he is unrealistic and, by turn, comic and noble; and Jim's inner conflict elevates him above the anti-hero of the twentieth century. But he is, nevertheless, doubly guilty. Although he does not intend to jump from the *Patna,* he does jump, and neither his public confession in court nor his private confession to Marlow can clear him. His suffering is enlarged by the very thing which creates his ideal self, his imagination. Patusan becomes his purgatory, where he almost succeeds in fusing the dreamer and the actor—but not quite: he rehabilitates himself, but he fails to realize that the values of the society of Patusan are different from those he had previously violated. Thus his sacrifice is as much self-punishment for his betrayal as it is an attempted redemption. His self-immolation separates him from the great tragic heroes: he is, after all, "one of us," a common, even a universal type of being.

2146 Hepburn, James (ed.). *Letters of Arnold Bennett, Vol II: 1889–1915* (London: Oxford University Press, 1968), pp. 81, 93–94, 188–89, 243, 281, 321–22.

Arnold Bennett thought JC's *The Nigger of the Narcissus* "magnificent"; he praised its style, JC's "attitude," and his "*synthetic* way of gathering up a general impression and flinging it at you." Unlike Kipling, JC is "so consciously an artist." *Romance,* though, he thought to be bad. To Bennett, Frank Harris was the first man he could consider an equal, because JC was "so damned clumsy, constructively." For Bennett, JC's greatest novel was *Nostromo,* with the mountain Higuerota "being the principal personage in the story"; it was, he thought, "the finest novel of this generation (bar none)." And all of *Under Western Eyes* was "superb" for him. "The Secret Sharer" was "about as fine as anything you've [JC] ever done."

2147 Hewitt, Douglas. *Conrad: A Reassessment,* second ed. (Chester Springs, Pennsylvania: Dufour Editions, 1968; London: Bowes & Bowes, 1969).

[Aside from a few factual corrections, the original edition of this book (1952), (C, I, No. 1266), has not been altered. The title is thus somewhat misleading, because since first publication of the book, much critical work has been done on JC. The present surplus of overly ingenious symbolic interpretations overlooks, however, the fact that the literal world is their source.]

2148 Hill, John S. "Henry James: Fitzgerald's Literary Ancestor," *Fitzgerald Newsletter*, XL (Winter 1968), pp. 6–10.

Henry James's role as a literary ancestor of Fitzgerald's has not been well evaluated because Fitzgerald's debt to JC has overshadowed any role James played. JC, James's disciple, strongly influences Fitzgerald, most obviously in his use in *The Great Gatsby* of a Conradian narrator, Nick Carraway, who watches Jay Gatsby sink to defeat and death as the price of upholding a "bankrupt" myth, the American dream.

2149 Himmelfarb, Gertrude. *Victorian Minds* (New York: Knopf, 1968), pp. 259–60.

John Buchan was not conscious of race as a "problem" to which racism provided a solution; both he and JC could write unselfconsciously of a "nigger." The familiar racist sentiments of Buchan, Kipling, and even JC, were a reflection of a common attitude: they were descriptive, not prescriptive, representing an attempt to express differences of culture and color in terms that had been unquestioned for generations.

2150 Holland, Norman N. *The Dynamics of Literary Response* (New York: Oxford University Press, 1968), pp. 44, 56, 226–37, 241–42, 258–60, 285, 289–99, 312.

The informing principle around which *The Secret Agent* finds its shape and inner logic is the unsuspected—a sense throughout the book that each character has a "doubleness or tripleness, a secret self." The characters bisect and trisect one another, each touching only a part of the others in a choas and maze of human relations, thus indicating the significance of Stevie's circles. The novel "fairly bristles" with geometric images, as if JC were attempting to "squeeze" some kind of order out of the choas. Light and dark are the key images in the novel, especially the dark city, London, which becomes inner madness rendered as outer setting, the "engulfing sea or maze of irrationality." Lustful, lazy, and fat, the men in the story "rest and feed complacently on the obvious"; *Agent* is, among other things, a study in sloth.

2151 Hollander, Robert B., and Sidney E. Lind. *The Art of the Story: An Introduction* (New York: American Book Company, 1968), pp. 159–97.

The contrasting characters of the two protagonists in "The Secret Sharer" initiate the action of the plot. The setting is important in establishing the mood of events, and the background, an intrinsic part of the plot, gives the information necessary to account for Leggatt's presence and the captain's conduct. [Includes a short biographical sketch, reprints the text of "The Secret Sharer," and supplies six general "Questions for Discussion and Writing."]

2152 Houle, Sister M. Sheila, B.V.M. "Kenneth L. Pike's Behavioremic Theory as a Model for Explicating the Imagery in Joseph Conrad's 'Heart of Darkness,'" *DA*, XXIX (1968), 248A. Unpublished dissertation, University of Iowa, 1968.

2153 Howe, Irving (ed.). "Introduction" [to "The Secret Sharer"], *Classics of Modern Fiction: Eight Short Novels* (New York: Harcourt, Brace and World, 1968), pp. 271–81.

"The Secret Sharer" may readily be seen as a story of action, meant to create suspense and excitement, as an extremely complicated account of the necessity of making a moral choice even when one cannot know what the consequences of such a particular choice will be, or as a study in depth psychology. And these are only three possible points of view, only "preliminary" explanations of the story. [Adds suggestions for further study.]

2154 Hynes, Samuel. "Reviews: Phenomenology," *Novel*, II (Winter 1968–69), pp. 179–81.

Edward W. Said's book, *Joseph Conrad and the Fiction of Autobiography* (1966), is about the connection between JC's life and his work. Both the letters and the tales are creations, according to the phenomenologist, of a consciousness ordering its perceptions. This approach makes possible a very successful theory of JC's developing sense of himself and his world. There are, however, some weaknesses in this method: JC had no actual philosophical ideas— he simply had a "melancholy inability" to find satisfactory meanings in experience, and his mind did not develop schematically. Furthermore, we do not know enough to make the connection between his life and his work categorically; but the major problem is abstractness, not arbitrariness, a basic objection to phenomenological criticism. [Important because of the phenomenological approach to JC.]

2155 Isle, Walter. "The Romantic and the Real: Henry James's *The Sacred Fount*," *Henry James*, ed. by Tony Tanner (London: Macmillan [Modern Judgements], 1968), p. 264.

Perhaps *The Sacred Fount* is closer in theme, in the delineation of the relationship between the romantic and the real, to a novel published only a year before it—JC's *Lord Jim*. For James's art is always of the world he lives in, of "the individual alienated from but struggling with his world."

2156 Jacobs, Robert G. "Comrade Ossipon's Favorite Saint: Lombroso and Conrad," *NCF*, XXIII (June 1968), pp. 74–84.

For years, readers have observed JC's careful detailing of the physical appearance of his characters. The reason is probably to be discovered in his understanding of Dr. Cesare Lombroso's theories of criminality. Lombroso theorized on the relationship of physical characteristics to the types of crimes committed by persons exhibiting those characteristics. He also speculated on the relationships between physical appearance, illness, and genius. Many of JC's characters and situations seem to be built upon Lombroso's conclusions. *The Secret Agent* presents a particularly complex and ironic understanding of them. And, insofar as Lombroso's theories assisted the "epileptic" JC to understand himself, they suggest that his claim in his prefaces to have written adventure stories is an expression of a wish to be considered "normal."

2157 Jacobs, Robert G. "H. G. Wells, Joseph Conrad, and the Relative Universe," *CON*, I, No. 1 (Summer 1968), pp. 51–55.

Under the influence of H. G. Wells and his science fiction narrative, *The Time Machine*, JC, in collaboration with Ford Madox Ford, turned his attention to time, the fourth dimension, in *The Inheritors*, which is reminiscent of Wells throughout. The fourth dimension, though, enters JC's fiction more directly in "Heart of Darkness" and *Lord Jim.* Jim's sensations on board the *Patna* during the crucial moments of his terror are very much like those of the Time Traveller in Wells's novel. For Jim, everything is out of its accustomed order; and Marlow, too, is concerned with the control of time. Like Wells' *The Invisible Man*, Jim also yearns for invisibility and achieves it in Patusan; he appears to Marlow, in fact, in various degrees of visibility. JC acquired from Wells the means to achieve his presentation of the phenomena of relativity. The complexities of Jim's romantic time sense are new in JC's fiction, and they account largely for Jim's success. JC made use of some of Wells' physical ideas, and by using his own imagination he "domesticated" them to the present in some of his major fiction, as with Decoud of *Nostromo*,

Razumov of *Under Western Eyes*, and the attempt to destroy time in *The Secret Agent*.

2158 Johnson, Bruce. "*Under Western Eyes*: Politics as Symbol," *CON*, I, No. 1 (Summer 1968), pp. 35–44; rpt. practically intact as chapter 9 in *Conrad's Models of Mind* (1971).

JC's Russia is not the subject of *Under Western Eyes*. In this novel, as in "The Secret Sharer" and *The Shadow-Line*, the problem of sympathy involves the hero's conception of his own identity. Razumov's hopes for a rational, central will to shape Russia are contrary to the "mystical irrationality" of that land and to the deepest reality of Razumov's own character. Because Razumov is an extremely complex protagonist, he is a "paradigm of all the ironies inherent in the kinds of sympathetic sharing" that are predominant in JC's works from the beginning. By the end of the novel, Russia becomes symbolic of the "inevitably unsatisfying and possibly tragic nature of the call to human community," and *Eyes* suggests the paradox that Razumov must identify with a nation whose "mystical essence" denies his aspiration to be a reasonable man. Here JC abandoned many of his earlier and somewhat easier versions of the relations between an individual and human community, and he also began to lose the self-confident irony that is justified in *The Secret Agent*. Much of the moral certainty JC had felt in his politics disappears in *Eyes*, which is, then, scarcely a political novel.

2159 Johnson, J. W. "Marlow and *Chance*: A Reappraisal," *TSLL*, X (Spring 1968), pp. 91–105.

An examination of the four Marlow tales establishes a biography of this narrator. As the protagonist of "Youth" at twenty, Marlow is adventuresome and idealistic; his outlook is heroic-epic or romantic. As the protagonist of "Heart of Darkness" at thirty and then its narrator at thirty-six, his vision changes from idealistic to one that transcends the tragic. As the narrator of *Lord Jim*, now in his late thirties, Marlow sees life as more ambiguous and complex than the heroic and tragic would permit. As the narrator of "Youth," at forty-two, Marlow has become a realist, and as the narrator of *Chance* at fifty-six, he is the tolerant man who sees life as a game of chance, who despite his sentimentality, is sane, realistic, and sympathetic. Here, Marlow balances the cynicism of the anonymous first-person narrator and the "innocent romanticism" of Powell. The tone of the novel is a mixture of "tragedy, comedy, adventure, and pathos" used to satirize Victorian ideals. Carleon Anthony represents the intellectual and didactic aspect of Victorianism and de Barral represents its middle-class, mercantile nature. By them, the sexual love between Captain Anthony and Flora is frustrated, and JC's theme of the sterility of Victorian prohibitions is dramatized.

2160 Jones, Charles. "Varieties of Speech Presentation in Conrad's *The Secret Agent*," *Lingua*, XX (August 1968), pp. 162–76.

In *The Secret Agent*, JC uses direct and indirect speech classifications to avoid rigidity and suggest the range of mixed types within the extreme. Much of the novel's strength lies in the author's use of shifting viewpoint, where the speech may represent the writer's narration, a character's direct or reported speech, or a mixture of the three. The subtle suggestions of the spoken or reported word also add to the tension of the novel and unconsciously alter the reader's viewpoint.

2161 Kagarlitzkii, Julius I., comp. "A Russian Conrad Bibliography," *CON*, I, No. 1 (Summer 1968), pp. 61–66.

[A list of thirty translations of JC's works into Russian and of sixty critical works on JC in Russian.]

2162 Karl, Frederick R. "Conrad–Galsworthy: A Record of Their Friendship in Letters," *Midway*, IX (Autumn 1968), pp. 87–106.

After JC met John Galsworthy in 1892, a correspondence between the two writers soon developed, and even in the early letters the misinterpretation each put on the other's work appears. JC perfunctorily praised Galsworthy's novels and the latter requested advice which he could not heed. JC was unstable and uncertain; Galsworthy held to steadiness of purpose. Essentially, Galsworthy's JC is the Victorian, moralistic JC, not the modern anguished victim of his own perceptions. Gradually, the two men grew further apart. The bifurcation that characterizes JC's entire career appears in the conflict, for example, between gentlemanly ideals based on duty and discipline, and dark knowledge that leads to destruction. Shown throughout the correspondence is the fact that Galsworthy does not really understand JC's intentions or his achievements, that JC's anarchic view of governmental process may be lost in Galsworthy's "liberal and orthodox public school view" of how politics or politicians function, that the "dark and uncontrollable" in JC will be compromised by the "light and genteel" in Galsworthy. After praising Galsworthy's novels and plays specifically, by 1908 JC wrote Galsworthy a long letter full of the tensions of a serious writer caught up by work, debts, personal troubles, hopes, fears, and accomplishments. After this "confession," the correspondence loses whatever literary flavor it had had, and neither correspondent could disguise the difference between the two. Because both were settling into middle and old age, both were at the end of their development.

2163 Karl, Frederick R. "Introduction to the *Danse Macabre*: Conrad's 'Heart of Darkness,'" *MFS*, XIV (Summer 1968), pp. 143–56; rpt. *JCC*, pp. 27–41.

Both Freud and JC were pioneers in stressing the irrational elements in man's behavior: the black of the jungle in JC's "Heart of Darkness" is the dark of the "sleeping consciousness" of Freud. For both men, the key word is "darkness." Pillar of truth and morality that he is, Marlow does Kurtz's work at the end of the story: he lies to protect the lie of Kurtz's existence, lies finally to protect his (Marlow's) own illusions. To create order from bits of nihilism, negativism, deception, and savagery, JC offers a "dubious" restraint, which marks the difference between civilization and capitulation to savagery. He makes Marlow, his Everyman, most of all courageous, yet sufficiently cynical at the same time. Marlow's "great revelation" comes when he sees that the world is not maintained by just men, when he notes that many men do not share his beliefs in an orderly, enlightened society but prefer one of chaos, anarchy, "unspeakable rights." A law-abiding morally sensitive man enters an avaricious, predatory "almost psychopathic world;" "the nineteenth century becomes the twentieth." The sense of human waste that pervades the novel is best seen in the ivory, from which Kurtz gains his power. Kurtz is Europe. The ultimate corruption is that Kurtz can go his way without restraint; only power counts. Kurtz is the "extremist" in JC's greatest insight into the politics of the twentieth century, and his kind of exploitation was the rule, not the exception. Ironically, Marlow, the twentieth-century European returning from the world of the dead, cannot admit the depth of indecency which he has witnessed; only JC can detect the truth and "triumph."

2164 Kashkin, Ivan. "Dzhozef Konrad" (Joseph Conrad), *Dlia Chitateliasovremennika* (Moscow: Sovetskii pisatel', 1968), pp. 301–25.

JC's early works are concerned with man's struggle with the elements; then come the writings in which man's inner world predominates over the sea and in which exotic themes appear. *Nostromo* is JC's only, but unconvincing, attempt to portray a broader picture of society. *The Secret Agent* and *Under Western Eyes* are not entirely successful excursions into the psychology of East European man, which in JC's hands becomes a lampoon on terrorists. Then comes a series of great novels in which the author deepens the psychological analysis and surveys man's defeat in the struggle with himself. He adopts the complex method of oblique narration in the spirit of Henry James. In the last two novels, JC turns from analysis to direct, dynamic narrative on historical themes. He lived half his life in the colonies and did not wish to praise imperialism. In the second half, he was increasingly accepted by London's cosmopolitan literary intelligentsia. JC's romanticism has two aspects: the first is that of the sea, of struggle with the elements, of the duty of simple men; the second is that of "the dark calls of life and death," which lead him into the psychological jungle. He achieves much in "making the reader see," hear, and feel by means of words and intonations which often strike an English reader as unusual. After 1905, his work bears the deep imprint of James. *Chance*, for example, was hailed by bourgeois critics as a discovery, though in it JC's mastery was merely a conventional variation on his old subject of man defeated by the elements. [In Russian.]

2165 Kauver, Gerald B. "Marlow as Liar," *SSF*, V (Spring 1968), pp. 290–92.

The standard interpretation of the last scene of "Heart of Darkness" is that Marlow is lying on principle, the principle of compassion. Considering the ambiguous and difficult nature of JC's moral conceptions, however, we should consider the possibility that Marlow is not lying as patently as we often assume. He speaks in *double entendre* to Kurtz's Intended, satisfying both her illusions and his own ironic sense of the truth. The name of the Intended does indeed correspond to "the horror" of moral vacuity.

2166 Kermode, Frank. "Novel, History and Type," *Novel*, I (Spring 1968), pp. 231–38.

The narrative of a novel is as like an historical novel as possible, with coherence that depends on plausibility imposed upon it. Historians rely upon fact for their major points, arranging minor events around a central incident; novelists may rely more on the situational logic, as JC does in chapter IV of *The Secret Agent*, where the accident at Greenwich belongs to a world with no coherence, a world which thus echoes early in the novel the hopes of the anarchists. The irrevelant "frescoes" of the filth and gloom of the city and the mechanical music of the player-piano establish "emblematically" the complete incoherence of the anarchists' world. This scene, chaotic as it may appear, is plausible; it makes us see; it explains. It takes the reader into a region of historical explanations which historians avoid because of their primary adherence to documents. Yet the scene is recognizably historical; JC is not simply leaves one to infer a theory or to collect what is said elsewhere in the novel about the structures of civilization and the darkness of evil. Whereas the historian gets his effects by explanations of which the narrative content is much reduced and by chronological "conflations," the novelist gets his effects more freely, as D. H. Lawrence does in *Women in Love*. But in spite of the many differences, JC is closer, in the "highly wrought" *Agent,* to the historian than to the poet.

2167 Killam, G. D. *Africa in English Fiction, 1874–1939* (Ibadan: Ibadan University Press, 1968), pp. ix, x, xi, 1, 8–9, 10, 11, 60–62, 85–95.

Some authors, like JC, detest suggestions of a deep and penetrating influence of Africa, seeing that Africa resembles the world as it was at its beginnings, as a "heart of darkness." Marlow, JC's spokesman, compares the Congo to the beginnings of the world. Although the Africans appear at first as inhuman, Marlow comes to feel a strong affinity with them. This close kinship is revealed by Kurtz's joining a primitive tribe and initiating tribal rites. Kurtz has been converted by the jungle from a humanizing agent to a high priest of the "devils of the land." Finally, Marlow finds in Europe the darkness symbolized by Africa. In "Heart of Darkness," JC has both sympathy for and understanding of the Africans, but both he and Marlow recognize their inferior station. JC offers an ironic comment on the hypocrisy of Leopold's Congo mission. [Discusses several well known themes of "Heart of Darkness."]

2168 Kirschner, Paul. "Conrad: An Uncollected Article," *N&Q,* XV (August 1968), pp. 292–94.

An article by JC in the *Daily Mail,* 18 September 1909, has not been collected. Entitled "The Silence of the Sea," it speculates on the fate of the ship *Waratah,* which left Durban for Capetown on July 27, 1909, carrying 300 passengers, and was evidently lost as sea. [The text of the article is reprinted here.]

2169 Kirschner, Paul. *Conrad: The Psychologist as Artist* (Edinburgh: Oliver & Boyd, 1968).

A Freudian or Jungian approach to JC is unnecessary because JC was a great psychologist who knew what he wished to say about human nature and expressed this well in his works. To think of him as a psychologist enables one to link his disparate writings by asking how the self is being studied. It is also advantageous to relate his works with his life.

JC felt that the basic drive of the self is towards power and significance. His works up to *Under Western Eyes* express the self as being involved in an "egocentric striving towards a dream of personal greatness and power." Between the writing of *The Nigger of the Narcissus* and *The Shadow-Line,* his fiction is concerned with the relationship between man and woman. *Chance* is the first work in which the feminine-masculine polarity is treated. In *Victory,* JC vindicates the feminine principle, and in *The Rover* the feminine self wins an even wider victory.

Several authors, such as Shakespeare, Flaubert, Maupassant, Anatole France, and Turgenev contributed seriously to JC's works. Dostoevski, for whom JC professed a strong dislike, actually shares certain similarities in his view of "the irrational element surrounding man" and in characters which stand as expressions of that idea. He was also influenced by Schopenhauer and Alfred Adler.

2170 Kott, Jan. *Theatre Notebook, 1947–1967* (London: Methuen, p. 116; New York: Doubleday, 1968), p. 118.

Both *Oedipus Rex* and *Lord Jim* are examples of human fate: Jim's fate turned out to be not much less cruel than that of Oedipus. *Jim* is not only a story of a merchant navy officer who failed in what was expected of him; it is also a considered reflection on that story. As the fictitious narrator, Marlow serves the function of the chorus in a Greek tragedy and also contemplates, as Pascal would have it, the "fragility of, and contradictions inherent in, the moral order." Unlike Sophocles, however, who inherited the story of Oedipus, JC created the character of Jim.

2171 Krieger, Murray. "Conrad's 'Youth': A Naive Opening to Art and Life," *Thirty-Eight Short Stories: An Introductory Anthology*, ed. by Michael Timko and Clinton F. Oliver (New York: Knopf, 1968), pp. 49–57.

Although JC's "Youth" is not the most artistic of his tales, when compared, for example, with *Lord Jim*, it makes use of some techniques and dramatizes a theme which appears in later fiction. The narrative point of view allows a double tone which permits Marlow to dramatize the freshness of romantic youth and the wisdom of middle age. The ambiguity of the ending corresponds with JC's idea of the complexity of moral reality. But the point of view is not developed into the subtle instrument it is in later works, and the symbolism adds little to the story because of its obviousness. It is, finally, difficult to take the young Marlow's story very seriously.

2172 Larson, Charles R. "Come to the Ship, Leggatt, Honey?'" *Atlantic*, CCXXI (March 1968), pp. 111–12.

A college freshman found that in JC's "The Secret Sharer" the captain and Leggatt are "queer" because they share pajamas, hide from the others on the ship, and sit on the john all day. Leggatt has left the *Sephora* because "they were all queer on that ship" and now he wants to leave the present ship because its captain is queer. Leggatt left his floppy hat on the water at the end of the story purposely because it was a bonnet to keep the sun from his eyes, "a mere fetish." It belonged to the captain's aunt; the captain was a transvestite. [Reminiscent of Bruce Harkness, "The Secret of 'The Secret Sharer' Bared," [C, I, no. 1877]. A spoof on critical interpretation—or, more likely, a pathetic comment on current education.]

2173 Laskowsky, Henry. "Joseph Conrad: Epistemology and the Novel," *DA*, XXVIII (1968), 1439A. Unpublished dissertation, Syracuse University, 1967.

2174 Las Vergnas, Raymond. "*Les Années de Mer de Joseph Conrad*" (The Sea Years of Joseph Conrad), *Nouvelles Litteraire* (12 September 1968), p. 4.

In *Les Annees de Mer de Joseph Conrad*, Jerry Allen provides a detailed account of all the lesser known sea adventures of JC. She has discovered the identity of some of the models for JC's main characters.

2175 LaValley, Albert J. *Carlyle and the Idea of the Modern* (New Haven and London: Yale University Press, 1968), pp. 175–81.

Although *Nostromo* is more sombre and skeptical toward imperialism than Carlyle's *The French Revolution*, the books have many similarities. History, though created by man, is sometimes out of his control, but this very difficulty makes both authors sympathetic with man's plight. Both writers are impatient with Utopian idealism that lacks the direction of historical knowledge and with primitive instincts that surface with brutalizing revolutions, yet both Carlyle and JC are moved by a hope that protects them from endless skepticism.

2176 Lee, Robin. "*The Secret Agent*: Structure, Theme, and Mode," *English Studies in Africa*, XI (September 1968), pp. 185–93.

The structure of *The Secret Agent* is largely dictated by JC's choice of theme and by the mode of treatment of that theme. The break in the chronological structure of the novel between chapters 7 and 8 is important. JC uses two kinds of time-shift: (1) the lesser, but not unimportant, flashback, employed twice, which stresses information and maintains the ironic mode of the book; and (2) the dislocation of the chronological sequences around the central event of the novel, Stevie's death, which JC refused to narrate. There are three major reasons for JC's tactics: the uncertainty and the mystery surrounding the Greenwich Park explosion helps to create suspense and interest in the outcome of the detective-story narrative; the comic and ironic mode may not be used to describe an act of destruction, especially not of an innocent victim; and the refusal to describe the central event contributes also to the quality of absurdity in violent political action.

2177 Leech, Clifford. "The Shaping of Time: *Nostromo* and *Under the Volcano*," *Imagined Worlds: Essays on Some English Novels and Novelists in Honour of John Butt*, ed. by Maynard Mack and Ian Gregor (London: Methuen, 1968), pp. 323–41.

The modern novel utilizes a free manipulation of events which is illustrated in JC's *Nostromo* and Malcom Lowry's *Under the Volcano*. Both exemplify different ways in which the twentieth-century writer may treat time with disrespect. In *Nostromo*, JC's movements backwards and forwards in time are "profoundly functional." The relations of the book's three parts provide a basis for a "superb" structure, the lingering with the past in the first two-thirds of the narrative hinting at the reluctance to plunge into the characteristic world of the twentieth century and the free movement between the past and present placing an insistence on the entrammeling of fully alive individuals within a partially hidden progression which is not within their control. It is chance that, in the concatenation of events, gives the entire concept of time a terrifying quality. Lowry and JC use different technical methods: *Nostromo* is far less centered in the personal than is *Under the Volcano*, and Lowry has given the broader sense of historical event and geographical setting. Both novels, however, are remote from simple progression in their narrative; both see the total process within the movement; both are tragic writings; and both illustrate the way in which our experience of the past and the future is being continuously shaped by our minds.

2178 Lester, John Ashby, Jr. *Journey Through Despair, 1880–1914: Transformations in British Literary Culture* (Princeton: Princeton University Press, 1968), pp. 186–93 and passim.

JC deeply shared in the disillusionment of the *fin de siècle* generation, and his major imaginative response in combating it lay in a willful construction of an internal sense of order and light, which he then sought to impose on the external darkness. To see this is not to resolve or dissipate the many ambiguities in JC's work, but to make those ambiguities more visible and acute.

2179 Liljegren, S. B. *Joseph Conrad as a "Prober of Feminine Hearts": Notes on the Novel "The Rescue"* (Upsala: A.-B. Lundequistska [Essays and Studies on English Language and Literature 27], 1968).

The Rescue is not merely a novel of adventure and suspense; the adventures simply form the setting for the "all-important men and women." Mrs. Travers is JC's only "full-length portrait of a woman and a very grandiose one," and the main plot is "the meeting of Lingard with Mrs. Travers." If JC's portrayal of psychology in Lingard needs to be questioned, his portrait of Mrs. Travers "rings true." What appeals to her in Lingard is the unselfishness of purpose, "the point of honor," which causes his difficulties and obtains for him the "blows" while others get the rewards. His passion, however, weakens him, and he refuses to go on when his honor has been forced to yield to it. He allows his native friends to be destroyed, he saves the strangers who have been the unwitting reason of the destruction of his friends, and he—like Mrs. Travers—has strength enough to look away as she is passing out of his sight. [Adds little to our knowledge of JC as "a prober of feminine hearts."]

2180 Lindstrand, Gordon. "Joseph Conrad's *Nostromo*: The Transmission of the Text," *DA*, XXVIII (1968), 3149A. Unpublished dissertation, University of Illinois, 1967.

2181 Lodge, David. "Waiting for the End: Current Novel Criticism," *Critical Quarterly*, X (Spring/Summer 1968), pp. 184–99.

Special about JC is the element of deliberately-invited risk in his early life in a full confrontation with what seemed most of the time to him a threatening and unpleasant world. What is more notable, though, is what he made of his experience artistically and imaginatively.

2182 Madden, David. "Romanticisim and the Hero-Witness Relationship in Four Conrad Stories," *Ohio University Review*, X (1968), pp. 5–22.

JC's four works, "Youth," "The Secret Sharer," "Heart of Darkness," and *Lord Jim*, have in common the theme of romanticism and disillusionment, enhanced by the hero-witness relationship in which Charles Marlow, in effect at least, is the central witness. The one most important event both JC and Marlow share is the journey into "the heart of darkness." As a double, Marlow is haunted by *his* own doubles. His ordering, selecting, and evaluating transform the "chaos of facts" into a metaphor of the human quandary.

Romanticism is no systematic philosophy. The Romantic acts more on impulse than on reason. In the hero-witness relationship, the common theme of these four stories is worked out. Marlow is a literary, thematic, and technical device, which supplies the point-of-view framework for each story and thereby provides the reader with a dynamic means of evaluating the theme of romanticism and disillusionment. "Youth" portrays mainly a test of physical endurance. In "The Secret Sharer," in which one can justifiably see the young captain as another Marlow, Marlow harbors Leggatt, the murderer, and so journeys into his "darker possibilities" as he becomes, more than ever before, a stranger to his ship and its crew. A greater test of his romantic "self-concept" arrives when Marlow, in "Heart of Darkness," journeys to the inner station of the Congo, where he finds Kurtz, the romantic who penetrates to the heart of "great enterprises" and discovers there the heart of darkness that "beats in every man." And in *Jim*, Marlow pieces together the enigma of Jim's character until now he and the reader are equals in that both study Jim together. In a way, Jim is Marlow's irretrievable self, and through Marlow, the reader identifies with Jim. Jim provides a good summation of the theme of romanticism and disillusionment in the four stories, each of which is a phase in a single mythic structure: each is an expression of the hero-witness relationship in which romanticism moves toward disillusionment. These stories project a triangular conflict: "civilized man is in conflict with himself, he is in conflict with the civilization that produced him, and his conception of himself conflicts with the everlasting, brute, indifferent forces of the natural environment." In these stories, it is always the witness, never the hero, who benefits from the hero-witness relationship.

2183 Markovic, Vida E. "Dzozef Konrad," *Engleski Roman XX Veku* (The English Novel of the Twentieth Century), (Belgrade: "Naucna kngija," 1968), I, pp. 49–59.

JC did not reach a wide reading public until 1914, when he published *Chance*, which is not one of his better works. But he did not write for the reading public. His themes are ethical dilemmas regarded from a new point of view. He struggled with a language which was not his own and gained a major victory; he is among the foremost stylists, in a language he learned as a mature person. [In Croatian.]

2184 Maurois, André. "Joseph Conrad," *Points of View: From Kipling to Graham Greene* (New York: Frederick Ungar, 1968), pp. 175–211.

JC was admired by sensitive writers concerned with form. His success is all the more remarkable because he wrote in English, a language he could speak less well than Polish or French. Better than most other writers, he expressed a stoic philosophy of life and interpreted better than others what is best in the English soul. In his books, man stands face to face with the universe, and particularly with the sea; JC propounds a philosophy of active pessimism akin to that of Chekhov. He admires common seamen who serve with loyalty and obedience as much as he admires their captains. He dislikes men who think only of their rights and never of their duties. Also, he does not believe that democracy will free men from war, but rather that the wars of democracies will cause men to yearn for earlier, more structured societies and values.

2185 McCall, Dan. "The Meaning of Darkness: A Response to a Psychoanalytical Study of Conrad," *College English,* XXIX (May 1968), pp. 620–27.

[Specifically, a response to Frederick Crews, "The Power of Darkness," *Partisan Review,* XXXIX (Fall 1967), pp. 507–25.] In his essay on "Heart of Darkness," Crews has fallen into several of the usual errors of "Freudian" criticism. The first is presenting as critical perception what is actually a summary of what the author explicity tells us. The second is creating false dichotomies and misleading distinctions. The third is misusing evidence, especially the biographical. Greater and more fundamental than these, however, is the error of the psychoanalytic approach itself, which is inherently reductive and which leads away from considering the tale itself to considering various hypothetical speculations about the assumed mentality of the author. Not only is literary criticism thus abused, but Freud himself is maltreated.

2186 McConnell, Ruth E. "Iterative Imagery in the Fiction of Joseph Conrad," *DA,* XXIX (1968), 267A. Unpublished dissertation, University of California, Berkeley, 1967.

2187 McCord, David. "Concerned with People," *NYTBR,* LXXIII (27 October 1968), p. 4.

JC is, like J. B. Priestley, "the rarest example" of crossing the border "from the essay to the novel, to the story, to the play"; and in *The Mirror of the Sea* is "distilled . . . the best" of JC. [Rev. of J. B. Priestley, *Essays of Five Decades.*]

2188 McDonald, Walter R. "Conrad as a Novelist of Moral Conflict and Isolation," *Iowa English Yearbook,* XIII (Fall 1968), pp. 34–43.

JC is a moralist concerned with human conflict and the duality of the human soul, which results in internal conflict. Neither extreme, "romantic idealization" nor "the socially oriented focus on adjustment," explains the dilemma of JC's protagonists, for JC believes that before assuming any sort of meaningful life in society, man must face the "personal forces" of his own soul and redeem himself. Thus human fidelity, beginning with oneself, is to JC the basis of experience in an isolating and unpredictable world. His "greatest theme" is the idea of "what happens to a man when he acknowledges from within the evil from without and fidelity is forced aside." Central to *Nostromo* is the moral conflict in the hero himself. The characters in *The Secret Agent* are "strangely non-heroic," finally demonstrating a complete breakdown of fidelity to themselves and others. *Lord Jim* is the story of a man's moral conflict as he lives with his breach of faith, anticipating redemption through faithful action. In *Victory*, Heyst's career proves that inaction is just as deadly as Jim's action. For JC, courage, acceptance, love, and most of all fidelity, must be the code of man in an imperfect world. The only victory worth winning is "the maintenance of one's personal integrity as he keeps faith with the community of man."

2189 McDowell, Frederick P. W. "The Most Recent Books on Joseph Conrad," *Papers on Language & Literature*, IV (Spring 1968), pp. 201-23.

JC does not consider truth to be "undifferentiated darkness"; rather, he associates it with deprivation, negation, evil, primitivism, and incapacity to feel. Although some elements of truth or reality can be found in JC's darkness, not all of them can.

2190 McGinnity, Mary L. "Forms and Function of Scepticism in the Fiction of Joseph Conrad." Unpublished dissertation, Loyola University (Chicago), 1968.

2191 Mellard, James. "Myth and Archetype in 'Heart of Darkness,'" *Tennessee Studies in Literature*, XIII (1968), pp. 1-15.

The multiplicity of mythic and archetypal, classic and psychological figures which some of the main characters in "Heart of Darkness" are meant to represent provides a problem for the critic. Some commentators say that Kurtz represents the id; others suggest a parallel between Marlow's journey up the river and Aeneas's descent into the underworld; some critics suggest that the basic pattern of the story resembles the Arthurian grail quest. Yet some order can be established in the interpretations if the story's thematic and structural patterns are viewed as a whole. Thus the story can be reduced to its common denominator—myth and archetype.

2192 Mellen, Joan C. "Morality in the Novel: A Study of Five English Novelists, Henry Fielding, Jane Austen, George Eliot, Joseph Conrad, and D. H. Lawrence," *DA*, XXIX (1968), 1543A. Unpublished dissertation, City College of New York, 1968.

2193 Meyers, Jeffrey. "The Agamemnon Myth and *The Secret Agent*," *CON*, I, No. 1 (Summer 1968), pp. 57-59.

A linking of the Agamemnon myth and *The Secret Agent* shows a diminishing of "the stature of [JC's] protagonists by a mock-heroic contrast to genuine heroes and tragedies." Agamemnon and Verloc, Winnie and Clytemnestra, and Stevie and Iphigeneia are parallels. The mythic framework "intensifies the subtle and disturbing mixture of tragedy and irony and accounts for the extraordinary power" of JC's novels.

2194 Michael, Marion C. "Conrad's 'Definite Intention' in *The Secret Agent*," *CON*, I, No. 1 (Summer 1968), pp. 9–17.

JC achieved a "tremendous growth" in *The Secret Agent* from the revisions of the holograph and the publication of the English book form, an examination of which demonstrates what he meant by comment to a friend of the establishment of "the solid basis of a definite intention" in his work. Some of his revisions tighten the complex time scheme of the novel and indicate his care in developing the details of Adolf and Winnie Verloc's domestic relationship; others emphasize the rapport between Winnie and her mother and complicate Winnie's somewhat elementary psychology. The variant states of *The Secret Agent* thus reveal JC's usual "meticulous care" for his texts and remind critics that they "should show a greater care for the accuracy of the texts upon which they built their theories."

2195 Mizener, Arthur. "Afterword," *Romance* (New York: New American Library [Signet Books], 1968), pp. 395–406.

An adult adventure story, *Romance* makes the accepted moral attitudes of its time, that is, about 1821, appear adequate to the "most testing—the most dangerous possible—occasions." Ford and JC took great pride in working well within a highly conventionalized form of this kind. They stressed frequently the fact that John Kemp, telling his story when he is an old man, remembers the past in a simplified and intense form so that experiences recalled can be convincingly recalled as adventurous. The idea of writing this story brought Ford and JC together in what was to be ten years of the closest kind of collaboration. Much of the time the writing of the two authors is inseparable, but the fourth part, which is the heart of the book, shows JC the storyteller at his best. JC often risked lifting the narrative out of Ford's adventure-story world into a much more complex realm of moral perception; the entire business of Sebright and the Williamses on board the *Lion*, for example, is "pure" JC.

2196 Moser, Thomas C. "The Division, by Chapters, of the Monthly Installments of *Lord Jim: A Sketch* in *Blackwood's Edinburgh Magazine*," *JCLJ* (1968), p. 306.

[Lists the chapters of *Lord Jim* contained in each monthly issue of *Blackwood's* from October 1899 to November 1900.]

2197 Moser, Thomas C. "Editor's Note on the Composition of *Lord Jim*," *JCLC* (1968), pp. 275–76.

JC's letters between 1898 and 1900 reveal such a life of "virtual chaos" that the artistry of *Lord Jim* in terms both of its moral and psychological complexity and of its formal excellence seems little short of miraculous. Intending his story at first to be only slightly longer than "Youth," JC saw it grow and grow from his envisioned four or five installments in *Blackwood's Magazine* to fourteen.

2198 Moser, Thomas C. (ed.). *Joseph Conrad, Lord Jim: An Authoritative Text, Backgrounds, Sources* (ed. by Norman Sherry), in *Essays in Criticism*, ed. by Thomas C. Moser (New York: Norton [A Norton Critical Edition], 1968).

Contents, abstracted under year of first publication: Thomas C. Moser, "Preface" (1968); Thomas C. Moser, "Textual History" (1968); Thomas C. Moser, "Textual Notes" (1968); Thomas C. Moser, "A *Lord Jim* Gazetteer and Glossary of Eastern and Nautical Terms" (1968); Alexander Janta, ["Tuan Jim: A Sketch"], from "A Conrad Family Heirloom at Harvard," Ludwik Krzyzanowski (ed.), *Joseph Conrad: Centennial Essays* (1960); Thomas C. Moser (ed.), "Correspondence Related to *Lord Jim*," [extracts from letters which dramatize how, to JC's consternation, *Lord Jim* "grew and grew and grew." The extracts are from *Joseph Conrad: Letters to William Blackwood and David S. Meldrum*, ed. by William Blackburn (1958); *Letters from Joseph Conrad, 1895–1924*, ed. by Edward Garnett (1928); and *Joseph Conrad: Life and Letters*, I, ed. by G. Jean-Aubry (1927), (C, I, No. 746)]; Thomas C. Moser, "The Division, by Chapters, of the Monthly Installments of *Lord Jim: A Sketch* in *Blackwood's Edinburgh Magazine* (1968); Norman Sherry (ed.), "Sources," [drawn upon materials contained in Sherry's *Conrad's Eastern World* (1966), (C, I, No. 1967)]; "Two Early Reviews" ["From the *New York Tribune*"], (3 November 1900), and ["From the *Spectator*"], LXXXV (24 November 1900); Hugh Clifford, ["From 'The Genius of Mr. Joseph Conrad'"], from *North American Review* (1904), (C, I, No. 71); Gustav Morf, ["*Lord Jim*"], from *The Polish Heritage of Joseph Conrad* (1965), (C, I, No. 913); Edward Crankshaw, ["Art vs. Didacticism in *Lord Jim*"], from *Joseph Conrad: Some Aspects of the Art of the Novel* (1963), (C, I, No. 1305); Dorothy Van Ghent, "On *Lord Jim*," from *The English Novel: Form and Function* (1953), (C, I, No. 1292); Albert J. Guerard, "*Lord Jim*," from *Conrad the Novelist* (1958), (C, I, No. 1470); Eloise Knapp Hay, "*Lord Jim*: From Sketch to Novel," from *Comparative Literature* (1960), (C, I, No. 1588); Murray Krieger, "The Varieties of Extremity:

Lord Jim," from *The Tragic Vision: Variations on a Theme in Literary Interpretation* (1960); Tony Tanner, "Butterflies and Beetles— Conrad's Two Truths," from *Chicago Review* (1963), (C, I, No. 1762); Bruce M. Johnson, "Conrad's 'Karain' and *Lord Jim,*" from *Modern Language Quarterly* (1963), (C, I, No. 1726); Donald C. Yelton, "Symbolic Imagery in *Lord Jim*" (1968); and Thomas C. Moser, "Selective Bibliography" (1968).

By JC, and not abstracted: *Lord Jim* [and some extracts from letters, listed above under "Correspondence Related to *Lord Jim.*"]

2199 Moser, Thomas C. "A *Lord Jim* Gazetteer and Glossary of Eastern and Nautical Terms," *JCLJ* (1968), pp. 266–71.

[This glossary to *Lord Jim* is especially useful for its explanations of terms in use around the time of JC's nineteenth-century maritime world.]

2200 Moser, Thomas C. "Preface," *JCJL* (1968), pp. vi–viii.

Lord Jim is a masterpiece in two separate and apparently conflicting genres: (1) "an exotic adventure story of the Eastern seas" in the popular tradition of Kipling and Stevenson, and (2) "a completely wrought 'art novel'" in the tradition of Flaubert and James. While melodrama abounds in the book, *Jim* explores moral and psychological questions with a complexity unknown in novels of adventure, and it refuses finally to provide clear-cut answers to difficult questions. JC accomplishes his effects by means of several narrative techniques never before employed in the English novel. If this work differs from ordinary adventure stories in the "actuality" of its materials, it differs still more in the artistry of its composition. Factual material related to the book provides information likely to have been known to a reader of 1900 but lost to us and reminds us that JC, an impressionistic novelist, had been "really a seaman" for twenty years, so that the authenticity of his fiction is almost unprecedented in the history of the novel.

2201 Moser, Thomas C. "Selected Bibliography," *JCLS* (1968), pp. 485–86.

[Lists a few biographical and general studies of JC and several that deal more directly with *Lord Jim.*]

2202 Moser, Thomas C. "Textual History," *JCLJ* (1968), pp. 255–58.

[Traces the revisions of the text of *Lord Jim,* which was much revised, especially in the first half of the novel. The copy-text for Moser's edition is that of the limited Heinemann edition of 1921, the third English edition.]

2203 Moser, Thomas C. "Textual Notes," *JCLJ* (1968), pp. 258–65.

[These textual notes to *Lord Jim* give, according to Moser, "every substantive change likely to have been made by Conrad after the periodical version." They are of great value.]

2204 Mursia, Ugo. "Appendix," *Romanzi della Malesia* (Malay Novels), (Milan: Mursia, 1968), pp. 879–83.

[Contains biographical sources and notes on the originals of Lingard, Almayer, and Jim.] [In Italian.]

2205 Mursia, Ugo. "Editorial Note," in *The Sisters, An Unfinished Story by Joseph Conrad* (Milan: Mursia, 1968), pp. 7–8.

First published in 1928 in New York in Vol. LXVI, No. 5, of *The Bookman* and re-published in book form in the same year by Crosby Gaige in an edition limited to 935 copies, *The Sisters*, one of the two novels left unfinished by JC, is now made readily available, especially to readers in Europe. This publication is an "exceptional event" because it provides the first European edition and offers what may be regarded as the "Editio princeps" of the work. The story itself is important because its biographical interest lies in the fact that the main character, Rita, appears in *The Arrow of Gold* and *The Mirror of the Sea*, and because its critical interest, taken together with "The Return," indicates the literary direction JC would have followed if he had not been dissuaded, chiefly by Edward Garnett.

2206 Mursia, Ugo. "La fortuna di Joseph Conrad in Italia: Inventario al 1968" (The Fortunes of Joseph Conrad in Italy: 1968 Inventory), *Annali di Ca' Foscari*, VII, 2 (1968), pp. 1–20; rpt. [trans. by Dominic J. Bisignano] as "Joseph Conrad's Works: An Italian Bibliography," *CON*, II, No. 2 (Winter 1969–70), pp. 133–51.

The translations of JC's works into Italian can be divided into two groups with diverse characteristics. The line of demarcation is World War II. The first group is filled with errors and absurd changes; the second group has produced work of much higher quality. Today, JC is approached with proper respect. [Contains a lengthy list of Italian translations of JC's individual works, 118 in all, with detailed information about each.] [In Italian.]

2207 Najder, Zdzislaw. "*Lord Jim*: A Romantic Tragedy of Honor," *CON*, I, No. 1 (Summer 1968), pp. 1–7.

Of the two protagonists of *Lord Jim*, Jim possesses the same basic ideals of conduct as Marlow. Marlow, though, is surprised by the consequence of adherence to these standards; whereas Jim has an exalted sense of responsibility. Two typically romantic concepts, imagination and dream, are opposed; imagination is a dangerous quality, but the dream is something positive. The problem of honor is brought into the latter part of the novel, and in contrast to the two men who understand Jim (the simple-minded lieutenant of the French gunboat and Stein), Marlow is amazed and confused by the ethics of honor. The essence of the psychological problem in *Lord Jim* is the conflict between social reality and an individual's notions and ideas. After the *Patna* incident, Jim's desire is to bring about a concurrence between his own concept of himself and the judgment of other people. The construction of the plot in the novel—introduction, development, suspension of the final catastrophe, and the pathetic finale—is suggestive of a classical tragedy. One of its basic elements is the inevitability of fate, and Jim's fate is a consequence of his principles. Tragic catharsis thus appears in a twentieth-century novel, but at the end, JC the romantic prevails over JC the realist, and *Lord Jim*, as a whole, is a romantic "drama of incomprehension."

2208 Najder, Zdzislaw. "Wstep" (Introduction), *Joseph Conrad, Listy* (Joseph Conrad, Letters), (Warsaw: Panstwowy Instytut Wydawniczy, 1968), pp. 5–17.

JC's letters are a valuable source not for his "intentions" but for his general views and processes of thought and for placing his work in intellectual, moral, and artistic systems. JC saw reality in purely human categories, but he lacked faith in the "original" goodness of human nature, though he was not antisocial. [In Polish.]

2209 Nicolaisen, Peter. "Die Darstellung der Wildnis in Joseph Conrads 'Heart of Darkness'" (The Representation of Wilderness in Joseph Conrad's "Heart of Darkness"), *Die Neuren Sprachen*, XVII (1968), pp. 265–81.

Before searching for hidden meanings in "Heart of Darkness," one should realize that JC describes a journey into the wilderness of Africa which is based on an actual trip. Between JC's diary entries and his fictional account of the journey, there are remarkable discrepancies, and JC obviously intends both to convey the impression of an empty, monotonous, alien country and to depict Marlow's emotional reactions. Rather than describing the landscape in detail, JC emphasizes a few general traits (silence, immobility) by repetition, thus accounting for Marlow's sense of nightmare and the dangerous, evil aspects of the wilderness. The result is a kind of abstraction that explains the diverging analyses of the past and, in some ways, is unsuccessful (if compared with similar descriptions by Stevenson and Kipling). While the diary presents many facts which the short story disregards, it does not contain such subjective impressions. Once again, one has to consider JC's dual nature. [In German.]

2210 Ordoñez, Elmer A[lindogan]. "Notes on the Revisions in *An Outcast of the Islands*," *N&Q*, N.S., XV (August 1968), pp. 287–89.

The revisions of *An Outcast of the Islands* attempt, for the most part, to improve rhythm and economy. They increase the material of Willem's introspective examinations.

2211 "Organic Attitudes," *TLS* (11 July 1968), p. 734.

JC writes basically about specific matters, such as colonial exploitation in "Heart of Darkness" and political relationships in an underdeveloped country in *Nostromo*, but he is not the usual stereotype of "an ironist denouncing radical causes."

2212 Orwell, George. *The Collected Essays: Journalism and Letters*, 4 vols. ed. by Sonia Orwell and Ian Angus (New York: Harcourt, Brace & World; London: Secker & Warburg, 1968), I, pp. 25, 26, 33, 227, 234, 506; II, pp. 199; III, pp. 387–89; IV, pp. 488–90, 506.

I. *Almayer's Folly* contains an underlying sense of the East which one cannot always perceive without actually having lived in the tropics, and that JC could have remained there as long as he did makes him an anomaly among writers. He is not popular now because of his florid language and redundant adjectives.

II. "Youth" is probably too long to be considered for inclusion in any modern periodical. "Typhoon" reveals JC in top form, but "The Planter of Malata" is of small value; it reveals the vulgar theatricality of JC's attitudes toward the *noblesse oblige* "The Partner" is basically a good story; its major flaw is JC's clumsy effort at narrating in third person. The descriptive passages in *The Nigger of the Narcissus* are good, but what is especially worth notice is the occasional appearance of JC's social and political ideas. At best, *The Shadow-Line* is an average tale.

III. JC is attractive for his extreme understanding of conspiratorial politics and for his writing style, which is clearly non-English and at times seems like a translation. Even his romanticism is non-English.

IV. JC has often been dubbed a writer of sea stories, but he had only an incomplete understanding of the East. [This seems to contradict statements made in I]. His greatest work involves political themes. His English is sometimes incorrect, but it has served to civilize English literature and to bring it back into contact with Europe.

2213 Palmer, John A. "'Achievement and Decline': A Bibliographical Note," from *Joseph Conrad's Fiction: A Study in Literary Growth* (1968); rpt. *JCC* (1975), pp. 139–45.

[Provides a short survey of JC's fiction and also supplies an overview of the current state of JC scholarship and criticism. Offers alternatives to the contentions of Douglas Hewitt through Thomas Moser and Albert Guerard that JC's literary quality declined precipitously in the last ten years of his life.]

2214 Palmer, John A. *Joseph Conrad's Fiction: A Study in Literary Growth* (Ithaca, New York: Cornell University Press, 1968).

Since the view of JC's writing career as a course of achievement and decline imposes a false symmetry on the JC canon, JC's works may be more usefully viewed as successive major achievements, each preceded by a period of experiment and partial success, thus showing his later works to be much better than commonly supposed. JC's career, then, revealing a "progress-of-awareness," consists of three stages: (1) a beginning, with the "presocial dilemmas of private honor and individual fidelity": the less important Almayer stories and *The Nigger of the Narcissus*, followed by "Heart of Darkness" and *Lord Jim* being the most important early works; (2) an expansion of the early works to a consideration of the individual in society and the moral contradictions imposed by social restrictions: the lesser political works, *The Secret Agent* and *Under Western Eyes* followed by JC's greatest achievement, *Nostromo*; and (3) an extension, with *Chance* and *Victory*, to the theoretical and metaphysical bases of any moral commitment. The works that follow these groups are largely anticlimactic. JC's moral concerns remain the same throughout his career—"individual responsibility; self-knowledge; man's near inability to cope with (or even discover) his own darkness, and yet the necessity of doing so." [Palmer's book deserves detailed attention; he may not be entirely successful in his view of the JC canon, but he provides very useful insights into the individual works.]

2215 Pinsker, Sanford. "The Conradian Hero and the Death of Language: A Note on *Nostromo*," *CON*, I, No. 1 (Summer 1968), pp. 49–50.

JC is consistently concerned with the inability of language to capture or assimilate adequately the meaning of external experience, and he uses language in a peculiar way in the downfall of Decoud and Nostromo. Even though Decoud, who *writes* a long letter to his sister and *writes* inflammatory material for the *Porvenir*, displays much ironic detachment, he betrays a "Western sensibility," a kind of mind that needs to talk, to write, to communicate, "no matter how impossible these things may be in the modern world" so that in his last days on the island he is unable to see himself as having any significance in the universe. Unlike Decoud, however, Nostromo receives his identity, "our man," from language so that his *name* creates the vanity and the subsequent illusion which leads to his sense of "betrayal" and eventual death: reborn into a world where Nostromo, both man and idea, has no place, he becomes the victim of his own vanity, his own illusion of being "their man."

2216 Pizer, Donald. "A Primer of Fictional Aesthetics," *College English,* XXX (April 1968), pp. 572–80.

JC, among others, developed a fictional aesthetic interest by forcing a criticism capable of coping with his complex novels. The new criticism forced an awareness of both past and present novels and allowed the novel to reach a new sophistication.

2217 Raban, Jonathan. *The Technique of Modern Fiction: Essays in Practical Criticism* (London: Edward Arnold, 1968; Notre Dame, Indiana: University of Notre Dame Press, 1969), p. 34.

The technique of the single, consistent point of view in a novel may be used in various ways. A narrator like Moll Flanders sees the world only in partial ignorance, which the reader shares. Again, the narrator may be a character who stands on the fringe of the events in the novel, observing and taking a minor role in the plot, like Marlow in "Heart of Darkness" and Nick Carraway in *The Great Gatsby.* This kind of narrator is the reader's representative in the action, allowing for a focus on the story from within.

2218 Rajiva, Stanley F. "The Singular Person: An Essay on Conrad's Use of Marlow as Narrator," *Literary Criterion,* (Mysore), VIII (Summer 1968), pp. 35–45.

JC invented Marlow. In "Heart of Darkness," Marlow comes as close as any character can to being protagonist and narrator in one person. There are, actually, three Marlows. The Marlow of *Chance* is the narrator so far removed from the story that he cannot "tell" it at all convincingly; there is the Marlow of *Lord Jim,* a "receiver and sifter of evidence collected from several sources"; and there is the Marlow of "Heart of Darkness" who, through the pattern of Kurtz's life, his own voyage to find Kurtz, and his tranquil "recollection" of the whole thing in its spiritual focus makes of the telling a spiritual journey into the heart of darkness. Both *Jim* and "Heart of Darkness" are tragic, but the latter alone contains JC's tragic irony which makes the theme, man's inhumanity to man, universal. JC needed his narrator, a man like Marlow, to keep both a grip on himself and the right distance from the experience. [The Marlow of "Youth" is virtually ignored.]

2219 Randall, Dale B. J. *Joseph Conrad and Warrington Dawson: The Record of a Friendship* (Durham, North Carolina: Duke University Press, 1968).

As a rule, JC disliked Americans because they lacked the "subtleties of civilization," but Warrington Dawson was an exception since he was a "thorough gentleman." JC and Dawson met in May, 1910, and the friendship continued throughout JC's life. JC was working on *Chance* at the time of their meeting, and Dawson provided background materials for the novel. JC apparently thought Dawson understood him, and Dawson came into his life at a time when JC especially needed assurance; Dawson's admiration helped restore JC's equilibrium. [One part of this study, the first, deals with the background, development, and decline of the friendship; the second presents 119 letters of which 51 are from JC to Dawson. Each part throws light on the other. Included, too, are 36 unpublished letters from Jessie Conrad to Dawson. This combination of biography and letters supplies a unique picture of JC's humanity and innate charity. The text and letters are copiously and carefully annotated, and they contain much that is fresh regarding the complex JC. One letter to Dawson (6/20/13) gives a statement of JC's credo as an artist expressed in a manner not hitherto published.]

2220 Randall, Dale B. J. "Some New Conrad Biographical Sources," *CON*, I, No. 2 (Fall 1968), pp. 69–70.

The unique JC items recently acquired by the William R. Perkins Library at Duke University include six scrapbooks of press cuttings "assembled" by JC's family and an old album containing photographs of some of JC's Polish friends and relatives. The Polish album is the "most precious" item of the group because it provides an important "means of ingression" into JC's Polish milieu. The six scrapbooks "devoted" to book review clippings and to JC's visit of 1923 to the United States and his death in 1924 contain many comments of general interest, such as those about the novelist's literary aims as he approached the end of his career. [Contains an appendage of seventeen titles from the scrapbooks which are not listed in Lohf and Sheehy, *Joseph Conrad at Mid-century* (1957).] [Randall's articles, based on JC's scrapbooks, listed in chronological order as they appear in *Conradiana*, are scattered through Vols. I–IV, as follows: "Conrad Interviews, No. 1: Perriton Maxwell," *Conradiana*, II, No. 1 (Fall 1969–70), pp. 17–22; "Conrad Interviews, No. 2: James Walter Smith," *Conradiana*, II, No. 2 (Winter 1969–70), pp. 83–93; "Conrad Interviews, No. 3: Thomas B. Sherman," *Conradiana*, II, No. 3

(1969–70), pp. 122–27; "Conrad Interviews, No. 4: Edward K. Titus, Jr.," *Conradiana*, III, No. 1 (1970–71), pp. 75–80; "Conrad Interviews, No. 5: Tracey Hammond Lewis," *Conradiana*, III, No. 2 (1971–72), pp. 67–73; and "Conrad Interviews, No. 6: Louis Weitzenkorn," *Conradiana*, IV, No. 1 (1972), pp. 25–32. I. M. Fitzrandolph suggests as a footnote in *Conradiana*, III, No. 1 (1970–71), p. 38, Ford Madox Ford's *Thus to Revisit* as a "plausible" source for recollections of the journalist James Walter Smith about a question posed by Randall in "Conrad Interviews, No. 2: James Walter Smith," *Conradiana*, II, No. 2 (Winter 1969–70, pp. 87, 92.]

2221 Raskin, Jonah. "*Nostromo*: The Argument from Revision," *EIC*, XVIII (April 1968), pp. 183–92.

The disagreement about the status of *Nostromo* begins with JC himself. A comparison of the version serialized in *T. P.'s Weekly* (1903–1904) with that of the first edition (1904) suggests that in the latter version JC became acutely aware of some of the novel's moral implications to which critics had objected and was attempting to add an extra dimension to what he had already written. The final version is "more humane, more positive, more liberal," at least in intention. In it, the last eighty pages were almost entirely rewritten. The people who have been betrayed by the old revolution form the nucleus for a new revolutionary party, and JC makes it clear that Nostromo's descendant, the working class leader of the future, will be a Marxist. JC disliked the Marxists, but he realized that the revolutions of the future would be Socialist. Through additional changes in his criticism of Decoud, JC asserts a belief that "man *must* be involved in social and political life, that he *must* reject isolation and seek human fellowship." At least, his intention is clear. [Preceded by Michael Wilding, "The Politics of *Nostromo*," *Essays in Criticism*, XVI (October 1966), pp. 441–56; and Ivo Vidan and Juliet McLauchlan, "The Politics of *Nostromo*," *Essays in Criticism*, XVII (July 1967), pp. 392–406; and followed by Michael Wilding, "The Politics of *Nostromo*," *Essays in Criticism*, XVIII (April 19680, pp. 234–36.]

2222 Raval, R. K. "*Lord Jim*: An Existential Analysis," *Journal of The Maharaja Sayaji Rao University of Baroda*, XVII (April 1968), pp. 57–70.

[Raval provides a complete and concise summary in the text of the essay itself: "Jim's character can be regarded as an epitome of existential philosophy. The theme of responsibility and its abandonment, the consequent abandonment of self and humanity, the resulting isolation, the sense of anguish and pain following isolation, a fresh commitment or a sense of new involvement in search of the lost self and a persistent pursuit of the ideal heroic conduct are worked out systematically in the character of Jim." This is a responsible reading of the novel from a well defined point of view.]

2223 Reichard, Hugo M. "The Patusan Crisis: A Revaluation of Jim and Marlow," *English Studies*, XLIX (December 1968), pp. 547–52.

The crises of the second half of *Lord Jim* are very different from those of the first half: in particular, they are strongly interracial. Jim seems to love Jewel much less than he loves the honor of the white men, and he puts his role of white champion of Brown above his role as guardian of the people of Patusan. And in the end, Jim seems to believe that he is doing better than the "benighted, bewildered" natives can do. His last acts, then, are so greatly affected by racism that he fails to purge himself from the shame of his first career; he is a hero manqué. Both Marlow and JC leave too many rifts and gaps; "both the protagonist and his Boswell prove unequal to their opportunities." But even great writers like JC sometimes produce works different from what they plan.

2224 Reid, B[enjamin] L[awrence]. *The Man from New York* (New York: Oxford University Press, 1968), pp. 73 and passim.

At the suggestion of Agnes Tobin, John Quinn and JC began corresponding in 1911. The resulting friendship led to mutual admiration and mutual benefit: the needy JC sold his manuscripts and Quinn made a successful investment, buying stories for £15 and novels for £80. By 1919, their friendship began to cool when JC started selling manuscripts elsewhere. In 1923, Quinn sold all his JC papers at auction, making a ten-fold profit on his $10,000 investment.

2225 Resink, G[ertrude] J[ohan]. "The Eastern Archipelago Under Joseph Conrad's Western Eyes," *Indonesia's History between the Myths: Essays in Legal History and Historical Theory* (The Hague: W. van Hoeve [Selected Studies in Indonesia, vol. 7], 1968), pp. 307–23, 385–87.

JC learned much about the "Eastern Archipelago" by reading the works of his predecessors (especially Multatuli's *Max Havelaar*, "the only great Dutch novel of the nineteenth century") but he traveled widely in the East between 1883 and 1888, thereby learning to know the area at first hand. He could thus create Patusan for Lord Jim, a "native state" which "can only be Achin"; and the old sultan of Batu Beru in "The End of the Tether," who hoped to die before the white man could take his country from him and lived in another such realm on the east coast of Sumatra. In these two instances appears the "reality" of the "noninterference policy" pursued by the Dutch with their ideal of future conquest.

JC's Indonesian novels and tales, set in the years between 1860 and 1915, include *The Rescue*, *Almayer's Folly*, *An Outcast of the Islands*, "The End of the Tether," *Lord Jim*, "Karain," "The Lagoon," and "Because of the Dollars." True to his Polish background, JC, who was opposed to the intra-European, continental imperialism of Russia, Prussia, and Austria, was also a "sharp critic" of the extra-European, overseas imperialism of the other Western powers. But the Eastern Archipelago so inspired him that as late as 1920 he maintained that the inhabitants of the archipelago "have kept to this day their love of liberty." [An excellent treatment of little known material.]

2226 Resink, G[ertrude] J[ohan]. "Samburan Encantada," *CON*, I, No. 2 (Fall 1968), pp. 37–44.

Sufficient evidence exists to conclude that Melville's *The Piazza Tales* of 1856 could have influenced JC's writing, especially *Victory* and *An Outcast of the Islands*. Melville's sketches entitled "The Encantadas: or Enchanted Islands," contain many similarities to JC's "Island Tale." Since his first-hand knowledge of the Indonesian Archipelago was from calls at some seven ports probably within a year's time, JC very much needed to familiarize himself with the region by extensive reading.

2227 Robb, Kenneth A. "Article Note," *CON*, I, No. 2 (Fall 1968), pp. 85–86.

[An annotation of an article, Charles Jones, "Varieties of Speech Presentation in Conrad's *The Secret Agent*," *Lingua*, XX (1968), pp. 162–76, makes a "substantial contribution" to the study of JC's style.]

2228 Rocks, James E. "The Christian Myth as Salvation: Caroline Gordon's *The Strange Children*," *Tulane Studies in English*, XVI (1968), pp. 149–60.

Caroline Gordon, having learned much from Flaubert, James, Ford Madox Ford, Joyce, and JC, insists upon the "informing techniques of these impressionistic novelists."

2229 Rosa, Alfred F. "The Counterforce of Technology on the Pastoral Ideal in *Nostromo*," *Massachusetts Studies in English*, I (Fall 1968), pp. 88–93.

Nostromo is a descendant of the literary strain established by Virgil in his pastoral *Eclogues*, with the counterforce to the pastoral being technology. Sulaco, with its pastoral environment and its foreign influences, displays in various ways the impact of technology. Perhaps the skeptic Decoud is best aware of the counterforce; through his heightened sensitivity to sounds he is unable to endure the serenity of the pastoral without the noise of mechanization. Nostromo, too, falls prey to the counterforce of the pastoral when he begins to steal the silver.

2230 Russell, Bertrand. *The Autobiography of Bertrand Russell, 1914–1944* (Boston: Little, Brown, 1968), pp. 32, 97, 208–10, 234–38.

H. M. Tomlinson owes much to "Heart of Darkness," in which one sees "how our generation . . . is a little mad, because it has allowed itself glimpses of the truth," which is "spectral, insane, ghastly." [Russell's "centre" of being, "a curious wild pain," is rare, but JC "especially" had it also.] [Contains letters from JC dated 2 November 1921, 18 November 1921, and 23 October 1922.]

2231 Ruthven, K. K. "The Savage God: Conrad and Lawrence," *Critical Quarterly,* X (Spring–Summer 1968), pp. 39–54.

JC's "Heart of Darkness" is "the *locus classicus* of savage primitivism," and thus a criticism of the values of European society. For JC and others, Europeans suppress the impulses of their id. Consequently, civilization, not "darkest Africa," and all that it symbolizes for the European mind is the enemy. The authentic and complete man is primitive man, and he can thrive only in a state of primitivism. Thus, in rejecting the values of European civilization to reach out to face the unknown impulses hidden by the veneer of civilization, Kurtz alone becomes the hero of JC's story. Unlike Marlow and the chief accountant, he submits to the "heavy, mute spell of the wilderness." For Marlow, a venture into Africa is a test of European integrity; for JC, this test is folly: his true heroes face the darkness and "live in the midst of the incomprehensible," as Kurtz does in undergoing "a sort of moral emancipation." Kurtz says that he is on the threshold of great things; Marlow, of course, interprets this statement as a reference to Kurtz's greed as an ivory-collector. But Marlow is not a reliable commentator; Kurtz lived in a "realm of experience . . . beyond the conventional scope of good and evil." Not in touch with the dark side of the mind, Marlow cannot understand Kurtz. Of course, Kurtz fails, but only because he dies before he is completely freed from European values. Near the end of the story, Marlow changes his mind and says that Kurtz's cry had "the appalling face of a glimpsed truth."

2232 Ryan, Patrick J., S.J. "Images of the White Liberal," *America*, CXIX (12 October 1968), pp. 316–17, 320–21.

Among the white liberals in England who cried out at the turn of the century against the exploitation of the Congo by European commerce were Sir Roger Casement and JC. The images of these two men suggest some "food" for the contemporary white liberal's "identity crisis." JC's "Heart of Darkness" is a powerful vision of the effects of colonization on both the colonized and the colonizer. As JC grew older, his dislike for colonialism gave way to his growing British identity until he remains as the image of the youthful white liberal of our day who fails to be consistently radical. But whereas JC withdrew into silence, Sir Roger Casement, a more consistent white liberal, finally defied the colonialist system "to its face" and was hanged in 1916. JC, then Captain Korzeniowski, first met Casement at Matadi, a river port on the Congo, in 1890. It is "curious and sad" that Casement's old friend, JC, refrained from signing a plea for clemency for the man who "may well serve as the tragic hero of the best white liberals in America today"; but JC spent his later years becoming "as English as he possibly could."

2233 Sarang, Vilas. "A Source for 'The Hollow Men,'" *N&Q*, XV (February 1968), pp. 57–58.

T. S. Eliot's line, "Life is very long," probably comes from JC's *An Outcast of the Islands*, which may have been as much in the back of Eliot's mind as "Heart of Darkness" when he wrote the poem.

2234 Schaefer, William D. "Recent Books: British Fiction," *NCF*, XXIII (September 1968), pp. 248–51.

[A brief review of the Meyer, Fleishman, and Rosenfield book-length studies of Conrad, all 1967]. ". . . if the total picture of Conrad's politics is not, in the final analysis, [because he did not have a consistent or rigorously applied political philosophy] a completely satisfactory one, the fault is mainly Conrad's."

2235 Schorer, Mark. "Technique as Discovery," *The World We Imagine: Selected Essays* (New York: Farrar, Straus and Giroux, 1968), p. 19.

What is needed in fiction is "a devoted fidelity to every technique which will help us to discover and to evaluate our subject matter, and more than that, to discover the amplifications of naming of which our subject matter is capable." Most modern novelists have felt this demand upon them. They responded differently to it: H. G. Wells, for example, with his large "blob of potential material," did not know where to "cut" it to the novel's taste; André Gide cut it, "of course—in every possible direction." None, perhaps, is more important than the inheritance from French symbolism which Huxley called "the musicalization of fiction." JC anticipated both, however, when he wrote that the novel "must strenuously aspire to the plasticity of sculpture, to the colour of painting, and to the magic suggestiveness of music—which is the art of arts." [Helps to explain JC's importance among other novelists.]

2236 Secor, Robert. "Conrad's American Secret Sharers," *CON*, I, No. 2 (Fall 1968), pp. 59–67.

There is a "spiritual affinity" between JC and the "American consciousness," but the assumptions and purposes shared by JC and Hawthorne, for example, are more the concern of the American than of the English novelist. Neither JC nor the American novelist was able to give the rich social context of the English writers to his works because both, living and writing without a long tradition behind them, turned inward, away from the novel of morals and manners, and looked for significance on a different level. JC's *Victory* and Hawthorne's *The Blithedale Romance* are analogous in that both contain the premise of the complexity of the human condition and the impossibility of evading this condition by altering social surroundings; both contain impossible Edens built on partial visions which oversimplify moral existence; both contain sanctuaries which are exposed as illusion; both have protagonists who refuse the commitment to life which would allow psychological health and lead to moral action; both display a certain identity between the novelists and their protagonists; and finally, both authors insist upon commitment to life even if the realities are "absurdity and horror, failure and tragedy." [Further comparative studies of JC and other American novels are needed as well as such studies of JC and other English novels.]

2237 Seltzer, Leon F. "The Vision of Melville and Conrad: A Comparative Study," *DA*, XXIX (August 1968), 613A–14A. Unpublished dissertation, SUNY, Buffalo, 1968; pub. as *The Vision of Melville and Conrad: A Comparative Study* (Athens: Ohio University Press, 1970).

Since Herman Melville and JC as artists responded similarly to human experience, their works contain certain "broad parallels" in philosophical and moral outlook expressed in common themes and techniques and with "substantial stylistic affinities." Both novelists recognized egoism as a basic part of the corrupt nature of man (for example, in Ahab and Kurtz), which is unchangeable, and both tended toward an ironic mode in their fiction because they disliked current social conditions and had no faith in any alternatives. Not only were they disillusioned by man's egoistic nature and by a society intrinsically corrupt, they were also disheartened by their concept of a hostile universe and their skepticism regarding a benevolent Deity and a distrust of man's reasons. These skeptical attitudes, in addition to a disbelief in the efficacy of art, created in both men a "stance of disillusionment" so that skepticism, manifested in irony as the method of their composition, became for them "the way of art." Melville and JC were unable to discern any fixed standards for evaluating the morality of human behavior: human life was "absurd." As a result they developed ambiguity as a theme or subject in their writings. The isolated or independent man is defeated; man in general needs a belief in human devotion. Thus, stoical resignation became for these two writers an important human value.

2238 Simmonds, Harvey. "John Quinn: An Exhibition to Mark the Gift of the New John Quinn Memorial Collection," *Bulletin of the New York Public Library*, LXXII (November 1968), pp. 568–87; rpt. *John Quinn: An Exhibition to Mark the Gift of the John Quinn Memorial Collection* (New York: New York Public Library, 1968), pp. 8, 9, 11.

[Simmonds lists JC's signed letters to Quinn and the manuscript of *Chance*, purchased by Quinn in 1912, as well as a signed letter from Jessie Conrad.]

2239 Smith, David R. "'One Word More' about *The Nigger of the Narcissus*," *NCF*, XXIII (September 1968), pp. 201–16.

A recently discovered written exchange between JC and William Leonard Courtney is illuminating because JC's part in it can be compared with his best known critical statement, the Preface to *The Nigger of the Narcissus*, which it clarifies. JC, world-wearied realist and seeming cynic, was confronted by an entrenched and slightly obtuse member of the Victorian establishment, imperial idealist, optimist, and conventional moralist, reviewing *Nigger*. JC's response in a previously unpublished letter to Courtney is significant for what it says about the methods and aims of *Nigger* and JC's writing in general.

2240 Sokolianskii, M. "Dzhozef Konrad o literature" (Joseph Conrad on Literature), *Voprosy Literatury* (Moscow), No. 7 (1968), pp. 202–206.

JC's themes, the originality of his settings, and the stylistic character of his prose have caused scholars to call him neo-Romantic. He admired Chekhov and Turgenev, though his attitude toward Dostoevski and Tolstoi was more complex, a fact which made him an interesting instance of difference between a writer's opinions of other writers and his own creative activity. [Pages 206–27 extracts from JC's prefaces, essays, and letters translated into Russian.] [In Russian.]

2241 Spalding, Alex. "*Lord Jim*: The Result of Reading Light Holiday Literature," *Humanities Association Bulletin* (Canada), XIX (Winter 1968), pp. 14–22.

The reader's view of Jim, in JC's *Lord Jim*, is blurred and refracted. His moral lapse on the *Patna* is the working of his imagination: he is still a boy who wants people to live like Sir Galahad or Jim Hawkins in *Treasure Island*. And Jim, still a creature of flesh and blood, cannot be reborn by his jump over the palisades into the world of Patusan. The natives there accept him only in the role of a protective god; we are not fooled by the sentimentality of Marlow and Stein. The traditional symbols, the ship and the island, the stable and the unstable states of society, do not allow us to take Jim's island role seriously any more than JC does, for we know his death is incongruous with his fairyland world. The image of the Eastern bride, associated often with the key words "side," "dream," and "opportunity," is obviously the kind of image a boy might obtain from reading fairy tales. Nor is Jim at all like Alexander the Great, to whom he is frequently compared. Also, Gentleman Brown is Jim's alter-ego: they are two halves of one Everyman, or of one "Everybody." Jim is a split personality, and neither of the halves will accept the other. *Jim*, then, is, in addition to other things, a grim reminder that all people must meet on more human levels than have yet been reached. The code of adventure books cannot be used in the intractable world of nature.

2242 Stallman, R[obert] W[ooster]. *Stephen Crane: A Biography* (New York: George Braziller, 1968), pp. 320–35, 418–19, and passim.

Crane and JC met in October, 1897, and were close friends as well as mutual admirers thereafter. H. G. Wells, Arthur Symons, and Ford Madox Ford noticed that despite JC's nervous and intense haughtiness, he was often servile and overly modest, especially in comparing his work with Crane's. Crane, on the other hand, was very frank with JC, but the two authors were quite similar in their fictional techniques of impressionism, symbolism, irony, and handling of point of view. Crane's *The Red Badge of Courage* influenced *The Nigger of the Narcissus*, "Youth," and *Lord Jim*. Crane once proposed that he and JC collaborate on a play, "The Predecessor," but they never began this project. JC spent much time, effort, and money in encouraging Crane, bringing him back to England from Havana and helping him out of financial difficulties.

2243 Stein, William Bysshe. "*Almayer's Folly*: The Terrors of Time," *CON,* I, No. 1 (Summer 1968), pp. 27–34.

For JC, time is not a spatial phenomenon but a state of being: in *Almayer's Folly,* Almayer experiences time *in* time; he relives the past in the present, with thoughts of the future. JC connects futurity with Western man's dominant notion of self-fulfillment, usually an aspiration for success and fame. Thus Almayer's expectations in the present are always determined by the past and its vague promises of fortune in the future. But eventually, when this illusion of achievement is dispelled, the protagonist's future vanishes and his life loses its direction and purpose. The incongruous collapse of Almayer's hopes and dreams represents a "fall out of time," and his subsequent addiction to opium exemplifies his inability to transcend the "absurd" experience. This course of events clarifies the basic theme of the novel: like Western man, Almayer lacks the religious, philosophical, or moral faith to bridge this "chasm in human finitude." The action proper of the novel spans only three days; JC creates the illusion, however, of the passing of more than twenty-five years by his finesse in telescoping and staggering his report of present and past events. Thus the novel is seen to be much more complexly executed than most readers realize.

2244 Stein, William Bysshe. "The Eastern Matrix of Conrad's Art," *CON,* I, No. 2 (Fall 1968), pp. 1–14.

In JC's Eastern tales, the mark of his unique cultural identity is Western man's infatuation with the "fruits of directed action"; that is, Western man, unlike the Oriental man, temporalizes his existence almost exclusively in the future. One adversity which he cannot cope with morally or emotionally is the loss of faith in a cherished aspiration. Almayer, of *Almayer's Folly,* for example, struggles to rehearse the scenario of Western man's endeavors to shape events into the image of his dreams; his "lesson" is a scathing but pitying indictment of Western man's "perilous optimism," his unsubstantiated belief that he is master of his own fate. "Karain" obliquely delineates the complacent self-deception of Europeanized man, and Marlow in *Lord Jim* is betrayed into moral nihilism by his "compulsive desire" to transform Jim's fantasies of heroism into the "collective aspiration" of Western man. The "pragmatic philosophy" of "Because of the Dollars" governs not only one particular episode in Davidson's life but also his entire course of life, and "A Smile of Fortune" is JC's analysis of the implications of his society's compulsive pursuit of success.

2245 Stephens, Robert O. *Hemingway's Nonfiction: The Public Voice* (Chapel Hill: University of North Carolina Press, 1968), pp. 12, 113, 132–33, 231–32.

Writing for little magazines in the capacity of man of letters, Hemingway produced his first prose elegy, in recognition of JC, for Ford Madox Ford's *The Transatlantic Review*. Adopting a "personal voice," Hemingway praised JC as a model for the novelist, while dismissing T. S. Eliot. He equated JC's skill and artistry with that of the bullfighter Garcia and gave a private account of how he read JC's novels, prudently saving them for times when they were needed, since he could not reread JC. Hemingway at the same time anticipated and rejected the standard encomiums: "remarkable story teller," "stylist," "deep thinker," and "serene philosopher," and in a review of the Nobel Prize award to Yeats, he noted the Nobel committee's neglect of JC, which it would have to live down.

2246 [Stevens, H. Ray.] "Bibliography," *CON*, I, No. 1 (Summer 1968), pp. 87–89.

[First in a continuing series in *Conradiana* of bibliographies of works about JC.]

2247 Stewart, J. I. M. *Joseph Conrad* (London: Longmans; New York: Dodd, Mead, 1968).

[To some degree an extension of Stewart's "Conrad" in *Eight Modern Writers* (1963), (C, I, No. 1760), this biography of JC seems intended for the general reader or the student, as the plot-summaries and the brevity of both the account of JC's life and the paucity of original interpretations indicate. Since *Under Western Eyes*, completed in 1910, is the last of JC's "unchallengeable masterpieces," Stewart accepts the achievement-and-decline attitude toward JC's work. The last novels, though, have a substantial interest for criticism because they make possible a comparison between "Conrad and the Conradesque." In his final phase as a writer, JC has relinquished his "unflinching gaze" into a heart of darkness and has come to move, "rather stiffly and painfully, in the light . . . of common day, a little softened by the veil of romantic sentiment." If Stewart is somewhat weak critically, we still have his urbane style and his occasional insights into familiar material.]

2248 Stirling, Nora. "Joseph Conrad," *Who Wrote the Classics?, II* (New York: John Day, 1968), pp. 213–46.

[A nicely written short biography of JC for high school sophomores.]

2249 Sutton, Maurice Lewis. "Introduction," *Joseph Conrad: "Heart of Darkness" and "The Secret Sharer"* (New York: Barnes & Noble, 1968), pp. 5–14.

Many critics complain that JC's powers declined in his later years, but part of his problem may be due to his learning English in his twenties. Some of his sentences, in fact, read like translations. At any rate, his work can be separated into three categories: sea stories, jungle stories, and political stories. The sea stories are purely adventure and are often so exciting that some readers do not discover the psychological tension in them. The jungle stories are about the moral and psychological conflicts arising out of one character's isolation.

JC's ideas about life and art center on his belief in duty and work. Man can protect himself from evil as well as from meaninglessness through proper conduct and hard work. "Heart of Darkness" and "The Secret Sharer" are basically the same. In the former, Marlow is the central figure, although the novel is firmly based on JC's own experiences in traveling up the Congo River in 1890. Marlow is, in a sense, the stabilizing force, the purveyor of the events. The central themes are restraint, isolation, and hollow men. In "The Secret Sharer," the central themes are again isolation and restraint. [Contains plot summaries, character sketches, study questions, critical opinions, a brief biography, and a brief bibliography. The analysis is uneven.]

2250 Tanner, Tony. "Introduction," *Henry James*, ed. by Tony Tanner (London: Macmillan [Modern Judgements], 1968), pp. 11–41.

Henry James was recognized "almost immediately" as a major writer "of some sort," and within his own lifetime he received the "genuinely appreciative acclaim of three very different but very important fellow novelists—William Dean Howells, Ford Madox Ford, and JC. In 1905, when people were not very much interested in what James was trying to do with the novel, JC wrote one phrase which all subsequent criticism of James has scarcely bettered: "Mr. Henry James is the historian of fine consciences."

2251 Tarnawski, Wit. "Conrad's *A Personal Record*," *CON*, I, No. 2 (Fall 1968), pp. 55–58. Trans. from the Polish by David Welsh, from "Apologia Conrada Korzeniowskiego," (Conrad Korzeniowski's Apology), *Wiadomosci* (News), (London), No. 1159 (16 June 1968), p. 2.

Although JC often touched on the theme of loyalty in his fictitious works, he wanted to clarify the question of betrayal to his country; therefore, at the peak of his creative years, he produced *A*

Personal Record, containing two main themes: the history of his leaving Poland and serving later in the British merchant navy, and the writing of his first novel in English. He wanted to illuminate and defend this "double departure" from his native country. As justification, he offered the defensive theses that he had left Poland under the influence of a mysterious inner voice; that the entire weight of his decision lay on his youthful quitting of his country, not the choice of a literary language; and that he had engaged in literature by accident and to make a living. The adoption of this attitude made JC immune to censure because of the irrationality of his youthful impulses. Most of these arguments appear in *Lord Jim. A Personal Record* served as a sort of catharsis in JC's "Polish complex" and brought inner liberation to the novelist. JC, however, wrote this memoir "with sealed lips" and "with inspiration in fetters," thereby producing his "least artistically successful work."

2252 Teets, Bruce E. "Book Reviews," *CON*, I, No. 2 (Fall 1968), pp. 103–105.

In writing *The Nigger of the Narcissus*, JC learned to be a novelist: the story speaks for itself by means of close description of the details of seamanship, of clearly portrayed characters, of some "superb surprises," and of the central mystery of Wait's hold on everyone on the ship. An inspection of the chronological development of JC's themes reveals a gradual broadening from a concern with the individual man to man's place in the world and the universe. In his greatest works, 1897 to 1915, JC intricately bound together theme and technique. In his later novels, his heroes fail in their attempts to avoid involvement with other people and finally learn to exercise compassion. [In a review of Neville H. Newhouse, *Joseph Conrad* (1966).]

2253 Thomas, J. D. "How Many Children Had Plain Mr. Jones?" *CEA*, XXX (May 1968), p. 3.

In *Victory*, Mr. Jones is not Satan himself, but a "portrait" of "Satan's only begotten son: Death," as all details of his picturing indicate. And Heyst has heretofore confronted death's surrogate in the person of his father, the "philosopher of universal negation." Lena's violent duel for Heyst's life is not with Jones, or Death, directly, but with his "vital" attendant, Martin Ricardo. Incapable of estimating the power of her adversaries, Lena, assured of "her tremendous achievement" because she is "convinced of the reality of her victory over death," fails. The victory is doubly ironic in that Lena understands very little of the net of evil in which she and Heyst have been entrapped and in that she senses only dimly the spiritual vacuum within him. Yet as she dies, Heyst's silent imprecations upon his soul's distrust of life is, after all, a measure of her triumph.

2254 Thorburn, David. "Conrad: The Use of Adventure," *DA*, XXIX (1968), 617A. Unpublished dissertation, Stanford University, 1968; developed into "Conrad's Romanticism: Self-Consciousness and Community," in *Romanticism: Vistas, Instances, Continuities*, ed. by David Thorburn and Geoffrey Hartman (Ithaca and London: Cornell University Press, 1973); developed into *Conrad's Romanticism* (New Haven and London: Yale University Press, 1974).

At this point JC, according to a "revisionist" survey of his works, has deep affinities with the *fin de siecle* tradition of the adventure story as found in such writers as R. L. Stevenson, Anthony Hope, and Rudyard Kipling, and ultimately with the Romantic poets, especially with Wordsworth. His Polish background, his early life, and his years at sea encouraged his interest in the world of danger and adventure. Both the typical adventure tale and many of JC's stories have in common a young, inexperienced hero and an older and more reliable "retainer figure," such as Dominic Cervoni in the *Tremolino* story in *The Mirror of the Sea*, and Marlow and Lord Jim in *Lord Jim*. But JC was able to achieve life from the dead clichés of the adventure character, as he did with *Nostromo* and *Jim*. JC's two autobiographies illustrate the distance gained between original aim and final achievement: *A Personal Record* (1912) supplies the subjective result of the free play of his memories, impressions, and feelings, whereas *The Mirror of the Sea* (1906) is less good, though important for the *Tremolino* episode. JC's characteristic and recurring story is a "Romantic bildungsroman," usually in the form of a voyage into an "uncluttered, elementary world" that appears to offer more promise."

Against the "fledgling voyager" are two (usually) older figures, the first, the retainer character, and the second, the "witness or observer," the teller of the story (as in"Youth," "Heart of Darkness," *Jim*, and *Eyes*). Since able critics (such as Geoffrey Hartman, Northrop Frye, M.H. Abrams, and Harold Bloom) have seen an essential continuity between modernism and the "Age of Wordsworth," JC's similarities to the Romantic poets emphasize the importance of his romanticism. And JC has also a fundamentally Romantic vision of art. The "gesture of community" present in a teller's decision to relate a story is lifted to a particular prominence by JC's drama of the telling, just as Wordsworth and Coleridge supply similar counterparts. And in works like "Youth," "Heart of Darkness," *Jim*, "The Secret Sharer," and *The Shadow-Line*, JC projects a world much like Wordsworth's. JC's best work has a double appeal: it is modern and Romantic simultaneously. [This "revisionist" view of JC is in some ways congruent with that in Edward Said's *Joseph Conrad and the Fiction of Autobiography* (1966) and Bruce Johnson's *Conrad's Models of Mind* (1971). It qualifies somewhat Thomas Moser's sharp distinction between JC's early and late work. It also opens some new possibilities for further exploration of JC's achievement.]

2255 Tucker, Martin. *Africa in Modern Literature: A Survey of Contemporary Writing in English* (New York: Frederick Ungar, 1968], pp. 10–15, 28–29, 152–54, and passim.

JC broadened the psychological tradition of the English novel about Africa in "Heart of Darkness," an initiation story, and thus influenced such writers as Graham Greene, C. S. Forester, G. B. Shaw, Elspeth Huxley, and André Gide. The journey to the dark place of the earth is used to shed light on the human psyche. Africa as a challenge is, however, ultimately rejected. The journey there allows one man to investigate primitivism and another degeneration. JC's missionaries do not enlighten; rather, they exploit Africa.

2256 Urnov, M. V. "Angliiskaia literatura" (English Literature), *Istoriia Zarubezhnoi Literatury Kontsa XIX Veka–Nachala XX Veka* (History of Foreign Literature at the End of the Nineteenth and the Beginning of the Twentieth Century), (Moscow: Moscow University, 1968), pp. 182–83.

JC's best books are those about the sea, with sailors as heroes, set on board ship in far away ports and distant lands. But JC is by no means a writer of sea stories and pays more attention to psychology than to adventures. His heroes struggle with the problem of self-identification. They (and JC himself) seem as if they are constantly awaiting some universal discovery which will suddenly illuminate the essence of their passions, strivings, and actions. Each acts alone: this situation, in JC's view, is the result of bourgeois progress.

Lord Jim occupies an important place in JC's work and in the development of English literature at the turn of the century. The influence of Dostoevski is unquestionable (JC could read him in Russian.) *Under Western Eyes* is not only of the school of Dostoevski, but also an imitation of *The Possessed*. In *Jim*, the hero, who deliberately tries to face moral experience and dangers, is reminiscent of Raskolnikov, the Karamazovs, and Stavrogin. And through JC, other English writers adopted Dostoevski, or his outlook and manner. [In Russian.]

2257 Ursell, Geoffrey. "Conrad and the 'Riversdale,'" *TLS* (11 July 1968), pp. 733–34.

JC's Certificate of Discharge from the *Riversdale* (17 April 1884) and other records indicate that his relationship with Captain L. B. McDonald was at least unsatisfactory and that he retracted an unfavorable statement made about the Captain to Dr. Daniel Thompson and publicly concurred with the justice of the bad report on his discharge. His experiences on this sailing ship are seen in *The Mirror of the Sea*, *Chance*, and "The End of the Tether." [For further comments on this matter, see Alan Villiers, "Conrad and the 'Riversdale,'" 1968, item 2268 and Robert Craig, "Conrad and the 'Riversdale,'" 1968.]

2258 Van Marle, A. "The Location of Lord Jim's Patusan," *N&Q*, N.S., XV (Vol. 213 of continuous series; August 1968), pp. 289–91.

In his cogent argument locating the settlement of Patusan in northwest Sumatra (*Notes and Queries*, CCXI [1966]), C. M. Armitage overlooked one detail making it possible to arrive at a still more specific location and suggesting why JC may have chosen a setting in a part of Sumatra he had never seen. In the novel, JC himself provided clues enabling us to identify Patusan with a settlement called Tenom, located at the mouth of the Tenom River. Widely publicized events of the early 1880s help explain why, out of a multitude of possibilities, JC set his novel in this remote district. Then, too, since JC used a complex method of juxtaposing and fusing sources, there is no real reason for assuming that Tenom alone was the model for Patusan.

2259 Vigini, Giuliano. "Il Conrad 'malese'" ('Malay' Conrad), *Letture* (Milan), XXIII, 8–9 (1968), pp. 565–68.

[Review of Italian edition of Malay novels: *Romanzi della Malesia* (Milan: Mursia, 1968).] [In Italian.]

2260 Villiers, Alan. "Conrad and the 'Riversdale,'" *TLS* (18 July 1968), p. 753.

Since JC needed a testimonial from Captain McDonald of the *Riversdale* in order to obtain another position, he apparently retracted, under duress, his unfavorable comment to Dr. Thompson about the Captain. [See a reply to Geoffrey Ursell, "Conrad and the 'Riversdale,'" 1968, Cf. item 2257 followed by Robert Craig, "Conrad and the 'Riversdale,'" 1968.]

2261 Walcutt, Charles Child, and J. Edwin Whitesell (eds.). "Conrad," *The Explicator Cyclopedia, Vol. III, Prose* (Chicago: Triangle Books, 1968), pp. 13–22.

[This collection of articles published on JC in *The Explicator* is abstracted in C, I, Nos. 1209, 1345, 1468, 1550, 1640, 1305, 1331, 1607, and 1601.]

2262 Watt, Ian. "Conrad, James and *Chance*," *Imagined Worlds: Essays on Some English Novels and Novelists in Honour of John Butt,* ed. by Maynard Mack and Ian Gregor (London: Methuen, 1968), pp. 301–22.

Although Henry James and JC knew each other fairly well for nearly twenty years, the relationship is elusive and obscure, mainly because JC usually destroyed his letters and James burned most of his papers before his death. JC read and admired James at an early date. They lived for some time near Rye, exchanging literary ideas, but after 1906 JC saw James very seldom. JC felt a "profound reverence" for James, and it is likely that James's example, more than anything else, helped him to evolve his mature technique. By 1913, it became clear to many critics that JC was James's chief rival for the position of the greatest contemporary novelist, and then in *Chance* JC came closest to writing a Jamesian novel. James's major objection to the novel was that it compromises the reader's sense of reality of the events by drawing attention to the narrators rather than to the narrative, but this view of *Chance* seems not to take into account JC's aims. Although James praised *Chance*, he also found fault with it. Apparently the two men confronted an "invincible difference" of temperament. If JC hoped for recognition from James, he finally found that James did not accept him as a peer. [Gives a clear account of the relationship between James and JC and contains some reasonable speculations about it.]

2263 Watt, Ian. "The First Paragraph of *The Ambassadors*: An Explication (1960)," *Henry James,* ed. by Tony Tanner (London: Macmillan [Modern Judgements], 1968), pp. 282–303.

For openings of novels that suggest something of James's ambitious attempt to achieve a prologue that is a "synchronic introduction of all the main aspects of the narrative," it seems that JC is his closest rival. But JC, whether in expository or dramatic vein, tends to an "arresting vigour that has dangers which James's more muted tones avoid, as seen, for example, in *An Outcast of the Islands,* which has such enormous immediate import that it surely gives too much away. This danger lurks also in the beginning of *Lord Jim.*

2264 Weinstock, Donald, and Cathy Radaman. "Symbolic Structure in *Things Fall Apart*," *Critique: Studies in Modern Fiction,* XI, No. 1 (1968), pp. 33–41.

Chinua Achebe's technique in *Things Fall Apart* is similar to that of JC, Joyce (in *A Portrait of the Artist as a Young Man*), and Lawrence, in that Achebe blends realistic modes and makes the symbolism a part of the realistic texture.

2265 Welsh, David. "Conrad's Copy of the Fredro Memoirs," *CON*, I, No. 2 (Fall 1968), p. 36.

A copy of Aleksander Fredro's *Trzy Po Trzy* (Topsy-turvey Talk), Fredro's memoirs of the Napoleonic period, is in the possession of the Library of the University of Michigan, Ann Arbor. JC probably knew this book: analogies in technique between it and *A Personal Record* have been noted.

2266 Wild, Bernadette. "Malcolm Lowry: A Study of the Sea Metaphor in *Under the Volcano*," *University of Windsor Review*, IV (Fall 1968), pp. 56–60.

In *Ultramarine*, Malcolm Lowry uses the sea metaphor in the traditional way established by writers like JC in *Lord Jim*, Herman Melville, and Conrad Aiken: the ship becomes a society, a microcosm of universal life. In *Under the Volcano*, Geoffrey Firmin, like Jim, almost passively accepts death. For Geoffrey, as for Jim, the sea becomes the teacher who prepares him for a manly acceptance of death, but it also encompasses the spiritual vision of the true brotherhood of man. In Lowry's novel, Mexico gives the protagonists an isolation from society that parallels isolation on board a ship.

2267 Wilding, Michael. "The Politics of *Nostromo*," *EIC*, XVIII (April 1968), pp. 234–36.

[Attempts to correct two "mistakes" seen by Juliet McLauchlan in his original article on politics in *Nostromo*. Preceded by Michael Wilding, "The Politics of *Nostromo*," *Essays in Criticism*, XVI (October 1966), pp. 441–56; Ivo Vidan and Juliet McLauchlan, "The Politics of *Nostromo*," *Essays in Criticism*, XVII (July 1967), pp. 392–406; and Jonah Raskin, "*Nostromo*: The Argument from Revision," *Essays in Criticism*, XVIII (April 1968), pp. 183–92.]

2268 Williams, Helen. *T. S. Eliot: The Waste Land* (London: Edward Arnold [Studies in English Literature No. 37], 1968), pp. 42, 50.

In T. S. Eliot's *The Waste Land*, the river "sweats" in terms reminiscent of JC's Thames in the opening pages of "Heart of Darkness," a work also in which a river becomes a symbol for the penetration of corruption, not vitality. Eliot, in fact, seems to be indebted in a number of ways to "Heart of Darkness," as in his evocation of the Thames estuary (11. 266–96).

2269 Williams, Porter, Jr. "Story and Frame in Conrad's 'The Tale,'" *SSF*, V (Winter 1968), pp. 179–85.

The central theme of "The Tale" is that of a critical moral decision made in uncertainty and doubt under the stress of conflicting codes. In the central story told by the captain, the protagonist agonizes over his decision during war to test a suspected traitor with a treacherous lie. The shadowy frame story bears a similar theme of the struggles of moral crisis and decision. In both cases, there is no ultimate appeal, only possible understanding and sympathy. The captain and the lady who requests the story are involved in a troubled, probably illicit, affair. The central tale can be seen as an evaluation of this relationship. The line of reasoning used by the captain in the sea tale is subtly linked to the frame story, and numerous asides link love and war. The captain is criticizing and voicing his doubts about a relationship clouded by suspected insincerity and secrecy. He emphasizes that in duty lies absolution; the lady is on leave of her duties and thus expresses a horror of duty. He asserts that in the name of victory ideals can be betrayed in both love and war. Both tales thus unfold from the same strand of moral philosophy, and both lead to an act of withdrawal; both call to duty, and both speak of the degradation of values in the name of victory. In fact, the sea tale might be seen as a parable serving to suggest a solution for a crisis on land. [It is interesting to note that JC was involved in wartime naval activities from September through May, 1916, and from August 1916 into 1917 showed an interest in Jane Anderson, a married American lady.]

2270 Woodruff, Neal, Jr. "The Structure of Conrad's Fiction," *DA*, XXIX (1968), 920A. Unpublished dissertation, Yale University, 1955.

2271 Wright, Walter F. "Ambiguity of Emphasis in Joseph Conrad," *On Stage and Off: Eight Essays in English Literature*, ed. by John W. Ehrstine, John R. Elwood, and Robert C. McLean (Pullman: Washington State University Press, 1968), pp. 90–96.

Ambiguities of emphasis arose when JC converted his nervous force into phrases that left much to chance. Since JC saw life as shifting images and impressions, he was forced into accounting for these sensations as they vied for emphasis. This emphasis often became nebulous, though, when assertions that could not be fully sustained were made. "The Secret Sharer," for example, often leaves unexplained ambiguities involving assertions of the subconscious.

2272 Yelton, Donald C. "Symbolic Imagery in *Lord Jim*," [composed especially for the Norton Critical Edition of *Lord Jim*, but derived "in large part" from Yelton, *Mimesis and Metaphor: An Inquiry Into the Genesis and Scope of Conrad's Symbolic Imagery* (1967)], *JCLJ* (1968), pp. 470–84.

The major strains of verbal metaphor in *Lord Jim* and the major natural images allied with them are related to the psychological and moral issues dramatized in the novel. One of the most important kinds of reference is the animal imagery, including JC's many uses of animal similes and metaphors such as the "yellow-dog" incident following the *Patna* inquiry, the basic "destructive element" passage, and Stein's butterflies and beetles. Another is JC's expressionistic metaphors, with the spectral, with the themes of enchantment, of haunting and exorcism, with the abyss, and with cosmic and meteorological manifestations, with their accompanying interplay of light and dark. If some of these images, like that of the moon of Patusan, do not reveal unambiguous answers to Jim's character and his problems, no doubt they indicate their peculiar fitness within their narrative context by exhibiting precisely the novel's "irreducible ambiguity."

2273 Young, W. J. "Conrad Against Himself," *Critical Review* (Melbourne), No. 11 (1968), pp. 32–47.

A fundamental ambiguity in the whole of JC's work consists of an impulse towards "a passionate involvement in the 'imagined life' of the novel and a withdrawal into regarding life as a 'sublime spectacle.'" Yet in some sense these two meet in the act of writing. "Detachment" is a key word. JC is tempted by the conviction that to be morally involved in the lives of other people necessarily brings despair. But something in his novels refuses to be tied down by detachment. *Victory* is a case in point, but in *Chance* Marlow's "curiously ragged" sense of society seems to influence JC's feeling for all people in the book. JC wants to believe that all evil is chance, not an essential part of experience, but his argument also works well the other way; no one can live solely on chance, with no guiding principle of action; chance, therefore, becomes an opportunity to do something. JC creates a "form of imagined life clearer than reality." A person's conception of himself or a "well-balanced" personality is for JC something too fragile to stand the pressures of life. *Chance* is quite disappointing: the glibness of Marlow's long sermon on the proper "life-enhancing" relationship avails nothing. But in *Victory*, JC provides the significance of the actual events. This novel is the one in which JC can no longer hold himself divorced from the violence and passion of active life, and yet he maintains an extraordinary control in his handling of them. The dilemma presented by *Victory* is given most finely in the lines from *Comus* that JC used as the epigraph to the novel.

2274 Zabierowski, Stefan. "*Lord Jim* w Polsce, 1904–1939" (*Lord Jim* in Poland, 1904–1939), *Zeszyty Naukowe Uniwersytetu Jagiellonskiego* (Scholarly Fascicles of the Jagellonian University), (Cracow), CLXVIII, No. 168, *Prace Historycznoliterackie, No. 14* (Works on the History of Literature, Fascicle 14), (1968), pp. 193–209.

Lord Jim is one of JC's most popular novels in Poland. Critical opinion has been paid to the moral issues raised by the novel, and the text has been analyzed as manifesting JC's feelings of guilt toward Poland and its associations with Polish Romantic literature. The moral patterns set forth by JC in his works, especially in *Jim*, have found supporters among representatives of various ideologies, although the line represented by journals and newspapers does not always conform to the attitude of JC's critics. [English summary, p. 209.] [In Polish.]

2275 Zabierowski, Stefan. [Review of Barbara Kocowna, *Polskosc Conrada* (Conrad's Polishness)], trans. by Adam Gillon and Ludwik Krzyzanowski, *CON*, I, No. 1 (Summer 1968), pp. 83–86.

JC wrote in English because of his early life in Poland, his exile in Russia, and his experiences in Lvov and Cracow. His "richly endowed nature" responded readily to his Uncle Tadeusz Bobrowski's "sterling character." He left Poland and adopted foreign citizenship as practical necessities. His entry into English literature lay in his "inner tragedy" caused by his uncle's insistence on his acceptance of British citizenship and his own desire to remain faithful to Polish tradition, even to write in Polish. JC's treatment of the heroes of his stories and novels, especially of the Malays and Negroes, makes them not only equal to the whites but morally superior to them, because JC's attitude toward them is the result of the analogy of their situation with the fate of the Poles under the Partition. [Kocówna's book is a revised and popularized version of her doctoral dissertation, "Conrad a Polska" (Conrad and Poland), completed in 1962 at the University of Warsaw. Zabierowski's review is generally considered to be as reliable as such a consideration of a book can be.]

2276 Zeigler, Sonia Labiner. "Language and Dramatic Purpose in Conrad's Shorter Fiction," *DA*, XXVIII (1968), 4652A–53A. Unpublished dissertation, University of Wisconsin, 1968.

2277 Zuckerman, Jerome. "The Motif of Cannibalism in *The Secret Agent*," *TSLL*, X (Summer 1968), pp. 295–99.

In *The Secret Agent*, JC, aware of the irrationality and violence which lurk beneath the veneer of civilized life, employs images and situations of cannibalism to suggest this as a pervasive theme. Cannibalism in the novel, basically a "morality of use and expediency," reveals the way a human being preys on or takes advantage of another for selfish motives. JC's language emphasizes food and eating. London appears as a personification of the cannibalism typical of a large modern city, as a "master cannibal." Inspector Heat's comment on seeing Stevie's fragmented remains ironically reduces Stevie to food, thereby suggesting that modern man has been dehumanized. Verloc, though, actually preys on Stevie and therefore engages in cannibalism. Whereas several implicit references to this subject appear in the novel, the central situation of the work strongly implies cannibalism—Winnie marries Verloc so she can gain financial security for Stevie and her mother. And from Winnie a great network of cannibals reaches out to penetrate all "corners" of society and to poison all human relationships.

1969

2278 Addison, Bill Kaler. "Marlow, Aschenbach, and We," *CON*, II, No. 2 (Winter 1969–70), 79–81.

In his voyage into the physical and psychological darkness of JC's "Heart of Darkness," Marlow was capable of controlling his id, "that conscienceless repository of wishes"; he would always be incapable of control of his unconscious. Gustave von Aschenbach, in Thomas Mann's *Death in Venice*, continually fell under the spell of his unconscious desires. Perhaps everyone contains a Kurtz, "an unconscious teeming with the most frightful lusts," a Marlow, an ego that may be relied on to sublimate those lusts, and an Aschenbach, developed from many years of denial.

2279 Allen, Jerry. "Conrad," *NYTBR*, 14 September 1969, p.19.

Although JC used variant spellings of his last name at different times, his sons have reported that in his home in England "he was always called J.C." Miss Allen found so much willing assistance in her six years of research on JC in Singapore that "Traveling" with JC is to her "more a matter of coming upon such amity" than finding buildings that JC once knew, "as Mr. Theroux has done," [Paul Theroux, in "My Travels with Joseph Conrad," 1969.]

2280 Astaldi, Maria Luisa. "Dostojevkij [sic] nel cassetto di Conrad" (Dostoevski in Conrad's Drawer), *Opinione*, 27 April 1969, pp. 54–55.

The extant chapters of *The Sisters* ("which he [JC] was tackling in 1924" [sic]) are written with intensity and contain poetic glimmerings. The dismay of the parents confronted with the son who, in words meaningless to them, explains his wish to go to Rome and Paris, is told very well. But when JC's pen comes to deal with Paris it grows heavy and sluggish; his prose is fettered, turgid and declamatory. According to Ford it is a sort of unconscious defense against that rough seaman slang which JC had heard for years. [Review of *The Sisters* (Milan: Mursia, 1968).] [In Italian.]

2281 Baldini, Gabriele. "Un Conrad di terra ferma" (A Terra Firma Conrad), *Corriere Della Sera*, 1 May 1969, p. 11.

[Short review of *Le sorelle* (The Sisters), (Milan: Mursia, 1968).] [In Italian.]

2282 Barks, Coleman B. "Joseph Conrad and the Short Novel," *DA*, XXIX (1969), 2247A. Unpublished dissertation, University of North Carolina, 1968.

2283 Barringer, George Martyn. "Joseph Conrad and *Nostromo*: Two New Letters," *Thoth, X* (Spring 1969), 20–24.

Two of JC's letters of 1918, about the time *Nostromo* was reissued by Dent, indicate clearly that JC believed in his novels and wanted others to understand their importance to him. [The letters, one to Mrs. Dummett and one to Sir Edumund Gosse, are part of the JC collection in the Rare Book Department of the Syracuse University Library.]

2284 Berenson, Bernard, M. D. Some Thoughts on Conrad's 'The Silence of the Sea,'" *CON*, I, NO. 3 (Summer 1969), 123–25.

JC frequently included in his writing commentaries which require a familiarity with the history of seafaring and of trades long since gone. For example, the article, "The Silence of the Sea," published 18 September 1909 in the *London Daily Mail*, refers to two ships, the *Waratah*, which was missing in 1909 and was never found, and the *President*, missing in 1841. [Gives several facts about these two ships.]

2285 Bernard, Kenneth. "Conrad's Fools of Innocence in *The Nigger of the Narcissus*," *CON*, II, No. 1 (Fall 1969–70), 49–57.

In *The Nigger of the Narcissus*, Singleton and Wait are the real antagonists, but Wait is the victor and JC does not ultimately approve of what Singleton stands for. JC's basic opposition of sea and land frames the action of the novel: the land is considered corrupt and the sea pure. The crew of the *Narcissus*, who initially live in an ignorance and innocence consistent with the purity of the sea, have the last vestiges of their innocence destroyed. In a metaphysical sense, the crew moves from the light to the dark, and James Wait is at the center of all the "blackness." Donkin is an intrusion from the land: he represents the obvious imperfections of man; Wait represents man's ultimate imperfection, his mortality. The innocent crew cannot survive because their innocence denies their bonds with humanity; JC believes that each man can live life properly only after he has knowledge of evil. The storm offers the crew a test by which they may redeem themselves as human beings, and because of their rescue of Wait they lose some of their innocence and begin to demonstrate some of the qualities heretofore associated only with the land. And they are lured, finally, by Donkin almost into an act of mutiny. Wait dies and is buried within sight of land, but his rescuing is a death blow to Singleton; his inner strength is gone. The captain, however, sees no difference between the sea and the land, between the purity and the corruption of human life. The crew, though, finds the transition at the end of the novel very difficult; no longer innocent children of the sea, they are fallen creatures who know their fate.

2286 Bishop, Morchard. "*Nostromo*," *TLS*, 2 October 1969, p. 1132.

In recent editions of *Nostromo*, in part III, chapter ix, Sotillo, in speaking of the killing of Señor Hirsch, uses the word "fractious." The original 1904 edition employed the word "factious."

2287 Blodgett, Harold W. "Mencken and Conrad," *Menckeniana*, XXIX (Spring 1969), 2–3.

As early as 1908, H. L. Mencken designated JC as "a very great man," and he continued his encomiums until 1925, the year after JC's death. His most memorable single tribute was his "lead-off" chapter for *A Book of Prefaces* (1917), a work which he knew to be his bid for serious attention as a major critic. His essay was "appreciation in the best sense—the recognition of greatness," and it came at the right time, since JC still needed a wider audience. For this achievement, JC expressed his warm thanks in a letter to Mencken. [Blodgett's comments follow JC's letter of 11 November 1917 to Mencken, printed in part 1 of this issue.]

2288 Bluefarb, Sam. "Samburan: Conrad's Mirror Image of Eden,"
CON, I, No. 3 (Summer 1969), 89-94.

Samburan, Axel Heyst's retreat from the world in *Victory*, reflects,
though reversed in several ways, a true image of Eden. Both places
are, for example, virtually self-contained "paradises"; Heyst, unlike
Adam, is impelled by a moment of pity into action; both locations are
isolated from the larger world; both contain peace until the advent of
changes wrought by circumstance; and both Adam and Heyst
possess tragic flaws which impel them toward their final destinies.
Contrasts, too, appear: whereas Adam was innocent of the
knowledge "that could kill," Heyst was not; Lena, unlike Eve, needed
no serpent to tempt her to sin; and, perhaps most important of all
(and proceeding from the reverse mirror image), the avoidance of evil
becomes Heyst's "sin" or tragic flaw. For Heyst, unlike Adam,
thinking accompanied by no action is bereft of conflict and
ultimately the enemy of life—or the mirror image of death.

2289 Bojarski, Edumund A., and Henry T. Bojarski. "Three Hundred
and Thirty-six Unpublished Papers on Joseph Conrad: A
Bibliography of Masters Theses and Doctoral Dissertations,
1917-1963," *Bulletin of Bibliography and Magazine notes*, XXVI
(July–September 1969), 61–66, 79–83.

An unannotated list. Based on incorrect information, a note was
included in JCI about a hardbound edition of this work, published by
the Pierian Press in 1971. Unfortunately, this work has presumably
not yet been made available in a hardbound edition.

2290 Bolton, W. F. "The Role of Language in *Lord Jim*," CON, I, No. 3
(Summer 1969), 51–59.

JC's use of language in *Lord Jim* is both "pervasive" and
"purposeful." The difference between Jim and Marlow, for example, is
indicated in their optimism about language as well as in their
employment of it: Jim's short and often incomplete sentences and
Marlow's long and involved ones are consonant with their attitudes.
Also, Jim's last name, never given, is both title and report; and when
Jim finally earns his name in Patusan, the natives deny it. JC also
concentrates on the relationship of what a thing is to what it is called
through his use of simile. Differences of style provide a powerful
instrument of characterization, too. JC ranges from "alien" style to
foreign language, including jargon. He thus imposes on his novel a
specialized organization of the normal patterns of language so that
language as medium and language as event begin to fuse.

2291 Braun, Andrzej. "Krolestwo do zdobycia" (Kingdom to be
Gained), *TW*, XXV, 12 (1969), 55–73.

JC's views of the Dutch Indies differ from English and Dutch views in being more penetrating and reliable, though he used facts from European literature on the region. Some anachronisms and alterations in chronology appear in *Lord Jim* and elsewhere when compared with the *Royal Malay Chronicles*. [Continued in Braun's "Singapur—wschodni port" (Singapore—An Eastern Port), *Osnowa* (Lodz), Summer 1969), 46–63. Not seen.] [In Polish.]

2292 Braun, Andrzej. "Sladami Conrada," *Zycie Literackie*, No. 5, 2 February 1969, pp. 8–9; trans in part by Elias J. Schwartz as "In Conrad's Footsteps," CON, IV, No. 2 (1972), 33–46.

[Braun gives an interesting account of some of his efforts to obtain information about JC and his early travels. In Amsterdam, he sees the place where JC waited in 1887 for cargo for the barge *Highland Forest*, of which he was the first officer. In Rotterdam, Braun, in talking later with the captain of his ship, tells all that is known about Berau, Almayer's "Sambir" on the "East River Pantai." So far, no single JC investigator has been able to reach this river.] [In Polish.]

2293 Bross, Addison C. "The Unextinguishable Light of Belief: Conrad's Attitude Toward Women," *CON*, II, No. 3 (Spring 1969–70), 39–46.

JC's attitude toward women is notable, at least in "Heart of Darkness," not as a total rejection of woman per se, but rather as an ambivalence toward a trait which JC had come to consider particularly feminine: the ambiguous "Kurtzian act of belief"; his female characters therefore do not represent his supposed misogyny or sexual neurosis; instead, they have a definite aesthetic function in the novel. Kurtz's hollowness, his universal capacity for belief, enables him to achieve his final vision of "the horror," which is, according to Marlow, a redemptive vision. Like Kurtz, the women in the story are presented as ardent believers whose idealism is "somehow prone" to involve them in evil. Marlow's aunt, the two receptionists of Marlow's employer, Kurtz's fiancée, and Kurtz's African mistress, fill the role of Kurtz's "equivocal" idealism and serve to deepen his ambiguity by sharing with him basically the same corruptible idealism. JC's attitude toward the female characters is not an attitude toward women alone, but toward that which the novel associates predominantly with women: "the human phenomenon of belief." JC may have been ambivalent toward this phenomenon because he believed his father to be fanatical, because of his own feelings of guilt for his expatriation, and because he may have had some justification for seeing women as the personification of idealism.

2294 Bufkin, E. C. "A Patter of Parallel and Double: The Function of Myrtle in *The Great Gatsby*," MFS, XV (Winter 1969–70), 517–24.

F. Scott Fitzgerald's reading of JC instructed him in the writer's craft. In *The Great Gatsby*, for example, Myrtle functions as Gatsby's double, repeating his trauma. The technique of chapter IV is Conradian: Myrtle as Gatsby's double provides a "structural instead of narrative comment on Gatsby," tempering the reader's sympathy towards him with an active and "impartial judgment."

2295 Carroll, Wesley B. "Recent Books on Modern Fiction: British," *MFS*, XV (Winter 1969–70), 571–76.

Ehrsam's bibliography of JC is practically complete, "a compendium of all or most of the printed data" on JC [even though innumerable items remain unlisted].

2296 "Conrad, Joseph," *Das Grosse Duden-Lexikon in Acht Bänden* (The Big Duden-Encyclopedia in Eight Volumes), (Mannheim, Vienna, and Zurich: Bibliographisches Institut, 1969), 2nd rev ed, II (C-D-E), 208.

[A brief survey of JC's life and works.] [In German.]

2297 "Contemporary Reviews: From *The Times Literary Supplement* (London), December 12, 1902," *JCHD* & SS, (1969), pp. 214–15.

JC's method in the three stories in *Youth* is " a little precious"; one notices "a tasting of the quality of phrases and an occasional indulgence in poetic rhetoric." The effect of the concluding scene of "Heart of Darkness"—a woman's ecstatic belief in a villain's heroism—is reached in an indulgence in the "picturesque horror" of the villain, his work and his surroundings, which is "quite extravagant according to the canons of art." "The End of the Tether" is the best story in this volume.

2298 Crawford, John. "Another Look at 'Youth,'" *Research Studies*, (Washington State University), XXXVI (June 1969), 154–56.

The contrast between old Captain Beard and the young Marlow with his first command permeates the plot of "Youth"; Beard serves as a parallel to the youthful second mate. The entire story reminds us that older men look back at their youthful days and long for their return, knowing all the while that such a return is impossible. And this is part of Marlow's eventual discovery. But Marlow still loves youth and what it represents. Marlow is "Youth," and Beard is "Old Age" reliving Youth.

2299 Cummings, David Earl. "A World of Secret Agents: Subversion and Survival in the Fiction of Joseph Conrad," *DAI*, XXX (October 1969), 1558A. Unpublished dissertation, University of Nebraska, 1969.

2300 Daiches, David. *Some Late Victorian Attitudes* (New York: W. W. Norton, 1969), pp. 26-28, 38.

In his attitude toward society, JC is ambivalent: he professed to find in the seaman's code of fidelity, loyalty, and endurance a sufficient basis for his ethics, but the insights provided by his finest works do not support his view. In *Nostromo*, for example, he presents the hopeless paradox of the necessity of human relationships but also the accompanying corruption of society and the desirability of loneliness, thus displaying a "deep and inescapable" pessimism. Social man is corrupt, destructive of others; individual man is self-destructive. If we subsume the needs of others to our own imaginative needs and impulses, we jump as Jim jumped; if we become trapped into trying to mediate between an isolated sense of identity and an outgoing sense of community, like Razumov in *Under Western Eyes*, we destroy ourselves and others; if we use our relations with others purely to serve our own "aloof purposes," like most of the characters in *The Secret Agent*, the final result is even more destructive. Moral idealism can sometimes produce the reverse of itself, as with Kurtz in "Heart of Darkness." Only the lonely, unimaginative, enduring Captain MacWhirr wins through without obvious disillusion or destruction; his kind of egoism saves. An "activist stoicism" emerges from JC's novels as the only way of confronting life. Only this attitude will enable man to come to terms with himself.

2301 Daiches, David. "The Twentieth-Century Novel," *A Critical History of English Literature*. Second Ed. (London: Secker & Warburg, 1969), IV, pp. 1155-57.

The "characteristic theme" of the twentieth-century novel is "the relation between loneliness and love," and JC, "a deeply pessimistic novelist," "tests" his characters accordingly. *Nostromo*, for example, is "a brilliant symbolic rendering of the inevitable fate of political animal, this means of the inevitable fate of man." *The Nigger of the Narcissus* "probes the necessary corruption of any kind of human society"; JC, indeed, explores again and again the theme that although society is necessary, it is inevitably corrupting. "Idealism corrupts" (as in "Heart of Darkness"), and loneliness can force a man into horrified awareness of his identity with his own moral opposite, "the secret sharer." How to come to terms with this "secret sharer" is another of JC's characteristic themes. *Under Western Eyes* is a study of the "ultimate in false positions, from which the only escape is self-destruction."

2302 Davis, Harold E. "Shifting Rents in a Thick Fog: Point of View in the Novels of Joseph Conrad," *CON*, II, No. 2 (Winter 1969-70), 23–38.

In experimenting with point of view, JC began with an attempt to follow Flaubert's shifting but consistent focuses, but was unable in *Almayer's Folly* and *An Outcast of the Islands* to maintain any real impersonality and perspective because of his sympathies with his characters and the resulting wavering points of view. His failure induced the introduction of a narrator, at first the anonymous voice of the crew in *The Nigger of the Narcissus* and then the living character, Marlow, who participated in the action as well as narrating it (*Lord Jim* and *Chance*). In two other full-length novels, JC focused his view through the first person: *Under Western Eyes*, with the teacher of language narrating or editing Razumov's journal, and *The Arrow of Gold*, with the use of the conventional device of a "discovered" journal. JC solved his problem of distance very skillfully in *Nostromo* by means of the "cinematographic" method, in which he carefully controls all the currents of the novel from a point outside them. *The Secret Agent* also contains an external point of view, with several interviews balanced against others and with two key scenes: the "curiously dead" exchanges between Verloc and his wife; here the objectivity and the distance provide the irony, the basic tone of the novel. In his most successfully focused novels, JC either used the narrator device or kept himself emotionally apart from his characters.

2303 Davis, O. B. "*The Shadow-Line:* A Confession," *Introduction To The Novel* (New York: Hayden Book Co, 1969), pp. 175, 261–64.

The Shadow-Line is different from *Daisy Miller* and "Benito Cereno" as to point of view: JC himself is the central character of his story.

2304 Dickson, Lovat. *H. G. Wells: His Turbulent Life and Times* (New York: Atheneum, 1969), pp. 71, 81, 136, 316.

H. G. Wells arrived on the literary scene when the last of the great Victorian writers were being supplanted by such remarkable authors as Kipling and JC, who were providing plenty of excitement for readers wanting that kind of fare. Among the publishers, Macmillan soon learned that it was not enough to have Kipling and Hardy if he did not also have Wells, Somerset Maugham or JC. By the end of his writing career, Wells had had stiff competition from the last Victorians, the Edwardians, and the post-war generation. If he is nearly forgotten now, when JC is more popular than ever, "is it that our times prefer the romantic prints of a forgotten time to the uncomfortable realization of our present?"

2305 Dolan, Paul J. "'Il Conde': Conrad's Little Miss Muffett," *CON*, I, No. 3 (Summer 1969), 107–11.

JC's story, "Il Conde," is "an exact analogue of the nursery rhyme tragedy of 'Little Miss Muffett,'" and the nursery rhyme and the story have a common theme, "the fragility and impermanence of comfort and security in this world," both stories being accounts of human comfort and security interrupted by the intrusion of "some unseemly aspect of reality." [Trivial, whether intended seriously or as a parody of some literary criticism.]

2306 Donoghue, Denis. *Jonathan Swift: A Critical Introduction* (Cambridge: Cambridge UP, 1969), pp. 24, 172, 175, 179–81.

If we read Jonathan Swift and then compare our experience of his work with our experience of Henry James, Dostoevski, Kafka, Lawrence, or JC, we are "scandalized" by the persistence of his disavowal of all the values for which modern writers strive: the sense of self, the autonomous imagination, the risks of freedom, the multiple demands upon life which appear in such works as *The Trial, Sons and Lovers, A Portrait of a Lady, The Brothers Karamazov,* and "Heart of Darkness."

In his description of the storm in "Typhoon," JC clearly says that the world is man: all the analogies are human, the ship is a living creature, the storm is a mob, the forces at work are functions of human passion. The storm ceases to be water and wind and becomes human passion. JC convinces us with language to enter into collusion with Nature and force it to receive man's soul. To Gulliver, however, a storm is merely a storm, a ship merely a ship. The only demand Swift makes upon Nature is Gulliver's survival.

2307 Dulles, Allen (ed). *Great Spy Stories From Fiction* (New York and Evanston: Harper & Row [A Ginger Book], 1969), pp. 74–85.

In *The Secret Agent,* JC holds up to ridicule both the Czarist autocracy and the disruptive "asinine machinations" of the anarchists. He successfully manages to give the flavor of an exchange between a supercilious intelligence officer and his unsatisfactory agent. [Summarizes briefly the situation in the novel and quotes form the scene between Mr. Vladimir and Mr. Verloc.]

2308 Duncan-Jones, E. E. "Some Sources of *Chance*," *RES*, XX (November 1969), 468–71.

For the character of Carleton Anthony, whose son is the hero of *Chance*, JC drew on his knowledge of Coventry Patmore. The origin of the heroine is probably literary. Flora de Barral suffers under an evil governess, reminding one of another Flora who suffered in a similar way in *The Turn of the Screw*.

2309 Dussinger, Gloria R. "'The Secret Sharer': Conrad's Psychological Study," *TSLL*, X (Winter 1969), 599–608.

The most essential criterion for a coherent reading of "The Secret Sharer" is that the action be seen to occur in a social vacuum. Ethical judgments and social considerations must be divorced from the story so it may be seen in an asocial laboratory environment created to intensify the captain's confrontation with himself. Imagery, characterization, setting, mood, and direct statement all bolster a strictly psychological reading. A stranger to himself and a novice who believes in the orderliness of the universe, the captain must meet Leggatt, who reveals to him the inadequacy of his view. Through Leggatt, the captain finds the amoral force within himself which has the power to save man by giving full selfhood or to destroy him through chaotic irrationality. Through self-knowledge and the truth of selfhood, the captain becomes a free man able to deal with chance. [An existential depth-psychology approach.]

2310 Ehrsam, Theodore G. *A Bibliography of Joseph Conrad* (Metuchen, N.J.: Scarecrow, 1969).

[Contains a chronology of the first publication of JC's books; an alphabetical listing by author of critical and biographical works on JC; an alphabetical listing of works by JC with references to reviews; an alphabetical listing by author, of works for which JC wrote prefatory material; an alphabetical listing of JC's translated works, some with reviews; an alphabetical listing by title, publisher, or author, of bibliographies of works by JC; an alphabetical listing by title, of reproductions of photographs, portraits, drawings, sketches, and caricatures appearing in periodicals; an alphabetical listing by JC's original title, of films made from his works; index. Contains too many errors to make it very reliable.]

2311 Faulkner, Peter. "Vision and Normality: Conrad's 'Heart of Darkness,'" *Ibadan Studies in English*, I (1969), 36–47.

As JC gives the account of Marlow's journey up the Congo in "Heart of Darkness," the focus is on Kurtz, and the significance of the story to the reader is the question of "vision" or "normality" as the surer source of values. Kurtz succumbs to the appeal of the darkness whereas Marlow is able to withstand it; but Marlow, the sensible, normal man, responds to the depraved and corrupted Kurtz with "emotions other than disgust," chooses to ally himself with Kurtz, and, after Kurtz's death, comes to believe that Kurtz deserves respect in his own right. Throughout the story, as Marlow searches for reality, he finds that "evil" and "truth," evidently the most permanent things he can think of, are united in Kurtz. He therefore maintains his allegiance to Kurtz when he lies to the Intended. Through Kurtz, JC disturbingly suggests the alarm of a sensitive writer who is becoming aware of the demands made upon him by his vocation. Our modern conception of the artist, originating in the Romantic movement, is that of a moral explorer, who is "open to life" in a way that most people are not; hence the actuality of his corruption. We expect the artist to take this risk for our vicarious benefit. JC was one of the earliest artists to become acutely aware of the demands made upon him in an "increasingly secularized and bewildered" society. The explorations of Kurtz may end in disaster, and the good sense of Marlow in complacency. This is the "poignant truth" which "Heart of Darkness" brings to our attention.

2312 Fleisman, Avrom. "Conrad's Last Novel," *ELT*, XII, No. 4 (1969), 189–94.

In several ways *The Rover* closely resembles *The Secret Agent*, which exhibits JC's stylistic mastery at its best, and it is organized by means of "a stream of imagery and an architecture of construction" as accomplished as that of the earlier novel. Concerned with vision as it is, *The Rover* has as hero Peyrol, whose heroism rests both on his "educated vision" developed from his experiences and on his "energetic imagination"—on both outward and inward sight. Peyrol generalizes from his mental pictures, a habit which helps to determine his fate. Arlette, too, provides a study of the powers and limits of sight. A set of visual activities and images which is the thematic center of the novel "deepens" the otherwise somewhat hackneyed actions of the main characters.; The world of the novel is intensely visual: the setting is "extensively and lovingly described," and the characters live "largely through the eyes." JC's "thoroughness of execution" and "consistency of theme" place *Rover* with his finest achievements and "belie any generalizations about his late falling-off." [This strong plea for the strength of *Rover* clarifies JC's achievement in his last novel but scarcely demonstrates that there is no decline in power.]

2313 "The Forgotten Lawyer Who Found the Dollars," *TLS*, 6 March 1969, p. 240.

[B. L. Reid's *The Man From New York*, a biography of John Quinn, points out that Reid concerns himself with the relationship between Quinn and JC, with the reasons for the eventual break between the two friends, and with Quinn's profits from his sale of JC's manuscripts.]

2314 Forsyth, R. A. "'Europe,' 'Africa,' and the Problem of Spiritual Authority," *Southern Review* (Adelaide), III, No. 4 (1969), 294–323.

In practically all the thought of the nineteenth century, there appears some version of a "drunken boat" construct, where the values of humanity, intelligence, or cultural or social tradition seem to toss precariously above a menacing and potentially destructive force. This is seen in Schopenhauer, in Darwin and Huxley, in Marx, in Freud, in Nietzsche. There arises, too, the conviction that Europe is being threatened by Africa, an idea that was not dispelled from Tennyson's mind. Robert Buchanan felt a source of alienation from a hostile universe governed by implacable "laws" indifferent to spiritual aspirations, and JC also shared this sense with Buchanan, picturing the universe as a self-evolved and indestructible knitting machine which has no thought, conscience, or foresight. Probably the most powerful presentation of the "drunken boat" construct seen in terms of Europe and Africa is JC's "Heart of Darkness."

The narrative of this story exists on two interrelated levels, just as it appears also in the destination of the journey, the Inner Station, and in the darkness of Marlow's "European" mind. JC's true theme is the imaginative investigation of what happens to a man when the evil without is acknowledged by the evil within. Marlow is a "modern" man in whom the mind and its self have begun a dialogue between the "European" and the "African" selves. [Places "Heart of Darkness" in a major cultural, social, and moral context.]

2315 Fox, Austin M. "Stephen Crane and Joseph Conrad," *Serif, VI* (December 1969), 16–20.

In spite of their difference in age and national background, Stephen Crane and JC show surprising parallels in their lives, and more importantly in their works. Both dealt with daring and unconventional subjects in their day, both utilized the theme of anti-imperialism, both considered chance basic in the universe, both disliked German militarism, and both frequently used similar plot situations. Each seemed to stimulate the other "symbiotically," with Crane being in some ways a catalyst for JC's imagination. JC greatly surpassed Crane in the maturity of his intellect, but Crane was probably the more original.

2316 Fradin, Joseph I. "Conrad's Everyman: *The Secret Agent*," *TSLL*, XI (Summer 1969), 1023–38.

The Secret Agent is pervaded with a sense of nonbeing, of a void, of a darkness which is diminished to that of sheer blankness. Any thread pursued in this novel leads to the same emptiness. For instance, Verloc's journey from his shop to the embassy and back is typical of the themes of the novel. Verloc possesses an animality which is a refusal of consciousness and a sleepy inertia which is an invasion by death. He lives by alternatives, not choices. If the paradigm of stillness is death, the paradigm of movement is an aimless identity-destroying journey. Verloc's journey takes place in a thoroughly dehumanized landscape, in the deeply alienated city, among things which threaten to assimilate the human. Men in the novel are often seen as faceless fragments. The abyss opens under Veloc when Vladimir destroys his past and puts his future in doubt. A subtle irony is expressed in the preoccupation of the characters with clock time, a form of death, in order to avoid looking within to the dark empty spaces which exist beyond time in the self. Men are ignorant of the secret self. They don't have the energy or the opportunity to create a present which opens to a true future. Verloc's journey goes full circle, from a bogus fresh start, to a disconnection from his environment, to a complete isolation, lying fearfully in the dark.

2317 Franklin, Rosemary F. "Death or the Heat of Life in the Handful of Dust," *American Literature*, XLI (May 1969), 277–79.

Line 30 of T. S. Eliot's *The Waste Land*, "I will show you fear in a handful of dust," is clarified when seen with its source, in the words of the young Marlow in "Youth," "the heat of life in the handful of dust." Whereas the young Marlow is "heroic and courageous," Eliot's speakers have never been other than "wizened and impotent." Eliot, in substituting "fear" for "the heat of life," is probably using his source ironically to show the "fear of life and its resurrection in the heat of spring."

2318 G., V. [Vigini, Giuliano]. "Le sorelle" (The Sisters), *Letture* (Milan), XXIV, 8–9 (1969), 637.

[Review of Italian translation of *The Sisters* (Milan: Mursia, 1969). These fragmentary pages confirm JC's art, and may be compared with Constant's *Adolphe* or Mann's "Tonio Kröger."]
[In Italian.]

2319 Gale, Bell. "Conrad and the Romantic Hero," DA, XXX (1969). 719–20A. Unpublished dissertation, Yale University, 1962.

2320 Garrett, Peter K. *Scene and Symbol From George Eliot to James Joyce: Studies in Changing Fictional Mode* (New Haven and London: Yale UP, 1969), pp. 13, 160–80, 181, 183, 253.

JC's fictional world is more persistently symbolic in quality than is Henry James'. Landscape in *Nostromo*, for example, conveys a setting alien to man and the values he produces. Against the large canvas of nature, society and human action are diminished and as human awareness is reduced, symbol assumes a greater responsibility in interpreting the "nature of the universe."

In "Heart of Darkness," sharp images of imperialism first appear, later to give way before a larger and more sinister experience, elusive, not fully definable, but implying meaning to Marlow. In terms of this character, the change is from a voyage to a wandering and circling quest as the contact with the jungle and Kurtz absorbs and engages his attention more energetically than the original contact with corrupt imperialism. The vagueness of the symbolism expresses Marlow's irresolution before the total meaning of his encounter with the hidden truth. These two varieties of symbolism communicate the two levels of experience, hidden truth and surface reality. And the vague, blurred, and rhetorical imagery reflects a metaphysical significance: the threat hidden truth poses to moral life. Marlow is spared Kurtz's fate because he does not reconcile in himself the two symbolic attitudes. Character is hence predominantly symbolic rather than psychological in motivation; character serves to reinforce symbol.

2321 Garst, Tom. "Beyond Realism: Short Fiction of Kipling, Conrad, and James in the 1890's," *DA*, XXX (1969), 1167A. Unpublished dissertation, Washington University, 1969.

2322 Geddes, Gary. "The Structure of Sympathy: Conrad and the Chance That Wasn't," *ELT*, XII, No. 4 (1969), 175–88.

Chance "operates" on two important levels: that of Flora's story, her "progress" through an unsympathetic world, and that of Marlow, who attempts to piece together a meaningful whole from the fragments of this story. Flora's history consists of a series of encounters between herself and other characters in the novel, such as de Barral's bourgeois cousin, a wealthy old maid, the German husband, Captain Anthony, and Powell, in which sympathy or understanding is shown to be central in the book. In addition to being an account of Flora's maturation, *Chance* is also Marlow's representation, as he attempts to bring under imaginative control the facts of Flora's story, of the ethical ideal of "imaginative sympathy which informs the whole novel." *Chance* also, from an external viewpoint, reflects JC's major preoccupations when he wrote the work: Flora's desire to be believed is, for example, a parallel to JC's own hope of eventually making himself understood to his readers. In writing *Chance*, JC was striving to express imaginatively an attitude toward reality, that of "imaginative sympathy." He therefore reasserted in this novel his faith in the role of the artist in society, and *Chance* is thus his portrait of the artist as "mature observer, as sympathetic worshipper of the spectacle of human life. JC's "vision of things" in *Chance* is closely allied to the style and structure of the novel.

2323 Gekoski, R. A. "*An Outcast of the Islands*: A New Reading," *CON*, II, No. 3 (Spring 1969–70), 47–58.

An Outcast of the Islands is more profitably understood if it is read with Tom Lingard, rather than Peter Willems, at the center. The plot, even more than that of *Almayer's Folly,* depends largely upon the actions of Lingard: it is impossible to account for the length of the novel if it is simply concerned with Willems; and just as Willems falls, so too will Lingard—and in his fall lies the major interest of the work. At the climactic confrontation of the two men (in part IV, chapter 5), Lingard recognizes the inescapable truth that he alone is responsible for what happens to him, that his confrontation with Willems is simply a confrontation with an obscure and deadly aspect of his own behavior. The novel should end with part IV; even JC knew that the last chapters were irrelevant to the basic thematic texture of the book. *Outcast* is, however, closer to greatness than most readers are aware of.

2324 Gillon, Adam. "Joseph Conrad and Shakespeare: Part III," *CON*, I, No. 3 (Summer 1969), 7–27.

Textually, many parallels to *Hamlet* appear in *Lord Jim*: Jim's problem, like Hamlet's, is basically his unpreparedness for the fate that awaits him, and both protagonists are helpless "victims and executors" of an inexorable fate. As *Jim* is thematically close to *Hamlet,* so is *Under Western Eyes* similarly close to *Macbeth*: in both works, the primary motif is the betrayal of a trusting guest, followed by a long, painful awareness of guilt, and subsequent punishment. The Shakespearean analogy with *Nostromo* is with *Othello* especially, since Nostromo yields to the lure of the silver and to the weakness in himself as Othello submits to the machinations of Iago. The epigraph in *Nostromo,* from *King John,* may have been designed to set the general mood of war and revolution in JC's novel. And Hirsch is an obvious Shakespearean presence, Shylock in *The Merchant of Venice.* [Preceded by Gillon, "Joseph Conrad and Shakespeare: Part I," *Conradiana,* I, No. 1 (Summer 1968); "Joseph Conrad and Shakespeare: Part II," *Conradiana, I,* No. 2 (Fall 1968); and followed by "Joseph Conrad and Shakespeare, Part Four: A New Reading of *Victory,* " *Conradiana* VII, No 3 (1975); and "Joseph Conrad and Shakespeare, Part Five: *King Lear* and 'Heart of

Darkness,'" *Polish Review*, XX, Nos. 2–3 (1975); rptd in *Joseph Conrad: Commemorative Essays*, ed by Adam Gillon and Ludwik Krzyzanowski (NY: Astra Books, 1975), pp. 133–39; all five articles collected in Adam Gillon, *Conrad and Shakespeare and Other Essays* (New York: Astra Books, 1976), pp. 41–141.]

2325 Gillon, Adam. "Polish and Russian Elements in Joseph Conrad," *Actes Du Ve Congress De L'Association Internationale De Littérature Comparée, Belgrade,* 1967 (Proceedings of the Fifth Meeting of the International Association of Comparative Literature, Belgrade, 1967), ed by Nikola Banasenic (Belgrade: Université de Belgrade; Amsterdam: Swets & Zeitlinger, 1969), pp. 685–94.

JC has said that what appears in his writing as the incomprehensible, the impalpable, and the ungraspable is really his Polishness; and he has maintained that only Poles can comprehend what he means. His Polish background includes a sense of earnestness which he learned from his homelife with his father. He also inherited from his father his pessimism and patriotism. From much of the Polish literature he had read, he acquired a complex romanticism composed of a preoccupation with guilt and expiation, with moral commitment to lost causes, with duty and honor, and with many different fictional devices. He further acquired much from his Russian background. Although he claims to have little knowledge of Russian matters, his political and literary pronouncements on Russians suggest that his knowledge is rather extensive. Accordingly, JC could write about Russians "without lapsing into caricature." Furthermore, his examination of Russians, of anarchism and of tyranny is related equally to his Polish background and to his Russian background. [A perceptive scholarly treatment of this much discussed subject.]

2326 Gilmore, Thomas B., Jr. "Retributive Irony in Conrad's *The Secret Agent*," *CON.* I, No. 3 (Summer 1969), 41–50.

Irony, fundamental in *The Secret Agent*, appears there in two different forms: (1) that which establishes at least a provisional balance between opposite emotions toward the characters, creating, for Verloc, for example, feelings of both pity and scorn; and (2) an irony of retribution, or retributive irony. The second kind complicates our judgments of the characters. The punishments of some characters seem relatively mild, particularly those of Yundt, Michaelis, Vladimir, the Professor, and Chief Inspector Heat. Much more severe punishments are reserved for Ossipon, Winnie, and Verloc. JC found this retributive irony of special value in *Agent* because in this novel the characters are incapable of true self-analysis and of recognizing moral principles, either within themselves or without. In nearly every instance, JC causes his retribution to be the natural outcome of some flaw of character, thus making his retributive irony one of the chief aesthetic virtues of his novel.

2327 Godshalk, William Leigh. "Kurtz as Diabolical Christ," *Discourse, XII* (Winter 1969), 100–07.

In "Heart of Darkness," Africa is associated with evil and Hell by Marlow's image of the snake; and Kurtz, met at the heart of the continent, is Lucifer, a diabolical Christ who, instead of self-sacrifice, sacrifices the natives. Kurtz's fiancée is a reincarnation of Mary Magdalene, and Marlow is a Peter figure who denies Kurtz. In the end, though, Marlow allies himself with Kurtz to obtain self-knowledge. [An example of striving too hard for an ingenious interpretation.]

2328 Graver, Lawrence. *Conrad's Short Fiction* (Berkeley and Los Angeles: University of California P, 1969).

A major problem of JC's was his desire to be a creator of original and artistic tales and his need to try to be a writer of popular stories. This conflict is largely compounded by the length of the stories he wrote. He created most of his early stories for publication in specific magazines. With *Blackwood's*, he discovered the editorial harmony and attractive fees which he wanted; with other periodicals he was forced to alter his stories to fit the public taste. Most of his major work appeared during a seven-year period beginning in 1898. The two collections of stories of this time are concerned with egoism and altruism, with egoism as the "moving force of the world" and altruism, its essential morality. Most of his characters are egoists rather than altruists. The harlequin in "Heart of Darkness" represents the natural egoist; the unimaginative type of egoist who is characterized by respectability, like Mitchell and MacWhirr, is ludicrously self-confident; de Barral and Brown belong to the rapacious type; Jim and Gould are obsessive egoists; and the "sequestered" egoist is seen in Heyst, Decoud, and Razumov. While JC was writing novels in order to have space for greater expression, he produced some very poor stories. "The Secret Sharer" is a fine tale, but it is too ambivalent to support any single meaning. *The Shadow-Line* contains all the qualities of his best short fiction. The best stories are in the tradition of "masculine" adventure stories with emphasis not on romance but on man's response to it. [A book necessary to the understanding of JC's short fiction.]

2329 Green, Robert. "Messrs Wilcox and Kurtz, Hollow Men," *Twentieth Century Literature, XIV* (January 1969), 231–39.

Forster's Wilcoxes in *Howard's End* embody English imperialism, and the author's understanding of the real nature and effects of imperialism was as deep as that shown by JC in "Heart of Darkness."

2330 Greenstein, David Merrall. "Conrad and the Congo," *DAI*, XXX (1969), 723A. Unpublished dissertation, Columbia University, 1968.

2331 Gullason, Thomas A. "The Letters of Stephen Crane: Additions and Corrections," *American Literature*, XLI (March 1969), 104–06.

A letter from JC to Stephen Crane's niece, Edith F. Crane, dated January 12, 1924, reaffirms the great respect JC always had for Crane. JC seems to be doing his share to counter the malicious gossip about Crane still circulated in 1924.

2332 Gurko, Leo. "*Heart of Darkness*" (New York: Limited Editions Club; New York: Heritage P, 1969), pp. v-xix.

JC's journey to Africa darkened his imagination, "exacerbated his already shaky nerves," and forced him into "emotional maturity" by disrupting his faith in civilization and civilized man. His earlier experiences had taught him how dangerous men are. "Heart of Darkness" reveals the duality of experience, the realistic detail of the narrative and its evocation of meaning and emotions lying beneath the surface. What redeems imperialism for Marlow, as for JC, is the idea behind it, like Kurtz's desire to elevate the native, which is nobler than the manager's lack of idea. Marlow admires Kurtz who, although fallen, has fallen from a great height; the manager has nowhere to fall to. In addition to his moral distinction, Marlow is also sustained by sheer physical work. "Heart of Darkness" is filled with deliberate oppositions: the hollow Kurtz and Marlow who at last tells the lie he hates, darkness and light, Negroes and Caucasians, Africa and Europe, the "coiling" Congo River and the "straight-flowing" Thames, but even these exchange roles and become their own opposites. Thus the theme of the story is the "indissoluble and organic oneness of all things that underlie the surface contradictions." The "lesson" of the tale is that one must descend into primitive darkness to achieve wisdom, but one must also return to the light, as Marlow, unlike Kurtz, does.

2333 Haack, Dietmar. "Stephen Crane und die 'kühne' Metapher" (Stephen Crane and the "bold" Metaphor), *Jahrbuch für Amerikastudien*, XIV (1969), pp. 116–23.

[Briefly discusses the use of strong colors and the cult of the sun in the literature in the Age of Transition. In JC's description of the sky in *Lord Jim,* it is "blood-red, immense, steaming like an open vein. An enormous sun nestled crimson against the tree tops."] [In German.]

2334 Hagan, John. "Conrad's *Under Western Eyes*: The Question of Razumov's 'Guilt' and 'Remorse,'" *SNNTS,* I (Fall 1969), pp. 310–22.

The "orthodox reading" of *Under Western Eyes* is that Razumov's confession stems from the guilt he suffers for his betrayal of Haldin. But Razumov never doubts the rightness or necessity of turning Haldin in to the authorities nor is he ever reconciled to revolutionary politics, which are anathema to him. Haldin thrusts revolutionary confidences upon a practical and lonely Razumov who is astonished at this unbidden act and who realizes, too, that his orderly-planned future—the only decent one for a man without birthright—has been destroyed. In order to revenge himself for Haldin's shattering of his life, he plots to destroy Haldin's sister by falsely marrying her to "steal her soul." But her innocent love for him—a man never before loved—converts his plan into love and makes him understand how hatred has corrupted him. Hence he confesses, first to her; and then as a second purging ritual to expiate his wrong intentions toward her, he confesses his moral failure to the revolutionary group, who are actually surrogates for the brother. And their ridiculousness satisfies his requirement for total abasement and humiliation. For this sacrifice, he is admired by the reader.

2335 Hamilton, S. C. "'Cast-Anchor Devils' and Conrad: A Study of Persona and Point of View in 'The Secret Sharer,'" *CON,* II, No. 3 (Spring 1969–70), pp. 111–21.

The general framework of "The Secret Sharer," its point of view, and its development of personas, provides the necessary organizational context of the story, and the levels of narration provide a means for interpreting the work. The simplest stage of narration is that of a story recollected and told by "I," the captain, who as narrator-agent, is the primary persona. Within the story, though, are an account by Leggatt and another version of the same matter by Archbold, skipper of the *Sephora.* The captain, a retrospective, self-conscious narrator lacking infallible and complete understanding, is so unaware of the intricate structures of the description and narration that he is included in the final sentence. The captain, we are informed by his older self, was so deeply involved psychologically with Leggatt that he may not be completely reliable. Thus good reasons exist to distrust all of the narrators created by JC because all of them lack total omniscience. The reader must, therefore, interpret the truth from many persons.

The simplest degree of complexity is the story as told by Archbold. Leggatt, a much more conscious storyteller than Archbold, is ideally suited to JC's purpose. The narrator-captain "de-dramatizes" himself but is entirely distinct from the captain during the story. It is JC who remains behind his puppets, telling a story of the nature of man and ships.

2336 Hay, Eloise Knapp. "Book Reviews: Paul Kirschner, *Conrad, The Psychologist as Artist*," *CON*, II, No. 1 (Fall 1969–70), pp. 107–11.

The "hallmark" of JC's egoists is not primarily an assertion of "needs, in love or politics," but their preservation of "an idea or code, lovable or hateful." JC suggests that reason, no less than imagination, passion, and will, operates both unconsciously and consciously. Martin Decoud's ego is weakened by a skepticism deeper than he is aware of, an intellect that has "eroded all moral conviction." His suicide is the antithesis of Jim's death, within reach of his "sustaining illusion." Eventually, JC may be grouped with those like Teilhard de Chardin who consider ego psychology less as a system of unchangeable biological forces than as a "blindfolded participant" in "cosmic strivings, noumenal and phenomenal." JC's interest in noumenal aspects of the universe appears in *The Nigger of the Narcissus*. JC borrowed heavily from several French authors who were "reweaving" both Pascal's metaphysical imagery and his wry observations on the bestiality of a creature who can believe himself to be superior to the stars.

2337 Hay, Eloise Knapp. "Joseph Conrad's Last Epigraph," *CON*, II, No. 3 (Spring 1969–70), pp. 9–15.

The epigraph heading JC's last completed novel, *The Rover*, Spenser's "Sleepe after toyle" passage, fits Peyrol from the beginning to the end of the novel. JC's epigraphs usually point at his own experience as well as at his main character's, as in *Within the Tides* and *Nostromo*. The epigraph of *Rover* (to become later the author's own epitaph) provides two kinds of "bifocal union": a "personal-fictional" one and an "external-internal, or straight-versus-ironic" meaning. If JC chose Spenser's lines with full knowledge of their undertones, they then lend to Peyrol's death a suggestion of suicide and of the more obvious sacrifice the old man makes for the girl he loves and for the country he has once again been compelled to serve. His character, indeed, becomes complex, like that of JC's other self-sacrificing heroes, Jim and Razumov, for example. Peyrol's death, though, like Jim's and Razumov's, is also ambiguous: it is part political and part sacrificial. It demonstrates, in addition, man's need to die if he is unable to live for something beyond himself.

2338 Heimer, Jackson W. "'Look on—Make No Sound': Conrad's *Victory*," *Studies in the Humanities*, ed. by William F. Grayburn (Indiana: Indiana University of Pennsylvania, 1969), pp. 8–13.

Victory is JC's "vitriolic" assault on the man who despairs and, as a result, "betrays the world" either by detaching himself from it or by "dilletantishly dabbling" in its affairs. Heyst moves through two definite, yet closely related, patterns: the basic one—act, confession, attempted redemption, and punishment; and the minor one—isolation, involvement, and isolation. His "act" is his failure to fulfill his role as a human being, a complete detachment from life based on a skepticism that relies on reason and rejects emotion. The bulk of the novel deals with Heyst's struggles to reconstruct his character, to become a human being; and by the end of the book he has acquired a new self-knowledge by advancing from the rational to the emotional. When confronted by Jones and his crew, Heyst cannot, though, cast off his attitude of detachment and he, therefore, succeeds only in partially redeeming himself. In death, he at last triumphs over his crippling philosophy. In no other work does JC so clearly indicate that isolation destroys those who seek it. Man has an obligation to all men, no matter how distasteful or revolting he may find it.

2339 Henighan, T. J. "Mr. Bransdon: A Ford Lampoon of Conrad?" *American Notes and Queries*, VIII (September–October 1969), pp. 3–5, 20–22.

Ford's *The Simple Life Limited* caricatures JC in the person of Bransdon, and the critics W. E. Henley and Edward Garnett in the character of Parmont. JC's coolness toward Ford may have resulted from his recognizing himself in Ford's malicious but funny portrait.

2340 Herrmann, John. "You Only Say," *CON*, II, No. 1 (Fall 1969–70), p. 88.

[A short, imagistic expression in verse of the spirit of JC's novels.]

2341 Hewitt, Douglas. *Conrad: A Reassessment* (London: Bowes & Bowes; Chester Springs, Pennsylvania: Dufour, 1969), second ed.

JC's reputation now is very different from what it was in 1952 [the date of the first publication of Hewitt's book.] JC has become established as a "modern classic," and he is now a part of the "academic critical industry."

The study of fiction in the past twenty years has shifted from interest in plot to interest in symbolic pattern, to the concept of long works as sustained metaphors, and JC is obviously attractive to critics who favor this method. There is now, though, too much emphasis on critical participation in a "quasi-creative process of discovery," in too much radical interpretation. But current criticism directs attention to the symbolic rather than to the literal sense of JC's work. *Lord Jim*, for example, is a novel mainly about moral dilemmas of a real kind, but the issues, familiar to JC, are not so to us. JC's deeply rooted interest in the literal world should be noted for its prophetic value: *Nostromo* and "Heart of Darkness" reveal the fact that JC knew much more about colonialism than anyone seems to have noted until the present time. "The Secret Sharer" has lost some of its importance: the literal and the symbolic meanings diverge, as they do not in JC's best work. [This republished book of 1952 contains a new "Preface to the Second Edition," which is a helpful review of the criticism of JC from 1952 to 1969.] [Add: C, I, No. 1266.]

2342 Higdon, David Leon. "Conrad's *The Rover*: The Grammar of a Myth," *SNNTS*, I (Spring 1969), pp. 17–26.

In his last five novels, but particularly in *The Rover*, JC moved away from the employment of his usual biblical allusions, images, and archetypes which appear in his earlier fiction and depended increasingly upon classical myth, a change which reveals a modification of his outlook toward man and a greater concern with allegorical presentation. The archetype most often utilized is the Galatea myth, with Galatea both as persecuted nymph and as Pygmalion's statue. For *The Rover*, the enchanted garden, Acis, Polyphemus, and Galatea provide a mythic framework for Peyrol, who is seen as an allegorical, not a biographical hero, whose personality is disintegrated into two characters, Scevola (emotional involvement) and Real (rational detachment), both transfixed before Arlette (Galatea), who symbolizes the enchantress of the enchanted garden (Escampobar Farm) and the suffering innocent which JC saw dualized in woman. The novel is finally uneven and disappointing because Peyrol is the protagonist in the earlier part of the novel and a detached observer in the latter part. JC found the Galatea archetype an excellent device; his vision was effective, but a desire for brevity weakened, at crucial moments, the presentation. Whether *The Rover* is considered realistic, romantic or allegorical, the main need of criticism is to consider it mythopoeic.

2343 Hodgson, Terry. "'The End of the Tether,'" *London Review*, VI (Winter 1969–70), pp. 15–24.

"The End of the Tether" is a powerful tale in several ways: JC renders "actuality" brilliantly, together with the "fugitiveness" of this actuality; he provides a rich symbolic structure; his writing is technically brilliant; the alternation of incident, description, and thought is deftly done; there are timeless moments in the story, although for JC they are illusory; imagination, reflection, disgust, imminent catastrophe, and especially a sense of isolation cause Captain Whalley to lose his sense of his own identity; and the story is capable of many interpretations, a quality which exists because of the combination of a realized actuality with "subtle psychological, moral, and philosophical analysis."

2344 Hoffmann, Anastasia Carlos. "Outer and Inner Perspectives in the Impressionist Novels of Crane, Conrad and Ford," *DA*, XXIX (1969), 2711A–12A. Unpublished dissertation, University of Wisconsin, 1968.

2345 Hoffman, Stanton de Voren. *Comedy and Form in the Fiction of Joseph Conrad* (The Hague: Mouton, 1969).

In "Heart of Darkness," burlesque and other forms of low comedy are used to define what the pilgrims represent and to serve as the metaphor of their "profound disorder." [Chapter II, about this story, is excerpted from Hoffman's article, "The Hole in the Bottom of the Pail: Comedy and Theme in 'Heart of Darkness,'" 1965.] The comic images have both objective and subjective uses: objective to serve as a correlative for a human being (Marlow) and to be part of the subjective use, that is, "part of Marlow's attempt to establish a relationship with that which he is encountering, and part of Marlow's being, his manner of perceiving and knowing."

In *Lord Jim*, the central incident in both Jim's and Marlow's experience, Jim's leap from the *Patna*, is "figured" in terms of "knock-about clowns, in terms of types and burlesque meanness"; and Jim jumps into a "ship of fools" which "flounders on a leaden sea." [Chapter III, on *Jim*, is expanded from Hoffman's article, "'Scenes of Low Comedy': The Comic in *Lord Jim*," 1964.] The low comedy in this scene is a symbol of disorder. [See Hoffman, "Conrad's Menagerie: Animal Imagery and Theme," 1964.] *Jim* is Marlow's tale of Jim and of himself as he responds to Jim and seeks self-knowledge. The novel reveals that all things are unclear and that absolutes must become relatives and doubts. Several of JC's other works employ various forms of improbable comedy to reveal this concept.

2346 Holberg, Stanley M. "Sound and Silence in *Victory*," *CEA*, XXXI (May 1969), pp. 3–5.

JC effectively uses repetition of images of sound and silence in *Victory* to attain a sustained symbolism. Following the sterile, uninvolved skepticism of his father, Heyst chooses isolation and silence as outward expression of his inner life-denying emptiness. The quietness of the islands suits him; the squalid uproar of Schomberg's hotel dismays him. He finds in Lena a lovely, fascinating voice, the affirmative power of love which can be the mediating force between noise and silence, between vileness and fastidiousness. In his failure to love Lena, Heyst chooses silence and succumbs to his own philosophy in the form of Mr. Jones, who mirrors Heyst in a diseased and intensified way.

2347 Houk, Annelle S., and Carlotta L. Bogart (eds.). "Joseph Conrad: 'The Secret Sharer,'" *Understanding the Short Story* (New York: Odyssey Press, 1969), pp. 149–202.

[After reprinting JC's stories, the editors include "study materials" (theme, symbols, point of view, etc.) for assisting the reader to increase his skill in understanding stories.]

2348 Howard, Patsy C. "Borys Conrad's Reminiscences," *CON*, II, No. 1 (Fall 1969–70), pp. 89–93.

In preparation for publication, Borys Conrad's biography of JC, his famous father, supplies a "flesh-and-blood" JC who is moody but "certainly not a senile, unapproachable old fool," as he was portrayed by Jessie Conrad in *Joseph Conrad as I Knew Him* (1926). Borys' recollections depict "a warm, sympathetic human being." [Borys Conrad's *My Father: Joseph Conrad*, published by Calder & Boyars (London) in 1970.]

2349 Hurwitz, Harold. "*The Great Gatsby* and 'Heart of Darkness': The Confrontation Scenes," *Fitzgerald-Hemingway Annual* (1969), pp. 27–34.

Fitzgerald in *The Great Gatsby* borrowed from JC's interview scene at the end of "Heart of Darkness." In both works, the narrators, Marlow and Nick Carraway, are confronted with the difficult task of attempting to tell the truth about complex characters (Kurtz and Gatsby) to listeners who have severe illusions about them. And the confrontation scenes in both books turn into apotheoses of the heroes by the speakers, followed by ambiguous or noncommittal replies by the narrator. Important differences between the two scenes underscore the varied purpose of each scene: Fitzgerald's ending serves to make his novel, unlike JC's, a social tragedy; JC's last scene deepens the nature of the tragedy.

2350 Hyde, H. Montgomery. *Henry James at Home* (London: Methuen; New York: Farrar, Straus & Giroux, 1969), pp. 120, 179, 183, 191–94, 195, 241, 250.

Early in 1899, Stephen Crane and his "wife," Cora Taylor, took Brede Place, a few miles from Rye, Henry James's residence. The fact that Brede was reputed to be haunted gave Crane the idea for a play to be performed at Christmas in the local village hall, but according to the program there were nine literary collaborators, one of whom was JC. One of the characters in *The Ghost*, Peter Quint Prodmore Moreau, appears to have been an amalgam derived from James's *The Turn of the Screw* and JC's *The Nigger of the Narcissus*. Neither James nor JC liked the other personally, but each respected the other's literary achievements.

2351 Hynes, Samuel. "Conrad and the Congo," *DAI*, XXX (1969), 723A. Unpublished dissertation, Columbia University, 1968.

2352 Iwanowska, Olga Klug. "Club Activities: Washington, D.C.," *Quarterly Review*, XXI (American Council of Polish Cultural Clubs), (April–June 1969), p. 7.

[A glowing account of Dr. (actually Mr.) Edmund A. Bojarski's lecture on JC on March 28, 1969, for the Polish-American Club of Washington, D.C.]

2353 "Joseph Conrad," *Menckeniana*, XXIX (Spring 1969), p. 1.

[Quotes a letter from JC to H. L. Mencken dated 11 November 1917. See Harold W. Blodgett, "Mencken and Conrad," 1969.]

2354 Karl, Frederick R. "Addendum, 1968," *PCK* (1969), pp. 47–48.

Recently discovered information indicates that the so-called duel with the American adventurer Blunt was more likely an attempt on JC's part to commit suicide. [Supplies evidence to support this conclusion.]

2355 Karl, Frederick R. "Bibliographical Note: rvsd., 1968, by Frederick R. Karl," *PCK* (1969), pp. 758–62.

[Omits some items from the latest printing of the book and adds some more recent ones.]

2356 Karl, Frederick R. "Conrad, Ford, and the Novel," *Midway*, X (Autumn 1969), pp. 17–34.

The essential interest in the collaboration of Ford Madox Ford and JC comes from their innovative ideas and techniques, developed at the turn of the century when English fiction seemed exhausted. The friendship falls into three main parts: first, the work of enduring value that resulted from the interaction of two lively and dedicated minds, the ideas and experiments that appeared in their fiction; second, the three early uneven and flat prose works which issued from their labor; and third, the personal relationship which endured for twenty-six years, until JC's death in 1924.

When JC first came to live on land, he needed someone to encourage him with his literary career, and he found this person in Ford, who sensed that his own development depended on association with other literary figures. The two writers worked out the idea of the "planned novel," with the technique of *progression d'effet*—in which the intensity increases as the story develops. Their object was to utilize appropriate technique to create a semblance of actual experience. Eventually, as the two began to drift apart, the division between them widened professionally more and more. JC saw that the collaboration had done him very little good. By 1909, his own career was only a "monstrous joke." Gradually, Ford moved out into wider circles while JC did his best work in the decade following the collaboration. At last, two such ambitious and "utterly different" men "could only count their differences."

2357 Karl, Frederick R. (ed.). *The Portable Conrad*, ed. by Morton Dauwen Zabel, rvsd. by Frederick R. Karl (New York: Viking Press, 1969), (C, I, No. 1186).

Contents, not included in C, I, No. 1186, abstracted separately under year of first publication: Frederick R. Karl, "Addendum, 1968," to Zabel, "Editor's Introduction," pp. 47–48 (1969); Morton Dauwen Zabel, "Note and Acknowledgment," pp. 48–49 (1947); Frederick R. Karl, "Bibliographical Note," rvsd. 1968, pp. 758–62 (1969).

By JC and not abstracted: "Prince Roman," "The Warrior's Soul," "Youth," "Amy Foster," "Typhoon," *The Nigger of the Narcissus*, "An Outpost of Progress," "Heart of Darkness," "Il Conde," "The Lagoon," "The Secret Sharer," ["The Condition of Art"] consisting of excerpts from several works by JC, and ["Letters"] consisting of letters and excerpts from letters by JC.

2358 Karl, Frederick R. *A Reader's Guide to Joseph Conrad*, rvsd. ed. (New York: Farrar, Straus & Giroux, 1969).

[Frederick R. Karl's revised edition of his earlier book of 1960 contains few changes, most of which are of little significance and therefore add little to the value of the revised work. The changes consist of such matters as slight corrections (on page 10 of the "Introduction," JC's age at the time of his enrollment at St. Anne's "High" [formerly "Secondary" School] becomes twelve instead of eleven; a few variations appear in the notes ("suggested" becomes "indicated"); three paragraphs are added to section I of chapter IV; and the bibliography is brought up to date and "important words" are marked with an asterisk. The revisions, most of which are of minor importance, require few changes in the pagination of the book; in fact, each chapter begins and ends on the same pages as those of the first edition. This kind of useless revision is similar to Karl's treatment of *The Portable Conrad* in 1969.]

2359 Karrfalt, David H. "Accepting Lord Jim on His Own Terms: A Structural Approach," *CON*, II, No. 1 (Fall 1969–70), pp. 37–47.

Lord Jim contains three major structural divisions: the first four chapters, told by the "public" JC as omniscient narrator, chapters five through thirty-five and chapters thirty-six through forty-five, the last two sections narrated by Marlow. The audience for the second part includes the unspecified number of Marlow's listeners on a verandah after dinner, and the audience of the third part is one "privileged man" to whom Marlow mailed his written account of the final episode of Jim's story. The junctures between the structural units indicate that JC is inviting the reader to penetrate imaginatively the significance of the story. Other aspects of the story also lead both the narrator and the reader deeper and deeper into an understanding of Jim; images of penetration especially indicate how to approach Jim's meaning. Jim's leap into the darkness is complemented by a development of light imagery; Jim's conviction that there is light is stronger than Stein's affirmation of darkness. The darkness and light interpenetrate each other, suggesting Marlow's developing understanding of Jim's "success" and, through Marlow, the reader's increasing understanding of Jim throughout the development of the whole novel. In JC's view, civilization is a lie and an illusion. Jim, however, refuses to accept the reality of evil, "the prime reality of the darkness," and thereby creates the greatest lie of all. The reader must finally accept Jim on his own terms.

2360 Katona, Anna. "A Hungarian Conrad Bibliography," *CON*, II, No. 1 (Fall 1969–70), pp. 133–34.

[Lists both translations of JC's works into Hungarian and critical studies.]

2361 Kemoli, Arthur, and David K. Mulwa. "The European Image of Africa and the Africans," *Busara* (Nairobi), II, No. 1 (1969), pp. 51–53.

The problem of the European image of Africa and the Africans as seen by Joyce Cary and JC is idealized and false. JC in "Heart of Darkness" sees Africa as something curious and mysterious, and he caricatures his natives. Kurtz realizes his idealism too late for his soul to be saved from "the horror, the horror!" Last comes the finality of the words that might spell a glimmer of hope for a changed attitude: "Mr. Kurtz, he dead."

2362 Ketterer, David A. "'Beyond the Threshold' in Conrad's 'Heart of Darkness,'" *TSLL* (1969), pp. 1013–22.

Three significant details in "Heart of Darkness" are the Buddha tableaux, the African woman, and the Russian harlequin figure. Marlow's comparison to an idol or Buddha links him with the world of ideals as opposed to the equally meaningless everyday world. Like the third fate, the black woman is described as an apparition and as the spirit of the wilderness. The Intended and the Negress are the black and white avatars of Atropos, and in this role both exude exultation and triumph at the moment of Kurtz's death, when the nature of idealism is seen to involve savagery and death. Kurtz's liason with these two women is an alliance with the powers of darkness. Word of Kurtz's death carried across the threshold of the Intended's door symbolizes the passing over the bordering area between the known and the unknown, the natural and the preternatural. In contrast, the Russian harlequin figure carries the suggestion of the possibility that there may exist "a plane of reality or an angle of perception at which practicality and idealism may be successfully combined." He, a preternatural figure beyond human possibility, is opposed, as Kurtz's guardian, to the African woman. He stitches while she cuts. Thus "Heart of Darkness" "reverberates not only through time and space but beyond."

2363 Kisner, Sister Mary Rosaline, A.S.C. "The Lure of the Abyss for the Hollow Man: Conrad's Notion of Evil," *CON*, II, No. 3 (Spring 1969–70), pp. 85–99.

According to JC, man in his own isolation is confronted with the evil of his own nature, and man's lack of restraint is his vulnerability which opens the way for his journey into "the abyss of total destruction by evil." JC's idea is that man must mold the materials of his existence out of the neutral cosmos and that the "moral law" dramatizes the necessity of human solidarity. In order to be saved, man must serve this idea, which ends in the service of love, without which man is "hollow, inhuman, and easily lured into destruction." Evil in "Typhoon," for example, is an outward conflict with nature, and by confronting the forces of evil with fidelity to duty and command, MacWhirr wins against them. In "Heart of Darkness," Marlow, through restraint, avoids becoming like Kurtz; but he, as a man who confronts evil without choosing a saving good, is an incomplete picture of man's confrontation. In *Victory*, JC demonstrates a deeper concern for the nature of evil and its confrontation: he suggests "satanic villains" who exemplify the many forms of evil man must confront. Heyst's tragedy is that of every man who mistrusts others; in contrast to him, Lena is a symbol of "pure love" who brings Heyst back to human solidarity in her "hour of glory." The darkness of JC's MacWhirr, Marlow, and Heyst is the "basic stuff of the universe," and only in solidarity and restraint can man confront the "blackness" and overcome it.

2364 Klotz, Günther. "Zwei Jahrzehnte englische und amerikanische Belletristik im Aufbau-Verlag und im Verlag Rütten & Loening" (Two Decades of English and American Fictional Literature Published by the Publishing Houses "Aufbau" and "Rütten & Loening"), *Zeitschrift für Anglistik und Amerikanistik*, XVII (1969), pp. 406–20.

[Refers to German translations of JC's novels published in the German Democratic Republic: *Nostromo* (1957), "Heart of Darkness" (1958), *Lord Jim* (1963), *Almayer's Folly* (1966), and *An Outcast of the Islands* (1968).] [In German.]

2365 Krakowski, Elizabeth Joanne. "The Theme of Isolation in the Novels of Conrad, Malraux and Camus," *DA*, XXIX (1969), 2267A. Unpublished dissertation, University of Colorado, 1968.

2366 Kramer, Cheris. "Parallel Motives in *Lord Jim*," *CON*, II, No. 1 (Fall 1969–70), p. 58.

Similar motives cause Brierly's suicide and Jim's acceptance of death. Brierly sees his own potential guilt and failure in Jim; likewise, Jim goes to his death after he sees the similarities between his background and that of Gentleman Brown.

2367 Kuehn, Robert E. "Introduction," Robert E. Kuehn (ed.), *TCLJ*, pp. 1–13.

A characteristic pattern is found in several of JC's works: such characters as Almayer, Kurtz, Charles Gould, Razumov, Heyst, and Jim are self-deluded exiles, estranged from their fellow men by a dream of special destiny, and by "the ineluctable logic of tragedy" they betray and even destroy those who have the greatest claim on their loyalty. JC was "profoundly skeptical." In both halves of *Lord Jim*, Jim is essentially the same man. It is Marlow who interprets him for us; his attachment to Jim forces him into an "agony of speculation" on human nature and its variance with fixed standards of conduct. Whereas Jim embodies a paradox, he is unable to understand it; therefore, he learns nothing about his character from the training-ship incident, he goes to sea for the wrong reasons, he fails to recognize his degradation among the other officers of the *Patna*, and he also fails to acknowledge his act of jumping from the ship. He makes too much of his disgrace and too little of his guilt. In Patusan, Jim's dream is nearly ended when, before Brown invades his domain, Jewel prevents his being slain; he is still the preoccupied young sailor in the fore-top. He has too much confidence in himself, too much faith in "benign circumstance," and entirely too little recognition of the evil in others. His death is "self-destructive, wasteful, and yet undeniably fine." He goes to his death in the egoistic belief that his sacrifice will atone for the death of Doramin's son. He remains for the readers, as he does for Marlow, "something of an enigma."

2368 Kuehn, Robert E. (ed.). *Twentieth Century Interpretations of Lord Jim: A Collection of Critical Essays* (Englewood Cliffs, New Jersey: Prentice-Hall [A Spectrum Book], 1969).

Contents, abstracted under year of first publication: Robert E. Kuehn, "Introduction," pp. 1–13 (1969); Part One—Interpretations: Eloise Knapp Hay, "*Lord Jim*: From Sketch to Novel," from *Comparative Literature* (1960), with revisions by the author (C, I, No. 1588); Jocelyn Baines, ["Guilt and Atonement in *Lord Jim*"], from *Joseph Conrad: A Critical Biography* (1960), (C, I, No. 1523); Paul L. Wiley, ["*Lord Jim* and the Loss of Eden"], from *Conrad's Measure of Man* (1954), (C, I, No. 1309); Tony Tanner, "Butterflies and Beetles— Conrad's Two Truths," from *Chicago Review* (1963), (C, I, No. 1762); Dorothy Van Ghent, "On *Lord Jim*," from *The English Novel: Form and Function* (1953), (C, I, No. 1292); Albert J. Guerard, ["Sympathy and Judgment in *Lord Jim*"], from *Conrad the Novelist* (1958), (C, I, No. 1470); Part Two—View Points: Joseph Conrad, "Letter to John Galsworthy" (1900), from G. Jean-Aubry, *Joseph Conrad: Life and Letters*, I (1927), [not abstracted]; Joseph Conrad, "Letter to Edward Garnett," I (1900), from G. Jean-Aubry, *Joseph Conrad: Life and Letters* (1927), [not abstracted]; Joseph Conrad, "Author's Note to *Lord Jim*," (nd), [not abstracted]; David Daiches, ["View Points"], from *The Novel and the Modern World*, rev. ed. (1960), (C, I, No. 1077); Robert B. Heilman, ["View Points"], from "Introduction to *Lord Jim*" (1957), (C, I, No. 1391); Douglas Hewitt, ["View Points"], from *Conrad: A Reassessment* (1952), (C, I, No. 1266); Frederick Karl, ["View Points"], from *A Reader's Guide to Joseph Conrad* (1960), (C, I, No. 1595); F. R. Leavis, ["View Points"], from *The Great Tradition* (1948), (C, I, No. 1106); Morton Dauwen Zabel, ["View Points"], from "Introduction to *Lord Jim*" (1958), (C, I, No. 1518); "Chronology of Important Dates," "Notes on the Editor and Contributors," and "Selected Bibliography," [not abstracted].

2369 Laskowsky, Henry J. "Joseph Conrad and N. G. Chernyshevsky," *CON*, II, No. 3 (Spring 1969–70), pp. 132–38.

The feasibility of analyzing historical backgrounds and possible literary sources for JC's *Under Western Eyes* is greatly increased by the publication in 1960 of an English translation of Franco Venturi's *Roots of Revolution: A History of the Populist and Socialist Movements in Nineteenth Century Russia*, which indicates that the image of Rousseau in JC's novel has great historical relevance to the Populist movement and makes clear that the English teacher's observation about a "violent revolution . . . in the hands of narrow minded fanatics" represents an acknowledged fear within the Populist movement itself. Venturi makes it clear that Chernyshevsky, a major figure in the Populist movement, had much in common philosophically with both the English teacher of languages and Razumov. There is, furthermore, both circumstantial and textual evidence that Cheryshevsky's life and his book *What Is To Be Done?*, a "crude propagandistic novel," were also important sources for *Eyes*.

2370 Lass, Abraham H[arold], and Norma L. Tasman (eds.). *"The Secret Agent" and Other Great Stories* (New York: New American Library, 1969), pp. 309–10.

"The Secret Sharer" is about the "lonely struggle for identity," a process which matures and frees the individual. It combines into greatness several of the qualities of JC's work: his exploration of man's moral being, his search for meaning in the universe, his powerful description of the sea, and his evocation of symbol and mood.

2371 Lee, Robert F[rancis]. *Conrad's Colonialism* (The Hague, Paris: Mouton [Studies in English Literature, 54], 1969).

Conrad's fiction reveals a belief in the superior administering ability of the British in the Orient. This "white man's burden" is to supply protection and control for the natives. The colonial leader, of whom Lord Jim is an example, though an imperfect one, is imaginative, dedicated, honorable, humanistic, and courageous; he is often portrayed as an individualistic merchant-adventurer rather than a government clerk. Kurtz is an example of the colonial who fails to fulfill the requirements though he recognizes his obligation to do so. James Wait is an example of the native as burden, behaving with lack of responsibility, of gratitude, of courage, and of self-reliance. In "Typhoon," Captain MacWhirr embodies the colonial qualities of British stolidity and responsibility for others. Impeccable dress, ideally white, is often a symbol of "keeping face," of pride in one's identity, discipline, and exclusiveness. Furthermore, the English colonial keeps apart from the natives and forms a tight bond with other colonials. The best example of the English colonial maintaining his identity in alien surroundings is Charles Gould. In *Nostromo*, the colonial obligation to improve the finances and life of native countries is well dramatized.

2372 Leech, Clifford. *Tragedy* (London: Methuen [The Critical Idiom 1], 1969), pp. 31, 46, 78, 81.

Although the tragic hero is not necessarily "virtuous" nor free from "profound guilt," he is, like Jim in *Lord Jim*, "one of us," a man who strongly reminds us of our own humanity. In some tragedies, the focus may shift from one character to another, as it often does in "tragic novels" like *Nostromo*, in which Nostromo, Charles Gould, Mrs. Gould, Antonia, and Decoud all share the tragic burden and thereby imply a universal demand for us to share it also.

2373 Lemon, Lee T. "Conrad's 'Heart of Darkness,'" *Approaches to Literature* (New York: Oxford University Press, 1969), pp. 192–231.

A "double romanticism" in JC's and Marlow's expressed desire to go to Africa leads them both to important lessons gained from their African journey: they learn to distrust boyish romanticism and to accept the need for facing the mystery that the explorer must ultimately conquer not land but truth and realize that at times the mystery destroys the explorer. The first narrator in "Heart of Darkness" serves subtly as a mediator between Marlow and the reader. Just as the African experience changes Marlow, hearing about it changes the first narrator: at the end of the story, he has lost his youthful optimism. He is a part of a complex series of parallel relationships: as Kurtz is to Marlow, so Marlow is to the first narrator, and so the first narrator is to the reader. The frame of "Heart of Darkness" also introduces the main motifs and the main thematic conflict of the novel. The latter may be stated as light versus darkness, civilization versus savagery, or the unconscious self versus the conscious self. As for the motifs, London on the Thames, enveloped in natural darkness, is an analogue to Kurtz and Marlow in the jungle. The darkness of the story is expanded to space and time and also to the mind of man. To indicate the existence of the primitive in all men, JC presents each of the listeners on the *Nellie*, except the first narrator himself, as having something in common with Kurtz and thereby prepares the reader to accept Kurtz's disintegration in the jungle. Marlow's victory is his recognition of Kurtz's action and his survival with that recognition. JC thus suggests that efficiency saves; principles do not.

2374 Lewis, John S. "*Nostromo*," *TLS* (23 October 1969), p. 1235.

Morchard Bishop ("*Nostromo*," *Times Literary Supplement* [London], [2 October 1969], p. 1132) is right about the use of the word "factious" in *Nostromo*. Also, the Spanish word, "*bribon*" was used without the accent in two American editions, and in another American edition without being italicized. And in chapter VI of *The Shadow-Line*, the word "exercising" was used incorrectly in place of the word "exorcising."

2375 Lincoln, Kenneth R[obert]. "Glass Beads: The American Edition of *Lord Jim*," *CON*, II, No. 1 (Fall 1969–70), pp. 69–72.

JC allegedly felt like a merchant "selling glass beads to African natives" when he sold his books to American publishers, and a textual comparison of the first English and American editions of *Lord Jim* reveals "intriguing flaws" in the American "bauble." A major break in revision occurs at the beginning of Chapter Thirty-six, the place where Marlow's narrative ends and the omniscient author reenters; thereafter the English and American book form variants increase greatly, with the American edition agreeing with the serial version of *Blackwood's Magazine*. Apparently JC did not revise the last ten chapters in time to send them to America for publication, and they were therefore set from JC's uncorrected proofs.

2376 Lincoln, Kenneth Robert. "Joseph Conrad: The Comedy of Perception," *DA*, XXX (1969–70), 3014A. Unpublished dissertation, Indiana University, 1969.

2377 Lincoln, Kenneth Robert. "Voice and Vision in Joseph Conrad," *CON*, I, No. 3 (Summer 1969), pp. 95–100.

JC uses visual scenery to revitalize language; his most vivid prose entails a visual description of character and setting. For him, seeing involves perceiving, and talking implies communication of one's perceptions: Marlow's frustrated imbalance of visual judgment and oral communication in his relationship with Jim, in *Lord Jim*, suggests, for example, the limitations of human awareness and exchange. JC's preoccupation with the visual seems a natural consequence of nineteenth-century interest in optics and epistemology, as well as an offshoot of his own philosophy of impressionism borrowed from Impressionist painters. As an early explorer of the psychological novel, JC dramatizes the attempt of a man to assimilate experience rationally; the artist, therefore, observes closely the associative processes of the mind as it moves about in the continuum of time and space. Thus in *Jim*, with its irresolutions, each individual is both "one of us" and at the same time painfully isolated by the burden of his past actions and his present consciousness. He belongs to his community, but he can never find his place in that community. As an artist, JC himself is aware of the limitations of the spoken and the written word, of the barriers hindering communication among individuals. The chronological pattern of the prefaces to the novels reveals a decline of sharp visualization, and there is a corresponding decline in the artistic intensity of the works themselves.

2378 Lindstrand, Gordon. "A Bibliographical Survey of the Literary Manuscripts of Joseph Conrad," *CON*, II, No. 1 (Fall 1969–70), pp. 23–32.

For the textual scholar preparing a critical edition, there has not yet been a coordinated effort to discover the appropriate literary documents, describe them, and thus complete the first step in making them available for scholarly purposes. The present survey "purports" to take that step for working with JC's literary manuscripts. [Introductory material includes manuscript description, authorial alterations, typescripts, titles, manuscript identification, the author's prefaces, designations for report origins, abbreviations used, and order of entry information. The manuscripts of JC are described from "Admiralty Paper" to "Foreword" to United Arts Gallery's Catalogue of *Landscapes of Corsica and Ireland* by Alice S. Kinkead. A second part of the survey appears in Lindstrand, "A Bibliographical Survey of Conrad's Literary Manuscripts, Part II," *Conradiana*, II, No. 2 (Winter 1969–70), pp. 105–14; and a third in "A Bibliographical Survey of the Literary Manuscripts of Joseph Conrad, Part III," *Conradiana*, II, No. 3 (Spring 1969–70), pp. 153–62.]

2379 Lindstrand, Gordon. "A Bibliographical Survey of the Literary Manuscripts of Joseph Conrad, Part II," *CON*, II, No. 2 (Winter 1969–70), pp. 105–14.

[Explains manuscript genealogy, original and authorial draft material, titling and cross indexing, symbols in the bibliographical description, abbreviations, and report origins. Lists JC items from "Freya of the Seven Isles" to *Romance*. Continued from Lindstrand, "A Bibliographical Survey of the Literary Manuscripts of Joseph Conrad," *Conradiana*, II, No. 1 (Fall, 1969–70), pp. 23–32; and concluded by "A Bibliographical Survey of the Literary Manuscripts of Joseph Conrad, Part III," *Conradiana*, II, No. 3 (Spring 1969–70), pp. 153–62.]

2380 Lindstrand, Gordon. "A Bibliographical Survey of the Literary Manuscripts of Joseph Conrad, Part III," *CON*, II, No. 3 (Spring 1969–70), pp. 153–62.

[Explains manuscript genealogy, original and authorial draft material, author's prefaces, titling and cross indexing, manuscript description, order of entry contents, abbreviations, and reports origin and present location designations. Lists JC items from *The Rover* to *Youth, A Narrative and Two Other Stories*, followed by a brief updating report and supplement. Preceded by Lindstrand, "A Bibliographical Survey of the Literary Manuscripts of Joseph Conrad," *Conradiana*, II, No. 1 (Fall 1969–70), pp. 23–32, and "A Bibliographical Survey of the Literary Manuscripts of Joseph Conrad, Part II," *Conradiana*, II, No. 2 (Winter 1969–70), pp. 105–14.]

2381 Lindstrand, Gordon. "Conrad's Literary Manuscripts: John Quinn and the New York Public Library," *CON*, II, No. 1 (Fall 1969–70), pp. 85–88.

Since the John Quinn Library sale of 1923–24, which included many first editions, rare issues of books, and manuscripts of JC's works, the New York Public Library has gradually acquired an enviable collection of materials essential to a study of the growth and transmission of JC texts. *Conradiana* has begun to make available to its readers additional sources of such materials for researchers, such as the Yale University Beinecke Rare Books and Manuscript library (which contains the largest single group of materials by and about JC), but many manuscripts from the John Quinn collection can no longer be traced. [Followed by Lindstrand, "A Bibliographical Survey of the Literary Manuscripts of Joseph Conrad, Part II," *Conradiana*, II, No. 2 (Winter 1969–70), pp. 105–14; and "A Bibliographical Survey of the Literary Manuscripts of Joseph Conrad, Part III," *Conradiana*, II, No. 3 (Spring 1969–70), pp. 153–62.]

2382 Lindstrand, Gordon. "An Unknown Conrad Manuscript and a Record Price Set for Conrad Typescript," *CON*, II, No. 3 (Spring 1969–70), p. 152.

In the *Times Literary Supplement* (London) for 25 June 1970, Norman Sherry reported finding a short and completely unknown autograph manuscript by JC; it consists of notes made on the siege and fall of Paris of 1870–71. More interesting, no doubt, is the offer for sale by the House of El Dieff, New York, of a typescript of *Almayer's Folly* with many holograph corrections and a typescript of *Chance*, also with many changes. Offered together for the high figure of $25,000, these manuscripts set a record. The reason for this phenomenal price setting is JC's enduring popularity among readers and collectors and his fascination for writers and scholars.

2383 Low, Anthony. "Drake and Franklin in 'Heart of Darkness,'" *CON*, II, No. 3 (1969–70), pp. 128–31.

Apparently the narrator in "Heart of Darkness" regards both Drake and Franklin as heroes of English imperialism, both in the story and elsewhere in JC's work as Belgian or continental imperialism. The two men are appropriate to "Heart of Darkness" for more than the knight-errantry of the sea expressed by the narrator. The account of the episode from Drake's life is ambivalent, suggesting that hints of the darker side of empire appear mixed with admiration, the dominant note.

2384 Low, Anthony. "'Heart of Darkness': The Search for an Occupation," *ELT*, XII, No. 1 (1969), pp. 1–9.

In "Heart of Darkness," the importance of work is ambivalent, but the concern with it is practically equivalent with one's role in life. Marlow suggests that to find one's work is to find oneself. He goes to Africa to "take on" an occupation and do a job, but he is troubled by the perversions of what is important to him there—"honest work." He finds that refuge in work is illusory because he himself, who serves the Company and works under the manager, cannot entirely escape implications, for the manager triumphs while Marlow—regardless of what he learns inwardly—fails. He is drawn by the sound of the savages singing and dancing because he feels a simultaneous attraction toward the natural, unspecialized vitality of the Africans and a repulsion from the European ideals of work and duty. Kurtz, however, even more than Marlow, is unsure of himself as he searches for the right profession. His freedom from convention and restriction concerns his relation to his work: as a man of many occupations, he actually has none. The Company, even more than Africa, corrupts Kurtz. Marlow, too, feels the attraction of the Company, and this is one reason why he associates himself with the "renegade Kurtz." For almost all the characters in "Heart of Darkness" other than Marlow, occupation means depersonalization and ultimately destruction; work somehow strengthens Marlow, however, and confirms him in his originally rather simplistic ideal about work. Thus, this story is Marlow's—and by reflection JC's—search for a real vocation in life.

2385 Marble, James Elton. "Joseph Conrad: A Structural Reading," *DAI*, XXX (December 1969), 2538A–39A. Unpublished dissertation, University of Washington, 1969.

2386 Marcus, Raymond. "Romantic Image in *Lord Jim*," *High Points* (Winter 1969), pp. 12–14.

Jim is a "self-created idol of heroism," a "charismatic ideal of a Conradian hero." He is also representative of the Victorian ideals of enlightenment and life; when he abandons the *Patna*, he chooses life, but only to reaffirm his idea of courage, because he submits to the Court of Inquiry and assumes the life of a hunted man. To Marlow,

Jim is the representative of the hero, for he abandons himself to his ideal, and he sacrifices himself for the truth of his illusions.

2387 Marsh, Derick R. C. "A Note on the *Otago*," *CON*, II, No. 1 (Fall 1969–70), pp. 33–35.

JC's first and only command, the *Otago*, was towed in 1931 to her last resting place on the eastern bank of the Derwent River seven miles above Hobart, Tasmania. In 1964, the stern section was cut from the hulk and shipped to the United States. The ship's wheel also made its way to this country. Soon nothing more will be left of the barque JC had in mind when writing *The Shadow-Line*.

2388 Matthews, James Harvey. "Particularity and Polarization: Realism in the Fiction of Hardy and Conrad," *DA*, XXIX (1969), 3147A. Unpublished dissertation, Vanderbilt University, 1968.

2389 Maxwell, J. C. "Mr. Stephens on 'Heart of Darkness,'" *EIC* (Oxford), XIX (October 1969), pp. 461–62.

R. C. Stephens is the victim of one "besetting sin" of criticism: "the ingenuity of the proposed solution sometimes seems to have generated the problem it claims to solve," as seen in some of his comments on "Heart of Darkness." [Articles by Maxwell and Stephens appear under the general heading, "The Critical Forum." A second article by Maxwell is found in "Mr. Stephens on 'Heart of Darkness,'" *Essays in Criticism*, XX (January 1970), pp. 118–19.]

2390 Maxwell, J. C. "*Victory*," *TLS* (4 December 1969), p. 1045.

[A very short letter pointing out a corrupt use of a comma in the Dent Collected Edition of *Victory*.]

2391 Maxwell-Mahon, W. D. "Joseph Conrad: 'Three Tales,'" *Crux* (Pretoria), III (February 1969), pp. 16–21.

There is little wonder that people strive to recapture what JC describes in "Youth" as "the romance of illusions"; even if Marlow rhapsodizes too much in this story, we can forgive him as we remember ourselves in him. In "The Secret Sharer" also, JC presents a conflict between youthful illusions and the substantiality of life, including the irony that accompanies it. And "Freya of the Seven Isles" is a tragic account of the consequences of a blind adherence to "the romance of illusions." [Written "for high schools"; contains much plot summary.]

2392 McLauchlan, Juliet. *Conrad: Nostromo* (London: Edward Arnold [Studies in English Literature No. 40], 1969).

Rich in nuance, *Nostromo* is innovative for its time. Symbolic overtones grow through aptness of imagery and gradually deepen as images are varied and developed. Ideas are superbly embodied in images; major themes are varied and enriched by words and ideas which recur as motifs. The events of the novel are seen with ironic detachment, in terms of a game with many individuals gambling desperately. The very essence of *Nostromo* is irony. Since the novel is greatly concerned with corruption through obsession by material interests, characters are either those primarily concerned with materialism or those not so concerned, and the book shows that obsession with material interests is the worst and most useless of all the illusions by which men try to live. [Each character is analyzed in effective detail. A brief but helpful study is made of the first four chapters of the novel, and a chronology of events is given for the entire work. A short bibliography completes this eighty-page but very helpful introduction to *Nostromo*.]

2393 Messenger, William E[dmund]. "Conrad and Melville Again," *CON*, II, No. 2 (Winter 1969–70), pp. 53–64.

JC's antipathy toward Melville, insofar as it is not simply a case of "like repels like," can be explained on technical grounds. JC, with his artistic detachment and formal control, naturally felt aversion for Melville's exaggerated absence of aesthetic distance and formal design. Still, there is much evidence that *Redburn* directly influenced the writing of *The Nigger of the Narcissus*—more evidence than previous scholars have noted. *Redburn* may have been more congenial to JC than his recorded remarks on Melville might suggest; in this instance, apparently, like attracted like.

2394 Messenger, William Edmund. "Conrad's Early Sea Fiction: A Study in Reputation, Convention, and Artistic Achievement," *DAI*, XXX (1969), 1175A. Unpublished dissertation, University of California, Berkeley, 1968.

2395 Meyers, Jeffrey. "Savagery and Civilization in *The Tempest, Robinson Crusoe* and 'Heart of Darkness,'" *CON*, II, No. 3 (Spring 1969–70), pp. 171–79.

JC's "Heart of Darkness" is the "mirror-image" of *Robinson Crusoe*: Defoe's novel is Apollonian, suggesting self-control, tranquillity, order; JC's is Dionysian, bursting with frenzy, intoxication, and chaos. As the reason and optimism of the Enlightenment are succeeded by the primitive and the irrational of the modern age, "Eden becomes Hell," civilization becomes savage, and the traditional justification for colonialism no longer exists. Defoe clearly distinguished between savage and civilized; JC has

Kurtz confirm the latent fear of nature's ultimate triumph over man. Crusoe's survival and Kurtz's destruction suggest a radical change in thought from the age of reason to the modern era. But even if "Heart of Darkness" presents a "deeply pessimistic" view of the nature of man, the story has two redemptive aspects, both of which have a parallel in Defoe's novel: Crusoe seems not to have learned much from his long stay on the island whereas Marlow represents the conscience abandoned by Kurtz, and the code of primitive honor of Marlow's cannibalistic crew, like Friday's, exemplifies the virtues lacking in the Europeans, particularly in Kurtz. "Heart of Darkness" reverses the major premise of *The Tempest*, which was shared by *Robinson Crusoe*, by Rousseau, and by the exotic works of Melville, Loti, Gauguin, and Stevenson, to return to a Hobbesian belief that civilization is corrupt. "Heart of Darkness" is the first significant work in English literature to question the very foundations of western civilization.

2396 Miyoshi, Masao. *The Divided Self: A Perspective on the Literature of the Victorians* (New York: New York University Press, 1969), pp. 81–82, 282n, 305, 320, 328, 336n, 337n.

In Mary Shelley's novel *Frankenstein*, Robert Walton understands Frankenstein, and the two men immediately recognize in each other the poles of deep sympathy with another mind and a longing for more "inward" knowledge and wisdom. This is a remarkable resemblance to JC's "The Secret Sharer," in which Leggatt and the captain meet and then become, by their identical quest, indistinguishable. There are also hints in JC's story of the Mariner's meeting with the Wedding Guest.

2397 Molinoff, Katherine. "Conrad's Debt to Melville: James Wait, Donkin and Belfast of the *Narcissus*," *CON*, I, No. 3 (Summer 1969), pp. 119–22.

From Melville's Sailor Jackson of *Redburn* JC took three characters for *The Nigger of the Narcissus*: James Wait, who is identical to Jackson; Donkin, whose evil originally appeared in Jackson; and Belfast, from Melville's Irish crew member. This is a curious relationship, especially since JC was apparently entirely unaware of his heavy debt to the American novelist.

2398 Momcilovic, Branko. "Znacrnje i funcija epizoda u Konradovom romanu *Lord Dzim*" (Meaning and Function of Episodes in Conrad's Novel *Lord Jim*), *Godishnik Filologskog Fakulteta* (Novi Sad), VII, 2 (1969), pp. 487–99.

JC uses episodes to represent a body of complex attitudes which give various views of Jim's dilemma. The choice of characters in the episodes faces the reader with several ethical codes, e.g., idealism, cynical realism, practical thinking. In some episodes, the moral view is given as a statement; elsewhere it is implicit in the dramatization. The episodes are not chronological, but grouped in an order which enabled JC to produce special effects such as a balancing of opposing views and involving the reader and forcing him to adopt an attitude toward every episode. The illustrative episode is a major device in JC's narrative art. [English summary, pp. 489–99.] [In Serbian.]

2399 Morley, Patricia A. "Conrad's Vision of the Absurd," *CON*, II, No. 1 (Fall 1969–70), pp. 59–68.

Like all of JC's novels, *The Secret Agent* is concerned with "the impenetrable mystery of the universe" and with man's basic problems of loneliness, isolation, and death, in a word, with the "Absurd." The London of the novel suggests a dream or a nightmare. The cab ride which Stevie, Winnie, and her mother take to the charity cottage symbolizes the absurdity of man's life on his journey to death. Wetness and darkness predominate in the imagery, connected with London, which symbolizes death and man's fear of death. The confrontation between Inspector Heat and the Professor in Chapter Five symbolizes man's confrontation with the absurd. JC often uses the technique of inverting the normal and the rational into the opposite: in an absurd world, for example, Ossipon's faith in women and in science is inverted to madness and despair. JC's vision of the absurd is not, however, pessimistic or cynical: he recognizes the importance of the tension between the mood of metaphysical anguish and man's vigor and love of life. His emphasis in *Agent* on the shadows need not be defended as the total truth of man's existence, but as only one truth.

2400 Munro, John M. *Arthur Symons* (New York: Twayne, 1969), pp. 48, 124–26, 133.

Near the end of JC's life, Symons was sensitive to the novelist's evocation of the forces lying behind man's everyday existence, but he was more deeply impressed by JC's supposed cynicism and his "Satanical" view of mankind. Although JC did not appreciate Symons' interpretation of his character as seen through his novels, the two men became close friends, perhaps because they were very much unlike each other. Both, however, shared a brooding intensity, as well as common interests.

2401 Najder, Zdzislaw (ed.). "Nieznany list Josepha Conrada do Karoli Zagórskiej" (Unknown Letter from JC to Karoli Zagorska), *Tw*, XXV, 8 (August 1969), pp. 106–107.

[A twelfth letter by JC in Polish has survived. Previous letters published in *Twórczosc*, 1962: 11, and 1963: 12. Dated March 1923, the letter deals with JC's departure for the United States.] [In Polish.]

2402 Nash, Christopher. "More Light on *The Secret Agent*," *RES*, XX (June 1969), pp. 322–27.

JC was considerably more familiar than he claimed to be with the writings of London anarchists, thereby knowing the "true story of Martin Bourdin" for the original of the "pathetic Stevie." He appears to have carefully reread newspaper accounts of the Greenwich Park explosion and the report on Bourdin's inquest. Apparently JC put much more solid research into this novel than his remarks indicate.

2403 New York Public Library. *Dictionary Catalog of the Henry W. and Albert A. Berg Collection of English and American Literature* (Boston: G. K. Hall, 1969), pp. 617–30.

[A list composed of 261 entries, citing individual holdings of JC materials, which consist largely of first English and American editions of books, privately printed articles and stories, holographs, and collections of letters.]

2404 Palmer, John A. "Introduction," *TCNN* (1969), pp. 1–17.

The Nigger of the Narcissus is an affirmation of human solidarity and of the "few very simple ideas" JC supplied as the ethical core of his work, but it is also an ambivalent work with a "deep-lying background of metaphysical skepticism." JC is romantic insofar as the men of the *Narcissus* achieve "self-discovery and self-purgation through direct interaction with the forces of nature,"; they fulfill a typical romantic aim; but JC's romanticism was so conditioned by all the discoveries of evolutionary science and a sense of alienation from a mechanistic universe that the voyage of the *Narcissus* is "projected against a backdrop which holds latent within itself all the despair of Conrad's most pessimistic visions." The essentially optimistic conclusion of the novel poses questions which have been answered in various ways. A persistent ethical ambivalence is raised, for example, by the narrative voice, which shifts from "they" to "us" and finally to "I"; the narrative voice oscillates between the limited view of a crew member and the unrestricted view of an omniscient narrator, and at the end of the novel, the ship itself seems to supplant the crew as the protagonist. The total narrative context appears to make acceptable the view of the men's tentative symbolic renditions of their experience as somewhat successful "essays" toward a final state of metaphysical and ethical understanding represented fully only by the outside narrator himself.

2405 Palmer, John A. (ed.). *Twentieth Century Interpretations of The Nigger of the Narcissus: A Collection of Critical Essays* (Englewood Cliffs, New Jersey: Prentice-Hall [A Spectrum Book], 1969).

Contents, abstracted under year of first publication: John A. Palmer, "Introduction" (1969), pp. 1–17; James E. Miller, Jr., "*The Nigger of the Narcissus*: A Re-examination" [with the first two paragraphs omitted], from *PMLA* (1951), (C, I, No. 1246); Vernon Young, "Trial by Water: Joseph Conrad's *The Nigger of the Narcissus*," from *Accent* (1952), (C, I, No. 1277); Cecil Scrimgeour, "Jimmy Wait and the Dance of Death: Conrad's *Nigger of the Narcissus*," from *Critical Quarterly* (1965), (C, I, No. 1907); Albert J. Guerard, ["The Nigger of the Narcissus"], from *Conrad the Novelist* (1958), (C, I, No. 1421); Ian Watt, "Conrad Criticism and *The Nigger of the Narcissus*," from *Nineteenth Century Fiction* (1958), (C, I, No. 1917); Avrom Fleishman, ["Conrad's Early Political Attitudes"], from *Conrad's Politics: Community and Anarchy in the Fiction of Joseph Conrad* (1967); Norris W. Yates, "Social Comment in *The Nigger of the Narcissus*," from *PMLA* (1964), (C, I, No. 1849); Paul L. Wiley, ["The Nigger and Conrad's Artistic Growth"], from *Conrad's Measure of Man* (1954), (C, I, No. 1309); Bernard C. Meyer, M.D., ["On the Psychogenesis of the *Nigger*"], from *Joseph Conrad, A Psychoanalytic Biography* (1967); John A. Palmer, "Chronology of Important Dates," pp. 117–18; and "Selected Bibliography," pp. 121–22 [not abstracted].

2406 Pappas, John J. "Victorian Literature of the Divided Mind: A Study of the Self in Relation to Nature," *DAI*, XXX (1969), 693A–94A. Unpublished dissertation, Columbia University, 1968.

2407 Paton, Jonathan. "The Unforeseen Partnership," *Crux* (Pretoria), III (January–March 1969), pp. 22–26.

On his journey up the Congo, in "Heart of Darkness," Marlow forms a number of partnerships: with the six black men chained together, with the accountant sporting a neat appearance, with Towson's book, *An Inquiry Into Some Points of Seamanship*, with his helmsman, and finally with Kurtz. Although he knows that Kurtz is "hollow at the core," he is unable to accept the shallowness of the inhabitants of the "sepulchral city" or the illusion of Kurtz's Intended, and thus makes Kurtz his choice of nightmares. JC also forces the reader into a partnership in the novel because no reader can escape completely from involvement with the "heart of darkness." [For high schools.]

2408 Pavlov, Grigor. "Two Studies in Bourgeois Individualism by Joseph Conrad," *Zeitschrift für Anglistik und Amerikanistik*, XVII (1969), pp. 229–38.

JC's novels deal with "betrayal, alienation, moral isolation and the disintegration of the human personality under the strains and stresses of a bourgeois world beginning to crack and split up." *Almayer's Folly*, "Heart of Darkness," and *Nostromo* are attacks on the immorality of imperialism. "Heart of Darkness" is JC's "macabre study of the self-annihilation of bourgeois individualism"; *Lord Jim* describes the "moral isolation of the bourgeois individual and the intense mental pain it entails."

2409 Peirce, William P. "An Artistic Flaw in 'Heart of Darkness,'" *CON*, I, No. 3 (Summer 1969), pp. 73–80.

"Heart of Darkness" is flawed by an inconsistency in JC's "finely wrought" pattern of image, symbol, and theme: whereas the white men in the story have the capacity for self-discovery, the African savages lack this ability. The Africans are merely symbols, with no humanity; having no social or moral reality, they are used as literary symbols. Thus the moral message of the novel is for white men only.

2410 Pilecki, Gerard A., and Masamichi Mizushima. "Joseph Conrad in Japan," *CON*, I, No. 3 (Summer 1969), pp. 127–28.

Since the early twenties, several of JC's stories and novels have been translated into Japanese. World War II and then the stringencies of life for ten years afterwards prevented the rapid growth of interest in JC scholarship in Japan. Scholarly interest began to surge in 1961; it now includes some books and many articles. In spite of the number of available translations, however, JC remains unknown to vast numbers of the reading public.

2411 Pizer, Donald. "A Primer of Fictional Aesthetics," *College English*, XXX (April 1969), pp. 572–80.

[Identifies JC as a contributor to an early interest in the aesthetics of the novel. JC, not "primarily" a critic, composed novels of such "complexity" that they demanded "the emergence of a criticism capable of coping . . . with the novel as a form."]

2412 Quinn, John. *Complete Catalogue of the Library of John Quinn*, I (New York: Lemma Publishing Corporation, 1969), pp. 164–213. [Reprint of the 1924 two-volume ed.]

[Contains a brief biography of JC and an explanation given by the Polish author on his "mastery of English" and presents a complete list of JC's autograph and typed manuscripts and early editions that were sold by Quinn at auction in November and December, 1923, and in January, February, and March, 1924. The JC material, numbered inclusively from 1780 to 2010, was sold on November 13, 1923, as a portion of the first of the five separate parts of the sale. Among the manuscripts are *The Nigger of the Narcissus*, *Nostromo*, and *The Secret Agent*. There are short descriptions of each item, commentary on some, and a few facsimiles.]

2413 Rael, Elsa. "Joseph Conrad, Master Absurdist," *CON*, II, No. 3 (Spring 1969–70), pp. 163–70.

Although critical evaluation of JC's art seems to run the gamut of many kinds of criticism, also pertinent in contemporary terms is the "absurdist" vision. A chronological study of "two major novellas," "Heart of Darkness" and "The Secret Sharer" reveals the absurdity "like a consistent thread," especially in the former work, a "gem of the genre." "The Secret Sharer," which describes an ascent from hell, does not have the same consistent wealth of absurd humor; but it contains "chunks of first-rate absurdity." [Since the chronological examination of these stories points out only the absurd elements of each, the "absurd" interpretation is naturally absurd in itself.]

2414 Rhome, Frances Dodson. "Headgear as Symbol in Conrad's Novels," *CON*, II, No. 3 (1969–70), pp. 180–86.

Since JC objectifies his use of images, the images gradually become a symbol because of their suggestivity. Viewing words as fixed images, JC successfully reveals idiosyncrasies of behavior, then a general state of mind, and finally, the reflection of the inner self. A discernible pattern appears in JC's impressionism which requires a character to appear bareheaded, as with Almayer, Wait, and Jim. During periods of decisive trial, a character is often stripped of his outer clothing, to be redressed in an eccentric fashion, as with Almayer, Jim, Nostromo, and Verloc. For JC, symbolically, divestment of outer garments represents an exposure of the inner man, and changes of outer clothing reflect a changed attitude. A search of eleven stories for significance in the use of a hat reveals little mention of hats in the early stories, a gradual increase in realistic use with symbolic suggestions during JC's middle period, and a final "structuring" of the hat within the action itself in the later works. The hat as symbol, then, does not fall into a particularly neat pattern and so becomes one of JC's "imponderables"; but the hat used as a surprising image results also in control of the reader's responses.

2415 Roberts, Louis Edward. "Conrad's Tragic Vision: A Study of Four Representative Novels," *DA*, XXIX (1969, 4017A). Unpublished dissertation, University of Massachusetts, 1968.

2416 Roody, Sarah I. "Teaching Conrad's *Victory* to Superior High School Seniors," *English Journal*, LVIII (January 1969), pp. 40–46.

[Explains a method of teaching *Victory*, using such authorial devices as leitmotifs, doubles, natural symbolism, and irony.]

2417 Rose, Allan Manuel. "Conrad and the Sirens of the Decadence," *TSLL*, XI (Spring 1969), pp. 795–810.

In his early period, JC was a writer of the Decadence, displaying the main manifestations which Arthur Symons gives of this movement, impressionism and symbolism. JC built his art on impressionistic goals: vivid rendering of sensory impressions, a color close to that of painting, unremitting care for form, and an attempt to arrest motion for a moment. The impressionistic technique, seen in the painters of this group, of "applying light filtered through the environment," was similar to JC's theory that knowledge comes "in a discontinuous manner filtered through someone's emotions." JC's prose has been considered langorous, enervating, artificial, world-weary, and fascinated with the cruel and exotic, all symptoms of the literature of the *fin de siècle*. JC can also be seen as a symbolist in that his form is the symbol which reveals the truth of existence. He was, though, never a thoroughgoing apostle of "art for art's sake"; he belonged only momentarily to the adherents of this trend.

2418 Sadoff, Ira. "Sartre and Conrad: Lord Jim as Existential Hero," *Dalhousie Review*, XLIX (Winter 1969), pp. 518–25.

In *Lord Jim*, the hero develops from a "lost youngster" into an existential hero as he confronts the "dilemmas of modern man": isolation, despair, meaninglessness, and guilt, and thereby "masters his fate." JC continually emphasizes the loss of the ultimate authority; and since there are only multiple views of truth, there is, in fact, no truth, because truth, in JC's novel, has become internalized. Jim, therefore, despite the great gulf between his visions of himself and what he is, must determine his own fate. Existentialism, according to Jean-Paul Sartre, puts everyone in a position to understand that reality alone, not dreams or imaginings, is real. Jim is not a hero because of his own awareness of the absurdity and chaos of the modern universe. He cannot remain in a state of senescence; he is aware of himself, of the fact that he is alone, and also that he must accept the responsibility for his own welfare. He therefore makes his abstract dreams into reality by acting, by following his dream. Related to Jim's committment to action is his ability, developed by the end of the story, to confront death and to confront it courageously. Like Meursault in Camus's *The Stranger*, Jim has also committed himself to others, to the people of Patusan and to Jewel, thereby fulfilling another of Sartre's requirements of the existential hero. Jim is thus "a man among men," "one of us," all of whom face the same fate, "the universality of the human condition."

2419 Saha, P. K. "Conrad's 'Heart of Darkness,'" *Explicator*, XXVII (March 1969), Item 55.

JC's comparison of the Congo river to an uncoiled snake in "Heart of Darkness" may, along with the obvious sinister implications, also have favorable overtones based on traditional Hindu-Buddhist imagery, which likens the growth of enlightenment to the unfolding of snake-like coiled spiritual power from the tip of the spine to the brain.

2420 Saveson, John E. "Spencerian Assumptions in Conrad's Early Fiction," *CON*, I, No. 3 (Summer 1969), pp. 29–40; rpt. in *Joseph Conrad: The Making of a Moralist* (Amsterdam: Rodopi NV, 1972), pp. 17–36.

JC's earliest assumptions about Malayan life involve more than a mere catering to a Victorian taste for the sentimental and picturesque; they are "scientific" in that they embody Spencerian evolutionary theories. Recognizing this fact is a necessary first step in any attempt to describe JC's character as a psychologist and moralist. Spencer's analysis in *Principles of Psychology* of the differences between the savage and the civilized mentalities is reflected in JC's treatment of character in *Almayer's Folly* and his other Malayan writings, including *Lord Jim*.

2421 Sawyer, Arthur Edward. "Tragedy in the Fiction of Joseph Conrad." Unpublished dissertation, University of Toronto, 1960. [Listed in Lawrence F. McNamee, *Dissertations in English and American Literature, Supp. I* (New York and London: Bowker, 1969).]

2422 Schaefer, William D. "Recent Books: British Fiction," *NCF*, XXIV (September 1969), pp. 248–49.

JC's sixty letters to Warrington Dawson, with very few exceptions, "disclose absolutely nothing of biographical importance or of literary interest," JC's friendship with Dawson does not seem to be very "close or significant," and Dawson was "not a very interesting man." [Rev. of Dale B. J. Randall, *Joseph Conrad and Warrington Dawson: The Record of a Friendship* (1968).]

2423 Schultheiss, Thomas. "Conrad Bibliography: A Continuing Checklist," *CON*, II, No. 1 (Fall 1969–70), pp. 135–46.

[A continuing list in *Conradiana* of works about JC.]

2424 Schultheiss, Thomas. "Conrad Bibliography: A Continuing Checklist," *CON*, II, No. 2 (Winter 1969–70), pp. 153–63.

[A continuation of Schultheiss's invaluable bibliography.]

2425 Schultheiss, Thomas. "Conrad Bibliography: A Continuing Checklist," *CON*, II, No. 3 (Spring 1969–70), pp. 63–76.

[As item 2424.]

2426 Schultheiss, Thomas. "Conrad's Letters: The Forgotten Fragments," *CON*, II, No. 3 (Spring 1969–70), pp. 59–62.

For nearly a half-century, excerpts from literally hundreds of unpublished letters written by JC have been appearing in the sales catalogs of book dealers and auction houses "around the world." The "forgotten fragments" contain a "goldmine" of unpublished materials. Frederick R. Karl and Zdzislaw Najder, currently editing a "comprehensive edition" of JC's letters, are printing only complete texts of letters. Schultheiss is collecting such fragments as he can find and obtain the right to publish. [Contains four fragments drawn from the catalogs of the Anderson Galleries (later merged with the American Art Association.)]

2427 Schultheiss, Thomas. "Cornelius the Nazarene: Anti-ambiguity in *Lord Jim*," *ELT*, XII, No. 4 (1969), pp. 195–96.

In addition to other allusions in JC's ambiguous use of the term "Nazarene" in *Lord Jim* (see Thomas Schultheiss, "Lord Hamlet and *Lord Jim*," 1966, and Dudley Flamm, "The Ambiguous Nazarene in *Lord Jim*," 1969), there is the Roman Cornelius, a Nazarene, in Acts, chapter 10, of the New Testament. The basic ambiguity in JC's use of the word is that the reader at once calls to mind Jesus of Nazareth, an incongruous comparison. But underlying this, the ambiguity is comprehended by the "literate" reader's recollection of Cornelius, the Roman centurion of the New Testament, and of Cornelius in *Hamlet*—an uncalled-for devious pattern of associations. [And perhaps equally uncalled-for by the critic.]

2428 Schwarz, Daniel R[oger]. "The Function of the Narrator in Conrad's Shorter Fiction," *DAI*, XXX (1969), 338A–39A. Unpublished dissertation, Brown University, 1968.

2429 Schwarz, Daniel Roger. "Moral Bankruptcy in Ploumar Parish: A Study of Conrad's 'The Idiots,'" *CON*, I, No. 3 (Summer 1969), pp. 113–17.

"The Idiots," a penetrating study of emotional and moral idiocy, hardly deserves the critical neglect it has received. It goes beyond mere naturalism in JC's use of the Bacadous' retarded offspring to symbolize a community where familial and social structures are undermined by the selfishness and hypocrisy of those who should provide moral leadership. The true focus of the story is not on the children themselves but on the moral and emotional idiocy of the adults. The community's lack of humanity is demonstrated by its failure to provide adequate care for the helpless children.

2430 Schwarz, Daniel Roger. "The Self-Deceiving Narrator of Conrad's 'Il Conde,'" *SSF*, VI (Winter 1969), pp. 187–93.

The narrator of "Il Conde" is another of JC's imperceptive speakers. He thinks he stands dispassionately outside the story, but, far more than he knows, he identifies and empathizes with the Count and becomes the "secret sharer" of the Count's plight.

2431 Sebezhko, E. S. "I. S. Turgenev i Dzh. Konrad: Iz istorii russko-angliiskikh literaturnykh sviazei" (I. S. Turgenev and J. Conrad: From the History of Russian-English Literary Connections), *Stranitsy Istorii Russkoi Literatury* (Kaluga: Tula State Pedagogical Institute, 1969), pp. 151–57.

In his preface to Garnett's *Turgenev* (1917), JC might have been writing about himself. It is difficult to estimate the influence of Turgenev on a writer as original as JC; it appears not in themes, but in the spiritual atmosphere in the works of both writers. Turgenev's lyricism was close to that of JC, and he absorbed it, especially in portraying women. [In Russian.]

2432 Seltzer, Leon F. "Like Repels Like: The Case of Conrad's Antipathy for Melville," *CON*, I, No. 3 (Summer 1969), pp. 101–105.

JC disliked what he knew of Melville's works (*Typee, Omoo*, and *Moby Dick*) mainly because he feared being linked with a writer known especially for his "sea stuff," because he disliked being associated with an "exoticist" (*Typee* and *Omoo* shared some of the exoticisim of JC's first two novels), because he deplored the form (or lack of it) in Melville's works, because he must have considered as pedantry Melville's "tremendous allusions" and display of learning, because he thought that books which could attain the level of art should have no didactic content, and because he disparaged Melville's "portentious mysticism." [Included in somewhat different form (pp. xxxi–vi) in Seltzer, *The Vision of Melville and Conrad: A Comparative Study* (1970).]

2433 Sherry, Norman. "Conrad's Ticket-of-Leave Apostle," *Modern Language Review*, LXIV (October 1969), pp. 749–58.

The Secret Agent marks a turning point for JC in that its subject seems to have had no source in his personal experience. The character Michaelis is a patchwork of various revolutionary sources, part Fenian, part socialist, part anarchist. The case of "The Manchester Martyrs," a Fenian police van hold-up and killing, parallels in many ways the police van break-in in which Michaelis is involved. Further, the most famous ticket-of-leave prisoner of the day, Michael Davitt, a Fenian gun-smuggler, is similar to Michaelis in many respects. Contemporary sources had abundant descriptions of several different types of anarchist; of the four types of anarchist in *Agent*, Michaelis is the perfect idealist. His political philosophy seems to derive from Kropotkin, Bellamy, and William Morris. One socialist pamphleteer was named R. Michaelis. Furthermore, the Russian anarchist Bakunin, called the "apostle of destruction," was changed in prison from a young dandy to an obese, bloated, toothless being, much like the change Michaelis experiences in prison. But the irony in the figure of Michaelis is achieved through the very complexity of method which created him, in that JC does not give in the case of any one source the full moral impact implied by that source.

2434 Sherry, Norman. "Sir Ethelred in *The Secret Agent*," *Philological Quarterly*, XLVIII (January 1969), pp. 108–15.

In his Author's Note to *The Secret Agent*, JC makes vague reference to a recorded meeting between the Assistant Commissioner of Police and the Home Secretary in the lobby of the House of Commons. This meeting is recorded in Sir Robert Anderson's *Sidelights on the Home Rule Movement* (1906). The Home Secretary was Sir William Harcourt. JC makes use of two incidents in this book: Harcourt's reference to keeping the chief in the dark and his solicitations over a new man at Scotland Yard while leaning on the arm of a friend. Sir Ethelred is patterned on the historical figure of Sir William. The belief that JC read contemporary newspaper accounts is supported by this use of Harcourt, who was constantly in the news. The fisheries issue in the novel is also patterned after news stories on a current fisheries bill.

2435 [Slade, Joseph W.] "Letter from the Markham Archives," *Markham Review*, II (September 1969), pp. 8–11.

[Reproduces a letter from JC to Edwin Markham dated 30 June 1920.]

2436 Sladits, Lola L. "New in the Berg Collection: 1962–1964," *Bulletin of the New York Public Library*, LXXIII (April 1969), pp. 233–34.

JC acquisitions between 1962–1964 in the Berg Collection are: MS of *The Return*, dated September 24, 1897, 113 pages; MS of "Tomorrow," with partial wrapping paper postmarked May 24, 1912, addressed to John Quinn, 81 pages; TS of *The Rover* with the author's corrections, 389 pages; and, associated with *The Rover*, a photostat of JC's pen sketch of Peyrol.

2437 Sladits, Lola L., and Harvey Simmonds (comps.). *Pen and Brush: The Author as Artist (An Exhibition in the Berg Collection of English and American Literature)*, (New York: The New York Public Library, 1969), pp. 42–43.

JC drew both characters engaged in daily activities and visual images of characters from novels. [Includes two illustrations of pen and ink drawings: the hiring of girls for the ballet and "The Birthday of Madame Cigale."]

2438 Smoller, Sanford J. "A Note on Joseph Conrad's Fall and Abyss," *MFS*, XV (Summer 1969), pp. 261–64.

Two related images, those of the fall and the abyss, appear consistently in JC's early and middle work; but in the novels from *Chance* to *The Rover* the usual fall or jump either does not occur or is harmless. In general, then, JC's implied attitudes changed from "fatalistic pessimism" in the early and middle work to "guarded optimism" in the later work.

2439 Solomon, Barbara H. "Conrad's First-Person Narrators: A Study in Point of View," *DAI*, XXX (July 1969), 341A. Unpublished dissertation, University of Pittsburgh, 1968.

2440 Sperber, Michael A. "Sensory Deprivation in Autoscopic Illusion, and Joseph Conrad's 'The Secret Sharer,'" *Psychiatric Quarterly*, XLIII (October 1969), pp. 711–18.

Autoscopic illusion is a term used to apply to a "complex psychosensorial illusory projection of one's own body onto another's corporeal substance"; it is allied to the hallucination of one's double. Autoscopic illusion occurs to the unnamed narrator in JC's "The Secret Sharer," caused, probably, by a number of factors acting singly or in association. One major factor is the role played by sensory deprivation in such phenomena, the results of which are explained by psychological and physiological theories, in addition to, in JC's story, intrapsychic conflict: the narrator, feeling inadequate to his task, senses in Leggatt the strength he seems to lack. The autoscopic illusion remits when the captain emerges from his self-examination and can see Leggatt as a separate human being. [An excellent example of jargon which says little about the literature it discusses.]

2441 Stephens, R. C. "Heart of Darkness: Marlow's 'Spectral Moonshine,'" *EIC*, XIX (July 1969), pp. 273–84.

There is a mystery in Marlow rather than in Kurtz in "Heart of Darkness" as he transforms the facts of the case into a parable of transcendent evil. JC's tale dramatizes, with different degrees of intensity and completeness, several different forms of self-delusion, but Marlow alone is impelled to make of it a parable of cosmic evil. His method is to envelope his story in haze made by the "spectral illumination of moonshine." There is no assurance in the tale that Marlow's story is at any time a reasonably objective account of what occurred. His words and his disordered rhetoric are blended gradually into the voice of Kurtz as his voice takes over Kurtz's voice; he distorts the voice of the real Kurtz because he does not want its truth, preferring instead his own "lie." His choice is the lie disguised as the truth, with the result that he never dispels his nightmare, and something of the same situation is repeated in his final "lie" to Kurtz's Intended. Marlow must be hiding his own guilt and complicity, and at the end of his story he remains in a state of mental confusion about the entire question of the Imperialist mission.

2442 Stephens, R. C. "Mr. Stephens on 'Heart of Darkness,'" *EIC*, XIX (October 1969), pp. 463–66.

[Stephens examines Maxwell's issues one by one and finds that his argument about Kurtz' "Exterminate the brutes" leaves him in "a curious position." The articles by Stephens and Maxwell appear under the general heading, "The Critical Forum."]

2443 [Stevens, H. Ray.] "Conrad Bibliography: A Continuing Checklist," *CON*, I, No. 3 (Summer 1969), pp. 188–92.

[Third in a continuing listing in *Conradiana* of works about JC.]

2444 Summers, Marcia Perry. "The Use of Subordinate Characters as Dramatized Narrators in Twentieth-Century Novels," *DA*, XXX (1969–80), 3024A. Unpublished dissertation, University of Illinois, 1969.

2445 Sutton, Maurice Lewis. *Joseph Conrad: Victory* (New York: Barnes & Noble, 1969).

JC was probably unknown for some time because his thought is too complex and his rhetoric highly stylized. Also he is too wordy; some of his description is so long that it interferes with the illusion of reality, and his vocabulary is so vague that the reader cannot understand what he means.

The sea stories are appreciated solely for their adventure. Sometimes the action is so exciting that the reader does not examine deeper than the surface of the characters' psychology. The jungle stories concern men who isolate themselves from society. These men are always able to escape from the forces of the world.

JC believed that work was the one activity which gives any meaning to life. Through work, man protects himself from evil. Moreover, JC believed the artist is one who seeks the truth. This search manifests itself in various motifs, one of which is the quest motif. Another is the initiation motif.

The structure of *Victory* is largely circular in that JC circles from past to present to past, and the characters move in circles. They do not mature. For example, JC shows Lena as shallow, and this lack of identity makes her an allegorical figure. Heyst is more interesting because he is complex, and he too is an allegorical figure, but he is the only one who truly changes in the course of the book. [This book contains an incomplete list of JC's works and a very brief summary of the novel.]

2446 Tarnawski, Wit. "From the Translator," *CON*, II, No. 1 (Fall 1969–70), pp. 80–81. Trans. by Jadwiga Zwolska Sell and S. Dwight Stevens, III.

JC's unfinished novel, *The Sisters*, is practically unknown both to Polish and English readers. Begun in 1896 as JC's third novel in succession, it was abandoned, first for the first version of *Victory*, then for *The Nigger of the Narcissus*. The present, complete translation was first published in *Tworczosc*, a Polish literary monthly in Warsaw, in 1964. *The Arrow of Gold*, a return to the subject of *The Sisters*, is surpassed in nearly every respect by this largely unknown work. The text of *The Sisters* seems to be waiting to be translated into Polish. [Accompanies Kazimierz Wyka, "An Island in the Polish Gulf," *Conradiana*, II, No. 1 (Fall 1969–70), pp. 75–80, 82–83.]

2447 Teets, Bruce E. "Conrad and Guides to Art as *Psychagogia*," *CON*, II (Fall 1969–70), pp. 127–31.

The massive accumulation of publications on JC necessitates a reliable and complete bibliography of this great body of secondary works. Theodore G. Ehrsam's *Bibliography of Joseph Conrad* (1969), though incomplete, is a step in the right direction.

In answer to the question why JC has attracted such devoted attention from readers and scholars, the best explanation is probably that his works exemplify the ancient Greek concept of art as *psychagogia*—a developing and leading forth of the soul toward the molding of human character. JC himself was apparently aware of this concept of art; and the high purpose of his art increases the urgency of having reliable bibliographical guides to the thousands of items purporting to understand and explain the process of *psychagogia* in JC's works.

2448 Theroux, Paul. "Speaking of Books: My Travels with Joseph Conrad," *NYTBR* (22 June 1969), pp. 2, 26, 28–29.

"Heart of Darkness" is about a quest for truth, but JC's tales of "crazed Belgians in trading posts and enslaved villagers shackled together" do not present the truth accurately: his Africa contains more mystery and strangeness than does the real Africa of today; and even Singapore is no longer JC's city. [For additional comments on a similar subject, see Jerry Allen, "*Conrad*" (14 September 1969).

2449 Thomson, George H. "Conrad's Later Fiction," *ELT*, XII, No. 4 (1969), pp. 165–74.

JC's earlier fiction, characterized by "sustained and unresolved tension," changes after 1907, beginning with *Under Western Eyes*, towards a "resolution of tension," and turns towards a new subject, "the role of woman as the source of reality and salvation." Three characteristics distinguish JC's later from his earlier work: (1) his hero is no longer trapped in an everlasting deep hole, but is necessarily drawn out into the world and attracted by the "reality represented by woman"; (2) the hero no longer suffers from a "debilitatingly enigmatic sense of futility and guilt" because these responses are now overtly reflected in the plot; and (3) life is no longer a "protracted striving, incomplete and unresolved," because now resolution comes through a woman. These characteristics are "perfectly illustrated" by *Eyes*, *Chance*, and *Victory*, and "less perfectly" in *The Arrow of Gold* and *The Rover*. In the later novels, the human condition has become ameliorated, but at a high price for the male—witness Razumov, Captain Anthony, Heyst, Monsieur George, and old Peyrol; but at least the deadly salvation is now willed. To the old narrative structure JC now adds the new theme of salvation through woman. Although JC's employment after 1907 of a conventional love theme and a traditional style of ending appears to be a retreat, the time has not yet arrived for a final judgment of his later fiction.

2450 Vidan, Ivo. "Saint-John Perse's Visit to Conrad: A Letter by Alexis Saint-Leger Leger to G. Jean-Aubry," *CON*, II, No. 3 (Spring 1969–70), pp. 17–22.

Saint-John Perse (Alexis Saint-Leger Leger) was one of the French writers who visited JC while he lived at Capel House. A handwritten letter from that poet, addressed to Jean-Aubry, is kept in the Beinecke Rare Book and Manuscript Library at Yale University. Although the personal relationship between the two men was scarcely intimate, they had some important points in common. The occasion of this letter, dated 19 September 1947, was apparently given by Jean-Aubry's *Vie de Conrad*, a copy of which he had sent to Leger when it appeared. Leger seems to have been impressed by JC's "ease, humor, tolerance, and human understanding." [The letter is reprinted here in its French original and in an English translation.] [In French.]

2451 Wagar, W. Warren. "Art and Thought," *Virginia Quarterly Review*, XLV (Autumn 1969), pp. 693–97.

JC awakened in H. G. Wells the desire to be an esthete. [Review of Lovat Dickson, *H. G. Wells: His Turbulent Life and Times* (New York: Atheneum 1969).]

2452 Walker, Franklin. "Introduction," *JCHD & SS* (1969), pp. vii–xiv.

In "The Secret Sharer," the captain's predicament resembles most closely the moral dilemma of Captain Vere in Melville's *Billy Budd*. In assuming responsibility for Leggatt, not a typical *doppelgänger* but a "very real person," the captain proves himself worthy of his command. In "Heart of Darkness," the use of Marlow as narrator allowed JC to comment on his story without using old devices like Thackeray's "dear reader," preserved a sense of immediacy, enabled the author to manipulate time freely, and controlled aesthetic point of view. [Contains a brief survey of the criticism of the two stories.]

2453 Walker, Franklin. "Joseph Conrad: A Biographical Sketch," *JCHD & SS* (1969), pp. 195–99.

JC "specialized in adventure stories, . . . but adventure stories in which characters were realistic and moral probing and psychological portrayal were constantly present." [A fairly reliable sketch of JC's life.]

2454 Walker, Franklin (ed.). *Joseph Conrad, "Heart of Darkness" and "The Secret Sharer"* (New York: Bantam, 1969).

Contents, abstracted under year of first publication: Franklin Walker, "Introduction," pp. vii–xiv (1969); Franklin Walker, "Joseph Conrad: A Biographical Sketch," pp. 195–99 (1969); Jocelyn Baines, ["Conrad's Experiences in the Congo"], from *Joseph Conrad: A Critical Biography* (1960), (C, I, No. 1523); John Dozier Gordan, ["The Making of 'Heart of Darkness,'"], from *Joseph Conrad: The Making of a Novelist* (1940), (C, I, No. 1096); ["Contemporary Reviews: From *Times Literary Supplement* (London, 12 December 1902)"]; ["Contemporary Reviews: From *Nation* (New York, 11 June 1903)"], (C, I, No. 57); ["Contemporary Reviews: From *Independent* (New York, 6 March 1913)"]; Joseph Warren Beach, ["Control of Point of View Through the Use of Marlow"], from *The Twentieth Century Novel: Studies in Technique* (1932), (C, I, No. 944); F. R. Leavis, ["'Adjectival Insistence' in 'Heart of Darkness'"], from *The Great Tradition* (1963), (C, I, No. 1106); Albert J. Guerard, ["The Night Journey in 'The Secret Sharer' and 'Heart of Darkness'"], from *Conrad the Novelist* (1958), (C, I, No. 1470); Harold R. Collins, ["Detribalization of Kurtz and the Second-Rate Helmsman"], from "Kurtz, the Cannibals, and the Second-Rate Helmsman," *Western Humanities Review* (1954), (C, I, No. 1299); Leo Gurko, ["Ecology in 'Heart of Darkness'"], from *Joseph Conrad: Giant in Exile* (1962), (C, I, No. 1674); and "Suggestions for Further Reading" [not abstracted].

By others, not about JC and not abstracted: "The Crime Which Suggested 'The Secret Sharer,'" from *Times* (London), (Friday August 4, 1882).

By JC and not abstracted: "Heart of Darkness," pp. 1-132; "The Secret Sharer," pp. 133-93.

2455 Walt, James. "Conrad and Mencken—Part II," *CON*, II, No. 3 (Spring 1969-70), pp. 100–110.

H. L. Mencken's enthusiasm for JC's work lasted more than half a century. Mencken's admiration for JC rested largely on the fact that he had set himself the "facile optimism" of William Dean Howells, H. G. Wells, and Arnold Bennett, and that JC's "tragic and sardonic" view of man was supported by such writers as Aeschylus and Shakespeare. Beginning in 1908, Mencken began his fifteen years of reviewing books for *The Smart Set*. For him, JC stood at the forefront of English writers, with no rival near him. Always a superior artist, thought Mencken, JC discarded the richest part of his heritage when he turned to the land. *Under Western Eyes* was "average Conrad," *A*

Personal Record was the portrait of "a real man"; but *Chance* was on a lower level, even if neither the "complex structure" nor the "aching emptiness" of the novel injured its sales. Mencken liked *Victory* for its "pure storytelling." *Within the Tides* showed a sharp diminution in "dramatic force" when compared to "Typhoon" and "Heart of Darkness." *The Shadow-Line* was "competent" and "moving"; *The Rover* was the "quite mediocre" product of an "exhausted mind." After an awkward start, in *Suspense*, JC settled down to touch this fragment with "perfection that recalled Schubert's *Unfinished Symphony*." [Follows Walt; "Mencken and Conrad," *Conradiana*, II, No. 2 (Winter 1969–70), pp. 9–21, and precedes Walt, "Conrad and Mencken—Part III," *Conradiana*, III, No. 1 (1970–71), pp. 69–74.]

2456 Walt, James. "Conrad and the *Saturday Evening Post*," *CON*, I, No. 3 (Summer 1969), pp. 129–30.

JC appeared in the late *Saturday Evening Post* only once, in 1906, with "Gaspar Ruiz" as a four-part serial. In this story, a "sardonic" twentieth-century skepticism seems to muffle the note of nineteenth-century romanticism heard again and again. JC's main skill lay in his "exploration of inwardness."

2457 Walt, James. "Mencken and Conrad," *CON*, II, No. 2 (Winter 1969–70), pp. 9–21.

Even if the relations between Mencken and Conrad appear to be amiable, there was a gulf between the two writers which could not be bridged. Through reading some of JC's earlier works, Mencken eventually became the Anglo-Polish novelist's "leading drum beater" in America. His reviews in *The Smart Set*, nevertheless, lack a certain "discriminating analysis." His chapter on JC in *A Book of Prefaces* (1917) reveals his praise of JC's pessimism as essentially in support of naturalism, which was still looked upon with some doubt in America. Pessimism, he argues, is itself a literary virtue. He also portrays JC as an agnostic in religion and morality, who finds life unintelligible; he considers JC as a "pure artist" for whom beauty is sufficient. Mencken, attracted to JC's masculine world, attributed the anti-feminism of the works to the typical American's touchiness about his "masculine image." He recognized the "deep cunning" of the artist in JC which caused him to reject simple, straightforward storytelling, and found justification for the violence and melodrama of JC's stories. Nine years after his essay in *A Book of Prefaces*, in trying to alter the conventional theory that humor is inevitably good-natured, Mencken printed a shorter study in which he advocated the view that JC "let lightning flashes of humor play through his fictional world." He also attributed the exoticism and the so-called "barbarism" of JC's style to his "profound originality."

2458 Walton, James. "Conrad, Dickens, and the Detective Novel," *NCF*, XXIII (March 1969), pp. 446–62.

At the end of the cab-ride in *The Secret Agent*, JC states the paradox which is central to his entire apprehension of urban misery: one kind of wretchedness must feed upon the anguish of another. This is the same paradox which concerned Dickens in his later career. JC attempted in *Agent* to treat broad social themes in the manner of Dickens. Searching for new subject matter and a wider audience, he used his usual theme, the self; his basic source of inspiration was his own inner tensions, and Dickens enabled him to impersonalize these tensions and to give them social magnitude and "public" form. He therefore used in *Agent* the anonymity of characters, as did Dickens in several of his novels. Like Dickens, too, he is mainly concerned with people who must identify themselves with their career, and these led to the pressure and importance of official interviews. And as a new kind of detective thriller, *Agent* extends a tradition established by *Bleak House*: the Assistant Commissioner performs Inspector Bucket's function of guiding the reader into lurid slum scenes and of implementing an intricate social satire. *Agent*, also like *Bleak House*, is a novel of multiple detectives and of multiple, though related, intrigues, all of which both establish the connections among disparate characters and reveal the secrecy of the hidden motives, the self-justifying illusions, and the double lives which keep them apart. Dickens and JC have in common the importance of professional standing in social life, the ironic treatment of unconscious guilt in bourgeois life, and the grotesque-comic rendering of domestic isolation.

2459 Ward, Herbert. "About the 'Falconhurst,'" *Sea Breezes* (London), XLIII (January 1969), p. 91.

[A short response to Edmund A. Bojarski's mention of the *Falconhurst* in "Slop Chest," *Sea Breezes* (London), XLII (November 1968), p. 276. Ward offers technical data about the *Falconhurst* and a history of its becoming stranded.]

2460 Watts, C. T. (ed.). *Joseph Conrad's Letters to R. B. Cunninghame Graham* (Cambridge: Cambridge University, 1969).

JC's friendship with R. B. Cunninghame Graham lasted from 1897 until JC's death in 1924. The friendship seems paradoxical: JC in England was "reserved, reticent, and reluctant to appear before the public," whereas Graham was "a flamboyant public figure" who by 1890 had already been the subject of magazine profiles and political cartoons. But JC had more in common with Graham, "temperamentally and ethically," than with Garnett, Wells, James, or any of his other literary correspondents. In a sense, Graham was JC's "secret sharer": both men were described as "aristocratic" in their bearing, appearance, and sense of chivalry, honor, and justice; both held in contempt the arrogant materialism of their era; between them the "masks of irony" could be lowered, if not entirely laid aside; and both men had accumulated experience during their youthful years of travel, labor, and adventure. JC attempted to curb the potentially subversive tendencies of Graham's romantic existentialism by reminding him of the existential premises they held in common. With few exceptions, JC affords consistently high praise to Graham's work. His judgments on the correspondence display greatest interest in the ironic temperament and acuteness of perception shown in Graham's work.

[This book consists of a forty-page "Introduction," a collection of eighty-one letters from JC to Graham, and various appendices.]

2461 Whitehead, Lee M. "Conrad's 'Pessimism' Re-examined," *CON*, II, No. 3 (Spring 1969–70), pp. 25–38.

In the development of JC's art up to *The Nigger of the Narcissus* and the creation of Marlow, the vision of life presented in his tales changes from an early pessimism very much like Schopenhauer's to a tragic vision much like Nietzsche's in *The Birth of Tragedy*. JC's most convincing expression of his conception of life is found in his fiction. In *Nostromo*, he states the "ideal values" of life as act; in *Lord Jim*, he "structured" the tension between life seen as spectacle and life graspable only as an act. Consequent upon considering life as an act is the realization that our "posturings" have no cosmic nor absolute meaning. Even isolation, a recurrent theme in JC, contains meaning and terror only because it is recognized against the contrasting background of human solidarity. But human existence conceived as art reveals, along with the precariousness of life, the possibilities of human meaning and existence. Often the tension between the view of others and one man's view of himself becomes the central dramatic conflict, as in *Nostromo*, in which the discrepancy between Nostromo's public role and his actions as his "own man" becomes the central symbol of the novel, as is Winnie's recognition about Verloc in *The Secret Agent*. Another consequence of life considered as art is that, as Mrs. Gould comes to recognize, for life to be "large and full," it must "contain the care of the past and the future." For JC, such care in every passing moment demands self-discipline, responsibility, and sacrifice.

2462 Whitehead, Lee M. "*Nostromo*: The Tragic 'Idea,'" *NCF*, XXIII (March 1969), pp. 463–75.

Nostromo is a rendition of JC's response to the tragedy of man's social nature. Charles Gould, representing civilization as an unfolding and evolving community of individuals, in which individual personality is a result of the fact of community and possible only through it, and finally realizing the "meaning" of his life only to have it opposed by a new, antagonistic idea, is like society: by the capacity of the opposing ideas to draw men into the societal process and thus into the realization of themselves, they have performed a service to life. For JC, though, the social process is tragic because individuals, who discover themselves by pursuing an ideal, find the pursuit of the ideal self-contradictory, and because the process of self-discovery is a fall from self-sufficiency and unity into a split and divided awareness. Nostromo's change from a "magnificent animal" to a "self-tortured man" aware of the role he must play among other people to hide his secret from them illustrates this paradoxical fall. Life, as JC renders it in *Nostromo*, is hopeless, but not therefore devoid of meaning. The illusion of hope, of something outside oneself to give shape and meaning to his life, is for JC a source of suffering and despair, but the illusion of "idea"—motivated as it might be by vanity, egoism, sentiment, or passion, and at any possible cost in responsibility, guilt, alienation, suffering—can be the source of the dignity possible to man. Therefore JC often emphasizes the value of pursuing the "lost cause" or the "idea without a future."

2463 Winstedt, Richard. *Start from Alif: Count from One* (Kuala Lumpur: Oxford University, 1969), p. 4.

Somerset Maugham and JC are witnesses that "the Malay archipelago pullulates with romance," but romance exists "less in the apes and the crocodiles of reality" in the mangrove swamps of the Malacca Straits than in *Almayer's Folly*, where "apes and crocodiles are subdued to human ends by a man of genius." In a sonnet on JC's death [by Winstedt], JC flew one signal to all, "'Fail not your trust before the last landfall.'"

2464 Withim, Philip. "Joseph Conrad—His Character and His Genius," *Psychoanalytic Review*, LVI (Summer 1969), pp. 242–46.

Dr. Bernard C. Meyer's book, *Joseph Conrad: A Psychoanalytic Biography* (1967), exhibits the similarity between the pattern of alternating creative thrust toward life and withdrawal from it in JC's life, and in varying degrees in each of his novels. This pattern of thrust and collapse corresponds also with a pattern of alternation between masculine and feminine identifications. And the typical Conradian hero traces the outlines of the author's life. But nowhere does Meyer include our major interest in JC: the great personality and the great artist. JC's artistry, ignored by Meyer, is seen clearly in

Victory and *Nostromo*, where we, unlike Meyer, can see JC's art as a vision, a "depicting and ordering of reality" as JC himself saw it.

2465 Wolff, Erwin. "Conrad: *Lord Jim*," *Der Englische Roman*, ed. by Franz K. Stanzel (Dusseldorf: August Bagel Verlag, 1969), II, pp. 289–316, 391–94.

Because of JC's moral sensibility, *Lord Jim*, his greatest novel, is a classic written in a time hostile to the values of classicism. The starting point of any analysis must not be JC's technique: the novelist was not interested in technical problems as such; he was concerned with the motif of guilt and atonement. Jim's guilt is a moral and metaphysical one: it resembles the concept of original sin, though the novel is not a Christian book. Jim's flight is a search for expiation. His sacrificial death is an act of mercy granted by the inscrutable powers of the universe. Like all great tragedies, the novel ends in an atmosphere of hope, a fact often overlooked by critics who fail to see the relations between JC and Shakespeare. JC's handling of the point of view does not aim at psychological exploration but at showing that man is incapable of grasping the metaphysical core of any situation completely. In terms of an international novel, *Jim* has Stein represent German idealism and Marlow British imperialism and social sense. Jim stands for the older British tradition of romantic heroism. Marlow has to overcome his distrust of imagination and does not seem to understand fully the meaning of Jim's fate. Jim illustrates the failure of the European dream of civilizing the world. [In German.]

2466 Woolf, Leonard. *The Journey Not the Arrival Matters* (London: Hogarth, 1969; New York: Harcourt, Brace & World, 1970), pp. 197–98.

Woolf's nostalgia and sentimental love of Ceylon and its people are comparable to his love of youth and the jungle, to JC's love of his youth and the sea, as when Marlow and JC, one voice, produce the "nostalgic voice and purple patch": "Ah! The good old time. . . . Youth and the sea. Glamour and the sea!"

2467 Wright, Edgar. "Joseph Conrad and Bertrand Russell," *CON*, II, No. 1 (Fall 1969–70), pp. 7–16.

Six of JC's eleven letters to Bertrand Russell have been published in *The Autobiography of Bertrand Russell, 1872–1914* (1967) and *The Autobiography of Bertrand Russell, 1914–1944* (1968); four hitherto unpublished letters are given here in full, and one is described. On the whole, the bond between the two men consisted of intensity of feeling rather than in "meetings and sociability." World War I interrupted their growing acquaintance, but some contact was maintained later. Both mentally and emotionally the bond was close between them. [The four hitherto unpublished letters, located in the Russell Archives at McMaster University, are dated 12 December 1913, 4 February 1914, 17 February 1914, and 5 October 1921. The letter described is dated 23 October 1922.]

2468 Wright, Walter F. "Lawrence Graver, *Conrad's Short Fiction*," *NCF*, XXIV (December 1969), pp. 370–72.

JC is treated as an artist and judged, quite properly, as a teller of tales, not as an "amateur anthropologist, seer, or case study." "The Secret Sharer," a study for most critics, is "essentially a simple narrative" with some excessive decoration. [Rev. of Lawrence Graver, *Conrad's Short Fiction* (1969).]

2469 Wyatt, Robert David. "The Aesthetics of Doubt: Three Studies in Ironic Narrative," *DA*, XXX (1969–70), 5007A. Unpublished dissertation, University of Oregon, 1969.

2470 Wyka, Kazimierz. "Czas powieściowy" (Time in the Novel), *O Potrzebie Historii Literatury* (Warsaw: Panstwowy Instytut Wydawniczy, 1969), pp. 63–94.

Only in *Nostromo* was JC concerned with depicting a broad environment. His aim was the truth about man, even though this was too complex to express in an epic succession of events. JC therefore had to construct a method of his own to satisfy his own aims as well as the unwritten laws of the novel as a genre. He did so by transferring events to various levels of time. His time is exclusively constructive time; he was a contemporary of such philosophers of his age as Bergson and Proust, though with differences. [In Polish.]

2471 Wyka, Kazimierz. "An Island in the Polish Gulf," *CON*, II, No. 1 (Fall 1969–70), pp. 75–80, 82–83. Trans. by Wit Tarnawski.

JC's unfinished novel, *The Sisters*, almost unknown to critics, belongs more to Polish than to English literature because it contains JC's only picture of his native land; its "emotional, unconcealed" autobiographical elements; its "apotheosis of non-material values"; and its "ringing romantic resources," as Tarnawski has stated. Only a Polish student of Polish literature can find its real qualities accessible; the reader's ear must be attuned to JC's "poetics of description." [Wit Tarnawski writes further about *The Sisters* in his "From the Translator," *Conradiana*, II, No. 1 (Fall 1969–70), pp. 80–81.]

2472 Yoder, Albert C. "Oral Artistry in Conrad's 'Heart of Darkness': A Study of Oral Aggression," *CON*, II, No. 2 (Winter 1969–70), pp. 65–78.

From a Freudian viewpoint, Falk's kind of oral aggression, in which one wants to devour other people but especially the object of love itself, appears to be typical in "Heart of Darkness". This approach to the story illustrates that it contains much imagery indicative of oral aggression, such as eating, food, hunger, and cannibalism; that oral aggression, in providing both atmospheric background and metaphysical commentary, helps greatly in understanding the story; and that this generalized approach both stays close to the text and remains comprehensive enough to assimilate many of the earlier interpretations.

The ivory, in which everyone is interested, creates an unusual cannibalistic environment in "Heart of Darkness." Kurtz's cannibalism seems very probable; Marlow's aggression, though, reveals itself not in eating other people but in "digesting" the words that express ideas and eventually using them to tell the story. This interpretation includes, from a new point of view, interpretations seen by Harold Collins, Jerone Thrale, Albert Guerard, Lillian Feder, Robert Evans, and Bernard Meyer.

2473 Zagorska, Karola. "Ze wspomnien o Conradzie" (From Reminiscences of Conrad), *TW*, XXV, 8 (1969), pp. 108–11.

[Notes made by Karola Zagorska (1884–1955) to supplement her essay, "Pod dachem Konrada Korzeniowskiego" (Under Conrad's Roof), *Kultura* (1932), pp. 2, 3, describing a visit to Oswalds of the American pianist, John Powell.] [In Polish.]

2474 Zgorzelski, Andrzej. "Funkcjonalnosc struktur w 'Lagunie' Conrada" (Functional Character of Structures in Conrad's "Lagoon"), *KN* (1969), pp. 401–409.

"The Lagoon" contains the most important features of JC's work, including the use of the smallest structures within its framework. The artistry and style (described by Guerard and others as "pretentious" and "artificial") are functional, starting with the exposition where the narrator provides a framework, and then following the basic coloring and suggested atmosphere, a feeling of mystery intensified by the descriptions, the idea that the appearance of the world does not correspond to its significance, a theme to which JC gives almost cosmic dimension. The time of the action is emphasized by epic, proverbial expressions, and observance of the three unities. Epic, dramatic, and lyrical elements complement each other and are used to analyze the hero's experiences by expressing, not showing or telling. [In Polish.]

1970

2475 Andreach, Robert J. *The Slain and Resurrected God: Conrad, Ford, and the Christian Myth* (New York: New York University Press; London: University of London, 1970), pp. 29–119.

Many of JC's heroes try to explain the mystery of life by means of supernatural causes, but the only effective way they dominate their fears is to suppress their pride and illusions and to make a painful introspective journey. Woman provides the introspective mirror, and failure to heed her leads to death, as in what happens to Jim when he rejects Jewell. Woman, who leads man to discover the god within himself, is another Virgin Mary. Man must accept his nature, the necessity to die in order to be reborn, and the desirability of union with the female.

Both JC and Ford Madox Ford conceive of reality as twofold: that literal or surface reality which contains another dimension called symbolic or allegoric, and that which, when we penetrate the surface, reveals the other dimension. Just as Beatrice is Dante's experience of grace on earth, so are the heroines in the works of JC and Ford the heroes' experience of a metaphysical reality. *The Inheritors* is the archetypal expression of this myth as dramatized in the fiction of these two novelists. After meeting a woman who affords an insight into another reality, the hero travels into a region of darkness to overcome evil and then returns to the heroine. The role of woman to reveal a superior reality is also dramatized in *Under Western Eyes*, *Victory*, and *Nostromo*.

2476 Anshutz, H. L. "Conrad," *CON*, III, No. 1 (1970–71), p. 25.

Recognizing the "ugly facts" man must live with, JC "crept to the edge of nihilism," but avoided this "escape, not a solution" because "He knew that life demands affirmative creation." [A well written, perceptive poem which assesses JC's "world view" fairly and effectively.]

2477 Babb, Howard S. *The Novels of William Golding* (Athens: Ohio State University, 1970), pp. 62–63n, 100–101.

In Golding's *Free Fall* and JC's "Heart of Darkness," both essentially first-person narratives which the tellers feel compelled to relate, the narrators are groping through their pasts and recalling events whose significance, though "portentous," often seems beyond decisive formulation by the tellers. Both tellers are involved in a kind of subjective experience which can be more readily lived through than analyzed and rationally comprehended by them. A major difference, though, is that whereas by the end of *Free Fall* the reader remains as limited in his knowledge as the narrator is, JC's reader understands more, or at least more clearly, than does Marlow.

2478 Beardsley, Monroe C. *The Possibility of Criticism* (Detroit: Wayne State University, 1970), p. 23.

The question for the interpreter of literature, unlike that for the biographer, does not concern the author's attitude toward a character, but the attitude of the narrator—of a novel, for example—and of the novel itself. Accordingly, it is not JC's attitude towards the Intended in "Heart of Darkness" that matters, but Marlow's. And information about attitudes contained in other novels, with other narrators, as with Rita in *The Arrow of Gold*, does not help in understanding the Intended, unless we accept the untenable position that the narrator's attitude and JC's attitude are identical.

2479 Bergonzi, Bernard. "The Advent of Modernism 1900–1920," *History of Literature in the English Language: The Twentieth Century* (XI volumes in preparation), ed. by Bernard Bergonzi, (London: Barrie and Jenkins, 1970), XI, pp. 20, 21, 28–31, 33.

With origins and background "romantically unlike" those of most English writers, JC is difficult to fit into convenient critical categories. His books are pervaded by a sense of values that is not English; certain of his strong convictions about the importance of chivalry, honor, and reputation are "positively feudal." His experience in the merchant service left him with "a thoroughly pessimistic view of existence," with something in common with the view of life of the existentialist philosophers which was far ahead of its time in Edwardian England. His scanty belief in the permanence of Western civilization appears as a collapse of conventional Western values in "Heart of Darkness." And one of his most compelling books, *The Secret Agent*, reveals London as not basically different from Central Africa: the novel leaves the reader with "a disturbing sense of any kind of organized society" and of "the absurdity of politics." JC's masterpiece, *Nostromo*, an "astonishingly modern" work, has throughout a "tension" between his belief in "the traditional virtues of order, fidelity and discipline" and "a deeper underlying scepticism about the viability of any human values at all." [In his introduction to this book, Bergonzi, although characterizing JC as "certainly one of the greatest English novelists," omits him from the august company of the four great writers of our time whose stature is "unshakeably established": Yeats, Joyce, Lawrence, and Eliot.]

2480 Biddison, Larry T. "The *Femme Fatale* as Symbol of the Creative Imagination in Late Victorian Fiction," *DAI*, XXX (1970),

4976A. Unpublished dissertation, Louisiana State University, 1969.

2481 Bloch, Tuvia. "Lena's Voice in *Victory*," *CON*, III, No. 1 (1970–71), p. 91.

Although in his fiction JC sometimes stresses the quality of a voice to help create the impression he wishes to convey of a character's nature, he uses this device notably in *Victory*: the seductiveness in Lena's voice clearly represents the physical appeal which she has for Heyst.

2482 Bojarski, Edmund A. "Wells on Conrad," *TLS*, 28 May 1970, p. 587.

H. G. Wells's review of JC's second book, *An Outcast of the Islands*, as "perhaps the finest piece of fiction" published in 1896 just as *Almayer's Folly* was one of the finest in 1895, was the cause of the "ambivalent friendship" between the two writers. JC recognized his debt to Wells even though he declared to his publisher that no one could alter his own style. [A reply to Patrick Parrinder, "Wells on Hardy," 23 April 1970.]

2483 Bojarski, Edmund A., and Harold Ray Stevens. "Joseph Conrad and the *Falconhurst*," *JML*, I (second issue 1970–71), pp. 197–208.

JC's association with the ship *Falconhurst*, although previously suspected, has been definitely determined only recently by JC's testimony in 1894 before the Board of Trade's Departmental Committee on the Manning of Merchant Ships and even more recently by the uncovering of the record of the *Falconhurst*'s passage from London to Cardiff, Wales (a reproduction of which accompanies this article), which lists JC's name, then Korzeniowski. Being in need of money in 1886, JC, even though having recently received his Master's Certificate, signed up as second mate for a five-day voyage on the *Falconhurst* from London to Cardiff. The voyage was apparently uneventful. The discovery of JC's service on this ship suggests that about this time he began to write his first prose fiction, "The Black Mate," and to consider his future as a writer, and it also makes a total of twenty ships on which he is known to have sailed. Although no photograph of the *Falconhurst* has been found, a model has been located. [A description and history of the ship are given.]

2484 Brooks, Harold F. "*Lord Jim* and *Fifine at the Fair*," *CON*, III, No. 1 (1970–71), pp. 9–25.

The symbolic butterfly is linked in both *Lord Jim* and *Fifine at the Fair* with the symbol of the swimmer, concerning, respectively, Stein and Don Juan, and equating in somewhat similar ways, the idea that one must rely more completely upon the water than upon the air. It thus appears that JC owed part of his inspiration to Browning, and other parallels between the two works strengthen this conclusion: both Jim and Fifine have a "shameful past"; at one point in their degradation, both Jim and Fifine are praised for one redeeming virtue, courage or frankness for the sake of truth; imagery "importing the ghostliness of what besets or confronts us in life" appears in both works; and Jim's refusal to accept his disgrace is the same as Fifine's attitude. Each writer, furthermore, makes clear that behind the concern with which he invests his characters and situation, there remains his interest, which he also makes that of his readers, in the "wider problem" of man's nature; and also, for each writer, the demand on "casuistical understanding" constitutes, largely, the richness of his subject.

2485 Carson, Herbert L. "The Second Self in 'The Secret Sharer,'" *Cresset* (Valparaiso University), XXXIV (November 1970), pp. 11–13.

In "The Secret Sharer," the young captain, suffering from uncertainty and loneliness, creates a problem: his hallucinations create (in his mind only) the nonexistent Leggatt. At the end of the story, it is the captain's own hat that is blown by the air onto the water. Evidence that the captain suffers from self-delusion and the concept that Leggatt is merely the reaction of a man who has temporarily become emotionally upset are provided by JC: the captain continually seems to see himself and those around him as if he were an observer of the action rather than a participant in the events. Since there is no tangible second self, this *legate* of the captain's insecure and lonesome mind sets up a counterpart for himself, a man with whom he can share the lonely hours of uncertainty as an excuse to avoid his own duties. Later, by taking the ship into the most extreme danger, he uses his delusion to test the secret self-image he has, and the unhealthy and deluded communion with Leggatt is replaced by successful responsibility. The stranger, the secret sharer, has been rejected.

2486 Chapple, J. A. V. *Documentary and Imaginative Literature: 1880–1920* (London: Blandford Press; New York: Barnes & Noble, 1970), pp. 13, 18, 62n, 123–24, 137, 152–56, 191, 192–201, 206, 208, 219n, 240, 267–68, 333, 376.

The egoism of Verloc in *The Secret Agent* is sublime: he fails to realize why Winnie marries him, fails to perceive the developing father-son relationship between himself and Stevie, fails to realize that Winnie entirely lacks affection not only for himself, and fails to see at last that she has full knowledge of his conduct with Stevie. In *Agent*, JC emphasizes the underworld and its connection with the normal world; he emphasizes the connection between the criminal and the respectable people who believe in their moral superiority. What JC actually reveals is the moral torpor of this part of society, the relationship existing only on the surface of society.

"Heart of Darkness" is a fictional account of JC's own experience in the Congo, but negative as it is of the attempts to colonize Africa, it is not cheap anti-imperialistic literature. JC repeatedly stresses the futility of the colonial effort and the weakness of its highest ideals. Ultimately he stresses that in man's heart of darkness there is only meaninglessness.

Nostromo is a great panorama of a fictitious country in South America. JC attempts to reveal the frequent revolutions and the connections between moral and material interests. While he says that part of the motivation for advanced countries to promote underdeveloped countries is pursuit of profit, he exposes the duplicity of other causes.

2487 Cheney, Lynne. "Joseph Conrad's *The Secret Agent* and Graham Greene's *It's A Battlefield*: A Study in Structural Meaning," *MFS*, XVI (Summer 1970), pp. 117–31.

Both JC and Graham Greene use structure to focus the attention of the reader; in both *The Secret Agent* and *It's A Battlefield*, structure indicates that the violence initiating the action is subordinate to the consequences of the violence. In JC's novel, the bombing, and in Greene's, the stabbing, happen offstage, thus involving not the event itself, but its effects, which become the real crisis in each novel. In JC's work, omitting the bombing indicates that the real center is elsewhere—not in the attempt to destroy an observatory but in the symbolic drive toward chaos and irrationaltiy present in modern life. In both works, structural devices relating to time serve to unify: JC's device is the time shift; Greene's, short scenes which move from action in one place to almost simultaneous action in another. The thirty-year time span between the two novels reveals that the chaos and the disorder Greene was attempting to communicate were of a more fundamental kind than JC was concerned with. But the structure of the earlier book, in mirroring these particular facts of existence, is not deficient; the deficiency lies in the universe when it is measured against the human desire for a harmonious and ordered cosmos.

2488 Conrad, Borys. *My Father: Joseph Conrad* (London: Calder & Boyars, 1970).

Borys Conrad, JC's elder son, learned quickly not to disobey his parents. His father demanded "absolute peace and quiet for his activities" by screwing his monocle "firmly in his eye" and assuming "an expression of truly diabolical savagery" while his mother achieved the same result by merely looking at him and forbidding an action in her typically gentle tone of voice. Mrs. Conrad was "the ideal wife" for JC: "with her rigid self-control she was impervious to his emotional outbursts." JC always worked "in complete seclusion," and no one except his wife dared intrude upon his privacy. His friends included such well known figures as John Galsworthy, Edward Garnett, Ford Madox Hueffer, H. G. Wells, and Henry James. In some respects, the Conrad family life revolved around motor cars, from the early hiring of a 1/2 h.p. De Dion, through purchasing various improved models, including a second-hand Model T Ford, to the eventual but inevitable Cadillac. [Having been in the motor car industry most of his life, Borys Conrad emphasizes the motoring adventures of his family. JC developed a very close relationship with Borys, with whom he indulged in pranks which had to be kept hidden from the less tolerant Mrs. Conrad. This unpretentious and often artless book contains anecdotes about trivial domestic pleasures and trials. With no illuminating insights into JC's works, it presents a picture of him very different from that of other biographers but one that will have to be taken into account hereafter.]

2489 "Conrad in Fashion," *TLS* (25 June 1970), pp. 673–74.

Ten books on JC, Borys Conrad, *My Father: Joseph Conrad* (1970), which gives an incomplete but lighter than usual portrait of JC; C. T. Watts (ed.), *Joseph Conrad's Letters to R. B. Cunninghame Graham* (1969), which includes some of JC's more important letters even if they do not illuminate his works; Dale B. J. Randall, *Joseph Conrad and Warrington Dawson* (1968), mainly a work of "local piety"; JC, *The Sisters* (1968), a high priced edition of JC's well known unfinished novel; Juliet McLauchlan, *Conrad: Nostromo* (1969), which emphasizes the richness and solidity of the novel studied; John A. Palmer, *Joseph Conrad's Fiction* (1968), a book containing such gross misunderstandings that its credibility is destroyed; Lawrence Graver, *Conrad's Short Fiction* (1969), perceptive but not very original; Stanton de Voren Hoffman, *Comedy and Form in the Fiction of Joseph Conrad* (1969), entirely too much about the small amount of comedy in JC's works; Robert F. Lee, *Conrad's Colonialism* (1969), which consists mainly of the author's own prejudices; and Theodore Ehrsam, *A Bibliography of Joseph Conrad* (1969), serves largely two purposes: (1) to demonstrate that the JC "critical-industrial complex" is scarcely intended for the common reader, "who may take up Conrad's works without examination, tenure or promotion in mind," and (2) to call attention to the great chasm between the author's works and the fashions of critics and reviewers.

2490 Cooper, Christopher. *Conrad and the Human Dilemma* (London: Chatto and Windus; New York: Barnes & Noble, 1970).

In the three main political novels, JC suggests an overall morality often very different from that of any one character. Using different techniques, he provides a stable morality for the entire "microcosmos" of the individual work of art, against which he measures the moralities of the characters. The central character of *The Secret Agent* is Winnie Verloc, but the "fourfold" structure of the novel (the police, the Foreign Embassy, Verloc's home, and the anarchical group which meets there) is unified by Verloc. As a character, Verloc is amoral: he fails completely to take other people into account. Stevie, the idiot, is the only character in the novel to have a complete, "worked-out" morality. After killing Verloc, Winnie, however "free," must fear society: she is the victim of both individuals and of society. All the characters center on the major trio, Stevie, his mother, and Winnie, all of whom are nonconformist and suffer, as a result, from a corrupt society.

In *Under Western Eyes*, JC uses the Professor to engage his reader with an absolute moral point of view. Razumov experiences all of the misfortunes of alienation, both physically and spiritually. As the central figure, he suffers from the misfortunes of environment and personal alienation, but his weakness lies basically in his morality, which takes into account only himself. So does Nostromo, in the novel of this name, also suffer spiritually and morally when his moral values become entirely confused. But each of these novels emphasizes the concept that only the denial of the self can bring moral wholeness and thus avoid pessimism.

2491 De Beer, Alan. "Conrad Questions," *TLS* (31 July 1970), p. 855.

Even writers of JC's eminence occasionally nod: when Richard Curle pointed out to JC [reported in Curle, *The Last Twelve Years of Joseph Conrad* (1928)] that in *Nostromo* Decoud did not have sufficient time to write his long letter to his sister, JC admitted that this was probably so, but added that "some people were always waiting to find one out in mistakes." [Preceded by John S. Lewis and Leonard Wayman, "Conrad Questions," 16 July 1970, and followed by Bernard Susser, "Conrad Questions," 7 August 1970, both in *Times Literary Supplement* (London).]

2492 Dowden, Wilfred A. *Joseph Conrad: The Imaged Style* (Nashville, Tennessee: Vanderbilt University Press, 1970).

It was JC's "constant concern to find the right word to produce the right image," and JC's conception of the function of imagery changed as he matured. [Both statements, made in Dowden's introduction, and true of every serious writer, are representative of many equally banal comments in his work.] All the early works display a simple, unambiguous use of imagery, although in these the novelist shows an increasing preoccupation with imagery as symbol. Many works contain controlling images—fog, mist, shadow, and moonlight in *Lord Jim*, silver in *Nostromo*, and snow in *Under Western Eyes*. To the end of his writing career, JC was preoccupied with "basic imagery as a means of developing various aspects of his fiction." [Dowden frequently fails to relate the overworked imagery he discusses to the larger meanings of the novels and stories. He reaches a qualified agreement with the achievement-and-decline theory of Guerard and Moser.]

2493 Eagleton, Terry. "Joseph Conrad and *Under Western Eyes*," *Exiles and Emigrés: Studies in Modern Literature* (London: Chatto and Windus; New York: Schocken Books, 1970), pp. 21–32.

As an emigré fleeing a lack of civilized order abroad, JC was able to survey English society from a broad perspective and grasp it in a complete pattern at a time when the indigenous English writers were fragmented and unable to "totalise" their culture. In *Under Western Eyes*, JC strives for a disinterested and impartial view of a violent episode of Russian revolutionary history by using an English observer. An antirevolutionary bias is discernible; the revolutionaries' traits are not mollified by the same understanding given the antirevolutionaries. Razumov is put in a position to judge the revolutionaries. By means of a technique of double detachment (both the narrator and Razumov are politically disengaged) the limitations of decent English empiricism can be satirized in its inability to comprehend passionate experience but, on the other hand, there is no succumbing to Russian cynicism and corrosive skepticism. There is, indeed, a "treble-detachment," for the novel, at the climax, detaches itself from the narrator. Razumov is portrayed as being more intense and perceptive than the narrator, but since he has the same political bias as the narrator he merely confirms, at a more profound level, the English conservative attitudes. This novel is unable to transcend English assumptions and gain a vantage point from which to probe or fully escape the conventions and habits of its own culture.

2494 "Eastern Europe Between the Habsburgs and the Russians," *TLS* (9 April 1970), pp. 374–75.

Charles Quénet, during the reign of Emperor Nicholas of Russia, wrote critically of the times: "Nous faisons lacune dans l'ordre intellectuel." Seventy years later, in "Autocracy and War," JC made much the same point, charging the despotic Russian aristocracy—a class without a human rationale and hence without origins and evolutionary historical meaning—with the destruction of the mind of the country. JC believed at the time, 1905, that tyrannic aristocracy had run its course. No historian has better envisioned the tragic cost that that class exacted, but the new Communist aristocracy has proved JC wrong.

2495 Edwards, Paul. "The Narrator's Voice in 'Goody Blake and Harry Gill,'" *English,* XIX (Spring 1970), pp. 13–17.

Wordsworth's problem in "The Thorn" is his unconvincing mixture of voices, one consciously "poetic" and the other that of an elderly but not very clever retired seaman who wants to describe his feelings but can't quite remain on his subject. The latter is perhaps an ancestor of Marlow in "Heart of Darkness," which can be understood only as dramatic monologue. Wordsworth had in mind problems of language which JC later examined—the search for a "rhetoric of inarticulacy," as he clearly reveals in his note on "The Thorn."

2496 Emmett, V. J., Jr. "'Youth': Its Place in Conrad's Oeuvre," *Connecticut Review,* IX (October 1970), pp. 49–58.

Various circumstances—a common narrator, chronology, and publishing plans—suggest that a "loose kind of unity" exists among "Youth," "Heart of Darkness," and *Lord Jim*; and thematic links imply a progress from the first story to the other two. Marlow, narrating "Youth," a story of his passage to maturity, prepares the way for the narrator of "Heart of Darkness" and *Jim*, whose secular interpretation of the world is formed in "Youth." In this early story, Marlow learns that the natural world is indifferent and unconsciously hostile to human nature. This knowledge derives from the sinking *Judea*, the loss of which, with its rising and falling action, assumes the essential form of a five-act tragic drama. It represents humanity struggling to survive in JC's cosmos, and it is a story of a failure without a cause. On the other hand, Marlow's growth is epic, with "faint overtones of symbolic death and rebirth." He learns to stop thinking romantically of his ego, but he also enacts the basic gestures of carrying out one's duties and obligations. The *Judea* story and the initiation of the young hero are intertwined; his story is the ship's and the crew's story. And if the ship is lost, Marlow reaches his Eastern destination with difficulty but under his command. His earned integrity is a contrast with Jim and Kurtz, whose stories he later tells. Yet, since the *Judea*'s bad ending proportionally outweighs Marlow's good end, a triumph is denied. The preponderance of one fact over the lesser success is Marlow's hard lesson.

2497 Faatz, Anita J. "An Illusion of the Experience of Change in Conrad's 'Secret Sharer,'" *Journal of the Otto Rank Association*, V (June 1970), pp. 31–37.

"The Secret Sharer" illustrates the experience of change in the authentic portrayal of growth in the course of which a young man, the new captain of a ship, takes at the end, in five short days, full command of himself, his ship, and his crew, but not until he has risked his ship, his life, and the lives of others. This story illustrates Otto Rank's conception of the artist, who is an individual of "richer emotion, more intense conflict, and heightened consciousness." But the artist, soon learning that this abundance cannot be lived out in real life, consequently transforms, with his creative personality, the chaos of his inner life into forms that convey the inner meanings. Art, unlike life, selects and heightens and shapes truths that are hidden in the "clutter" of everyday living. It is perhaps best not to analyze too closely the meaning of such a story, but instead to yield oneself to the "shimmering ambiguity" of the whole, which then bewitches us. Also, this story includes the mythical belief developed by Jung, that every man in order to grow must somehow be tested, must risk his life in order to gain it.

2498 Fitzrandolph, I. M. "James on Conrad: A Footnote to 'Conrad Interviews,' No. 2: James Walter Smith," *CON*, III, No. 1 (1970–71), p. 38.

Ford Madox Ford's *Thus to Revisit* provides a plausible source for the recollections of the journalist James Walter Smith about Henry James's reaction to JC's Marlow. [Dale B. J. Randall posed the question in "Conrad Interviews: No. 2: James Walter Smith," *Conradiana*, II, No. 2 (Winter 1969–70), p. 87, 92.]

2499 Furst, Henry. "Joseph Conrad: Studio" (Joseph Conrad: A Study), *Il Meglio di Henry Furst* (The Best of Henry Furst), ed. by Orsola Nemi (Milan: Longanesi, 1970), pp. 74–111.

[Reprints in a slightly revised form two articles originally published in *L'Idea Nazionale* (19 April and 12 August 1924).] [In Italian.]

2500 Gallagher, Michael P. "*The Nigger of the Narcissus*: Two Worlds of Perspective," *CON*, III, No. 1 (1969–70), pp. 51–60.

Unlike *Lord Jim* with its relativistic network of time-shifts and converging evidence, *The Nigger of the Narcissus* is not fully a perspectivist work. It represents, though, a transition between Victorian and modern fiction, "between omniscient narration" and "perspectivist suggestion" of hidden horizons. It is clearly intended to carry "reverberations" of meaning beyond the events described, to present an image of the human condition. The action of the novel lies in the conflict in the crew between the two worlds of experience, the "daylight world of duty and order" best symbolized by old Singleton and the "nightmare" world of the irrational and the unknown symbolized by James Wait. Ultimately, Wait becomes the crew's point of entry into "an ambiguous world of multiperspectival imaginings and fictions"; Wait is a "mirror" for the crew of the *Narcissus*, revealing a darkness in both themselves and in human life as a whole. In the novel, the two worlds are inextricably mixed, and the Negro is the chief catalyst for the confusion which results. The action of the novel, an education in a perspective other than that of the ordinary living, is both hard to find and hard to bear. The story is, for the most part, told in the Victorian manner, but as a novel about people experiencing a double perspective, people living and working in a ship's community while aware for a time of another and darker vision of themselves, it is modern.

2501 Garmon, Gerald M. "'Conrad, Our Contemporary': The MLA Seminar," *CON*, III, No. 1 (1970–71), pp. 129–32.

At the first annual JC seminar at the 1970 convention of the Modern Language Association in New York City, a number of well known JC scholars made important comments about JC and his writings. Adam Gillon believes that it is JC's appeal to the present that accounts for the great amount of critical writing about him, but he urges scholars to go back from "critiques on critiques" to the influence on JC of such authors as Cooper, Balzac, Shakespeare, Dostoevski, Dickens, Maupassant, James, Turgenev, and Flaubert. Frederick Karl, who is editing JC's letters, believes that the newly found letters will not substantially alter our ideas of JC's personality, but will add information about several specific incidents in his life and will also establish the text of the letters. Zdzislaw Najder, now in the process of compiling the complete works of JC in Polish, points out that JC, with a background of the landed gentry, is difficult to classify politically; but it is known that he was opposed to any kind of democracy based on material wealth, urban civilization, all kinds of political tyranny, the bourgeoisie, capitalism, and mercantilism. Kenneth Newell reveals the fact that even if many of

JC's manuscripts are readily available, little use has been made of them by scholars. Bruce Harkness is concerned about the lack of teaching Conrad, thinking students and young instructors see him as a racist. Ian Watt believes that *The Secret Agent* reflects much of the negativism of current thought, that this novel, often believed to be satirical, has been shown to contain JC's view accurately.

2502 Gilbert, Elliot L. *The Good Kipling: Studies in the Short Story* (Athens: Ohio University, 1970), pp. 112, 121, 190n, 197–98.

Kipling and JC were similar in several ways, but in different degrees: both were foreigners in England; for both, the English language was a second tongue; both possessed "stylistic brilliance and inventiveness and a concern for what sometimes seems pure verbal display"; both utilized similar subject matter; both dealt seriously with "sensational materials"; and both attempted to establish moral and ethical codes in their fiction. JC believed in the possibility of "human response" to the "absurd" universe, and in this belief he, unlike Hardy, shared a philosophical position closer to Kipling's than did most serious writers of the time. But however much alike the two writers were in doctrinal terms, they differed on at least one important issue: whereas JC's response to the challenge presented by life was basically an "aristocratic" one Kipling's was "largely egalitarian."

2503 Goodin, George. "The Personal and the Political in *Under Western Eyes*," *NCF, XXV* (December 1970), pp. 327–42.

In *Under Western Eyes*, JC "uses character, action, and imagery to suggest the political realities underlying Russian life, and . . . this political content figures forth the moral realities he found in human life itself." In order to connect the background to the action, JC takes a young man with an unformed character and places him in a situation "so charged with politics" that ordinary moral choices which form his mature character are also political choices. The political influence on Razumov's character development is best seen through the decisions he makes: from neutrality he moves to the position of considering alternatives, and eventually to rejecting revolution; but in rejecting revolution he chooses the political opposite, thus acting to protect his future freedom of action and to avoid overchoosing—and overchoosing builds a strong character by diminishing the number of actions it is capable of. To be a person, Razumov needs love, and Natalia is a way of fulfilling this need. The love of Natalia and the "true Razumov" results from the relation of Victor Haldin to each of them, and Haldin is thus a kind of second self to each one. When Razumov confesses to Natalia, his act is a personal triumph over politics, but one made possible only by politics. As long as Razumov chooses the freedom which prudently protects his future, he is not free; when he sacrifices his future and his safety, he is free.

2504 Guérin, Yves. "Huit lettres inédites de Joseph Conrad à Robert d'Humières, traducteur du *Nigger of the Narcissus* en français" (Eight unpublished letters by Joseph Conrad to Robert d'Humières, translator of *The Nigger of the Narcissus* into French), *Revue de Littérature Comparée*, XLV (July–September 1970), pp. 367–92.

Robert d'Humières, an active writer and translator who flourished in France between 1890 and 1914, translated *The Nigger of the Narcissus* for the journal *Correspondent*, which published it in four installments on 25 August 1909, 10 September 1909, 25 September 1909, and 10 October 1909. In 1910, the translation appeared in a single volume published by Mercure de France. The eight letters of JC to d'Humières reveal JC's ungrammatical though often idiomatic French, his financial anxiety, his insecurity, and his justified concern about the censorship exercised by the *Correspondent* on d'Humières' translation. A comparison of *Nigger* and Flaubert's *Salammbô* reveals the influence of the latter, particularly on JC's handling of the description of the sailors. [The eight letters are reproduced here in printed form.] [In French.]

2505 Haltrecht, Michael. "Characterization, Symbol, and Theme in Conrad's *Nostromo* and *The Secret Agent*," *DAI*, XXXI (1970), 2385A. Unpublished dissertation, Emory University, 1970.

2506 Hay, Eloise Knapp. "Joseph Conrad," *Contemporary Literature*, XI (Summer 1970), pp. 435–48.

The "queer friendship" with Warrington Dawson illuminates several important motifs in JC's development: his passion for a "new form" in the novel was not Ford Madox Ford's but his own, the composition of *Chance* developed under Dawson's influence, Dawson served as the model for Blunt in *The Arrow of Gold*, and 1913 seems to be a more crucial beginning for the decline of the friendship of the two men than 1919 (Randall's date). Watts's collection of letters indicates that JC must have noted that Graham's family history and nobility, like his own, were a "dead letter" which still made more sense, in the year of his first return to Poland after his marriage twenty years earlier than most current history. JC's defense of Kipling's artistry is still unclear; unlike Wilde, Ford, Shaw, and Galsworthy, who appealed chiefly to the English upper classes, Kipling and JC wrote for the entire English nation. Two of JC's letters, his so-called "peace and brotherhood letter" of 1899 to

Cunninghame Graham and his "egoism and altruism" letter of 1901
to the *New York Times*, show how much more profound JC was in
writing to his friend than to the newspapers. [Rev. of B. J. Randall,
Joseph Conrad and Warrington Dawson: The Record of a Friendship
(1968); C. T. Watts, *Joseph Conrad's Letters to R. B. Cunninghame
Graham* (1969); John A. Palmer, *Joseph Conrad's Fiction: A Study in
Literary Growth* (1968); and Lawrence Graver, *Conrad's Short Fiction*
(1969). Much more than a review, this article supplies new
information in abundance about JC and his work.]

2507 Hepburn, James. *Letters of Arnold Bennett*, Vol III: *1916–1931*
(London: Oxford University, 1970), pp. 4, 17, 52, 69, 86, 135, 141,
152, 224.

Arnold Bennett thought JC's *Victory* not at all "first-rate
Conrad," but considered *Chance* among his best works. He would
have liked to chat with JC about Hugh Walpole's theories, thinking
they would not agree. About 1923, Bennett, who had not seen JC very
often for a few years, found him on one occasion "simply
magnificent."

2508 Herling-Grudzinski, Gustaw. "Under Conrad's Eyes," *Kultura
Essays*, ed. by Leopold Tyrmand (New York: Free Press in
cooperation with The State University at Albany, 1970), pp. 177–
91.

Under Western Eyes has a serious artistic flaw, centering in five
Conradian voices. The first voice is that of JC the Pole, which
vehemently denies Russia's history and literature. The second voice
is that of JC, the Englishman who takes up arms against Russian
tyranny and who presents himself as public defender of English
society. The third voice is that of JC, the skeptical conservative who
is terrified by the ideas that the Russian terrorists are the product of
their own time and place. The fourth voice is that of JC, the tragic
pessimist for whom life is but a jungle and who scorns any
desperation as an answer to tyranny. The last voice is that of JC, the
stern moralist who condemns Razumov. In the first two voices, the
interpreter predominates. In the third voice, the conviction of
utopianism takes on Russian attributes. The last two voices reveal
JC's philosophy of life, and the flaw in Razumov's story enters here:
JC fails to use Russia as the background for the story and instead
treats it as the main subject. In this sense, the interpreter of the first
voice overcomes the writer himself, and the book becomes nothing
more than an historically topical story. Had JC not meant the novel
to be a handbook of Russian psychology, it would have been a
successful piece of literature, but because the first voice
predominates, only JC sees the profound and the immutable; his

Western audience sees only the superficial and transitory. The result is a Polish atavism passing through an English filter.

2509 Hervouet, Yves. "Conrad and Anatole France," *Ariel*, I (January 1970), pp. 84–99.

For *Nostromo* (1904), JC drew from Anatole France's *L'Anneau D'Améthyste* (1899) for his view of the importance of work, for the characterization of Pedrito Montero, and for his treatment of the love scene between Nostromo and Giselle. Both France and JC had in common a distrust of thought because it corrodes belief. JC found inspiration in France when, in 1904, he was writing his essay on Maupassant, whom both greatly admired, and he also found a model in France's criticism. JC "borrowed" boldly several passages and used many phrases from France. The latter's influence is seen in *Chance*, "The Planter of Malata," and *The Arrow of Gold*, as well as in several other places. And JC's vision of the universe was strikingly similar to that of France. France had, indeed, a considerable intellectual influence on JC and helped to shape some of his ideas on life and human nature.

2510 Hosillos, Lucila. "A Reliable Narrator: Conrad's Distance and Effects Through Marlow," *Diliman Review*, XVIII (April 1970), pp. 154–72.

In "Youth," "Heart of Darkness," and *Lord Jim*, JC uses Marlow to convey the effects he intends to invoke in his reader, the sense of bewilderment in life through a sensitive person able to contemplate his own reaction to "life situations" to render human existence explicable. In "Youth," Marlow is a reliable narrator: he fuses narrator and author, he imparts no sentimental note in spite of the nostalgia, and he achieves distance from his material by means of his ironic tone. In "Heart of Darkness," Marlow's reliability is qualified: JC solves the problem of distance and objectivity, though, by having Marlow subscribe to Kurtz's values and ideals, which are his own. JC's distance from us, through Kurtz and Marlow, draws us into involvement with the experience. At the end, Kurtz's norms are identifiable with JC's but only after they have been qualified by Marlow. *Lord Jim* reveals JC's greater artistic maturity through his more complex use of the Marlow device. Although Marlow is a necessary narrator, he has to maintain distance from Jim for his own objectivity of judgment. At the end, Jim rejects the code of the "craft" to embrace a larger universal code for the individual. But Marlow is uncertain, and herein lie his limitations as a reliable narrator. But however unreliable he may be, he is necessary to provide logical coherence for the reader.

2511 Howarth, Herbert. "The Meaning of Conrad's *The Rover*," *Southern Review*, N.S., VI (July 1970), pp. 682–97.

In his last completed novel, JC makes lawlessness the "natural mode of a clean life," despite his previous disgust for killers. Through Peyrol, he releases the primitivism of his own nature which he had heretofore repressed. In *The Rover*, however, JC discriminates between Peyrol's vital lawlessness and the politicians' "anti-vital" lawlessness. The politicans are brutal in the name of humanity; whereas Peyrol is honest. JC deplores killing for "Principles" but condones killing "in heat and vigor." Implicit in the contrast between the hunchback and Scevola is JC's view that even if life is not to be changed, its inequities are not to be hated. Love is born of action (e.g., the relationship of Peyrol and Michel), even of fighting (e.g., Peyrol and Lieutenant Réal), although "fraternity" is perhaps a better word than love. Peyrol, however, having known fraternity and passion, must come to know sentiment, and he finally makes his life a kind of sentimental gift to Arlette. In *The Rover*, JC finds life difficult but "lustrous" ; he teaches "how to answer the symptoms of age and die well" ; and he finishes the "campaigns of his writing life" with an act of "perfect professionalism." Peyrol dies in his last race "rejoicing in the variety of his powers and their coordination," "beautiful equivalents of the power and suffering" with which JC executes the novel.

2512 Huntley, H. Robert. *The Alien Protagonist of Ford Madox Ford* (Chapel Hill: University of North Carolina Press, 1970), pp. 13, 19–20, 22, 24–25, 30–31, 51–60, 66–68, 75–76, 84, 106, 113, 127, 137, 155, 169, 170, 174, 178.

In Edwardian England, when many people were assured of the benefits of "Progress," a few like Ford Madox Ford and JC saw the "dark side" of the situation as well, and while John Davidson, Kipling, and Wells played into the hands of the jingoists, others—like Bennett, George Moore, Ford, and JC—were shocked at the numerous expressions of national insularity. In *The Inheritors*, Ford and JC allegorized the increasingly technocratic society of the time; this novel belongs to the dying genre of the evolutionary romance. Both novelists, though, were aware of the Nietzschean implications of *Inheritors*, which Ford in later years dismissed as hack work despite JC's insistence that it was "a damn good book." Speaking for Ford, Henry James, and himself, JC suggested that the contemporary Edwardian novelist had become of necessity a historian. Stevenson's psychological portrait of power politics in *Prince Otto* (1885) and the symbolic interplay between states of mind and natural settings suggests JC's better short fiction. A new Edwardian emphasis on irrational motivation is what ultimately lies between the "network of farce and tragedy" in JC's *The Secret Agent*, for which Ford apparently supplied the central circumstances.

2513 Inniss, Kenneth. "Conrad's Native Girl: Some Social Questions," *Pacific Coast Philology*, V (April 1970), pp. 39–45.

The native girl, who appears early and late in JC's fiction (in addition to a sketch of an "Eastern" girl drawn while JC was completing his first novel), Nina Almayer of *Almayer's Folly*, Aissa of *An Outcast of the Islands*, Jewel of *Lord Jim*, Alice Jacobus of "A Smile of Fortune," and Lena of *Victory*, is "compounded" of the kind of wish-fulfillment evident in the early sketch and of some "anxiety at the threat to self and social order which resides in her appeal." In JC's world, a native carries a "taboo" which no one breaks with impunity; JC worked, perhaps somewhat consciously, "within the terms of a prevailing racial mythology which met the subliminal expectations of his adopted culture," keeping the imagined native an outsider. However much the native girl may appeal, even ambivalently, because of her "otherness," the pressure of tradition helped to enforce in JC a "grim statute against miscegenation."

2514 Irvine, Peter L. "The 'Witness' Point of View in Fiction," *South Atlantic Quarterly*, LXIX (Spring 1970), pp. 217–25.

An effective narrative device in fiction, that of the witness, which enables the person to grow to maturity because of his story, is seen in Welty's "Why I Live at the P. O.," Wescott's *The Pilgrim Hawk*, some of Browning's dialogues, *Moby Dick*, *The Good Soldier*, *The Great Gatsby*, and *All the King's Men*. JC's *Lord Jim* and "Heart of Darkness," two works of this kind, raise the question as to who the central character is. The most evident link among such works rests in the romantic temperament of the witness: Nick, Marlow, Jack Burden, Ishmael, and John Dowell all appear complex personalities near the end of their narratives. In each instance, this complexity has grown and shifted during the novel, and all are careful to let the reader know that their perspective is unique. Even at the end, narrator and reader have difficulty in fixing the central figure's total reality into the lines of the narrative. The hero's very existence belies the normal life. What is affirmed is the power and validity of the romantic dream as a means whereby fairly normal people are transfigured. This form of narrative is very flexible and fruitful. Later users of this technique in fiction are indebted to Fitzgerald and JC.

2515 "Jessie Conrad, Harold Frederic and Kate Lyons: An Unpublished Letter," *CON*, III, No. 1 (1970–71), pp. 6, 8.

[Publishes for the first time a letter of 28 April 1935 from Mrs. Jessie Conrad to Paul Haines, about Harold Frederic and Kate Lyons.]

2516 Johnson, Bruce. "Names, Naming, and the 'Inscrutable' in Conrad's 'Heart of Darkness,'" *TSLL,* XII (Winter 1970), pp. 675–88.

In "Heart of Darkness," Marlow spends much of his time trying to read a message which is no longer legible; the symbols of nature are inscrutable, and language is practically useless in gathering meaning from his surroundings. For Marlow, names often betray the difficulty of using them. Everything associated with the natives is an unreadable symbol to him, and one of the chief oppositions in the story is between nature, which can neither talk nor hear, and Kurtz, who is the archetypal talker. Speech is the only proper response to nature and to the essentially preverbal character of experience: it is Kurtz's achievement. His last act of naming, "The horror!" comes when he has shaken off all acquired values. Marlow discovers that Kurtz has become an "unchallenged namer and definition-giver," and Kurtz's "The horror!" is the statement of a man who knows that he himself is the myth-maker. In his lie to Kurtz's Intended, Marlow intimates that he has moved on to a fuller appreciation of Kurtz and that this lie is his first "almost intentional" attempt to create myth in the way Kurtz had.

2517 Johnston, John H. "*The Secret Agent* and *Under Western Eyes*: Conrad's Two Political Novels," *West Virginia University Philological Papers,* XVII (June 1970), pp. 57–71.

The Secret Agent and *Under Western Eyes* are unique among JC's fourteen completed novels in that they lie totally outside the physical and social world established by the other novels and also in that they are both political novels based on contemporary political events. Both *Agent* and *Eyes* reflect an extremely conservative political outlook. *Eyes* has in common with *Agent* the central and precipitating act, the assassination of de P—, and the employment of satire in portraying a set of characters who are antipathetic and opposed to a group of sympathetic characters. For to have some tragic weight and effect beyond mere caricature, JC has to establish two conflicting centers of interest: one of naive domestic innocence, which is destroyed by the other center, that of "cynical intrigue, senseless revolutionary action, and irresponsible force." The political problem of autocracy and revolution and the more personal problem of trust and betrayal are brought together in *Eyes*; the two themes are more carefully handled than the two similar themes in *Agent.* The moral discovery of Razumov is too basic and too universal to bear any suggestion of ironic sideplay. Even if JC's basic political views remain unchanged from *Agent* to *Eyes*, in the later novel he discriminates among individual personalities and motives, a concession which is, at the same time, a recognition of the shortcomings of the earlier novel and of his dogmatic and illiberal political views.

2518 Karl, Frederick R. "Joseph Conrad's Letters to the Sandersons," *Yale University Library Gazette*, XLV (July 1970), pp. 1–11.

The letters to the Sandersons are important because they reflect the early years of JC's writing career, describe his routine life, and imply his desire for a life uncomplicated by economic worries. Edward Lancelot (Ted) Sanderson met JC aboard the *Torrens* in 1893, and the two became friends. JC visited Sanderson and Galsworthy at Elstree, where the former was an assistant master and later headmaster. The letters reflect JC's admiration for Sanderson, who possibly represented for the elder man the type of Englishman he would have liked to be.

2519 Karl, Frederick R. "Three Conrad Letters in the Edith Wharton Papers," *Yale University Library Gazette*, XLIV (January 1970), pp. 148–51.

JC's ALS to Henry James, "Très cher Maître," 24 July 1925, maintains a friendly if not confidential tone, as if overlooking James's too temperate review of *Chance*, and agrees "to try to do" a piece for *The Book of the Homeless*, which Edith Wharton is editing. He submitted the essay, which was printed. In one ALS to Wharton, 24 December 1912, JC feels fascination and fright at the prospect of translating into French "The Secret Sharer," "so particularly English," but is willing to attempt it if he somehow gets a "mere mot-à-mot rendering." This plan was not realized. In another ALS, 1 October 1917, JC thanks Wharton for a presentation copy of *Summer*, praising it, but mechanically. JC thought, perhaps, *Summer* too little "worked," as James thought *Chance* too much so.

2520 Kitonga, Ellen M. "Conrad's Image of African and Colonizer in 'Heart of Darkness,'" *Busara* (Nairobi), III, No. 2 (1970), pp. 33–35.

Marlow's attitude toward the Africans in "Heart of Darkness" changes as he moves towards self-discovery, but from the beginning he realizes the basic humanity of these people who have been branded as enemies or criminals "solely for the sake of exploitation." With the death of the helmsman, Marlow no longer accepts the African as a resourceful worker, but views him as a "fellow mortal." Later, JC presents the African as a natural savage, and thus as a foil to Kurtz. This unrealistic portrait, however, is contrasted with the less flattering, realistic picture of the African's "civilizers." Those who are civilized remain oblivious to the horrifying realities they create. Hope lies, finally, in the ability of the individual to come to terms with his own savagery and to "present the heart of darkness to others that they too might face and conquer it."

2521 Korg, Jacob. "Recent Books: British Fiction," *NCF*, XXV (December 1970), pp. 377–79.

In *The English Novel from Dickens to Lawrence* (1970), Raymond Williams directly attacks the critics' "'endless reduction of deliberately created realities'" in JC "'to analogues, symbolic circumstances, abstract situations'" and returns the novelist to "specific realities," thereby treating his works concretely and emphasizing the difference "between creative seriousness and a now fashionable game." [A timely appeal to treat JC as he deserves to be considered.]

2522 Kronsky, Betty J. "Joseph Conrad: A Psychoanalytic Biography," *Literature and Psychology*, XX, No. 1 (1970), pp. 37–41.

Bernard C. Meyer, M.D., illustrates in his book *Joseph Conrad: A Psychoanalytic Biography* (1967), the dangers of a purely psychological view of art. Since statements about JC's characters as referring to the author himself are excessive, there is no way to distinguish good art from bad art. The medical psychoanalyst is most at home when discussing psychopathology; Dr. Meyer is more effective when writing, for example, about JC's suicidal impulses, his psychosomatic disorders, and his serious nervous breakdown in 1910—about JC's complex personality—than when writing about his works. But the mystery of JC's personality will send the reader to the works with a new sensitivity to the personal references there.

2523 Lafferty, William Lewis. "Moral Problems in the Short Fiction of Joseph Conrad," *DAI*, XXX (March 1970), 3910A. Unpublished dissertation, University of Wisconsin, 1969.

2524 Lewis, John S. "Conrad: A Son on His Father," *ELT*, XIII, No. 3 (1970), pp. 246–47.

In his son's eyes, JC's humor, unlike that of JC's biographer, Jocelyn Baines, seemed "spontaneous and light-hearted." JC remained calm in sudden emergencies. [Borys Conrad adds little to what is already known about JC and his life and works, but his portrait is most distinct of the years preceding World War I, the time of JC's greatest achievements. He does, though, make JC's character "more distinct" than his mother's books did.] [Rev. of Borys Conrad, *My Father: Joseph Conrad* (1970).]

2525 Lewis, John S. "A Conrad Reprint: *The Sisters*," *ELT*, XIII, No. 3 (1970), pp. 245–46.

JC's unfinished novel, *The Sisters*, put aside in 1896, seems to be "a search for precision of utterance." JC may have written *The Arrow of Gold* "as an act of contrition" for having abandoned *The Sisters* twenty years earlier. The question of his intentions for completing the novel is "unanswerable." [Rev. of *The Sisters*, ed. by Ugo Mursia (Milan: Mursia, 1968).]

2526 Lewis, John S., and Leonard Wayman. "Conrad Questions," *TLS* (16 July 1970), p. 775.

[In letters to the editor, Lewis provides evidence that JC wrote, in the manuscript of *Nostromo*, "factious" and "bribon" (words which had been previously questioned [Lewis, "*Nostromo*," 1969]), leaving off the accent mark in the Spanish word "bribón." Wayman asks how Singleton in *The Nigger of the Narcissus*, who was unable to sign his name, could read *Pelham*, even by "spelling through" it "with slow labour" ; "Is it possible to be able to read a novel . . . without being literate enough to write your own name?" (For replies, see Alan De Beer, "Conrad Questions," 31 July 1970, and Bernard Susser, "Conrad Questions," 7 August 1970).]

2527 Lincoln, Kenneth Robert. "Joseph Conrad: The Comedy of Perception," *DAI*, XXX (1970), 3014A. Unpublished dissertation, Indiana University, 1969.

2528 Markovic, Vida E. "Jim," *The Changing Face: Disintegration of Personality in the Twentieth-Century British Novel, 1900–1950* (Carbondale and Edwardsville: Southern Illinois University Press, 1970), pp. 1–18, passim.

In *Lord Jim*, no one can understand the central figure because he does not understand himself; living in a world of dreams, he tries, by violence, to adapt the world of reality to it. Since he has no courage to look into himself and to admit the existence of a "dark side" to his personality, there is a profound gap in his being, even though his existence depends on internal continuity. Since Jim ignores the elementary principle of the "tragic necessity of self-knowledge," he is eventually overtaken by his own darker self. Being divided thus against oneself is, according to JC, universal: in treating Jim, JC does not separate him from the rest of mankind and watch him as apart; rather, he considers him "one of us," and by identifying himself with him, the author begins to understand him. Jim's entire life is a prolonged attempt to conceal himself from himself, and his ultimate refusal to accept himself is tantamount to a rejection of life, to an acceptance of death. But with Jim, death is a triumph after failure in life: death, his supreme opportunity, comes to him "veiled," but he recognizes it and follows it. Like Jim, all people contain both constructive, life-giving urges and destructive, negative ones; but JC goes below this obvious commonplace to realize that the irrational pervades every human being. For JC, human destiny is preordained in consciousness and always remains at the mercy of consciousness; and each person's destiny is determined by an awareness of whether or not one has lived up to its standards.

2529 Martin, Graham. "Manuscript Letters," *TLS* (2 April 1970), p. 362.

The Victoria and Albert Museum holds a collection of manuscript letters (catalogue no. RC/EE3) which includes letters from JC, with a comment on Wilfrid Blunt's diaries.

2530 Maxwell, J. C. "Mr. Stephens on 'Heart of Darkness,'" *EIC*, XX (January 1970), pp. 118-19.

[Refutes R. C. Stephens's claim that Marlow in "Heart of Darkness" does not tell everything about the "vileness of the Congo set-up" but that he "tells enough." A reply to R. C. Stephens, "Mr. Stephens on 'Heart of Darkness,'" *Essays in Criticism*, XIX (October 1969), pp. 463-66.

2531 McDowell, Frederick P. W. "Joseph Conrad: Current Criticism and the 'Achievement and Decline' Question," *JML*, I (second issue 1970-71), pp. 261-72.

The theory that JC underwent a period of achievement followed by one of decline, the "most pressing" issue confronting both scholars and readers at the present time, is accepted by Lawrence Graver in *Conrad's Short Fiction* (1969) and challenged by John A. Palmer in *Joseph Conrad's Fiction: A Study in Literary Growth* (1968), the latter of whom insists that JC's development was continuous throughout his career. Although there is no doubt of JC's "achievement and stature," the existence and the extent of his so-called decline remain to be determined. [An essay-review, considering two lesser books on JC, loosely held together by the "achievement and decline" theme.]

2532 McLauchlan, Juliet. "Studies in English Literature," *TLS* (9 July 1970), p. 750.

[This letter to the editor adds nothing new about JC, but it recognizes Tony Tanner's book, *Conrad: Lord Jim*, 1963, as a "definitive assessment" of *Jim*.]

2533 Mensforth, Douglas L. *Lord Jim (Conrad)*, (Oxford: Basil Blackwell [Notes on English Literature], 1970).

In *Lord Jim*, JC's technique of ignoring chronology and of concentrating upon the apparently trivial or irrelevant as an index of significance is a part of the general confusion of the accepted, which is a theme in the novel, part of the general departure from normality, which is a feature of Jim's character. It is useful also as a technique of suspense, and it seems to redirect the reader's suspense and attention away from the obvious features towards the meaning or towards the manner of an incident. JC's technique serves, too, to leave Jim at the end of the novel as cut off from the world, from the society around him, considering himself a being apart, whereas he is in fact "one of us." A principal method of universalizing the meaning of Jim is to set him in situations where he is compared and contrasted with others who are expressions of his own characteristics writ large, made gross, carried to the ultimate end, as with Chester and Brown. Several important notions serve as standards, as principles by which the reader judges the characters and their actions: isolation and community, individualism and solidarity, duty and imagination of the individual. [Contains materials for teaching the novel, but is worthy of some attention for specialists in JC.]

2534 Michel, Laurence. "Conrad: Romance and Tragedy," *The Thing Contained: Theory of the Tragic* (Bloomington: Indiana University Press, 1970), pp. 86–106.

JC was a Romantic with a vision of evil who could write novels in English about "the predicament of the modern European." In *Lord Jim*, JC's dream of romantic sentiment is confronted by the fact of tragic logic and has acquiesced in it; the dialectics of reality-illusion and good-evil are amorphous conceptualizations, each element of a pair difficult to delimit, but each necessary for the other. Tragedy is consummated when the dream of innocence is confronted by the fact of guilt and acquiesces therein. *Jim* is a paradigm of this action. JC utilizes what is, after the Dostoevskian double, perhaps his most important contribution to the tragic method, the idea of the author as hero. JC is among those who listen to Marlow's tale and the only listener "who was ever to hear the last word of the story." Jim's purpose, his "dream of innocence," egoism, came out in Gentleman Brown. Jim's real test was that confrontation with Brown, in which his perception was the tragic one that "altruism is egoism, egotism, solipsism; that excessive philanthropy is misanthropy; that truth is falsehood." Jim was "romantically true to his own self, tragically false to all men."

2535 Miller, J. Hillis. "The Interpretation of *Lord Jim*," *The Interpretation of Narrative*, ed. by Morton W. Bloomfield (Cambridge, Massachusetts: Harvard University Press [Harvard English Studies], 1970), pp. 211–28.

Lord Jim has no center, no origin, no end; it has no kernel. The tale lacks an ostensible meaning beyond the outward developing tale. It is not modelled on the cosmos or "an externally existing divine center," and it has no structural principle that will permit the reader to interpret and to understand the universe of the novel. Since Jim threatens society's belief in a sovereign power, one of Marlow's main purposes is to find the means for explaining Jim's action in terms of this power. One way he tries to do this is by discovering any extenuating circumstances and by suggesting that Jim is the victim of the dark powers. The problem here actually has no acceptable answer. Not only does Marlow fail to find a solution for Jim's action, but the reader also inevitably fails to do so as well because of the ending of the novel, because of the point of view, because of Stein's cryptic advice, and because of the complex use of language. [One of the most perceptive essays to appear on *Lord Jim*.]

2536 Miller, J. Hillis. *Thomas Hardy: Distance and Desire* (Cambridge, Massachusetts: Belknap Press, Harvard University Press, 1970), pp. 23, 29, 31–32.

Both Hardy and JC, as in *Far From the Madding Crowd* and *Victory*, utilize a theme which has grimly comic aspects: the story of a man who, having accidentally or purposely held himself apart from other men and women, is in spite of his aloofness led into involvement and suffering (Boldworth and Heyst): safety cannot be surely found even in passivity. Since all ways of living are "modifications of the periodically given human situation, which is to be inextricably involved in the world," writing novels was for both Hardy and JC a "strategy" for dealing with the situations in which they found themselves. Neither one was able to remain a silent, detached spectator of life because "spectatorship" is a mode of involvement in which the watcher is still vulnerable to the attractions of the world; and neither one chose to leave the world altogether, to choose death: instead, both chose to cover sheets of paper with words, thus remaining alive.

2537 Mitchell, Mary Virginia. "Joseph Conrad and 19th Century Aesthetic Tradition," *DA,* XXXI (1970–71), 1235A. Unpublished dissertation, University of Minnesota, 1969.

2538 "Morals Matter," *TLS* (11 September 1970), p. 993.

[Rev. of Christopher Cooper, *Conrad and the Human Dilemma* (1970). Cooper's concern is with what is most fundamental in *The Secret Agent, Under Western Eyes,* and *Nostromo,* "the exploration of moral dilemmas" and a firm concern for moral judgments, and includes a serious consideration of JC's characters and techniques.]

2539 Mroczkowski, Przemyslaw. *Conradian Commentaries* (Krakow: Nakladem Uniwersytetu Jagiellonskiego, 1970).

The "neat" scheme of the introduction of "The Lagoon," a short voyage and the lagoon itself, serves as both a physical and a metaphorical frame. The actual telling of the story contains the European receiver's skepticism and the romantic attitude of the speaker and of the protagonist in his tale. Contrasted with the telling is the sequence of dramatic happenings, with possible minor clashes between the solemnity of epic devices and the quick, short action. In "Heart of Darkness," JC's lasting achievement lies, in part, in his style. A partial failure of this story is the indirectness of approach. The tale is a manifestation of the author's personality: romanticism and realism, imperfectly welded in the man, are also imperfectly united in the work. *Lord Jim* contains as a latent feature the "stamp" of the nineteenth century. Stylistically, the adjectives, the quality of the metaphors and similes, the frequency and the suggestiveness of the placing of emphasis within a sentence, the occurrence of visual and auditory effects, and the movement in the narration or description which these contribute to the pleasure of the reader are offset by the involved quality of the same style and its frequent overelaboration and "nervousness." Marlow, as well as Brierly, Chester, and Robinson, helps to keep the moral and intellectual atmosphere somewhat "foggy," especially in that he is not able to explain to the young man the right concept of rehabilitation. The fatalistic helplessness recedes in the last part of the book, and the basic values seem to be assumed again until the end, after Brown's invasion.

2540 Mudrick, Marvin. "Conrad," *On Culture and Literature* (New York: Horizon Press, 1970), pp. 93–107.

The effect of JC's very best work is "obstruction and deadlock, an opposition of matched and mutually paralyzed energies," and both effects may be found together, as in "Heart of Darkness." Whereas

"Typhoon" displays an "unobstructed intensity of observation,"
"Youth" is weakened by Marlow's "yeasty apostrophizing" as moral
illumination, and *The Shadow-Line*, which suffers from "comparable
leakages of facile skepticism," takes an "awkward . . . fling" at the
quasi-supernatural and disappoints principally by its unreserved
endorsement of the concept of duty. JC's "solipsistic temperament"
solves the problem of morality by the "doctrine of extremity" : man
proves his moral nature by enduring catastrophic and lonely
circumstances which "wring out of him all possible insincerities,"
including that of a consoling rhetoric. *The Secret Agent* is a
"masterly, if somewhat fatigued Flaubertian exercise in the form of a
thriller." *Nostromo*, full of "astute, even aphoristic observations" and
"brilliantly put together," is "hollow." By the time of *Chance* and
Victory and JC's "fag-end adventure stuff," even his rhetoric is
"shabby and hurried," and his plots creak. JC is not a novelist, but a
writer of "novellas," among the best of which are "An Outpost of
Progress," "Heart of Darkness," "Typhoon," and *Lord Jim*, which is
essentially an expanded short story.

2541 Mueller, William R. "Man and Nature in Conrad's *Nostromo*,"
Thought, XLV (Winter 1970), pp. 559–76.

The most pervasive of the various epic struggles in *Nostromo* is
that between man and nature. Utilizing the central theme of the
"motions and countermotions of the human and the natural orders of
creation," JC proffers an ontological comment on the "structural
economy of the universe." Impelled by a variety of reasons, noble and
ignoble, the inhabitants of Costaguana are led to plunder the San
Tomé silver mine, their insatiable passions leading, in turn, to the
mine's "unremitting resistance" to its human invaders. The main
motivating source of the massive struggle is seen in the competing
claims for the great attractor of "material interests," the San Tomé
mine. Most of the characters are bound to the mine through common
interest, including the novel's five main characters, each deeply
affected by the mine. San Tomé weights Decoud to the bottom of the
sea, adding grief to the already oppressed Dr. Monygham and making
a total failure of Charles Gould's fervent idealism, robbing Emma
Gould of a husband, and corrupting the "incorruptible" Nostromo.
The common denominator which links *Nostromo*'s widely diverse
characters is their interest, for whatever reason, in the successful
working of the mine. The novel displays a vision between the human
characters seen as a kind of communal protagonist with San Tomé
as antagonist. JC's basic ontological position in the novel seems to
be the incalculable virtue of self-restraint in a universe which
demands man's "wise, humble, and compassionate sovereignty, not
his manic tyranny."

2542 Nadelhaft, Ruth Levy. "Character Doubles in the Works of Joseph Conrad," *DAI*, XXXI (1970), 1236A. Unpublished dissertation, University of Wisconsin, 1970.

2543 Najder, Zdzislaw. "Joseph Conrad: A Selection of Unknown Letters," *Polish Perspectives* (Warsaw), XIII (February 1970), pp. 31–45.

[Prints eight hitherto unpublished letters of JC in their original English. They are being included in a forthcoming edition of JC's letters being prepared by Frederick R. Karl and Zdzislaw Najder.]

2544 Newell, Kenneth B. "The Destructive Element and Related 'Dream' Passages in the *Lord Jim* Manuscript," *JML*, I (first issue 1970), pp. 30–44.

An examination of JC's manuscript of *Lord Jim* reveals that some of the novelist's revisions for the published version of Chapter Twenty cause great confusion; the original version is much clearer. Stein's answer to the question "how to be?" is, for example, *not* "follow the dream," as most critics seem to believe. On the whole, Stein, though, is a dependable narrator because (1) his destructive-element speech is consistent and understandable, (2) his words as he returns from the shadows to the lamplight are "figuratively associated with ultimate truth" and are therefore reliable, and (3) his failure to speak ultimate truth is caused as every man fails—because of human limitations. Stein's prescription of the "way"—and Marlow's and JC's too—is romantic, a way which is ambivalent: "it gives pain and suffering but also illumination and meaning." Stein thus comes near, if anyone in *Lord Jim* does, to being JC's spokesman; unlike the other character-observers, he transcends the ethical view and understands Jim's "case" metaphysically. [This article exemplifies the importance of basic scholarly research.]

2545 Nowak, Jadwiga (comp.). *The Joseph Conrad Collection in the Polish Library in London* (London: The Polish Library, 1970).

[This "up-dated" catalogue of the Joseph Conrad Collection of the Polish Library in London, with an exemplary preface by Maria L. Danilewicz, contains a listing of 399 items, at least 320 of which are books. Classifications of these include "Bibliographies & Catalogues," "First Editions," "Later Editions in English," "Translations," "Letters," "Works on Conrad," "Essays on Conrad and References to Conrad in Various Authors' Works," and "Periodicals." The catalogue is especially valuable for the inclusion of many items in Polish.]

2546 O'Connor, Peter David. "The Developing Pattern: Imagery in Five of the Novels of Joseph Conrad," *DAI*, XXX (1970), 3472A. Unpublished dissertation, Lehigh University, 1969.

2547 Odden, Edmund S. "Action and Idealism in the Novels of Joseph Conrad," *DAI*, XXXI (1970), 2395A. Unpublished dissertation, University of Wisconsin, 1970.

2548 Ordoñez, Elmer Alindogan. "Notes on the 'Falk' Manuscript," *Twenty-Seven to One: A Potpourri of Humanistic Material Presented to Dr. Donald Gale Stillman on the Occasion of His Retirement from Clarkson College of Technology by Members of the Liberal Studies–Humanities Dept. Staff, 1949–1970*, Foreword by John W. Graham, Jr., ed. by Bradford B. Broughton (Ogdensburg, New York: Ryan, 1970), pp. 45–51.

In the formative years of his writing, JC was primarily concerned with stylistic matters; he desired more to improve various verbal elements in his writing than he did to make large changes in structure or plot. [Discusses the significance of many passages deleted from the holograph of "Falk."]

2549 Parrinder, Patrick. "Wells on Hardy," *TLS* (23 April 1970), p. 455.

Prospective editors of the contemporary reviews of such writers as Meredith, Stevenson, Gissing, and JC should note the anonymous fiction reviews of H. G. Wells in the *Saturday Review* between 1895 and 1897. [See Edmund A. Bojarski, "Wells on Conrad," (28 May 1970).]

2550 Pasqualato, Roberto. "L'uso del narratore in *The Nigger of the Narcissus* (Use of the Narrator in *The Nigger of the Narcissus*), *Annali della Facoltà di Lingue e Letterature Straniere di Ca'Foscari* (Annals of the Ca'Foscari Faculty of Foreign Languages and Literatures), (Venice), IX, 2 (1970), pp. 49–62.

Shifts in points of view start in *The Nigger of the Narcissus* on the personal level, from that of the anonymous narrator to that of the collective "we," then to the more personal "I," with various moral rather than structural implications. On a stylistic level, the narrative passes from "restless impatience with nominal objectivity to magniloquent, often intrusive passages, and from visible to invisible" (scenes which the narrator could not have observed and thoughts of other characters). This is often of disputable value on a technical level. The narrative occurs not in the dramatic present but in a phase immediately preceding it, producing tension between present and past and between the ironical narrator's "knowledge of life" and the human folly exemplified in the story. [In Italian.]

2551 Pollard, Arthur. "Thackeray and Trollope," *The Victorians*, ed. by Arthur Pollard (London: Barrie & Jenkins; Sphere Books [History of Literature in the English Language], 1970),, pp. 132–33.

Trollope portrays the kind of society described by JC in a letter [presumably unpublished] of 1924 as "highly organized, if not complex," and he has what JC called, in the same letter, a "gift of intimate communion with the reader," indicating the importance [for both Trollope and JC] of the ordinary man or woman. [A significant example of JC's criticism.]

2552 Priestley, J. B. *The Edwardians* (New York and Evanston: Harper & Row, 1970), pp. 48, 127.

Even if JC, in the years 1904 to 1907, had not reached a large public, shortly before World War I, several "youngsters" (including J. B. Priestley) were "very enthusiastic" about him. The importance of his works is difficult to estimate because "at some time in our lives we are completely fascinated by them, and then later, because we have already taken so much from them, we miss this first enchantment." JC is best when working on a small scale and "rather unsatisfying and irritating" when he is "more ambitious, complicated, suggesting psychological depths we find we cannot explore."

2553 Pulc, I. P. [pseud. of Irminia Pulc Plaszkiewicz]. "Two Portrayals of a Storm: Some Notes on Conrad's Descriptive Style in *The Nigger of the Narcissus* and 'Typhoon,'" *Style*, IV (Winter 1970), pp. 49–57.

Whereas JC's rendering of the storm in *The Nigger of the Narcissus* is a "magnificent triumph," his depiction of the hurricane in "Typhoon" is almost a total failure. In *Nigger*, the monosyllabic finite verbs singly or in "staccato series" evoke the swiftness of the elemental attack. JC's vocabulary animates and personifies the elements, at the same time depicting their fury. JC gives the tempest a tangible reality and also makes manifest his concept of nature as a predatory force bent on man's destruction. But in "Typhoon," the verbs and the subjects do not mix, predicates are usually copulative verbs rather than verbs of action, verbs are often used in the passive voice, and the use of similes loses vividness and immediacy. Significantly, after "Typhoon," JC did not again attempt an extensive and sustained description of a storm.

When the problem of conduct is absent from or ambiguous in any of JC's works, as in "A Smile of Fortune," "Heart of Darkness," and "The Secret Sharer," such work often lends itself to "pretentious symbolistic interpretation."

2555 Read, J. V. "Graveyard Removal," *Mercury* (Hobart), 28 August 1970, p. 4.

The Hobart Marine Board plans to remove the "Old Ships Graveyard" containing the remains of JC's only command, the *Otago*.

2556 Renner, Stanley William. "Joseph Conrad and the Victorian Religion," *DAI*, XXXI (1970), 1289A–90A. Unpublished dissertation, University of Iowa, 1970.

2557 Roberts, Cecil. *The Bright Twenties: Being the Third Book of an Autobiography, 1920–1929* (London: Hodder and Stoughton, 1970), pp. 13, 66, 83, 92, 148, 151, 255, 305, 310, 366–67, 389.

Cecil Roberts dedicated his play, *A Tale of Young Lovers*, to JC; and he received from JC a complimentary letter when he published his book, *Scissors*, in 1923. Norman Douglas's "paedophilia" brought him into difficulty with both the British and Italian authorities so seriously that JC and others broke off their friendship. [Slight references to JC, but always with respect.]

2558 Robson, W. W. *Modern English Literature* (London: Oxford; New York: Oxford University Press, 1970), pp. xv, 14, 29–36, 106, 139.

JC is the only great artist in Edwardian fiction. Whereas Kipling's imperialism made him ideologically hateful to many people, JC supported colonialism. JC's interest in violence and conflict, in isolation and guilt, link him with Malraux, Koestler, and Silone, with Hemingway and Sartre, rather than with his English contemporaries. His worst fault is overwriting. He always believed that modern man takes too much for granted, above all, his safety. He remains aloof from his characters, seeing them at a distance. A "troubled, neurotic man," JC wanted to be free from illusions; hence his liking of irony in his works. [Sketchy biographical and critical details.]

2559 Rogers, Robert. *A Psychoanalytic Study of the Double in Literature* (Detroit: Wayne State University, 1970), pp. 41, 42–45, 84.

The characters representing doubles in Hawthorne's "Alice Doane's Appeal" and JC's "The Secret Sharer" exist more or less autonomously on the narrative level and are also fragments of one mind on the psychological level of meaning. These stories bridge the gap between overt doubling and the unconscious fragmentation of the soul which represents a basic secret kinship between two or more characters. In "Heart of Darkness," Marlow and Kurtz share a "secret sympathy" which transcends the normal bounds of friendship: the reasonable and self-disciplined Marlow finds deep within himself a "mad, monomaniacal soul." Likewise, Marlow in *Lord Jim* has much the same kind of relationship with "that other admirable criminal," Lord Jim.

2560 Ryf, Robert S. *Joseph Conrad* (New York and London: Columbia University [Columbia Essays on Modern Writers], 1970).

By means of his fiction of "dramatic embodiment," JC raises the "right questions" about the nature of human experience and concludes, not nihilistically but courageously, that man's way of life is one of commitment to, of total engagement in, life. Behind the exemplification of the necessity of this engagement in his writings lie his aesthetic theory and the central events and traumas of his life. Although JC shows, in his later works, a definite decline, a more important matter is the correlation between quality and visual scene. One central visual pattern in the novels is the leap or fall by which such characters as Jim, Kurtz, Wait, and Nostromo sever the necessary (necessary for JC) bond of solidarity. Another such pattern concerns the intrusion of reality or evil, or both, into the small world of egocentric or untested illusion, or both, illustrated by persons like Wait, Marlow in "Heart of Darkness," and by the ship in *The Shadow-Line*. The more effectively JC was able to embody his material visually, the stronger and more effective is his fiction; the more he could "see," the more he could make his reader "see." A major theme in JC's fiction is the relationship between man and his environment; JC never fully answers the question as to what extent man is master of his destiny. Man must make what he can of his own values, but activism for its own sake is inadequate. Aesthetic and activist impulses merge in the ideals of fidelity and solidarity. Man cannot live for himself alone.

2561 Said, Edward W. (ed.). "Introduction," *Three Novels by Joseph Conrad: The Nigger of the Narcissus, "Heart of Darkness," "The Secret Sharer"* (New York: Washington Square, 1970), pp. vii–xvi.

JC's life is characterized by two major stages, the sea years and the full-time writer years. Much of his work constitutes his attempt to reconcile these two stages, but this was difficult for him. Even though he maintained a belief in duty and fidelity, he was reluctant to accept abstractions. Instead, he emphasized action as it was dramatized in various aspects of a recollecting unconsciousness. This emphasis on action enabled him to reconcile his life as a sailor with his life as a writer, and consequently the reader of his work receives the impression of unity in JC the man and JC the artist. But, too, there is a sense of irony in JC because of the completely separate aspects of his experience; in his work, he portrays the process of the reconciliation. *The Nigger of the Narcissus,* "Heart of Darkness," and "The Secret Sharer" in effect contain a kind of shadow-line: the crew of the *Narcissus* must overcome the effect of James Wait, Marlow must overcome the effect of Kurtz, and the captain must overcome Leggatt and finally *be* captain. In each instance, JC reveals his need to overcome his history. In *Nigger* and "Heart of Darkness," the imagery is resonant and dense and both stories have villains who act as direct challenges to others. The theme of *Nigger,* "the effort to maintain life at a level with duty," makes this tale an important prelude to "Heart of Darkness," and "The Secret Sharer" is another tale of the realms of silence and darkness. All of these chart out a significant part of JC's career and growth as a writer.

2562 Saveson, John E. "Conrad's View of Primitive Peoples in *Lord Jim* and 'Heart of Darkness,'" *MFS,* XVI (Summer 1970), pp. 163–83; rpt. Saveson, *Joseph Conrad: The Making of a Moralist* (Amsterdam: Rodopi, 1972), pp. 37–63.

Before JC wrote *Lord Jim,* some serious influence changed his early assumptions about primitive peoples as he had depicted them in his first two novels: he moved away from the Spencerian distinction between savage and civilized. His chief source for *Jim,* writings about Sir James Brooke, the White Rajah of Sarawak, serve as an explanation of the change. JC was apparently familiar with some of the common views in nineteenth-century works by men like W. E. H. Lecky, St. George Mivert, and Alfred Russell Wallace; in fact, the "post-Spencerian" quality in *Jim* corresponds in general to the same kind of quality in the descriptions of Mivart and Wallace especially. And, too, Marlow's pessimistic uncertainty about the future of the people in Patusan may have come from JC's reading of Eduard von Hartmann's *Philosophy of the Unconscious.* "Heart of Darkness," though, suggests Hartmann's influence more strongly than *Jim* does. Here JC treats a kind of nineteenth-century humanitarianism, and several implications in the story seem a "transliteration" of Hartmann's theory of the world's process. Marlow senses a universal darkness somewhat like Hartmann's metaphysics. In these two of JC's works, Marlow is educated in the fact of the Unconscious and he often views events from the viewpoint of someone familiar with pessimistic concepts.

2563 Saveson, John E. "Contemporary Psychology in *The Nigger of the Narcissus*," *SSF*, VII (Spring 1970), pp. 219–31; rpt. *Joseph Conrad: The Making of a Moralist* (Amsterdam: Rodopi NV, 1972), pp. 109–15.

Utilitarian psychological assumptions in *The Nigger of the Narcissus* correspond to those of such psychologists as Alexander Bain, James Scully, and especially the widely translated French writer Théodule Ribot. That JC had read their works or was familiar with their theories is very likely, because they were well known to H. G. Wells, with whom JC was intimate while writing *Nigger*. JC must have meant Wait to embody egoistic debility, an important principle or analysis in the dominant Utilitarian psychology of the time; the correspondence is "exact." And as Wait represents one aspect in its extreme form in the psychology of the crew, Donkin represents another, including natural viciousness and malevolence. Donkin's "progress" into malevolence, like Wait's progress towards a denial of the will to live, is also governed by certain psychological principles found in Ribot.

2564 Saveson, John E. "Marlow's Psychological Vocabulary in *Lord Jim*," *TSLL*, XII (Fall 1970), pp. 457–70; rpt. in *Joseph Conrad: The Making of a Moralist* (Amsterdam: Rodopi NV, 1972), pp. 89–107.

Comparison of Marlow's terms in *Lord Jim* with those of psychologists known to H. G. Wells, such as James Sully, reveals that JC's psychological vocabulary is "contemporary and informed." Marlow's terms particularly are almost the same as Sully's: egoism, ideas, imagination, illusion, sensibility. Marlow describes a Kantian alteration of the will, but his intricate descriptions convey a Utilitarian view of the Kantian moralist. Jim illustrates Sully's psychology and morality of illusion, with its origin in the egoistic feelings. JC traces in great detail the genesis of an intuitionist ethic in *Jim* and maintains egoism with great consistency as the basic term and principle in characterizing his hero. Egoistic feeling in Sully affects the imagination and distorts reality in perception, and Jim's mind so conditions itself to will illusory and ideal achievements that inevitably he loses his ability to will the actual. The similarity between Sully's and JC's descriptive terms is striking. Sully, however, was not necessarily a direct influence upon JC; if the terms used by both are comparable, Marlow's psychological vocabulary is "technical, allusive, and contemporary."

2565 Schultheiss, Thomas. "Conrad Bibliography: A Continuing Checklist," *CON*, III, No. 1 (1970–71), pp. 93–109.

[A continuation of Schultheiss's invaluable bibliography.]

2566 Schultheiss, Thomas. "The Search for *The Sisters*: A Chronology of Ownership," *CON*, III, No. 1 (1970–71), pp. 26, 50, 68, 90, 92.

A careful search for the whereabouts of the manuscript of JC's unfinished novel, *The Sisters*, revealed the existence of two "*Sisters*," a manuscript and a typescript, both of which have now disappeared. The manuscript, however, is traced "between 1913 and the mid-40s from Conrad to [John] Quinn, from Quinn's executors to [Burton] Rascoe, from Rascoe to [Crosby] Gaige, and from Gaige to Scribner's Book Store," where the trail ends.

2567 Sebezhko, E. S. "Khudozestvennoe svoeobrazie romana Dzhozefa Konrada *Nostromo*" (Artistic Originality of Conrad's Novel *Nostromo*), *Istoriko-Literaturnyi Sbornik* (Kaluga: Tula Pedagogical Institute, 1970), pp. 147–62.

JC's attention throughout *Nostromo* is on the characters, not the incidents, and the psychological sub-text makes it an important phenomenon in English literature of the early twentieth century. [In Russian.]

2568 Secor, Robert Arnold. "Conrad's Rhetoric of Shifting Perspectives," *DA*, XXXI (1970–71), 402A. Unpublished dissertation, Brown University, 1969.

2569 Secor, Robert Arnold. "The Function of the Narrator in *Under Western Eyes*," *CON*, III, No. 1 (1970–71), pp. 27–38.

In *Under Western Eyes*, the language teacher, JC's spokesman, is treated ironically. In the contrast between the narrator's role in the first and last sections of the novel, JC depends most on the teacher to control our judgment of and final sympathy for Razumov. In Part First, JC uses the teacher to establish the word as "structuring symbol" and to "mirror" through his own struggles with rhetoric the moral and psychological struggle of Razumov. The basic assumption of the opening section is that words, the articulation of the rational self, are the agents of deception and self-deception; the secondary assumption is that humans as rational and conceptualizing beings must nevertheless depend on words. The struggles of the narrator are, of course, those of the novelist, who must first conceive and then verbalize his characters. In Part First of the novel, Razumov tortures himself because while constantly thinking that he is being mistrusted, he is actually only being misunderstood. In Part Four, Razumov's relevance to his surroundings is restored and the language teacher becomes increasingly irrelevant. The teacher is thus the one fully ironic figure in the novel. It seems that Henry

James had the greatest influence upon JC here: in *Eyes*, the troubled vision of Razumov is reflected through that of the language teacher, who therefore serves as a Jamesian ficelle largely peripheral to the novel.

2570 Sherry, Norman. "A Conrad Manuscript," *TLS* (25 June 1970), p. 691.

A short but completely unknown manuscript by JC dated February 12, 1898 [reproduced] consists of notes on the Siege and Fall of Paris, 1870–71. The style of the notes suggests that JC was making a precis of a contemporary account. He may, in fact, have been trying to find a subject on which he and Stephen Crane could collaborate in the writing of a novel. This manuscript is important because the notes "indirectly illuminate" JC's method of work and add to our knowledge of his life at the time they were written.

2571 Silkowski, Daniel R. "*Lord Jim*: 'Big Deal,'" *English Journal*, LIX (September 1970), pp. 780–81.

The possibilities of group discussion on the contemporary relevance of *Lord Jim* evolve after the baby-sitter irreverently says "big deal" to Jim's jump. [Scarcely profound.]

2572 Sinha, S. Murari. "Joseph Conrad," *CON*, III, No. 1 (1970–71), p. 118.

JC, a "dreamer" and a "realist" who "always lived alone," "belonged with the Immortals above –." [A poem.]

2573 Speaight, Robert. *The Property Basket: Recollections of a Divided Life* (London: Collins & Harvill Press, 1970), pp. 307, 375, 376.

JC admired Sir William Rothenstein just "this side of idolatry," both as an artist and a man. Rothenstein made a well known portrait drawing of JC.

2574 Spence, G. W. "The Form of Part III of *Nostromo*," *CON*, III, No. 1 (1970–71), pp. 81–86.

Albert J. Guerard's "irreverent comment" that *Nostromo* is at least two hundred pages too long (*Conrad the Novelist*, 1958), is inaccurate: the novel is actually about one hundred pages too short. The thematic relevance of the scenes in the Custom House is distinct from their function in the development of the action of the book: these scenes are not balanced by an adequate development of the historical process near the end of Part III, after the victory of General Barrios's troops. The events of Part III, chapters i to ix, mark a crisis and a transition to what should be called Part IV, in which the political and economic situation, which has been seriously treated, is dealt with too perfunctorily. In "Part IV," after material interests are triumphant, there is little study of these interests or of Gould's faith in them. The expectations raised earlier about the moral question of such interests are not satisfied with the completion, Mitchell's narrative, in Part III, chapter x, of the main historical action. It is in success rather than in failure that Charles Gould's illusion is harmful, but this concept is not made real in any sequence of public action; it appears only in a scene of private distress involving Mrs. Gould.

2575 Stoehr, Taylor. "Words and Deeds in *The Princess Casamassima*," *ELH*, XXXVII (March 1970), pp. 95–135.

Henry James is in the tradition of political novelists whose works include *Sentimental Education* (1869), *The Possessed* (1872), *Virgin Soil* (1877), and *Under Western Eyes* (1911), a conservative tradition that tests the claims of political life against those of the artistic. In *Eyes*, JC's narrator is safe from the dangers of imagination and insight, through overexposure to words. Only his confession, which his diary fully becomes, allows "his escape from the prison of lies." But if words have led Razumov to suicidal isolation, they have also saved him from it at the end. His elaborately fabricated identity is replaced by the true "story" of his part in the betrayal of Haldin, both of which are mere structures of words. And neither is entirely free from illusion, since neither is reality itself. The action of James's *The Princess Casamassima* may also be reduced to a sequence focused on the nature of the relationship between language and reality.

2576 Summers, Marcia P. "The Use of Subordinate Characters as Dramatized in Twentieth-Century Novels," *DAI*, XXX (1970), 3024A–25A. Unpublished dissertation, University of Illinois, 1969.

2577 Susser, Bernard. "Conrad Questions," *TLS* (7 August 1970), p. 879.

It is possible to be able to read a novel without being literate enough to write one's own name [like Singleton in *The Nigger of the Narcissus*], as evidenced by the fact that many thousands of Jews in the diaspora "learn to read and translate the Hebrew of the Pentateuch and prayer book with some degree of fluency, and yet are quite unable to write Hebrew." [Preceded by John S. Lewis and Leonard Wayman, "Conrad Questions," (1970).]

2578 Thomaier, William. "Conrad on the Screen Poses Cinematic Difficulties Which Haven't Yet Been Overcome," *Films in Review,* XXI (December 1970), pp. 611–21.

JC's visual sense and his facility of vivid description of people and their backgrounds make his work seem "made to order" for the motion picture medium, but the depths of his characterizations and his subjective preoccupations with moral and philosophical issues make his work difficult to present successfully on the screen. The story in a work by JC is always easy to put on film; its significance is not. Of the fourteen films made from JC's novels and stories, the most ambitious to date, Richard Brooks' *Lord Jim* (1965), is only a travesty of JC. The ending of Carol Reed's *Outcast of the Islands* (1951) is one of cinema's "great scenes" which of itself makes this film the most faithful screen adaptation of JC "not so much of letter as of spirit." [Constitutes a survey of films made from works by JC, with descriptive and critical information about each one.]

2579 Thomas, Edward. "'Truer Than History,'" *Ariel,* I (January 1970), pp. 65–72.

JC's ideas have a coherence in both his fiction and his other writings. An "objectivist" interpretation of JC reveals much in common with a Marxist approach, and Marxist criticism is helpful because it concentrates our attention on the material of the novels and away from the psychology of the author. JC was concerned basically with the histories of individuals and of groups, or, with "History." He attempted to render the "internal" meaning of history, which also suggests a Marxist interpretation. But this suggestion is only superficial: JC does not discover an existing objective structure in history; instead, he makes the meaning by the power of his imagination. He is thus in the tradition that goes back through Shelley and Sidney to Aristotle, the tradition that asserts the "sovereignty" of the artist's kind of truth. The artist, JC believed, was writing something "truer than history" because it was the "highest and most comprehensive" kind of history.

2580 Urnov, M. V. "Dzhozef Konrad" (Joseph Conrad), *Na Rubezhe Vek. XX: Ocherki Angliiskoi Literatury* (Turn of the Century XX: Sketches in English Literature), (Moscow: "Nauka," 1970), pp. 395–405.

Lord Jim occupies an important place in JC's work and in the development of English literature at the turn of the century. It is characteristic of his productions, including the choice of protagonist, setting, and construction. The influence of Dostoevski (whose work JC was able to read in Russian) is undoubted in *Under Western Eyes* and *Jim,* with characters deliberately testing the limits of their nature in a manner reminiscent of Raskolnikov and the Karamazov brothers. Other English writers learned Dostoevski through JC, without knowing his works in the original. JC may be described as a "romantic by nature" only with serious reservations. He has now been canonized as one of the most contemporary of writers, whose importance is only beginning to be discovered. He learned from Henry James how to construct narratives with contrasting rhythms, deliberate use of details in rendering experience, and also the use of point of view. Without denying JC's importance, one characteristic of his work is affected complexity, beneath which there is no real complexity, and a tendency to depict problems in experimentally inflated situations. [In Russian.]

2581 Ursell, Geoffrey. "Conrad: Two Misdated Letters," *N&Q*, N.S. XVII, No. 1 [Vol. 215 of continuous series] (January 1970), pp. 36–37.

A letter from JC to Stephen Crane dated "5th Febr. 98" appears in *Stephen Crane: Letters*, ed. by R. W. Stallman and Lillian Gilkes (New York, 1960). But events during this period of his life indicate that JC erred in writing down the month. The correct date is "5 *March* 1898*." Likewise, a letter from JC to David S. Meldrum dated "Friday 10 Aug 98" appears in *Joseph Conrad: Letters to William Blackwood and David S. Meldrum*, ed. by William Blackburn (Durham: North Carolina, 1958). The correct year is probably 1899.

2582 Van Domelen, John E. "Conrad and Journalism," *Journalism Quarterly*, XLVII (Spring 1970), pp. 153–56.

Journalists and journalism are "invariably" treated unfavorably by JC, as seen in such works as "An Outpost of Progress" and "Heart of Darkness," through *Victory*, *The Shadow-Line*, "The Planter of Malata," and "Because of the Dollars." His dislike of journalism seems to be that it takes men away from reflection and that newspapers do not adequately represent public opinion. But journalism, he thought, does sometimes provide quality in information and in interpretation of news. JC must have feared that such a strong force as the power of the word could be easily perverted.

2583 Van Domelen, John E. "In the Beginning Was the Word, or Awful Eloquence and Right Expression in Conrad," *South Central Bulletin*, XXX (Winter 1970), pp. 228–31.

JC's concern with man's abuse of language is evident throughout his fiction. In "Heart of Darkness," JC plays off the vicious backbiting of the traders against the elevated rhetoric of their aspirations. Marlow's delight in finding the book on seamanship is due partly to the fact that he sees it as an example of a rhetoric which is grounded in reality. In that his language is based on fantasy rather than on "objective or moral reality," Kurtz is very much like the other traders. But Kurtz finally speaks in terms which represent his reality: "the horror, the horror." In *Nostromo*, there is a difference between the rhetorical modes of the Anglo-Saxons and the Latin Americans. Although Charles Gould couches his actions in romantic, idealistic terms, he perceives the ways of dependence of expression upon the realities of the economic structure of society. Both Decoud and Nostromo are "addicted to fine, empty words." Because Decoud's brilliance is divorced from any comprehensive moral vision, he pursues a life of incessant, and unrelated, actions. His unrealistic eloquence demonstrates his egoistic isolation. Because he can perceive the gap between language and reality which so often characterizes the world of action, Axel Heyst withdraws from active life. But he ironically brings down upon himself "the avenging furies from the devilish world that will not tolerate the withdrawal of a good man." Thus, *Victory*, *Nostromo*, and "Heart of Darkness" demonstrate JC's belief that one must retain his vision, which must always be corrected by relating it to reality, and "which one must labor to translate into action."

2584 Van Domelen, John E. "A Note on the Reading of Conrad's Characters," *CON*, III, No. 1 (1970–71), pp. 87–89.

At times, JC provides insights into his fictional characters by means of their reading, as he does with old Singleton in *The Nigger of the Narcissus* and Captain MacWhirr in "Typhoon." Throughout his works, JC reveals a preference, like Faust in Goethe's poem, for the deed to the word, for the act to the thought, as he does with Marlow in "Youth." In *Lord Jim*, Stein is reminiscent of Goethe and may have been modeled on him. JC's ideal balance between intellect and action is symbolized in *Nostromo* by Charles Gould's two bookcases, one filled with books and one lined with firearms. In JC's writings, simple sailors like Singleton and unimaginative ones like MacWhirr can endure life with their ideals intact, but those characters who "read and ponder"—like Martin Decoud and Axel Heyst—are led toward nihilism. JC admitted the power of words only "with the most profound misgivings."

2585 Verschoor, Edith E. N. "Joseph Conrad's World," *Unisa English Studies*, VIII (June 1970), pp. 12–18.

JC's vision of life is somewhat somber because he has a strong sense of the existence of evil both within man himself and in the world around him. His greatest value seems to lie in the fact that he is never dogmatic. His technique consists of a dispassionate and balanced appraisal of facts, seen by the light of irony. His themes include the idea that although idealism is a fine thing, it is possible for a man to hold lofty ideals and intentions which he himself may betray through man's tragic fallibility, which may not be viable in this material world and which may lead to a dangerous physical or moral isolation. [An attempt to present "a general picture" of JC's world and how he creates it.]

2586 Vidan, Gabrijela, and Ivo Vidan. "Further Correspondence Between Joseph Conrad and André Gide," *Studia Romanica et Anglica Zagrebiensia*, No. 29–32 (1970–71), pp. 523–36.

[Reprints ten letters exchanged between JC and André Gide from 1913 to 1922, most of them dated 1919, concerning the translation of *The Arrow of Gold*. These letters add important information to the thirteen letters from Gide to JC published in 1967 (Ivo Vidan, "Thirteen Letters of André Gide to Joseph Conrad,") and G. Jean-Aubry, *Joseph Conrad: Lettres Françaises* (Paris, 1930). Eight of these letters go a long way in satisfying our curiosity about the way in which Gide and JC resolved the "one small argument between them of which we know."]

2587 Vidan, Ivo. "Conrad for the Magazines," *ELT*, XIII, No. 1 (1970), pp. 79–81.

Two conflicting desires in JC's literary work affected the results of his efforts: to write well according to his inclinations and to be able to sell his works as favorably as possible. Writing novels was his real ambition, and some of his stories were therefore deliberate potboilers. Important in understanding JC is his "all-pervasive" theme of conflict between egoism and altruism.

2588 Vidan, Ivo. "Conrad to a Friend," *ELT*, XIII, No 1 (1970), pp. 77–79.

In *Joseph Conrad's Letters to R. B. Cunninghame Graham* (1969), C. T. Watts, unlike G. Jean-Aubry in *Joseph Conrad: Life and Letters* (1927), publishes all of JC's letters to his friend and includes, in addition, the complete forms. But of greater value is his "exhaustive commentary" about relevant public and private events and about allusions and other pertinent materials. These letters to Graham contain a "peculiar quality" which is absent from JC's letters to other close literary friends, a quality that is "vivid and life-asserting" in contexts which otherwise contain "the most absolute statements of nihilism and despair" of all of JC's correspondence.

2589 Vidan, Ivo. "New Approaches to Conrad," *Massachusetts Review*, XI (Summer 1970), pp. 545–63.

JC's biography offers more problems than that of other authors of English literature, as a number of recent books shows. Jerry Allen, in *The Sea Years of Joseph Conrad*, a book worth having, does not demonstrate how JC transmuted actual events into fiction. Norman Sherry's book on JC's sources, useful for criticism, does not explain JC's basic uses of his source material. Dr. Bernard Meyer presents the least amiable features of JC, and his analysis does not account for the positive aspect of JC's art. Edward W. Said's philosophical attempt to explore JC's consciousness establishes no direct relationship between JC's letters and his shorter fiction. The "dual heritage" discussed by Ralph Hodges is that of the "impulsive yet melancholic national romanticism" of JC's father and his maternal uncle; Hodges sees JC's greatest fiction appearing when the two urges were not resolved. Eloise Knapp Hay's "ambitious" volume on JC's political works leaves some disappointment because "her interpretations rarely stress the imaginative value" of the fiction. Avrom Fleishman, however, reaches "a level of generality" which would account for all of JC's various, often contradictory attitudes and "amount to a coherent, comprehensive judgment." Claire Rosenfield fails to build mythical wholes in her archetypal approach to JC's political works. The overall effect of these volumes is "sobering." Hopefully they mark the beginning of a period in which JC will be assimilated by established techniques of learning. [A perspicacious assessment of recent scholarship on JC and his works.]

2590 Wagner, Geoffrey. "The Novel of Empire," *EIC*, XX (April 1970), pp. 229–42.

The commercial background lies close behind any clear concept of English "Empire" and the fiction written around it. For most of the nineteenth century, the period of the novel's greatness, England was a manufacturer selling products to Empire suppliers of cheap food and raw materials. JC placed Arabs in his Malaysian fiction because they traded in the archipelago at the time. Then, the word "white" did not carry primary connotations of skin color nor a racial theory in the British Empire. JC's Malaysian "construct" is a mixture of the hierarchical and mercantile, according to the custom of the time. The hierarchy, one of moral values more than social issues, is best seen in operation in *The Rescue*, where humanity comes before skin color. JC was realistic in expressing life in and around the Malay peninsula as it was then stratified. In JC, the mercantile novel operates at its best on the colonial scene. He romantically suspected the machine age and saw Whitehall as a "brake" on endeavor in a way that is reversed today.

2591 Walch, Günter. "Roman und Wirklichkeit: 1880 bis zum ersten Weltkrieg" (Novel and Reality: 1880 to the First World War), *Zeitschrift für Anglistik und Amerikanistik*, XVIII (1970), pp. 88–110.

[More or less a review essay, dealing with Paul Goetsch, *Die Romankonzeption in England 1880–1910* (1967); Samuel Hynes, *The Edwardian Turn of Mind* (1968); William Larrett, *The English Novel from Thomas Hardy to Graham Greene* (1967); and Hans-Joachim Müllenbrock, *Literatur und Zeitgeschichte in England Zwischen dem Ende des 19. Jahrhunderts und dem Ausbruch des Ersten Weltkrieges* (1967). Consideration is given to JC's attitude toward colonialism, the theme of isolation in his novels, the topicality of his art, and his apocalyptic vision.] [In German.]

2592 Walker, Warren S. *Twentieth-Century Short Story Explications: Supplement I to Second Edition, 1967–69* (Hamden, Connecticut: Shoe String Press, 1970), pp. 44–54.

[A bibliographical tool listing "all of the significant interpretative studies of short fiction" published in 1967, 1968, and 1969. The short story is defined as narrative fiction not exceeding 150 pages. An interpretative study explicates such matters as meaning, theme, structure, and symbol. Twenty-nine JC stories are listed, including "Heart of Darkness," "Typhoon," *The Shadow-Line*, "The End of the Tether," "Falk," "Youth," but not *The Nigger of the Narcissus*.]

2593 Walt, James. "Conrad and Mencken—Part III," *CON*, III, No. 1 (1970–71), pp. 69–74.

In the fall of 1916, Mencken published four articles on JC in the Baltimore *Evening Sun*, according JC the position of the supreme novelist on the English scene except for Thomas Hardy, emphasizing the lurid features of JC's political novels, declaring that it was in the Malayan stories and sea fiction that JC "struck his truest note," and commending Wilson Follett's book on JC while damning Richard Curle as tiresome and awkward. The personal relationship between Mencken and JC was limited to correspondence, only one letter of which has been located. JC appreciated the services rendered him by his American critic: his letter to Mencken of 11 November 1917 makes this clear; but he later questioned Mencken's emphasis on his "Slavonism." Few recent studies of JC recognize Mencken's contribution to making the Anglo-Pole known. This is no doubt at least partly Mencken's fault, because he could not keep his literary criticism free from "jesting asides and invective." [Preceded by Walt, "Mencken and Conrad—Part I," *Conradiana*, II, No. 2 (Winter 1969–70), pp. 9–21; and Walt, "Mencken and Conrad—Part II," *Conradiana*, II, No. 3 (Spring 1969–1970), pp. 100–110.]

2594 Walz, Lawrence Arnold. "From the Heroic Age: The Theme of Decline Through Time in the Fiction of Joseph Conrad," *DAI*, XXXI (1970), 406A–407A. Unpublished dissertation, University of North Carolina, Chapel Hill, 1969.

2595 Warner, John M. "Tragic Vision in B. Traven's *The Night Visitor*," *SSF*, VII (Summer 1970), pp. 377–84.

Two views on human existence are revealed in B. Traven's collection, *The Night Visitor and Other Stories*. Whereas the first view is that of man successfully adapting himself to life, the second reveals the darker side of life, comparable in its tragic suggestions to those found in JC's works.

2596 Watt, Ian. "Conrad's *Secret Agent*," *Listener* (London, 9 April 1970), pp. 474–76, 78.

The posthumous topicality of *The Secret Agent* makes it particularly valuable for noting some of the conflicting tendencies of modern literary criticism. In 1948, F. R. Leavis argued for the connection between JC's literary form and the moral content of the work. Since that time, romantic critics such as Irving Howe, Eloise Knapp Hay, and Norman Sherry have emphasized the political, sociological, and psychological aspects of the novel. First, Leo Gurko, then others, stressed the theme of a vision of an enormous, dark city, with the setting fitted to the presence of the anarchists. Most of the psychological approaches have been psychoanalytic, as in Albert Guerard, Thomas Moser, and Bernard Meyer. Descriptive or exegetic critics, who include the symbolic and the existential or phenomenological, have more modest aims which help to clarify our reading of the work. Symbolical in approach is Robert Stallman's "Time and *The Secret Agent*" (1959), (C, I, No. 1561). Avrom Fleishman's book of 1967 uses symbolic interpretation to synthesize a metaphysical world-view from the details of JC's texts. And J. Hillis Miller argues that JC uses both the narrator's ironic detachment and the whole action to make the characters move towards detachment from their normal view of the world. In its own way, however, *Agent* is a precursor of modern black humor, which is JC's conflict between the two opposite aspects of his personality—the conservative and the anarchist. *Agent*, then, along with Yeats, Eliot, or Joyce, assumes that only the artist's voice can impose some order on the "vulgar folly" of our world. JC seems to have found that "anger and evil have no more final efficacy than laziness or love" in his darkest look at modern urban civilization.

2597 Whalen, Terry. "Heyst's Moral Oddity: A Reading of *Victory*," *CON*, III, No. 1 (1970–71), pp. 39–48.

Heyst is "odd," not mad or neurotic. His unconventional behavior is finally based on a "legitimate" moral difficulty: he feels two impulses to action, "compassion" for Lena, a kind of pure attraction, and his physical attraction for her. JC's language about the latter is evasive but clear enough. Much of the "ostensible sloppiness" of *Victory* exists because of JC's attitude toward the meaning of sex. By the middle of the novel, Lena is Heyst's only attraction to the outside world, but she involves him in a "corruptive tie" that "mangles" his moral sensitivity by involving him in action and, even more seriously, by involving him specifically in sexual relations, a kind of action which implicitly affirms, in opposition to his skepticism, the continuation of the human race. His moral qualm is that he is skeptical about the worthiness of even this. His conscience recognizes that procreation is perhaps one of the most profound moral acts available to man. But he (and perhaps JC also) endorses what Paul Tillich would call "biological skepticism"—the lack of courage to father children into a life of adversity. To a great extent, *Victory* is thus a novel about fatherhood; the question raised is: Is it proper to propagate life without conviction? JC himself may have been directly involved in Heyst's moral qualm. An interesting question arises: Is Lena's "victory over death" a "victory" merely because it is paradoxically a victory over life—her own and the children Heyst will never have?

2598 Williams, Raymond. "Joseph Conrad," *The English Novel: From Dickens to Lawrence* (London: Chatto & Windus; New York: Oxford University Press, 1970), pp. 120, 123, 140–54, 187.

JC is usually described as being concerned with isolation and struggle, with man against Fate; but more accurate is his interest in man's necessity to live with social values. *Lord Jim*, for example, examines conduct within an agreed upon scheme of values. For JC, the ship provides a knowable community of a "transparent" kind, as in *The Nigger of the Narcissus*, "The End of the Tether," and *Lord Jim*. "Heart of Darkness" extends the community away from the ship, as does *The Secret Agent*. The last, however, as well as *Under Western Eyes*, is weak because JC deals with English and Russian literature instead of imagining and creating from his own experience. *Nostromo*, though, best recalls the seriousness of the loss of a social value: Decoud's isolation removed his "sane materialism," and Nostromo, "our man," learns tragically that the silver cannot replace his relationships with his fellow men; in the end, there is no order, no society, in which he can set it to work.

2599 Zeigler, Sonia Labiner. "Borys Conrad's Visit to Poland: Some Reflections on the Nature and Significance of Conrad's Polishness," *CON*, III, No. 1 (1970–71), pp. 61–67.

In 1967, Borys Conrad's visit to Poland in connection with the forthcoming book on his father elicited several newspaper articles which reveal, along with a "jealous veneration" of JC's work, an obsession with the matter of his "Polishness," a "bitter resentment" because of his departure from his own country, and his refusal, in exile, to work as a partisan of the "Polish cause." But JC's Polishness is very different from these reactions. His disavowal of Slavonism was an expression of a life-long hatred of classifications of people by colors, or "mystical 'national characteristics.'" "Autocracy and War," for instance, contains his conception of the nature of his Polish heritage; he prefers an impartial view of humanity as a whole with a special regard for the underprivileged, an ideal which appears most exhaustively in *Lord Jim*. JC's insistence on the "strength and spirituality" of national temperament is a "disguised reminder" to the Western powers that conquered nations "have a way of persisting, of being disruptive to the conquerors." The theme of Poland's "miraculous rebirth," found in "The Crime of Partition," is attached to a larger theme, one which is central to JC's vision: the issue for which men really fight—not ideas, systems, creations of states, nor "abstract justice"—but, as Jim says, for something "too mighty for the common standards by which reason measures the advantages of life and death."

1971

2600 Amur, G. S. "'Heart of Darkness' and 'The Fall of the House of Usher': The Tale as Discovery," *Literary Criterion* (University of Mysore), IX (Summer 1971), pp. 59–70.

Edgar Allan Poe's story, "The Fall of the House of Usher," and JC's "Heart of Darkness" resemble each other in theme and technique. Striking parallels are the concrete point of view realized through the narrators, both of whom discover the heart of darkness. Also, the use of symbolic devices to create fictional meaning appears in both stories: the poem, 'The Haunted Palace,' performs a function similar to that of the struggle between light and the historical correlation of the imagined career of the Roman citizen in JC's tale. And the structure in both stories contains the narrator's approach to the central character, his involvement in the crisis and catastrophe of the protagonist's life, and his final withdrawal or escape. The analogy of technique is equated by an analogy of theme: as darkness is the pervasive theme and symbol of JC's story, so does "Fall" provide the controlling thematic interests in Poe's, and both are in a way stories about fall through surrender to darkness. Poe and JC illustrate a difference between the English and the American traditions in fiction: JC, making in "Heart of Darkness" the power of his story largely through the unmasking of European civilization and the exposure of the hollowness of its representatives, was unable to probe the nature of "Darkness" as Poe did in "The Fall of the House of Usher" by means of the "concentrated spiritual intensity" achieved by the author "under the shadow of an imminent apocalypse."

2601 Begnal, Michael H. "The Ideals of Despair: A View of Joseph Conrad's *The Arrow of Gold*," *CON*, III, No. 3 (1971–72), pp. 37–40.

The Arrow of Gold has much merit as a literary work: it has a carefully defined structure and form and underlying motifs. The central concern is the romance of Rita de Lastaola and Monsieur George, who want to remain children playing grownup games but who are, ironically, saner and more mature than those who, like the Pretender and Blunt, are the most entangled with romantic illusions. If a political statement exists in the novel, it is that the policies and machinations of governments and societies are ultimately meaningless. The destruction of the idyllic relationship of the lovers, which is caused by pressures from beyond their world, is basically a "victory for the forces of bitterness and failure." Thus JC ends this late literary production with what may be his most pessimistic thematic statement, that ideals cannot be implemented in contemporary society.

2602 Beja, Morris. *Epiphany in the Modern Novel* (Seattle: University of Washington Press, 1971), pp. 52–54, 117–18, 130–31.

Like Henry James, JC stresses the "moment of vision." Starting from a critical position like James's, JC, in the preface to *The Nigger of the Narcissus*, presents an effective view of aesthetic experience: art causes the perceiver to act. For JC, it is not enough to cause one to *see*; the writer must also hold "the rescued fragment before all eyes in the light of a sincere mood" and "disclose its secret." Moments of vision, however, can be the origin of art as well as its result. These moments occur for JC as he glimpses a figure upon whom he models Almayer and Jim. Such moments come to characters as well, especially to Marlow. The one unique use of the epiphany for JC is that the moment often has unfortunate consequences; indeed, the idea that the epiphany is undesirable seems to be JC's alone.

Virginia Woolf's reservations about Joyce's use of the epiphany are revealed by her preference for Hardy's and JC's use of the device. She believed JC's "moments of vision" to be the best sections of his books. She thought, though, that his character portrayal is deficient, resting, as it does, on one or two qualities revealed in flashes.

2603 Bellamy, William. *The Novels of Wells, Bennett, and Galsworthy: 1890–1910* (London: Routledge & Kegan Paul; New York: Barnes & Noble, 1971), pp. 27, 29, 30, 47–48, 70, 93, 94, 98, 101, 175, 187, 188, 190, 195–98, 199, 211, 212, 227, 230–31, 232.

In the few important English novels of the 1890s, the predominant theme seems to be the sense of crisis in the life of isolated and alienated individuals. Writers like Henry James and JC must be seen in the Edwardian decade in order to be understood; the great technical triumph of *The Ambassadors* and *Nostromo* must be noted in relation to their authors' earlier stories. JC's preface to *The Nigger of the Narcissus* is a "characteristically *fin-de-siècle* vulgarization of what is already a quite vulgarized tradition." The emergence of impressionism in the novel shows why JC emphasized strongly the "*secret* spring of responsive emotions," the "*magic* suggestiveness of music," the *latent* feeling of fellowship with all creation," and the "solidarity of *dreams*." The unconscious is here related to the cosmos very directly, and the distinction between "Unconsciousness" and "Cosmic Consciousness" becomes the source of "reunion." The *fin-de-siècle* fascination with human attenuation and "hollowing out," which is implicit in JC's fascination with the skeletal Negro "criminals" in the grove of death in "Heart of Darkness," seems to be taken up as the underlying pretext for a new provisional community in social therapies of various kinds. JC's images from fantasy and fear are a kind of subversive surreality intended to undermine the autonomy and the security of any one level of socially accepted reality.

2604 Bellis, George. "Fidelity to a Higher Ideal: A Study of the Jump in Conrad's *Lord Jim*," *Erasmus Review*, I (September 1971), pp. 63–71.

Jim's jump from the *Patna*, in *Lord Jim*, is the beginning of Jim's pursuit of a dream. When he jumps, he is prepared to judge his own conscience. He intends to seek a new opportunity within the civilized world, but later circumstances force him to go outside. Jim jumps into the sea, which is Stein's metaphor for the dream, and he is willing to accept the consequences until opportunity appears again. By remaining on board, he could achieve only a cheap heroic reputation because it would have been based on passive response rather than active toil. His jumping exhibits a great amount of

courage: he instinctively defies convention in order to save himself
not for life only but for the fulfillment of life. The fact that he
maintains his self-control afterwards indicates the quality of his
courage. This view of Jim's jump conforms to the total context in
which JC places the jump. Whether we agree with him or not, JC
suggests that Jim is admirable because he deserts a sinking ship in
order to pursue his own ideal of human perfection. [Although well
supported, this view of Jim may overemphasize his egotism.]

2605 Berman, Jeffrey. "Joseph Conrad and the Self-Destructive
Urge," *DAI*, XXXII (1971), 2674A–75A. Unpublished dissertation,
Cornell University, 1971.

2606 Bidwell, Paul. "Leggatt and the Promised Land: A New Reading
of 'The Secret Sharer,'" *CON*, III, No. 2 (1971–72), pp. 26–34.

In "Echo Structures: Conrad's 'The Secret Sharer,'" *Twentieth
Century Literature*, V (January 1960), pp. 159–75 (C, I, No. 1598),
Louis H. Leiter unravels JC's intricate use of the Cain-Abel and the
Jonah motifs in "The Secret Sharer." A third Old Testament theme in
the story, that of most of the important events in the life of Moses,
helps to provide significant pattern to the basic elements of Leggatt's
dilemma and its counterpart, the narrator's attempt to manage his
difficult new role as commander of ship and crew. In the Book of
Exodus and in Job's story, both Moses and Leggatt must escape
inexorable law by entering the water, and both fugitives are saved by
accidental and sympathetic discovery by a person who might be
expected to be an enemy. Symbolically, the threat which the
Israelites represented to Pharaoh is "reorchestrated" as the threat
which Leggatt poses to Archbold's authority over his ship and crew.
A Leggatt-Moses identification suggests the nomad tribe as an
allusion to the wandering Israelites: the vertical fishing stakes of the
story recall the bullrushes where the infant Moses was hidden. The
crucial scene in which Archbold invades the narrator's cabin in
search of Leggatt suggests the likelihood that JC had the Moses-
Aaron brotherhood in mind as the context for the "double" in his
story.

2607 Boebel, Charles E., Jr. "The Art of Joseph Conrad," *DAI*, XXXI
(1971), 6046A. Unpublished dissertation, University of Arizona,
1970.

2608 Bojarski, Edmund A. "Wild Woman," *CEA*, XXXIV (1971), p. 30;
entitled "Conrad's 'Wild Woman,'" *Polish American* (Chicago, 1
May 1971); rpt. *Quetzal* (Pembroke State University), I (Summer
1971), p. 53.

[A short poem on Kurtz's African woman in "Heart of Darkness."
Of no critical value.]

2609 Bonney, William Wesley. "The Artistic Functions of the Device
of Inconsistent Point of View in Selected Novels of Joseph
Conrad," *DAI*, XXXI (April 1971), 5389A. Unpublished thesis,
University of Pennsylvania, 1970.

2610 Bradbury, Malcolm. *The Social Context of Modern English
Literature* (New York: Schocken Books, 1971), pp. xxiii, xxiv, 22,
40n, 50–51, 53, 54, 73, 84, 89, 93–94, 142, 254.

The great writers of the twentieth century, especially the literary
revolutionaries at its beginning (Lawrence, Joyce, Forster, Yeats,
Pound, Eliot, JC, and others), responded strongly to an infinitely
complex cultural and emotional situation. Appropriately, in
conceiving his most ironic, impressionistic, and "modern" novel, *The
Secret Agent*, a novel about the anarchy and the existential exposure
that lies behind the veneer of civilization, one which contains no
hero, no real plot, and no real center of positive value, JC used an
image of London, a classic reversal of the city as the locus of
civilization. It is in line with the "fourmillante cité" of Baudelaire, the
heart with "no pulsation" in Forster, and the "unreal city" that
dominates Eliot's *The Waste Land*. The model of the artist tended,
however, to become that of the urbanized intellectual, as with
Gissing, Henry James, and JC, the last of whom saw the city as an
ironic masterpiece of modern civilization. The literary generation
which seems to carry the experience of modernism most, the
generation that came to maturity and notice in a few brief years
before World War I, contains the years of the early works of such
writers as Pound, Eliot, Yeats, James, Forster, D. H. Lawrence,
Wyndham Lewis, Joyce, and some of JC's finest fiction.

2611 Bross, Addison C. "Beerbohm's 'The Feast' and Conrad's
Early Fiction," *NCF*, XXVI (December 1971), pp. 329–36.

Although most current commentators on Max Beerbohm's
parody, "The Feast by J*s*ph C*nr*d" in *A Christmas Garland* tend to
identify its object as JC's story "The Lagoon," Beerbohm, as he
burlesques JC's style, atmosphere, diction, a character type and
situation (the duping of a provincial white man by a shrewd savage),
and a tone of "world-weariness," draws on several other works of JC,
especially "Heart of Darkness," *Almayer's Folly, An Outcast of the
Islands*, "An Outpost of Progress," and "A Smile of Fortune."

2612 Brown, Harry. "Poem," *CON*, III, No. 2 (1971–72), p. 81.

[Short poem based on JC's observation in *The Secret Sharer* that "it is only the young who are ever confronted by such clear issues."]

2613 Brown, P. L. "'The Secret Sharer' and the Existential Hero," *CON*, III, No. 3 (1971–72), pp. 22–30.

Limitations of a psychological interpretation of "The Secret Sharer" can be overcome by expanding the frame of reference to include the relationship of the narrator and Leggatt from the common ground of existential action shared by the two men. Leggatt becomes a part of the narrator's subjective self because both men have common "philosophical" goals: both rebel against traditional values and desire to prove themselves, and to gain mastery over themselves and their worlds. Leggatt came to terms with such a world before reaching the narrator: he had acted in a way Sartre would approve—"freely, individually, responsibly." At the end of the story, he swims away from the narrator's ship, not determinedly but gratuitously. The narrator hides Leggatt on the ship and identifies with him for the same reason he dares sail so close to Koh-ring: he wants to prove himself, to have the kind of freedom, independence, courage, and self-reliance he sees in the mysterious sailor who becomes his own "existential ideal." In the act of sheltering Leggatt, the narrator initiates the existential committment of the man whose accomplice he becomes. At the end of the story he makes his ultimate attempt to prove himself: he defies death then because Koh-ring provides him with a symbol as ambiguous as Leggatt has become for him. It provides the narrator an appropriate test of his ability to gain mastery over himself, his ship and his world, over "life itself."

2614 Brufee, Kenneth A. "Elegiac Romance," *College English*, XXXII (January 1971), pp. 465–76.

Several novels of the nineteenth and twentieth centuries fall into the group called "elegiac Romance," of which two are "Heart of Darkness" and *Lord Jim.* As to narrative, each story is a pseudo-biography of an obsessively active, questing hero, which comes to be seen as a pseudo-autobiography of the narrator: Marlow, for example, tells the story of Kurtz and of Jim. The central action is an imaginative reconstruction of a one-way relationship which has once developed between the two central figures. This relationship is fundamentally corrupt. In "Heart of Darkness," Marlow is disgusted by Kurtz's corruption and yet drawn to him. The narrative structure is a dynamic metaphor which expresses the emotional predicament in which the will of the present is imprisoned by the persisting will of the past. A key seems to be the need of the younger man to identify with the older, as Marlow in his youth seems to have passionately needed to identify with the hero. Marlow's lie in "Heart of Darkness" is his means of breaking the hold of the past and reestablishing a condition of truth in the self. [Brufee has introduced this line of thought in "The Lesser Nightmare: Marlow's 'Lie' in 'Heart of Darkness,'" *Modern Language Quarterly*, XXV (Summer 1964), pp. 322–29 (C, I, No. 1784).]

2615 Bruss, Paul Samuel. "The Spaces of Death—A Study of the Early Conrad," *DAI*, XXXII (September 1971), 1504A. Unpublished thesis, University of Rochester, 1971.

2616 Butler, Richard E. "Jungian and Oriental Symbolism in Joseph Conrad's *Victory*," *CON*, III, No. 2 (1971–72), pp. 36–54.

Clues to the understanding of *Victory* lie in Jung's commentary on the book of Chinese philosophy, *The Secret of the Golden Flower*, and in the explication of the anima and the shadow archetypes in his *Aion*. The structure of the novel may be seen as circular, or perhaps more suggestively, as a mandala form. As the novel progresses, the story is told and retold on progressively deeper and more complex levels. In part III, a new presence, Lena, has begun to challenge Heyst's image of his father: in apparently breaking the spell of his father's dominance, he has brought into play the potentially dangerous anima. His implicit destiny is therefore about to become manifest. The peace of the island retreat is broken by the arrival of the melodramatic villains, one of whom, Jones, is a projection of the "shadow" archetype in Heyst's unconscious. The reality of Heyst's conscious undefiled gentlemanliness implies a "black alter-ego" in his unconscious: this duality theme assumes great importance in the novel. For the Christ-like Heyst, the Satanic Jones is the projection of the shadow figure in the unconscious. The savage trio of invaders, really one, a trinity, constitute Heyst's alter-ego, and they, with Lena, compose the quadripartite structure, which suggests again the mandala. In a sense, *Victory* represents the philosophical concept of solipsism; it is a very "Eastern" book but not an "awkward popular romance."

2617 Carter, Ernest. "Classical Allusions as the Clue to Meaning in Conrad's 'Il Conde,'" *CON*, III (1971–72), pp. 55–62.

At the close of "Il Conde," the "sedate aristocrat" is forced by a profound shock to his moral nature to leave his "beloved shores" and the serenity they represent because his confrontation with the reality of his inner emptiness has robbed his life of its illusory value. The Count's condemning himself to death is his single authentic act. The narrator of the story first meets Il Conde in Naples, where the two converse "over the celebrated Resting Hermes," the Count understanding nothing of the powerful forces of fertility and death the statue symbolized for the classical world. The young god of late classical literature was also regarded as the patron of thievery and duplicity. Quite fittingly, therefore, Il Conde is robbed—but of nothing of real value—by an unidentified "type" who is representative of Hermes. Thus this god fittingly presides throughout the story of a man who awakes to discover his invalid existence. The situation in "Il Conde" is basically that presented by several of JC's longer works (*Lord Jim, Nostromo, The Secret Agent*) in which outer chance or fatality combines strangely with inner weakness to provide the inevitable catastrophe through which, as Morton Zabel has said, "The terms of life are reversed."

2618 Cecchi, Ottavio. "Nota introduttiva" (Introductory Note), *Racconti di Mare e di Costa* ('Twixt Land and Sea), (Milano: Mondadori, 1971), pp. v–xix.

[Brief notes on JC's life and works, with a selection of critical judgments and a select bibliography.] [In Italian.]

2619 Chwalewik, Witold. "Conrad in the Light of a New Record," *KN*, XXVIII, I (1971), pp. 51–55.

Bobrowski's letter to Buszczynski (1879, discovered in 1911) reports an attempted suicide by JC, not a duel, in Marseilles. Edwin Pugh, in a serialization of his memoirs (*The New Witness*, 1919), records meeting JC, who described the "duel" as motivated by "romantic honour and intended to shield a woman." The explanation is thus rather that of a detective story than a case study in psychology.

2620 Cook, William J., Jr. "More Light on 'Heart of Darkness,'" *CON*, III, No. 3 (1971–72), pp. 4–14.

In "Heart of Darkness," there are three thematic levels—all supported by the central image of light and darkness: (1) the doubly ironic contrast of the civilized with the uncivilized countries, in which JC identifies civilization with light; (2) Kurtz and his "Western" aspirations for "great things" for both himself and the world, and Kurtz's moral struggle and eventual fall or submission to the darkness; and (3) the story of Marlow's descent into self, his examination of the dark possibilities of his own psyche and that of all men, after which he is no longer a "hollow" man. In learning that beneath the veneer of righteousness and morality there lies a potential darkness common to all men, Marlow chooses Kurtz and savagery over the "pious" civilized hypocrites and finally accepts the world and its people for what they are, weak beings who cannot live without saving illusions.

2621 Davis, W. Eugene. "Review: Image-Hunting," *ELT*, XIV, No. 1 (1971), pp. 53–54.

In *Joseph Conrad: The Imaged Style* (1970), Wilfred S. Dowden fails to provide either a much-needed analysis of the "interplay of style and imagery," an analysis that shows how aspects of style affect the significance of JC's images, or a careful consideration of "the rhetorical or syntactical" aspects of style in JC's works.

2622 Edwards, Paul. "Clothes for the Pilgrimage: A Recurrent Image in 'Heart of Darkness,'" *Mosaic* (University of Manitoba), IV (Spring 1971), pp. 67–74.

In "Heart of Darkness," "a study of the world at its least reassuring," JC uses images of dress to explore and reveal the thoughts and feelings of the people in the story. In throwing his shoes overboard, Marlow, for example, performs an unreasoning but symbolic act: he unconsciously assumes the role of barefoot pilgrim. And Marlow recognizes the "bepatched" Russian as another journeying man. The patched costume both reveals and perplexes; the Russian is, in one sense, a kind of fool and, in another, one of the hollow men of the tale. Marlow knows well that the patches and the dressing up of the accountant are only temporary, that in the end every man must face his own nakedness, "what he is, his inner being." Clothes as lies also appear in the story, though eventually they still reveal the corruption they seem to hide. And in the accountant one can see a "ghostly outline" of Marlow himself. Finally, Kurtz suffers from the same inner sickness—hollowness—as does Brussels, the dark center of the imperial enterprise: the "acquisitions, clothes, pretty rags" are torn away and Kurtz is stripped "down to the naked flesh," soon to be stripped "to the bone."

2623 Feaster, John William. "The Relationship Between Philosophical Scepticism and Aesthetic Form in the Novels of Joseph Conrad," *DAI*, XXXI (1971), 5398A. Unpublished dissertation, Purdue University, 1970.

2624 Fernando, Lloyd. "Literary English in the South-East Asian Tradition," *Westerly*, No. 3 (September 1971), pp. 7–13.

As the relationship of the various Commonwealth literatures in English to the great native British tradition may no longer be assumed, as formerly, those found in Asia do not obviously belong to a native Asian heritage, either. The only clear matter is that long after the Commonwealth itself vanishes—as it seems to be doing—some sort of general label may still continue to be a convenient way of referring to the literatures in English which have sprouted in spite

of orthodox ideas about the ways in which literature and tradition
evolve.   Tradition in South-East Asia, where four great traditions
have intermingled—texts and studies of traditional Malay life and
culture; a considerable body of minor writing by English visitors,
administrators, sailors, botanists, and casual residents; and the
other major communities of Malaysia, Chinese and Indian—is
difficult to piece together.   No "really outstanding" writers of
autobiography of fiction have emerged, with the exception of JC, and
to a lesser extent, Somerset Maugham, and they were not, in a
relevant sense, even temporary residents.   JC, of course, did not try to
delve into his Asian characters deeper than his "novelistic instinct"
told him was necessary or safe.   As a result we know very little about
the inner lives of such characters in *Lord Jim* as Jewel, Tamb' Itam,
Doramin, and Dain Waris.   JC "steered deftly" round the realities of
Asian life.

2625 Fink, Howard. "The Ambiguous Mirrors of Nabokov," *Canadian
Slavic Studies*, V (Spring 1971), pp. 85–89.

The "fictions" of B. Sirin, the name under which Vladimir
Nabokov published his Russian writings, perform the same function
as those of Konrad Korzeniowski (JC): to reveal "the exotic and
ambiguous realities behind our dull apprehension of our Western
world" by applying to that world "the insights of the Slavic exile and
the artist."   Both writers utilize in their fictions aesthetic strategies
which in themselves reveal the authors' philosophical vision. But
Nabokov, writing in a later age, goes far beyond JC's multiple views of
fictional reality.

2626 Fleishman, Avrom. "Experiment and Renewal: Conrad," *The
English Historical Novel: Walter Scott to Virginia Woolf*
(Baltimore and London: The Johns Hopkins University Press,
1971), pp. 115, 141, 208, 211, 212–32.

JC was committed to the idea that history is the shaping power
in modern experience, but he considered recent developments to
have made so sharp a break with the political values of the past that
"History may be said to have ended and an era of anarchy to have
been ushered in."   For JC, too, there was the "antiquarian tendency,"
the urge to recollect the things of the past because they slip away,
because they are not recognized by the young, because they give
pleasure to "that faculty of late-blooming romanticism—the
memory."   JC, for example, displayed a life-long interest in the
Napoleonic era; the "essential fable" of *The Rover* is the necessity of
engagement, if not to abstract political ideals, at least to the moral
beings such as Peyrol and Arlette. The greatest strength of *Rover* is
an evocation of the "Spirit of the Epoch" in the descriptions of the

Terror as it was felt in Toulon. In *Suspense, A Napoleonic Novel,* every character holds an attitude toward Napoleon, and this set of attitudes creates not a portrait of the man but an image of historical reality. Although dealing with a roughly contemporary situation, of JC's works *Nostromo* most fully realizes the spirit of an epoch. The action of the novel allows us to trace the circuitous course by which historical changes actually come about.

2627 Fletcher, Ian. "Can Haggard Ride Again?" *Listener,* LXXXVI (29 July 1971), pp. 136–38.

H. Rider Haggard, the popular romancer, has been related to both Kipling and JC through his interest in the relativity of cultures. Although he is a much more naive writer than either, he worries "over the same questions as the more profound writers of his time." He shares the "end-of-the-century fascination" with the "quirkily supernatural," second sight, primitive magic, and reincarnation, the last of which, though a part of the tradition of romance, is "a measure of the distance from, say, Conrad in that he rarely gives it a muted secularized form."

2628 Folsom, James K. "The Legacy of the Secret Sharer," *Bulletin of the Rocky Mountain MLA,* XXV (March 1971), pp. 16–21.

In addition to using the sea as a foil for the land in his fiction, JC also visualizes the sea as a place of testing. The narrator of "The Secret Sharer" achieves from Leggatt, during the course of the story, an insight which enables him to assume the role of commander of his ship, and his successful assumption of this role is then metaphorically expressed in his ability to execute a difficult nautical maneuver. A detailed knowledge of what actually happens in the story reveals the fact that Leggatt's killing of a sailor on the *Sephora* may not have been murder, because his victim had refused to obey a legitimate order given by his captain and was therefore technically a mutineer. Also, the captain, fearing to be involved, shirks the responsibilities of command. In a way, each captain is confronted with the problem of being a real commander. The ending of the story is not about how to avoid having gotten into the predicament at Koh-ring but how to get out of it; JC's point seems to be that peril is the basic fact of life on the sea and that no one can ignore it. That it can be overcome if one knows what he is doing is the significance of the hat which Leggatt leaves on the water: the hat lets the captain know exactly when he needs to shift the helm.

2629 Foulke, Robert. "Postures of Belief in *The Nigger of the Narcissus*," *MFS,* XVII (Summer 1971), pp. 249–62.

Three modes of perception are apparent in the language of the text in *The Nigger of the Narcissus*: (1) that which is most closely allied to usual notions of verisimilitude because it comes from the narrator's direct observation, (2) abstract judgments about men and events in the narrator's voice, "with obvious explicit meaning but no clear authority in events," and (3) that which emerges from clusters of metaphor suggesting a mythic voyage, with archetypal motifs and polarized characters." As his techniques evolved, JC developed increasingly sophisticated "strategies"; in "Youth," all the perception appears in the older Marlow telling the story, all the mimesis in the young, acting Marlow; in *Lord Jim*, the old Marlow identifies with young Jim, thereby making the tensions between the experience of the teller and the innocence of the actor stronger and more explicit; and in later versions there appears the Doppelgänger of "The Secret Sharer" and *The Shadow-Line*, where all the conflict of perception is built into the "schizophrenic" young captains who tell their own stories. This evolution of JC's narrative technique can also be seen as a movement away from mimesis toward fantasy, toward solipsism. In *Nigger*, there is a human voice which cannot be held accountable for all of its pronouncements, an elusive narrator who is unreliable when he generalizes, who consists of a "wise" narrator and a naive one who do not support simplified interpretations of *Nigger*.

2630 Foye, Paul F., Bruce Harkness, and Nathan L. Marvin. "The Sailing Maneuver in 'The Secret Sharer,'" *JML*, II (September 1971), pp. 119–23.

JC's fiction seems to contain a deliberate blurring of the distinctions between realism and symbolism; his world is paradoxically very real and at the same time insubstantial. In considering his fiction, readers have increasingly moved from an emphasis on the realistic detail to the symbolic element, as demonstrated in the many symbolic interpretations of "The Secret Sharer." Yet, many details that *seem* to be clear are not so, like the episode in this story in which the Captain takes his ship dangerously close to the island of Koh-ring and then allows Leggatt to slip away, after which he saves his ship only by virtue of Leggatt's leaving his white hat in the water. JC does not include enough detail for today's readers to grasp the peril of this maneuver. It is "very similar to driving your car up and beyond your driveway, coasting into the driveway backwards and coming out and going back in the direction that you first came." This extremely risky series of movements typifies "the daring and precision of Conrad the sailor as well as of Conrad the writer."

2631 Freeman, Leslie J. "The Integrity of *The Secret Agent,*" *DAI,* XXXII (1971), 428A. Unpublished dissertation, Columbia University, 1970.

2632 Geddes, Gary. "Conrad and the Darkness Before Creation," *Antigonish Review,* No. 7 (Autumn 1971), pp. 93–104.

When JC finally "put flesh and blood" on the creatures of his imagination, he was responding to a deep need in himself, the record of extreme anguish that drove him from the sea to his writing desk. *Almayer's Folly* and *An Outcast of the Islands,* with the letters while JC was writing these novels, are useful indicators of JC's preoccupations and general state of mind in his early years: he recognized the "dark vision of the world of human affairs" and the meaninglessness of the universe. His existential awareness seems prophetic of attitudes that have come to prevail in the twentieth century in such writers as Henry Miller, Camus, and Robbe-Grillet, with whom he shares the spiritual anguish because of the disappearance of ethical and intellectual standards. "Heart of Darkness" laid bare the raw facts of colonial exploitation, *Nostromo* charted the inevitable "collision course" of material interests, and *Under Western Eyes* questioned the effectiveness of political institutions as vehicles of reform. For Decoud, annihilation is preferable to an existence without structure or meaning. JC came to realize the importance of ignoring or transcending the self, since such a transcendence may free one for a creative existence. In "Books," he recommends a precarious balance between an artistic sense and believing that the world is good. For JC, art could fill the void left by the "clean sweep" of his intellect over the half-truths of life.

2633 Gerver, Elizabeth. "Facts into Fiction: Conrad's Creative Process," *Dalhousie Review,* LII (Summer 1972), pp. 295–302.

Norman Sherry in *Conrad's Western World* (1971) demonstrates convincingly that JC's technique of composing fiction was a "complex" transformation of facts into fiction. The major sources for *The Secret Agent,* "Heart of Darkness," and *Nostromo,* as Sherry shows, are public facts primarily in the form of "'underground' written sources" and personal experiences "derived . . . from his own marital" relationship. Sherry, however, neglects to discuss in detail a third and equally important type of source—namely, that of JC's use of "fiction to make fiction." For instance, *Agent* "bears interesting similarities" to Henry James's *The Princess Casamassima,* Turgenev's *Fathers and Children,* and Dostoevski's *The Possessed.*

2634 Goetsch, Paul. "Neure Arbeiten über Joseph Conrads Verhältnis zur Politik" (New Publications on Joseph Conrad's Attitude Toward Politics), *Die Neueuren Sprachen*, XX (1971), pp. 19–27.

[A review essay which centers on Avrom Fleishman, *Conrad's Politics: Community and Anarchy in the Fiction of Joseph Conrad* (Baltimore: The Johns Hopkins Press, 1967); Robert F. Lee, *Conrad's Colonialism* (The Hague, 1969); Claire Rosenfield, *Paradise of Snakes: An Archetypal Analysis of Conrad's Political Novels* (Chicago: University of Chicago Press, 1967). On JC's attitude towards ideology, class warfare, imperialism, and colonialism. Discusses some key terms of JC's "philosophy such as 'solidarity' and 'community.'" Interesting suggestions for further research.] [In German.]

2635 Gogol, John M. "Joseph Conrad and Johannes Bobrowski, Two Exiles from Sarmatia," *CON*, III, No. 2 (1971–72), pp. 77–80.

The "great" German lyric poet, Johannes Bobrowski, dedicated a biographical poem, "Joseph Conrad," to JC, his fellow Sarmatian, with whom he had an "affinity." Bobrowski's Sarmatia is the "central core" of the European territory, what was once the medieval Lithuanian Empire and also once a part of Poland. A mystique similar to that of the American West grew up around this "borderland" area in the nineteenth century under the influence of the historical novels of Henryk Sienkiewicz. From this region came JC and several other great Polish writers. Some lines of Bobrowski's poem, "The Tomsk Road," are the words of the Russian exile Alexander Herzen and also, coincidentally, the exact words used by Jerry Allen to describe the exile of JC's father and his family in her biography of JC, *The Thunder and the Sunshine* (1958). The "dark shadows" of Sarmatia appear in the exotic landscapes of JC's stories of the Congo and the Malay Archipelago, just as they reecho throughout the lyric poetry of Bobrowski. In *The Sisters*, where JC described this "shadowland" of his origins, his images are similar to those of Bobrowski in his poem, "The Sarmatian Plain."

2636 Goonetilleke, D. C. R. A. "Conrad's African Tales: Ironies of Progress," *Ceylon Journal of the Humanities*, II (January 1971), pp. 64–97.

"An Outpost of Progress" was, according to JC, "the lightest part of the loot" which he carried away from Central Africa. The story plays off the conventional, lofty associations of the title against the squalid, perilous reality, suggesting the irony prevalent in the tale. JC exposes several aspects of petty trading in imperial outposts, among them the insincerity of directors and the inhuman use of certain employees by imperial countries. The theme is the perils of petty trading on the edges of an empire. But JC does not go deep into his subject; he has not yet developed his power to explore psychology without a mediating narrator. In "Heart of Darkness," JC presents the imperial entanglements of Western civilization and primitive culture as these are skirted by a certain type of Englishman, Marlow. Detachment is the necessary essence of JC's technique. One reason why we accept his narrative as authentic is that his tone always sounds like that of an honest man. JC suggests through the ritual connotations of Marlow's concluding words that an ideal of imperialism is an essentially primitive justification of inhumanity, common to both civilized and primitive societies. JC records the entanglements of Western civilization and primitive culture in "lurid imperial prose," not in the "conversational idiom" of Marlow. Since there is something conventional in his view of Negroes, he cannot portray them deeply. But Kurtz's cry of horror is a recoil from the "mess of European rapacity."

2637 "Graham Greene Re Conrad," *CON*, III, No. 3 (1971–72), p. 32.

The *Listener* (London) carried for April 23, 1970, a published radio interview with Graham Greene. Greene stated that his last book to be seriously influenced by JC was *It's a Battlefield*, in which the second chief character, the assistant commissioner of police, seems to be "as it were, an uncle of mine transformed a little into a Conrad character. It is a conflict between experience and literature."

2638 Greene, Graham. *A Sort of Life* (London: Bodley Head; New York: Simon and Schuster, 1971), pp. 154, 206.

In his early novels, Graham Greene had to get JC and much belated romanticism out of his system. In writing about work on his second novel, he notes that "Conrad was the influence now, and in particular the most dangerous of all his books, *The Arrow of Gold*." Greene had removed himself almost entirely from his novels so that "all that was left in the heavy pages of the second [*Rumour at Nightfall*] was the distorted ghost of Conrad." [A revealing insight into JC's influence on later novelists.]

2639 Haltresht, Michael. "Disease Imagery in Conrad's *The Secret Agent*," *Literature and Psychology*, XXI, No. 2 (1971), pp. 101–105.

Many of the diseases afflicting characters in *The Secret Agent* are symbolic of or symptomatic of emotional problems. Karl Yundt's impotence suggests his psychic sterility. Skin conditions symbolize the moral repulsiveness of the Professor, Wurmt, Michaelis, Sir Ethelred, and the cabby. Mental blindness is reflected in eye disorders; physical laziness reflects mental intertia. Michaelis's obesity implies the oral craving of an unloved baby, and his asthmatic wheeze suggests a suppressed cry for affection. Likewise, the fatness of Winnie's mother may result from her frustration at not being loved. The Assistant Commissioner's "biliousness" results from his resentment of his job.

2640 Hardesty, William Howard. "Joseph Conrad: The Last Seven Years," *DAI*, XXXI (1971), 5403A. Unpublished dissertation, University of Pennsylvania, 1970.

2641 Harkness, Bruce. "The Light in the Darkness," *"Heart of Darkness" and Other Stories* (Boston: Houghton, Mifflin, 1971), pp. vi–xiv.

"The Secret Sharer," *The Shadow-Line*, "An Outpost of Progress," and "Heart of Darkness" share a single theme: the trials of a soul in isolation. Each deals with the problem of self-knowledge. The two Europeans in "An Outpost of Progress" cannot come to learn about themselves and are simply destroyed. The captain in "The Secret Sharer," Leggatt, and Marlow, however, do acquire self-knowledge, recover, and go on. They come to recognize the unavoidable darkness in the heart of man, but can continue because they know that one must live as if man were good, in order to preserve society. All four stories demonstrate that the individual can only rely on himself and that he must act when confronted by evil. These stories reflect JC's consistent view that men are neither good nor strong, but one must love them nonetheless. [Also contains "Suggestions for Reading and Discussion" by Gladys Veidemanis (pp. 257–271).]

2642 Hesla, David H. *The Shape of Chaos: An Interpretation of the Art of Samuel Beckett* (Minneapolis: University of Minnesota Press, 1971), p. 172.

Put briefly, according to the phenomenology of Husserl, we should "bracket" or disconnect from the world as it is all the values we have associated with real things in order to reach the "phenomenological residuum," and by making this reduction reach a new region of Being, the realm of "pure experiences," which we are to study and describe. Our task is to become conscious of consciousness. We thus, according to Merleau-Ponty, relearn how to look at the world, as the works of Balzac, Proust, Valéry, and Cézanne demonstrate; by "the same kind of attentiveness and wonder, the same demand for awareness," meaning comes into being. To these artists we must add JC, because of his claim that the artist "speaks to our capacity for delight and wonder, . . . [and] the sense of mystery surrounding our lives," and also because he justified the artist's mission by an appeal to awareness. And JC certainly did try to show us the world more clearly. [Seems to be one of the few attempts to apply phenomenology to JC.]

2643 Higdon, David Leon. "Chateau Borel, Petrus Borel, and Conrad's *Under Western Eyes*," *SNNTS*, III (Spring 1971), pp. 99–102.

JC may have named Chateau Borel, dominant in Parts II and III of *Under Western Eyes*, after the French republican and romanticist Petrus Borel (Pierre Joseph Borel d'Hauterive, author of books containing Gothic excesses), and he used in his novel romantic conventions similar to those of writers connected with or influenced by Borel (Gautier, Baudelaire, Huysmans). Although there is no evidence that JC knew Borel's works, he must have known his reputation. His choice of this name indicates the extent of his disapproval of romanticism and even his own use of its conventions in the same novel.

2644 Howarth, Howard. "Conrad and Imperialism: The Difference of *The Rescue*," *Ohio Review*, XIII (Fall 1971), pp. 62–72.

Three of JC's works conceived at the same period offer incompatibly different views of imperialism: "Heart of Darkness" condemns the imperial mission, *Lord Jim* vindicates it, and *The Rescue* displays its dislike of the English elite and western colonialism and its choice of a hero from below, Lingard, who is not "one of us," but has risen from poverty and become, through adventure, a "New Man." *Rescue* considers Lingard honorable as long as he loves the Wajo princess and the energy of the New Man is correlated with his fidelity to Asia. But the desirable dream is shattered: Lingard betrays Asia and himself for a poor man's illusion of the desirability of the "Great Lady," Mrs. Travers. The latter wins: if the primitive woman had emerged and given herself completely to the man, had accepted Hassim and Immada, by that choice the "two nations" of England would have been reconciled and the "mystic marriage" of East and West would have been celebrated. By most Conradian tests she has failed, but Lingard exonerates her. In filling in the background of *Rescue*, JC enlarged a childhood fight against handicaps of both to an obstinate redressing of the inequities of the world. His account of imperialism is here subordinated to his analysis of English society—a society split like his own personality.

2645 Howell, Elmo. "The Concept of Evil in Conrad's *Victory*," *Ball State University Forum*, XIII (Spring 1971), pp. 76–79.

Since in JC's world evil is inescapable, man must be able to recognize it and be prepared for it. To balanced minds, though, evil is not the occasion for despair. Rather, the awareness of its mystery creates a sense of participation in a cosmic drama. In *Victory*, the evil of the world is incarnated in Ricardo, evil intelligence in Jones, brute force in Pedro. In combating these forces JC's protagonist must realize that the only victory is participation in the drama and a gallant facing up to heavy odds. The novel dramatizes man's failure to discriminate and the resulting invitation to self-destruction.

2646 Hummel, Madeline. "Fifty Unpublished Letters from Joseph Conrad," *Library Chronicle of the University of Texas*, ns, No. 3 (May 1971), pp. 52–57.

When JC visited Norman Douglas in Capri in 1905, a long, satisfying friendship began. Of the fifty letters which JC wrote to Douglas between 1905 and 1913, most deal mainly with efforts to launch Douglas's career, but the letters also indicate JC's complex personality, the emotional energy which *Under Western Eyes* caused him, and some of the themes which dominated his early stories. [Contains a checklist of fifty autograph letters, 1905–1913, from JC to Douglas in the Academic Center Library at the University of Texas at Austin.]

2647 Hussey, William R. M. "'He Was Spared That Annoyance,'" *CON*, III, No. 2 (1971–72), pp. 17–25.

Certain parallels in the structure of "Typhoon" make it more than a mere adventure story. There is an internal hurricane which threatens the *Nan-Shan* almost as much as the external one. Captain MacWhirr, the central figure of the novel, is the eye of the social storm—the one person who remains calm. He is an admirable character, of a type seldom given close fictional treatment.

2648 Jeffrey, David K. "Conrad's *The Secret Agent*," *Explicator*, XXIX (February 1971), Item 53.

The imagery which pervades *The Secret Agent* indicates that man is not merely the villain which Hamlet dubs him; he is "a beast in the jungle" of London, a city as "monstrous" as its inhabitants.

2649 Johnson, Bruce. *Conrad's Models of Mind* (Minneapolis: University of Minnesota Press, 1971).

His fundamental beliefs, or models of mind, allow JC to organize and come to grips with the ultimately mysterious phenomenon of mind itself. Steadily he moves away from deductive psychology toward a flexible new psychology (at the time) that has implications for his entire development as a writer. He obtained his models from his affinities with other writers—Pascal, Sartre, and especially Schopenhauer—beginning with the metaphor of the paralyzed will in his early novels and breaking, in *The Nigger of the Narcissus*, with much of his earlier work. The basic structural principle of *Lord Jim* is to imagine a young man who, having violated a fixed standard, attempts to transfer it to a human community significantly unlike that of the ship in *Nigger* and to decipher what being faithful to it means in such a new situation. "Heart of Darkness" implies radical changes in JC's "root conceptions" of mind; both this story and *Jim* are about "the man who would be king" in Sartre's sense of God. In *Nostromo*, political maneuvers and ideals, apparently the source of value for many men, are seen as masks consciously and unconsciously used to disguise and reveal simultaneously the true source of value. In "The Secret Sharer," JC exploits an almost Freudian model developed in earlier stories, and *The Shadow-Line* was written as a counterpart to it. What may have begun as something of an indictment of Russia in *Under Western Eyes* develops into an extraordinary further view of sympathy. In *Chance* and *Victory*, sympathy very nearly remains in its lowest form—pity. The later works lose the potency of the earlier ones.

2650 Karl, Frederick R. "Joseph Conrad, Norman Douglas, and the *English Review*," *JML*, II (Third Issue 1971–72), pp. 342–56.

The more than fifty extant letters from JC to Norman Douglas reveal a neglected side of JC, his desire to foster good writing in others even when his taste differed from theirs. Wanting to help the struggling Douglas find a place of publication, he turned to the *English Review*, whose editor was Ford Madox Ford. The years 1908 to 1912 were the high point of the remarkable ten-year friendship of the two men and, in spite of JC's consideration of Douglas' work as saleable items rather than an artistic achievement, he assisted Douglas until he became an assistant editor of the *English Review*. Eventually the two friends drifted apart: the *Review* was failing rapidly, JC was becoming a wider selling novelist and was acquiring a new set of admirers, and the two men fell out personally. The relationship was actually one-sided: Douglas was neither the kind of man nor the kind of writer JC could respect.

2651 Kartiganer, Donald M. "Process and Product: A Study in Modern Literary Form [Part 1]," *Massachusetts Review*, XII (Winter 1971), pp. 297–328.

Modern writers are aware of the disparity between "movement and design, of contingency and form, image and abstraction, process and product." This awareness arises from a general consciousness of two distinct kinds of illusion possible in literary form: the work which appears to contain experience within "a deliberately structured form" and the work which creates "an impression of unmodified spontaneity," of experience met more directly by the refusal to impose traditional notions of form upon it. William Carlos Williams's *Paterson* illustrates the use of process in a comparatively pure form. The fusion of process and product distinguishes the best work of Joyce, Yeats, Eliot, Faulkner, Stevens, and JC. [Followed by Part 2 of the same essay (Autumn 1971).]

2652 Kartiganer, Donald M. "Process and Product: A Study of Modern Literary Form [Part 2]," *Massachusetts Review*, XII (Autumn 1971), pp. 789–816.

In Faulkner and JC, the "agonies" of an art suspended between the two poles of process and product are "definitively" explored. The major difference between these two writers is that the need for process is a need which JC arrives at only in despair, whereas for Faulkner it comes to represent the highest possibilities of human and moral engagement. The need to create meaning in *Nostromo*, for example, is an invitation only to illusion, usually a destructive kind. The "intense pessimism" of this novel is a consequence of the failure of any illusion to arrest or even approach the reality which occasionally lurks behind the novel's maze of illusions. Decoud's vision forces him to suicide, and every other character in the book is forced into the frailty of JC's version of the mythic mode, only out of fables of order can they survive. Even Dr. Monygham and Nostromo are alike in their need for illusion and a sustaining ideal. JC goes far in the matter of the dangers of the illusion; the novel's basic theme is the total isolation into which dreams may plunge a man. Nostromo himself is the center of the novel because the relationship between the impact of events and the creation of a saving illusion is the clearest and least sophisticated in him. In *Nostromo*, there is a sequence of products but no projected pattern as in *Paterson*, Whitman's *Song of Myself*, or Faulkner's *Absalom, Absalom!* [Preceded by Part 1 of the same essay (Winter 1971).]

2653 Kelley, Robert E. "'This Chance Glimpse': The Narrator in *Under Western Eyes*," *University Review—Kansas City*, XXXVII (June 1971), pp. 285–90.

The function and personality of the narrator in *Under Western Eyes* may be approached by considering recurring patterns and attitudes, called "constants," such as the narrator's remaining nameless and the narrator's style, which are among the prominent features of the book. It is from the interplay among these constants that the particular quality of the novel is derived.

2654 Kermode, Frank. "Joseph Conrad," *Atlantic Brief Lives: A Biographical Companion to the Arts*, ed. by Louis Kronenberger (Boston: Little, Brown, 1971), pp. 175–77.

Nearly always "at the end of his tether," JC brought to his writing "a gloomy dedication" well represented by the tortuous composition of *Nostromo*. Believing that man is a worker or nothing, he strove for the utmost precision. He had at least one negative qualification for producing good art: a complete inability to repeat himself. His terrain is the world seen by one who loved its humanity but renounced action and saw in it the pattern of evil. For him, to be conscious was tragic. Like one of his characters, JC "sees to" his beautiful chronometer before jumping overboard—then does not jump. [Preceded by a short biography and list of works, this "brief life" presents an unnecessarily dour portrait of JC.]

2655 Kermode, Frank. "Joseph Conrad Never Jumped," *NYTBR* (11 April 1971), p. 2; rpt. Louis Kronenberger (ed.), *Atlantic Brief Lives: A Biographical Companion to the Arts* (Boston: Atlantic—Little, Brown, 1971), pp. 175–77.

Believing in the value of work, JC brought to his writing a "gloomy dedication." He saw the world as one who, "having loved the humanity of it," renounced action and saw in it instead "the pattern of evil": Jim's need was *not* to jump, but "to be a convict rather than an idiot." So JC labored, a visionary who despised visionaries, saved by work and fidelity as he expiated "the curse of consciousness." Sometimes he extolled the simple man, like the sea captain; but he also recalled the young officer (himself) confronted with his "criminal double, his *semblable*," and the old man "tormented by fate and his own nobility." In his own life, he knew these tensions, but he did not quite kill himself; he did not jump.

2656 Kimbrough, Robert. "Preface to the Second Edition," *JCHD* (1971), p. ix.

[Explains the changes made for the revised edition of this book.]

2657 Kimbrough, Robert (ed.). *Joseph Conrad: "Heart of Darkness": An Authoritative Text, Backgrounds and Sources, Criticism*, rvd. (New York: Norton [A Norton Critical Edition], 1971), (C, I, No. 1731).

Contents, abstracted under year of first publication: Robert Kimbrough, "Preface to the Second Edition (1971), p. ix; Robert Kimbrough, "Preface" (1963), (C, I, No. 1733); Robert Kimbrough, "Note on the Text," pp. 80–81 (C, I, No. 1732); Muriel C. Bradbrook, ["Conrad: A Sketch"], from *Joseph Conrad: Poland's English Genius*

(1941), (C, I, No. 1102); Albert J. Guerard, ["From Life to Art"], from *Conrad the Novelist* (1958), (C, I, No. 1470); G. Jean-Aubry, ["From Sailor to Novelist"], from *Joseph Conrad: Life and Letters,* I (1927), (C, I, No. 746); Edward Garnett, ["Art Drawn from Memory"], from "Introduction," *Letters from Conrad 1895–1924* (1928), (C, I, No. 805); Richard Curle, ["His Piercing Memory"], from *The Last Twelve Years of Joseph Conrad* (1928), (C, I, No. 794); Ford Madox Ford, ["The Setting"], from "Heart of Darkness," *Portraits From Life* (1937); Ford Madox Ford, ["The Ending"], from "Heart of Darkness," *Portraits From Life* (1937); Robert F. Haugh, ["'Heart of Darkness': Problems for Critics"], from *Joseph Conrad: Discovery in Design* (1957), (C, I, No. 1390); Albert J. Guerard, "The Journey Within," from *Conrad the Novelist* (1958), (C, I, No. 1470); Jerome Thale, "Marlow's Quest," from *University of Toronto Quarterly* (1955), (C, I, No. 1334); Lillian Feder, "Marlow's Descent into Hell," from *Nineteenth-Century Fiction* (1955), (C, I, No. 1320); Marvin Mudrick, "The Originality of Conrad," from *Hudson Review* (1958–59), (C, I, No. 1496); Stewart C. Wilcox, "Conrad's 'Complicated Presentations' of Symbolic Imagery," from *Philological Quarterly* (1960), (C, I, No. 1613); Leo Gurko, ["Conrad's Ecological Art"], from *Joseph Conrad: Giant in Exile* (1962), (C, I, No. 1674); Paul L. Wiley, "Conrad's Skein of Ironies" (1971); Ralph Maud, "The Plain Tale of 'Heart of Darkness,'" from *Humanities Association Bulletin* (1966); Donald R. Benson, "'Heart of Darkness': The Grounds of Civilization in an Alien Universe," from *Texas Studies in Language and Literature* (1966); Robert O. Evans, "Conrad's Underworld," from *Modern Fiction Studies* (1956), (C, I, No. 1344); William Bysshe Stein, "The Lotus Posture and 'Heart of Darkness,'" from *Modern Fiction Studies* (1956–57), (C, I, No. 1355); Seymour Gross, ["The Frame"] from "A Further Note on the Function of the Frame in 'Heart of Darkness,'" *Modern Fiction Studies* (1957), (C, I, No. 1388); Robert O. Evans, ["No Easy Clue"], from "A Further Comment on 'Heart of Darkness,'" *Modern Fiction Studies* (1957–58), (C, I, No. 1379); R. Kerf, "Symbol Hunting in Conradian Land," from *Revue des Langues Vivantes* (1966); Kenneth A. Bruffee, "The Lesser Nightmare," from *Modern Language Quarterly* (1964), (C, I, No. 1784); Ted E. Boyle, "Marlow's Lie," from *Studies in Short Fiction* (1964), (C, I, No. 1782); Gerald B. Kauvar, "Marlow as Liar," from *Studies in Short Fiction* (1968); C. F. Burgess, "Conrad's Pesky Russian," from *Nineteenth-Century Fiction* (1963), (C, I, No. 1707); Mario D'Avanzo, "Conrad's Motley as an Organizing Metaphor," from *College Language Association Journal* (1966); and John W. Canario, "The Harlequin," from *Studies in Short Fiction* (1967).

By others, not about JC and not abstracted: "A Map of the Congo Free State, 1890" p. 85; "The Congo," containing three brief quotations by King Leopold II, of Belgium, H. M. Stanley, and Mark

Twain, p. 86; Maurice N. Hennessy, ["The Congo: A Brief History, 1876–1908"], pp. 86–90, from *Congo* (1961); Sir Harry Johnston, ["George Grenfell: A Missionary in the Congo"], pp. 90–91, from *George Grenfell and the Congo*, I (1910); John de Courcy MacDonald, ["The Visionary King"], p. 92, from *King Leopold II: His Rule in Belgium and the Congo* (1905); Richard Harding Davis, ["His Brother's Keeper"], pp. 92–93, from *The Congo and the Coasts of Africa* (1907); King Leopold II, ["The Sacred Mission of Civilization"], pp. 93–94, from Guy Burrows, *The Land of the Pigmies* (1898); H. R. Fox-Bourne, ["New Forms of Slavery"], pp. 94–96, from *Civilization in Congoland* (1903); E. D. Morel, ["The Testimony of the Kodak"], pp. 96–98, from *King Leopold's Rule in Africa* (1904); and "Conrad in the Congo," containing two brief quotations by Henry M. Stanley and André Gide, p. 98.

By JC and not abstracted: an "authoritative" text of "Heart of Darkness"; "Geography and Some Explorers," from *Last Essays*, ed. by Richard Curle (1926); ["When I Grow Up I Shall Go There"], *A Personal Record* (1912); ["Extracts from Correspondence, January 16–June 18, 1890"], from *Letters of Joseph Conrad to Marguerite Poradowska*, ed. by Gee and Sturm (1940), and from G. Jean-Aubry, *Joseph Conrad: Life and Letters*, I (1927); "The Congo Diary," from *Last Essays*, ed. by Richard Curle (1926); ["Stanley Falls, Early September 1890"], from "Geography and Some Explorers," *Last Essays*, ed. by Richard Curle (1926); ["Extracts from Correspondence, September 6–December 27, 1890"], from G. Jean-Aubry, *Joseph Conrad in the Congo* (1926), G. Jean-Aubry, *Joseph Conrad: Life and Letters*, I (1927), and *Letters of Joseph Conrad to Marguerite Poradowska*, ed. by Gee and Sturm (1940); "Two Final Notes," from *A Personal Record* (1912) and "Author's Note," *Tales of Unrest* (1921); ["Extracts from Correspondence, December 13, 1898–February 12, 1899"], from G. Jean-Aubry, *Joseph Conrad: Life and Letters*, I (1927), *Joseph Conrad: Letters to William Blackwood and David S. Meldrum*, ed. by William Blackburn (1958), *Letters from Conrad 1895–1924*, ed. by Edward Garnett (1928), and *Lettres Francaises*, ed. by G. Jean-Aubry (1929); ["Conrad's Manuscript of 'Heart of Darkness'"], a reproduction of four pages: a section titled "Conrad on Life and Art," as follows: ["Fidelity: Four Notes"], from "A Familiar Preface" (1912), *Conrad's Prefaces*, ed. by Edward Garnett (1937), "Tradition" (1918) and "Well Done" (1918), and *Notes on Life and Letters* (1921); ["The Cruel Sea"], from *The Mirror of the Sea* (1905); ["The Faithful River"] from *The Mirror of the Sea* (1905); ["The World of the Living"], from "Author's Notes," *The Shadow-Line* (1920); ["'To Make You See'"], from the Preface, *The Nigger of the Narcissus* (1897); ["Books"], from "Books," *Notes on Life and Letters* (1905); ["Fiction Is Human History"], from "Henry James: An Appreciation" (1905); *Notes on Life*

and Letters (1921); ["The Symbolic Character of Fiction"] from G.
Jean-Aubry, *Joseph Conrad: Life and Letters*, II (1927);
["Explicitness Is Fatal to Art"], from Richard Curle, *Conrad to a
Friend* (1928); ["My Manner of Telling"], from Richard Curle, *Conrad to
a Friend* (1928); ["Every Novel Contains Autobiography"], from Arthur
Symons, *Notes on Joseph Conrad: With Some Unpublished Letters*
(1925); and ["On Marlow and 'Heart of Darkness'"], from "Author's
Note" (1917), *Youth* (1921). [The major changes in this revised edition
are the omission of six critical articles and the inclusion of nine
more recent or more appropriate ones, (C, I, No. 1731).]

2658 King, William E. "Conrad's *Weltanschauung* and the God of
Material Interests in *Nostromo*," *CON*, III, No. 3 (1971–72), pp.
41–45.

The most powerful force in the world picture of *Nostromo* is
material interests; the most overt association of these interests with
deity is through the "evangelical" businessman Holroyd, who
blatantly states the doctrine of manifest destiny. The triviality of this
situation is shown in Mrs. Gould's "horrified" description of
Costaguana politics as a children's game, in the Garibaldino's
"pensive" description of it as a dwarf's game, and in Martin Decoud's
laughing comparison of it to the opera-bouffe. Both the power of the
god of material interests and the faith this god inspires are
demonstrated by the San Tomé mine, with Charles Gould as the chief
representative of JC's *Weltanschauung*. Exceptions to this pattern
provide a certain melioration of this rather "rough" statement: the
Garibaldino is a minor example, Mrs. Gould is a martyr to the god of
material interests, and Dr. Monygham, who remains somewhat out of
the system, is the most valid commentator in the novel.

2659 Knoepflmacher, U. C. "*The Secret Agent*: The Irony of the
Absurd," *Laughter and Despair: Readings in Ten Novels of the
Victorian Era* (Berkeley, Los Angeles, London: University of
California Press, 1971), pp. vii, ix, xiii, xiv–xvi, 25, 27, espec. 240–
73.

The Secret Agent is a modern novel which is a tale of the
nineteenth century. JC applies a new form and treatment to an old
question: how can man adhere to a moral code in a world that seems
anarchic and devoid of meaning? His novel relies on an
accumulation of fragments which at first seem to lack any coherence
but which eventually, in the thirteenth and last fragment of the book,
reveal the work to be a tragedy, with Winnie Verloc—not her husband
nor her brother—as its central figure. In the person of the corpulent
and inert Mr. Verloc, JC conveys to the reader the facts he wants
known: the fat man's uselessness, the absurdity of his role as

Vladimir's agent, makes this "spurious" anarchist an apt agent for JC's vision of a truly anarchic existence. In the triangle formed by Mr. Verloc, the triple agent, Stevie, his brother-in-law, and Mrs. Verloc, the last is the true protagonist of the work.

For JC, the world is divided into seers and nonseers. For him, too, the task of seeing involves a "confrontation" with an existence painfully devoid of such higher laws as those Dickens provided in some of his novels. Winnie's tragedy is that she is too abruptly moved from the position of those persons who feel but do not see to that of those who see.

2660 Krieger, Murray. *The Classic Vision: The Retreat from Extremity in Modern Literature* (Baltimore and London: Johns Hopkins Press, 1971), pp. 7n, 26, 33–35, 45, 47, 299, 301, 302, 303n, 306, 333n.

JC's Marlow in "Heart of Darkness" desires to see, if only vicariously, without undergoing the "awesome risks" of real vision. He instructs us that the vicarious and partial "tragic visionary" must, when he chooses an order of existence, choose the ethical, even if warily and skeptically. The poet chooses the "veil of falsely imposed universals," as Marlow chooses "the fixed standard of conduct"— knowing the universals to be nothing but veil and aware of the "brawling turmoil" they seek to cover. In Robert Penn Warren's *All the King's Men*, Jack Burden plays, in effect, Marlow to Willie Stark's Mr. Kurtz; Warren often parallels JC. The struggle against the community in Warren's novel is an echo of Ivan and Smerdyakov in *The Brothers Karamazov*, Jim and Brown in *Lord Jim*, and the captain and Leggatt in "The Secret Sharer." Hightower's need to remain disengaged from action out of the fear that to act is to act immorally is similar to Heyst's reticence in *Victory*.

2661 Kubal, Davil L. "*The Secret Agent* and the Mechanical Chaos," *Bucknell Review*, XV, No. 3 (1971), pp. 65–77; rpt., slightly rvd. in *Makers of the Twentieth-Century novel*, ed. by Harry R. Garvin (Cranberry, NJ and London: Associated University Presses, 1977), pp. 91–102.

Although JC does not "handle" a new idea in *The Secret Agent*, he treats the theme of his forerunners in a manner significantly different from theirs. The metaphor of "mechanical chaos" and a radical departure from the traditional conception of the individual link *Agent* to Orwell's *1984* and results in one of the first full expressions of "our civilization's political despair." In *Agent*, JC creates a chaotic world in which everything and everybody in the novel appear essentially the same under the narrator's ironical gaze. Holding this world together is the machine; even Stevie's circles fail to create any organic design. JC achieves thematic and structural unity through the paradoxical images of mechanism and chaos. The sequence of the chapters reflects the confusion of the characters and their existence; the concept of time lacks reason. A metallic imagery pattern appears throughout the novel, suggesting the "machine-lime gloss" of the city. The best illustration of the nether world that is London is the hackney carriage that takes Winnie's "bloated" mother away. Stevie is closest to being the moral center of the novel, but his crippled mind weakens his gestures toward reform. In this novel, only the machine, not anarchy, succeeds.

2662 La Cour, Tage, and Harold Mogensen. *The Murder Book: An Illustrated History of the Detective Story* (New York: Herder and Herder, 1971), pp. 122–23.

One of the first works of importance in the spy genre is JC's *The Secret Agent*, which has "a clear-cut anti-czarist tendency" resulting from the author's "first-hand experience of political underground activity." It is probably not as brilliant as Somerset Maugham's *Ashenden: Or the British Agent.* [Indicative of ways in which JC is sometimes misunderstood.]

2663 Larbaud, Valéry, and G. Jean-Aubry. *Correspondance, 1920–1935,* ed. by Frida Weissman (Paris: Gallimard, 1971), pp. 12, 14, 15, 16, 17, 20, 24, 27, 28, 29, 30, 31, 32, 33, 34, 35, 39, 40, 42, 43, 48, 56, 58, 59, 62, 63, 64, 65, 66, 68, 87, 91, 98, 102, 105, 125, 137, 139, 141, 143, 150, 154, 164, 180, 183, 194, 199, 203.

[This collection contains 150 letters with detailed notes and index. The contents of the letters reveal Jean-Aubry's friendship with JC and portray his work as translator into French of many of JC's works and as editor of a volume of JC's letters written in French. The book also provides evidence of Larbaud's admiration for JC and recalls Larbaud's note on *Chance* and his offer to contribute a photograph of André Gide, JC, and himself taken at JC's house to the special number of *La Nouvelle Revue Francaise* devoted to JC, published in 1924. Finally, the letters also document JC's admiration for Larbaud's work and refer to such anecdotes as the story of JC's finding the model for Lena in *Victory* in a girl who played in an orchestra at the Café Riche in Paris.] [In French.]

2664 Lewis, John S. "Conrad's Principal Source for 'The Lagoon,'" *Unisa English Studies,* IX (June 1971), pp. 21–26.

Two important sources for "The Lagoon" are Major Fred. McNair's *Perak and the Malays* (London, 1878) and Captain Henry Keppel's *The Expedition of H.M.S. "Dido" for the Suppression of Piracy* (London, 1846, 2 vols.). Keppel's book is of major importance because much of it consists of extended extracts from James Brooke's journal, from which JC drew the plot of his story. These two obscure books by English visitors to Malaysia demonstrate JC's precise care with his materials.

2665 Lodge, David. *The Novelist at the Crossroads and Other Essays on Fiction and Criticism* (Ithaca: Cornell University Press, 1971), pp. 40–42, 254–55.

Edward W. Said in *Joseph Conrad and the Fiction of Autobiography* (1966) argues that a close but devious relationship exists between JC's fiction and his own psyche.   The argument, though, is made unclear by jargon and by an abundance of "extraneous allusion."   What makes JC unique is the artistic and imaginative use to which he put his experiences.   The Modern movement in art is the product of European Romanticism.   It was suppressed by the Victorians, but was assimilated late in the nineteenth century by writers like Henry James, William Butler Yeats, and JC.   But the movement was also taken up by lesser talents and then went into disrepute, causing a reversion to Victorian standards of moral health.   This reversion caused James and JC to be neglected.

2666 Lowndes, Marie Belloc. *Diaries and Letters of Marie Belloc Lowndes 1911–1947*, ed. by Susan Lowndes (London: Chatto & Windus, 1971), pp. 93, 217, 256.

[In one of her letters, Marie Belloc Lowndes says that though she never met JC, she had received letters (or perhaps a letter) from him. In a diary, she mentions him as having lived in an atmosphere of adulation.   In a letter from Edward Marsh, Marsh mentions that he has lately acquired JC's autograph.   Contains nothing of critical interest, but may assist in a collection of JC's letters.]

2667 "The Man Within," *TLS* (17 September 1971), pp. 1101–1102.

The introductions to the new Collected Edition of Graham Greene's works (seven volumes published by Bodley Head) are "very like" JC's in that they are "personal and anecdotal, and focus on the occasions of the novels rather than on the creating mind," and they are therefore "minor and supplementary."   [No new information about JC's introductions, but a timely reminder not to take them too literally.]

2668 Martin, W. R.   "Gaspar Ruiz: A Conradian Hero," *CON*, III, No. 3 (1971–72), pp. 46–48.

"Gaspar Ruiz" dramatizes a conflict between the love of a man for a woman and his child and the "sanguinary imbecilities" of political hatred in war. In the end, he sacrifices everything for Erminia and the child and dies knowing that the woman at last loves him. The narrator of the story, General Santierra, serves to underline Gaspar Ruiz's conflict. In returning to his "radical innocence," Gaspar Ruiz bears some resemblance to such other Conradian heroes as Singleton in *The Nigger of the Narcissus*, MacWhirr in "Typhoon," and Peyrol in *The Rover*: the strength of JC's strong men is in their simplicity and their sincerity.

2669 McDonald, Captain P. A. "The *Otago*," *Clipper* I (The Johnson & Johnson Company, San Francisco), I (February 1971), pp. 1–2, 4.

[A brief history of the *Otago*, recounting some of the major events which occurred while JC commanded it.]

2670 McLaughlin, Frank. "Critics Didn't Like 'em, but the Kids Did," *Media & Methods*, VII (May 1971), p. 52.

The film, *Lord Jim*, running 154 minutes and starring Peter O'Toole as Jim, can reach those students who are unable to understand the novel's concerns of honor, loyalty, courage, and duty. [Includes a brief survey of the reception given to the film by some critics, but does not mention any literary critical response nor the film's fidelity to JC's text.]

2671 McMaster, Juliet. *Thackeray: The Major Novels* (Toronto: University of Toronto Press, 1971), p. 54.

JC's Jim, in *Lord Jim*, "sicklied o'er with the pale cast of thought" like Hamlet, is, like Mr. Batchelor in Thackeray's *Lovel the Widower*, unable to act at the crucial moment.

2672 Messenger, Ann P., and William E. Messenger. "'One of Us': A Biblical Allusion in Conrad's Lord Jim," *English Language Notes*, IX (December 1971), pp. 129–32.

The phrase "one of us," applying in Genesis 3:22 to Adam and Eve after they have eaten the forbidden fruit ("the Lord God said, Behold, the man is become as one of us, to know good and evil"), means simply that in losing his original innocence man becomes a moral being, able to distinguish between good and evil. Jim, therefore, in *Lord Jim*, unlike his fellow officers of the *Patna*, unlike Gentleman Brown, and very much like Marlow, is a moral being. As such, he can be broken, be tragically destroyed. By extension, then, "suffering humanity" in general is "in the same boat"; in his novel, JC emphasizes the strong sense of human community. The significant use of the phrase "one of us," from the Bible, enriches the meaning of the work and also enables it to embrace the various meanings ascribed to it by critics and also to resolve apparent contradictions among them.

2673 Meyers, Jeffrey. "'At the End of the Passage,'" *Kipling Journal*, XXXVIII (June 1971), pp. 20–22.

Both Kipling and JC write about the disease and madness that threaten the white man in the tropics, but each has a different conception of these dangers. JC, unlike Kipling, is aware of the dangers that lie within man, "his personal weakness and 'civilized' values" that are unable to sustain him in a hostile environment. In "At the End of the Passage," Kipling makes clear the fact that his characters are living "in an earthly Hell" and that Hummil should have been destroyed without the aid of the supernatural. In "An Outpost of Progress," JC indicates the existence of "things vague, uncontrollable, and repulsive" which threaten everyone alike.

2674 Meyers, Jeffrey. "Recent Books on Modern Fiction: British," *MFS*, XVII (Winter 1971–72), pp. 597–604.

Wilfred S. Dowden's book, *Joseph Conrad: The Imaged Style* (1970), does not do justice to some interesting possibilities on the subject of JC's style. Forster noted years ago that JC's language tends toward abstraction through which he achieves both powerful poetic effects and some "unpleasant fussiness." It would be helpful to study this abstract language to determine precisely what JC means in such passages as his description of Singleton "standing meditative and unthinking, . . . —a sixty-year-old child of the mysterious sea," and his description, in *The Secret Agent*, of the cab ride, which contains all the "poignant" themes of the novel.

2675 Montag, George E. "Marlow Tells the Truth: The Nature of Evil in 'Heart of Darkness,'" *CON*, III, No. 2 (1971–72), pp. 93–97.

Marlow, in "Heart of Darkness," contrary to general opinion, is not a liar. In telling his story in retrospect, he admits approaching a lie, but not telling one, not even to the Intended at the end of the novel. Kurtz's Intended is a European; in this story, all the Europeans except Marlow are evil: they are the living "lies" who continually appear to be what they are not. All end in a "hollow" state, but only Kurtz has not always been hollow; he has lost a "fullness" unapproached by any other character in the story, including Marlow. While Kurtz relinquishes his goodness and chooses to do evil, he *does* choose. The other Europeans do nothing. Marlow saves himself by identifying himself with Kurtz, by remaining "loyal" to him. During the final scene with the Intended, Marlow is aware of the cause of Kurtz's failure: feeling first anger, then pity, and knowing that all around him in the sepulchral city the "horror" is pervasive, he "bestows on her all of the terror, pain, despair—Horror! which Kurtz experienced and which rightfully belongs to the European society." And the heavens do not fall for the telling of the truth; instead, all the principals are benefited. The ending of this story is thus consistent with its entire development and among the most skillful conclusions to be found.

2676 Mudrick, Marvin. "Bearding Conrad," *Hudson Review*, XXIV (Winter 1971), pp. 711–15.

"Heart of Darkness" is unique among JC's novels in that it is "almost nothing except invention—a perverse sort of invention—consisting as it does mainly in distortion, omission, misrepresentation with the aim of denying the apparent and probable nature of the objects described." [Review of Norman Sherry, *Conrad's Eastern World* (1966) and *Conrad's Western World* (1971).]

2677 Muller, Herbert J. "The Uses of Tragedy: Interlude: Joseph Conrad's *Nostromo*," *In Pursuit of Relevance* (Bloomington and London: Indiana University Press, 1971), pp. 164–76.

In *Nostromo*, JC condemns capitalism and its effects on his protagonists. Charles Gould is the unwitting victim of material interests and causes his wife to suffer from solitude. Likewise, Nostromo and Don José Avellanos suffer from the disillusionment that materialism brings to their idealism. In fact, all the major characters are victims of frustration in the face of cosmic indifference, and they endure their fates alone. Yet, despite this pessimism, *Nostromo* is a moving tragedy impressing on us a vision of a common fate and the dignity of man.

2678 Mursia, Ugo. *Il Vero 'Scopritore' del Talento Letterario di Joseph Conrad e Altre Note di Bibliografia Conradiana con Tre Lettere Inedite* (Milan: [Mursia], 1971); partly rpt. as an appendix in the Italian edition of Jocelyn Baines, *Joseph Conrad: Biografia Critica* (Milan: Mursia, 1974), pp. 551–58 [In Italian]; rpt. *The True 'Discoverer' of Joseph Conrad's Literary Talent and Other Notes on Conradian Biography, with Three Unpublished Letters* ([Milan: Mursia], 1971); rpt. *CON*, IV, No. 2 (May 1972), pp. 5–22. [In English.]

Three undated letters by JC, recently come into possession of Ugo Mursia, seem important for the novelist's biography. With other relevant materials, they seem to establish W. H. Chesson, a reader for T. Fisher Unwin in 1894 (with Edward Garnett as reader also), as the actual discoverer, instead of Garnett, of JC's talent as a writer. One letter, presumably written between October 18 and November 15, 1894, to Chesson, and the other, apparently written January 9, 1895, also to Chesson, make clear that Chesson himself edited *Almayer's Folly*. A third letter by JC, seemingly written about 1922 to Frank Savery, the writer of the first German translation of *Under Western Eyes*, suggests that the young JC studied at St. Anne College in Cracow rather than at St. Jacek's Gymnasium, as some JC scholars maintain.

2679 Najder, Zdzislaw. "Conrad in His Historical Perspective," *ELT*, XIV, No. 3 (1971), pp. 157–66.

JC's place in the history of literature can be determined in that, first, the intellectual and artistic traditions which "nursed" his creative talent left their mark on his achievement. His "exceptionality" as a writer stemmed from his immediate French literary predecessors, from the tradition of Polish romantics, and from his Polish inheritance. Also, the position of JC's work within the contemporary and spiritual trends and movements was unusual. Very much aware of the current crisis in morality, he was probably unique in his response to it by his acceptance of the well known "simple principles"—fidelity, honor, friendship—by pitilessly confronting these principles with the way in which they actually worked in life, and by accepting the fact that whatever man may do the surrounding universe is indifferent both to his heroic efforts and his failures. In addition, JC left his followers and his legacies, some of which appear in Scott Fitzgerald, Faulkner, Hemingway, Antoine de Saint-Exupéry, and Camus. Aware as he was of the solitude of the human condition, he seems to be a prophet, but not a despairing one, of our present preoccupation with alienation and with the loneliness of the individual in mass society.

2680 Newell, Kenneth B. "The Yellow-Dog Incident in Conrad's *Lord Jim*," *SNNTS*, III (Spring 1971), pp. 26–33.

The yellow-dog incident, which occurs in chapter 6 of *Lord Jim*, brings Jim and Marlow together and provides the latter with the opportunity of gaining first-hand knowledge of Jim and his story. But this incident also serves as one in a pattern of incidents through which the apparently malevolent universe reveals its nature and causes Jim to expose his innermost self. Further, the incident establishes through Marlow's initial understanding of Jim a familiar JC theme: the inability of one man ever to know another.

2681 Park, Douglas B. "Fictional Reality in the Novels of Joseph Conrad," *DAI*, XXXII (1971), 448A. Unpublished dissertation, Cornell University, 1971.

2682 Pindell, Richard P. "The Ritual of Survival: Landscape in Conrad and Faulkner," *DAI*, XXXII (1971), 3324A. Unpublished dissertation, Yale University, 1971.

2683 Pinsker, Sanford. "'The End of the Tether': Joseph Conrad's Death of a Sailsman," *CON*, III, No. 2 (1971–72), pp. 74–76.

Henry Whalley of "The End of the Tether" exchanges a physical blindness for a moral one and plunges to his death with all his illusions intact. His problem is very similar to that of Arthur Miller's Willie Loman: both men seem "to whine with a single voice . . . against a modern world that has passed their values by"; both destroy themselves in a desperate effort to "make their dreams ring true." JC's story is much more pessimistic than Miller's because Willie leaves Biff having learned something whereas Whalley leaves no one to give his death either meaning or a "redemptive character."

2684 Pinsker, Sanford. "Joseph Conrad and the Language of the Sea," *CON*, III, No. 3 (1971–72), pp. 15–21.

JC succeeded in discovering the source of his richest material— the microcosmic world of sailing ships—and in so doing he altered the shape of English prose. [Generalizations and praise, both routine.]

2685 Pinsker, Sanford. "Selective Memory, Leisure and the Language of Joseph Conrad's *The Nigger of the Narcissus*," *Descant*, XV (Summer 1971), pp. 38–48.

[This essay seems to argue that JC (or the narrator?) uses language which tends to falsify and romanticize the situation in *The Nigger of the Narcissus*; however, the nonverbal language of the sea (employed by JC?) confronts and balances this, suggesting that "the juxtaposition of men and Nature is a function of sensibility rather than fact." Pinsker builds his argument on particularly vague implications, which leaves the reader wondering whether, in fact, there is an argument.]

2686 Pitol, Sergio. "Conrad en Costaguana" (Conrad in Costaguana), *Cuadernos Hispano Americanos* (Madrid), LXXXVI, No. 256 (1971), pp. 58–73.

JC's fiction is no less exotic than Stevenson's empty tales, but his ability to convey visual effects was more acute, and the exoticism is only important in that it expresses a different, external world, contact with which results in a crisis that ends either in salvation or irrevocable condemnation. JC's individual lives in a state of permanent tension between temptation and the struggle to remain steadfast in a moment of weakness. One of his great themes is the isolation of the individual, which is often voluntary, a kind of expiation. The "Costaguana" of *Nostromo* is a country which reproduces exactly the Latin American countries in search of national independence. [In Spanish.]

2687 Ramsey, Roger. "The Available and the Unavailable 'I': Conrad and James," *ELT*, XIV, No. 2 (1971), pp. 137–45.

Although no available evidence seems to indicate that JC read James's *Turn of the Screw* before achieving greatness with his stories having Marlow as narrator ("Youth," "Heart of Darkness," *Lord Jim*), both authors display similarity of intent especially in *The Turn of the Screw* and "Heart of Darkness." Both works are psychological mystery stories. As to the form of each, the "I" of James's story, devious, impertinent, and autonomous, disappears after the prologue, thus taking with him all recourse for the reader; the "I" in "Heart of Darkness," however, remains in the story and, continuously aware of what is happening, actually develops with Marlow's story. The similarities of the two formats are limited, though: the omniscient narrator is dismissed for a "frame" in which an anonymous but characterized "I" sets the tone (one of mystery), creates the scene, and introduces the person who will retail a complete experience. Certain differences between the two stories are apparent: when the "I" of *The Turn of the Screw* disappears, he creates the condition of "infinite perspective" and leaves the reader wondering ever afterwards about the validity of what he says; on the other hand, the "I" of "Heart of Darkness" creates the condition of "omnipresent perspective" and guides the reader to Marlow, keeps him fixed in the actual setting, challenges him for the reader, and is evidently, like the reader, enlightened by his story. James's story is a game of horror; JC's makes the horror real. James has his diversion; JC has his truth.

2688 Raskin, Jonah. *The Mythology of Imperialism: Rudyard Kipling, Joseph Conrad, E. M. Forster, D. H. Lawrence, and Joyce Cary* (New York: Random House, 1971), pp. 126–221.

For JC, "without contradictions nothing would exist"—struggle is found everywhere. JC's work is accounted for by the differences between the two men in one, Mr. Joseph Conrad and Mr. Korzeniowski: contradictions account for the "trash" in JC's work, *The Rescue, The Arrow of Gold*; the mediocre work, *The Secret Agent* and *The Nigger of the Narcissus*, and the "works of power," "Heart of Darkness" and *Nostromo*. "Heart of Darkness" is a story about Marlow's education in which the white man finds out about the "Third World, the Black man." This story is an epiphany: taking us behind the words "civilization" and "empire," it reveals European barbarism, death, disease, exile. But JC leaves a paradox in this story: he seems to say that imperialism is responsible for the evil, but at last he turns away and says it is in the Black man. Lord Jim is a lord without power: he "has a love affair with a Brown woman, acts kindly and gives up." He does not fight for "colonial liberation." In all its ugliness, "the romanticism of imperialism is transparent in *Lord Jim*." In the silver mine of *Nostromo*, JC creates a "Frankenstein," but he never realizes "what a monster he has brought to life." In *Under Western Eyes*, JC's sense of extremes blinded him to what happened in Russia; his sense of polarities prevents him from seeing that "direction comes through destruction," "that history and theory are dialectically connected." JC leaves "no place for the revolutionary party which combines armed struggle and mass work." [But this is enough of ranting with little substance beneath it.]

2689 Robinson, Rose B. "Imagery and Motif in the Stories of Conrad: A Computer-Aided Study," *DAI*, XXXII (1971), 2704A. Unpublished dissertation, Wayne State University Press, 1969.

2690 Roussel, Royal. *The Metaphysics of Darkness: A Study in the Unity and Development of Conrad's Fiction* (Baltimore and London: The Johns Hopkins University Press, 1971).

In JC's world, the ultimate reality is "inert matter," "the darkness." Since for JC consciousness must always turn outside itself to find the source of its existence in some ground which does not share its own nature, man has an "orphaned quality," and thus all of JC's characters are, "in a fundamental sense," orphans. JC is concerned with man's need to find a "social or intersubjective ground" for itself, but in his world this search always occurs within the context of the "fundamental alienation of consciousness from its metaphysical source." Consciousness is, for JC, an accidental property. For most of his characters, the experience of vulnerability marks the real beginning of their voyage toward destruction, as with Marlow in "Youth," Lord Jim, Razumov, and the narrator of *The Shadow-Line*. Two general alternatives are open to man: (1) perhaps mind can confront the darkness directly and master it, and (2) perhaps man can escape destruction by accepting the fact that it does not invalidate existence, and in this manner one's life comes to possess a certain stability. From this initial encounter with the darkness, JC's characters may then either return to commit themselves to the world and the men who inhabit it, thus affirming at least the possibility that man, through his own will, can master the darkness and win for himself a "stable identity," or he can accept the darkness as final and thereby come to terms with the "ephemerality of [his] own [self]."

2691 Roy, V[irenda] K[umar]. *The Romance of Illusions: A Study of Joseph Conrad* (Delhi: Doaba House, 1971).

JC was a moralist who sought for "the inscrutable region of the human psyche" and attempted to enter into that mysterious region and "emerged as a successful diver with pearls of uncertainty and inscrutability." For him, the universe is a vast arena in which man is to prove his worth and continue to develop his powers. In the struggle between man and the universe, it is the man who is defeated, but his glory lies in the strength with which he struggles in order to conquer the evils around him. JC is neither a nihilist nor a pessimist; he is an artist who makes every possible effort to grasp the essence of human existence even if it is not always "full of bright colours of happiness and joy." Through his characters, JC perceives various aspects of reality without arriving at any final conclusions. His greatest achievement in character portrayal is his presentation of his characters without "delving into any psychological jargon." The atmosphere of the novels exemplifies the irony of life—how his tragic protagonist lives in a world of illusory ideals, hopes, ambitions which, after some time, prove to be ironically otherwise. *Lord Jim* and "Heart of Darkness" display very well JC's "romance of illusions": in *Jim*, JC dramatizes man's fondness for lofty ideals, noble aspirations, and high ambitions, and then his crumbling to pieces when he is confronted with reality; the shorter novel is a commentary on the "splitting up of human personality under the pressure of the double claims of an ideal, first, its abstract principles and, second, its practical form."

2692 Saveson, John E. "The Intuitionist Hero of *Lord Jim*," *CON*, IV, No. 3 (1971-72), pp. 34–47; rpt. *Joseph Conrad: The Making of a Moralist* (Amsterdam: Rodopi NV, 1972), pp. 65–83.

In *Lord Jim*, a large ambivalence results from JC's narrative technique: Jim appears as both antagonist (in which his "romantic" attitude toward life is considered unfavorably) and protagonist (in which Marlow's uncertainties allow the "romantic" to recommend itself to the reader). The Spencerian and Utilitarian point of view is never strong enough in this novel to restore the assumptions of Spencerian anthropology common to JC's first novels. The change from bias to ambivalence reflects accurately JC's intellectual development between his second and third novels. Suggestions of

Jim's type appear in Galton and Lecky, but T. H. Green, JC's contemporary, offers a closer parallel. Jim's rationalizations are essentially those Green describes, and the milieu of Patusan is especially suited to produce in Jim the chief characteristics of Green's ideal type. Moreover, Green's philosophy enables the reader to discern a coherent relationship between the two parts of *Jim*, which are often considered disconnected. All parts of the novel have in common the belief that life is illogical and that ordinary objects of human desire do not achieve happiness. The psychology of the Unconscious obtrudes itself into the passages in which Marlow muses upon Jim's motives and in Jim's escape from the Rajah's stockade. It seems that JC was deeply affected by the most important English Utilitarians and Spencerians at the turn of the century.

2693 Scholes, Robert. "Editor's Introduction," *Some Modern Writers: Essays and Fiction by Conrad, Dinesen, Lawrence, Orwell, Faulkner, Ellison* (New York: Oxford University Press, 1971), pp. xi-xiii.

All six of the writers included in this book have experienced "that violent shock which occurs when White Western culture encounters Asian, African, or American Indian cultures." In JC, we get "a glimpse of Blacks in an Africa which has been subdued by White imperialism," and if we take the word "politics" in its broadest sense, we see in "Heart of Darkness" "how men relate to one another, how they serve and rule one another."

2694 [Schultheiss, Thomas]. "Conrad Bibliography: A Continuing Checklist," *CON*, III, No. 2 (1971-72), pp. 111-16.

[A continuation of Schultheiss's invaluable checklist.]

2695 [Schultheiss, Thomas]. "Conrad Bibliography: A Continuing Checklist," *CON*, III, No. 3 (1971-72), pp. 60-65.

[A continuation of Schultheiss's invaluable checklist.]

2696 Schultheiss, Thomas. "Conrad Bibliography: A Continuing Checklist," *CON*, IV, No. 3 (1971-72), pp. 62-66.

[A continuation of Schultheiss's valuable bibliography.]

2697 Schwab, Arnold T. "Joseph Conrad and Warrington Dawson," *Modern Philology*, LXVIII (May 1971), pp. 364-74.

The most valuable of JC's letters reprinted here are those dated June 20, 1913 and June 2, 1922: they contain important statements by JC concerning his "credo as an artist and as a critic." The most "significant contribution" of the study is "Randall's discussion of the extent to which Conrad drew on the Humbert swindle of 1902 for the plot and characterization of *Chance*." [A review article of Dale B. J. Randall's *Joseph Conrad and Warrington Dawson: The Record of a Friendship* (1968), which thoroughly explores a hitherto unknown part of JC's life.]

2698 Schwarz, Daniel R. "The Lepidopterist's Revenge: Theme and Structure in Conrad's 'An Anarchist,'" *SSF*, VIII (Spring 1971), pp. 330–34.

The narrator of "An Anarchist," a lepidopterist who has been severely frustrated by his inability to deal with his enemy, Henry Gee, presents sympathetically the anarchist who has also been a victim of Gee's barbarism. The narrator's perspicacity is so limited, however, by his own indignation and wounded feelings that he unconsciously creates a self-portrait very different from the impression he wants his audience to create of him. Like "Il Conde" and "The Informer," his story is a dramatic monologue told by an "imperceptive and self-deluded" narrator whose effort to impose a specific interpretation on the events he reports is undermined by the obvious inadequacy of his version of the events. When he relates how Paul has murdered his enemies, he works out his repressed desire for revenge by verbalizing his own unconscious fantasy of dealing violently with the adversary he hates. In "The Anarchist," telling a story thus becomes a method of both conscious and unconscious revenge.

2699 Schwarz, Daniel R. "The Significance of the Narrator in Conrad's 'Falk: A Reminiscence,'" *Tennessee Studies in Literature*, XVI (1971), pp. 103–10.

The principal interest for the reader of "Falk: A Reminiscence" is the middle-aged narrator's struggle to come to terms with and communicate the meaning of a crucial experience of his youth. The subtitle of the story intimates that the major focus is on the *"narrator's recollection of his encounter with Falk."* The process of "getting in touch with the real actuality"—of going back to man's savage origins and seeing man's primitive needs as the source of his civilized social relationships, even back to cannibalism—is repeated in the telling. At first, the narrator introduces the personae of the tale as "my enemy Falk and my friend Hermann," but the telling of the story turns the epithets inside out as the narrator reveals that he "admires and identifies with Falk while he despises Hermann's values." The odyssey through the Eastern seaport was necessary for the alteration of the captain's attitude toward Falk and Hermann: it displayed the crude level to which man's primitive instincts have been warped by his social organization. What the captain learned from his confrontation with Falk and his recollection of that experience is that man's civilized relationships have their source in man's primitive origins and that there is a splendor and magnitude to these unrestrained instincts.

2700 Sebezhko, E. S. "Problematika i khudozhestvennoe svoeobrazie romana Dzh. Konrada *Tainyi agent*" (Problems and Artistic Originality of Conrad's *The Secret Agent*), *Voprosy Russkoi i Zarubezhnoi Literatury* (Questions of Russian and Foreign Literature), (Tula: Tula State Pedagogical Institute, 1971), pp. 215–31.

JC's novels between 1904 and 1914 depict the bankruptcy of bourgeois ideology and the collapse of the individual under the influence of that ideology. But while depicting this process, JC sought ways of unifying mankind. The first Russian Revolution of 1905 confronted him with the problem of reviewing his previous convictions. *The Secret Agent* has factual and symbolic levels, and in it JC describes England as a country with a highly developed revolutionary working class; but JC did not believe it, hence the caricatures and the sarcasm in the novel. As Thomas Mann pointed out, *Agent* is inconceivable without Dostoevski's *The Idiot*. Steve and Prince Myshkin represent the contrast between intellect and heart, though Steve is more insignificant than Prince Myshkin. The latter was Dostoevski's idea of a positive hero, whereas Steve is merely feeble-minded. [In Russian.]

2701 Secor, Robert. *The Rhetoric of Shifting Perspectives: Conrad's Victory* (University Park: The Pennsylvania State University [The Pennsylvania State University Studies No. 32], 1971).

Victory displays a "mature" JC. Part I of the novel begins to establish his cognitive assumptions about the limitations of vision and knowledge; the narrator represents "the modern, scientific, materialistic age," with Schomberg's hotel the metaphor for this modern world and with Heyst a sacrificial victim "who fulfills the need of a guilty society to objectify its guilt." Schomberg himself is this world's "exaggerated caricature." By adopting two different perspectives, JC makes his case, in detailed creation of character and in the significant flow of narrative and imagery, against Heyst. In his meeting with Morrison, Heyst, in crushing Morrison's dream, is strongly responsible for the latter's death; in his meeting with Lena, Heyst reveals his philosophy in its morally and psychologically unsound effects upon others. Because of the involved perspectives used, the entire novel tests and judges the nihilistic philosophy of Heyst's father. Since Heyst himself virtually denies all validity to a world of external reality, he loses the necessary sense of reality established by social involvement. Samburan is therefore a "manifest dream world," and the reader, who must enter Heyst's dream to sense it, encounters the perspective of unreality. Chapter 9 of part III of *Victory* marks the point of the shift in perspective from Heyst's consciousness to Lena's, and part IV, essentially her book, charts her action and reveals her victory as the roles between savior and saved are reversed. Heyst's world, having no garden, partakes of the demonic rather than of the apocalyptic.

2702 Shadoian, Jack. "Irony Triumphant: Verloc's Death," *CON*, III, No. 2 (1971–72), pp. 82–86.

JC's careful and ironic descriptions of the death of secret agent Verloc at the hands of his wife in *The Secret Agent* is appropriate to Verloc's character, which is developed in the novel as a caricature. Verloc dies as he has lived, without self-awareness. JC's slow-motion description of his murder is funny; Verloc's self-developed lethargy kills him. But the description "patterns" the moment of death into a mechanical process, and the "grand rhetoric" collapses into verbal melodrama, as JC intended it to do. To get this close to a man's death and to realize that these final moments are merely a climax to a life of "hideous and sorrowful waste" cannot be "purely amusing": JC plays off style against content with "enviable skill." The irony is adequate to the author's aim in the novel.

2703 Sherry, Norman. *Conrad's Western World* (Cambridge: At the University Press, 1971).

[A "sequel" to Sherry's *Conrad's Eastern World* of 1966, this book on Conrad's western world ranges over the period 1896 to 1906 in terms of composition of JC's works, and only one short story, "An Outpost of Progress," and one major work, "Heart of Darkness," look back to JC's personal experience. The works dealt with in this volume rely less on the biographical element than do those in the earlier works because JC's source material moved away from "inspired analyses of personal experience or the related experience of others." JC thus moved away from the mark of an amateur to that of a professional.] In "Heart of Darkness," Kurtz is a combination of Klein and Hodister, whom JC met or learned about in his voyage to the Congo. The origins of *Nostromo* are more historical than autobiographical. Garibaldi was important for JC's depiction of Giorgio Viola, and Decoud is probably modeled on Dominic Cervoni, who had been with JC in a gunrunning expedition. The original source of Decoud, though, was Juan Decoud, a writer described in R. F. Burton's *Letters from the Battle Fields of Paraguay* (1870). In Decoud, however, JC presented something of his own nature. In *The*

Secret Agent, JC places his attention on the "unreason" [his word] back of the events. The basis of his plot is the incident of 1894 in which the anarchist Martial Bourdin, in carrying a homemade bomb across Greenwich Park, apparently tripped and killed himself. JC's movements in these works away from his own experience was from a strong idealism to a moving from his own experiences to "the general truths of human nature."

2704 Szladits, Lola L. "New in the Berg Collection: 1965–1969," *Bulletin of the New York Public Library*, LXXV (January 1971), pp. 9–29.

[Notes the acquisition of the John D. Gordon Collection, which includes letters, manuscripts, and corrected typescripts of JC.]

2705 Tanner, Tony. *City of Words: American Fiction 1950–1970* (New York, Evanston, San Francisco, London: Harper & Row, 1971), pp. 84, 127, 152, 170–71, 289.

The dread of "entropy" seems to haunt many contemporary writers: Yossarian in Heller's *Catch 22* is ultimately in flight from his own death and "the great sinking to waste and garbage that he sees around him." Ellison, Bellow, and Heller "celebrate" a "sort of private dance of life"; like JC's Axel Heyst in *Victory*, they aim to be "invulnerable because elusive." William Burroughs has "cut up" Shakespeare, Rimbaud, Eliot, Joyce, and JC, along with others, and folded selected bits into his writings, as if cutting up a great writer will release new potency from his work as cutting up a newspaper renders one immune from its "mind-numbing and artificial cliches." In *V*, Thomas Pynchon systematically and stylistically evokes, in a parodic manner, previous writers like Melville, Henry Adams, Nathanael West, Djuna Barnes, Evelyn Waugh, Lawrence Durrell, and JC, seeming to suggest that there is no one suitable "truth" about history and experience, only a series of versions.

2706 Teets, Bruce E., and Helmut E. Gerber (eds.). *Joseph Conrad: An Annotated Bibliography of Writings about Him* (DeKalb: Northern Illinois University Press [An Annotated Secondary Bibliography Series on English Literature in Transition, 1880–1920], 1971).

This book contains "1,977 studies, dated between 1895 and 1966," of all varieties and in all formats, about JC, in fourteen languages. Almost all are abstracted, as honestly in tone and content as is possible. Honors and M.A. theses are excluded, and dissertations are listed without abstracts, except in instances of foreign dissertations. Excepted from abstraction also are reviews of secondary books unless critical statements are voiced independent of the works under review. With certain specified works such as Jessie Conrad's and Norman Sherry's, evaluative reviews are given. Abstractors' critical comments have "in most cases" been bracketed. Errors, many with a long history, that have been discovered are corrected. Entries are chronicled annually and within each year arranged alphabetically by author and provided with abstracts. Five indexes facilitate reference. [Although the ideal of total inclusion can only be reasonably approached, the editors have done their "human best." For the present, Thedore Ehrsam's *Bibliography of Joseph Conrad* (1969), despite many inaccuracies, is useful.]

2707 Tomlinson, T. B. "Conrad's Trust in Life: *Nostromo*," *Critical Review* (Melbourne), XIV (1971), pp. 62–81.

Despite Conrad's near approach to skepticism or despair in *Nostromo*, several passages reveal the author's trust in life, his realization that neither the unstable political future of Costaguana, nor even the deeper despair of Decoud and Mrs. Gould, will destroy the "sheer reliability of ordinary daily existence." JC writes, with an assured, "crisp" comedy such scenes as the one about Captain Mitchell, surrounded by looting and torture, calling out indignantly that his watch has been stolen. If there is a part of JC in this novel that seems to avoid life, there is also an acceptance even of modern life, grudging perhaps, but certainly displaying interest and trust in it. The central surviving characters in this regard at the end of the book are Charles and Emilia Gould and Dr. Monygham. JC's triumph with the Goulds is that he keeps both of them linked throughout to the larger world of business and politics. And his treatment of Monygham's loyalty is finer than George Eliot's admission in *Middlemarch* that her hero has "fallen short of his task." If JC's writing in *Nostromo* reveals fear, loneliness, and physical pain as facts of modern life, it also presents these facts with a strength and resilience few other writers can match.

2708 "Tracking Down Conrad's Originals," *TLS* (28 May 1971), p. 615.

In *Conrad's Western World*, Norman Sherry has greatly enlarged our knowledge of JC's sources for such works as "Heart of Darkness," *Nostromo*, and *The Secret Agent*, but his book raises the question common to all biographical criticism: What can be made of the results of literary detection? In "Heart of Darkness," for example, if Sherry is correct, JC, in depicting the manager of the Central Station, is "paying off old scores and indulging in retrospective self-justification"; but this information, while contributing to our knowledge of the novelist, adds nothing to our understanding of

Marlow. [This criticism applies equally to Sherry's *Conrad's Eastern World* (1966).]

2709 "*Victory* Opera," *CON*, III, No. 2 (1971–72), p. 63.

Richard Rodney Bennett's opera based on JC's *Victory*, which was presented at Covent Garden on April 13, 1970, was reviewed widely in the British press. A few opinions were that the music differentiates the many characters in the plot, "even if not as strongly as one might wish"; the demands of "operatic feasibility" have reduced JC's "poetic" novel to "the level of a glib Maugham story"; and conductor Edward Downes and the stagers of the opera, Colin Graham and Alix Stone, have done especially well with their work.

2710 Walt, James. "Conrad's Reception in Yugoslavia," *CON*, III, No. 2 (1971–72), pp. 7–16.

During the four decades that JC's works have been published in Yugoslavia, JC has remained, for several reasons, only a coterie author. Ivo Vidan, the most ardent of JC's admirers, has been writing about him since 1951, and has made substantial contributions to JC scholarship. [Herein summarized.]

2711 Wright, Walter F. *Arnold Bennett: Romantic Realist* (Lincoln: University of Nebraska Press, 1971), pp. 70, 72, 101, 105, 111, 112, 141.

When Arnold Bennett concluded that JC's *The Secret Agent* gave a "disappointing effect of slightness," one wonders how well he understood what JC was doing, but he does describe the "melancholy charm" of the novel.

2712 Yanko, Helen M. "The Modern Sisyphus: Nihilism in the Works of Joseph Conrad," *DAI*, XXXII (August 1971), 990A. Unpublished thesis, University of Pennsylvania, 1970.

2713 Zabierowski, Stefan. *Conrad w Polsce: Wybrane Problemy Recepji Krytycznej w Latach 1896–1869* (Conrad in Poland: Selected Problems of Critical Reception in the Years 1896–1969), (Gdansk: Wydawnictwo Morskie, 1971).

Several early Polish critics became zealous, at times lapsing into sheer chauvinism, as they appraised JC's literary work in relation to his Polishness. To some extent, this biographical emphasis represented an aspect of Young Poland, a literary movement which coincided with JC's early creative years. Also, from the first, JC's work was regarded by several outstanding scholars as Polish literature. During World War II, JC's life and work became an existential experience, but there were no critical breakthroughs. After the war, there were no significant changes. The post-war period is marked by the emergence of Polish specialists in English literature who sought to present JC's personality in terms of the Polish Positivist tradition, rejecting the old Romantic-Modernist approaches.

JC's successful career in Poland can be attributed to his Polish origin and to the appeal of his work itself. It began quite early in 1896. The initial impact of JC's work was as that of a sea-writer. During the twenties, Polish critics were primarily interested in JC the thinker, the moralist. The thirties saw some decline in JC's repute: he was then seen as an "incorrigible" conservative. During the years of war and occupation, JC's fiction appeared to the Polish readers as more than literature: it was read with a special kind of reverence reserved for works revealing the true nature of surrounding reality. In 1946, a new quarrel arose about JC's ethical view of the universe: Jan Kott's essay, "O laickim tragizmie" (On the Lay Tragedy), struck a severe blow at JC's ethos without, however, negating his artistic achievement. The following years were marked by a flowering of Conradian critics, with major studies by Najder, Jablkowska, Kocówna, A. Busza, W. Chalewik, Wyka, Mroczkowski, and A. Braun. [This major work should be studied in its entirety.] [In Polish.]

2714 Zuckerman, Jerome. "The Architecture of *The Shadow-Line,*" *CON,* III, No. 2 (1971–72), pp. 87–92.

As in *Chance* and "The Secret Sharer," in *The Shadow-Line* JC uses the command or rule theme to cause the reader to "see" a psychological condition. The command situation is equated with the test of selfhood and the gaining of self-knowledge: from his inner growth the narrator develops into an effective captain. The captain's background of indolence serves as a counterpoise to his development of command. In this background, Captain Giles is the exception to the narrator's prevailing meaninglessness and irresponsibility. The captain is tested by calm, disease, and storm until he eventually reaches an ambivalent success so that he has triumphed over his spiritual malaise. In his achievement of maturity, Giles serves as his mentor, and Ransome the steward, with his weak heart, is his example. Despite some flaws, *Shadow-Line* maintains its place among the best of JC's later fiction.

1972

2715 Ackley, Randall. "For the Captain," *CON,* IV, No. 1 (1972), p. 71.

[Verse. About JC's knowing "the magic reality of words, / of language," and of his writing in English.]

2716 Adicks, Richard. "Conrad and the Politics of Morality," *Humanities Association Review*, XXIII (Spring 1972), pp. 3–7.

JC's novels display a political awareness which has little to do with the ways in which actual governments run. His concern is to demonstrate the need for man to govern himself with "compromise and self-renunciation." He is concerned not with statesmanship, but with man's ability to adhere to communal moral sanctions in the face of forces which seem to invalidate these sanctions. JC develops his understanding of right action by presenting situations in which small groups of men are forced to make moral decisions.

In *The Nigger of the Narcissus*, the crew must face the eventuality of Jimmy's death. Their banding together to push aside this eventuality is unsuccessful. The failure of this communal endeavor demonstrates the inadequacy of the sanctions upon which the crew acted, which were entirely narcissistic. In *Nostromo*, by providing a "moral test for most of the major characters," the silver of the San Tomé mine functions as James Wait functions in *Nigger*. Because he is entranced by the silver, Charles Gould surrenders the love of Emilia. Because of his total alienation from society, Martin Decoud acts upon motives which are totally unrealistic. Nostromo's only sanction is his concept of honor, which fails when he calls it into question. JC's political understanding demonstrates the dangers of a narcissistic creation of sanctions for action which are not based on a communal and natural understanding.

2717 Allen, Mary. "Melville and Conrad Confront Stillness," *Research Studies* XL (Washington State University), (June 1972), pp. 122–30.

Whereas Melville views stillness as a sign of the incommunicability of the human soul, JC views stillness as a debility to be overcome. Struggle, which is preferable to passivity, is found more often at sea than on land. In "Heart of Darkness," *The Shadow-Line*, and *The Nigger of the Narcissus*, life becomes weary when land is neared. But when the open sea is reached, the movements of the ocean restore life.

2718 Argyle, Barry. *An Introduction to the Australian Novel, 1830–1930* (Oxford: At the Clarendon Press, 1972), p. 230.

Richard Mahoney, in Henry Handel Richardson's *The Way Home* (1925), with his passion for music, sailing, and bathing, is happy to follow Stein's advice to Jim, "in the destructive element immerse."

2719 Armstrong, Robert M., M.D. "Joseph Conrad: The Conflict of Command," *The Psychoanalytic Study of the Child*, Vol. XXIV, ed. by Ruth S. Eissler, Anna Freud, Marianne Kris, Lottie M. Newman, and Albert J. Solnit (New York and Chicago: Quadrangle Books, 1972), pp. 485–534.

The major theme in JC's works—the political, man's relationship to the community of men, and the personal, man's need to integrate all aspects of his personality—meet in issues of authority and autonomy. The theme of command in JC's greatest works contains biographical material with insights into the "divided" man which make him seem contemporary. From his father, JC received a strong internal conflict: his desire to become like his father threatened "super ego" guilt because of the realization of hostile wishes in the father's early death and rage over frustrated dependency. The rebellious young JC therefore left Crakow for Marseilles and the sea. A second major "identity crisis" seems to have begun for JC when he became captain of the *Otago*, which was resolved only after many more years when he left the sea to struggle for a new identity as a writer of serious fiction. After his marriage, JC settled down to become less active, but the adventures ahead of him were in himself.

For JC, the autonomy of the function of writing, closely identified with his father, must have been precarious at best. He endured periods of paralysis and creative sterility, and as he committed himself to the identity of an English author, his difficulties became worse for him. But in spite of his handicaps, two of his greatest novels, *Lord Jim* and *Under Western Eyes*, deal with such material.

2720 Barrett, William. *Time of Need: Forms of Imagination in the Twentieth Century* (New York, Evanston, San Francisco, London: Harper and Row, 1972), p. 310.

In *A Passage to India*, E. M. Forster tells little about his despair, even in the matter of the Marabar caves; even the Marabar echoes must be kept in place in the balance of things. But this amiable surface is deceptive: Forster has rebuked T. S. Eliot and JC for being too forbidding and for placing barriers between themselves and the reader.

2721 Bedient, Calvin. *Architects of the Self: George Eliot, D. H. Lawrence, and E. M. Forster* (Berkeley, Los Angeles, London: University of California Press, 1972), pp. 19–20, 22, 24.

JC became the "supreme novelist" of the "new morbidity" of the period 1890 to 1910 and later. If one chooses his texts carefully, he may claim that JC is a late, if almost too late, Victorian idealist of selflessness, one who struggled to believe in "the idea of Fidelity" ; but nonetheless, in JC this ideal is "withered," "shaken with illness," and "dreadfully disabused and prone to a radical irony." In "Heart of Darkness," for example, Marlow sits apart in the yawl on the Thames, in the pose of a Buddha, because he is disillusioned with desire and

because its "treacherous subversion of virtue" has cast over all of life
for him a "dreamlike insincerity." JC's prose is heavy and hopeless.
And JC shares a "morale-crushing fatalism" with Ford Madox Ford
(*The Good Soldier*) and Thomas Hardy (*Tess of the D'Urbervilles*).
Before the self could be revived as an ideal, the "forces of life" had to
break through the "impacted crust" of a "defeatist determinism" ; the
universe had to seem more "friendly" than it does in Ford, Hardy, and
JC. And this it did in Joyce, Lawrence, and Forster, who saw, not the
perfidy, terror, and violence that JC saw, but rather "the most radiant
of the gods, Eros and his expansive positivity."

2722 Bell, Quentin. *Primitivism* (London: Methuen [The Critical
Idiom 20], 1972), pp. 38–42, 48–49, 61.

Unlike D. H. Lawrence in *The Plumed Serpent*, JC in "Heart of
Darkness" recognizes the necessary isolation, both cosmic and
human, of the primitivist hero, Kurtz, and implies that the primitivist
urge, if indulged, can lead only to the destruction of the "civilized self"
and that such a possibility is necessarily evil. Since JC's criticism of
social and political life is from within that of the moral assumptions
of western civilization, he sees the primitive as an undesirable
extreme. The "narrative strategy" of "Heart of Darkness" makes Kurtz
essentially the catalyst for the creation in Marlow's mind of an
imaginative symbol for a moral truth; it constructs a qualifying
context for its primitivist sympathy as opposed to the open ended
structure of Lawrence's novel. JC's work provides a representative
instance of the basic dilemma of primitivist literature: primitivism in
the sense of the endorsement of a return to a precivilized way of life
is always in danger of "bad faith" in that the primitivist urge can
never actually be realized or tested in real life. JC, Eliot, Joyce, and
Yeats are four major modern writers who have displayed an interest
in primitive life or ancient myth from the standpoint of their own
civilization: one can move from Lawrence's "direct affinity" with the
primitivism of the romantic tradition through JC's "horrified
fascination" for the instinctual towards the "distinctly anti-
romantic" attitudes of Eliot in *The Wasteland* and of William Golding
in *The Inheritors* and *Lord of the Flies*.

2723 Bell, Quentin. *Virginia Woolf: A Biography.* Volume 2: *Mrs.
Woolf, 1912–1941* (London: Hogarth Press; New York: Harcourt
Brace Jovanovich, 1972), p. 50.

When JC published *Victory*, though many people hailed it as a
masterpiece, Virginia Woolf expressed doubts, finding the book
below JC's best achievement—perhaps the moment had come to
disparage him: "one must tack, shift, reinsure, turn and come about."

2724 Bloch, Tuvia. "The Wait-Donkin Relationship in *The Nigger of the Narcissus*," *CON*, IV, No. 2 (1972), pp. 62–66.

The heretofore unresolved reason for Jimmy Wait's intent on gaining a contemptuous ascendancy over the crew of the *Narcissus* while excepting from his intention its most contemptuous member, Donkin, is that what sustains Wait in the first four chapters of the novel, what checks his defeat by his fatal illness, is his feeling that he is imposing on the crew. Without powerful confirmation of this view, confirmation supplied by Donkin, Wait could not submerge his fears by means of his self-deceiving, but life-giving, view of himself as a malingerer. Donkin's vilification is thus precisely what Wait requires as assurance from the best authority that he is taking the crew in, that he is not really ill. Eventually, when Donkin collapses like a crutch for Wait, Wait's life too collapses. The motif that a man may be able to survive as long as he believes his notion that his state is supported by a judgment on which he can rely is found also in *Lord Jim*, *Nostromo*, and *Razumov*.

2725 Bogard, Travis. *Contour in Time: The Plays of Eugene O'Neill* (New York: Oxford University Press, 1972), pp. 7, 16, 24, 31, 38–42, 52, 59, 93, 106, 126, 135, 139, 154n, 158–59, 161n, 203.

Eugene O'Neill seems to have been guided in several early one-act plays by O. Henry, Maupassant, Jack London, and JC, with the result being "hodgepodge." Most of them were unproduced. Although O'Neill's experiences at sea enabled him to confirm the truth of JC's account of the sailor's life, he learned to give them dramatic reality through JC's artistry. At least through 1920, with the writing of *Anna Christie*, the impact of JC on O'Neill's works was deeper than that of any other writer. In JC, the dramatist found, for the first time, a mature articulation of his instinctual sense of man's destiny—"the concept of men moving in the pattern established by an elemental force to which they belong by which they are controlled in spite of the pressure of their individual wills." In depicting the lives of men bound in life and death to the sea, O'Neill relies on JC for the suggestion that men caught in a common destiny find their relationship with one another a bond that gives value to their existence. O'Neill, however, makes no generalization such as JC does, that there is a savagery in the hearts of men. JC helped in various ways to make smooth the road O'Neill was to travel.

2726 Bojarski, Edmund A. "Beerbohm and Conrad," *CON*, IV, No. 1 (1972), pp. 60–62.

Of the series of caricatures of well known figures entitled "The Young Self and the Old Self," by Sir Max Beerbohm, only one, "Joseph Conrad: The Old Self and the Young Self," is now known. It was sold

recently at auction at Sotheby's in London to D. Kay for £320. [The
watercolor, unlikely to be seen again until another estate is
auctioned, is described and reprinted here.]

2727 Bonney, William Wesley. "Joseph Conrad and the
Discontinuous Point of View," *Journal of Narrative Technique*, II
(May 1972), pp. 99–115; rpt. with revisions in *Thorns and
Arabesques: Contexts for Conrad's Fiction* (Baltimore and
London: The Johns Hopkins University Press, 1980), pp. 151–94.

The discontinuous point of view in many of JC's works has
generally suffered negative criticism. JC, however, consciously
develops the third-person narrative voice as a negative qualifier of
the optimistic and ordered perceptions of the first-person,
subjectively limited persona. He thereby demystifies the universe in
which his characters function and establishes a normative vision,
consistent throughout much of his work, of a metaphysically neutral
world in which all ethics and values are invalid projections of the
human mind. In *The Nigger of the Narcissus*, for example, the third-
person narrative voice cuts through the narrator's visionary
elaboration of the mythical, mystical character of James Wait and
exposes him as simply a pathetic, vulnerable, and terrified human
being.

Youth and Other Stories must be read as a single, unified work in
which the progressive relationships of Marlow, the anonymous
narrator, and finally the third-person narrative voice expose
Marlow's subjective fallibility, cancel out his moral vision, and argue
a bleakly neutral universe. The trilogy, by means of shifts in narrative
perspective, frees the phenomenal world from the impossible
responsibility of articulating human values.

2728 Borges, Jorge Luis. "Guyaquil," *Periscopio* (4 August 1970); rpt.
Doctor Brodie's Report, trans. by Norman Thomas di Giovanni
(New York: E. P. Dutton, 1972), pp. 99–107.

One cannot write about the "Estado Occidental" without
recognizing the fact that he consciously reproduces JC's style;
perhaps, indeed, one cannot speak of JC's "Caribbean republic"
without echoing the "monumental" style of "its famous historian,
Captain Joseph Korzeniowski." One especially important letter
written by General Bolivar and found among the papers of Dr. José
Avellanos, whose *History of Fifty Years of Misrule*, thought to be lost,
has been ultimately "unearthed" and published by his grandson, Dr.
Ricardo Avellanos. [A fascinating instance of a novel by JC making
its way into one of the *ficciones* of Borges.]

2729 Bruecher, Werner. "The Discovery and Disintegration of Evil in the Fiction of Joseph Conrad and Hermann Hesse," *DAI*, XXXII (March 1972), 5221A. Unpublished dissertation, University of Arizona, 1972.

2730 Bruss, Paul Samuel. "Conrad's *The Nigger*: The Narrator and the Crew," *English Record*, XXIII (Fall 1972), pp. 16–26.

In *The Nigger of the Narcissus*, there is no journey "home" (" to wisdom and solidarity"). The sailors' narcissism prevails throughout their voyage to England, and this narcissism complicates the usual "light-good and dark-evil" patterns of metaphor. In this novel, the pursuit of narcissism is generally associated with the light, and the fear of contingency generally with the dark. Consequently, for JC the usual value equations tend to be reversed: "light-good and dark-evil become light-evil and dark-good." JC both values the association with the contingent and the dark, because such association liberates and "warns against insistent pursuit of narcissistic self-justification and of light because that pursuit ossifies." The crew generally does not achieve solidity, but the narrator (himself a member of the crew) does achieve resiliency and fertility: he becomes the artist who deals in contingencies, not in absolutes. He insists that "all of us, as sailors of uncertain and turbulent seas," find ourselves embroiled in the primary task of fashioning a meaning for our lives, and that we are "good" men as long as we struggle in the face of overwhelming odds and in moments of despair renew that meaning. The narrator discovers his own voice and tells the tale of maturation, thus becoming the prototype of the most mature of JC's narrators— Marlow.

2731 Burgess, C. F. "Of Men and Ships and Mortality: Conrad's *The Nigger of the Narcissus*," *ELT*, XV, No. 3 (1972), pp. 221–31.

The focus of *The Nigger of the Narcissus* is on the crew, who are in several senses children, a band of innocents; and into this band Jimmy Wait is abruptly thrust. The crew accept and protect Jimmy, even during the story, because of their commitment to him in his fight against death. The crew, however, must eventually turn from this commitment to their second commitment, their obligation to the *Narcissus*, especially during the storm: if they would save themselves, they must save the ship. It is the crew's dual commitment to Jimmy Wait and to the *Narcissus* that makes one story of two, that unifies the novel. The hurricane tests the two commitments to the utmost, so that clearly the novel is about both man and ship. The crew are motivated by the "grandest of design" —to prove that neither Jimmy nor the ship has to die, to prove that human capacity can will life and cheat death. For a time, this grand design is successful, but in the later part of the novel Jimmy dies within sight of the land and at last the ship also dies when it reaches harbor; in each instance, then, the land proves fatal. It appears that only the narrator of the story learns the lessons of the work: only through commitment can the Conradian "sin" of isolation and alienation be averted—but both ships and men are fated to die. Only the sea is immortal.

2732 Burstein, Janet. "On Ways of Knowing in *Lord Jim*," *NCF*, XXVI (March 1972), pp. 456–68.

The theoretical work of Ernst Cassirer, Susanne K. Langer, and Owen Barfield helps us to explain the tension in *Lord Jim* between the mythic way of knowing and that of discourse or abstraction. In the world of the *Patna*, in which the nature of discourse allows one to deal reasonably with facts, one cannot conceive the "pervasive ambience" of human feeling; in the mythic mode of Patusan, the mythic word-symbol fuses feeling with other aspects of experience. Jim's characteristic "leap" from sensory fact to emotional conclusion, as in the *Patna* incident, is very unlike Marlow's more logical, analytical processes of thought: "Thus where Marlow reasons, Jim—jumps." Reasoning and feeling, ways of knowing and modes of language, reveal that Jim's way of knowing displays the characteristic movement of mythic thought, the jump from inner to outer world, and helps explain several aspects of Jim's personality. The ability to reflect upon and to organize his perceptions of emotional reality make Marlow perform, to some extent, the function of the poet. The poet relates his awareness of emotional reality to other experiential truths. Near the end of the novel, Marlow abandons to some extent his original heavy narrative method and tries to allow the complex poetic fact to speak, unanalyzed, for itself. The novel presents both the inadequacies of discourse and myth, and as a poet Marlow moves between the two worlds, using them both to tell *Jim.*

2733 Calderwood, James L., and Harold E. Toliver (eds.). *Forms of Prose Fiction* (Englewood Cliffs, New Jersey: Prentice-Hall, 1972), pp. 36, 37, 181, 297, 398, 417–18 .

JC's "Heart of Darkness" is a version of demonic romance. The historical instruments of JC's darkness are imperialism and African savagery, both "explainable social elements." Part of the meaning of this story is that the demonic element lies at the heart of the commercial and the social world. The surface of life on the ship remains, however, logical and well ordered in spite of the underground reality that haunts it. The secret sharer both collaborates with and contrasts to the surface life of the captain: he does not destroy it. Eventually, the psychological doubles assist each other in resuming their separate courses. JC's London of *The Secret Agent* is a good example of the "demonic" city, a city near an extreme opposed to the romance utopia. JC, with such writers as Kafka, Borges, and Faulkner, in using the parable and the romance, has absorbed some of the techniques of the realist tradition. Just as heroes of epic and romance encounter enduring powers of some scope that make large demands upon them (like those of Homer, Milton, and Malory) so that their individual tempos must be fused with a very large destiny and a very general pattern that universalizes their actions, so do such modern novelists as Joyce, Hardy, Barth, Vonnegut, and JC utilize myth or romance so that several layers of cycles of time reflect each other and influence the particular course the hero takes. He must necessarily negotiate among them.

2734 Cap, Jean-Pierre. "Une lettre inédite de Joseph Conrad à Henri Ghéon" (An unedited letter by Joseph Conrad to Henri Ghéon), *Revue de Littérature Comparée*, XLVI (April–June 1972), pp. 258–60.

Only immediately before World War I did JC enter into amicable relationships with French writers such as Paul Claudel and André Gide. Henri Ghéon, a close friend of Gide's, sent his book of criticism, *Nos Directions*, to JC, who atypically replied very quickly to express his gratitude and his sympathy for the critical principles of Ghéon and *La Nouvelle Revue Française*. [This letter is in the hands of Mr. and Mrs. François Corré, Henri Ghéon's heirs, and of the editors of J. M. Dent & Sons, Ltd., executors of the JC estate.] [In French.]

2735 Cash, Joe Lynn. "The Treatment of Women Characters in the Complete Works of Joseph Conrad," *DAI*, XXXIII (1972), 2925A. Unpublished dissertation, Texas Tech University, 1972.

2736 Citati, Piero. "Un cuore di tenebra" (A Heart of Darkness), *Il Te' del Cappellato Matto* (The Tea of the Mad Hatter), (Milan: Mondadori, 1972), pp. 24–29.

After a long seafaring life, JC locked himself in his rooms in the heart of London and started to sound the depths of his own heart of darkness, remembering the East, Africa, and the oceans, trying to recapture their music and their suggestions, undergoing fits of depression and melancholia, indulging in self-denigration, fighting his own inner self. [A rather impressionistic piece of creative writing more than a critical essay.] [In Italian.]

2737 Cohen, Hubert. "The 'Heart of Darkness' in *Citizen Kane*," *Cinema Journal*, XII (Fall 1972), pp. 11–25.

Although evidence for JC's "influence" on the film, *Citizen Kane*, is only "circumstantial and inferential," the movie and JC's "Heart of Darkness" provide some interesting parallels, specifically in the conception, the shaping, and the shooting of the film. There may be evidence that JC's character, Kurtz, was a partial source of the film's Charles Foster Kane, that other characters in the JC story suggested, either wholly or in part, characters in the film, and that there are similarities between the film and the novel in structure, points of view, and details of action and style. [Much ado about nothing?]

2738 Cohn, Lowell Arthur. "Dramatized Narrators and the Quest for 'Solidarity' in Joseph Conrad," *DAI*, XXXIII (1972), 2319A. Unpublished dissertation, Stanford University, 1972.

2739 Cooke, Michael. "Trying to Understand Victorians," *Yale Review*, LXI (March 1972), pp. 433–41.

[U. C. Knoepflmacher's viewing of Victorian novels as entities in themselves, "independent of any historical considerations," succeeds as an "elliptical" history of the novel from Dickens to JC, in *Laughter and Despair: Readings in Ten Novels of the Victorian Era*.]

2740 Coolidge, Olivia. *The Three Lives of Joseph Conrad* (Boston: Houghton Mifflin, 1972).

JC's life falls into three amazingly different parts: his life as a "Polish prisoner," his life as a "sea wanderer," and his life as an English novelist. The first demonstrated his powers of survival; the second, his gradual adaptation to the human community that came from life on shipboard; the third, his becoming known and loved by a wide circle of people in a country not his own and becoming a major writer in a language not his own. [A biography of JC for young people, reasonably accurate and as critically fair as such a work can be.]

2741 Debo, Elizabeth Lea. "The Narrator in Henry James, Joseph Conrad, and Ford Madox Ford," *DAI*, XXXII (January 1972), 3946A–47A. Unpublished dissertation, University of Nebraska, 1971.

2742 Deurbergue, Jean. "*Lord Jim*, roman du nébuleux?" (*Lord Jim*, Novel of the Nebulous?), *Etudes Anglaises*, XXV (January–March 1972), pp. 148–61.

The ambiguity of *Lord Jim* is evident in its ending, where JC refuses to judge Jim's life as a victory or a defeat. The purpose of the novel's ambiguity is to engage the reader in an interpretation of Jim's life and his own, to be "one of us," both actor and judge. To create the ambiguity necessary for reader participation, JC uses various devices: structural, in the dialectic opposition between the early Jim and the later Lord Jim; narrative, in the use of the objective and sympathetic Marlow and the differing opinions of other narrators on Jim; symbolic, in the system of opposing images; character, in the opposition of solitude and solidarity; and thematic, in the contrast between the real and the imaginary. The novel teaches us that man is too complex to be judged hastily. [In French.]

2743 Deurbergue, Jean. "Récit et roman dans deux oeuvres de Conrad: *Lord Jim* et *Nostromo*" (Story and Novel in Two Works by Conrad: *Lord Jim* and *Nostromo*), *Récit et Roman: Formes du Roman Anglais du XVI Siècle au XXe Siècle* (Story and Novel: Forms of the English Novel of the Sixteenth Century to the Twentieth Century), (Paris: Didier, 1972), pp. 63–74.

In *Lord Jim* and *Nostromo*, the point of view takes three forms: an anonymous, impersonal narrator, a narrator revealing the mind of one character, and a first-person narrator. First-person narration may be divided into oral or written communication. Four other variations of narratives within narratives may be used: an oral tale within an oral narration, as in Jim's confession to Marlow in *Lord Jim*; a written narration within an oral narration, as in Marlow's quotations from Jim's letters; an oral tale within a written one, as in Brown's story transcribed in Marlow's letter; and a written narration within another written narration, as in Jim's father's letter quoted in Marlow's letter. Other variations also occur. Besides the complexity of point of view in these novels, there is also one of time: the narration makes use of flashforwards and flashbacks, time shifts equivalent to the spatial shifts afforded by the pattern of changing points of view. Furthermore, ellipses—notably one involving Jim's jump from the *Patna*—occur both in the narrative and in sentence structure. These techniques integrate geographical space into both historical and mythic time, provide illusions of the real by providing narratives told by witnesses, and provide irony by juxtaposing closely in the plot extremely different actions that are separated by a great deal of historical time. The chronologically related tales placed in atemporal structure are unified by thematic order. [*Nostromo* is omitted here because of lack of space.] [In French.]

2744 Dietiker, Don Wieland. "Joseph Conrad: The Novel of Process,"
DAI, XXXII (1972), 6970A–71A. Unpublished dissertation,
University of Wisconsin, 1972.

2745 Engelberg, Edward. *The Unknown Distance: From
Consciousness to Conscience, Goethe to Camus* (Cambridge,
Massachusetts: Harvard University Press, 1972), pp. 6, 46, 144–
45, 147, 172–85, 206, 227–29, 235, 244.

"Consciousness to Conscience is the only solution—however
risky—that men can find, provided they want to speak either of the
one or the other. . . . Men cannot possess a Conscience (whatever
they may mean by it), or anything else, without having a full
awareness, a full consciousness first." JC definitely has a place in
this conclusion. Lord Jim is JC's hero enslaved by conscience. Jim
neither resigns nor renounces: he resists. Within that resistance
both resignation and renunciation operate, but they are symptoms,
not aims, and there is no approval of Jim's final controversial act,
which is, in effect, suicide. Jim's false sense of martyrdom is seldom
stated explicitly, but JC's young man is conspicuous for his constant
effort directed towards vindication, not expiation. As the book
progresses, Jim's consciousness tends to inflate the wrong kind of
conscience. In his youthful dreams, Jim makes of himself exactly the
hero he will fail to be, and the *leitmotif* of his story is the pain of
conscious defeat; he never frees himself long enough to discover
other options that the abuse of self and supererogatory demands on
the ego. Imagination is Jim's enemy because he uses it toward
destructive ends. To err is human: Jim takes full advantage of this
concept and to the very end he concentrates on the error rather than
on the man who erred. "Heart of Darkness" is the analysis of the
"horror" implicit in an exchange in which conscience is swept away.

2746 Emmett, Victor J., Jr. "The Aesthetics of Anti-Imperialism:
Ironic Distortions of the Vergilian Epic Mode in Conrad's
Nostromo," *SNNTS*, IV (Fall 1972), pp. 459–72.

In writing both "Heart of Darkness" and *Nostromo*, JC had the
Aeneid in mind. Stories of men who go through an underground
journey and emerge worse instead of better cannot, however, rightly
be termed "Virgilian." The ironic undercutting of Virgilian epic occurs
in both "Heart of Darkness" and *Nostromo*, but more complexly in the
latter. In this novel, JC has provided all the elements of epic
described by E. M. W. Tillyard except for the heroic central character.
The novel presents time shifts, a tragic theme, suggestions of the
fabulous, and the journey to the underworld. Many of these elements
are, however, ironically distorted in a way that portrays the world as
a place in which heroism is no longer possible. JC has thus given us

the "accidents" of the epic without the "essence." The characters of the novel are unheroically corrupted by silver, which is itself an economic force beyond the power of heroic action. *Nostromo* is related to the epic "as *Brave New World* and *1984* are related to utopian literature."

2747 Espey, David B. "The Imperial Protagonist: Hero and Anti-Hero in Fiction of the Late British Empire," *DAI*, XXXII (1972), 6423A. Unpublished dissertation, University of Michigan, 1971.

2748 Feaster, John William. "Joseph Conrad: The Limits of Humanism," *Cresset* (Valparaiso University), XXXV (January 1972), pp. 9–12.

JC's letters to R. B. Cunninghame Graham demonstrate that in spite of the "public" JC's insistence on the rewards of such humanistic ideals as fidelity, honor, and solidarity, the "private" JC's vision of the human condition was far from optimistic. His sense of "the meaningless and the unknowable" underlying common experience infuses his work with what we call the "Conradian" element. At the center of JC's skepticism is a recognition of the limits of man's perception of and capacity for truth, and acknowledgment of the "severe limitations" of humanism itself. In his novels, though, JC is tormented by the unreality of words and the mendacity of language; his art creates a major paradox. In his doubts of ultimate truth and the nature of reality lie the ingredients of both his complex humanity and his modernism. His fullest claim to our attention is that of a novelist of "distinctively modern ideas and temperament."

2749 Feaster, John William, Bruce Johnson, Marion C. Michael, and Thomas C. Moser. "Currents in Conrad Criticism: A Symposium," *CON*, IV, No. 3 (1972), pp. 5–21.

In the interpretation of literature, the literary work itself should remain the center of interest, but all pertinent knowledge available must be brought to bear in the cumulative understanding of literature. In JC studies, we need definitive texts, a collected edition of JC's letters, a study of JC's humor, more scholarly research, and a "determined voice of dissent—maybe many voices."

After the production of a great amount of JC criticism (with the history of the JC revival marred by excesses of the New Criticism), the entire idea of investigating JC's proper context is still fascinating. We need to see JC as the Later Victorian he was, to appreciate his place in the technical evolution of the English novel, and to see his texts in relation to a whole new set of perspectives.

Some knowledge of the many levels of revision which JC's texts underwent could have "sobered or altered" critical commentary and interpretation: the different points of view in *The Nigger of the Narcissus* provide a good example. Modern reprints of JC's works reveal some shocking instances of "careless editing and deliberate corruption."

Needed for further study of JC are his letters, "every scrap" ; a complete, definitive edition of the works; a "profound" study of JC and literary impressionism; and another biography. [From the proceedings of the annual meeting of the Modern Language Association (Chicago, 1971).]

2750 Fichter, Andrew. "Dramatic Voice in *Lord Jim* and *Nostromo*," *THOTH*, XII (Spring–Summer 1972), pp. 3–19.

The ironic technique common to *Lord Jim* and *Nostromo* is having the principal dramatic interests, the stories of Jim and Nostromo, evolve with a characteristic rhetoric that is undercut by a more reflective consciousness. Marlow constantly resists the influence of Jim's imagination, and Martin Decoud and Dr. Monygham, in their fundamental skepticism, are opposed to the resounding influence of Nostromo's reputation. As the distance between the reflective, moral consciousness and the region of dramatic, rhetorical egoism widens from *Jim* to *Nostromo*, JC seems to allow more expression of irony and melodrama. The resulting relativism, present stylistically in more than one narrative voice, is a manifestation of a deeper metaphysical issue: the struggle between characters in the novel to locate for themselves "the reality of . . . existence." As narrator, then, Marlow is involved in a quest corresponding to Jim's own quest for redemption, but the modern, metaphysical question of Marlow's is his doubt of the existence of "sovereign power" informing reality. In a sense, for both Jim and Nostromo, character is speech. And just as Nostromo's death is perhaps ironically justified, the main themes of the novel may be taken as ironical: the triumph of "material interests" over ideals, or the way in which political events seem to move in defiance of the designs of political men.

2751 Garmon, Gerald M. "*Lord Jim* as Tragedy," *CON*, IV, No. 1 (1972), pp. 34–40.

Although *Lord Jim* contains striking classical elements of tragedy, "the sensitive modality of the novel is ineluctably tragic." JC seems to be attacking the myth of the hero because he knows that such ideal people do not exist and never did: he adorns Jim, a coward, with the "princely virtues of the classical and romantic hero" and also keeps before the reader the facts of Jim's very fallible humanity:

"He is one of us." But Jim is "distinctly modern and realistic." The novel is cynical: men like Jim, men who can do heroic things but are not always heroic, men who are complex and inexplicable, exist as ordinary mortals. Jim has rather ordinary shortcomings, but he is extraordinarily sensitive to his failures. JC's primary concern is with the "fellowship of men, the human community" and Jim obviously fails in his obligation to that ideal. At the end of the novel, Jim has followed the dictates of his conscience and he has not knowingly or willingly endangered the welfare of Patusan, and that is adequate. His death is tragic because the death of a good man, striving to do what he thinks is right, is always tragic. We readers are fond of him because his ailments are our own.

2752 Genette, Gérard. *Figures III* (Paris: Editions du Seuil, 1972), pp. 205, 207, 227, 242, 253.

In *The Nigger of the Narcissus*, JC restricts the point of view to make the principal character more mysterious; in *Lord Jim*, a "baroque" novel with a "Chinese-box" narration (tales within tales) reaches its limit. [In French.]

2753 Gertzman, Jay A. "Commitment and Sacrifice in 'Heart of Darkness': Marlow's Response to Kurtz," *SSF*, IX (Spring 1972), pp. 187–96.

The structure of "Heart of Darkness" is based on Marlow's journey from detachment to commitment and echoes epic voyages. Kurtz as Lucifer has descended into the depths of an anti-western value system. His example encourages Marlow to accept compromise and commitment, symbolized by his lie, when he suddenly realizes Kurtz's heroism and the Intended's beautiful vision.

2754 Gillespie, Robert. "Conrad Dark and Hollow," *Novel*, VI (1972–73), pp. 89–91.

The narrators of both *The Nigger of the Narcissus* and "Heart of Darkness" simultaneously create a world and deny its reality, an act of self-denial. JC had to move to an "ironic detachment from both life and art." Culminating in ironic detachment in *Lord Jim*, "writing-as-adventure" causes JC to abandon any hope of a positive commitment to life. Books on JC and his work are "slants" on his productions; slants are all we can have on great writers. Each person makes his own "voyages" into their work.

2755 Gilliam, Harriet. "The Novel as Fictive History: Conrad's *Under Western Eyes*," *DAI*, XXXII (1972), 6975A. Unpublished dissertation, Yale University, 1971.

2756 Glassman, Peter [Joel]. "Language and Being: Joseph Conrad and the Literature of Personality," *DAI*, XXXIII (1972), 5722A. Unpublished dissertation, Columbia University, 1972.

[Developed into *Language and Being: Joseph Conrad and the Literature of Personality* (New York and London: Columbia University Press, 1976.]

2757 Goonetilleke, D. C. R. A. "Forgotten Nineteenth-Century Fiction: William Arnold's *Oakfield* and William Knighton's *Forest Life in Ceylon*," *Journal of Commonwealth Literature* (University of Leeds), VII (June 1972), pp. 14–21.

Although William Arnold's *Oakfield* (1853) and William Knighton's *Forest Life in Ceylon* (1854) are not artistically outstanding, they are valuable because in mid-Victorian times no Englishman thought and felt as creatively about "undeveloped" countries in their own right as these authors did. Both novelists are "immediate forerunners" of Kipling, Forster, Joyce Cary, Graham Greene, and JC, on the one hand, and of Mulk Raj Anand, R. K. Narayan, Chinua Achebe, James Ngugi, and V. S. Naipaul on the other. Colonial officials such as they set up the tradition which leads to these writers of literature in English that concerns situations in the Third World.

2758 Gose, Elliott B., Jr. "Artist and Magician" and "Lord Jim," *Imagination Indulged: The Irrational in the Nineteenth-Century Novel* (Montreal and London: McGill-Queen's University Press, 1972), pp. ix, 13, 21, 42, 47, 99, 127–66, 168, 170–76.

JC's attempt to give full recognition to the demands of both outer and inner nature created a tension between the demands of the romantic ego and those of the physical world and the community of men. The central theme of *The Nigger of the Narcissus* is the plight of egocentric man in a ruthless universe; here JC withheld sympathy from James Wait, the character with pronounced ego. JC also drew upon the folklore of the sea and went to the depths and forces which the seaman's conscious will cannot fathom, to the depths of Jung's archetypes. Any work of art is "satanic" insofar as it attempts to create another universe, especially one operating on laws different from God's. In *Lord Jim*, JC tried to embody this dilemma: in the first half of the novel, he presents an egoist trying to cope with the social world; in the second half, he allows the egoist to withdraw into himself and satanically set up his own kingdom. Thus the irrational in *Jim* is associated with uncivilized Patusan, to which Jim brings the standards of honesty and consistency, to be destroyed by Brown, an outcast from the civilized world. For JC, Patusan and England are opposite poles, but the sea provides a place of meeting of dream and reality. Jim's tension consists of the need to develop a "personal identity" and an equally necessary archetypal identity. For him to be born again, he must die and be born again, thus displaying the "truth" that lies behind the emphasis on rebirth.

2759 Graver, Lawrence. "Conrad for the Seventies," *Virginia Quarterly Review*, XLVIII (Spring 1972), pp. 315–20.

On the whole, JC has not been lucky in his critics. Long ago, they exploited the spinner of tales and ignored the "historian of moral compromise"; even after World War II, when Zabel, Guerard, and others established more accurately the "substance" of his greatness, JC still elicited "foggy and diversionary" responses from his critics. The reasons can, in part, be found in the very nature of his genius: he was at times maladroit and he also worked at times with a "stupefying conventionality." Recent critics such as Royal Roussel, Bruce Johnson, and Norman Sherry have not gone very far into how JC the artist used his materials for creating his works.

2760 Gray, Virginia R. "Young Jósef Teodor Konrad Korzeniowski," *Duke University Library Notes*, XLIII (1972), pp. 42–52.

The collections of manuscripts and pictures of JC in the William R. Perkins Library of Duke University includes a photograph album illustrating the early years of his career in Poland. The forty-three photographs reveal his personal ties to Poland from 1860 to 1890. It is highly probably that this album was a personal possession of JC's mother, begun at the time of her arrest and exile in 1861–62. [Lists the photographs, most of which can be identified, and reproduces seventeen of them.]

2761 Haltresht, Michael. "The Dread of Space in Conrad's *The Secret Agent*," *Literature and Psychology*, XXII, No. 2 (1972), pp. 89–97.

JC's restlessness assumed the form of a "*double* phobia"—his inability to tolerate confined spaces as well as an opposite, and even stronger, dread of open spaces. His aversion for the out of doors is reflected in the dread that open space arouses in *The Secret Agent*. Vastness and emptiness produce frustration and anxiety because they bring to mind "a cosmic time-space continuum" that reduces the individual to utter insignificance; examples in the novel are Stevie's penchant for circles, which reveals space as being without bounds, center, animation, or meaning; a dread of falling, seen in much of the imagery; a sense of persecution, seen in Vladimir; the fear of being overwhelmed and absorbed by something monstrous, as in the Professor's fear of crowds; and the fear of entrapment, seen best in the Verloc tenement. This fear brings a feeling of entrapment to Ossipon when he discovers Verloc's corpse. Vicious circles, also as with Ossipon, are one kind of the anxieties projected upon the physical environment. Also, outdoor nature represents the inanimate environment into which every human being will be reabsorbed; therefore instances of "acrophobia" in the novel must be the author's fear of "falling (or exiting)" with dying. These phobias help greatly in accounting for the complexities of *Agent*.

2762 Haltresht, Michael. "The Gods of Conrad's *Nostromo*," *Renascence*, XXIV (Summer 1972), pp. 207–12.

JC's ambiguities and tensions in *Nostromo* are the manifestations of an equilibrium in his mind between his conscious rebellion against his austere Roman Catholic upbringing and his continuing "unconscious" allegiance to what he referred to as "the faith of his fathers." The desired spiritual yearnings, loyalties, and convictions gain indirect, symbolic expression in this novel and are at least as real as the "personal skepticism" of the surface. Several passages which deal with religion suddenly freeze the novel's action into stylized tableaux which expose to the reader meanings that JC's conscious mind may have scorned. In these, since women are often seen worshiping, the model for Teresa and Miss Lopez, for Mrs. Gould, Antonia, and Linda, is Saint Mary, the *Mater Dolorosa*. Although JC seems uncommitted in such passages, they assume the transcendent quality and the rich suggestiveness of iconography. Also, the first chapter of the novel presents a vast imaginary circle, the center of which is Sulaco. In time, the pattern is cyclical so that the "light-and-darkness" conflict of the central portion is resolved. A circle in space and a cycle in time provide excellent imagery of the divine, and the visual imagery of the first chapter suggests an "intuitively religious" world opposed to the "occasional conscious cynicism" of the novel.

2763 Hampshire, Stuart. "Figures in the Carpet," *New Statesman*, LXXXIV (4 August 1972), pp. 162–63.

That Henry James had no gift for abstract thought and no philosophical interests separates him from Hardy and JC. The latter's account of him is still the "most penetrating."

2764 Hartsell, Robert L. "Conrad's Left Symbolism in *The Secret Agent*," *CON*, IV, No. 1 (1972), pp. 57–59.

Of the twenty references in JC's *The Secret Agent* to a character's hand or to a direction, fifteen are to the left, suggesting the "sinister" or "leftist" anarchists of the novel. Winnie's mother and Stevie, the innocent pair, have a "right" relationship. Winnie has both "left" and "right" connections. In this way, JC tells his story on two levels simultaneously.

2765 Hay, Eloise Knapp. "Conrad, Between Fact & Fiction," *Encounter*, XXXVIII (April 1972), pp. 72–76.

The East in JC's fiction is paradoxically "passive and virile, . . . redemptive and degenerative"; equally paradoxically, the West is "atavistic and effete, . . . messianic and egocentripetal." For JC, imagination was the "primary act," but it had to act on materials that were not invented. For him, Aristotle's and Sidney's "higher truth" no longer resided mainly in myths: if there was any higher truth, JC had to find it in rendering the widest possible "justice to the visible universe."

2766 Hazelrig, Jack Octa. "The Moral Dilemma in Selected Fiction of Joseph Conrad," *DAI*, XXXII (1972), 5229A. Unpublished dissertation, Texas Tech University, 1971.

2767 Heath, Steven. *The Nouveau Roman: A Study in the Practice of Writing* (London: Elek, 1972), p. 130.

Whereas JC's *Lord Jim*, with its intricate and complex narrative organization, contains a basic narrative sequence which the reader can reassemble, Robbe-Grillet's novels (*La Jalousie*, for example) are not available to this kind of reading.

2768 Hernadi, Paul. *Beyond Genre: New Directions in Literary Classification* (Ithaca and London: Cornell University Press, 1972), pp. 141–42.

Northrop Frye's historical account of the "themes" of literature in his *Anatomy of Criticism: Four Essays* (1957) as displaced versions of their archetypes is not entirely convincing; but his general remarks on theme—Frye's term for Aristotle's *dianoia*, usually translated as "thought"—seem to be highly stimulating. Frye argues that while plot or *mythos* determines the temporal shape of a work as the consequence of hypothetical events, theme or dianoia holds the work together in a simultaneous quasi-spatial pattern of meaning. The relative prevalence of plot or theme will make some works primarily "fictional," others primarily "thematic." Yet *mythos* and *dianoia* emerge as complementary aspects of literature. Works in which the poet addresses his audience belong to the genre of *epos* or direct address, whereas *fiction* appears to be designed for the printed page. The "singer" of *lyric* poems pretends to be communing with himself or with someone other than his actual listener or reader who overhears rather than hears the lyric utterance. And the unmediated presence of hypothetical figures indicates acting as the "radical of presentation" characteristic of *drama*. Although all genres may and, since the invention of the printing press, increasingly do exist in written form, Frye's concept of the radical of presentation as the criterion for generic distinctions appears convincing in the light of his analogy of the keyboard.

In JC's novels, the "genre of the written" is being assimilated to that of the "spoken" one through the introduction of internal narrators. Frye thus considers each of the four genres (*epos, fiction, lyric,* and *drama*) as "an approximation or *mimesis* of the verbal 'rhythm' underlying direct address, assertive writing, mental association, and conversation, respectively." [The usual interpretation of mimesis as imitating the universe or some specific part of it is now being limited more fully to uses of language and is thereby moving beyond the four usual orientations of literary criticism into the realm of the poststructuralist uses of criticism. Frye explains that when JC "employs a narrator to help him tell his story, the genre of the written word is being assimilated to that of the spoken one." The emphasis is being shifted from Plato's forms or ideas to a consideration of language only—JC is seen as a forerunner of poststructuralism.]

2769 Hewitt, Douglas. *The Approach to Fiction: Good and Bad Readings of Novels* (London: Longman, 1972), pp. 49, 58, 59–60, 66n, 69, 111, 118n, 136, 137, 138, 141–45, 175, 184–85, 189–90, 191, 192.

Literary conventions, such as that of plot, should not disturb us by their artificiality; art, including realistic art, allows a very wide range of acceptable degrees of stylizations from the "highly artificial" plot structure of Hardy and JC to the looser organization of Tolstoy or Charlotte Brontë. The aim of major novelists to give an account of a complete society, like JC's in *Nostromo*, need not militate against formal order, because JC's view of human behavior is essentially determinist so that he can organize his novel around a key symbol, the silver. Since the supply of novels worth serious discussion has not kept pace with the supply of criticism, it is difficult not to feel that the extant criticism of any work by Melville, Faulkner, or JC is caused by placing more and more weight on smaller and smaller matters. Albert Guerard's desire to see "Heart of Darkness," for example, in terms of the Jungian archetypes leads to a number of distortions, "surprising in a critic of Guerard's powers"; he admits the possibility of two incompatible interpretations, rejection of the savage or rejection of the "civilized-rational," an interpretation which leads towards ambiguity and special pleading. One of the sources of strength in *Nostromo* is a recognition that a serious intellectual conflict is present.

2770 Hinz, Evelyn J. "Rider Haggard's *She*: An Archetypal 'History of Adventure,'" *SNNTS*, IV (Fall 1972), pp. 416–31.

In Rider Haggard's famous romance *She*, years before JC's Marlow, Horace Holly comes to realize how dependent is the "moral sense" upon circumstances. In his use of a kind of "reverse metamorphosis" to emphasize a journey backward into time, Haggard also appears as a forerunner of JC, for, as in "Heart of Darkness," Haggard's theme is that progress is an illusion. "There is what I shall be remembered by," Haggard is supposed to have said when he completed *She*. It seems that there are good reasons why this should be so, and it also suggests what such writers as D. H. Lawrence and JC—"and the immense audience which to the present has kept *She* in print in at least nine British-American editions in at least nineteen translations, and in eight film adaptations"—may have seen, or sensed, in the work.

2771 Hoben, John B. "*Lord Jim*: Marlow's Bewildered Voice," *Philobiblon: The Journal of the Friends of Colgate University Library*, No. 9 (Spring 1972), pp. 3–8.

Many recent critics praise JC for his digressive and open-ended handling of *Lord Jim*. They see the novel as a pioneer in modern impressionistic techniques. Consequently, while much attention has been given to Marlow's role as narrator, insufficient comment has focussed on whether or not Marlow's presence is an advantage to the story. Marlow is a flaw, not for talking so long but for saying so little. His presentation of Jim's death is unsatisfactory both to common sense and fancy. JC should have used a third person omniscient or a multiple point of view. Marlow's bewildered voice may be a reflection of JC's own state of mind as he struggled to create the novel.

2772 Hodgson, John A. "Left-Right Opposition in *The Nigger of the Narcissus*," *Papers on Language and Literature*, VIII (Spring 1972), pp. 207–10.

In *The Nigger of the Narcissus*, JC consistently opposes left and right: right is associated with the land and dark and negative values; left, with the sea and positive ones. JC also equates the values of good and evil with these oppositions.

2773 Hopwood, Alison L. "Carlyle and Conrad: *Past and Present* and 'Heart of Darkness,'" *RES*, XXIII (May 1972), pp. 162–72.

Themes from *Past and Present* occur in "Heart of Darkness" like echoes, but are largely ironic: the basic imperialism of *Past and Present* considered by Carlyle as a moral "Conquest over Chaos" is actually, JC shows, chaotic and evil. JC sometimes displays the reality behind Carlyle's abstractions and turns them into something different, as with the doctrine of the value of work, but at other times he reveals thoughts and attitudes similar to Carlyle's. Whereas Carlyle praises imperial expansion, JC finds it "not a pretty thing." Although JC proves his awareness of his critical attitude to Carlyle, his method is that of the imagination; his feelings provide the unifying force that combines materials from many sources into a coherent whole. But underlying his story is his rejection of the Carlylean view of imperialism.

2774 Howe, Irving. "Introduction," [to "The Secret Sharer"], *Classics of Modern Fiction: Ten Short Novels*, ed. by Irving Howe. Second ed. (New York: Harcourt, Brace, Jovanovich, 1972), pp. 273–83.

Three views of "The Secret Sharer" are those of (1) "The Lover of Adventure," who sees the story as a tale of action in which the captain must fulfill his responsibilities of command while Leggatt is attempting to avoid the consequences of a failure in responsibility; (2) "The Moral Realist," who cannot decide whether the captain is right in hiding Leggatt in his ship; and (3) "The Depth Psychologist," who sees Leggatt as the captain's "secret sharer" in "the way our guilt shares in our conscious life." [Raises more questions than can be readily answered. Is somewhat typical of an introduction to the story in a good textbook, like this one.]

2775 Hynes, Samuel. *Edwardian Occasions: Essays on English Writing in the Early Twentieth Century* (New York: Oxford University Press, 1972), pp. 25, 26, 58, 64–65, 66, 73, 78, 195.

Most of Arnold Bennett's judgments of writers like James, Galsworthy, and JC will last without revision because he had what might be called "*modern* intuitions." His best criticism, like his best work, resembles the views, and even the phrases, of Edwardian writers with whom he is not usually associated—James, Ford, and JC. In Ford's *The Good Soldier*, the real events of the novel are Dowell's thoughts about what has happened, not the happenings themselves. The reader is never "thrown back into the stream of events" as he is in the narratives of JC's Marlow. Ford's fiction is often more accurate than his facts, his personal remembrance of JC, is flatly described in the preface as a novel. The book on JC understandably annoyed readers like H. G. Wells, who held verifiable truth in higher esteem and who believed that a remembrance should not be quite frankly fiction. Even if Ford was more productive in his than JC, the latter came to Ford for a collaboration which now seems to have been the desperate, impossible scheme of an "impractical, penniless artist" who wanted a way of making some money by gaining for his own kind of work something more marketable. But if JC learned from Ford, Ford also learned much from JC. [Included also is "Conrad and Ford: Two Rye Revolutionists," pp. 48–53 (C, I, No. 1881).]

2776 Izsak, Emily. "*Under Western Eyes* and the Problems of Serial Publication," *RES*, XXIII (November 1972), pp. 429–44.

Under Western Eyes was first conceived as a novella suited for serialization. JC was in debt, and hoping to lessen the amount he owed, undertook the project with a strict deadline in mind. The story grew into a novel of 150,000 words and took more than two years to complete. But due to the pressures of serialization JC could not resolve the ambivalence he felt toward the novel's central issues.

2777 Jacobs, Robert G. "*Gilgamesh*: The Sumerian Epic That Helped *Lord Jim* to Stand Alone," *CON*, IV, No. 2 (1972), pp. 23–32.

Most of the epic poems which make up *Gilgamesh* were in existence by 2000 B.C., but the story of the king of ancient Uruk appears to have been, in due time, of help to JC in writing *Lord Jim*. *Jim* was first planned as a short story to accompany "Youth" and "Heart of Darkness"; but "The End of the Tether" appeared there instead. In due time, *Jim* became a single novel with an unusual plot structure. Much of the Patusan material resembles the ancient Sumerian epic. Both Gilgamesh and Jim have a close friendship with a native; both works end with the death of that native initiating the final action; Jim's search for a place involves a wise man, Stein, who is like Utnapishtim; both Utnapishtim and Stein are the master of a magical garden; in both stories the mountain slopes burn before the end; and Mashu, like Jim's mountain of Patusan, is a single peak split in two. Perhaps JC used the oldest epic tale in existence as a means to resolve his dilemma in writing *Jim*.

2778 Jacobson, Sibyl C. "Structure of 'Heart of Darkness': A Study in Narrative Technique and a Concordance to 'Heart of Darkness,'" *DAI*, XXXIII (1972), 2379A. Unpublished dissertation, University of Wisconsin, 1972.

2779 Janta, Alexander. "Conrad's 'Famous Cablegram' in Support of a Polish Loan," *PolR*, XVII (Spring 1972), pp. 69-77.

Although JC's "famous cablegram" of 26 April 1920, "An Appeal for Poland," addressed to the National Campaign Committee, Polish

Government Loan, in the United States, showing that Poland deserved American support in her crucial struggle with Russia and that JC was unswervingly attached to the country of his origin, has been known for many years, no autograph of the text has hitherto been located. An article by Maurice Francis Egan of 28 July 1921 in the *Outlook* contains the text of JC's appeal, with comments explaining each sentence. When JC was approached in April, 1920, to give Poland the support of his "illustrious" name, he responded "with generosity and feeling." [Contains an account of the Polish political situation of the time. For a further comment on this matter, see Juliet McLauchlan, "Conrad's 'Famous Telegram'—An Article Note," *Conradiana*, X, No. 2 (1973), pp. 85–86.]

2780 Johnson, Bruce. "'Heart of Darkness' and the Problem of Emptiness," *SSF*, IX (1972), pp. 384–400; rpt. *Conrad's Models of Mind* (Minneapolis: University of Minnesota Press, 1971).

Schopenhauer's conception of man's ability to transcend the egoistic demands of Will by affirming, either in art or in Buddha-like aesceticism, the selfless unity of all men, seems to have great bearing on JC's characterization of Marlow in "Heart of Darkness." Yet if Marlow is indeed employing Schopenhauerian defenses against the Will, he has misread his experience with Kurtz, for Kurtz is not simply a figure of Will. There is an "emptiness" to Kurtz which goes far beyond the emptiness of supreme egoism. His sense of the emptiness of life is analogous to the emptiness which permeates other late-Victorian stories, such as Kipling's "The Man Who Would Be King," which deals with white Europeans' attempts to play God for the members of a primitive tribe. Kurtz's final words indicate his acceptance of the emptiness within him when he suggests the possibility of a "radical freedom," which will enable man to move beyond the illusions which enchain him. If Marlow understands the value of Kurtz's sense of the horror—and his emphasis upon Kurtz's "victory" indicates that he does—then we can see his acceptance of an austere, Buddha-like stance as a duplication of Kurtz's final authority. Marlow's re-creation of his experience with Kurtz is not a repudiation of the ego, but is rather the attempt to bring a new ego into the world. JC alludes to Schopenhauer in order to reverse Schopenhauer's conclusions.

2781 Joy, Neill R. "The Joseph Conrad Collection at the Everett Needham Case Library," *Philobiblon: The Journal of the Friends of the Colgate University Library*, No. 9 (Spring 1972), pp. 10–17.

In 1958, a large and assorted JC collection—MSS, TSS, author's copy and proof, first and private printings, correspondence, and memorabilia—gathered and bequeathed by the bibliophile, Henry A.

Colgate, passed into the possession of Colgate University. This memorial library, drawing on the great sales of Quinn, Jessie Conrad, Curle, and Kern, is so rich as to place it with other distinguished collections at Harvard, Yale, Dartmouth, Duke, the University of Illinois, the British Museum, the Berg Collection in the New York Public Library, and the Rosenbach Foundation in Philadelphia. The number of separate publications well exceeds two hundred items. MS and TS correspondence, including letters to Garnett, Pinker, Norman Douglas, Unwin, and a unit of letters to MacDonald Hastings regarding the adaptation of *Victory* to the stage runs upward of one hundred twenty items. The accumulation of material describes the arc of JC's literary career, from *The Nigger of the Narcissus* to *Suspense*. This bibliographical collection helps to chart not only the transmission of the text but also—"biological in its implication"—the evolution of a literary aesthetic designed to make new discoveries. [In a paper read at the annual 1975 MLA meeting, Joy corrects the statement here that the TS "Preface" to *Nigger* corroborates "every detail of the text as it is now printed."]

2782 Keppler, C. F. *The Literature of the Second Self* (Tucson: University of Arizona Press, 1972), pp. 45–50, 56, 86–91, 99, 112–15, 119, 196.

There is in *Lord Jim* an atmosphere of the second self. Accordingly, the disgrace that Jim feels after leaping off the *Patna* has a profound effect on him, for he is not merely an officer who ran from his duty, but he is also a representative of all the men who attend his trial. They all realize that they have not yet been caught; appropriate examples are the French lieutenant and Brierly. Once Jim reaches Patusan, he redeems himself and so becomes Lord Jim. When Brown comes to Patusan, he strikes a responsive chord in Jim because he functions as Jim's second self. Later, when he dies and speaks to Marlow about Jim, he functions as the second self revealing secrets about the first self.

The clearest instance of JC's use of the relationship between the selves is "The Secret Sharer." Here, there are two processes: (1) the first self, the captain, saves the second self, Leggatt; (2) the second self saves the first. This story, though, is not about mistaken identity; the physical parallels merely serve as manifestations of the deeper internal activity.

Victory is a story containing a relentlessly pursuing self. Heyst actually owes allegiance to two fathers: his actual father, the elder Heyst, and the old Adam urging on his flesh. His tragedy results from his inability either to accept or to reject one or the other.

2783 Kiely, Robert. *The Romantic Novel in England* (Cambridge: Harvard University Press, 1972), p. 148.

Edward Waverley in Walter Scott's novel *Waverley* is no tormented protagonist of later romantic literature, like Lord Jim, to agonize over inconsistencies within himself. Scott stops, with his hero, where JC would have begun.

2784 Kirk, Carey H. "The Challenge of Involvement: A Response to Melville and Conrad," *DAI*, XXXIII (1972), 1731A. Unpublished dissertation, Vanderbilt University, 1972.

2785 Kirschner, Paul. "Conrad's Missing Link with Kipling," *N&Q*, XIX (September 1972), p. 331.

In his *A Bibliography of Joseph Conrad* (1969), Theodore G. Ehrsam attributes to JC an unsigned article, "Kipling, Rudyard—a criticism on his poems," which appeared in *Outlook* (London), 2 April 1898, and which JC described as "a chatter about Kipling provoked by a silly criticism." But Ehrsam is wrong: JC was replying to a remark in the *Saturday Review* by Arthur Symons.

2786 Knoepflmacher, U. C. "Recent Studies in the Nineteenth Century," *Studies in English Literature*, XII (Autumn 1972), pp. 801–24.

[Points out the fact that critics have yet to assess Walter Pater's relation to the Preface of *The Nigger of the Narcissus* or to investigate connections between JC's racial stereotypes and Herbert Spencer's belief that racial instincts are formed by the repetition of reflex actions lost in higher civilizations. Also notes that whereas Bruce Johnson in *Conrad's Models of Mind* (1971) argues that JC's delay in completing *The Rescue* was due to his altered "model of mind," Wilfred S. Dowden in *Joseph Conrad: The Imaged Style* (1970), a more traditional examination of JC's imagery, argues that JC's delay was caused by the novelist's "changing concept of the purpose and function of imagery"; the two views are hardly incompatible.]

2787 Kocowna, Barbara (ed.). "Korespondencja Ambasady Polskiej w Londynie z Josephem Conradem" (Correspondence of the Polish Embassy in London with Joseph Conrad), *KN*, XIX, 2 (1972), pp. 213–20.

Four JC letters are in the Archiwum akt nowych (Archives of New Documents, Warsaw) dated 20 February, 28 July, 1 August, and 22 September 1920. They deal with (1) a proposal made to JC to participate in the organization of an Anglo-Polish Society in London, which he declined on account of age and health, and (2) the translation rights into Polish of his works after his death. He signed over the rights to Aniela (Angela) Zagórska. Her translations are those used for the fiftieth anniversary edition (Warsaw), with some corrections in maritime terminology. [In Polish; JC's letters in English.]

2788 Krugliak, M. T. *"Kapriz Olmeiera* D. Konrada" (Conrad's *Almayer's Folly*), *Uchenye Zapiski Permskogo Gos. Universiteta* (Perm), No. 270 (1972), pp. 110–19.

In his portrayal of Dain and Nina in *Almayer's Folly*, JC the Romantic prevailed over JC the realist, since the portrait of Almayer is drawn realistically. This novel occupies an important place in JC's work, for with it he entered English literature a fully mature artist. The book deals with many important questions characteristic of English literature at the turn of the nineteenth century. [In Russian.]

2789 Krugliak, M. T. "Konflikty i geroi v romane Dzhozefa Konrada *Otverzhennyi s ostrovov*" (Conflicts and Heroes in Joseph Conrad's Novel *An Outcast of the Islands*), *Uchenye Zapiski Permskogo Gos. Universiteta* (Perm), No. 270 (1972), pp. 120–32.

JC depicts the degradation of the human personality in conditions of bourgeois reality. The theme of money and its destructive effects is in the forefront. Although praised by Western critics, *An Outcast of the Islands* has not been analyzed with regard to the social conditions which forced the characters into the erroneous paths and led to the tragic conclusion of the novel. Objectively, *Outcast*, entirely directed against bourgeois reality, is a step forward from *Almayer's Folly*, with a marked increase in psychological mastery and in JC's critical attitude towards the cruel, soulless world of money. [In Russian.]

2790 Laine, Michael. "Review," *Queen's Quarterly*, LXXIX (1972), pp. 421–22.

[Review of Royal Roussel, *The Metaphysics of Darkness* (1971) and Bruce Johnson, *Conrad's Models of Mind* (1971). Roussel sees *Lord Jim*'s "adventurous voyage . . . as a metaphor for the act of writing," and he sees JC as a nihilist. Johnson sees JC "embracing a vision of darkness and silence stemming from . . . the Victorian . . . 'death of God.'" He seems to bend the literature to fit the philosophic models he attributes to JC.]

2791 Lincoln, Kenneth R. "Comic Light in 'Heart of Darkness,'" *MFS*, XVIII (Summer 1972), pp. 183–97.

In "Heart of Darkness," Marlow maintains a comic sense of his nightmare in recounting many scenes of comic incongruity, and JC himself bares with ironic humor problems we prefer not to face. His narrative undercuts baseness and hypocrisy, and the tone of the fiction implies a personal sense of humor which enables the author to encompass and eventually transcend "'the horror' of civilized folly." One means to this end appears in Marlow's assurance to Kurtz's Intended that the last name the dying Kurtz had uttered was "your name"; that is, the real word *horror* is a pun of the real nature of woman, *whore*. Conceptually, this story involves several kinds of compromise; general prostitution covers these compromises in which appearance eclipses reality. And both psychologically and symbolically, JC links Kurtz's depravity with prostitution. The Intended symbolizes the disparity between intentions and deeds; the pun reveals a naive decadence in the heart abandoned by Kurtz, and "Heart" of darkness undercuts the Intended herself, "a madam in mourning," since her heart symbolizes "a universal prostitution of love, altruism, philanthropy, and human nature itself." JC suggests that the domination of one person over another approximates the imperialist exploitation of an entire continent. Kurtz's "tragic queen" is the Intended's double. The "horror" "leers" at Marlow wherever he goes, and he finds himself in the ambiguous role of "civilization's gigolo" in its "rape" of Africa.

2792 Marenco, Franco. ["A Critical Introduction"], *Conrad, Romanzi Occidentali* (Conrad, Novels of the West), (Milan: Mursia, 1972), pp. 1–22.

This work, the third in a series of Italian translations of the works of Joseph Conrad, includes four novels which share a non-Oriental setting: *Nostromo, The Secret Agent, Under Western Eyes,* and *Chance*. In *Nostromo,* the book's architectonic interplay of the actions and ethics of the main characters results in the gradual perversion of the man before whom all illusions of justification and idealized fantasies disappear. *Agent* involves the treatment of time and accident, which "introduce us to a permanent variation in Conrad between nature and the instruments which man has developed to use it." *Eyes* is a parable in the form of a *Bildungsroman*. The experiments with point of view serve to emphasize, for JC, the difference between Western and Eastern mentalities, which forms one of the bases of the novel. The confusion in *Chance* is not in JC, but in Marlow, because JC is always in complete control of his material. [Marenco makes a significant contribution to JC scholarship.] [In Italian.]

2793 Marten, Harry. "Conrad's Skeptic Reconsidered: A Study of Martin Decoud," *NCF*, XXVII (June 1972), pp. 81–94.

Martin Decoud, a supreme egoist, is perhaps the most important character in *Nostromo*, because he embodies one of the major thematic statements of the novel: man must base his actions on some belief in an external ideal if he is to survive the "crushing effects of a blank, uncaring universe." Decoud, skeptic, lover, half-patriot, plays his roles so others may regard him as important; but he becomes JC's successful emblem for the man without faith in any external ideal, without even the commitment to a negative outlook which a true skeptic must have. We have serious doubts about the real depth of love he feels for Antonia, and the sincerity of his work in Costaguana is questionable. After JC has revealed the many levels of Decoud's dependence upon the reactions of others, he gradually separates him from all contact with the external world to a "fatal condition of isolation" in which his ego has nothing to respond. Eventually, the man whose sole aim in life is to feel important is overwhelmed by his sense of insignificance—and shoots himself.

2794 Martin, David M. "'Victorian' Conrad: A Study of His Early Phase in Relation to the Nineteenth-Century Problems of Belief," *DAI*, XXXII (January 1972), 4009A. Unpublished dissertation, New York University, 1971.

2795 Martin, Joseph J. "Conrad's Literary Conscience: The Guiding Influence of Edward Garnett," *DAI*, XXXII (1972), 6437A–38A. Unpublished dissertation, The Pennsylvania State University, 1971.

2796 McGrail, David B. "The Narrator in the Fiction of Joseph Conrad," *DAI*, XXXII (1972), 6988A. Unpublished dissertation, University of Pennsylvania, 1971.

2797 McMillan, Dougald. "*Nostromo*: The Theology of Revolution," *The Classic British Novel*, ed. by Howard M. Harper, Jr., and Charles Edge (Athens: University of Georgia Press, 1972), pp. 166–82.

Certain Christian parallels reinforce the meaning and structure of *Nostromo*: the guilt and redemption which dominate the novel are worked out specifically in terms of Christian myth and theology. Nostromo, who becomes the "agent of mercy protecting vulnerable humanity," takes the curse of the silver upon himself and, like Christ, who "undoes" the curse brought upon the world by Adam and Eve, performs an act of vicarious atonement. Though Nostromo assumes the guilt of others and suffers symbolically in doing so, the guilt with which the novel is charged is not purged until the end of the book; before the curse can be permanently removed, Nostromo has to find absolution, and those for whom the sacrifice is made must demonstrate their belief so the vicarious atonement can be effective. Nostromo's confession to Mrs. Gould and Dr. Monygham's act of faith in believing that Nostromo has somehow saved the silver that was lost effect Nostromo's absolution. The evidence of the novel indicates that neither the popular revolution nor the imperialist expansion will change Costaguana, but the reader somehow disregards all the historical details and at least hopes that reunification is possible and that everyone will eventually benefit from the silver mine. The faith demanded contains the awareness that all humanity is involved in a "desperate affair," but the anguish of man is combined with a spirit of love that binds men together in spite of the infidelities they commit. [More optimistic than most views of *Nostromo.*]

2798 Meisel, Perry. *Thomas Hardy: The Return of the Repressed* (New Haven and London: Yale University Press, 1972), pp. 105, 138–39.

Henchard's tragedy in *The Mayor of Casterbridge*, before it is recognized by the protagonist, displays both a personal and a historical aspect, a private and a public; so does JC in *The Nigger of the Narcissus* reveal the bonds of the crew of the ship to James Wait. A juxtaposition of passages from the two novels illustrates the similarity between the two: the setting of Jude's abortive suicide attempt in which the ice cracks under the protagonist's weight is very much like Stein's words in *Lord Jim*: it is as though the water is "still frozen enough for Jude to live until the thaw of discovery."

2799 "Il mondo di Conrad: Fallimento e nobiltà" (Conrad's World: Failure and Nobleness), *Intimita'*, 1386 (29 September 1972), p. 16.

[Review of some TV adaptations from JC's works.] [In Italian.]

2800 Morris, Robert K. *Continuance and Change: The Contemporary British Novel Sequence* (Carbondale and Edwardsville: Southern Illinois University Press, 1972), pp. 71–72.

"One of two pieces" by JC, with a few items by Kipling, Waugh, Forster, and Orwell, indicate clearly the "pockets of cultural confusion" caused by imperialism. A common theme in these works, that the social, political, and mental "attrition" of an "effete" ruler (effete "through iron-fisted tactics or humanitarianism") must eventually yield to the will of the ruled, is discovered by the author of

"Shooting an Elephant," Mrs. Moore of *A Passage to India*, and Kurtz of "Heart of Darkness."

2801 Mueller, William R. "*Nostromo* and the Orders of Creation: An Ontological Argument," *Celebration of Life: Studies in Modern Fiction* (New York: Sheed & Ward, 1972), pp. 77–97, 275.

In *Nostromo*, conflicts are acted out on many levels: there are the inner turmoils of such introspective characters as Martin Decoud and Dr. Monygham as well as the vast, politically oriented battle between armed men who lay claim to a relatively primitive South American territory and its treasure, the silver. But the real fascination of the novel lies in the continuing confrontation between the human and the natural orders of creation—between man who would "unrestrainedly rape the earth" and those natural forces that would destroy him for his intrusion. In *The Nigger of the Narcissus*, the gale is seen as "an avenging terror" and the sea as demanding its own; in *Lord Jim*, nature seems to make a conscious effort to destroy people who sail the seas; "civilized" man becomes more and more unwelcome as Marlow goes into the heart of the dark Congo and Kurtz's mission becomes an unwelcome invasion of the wilderness. Kurtz's unrestrained pursuit of ivory suggests the unrestrained pursuit of silver in *Nostromo*. JC seems to proffer an ontological comment on the structural economy of the universe. The characters in this novel are most clearly bound through common interest in the San Tomé mine; even the five main characters fall, through involvement with the mine, to death or living in misery. Poetic justice in this novel is not justice allotted each man according to his deserts; it is a judgment upon all of man seen in its communal aspect. The protagonists agree that San Tomé exists only to serve mankind and is their only human solidarity.

2802 Mukerji, N. "The Problem of Point of View in *Under Western Eyes*," *Bulletin of the Department of English, Calcutta University*, VIII, No. 3 (1972–73), pp. 73–80.

The story of *Under Western Eyes* is told from the point of view of the English teacher of languages, who embodies the Western point of view and enables JC to have a kind of double focus—the Russians as seen by themselves and as seen and understood, or misunderstood, through Western eyes. The nameless narrator embodies the emotional imperceptiveness of the West. JC's success lies in dramatizing, in a meaningful way, the barrier between the East and the West. The use of a mask in the form of the narrator's point of view fulfills JC's need for impersonality. His greatest achievement in using this point of view lies in his successful dramatization of the major scenes.

2803 Mursia, Ugo. "Note a *Nostromo*: Riferimenti autobiografici e fonti," *Conrad, Romanzi Occidentali* (Conrad, Novels of the West), (Milan: Mursia, 1972), pp. 1067–72; rpt. in part as "The Italian Source of *Nostromo*" in *JCCP* (1975), pp. 93–99.

Generally speaking, JC's source for *Nostromo* is the life of Giuseppe Garibaldi, particularly as it is recounted in his *Memoirs* translated by Alexandre Dumas in 1860 and rendered into English and published in London the same year. JC apparently also used one or more biographies; close analogies exist between Giorgio Viola and one of Garibaldi's faithful followers, Gian Battista Culiolo. Also, some peculiar aspects of the character of Viola are modeled on Garibaldi himself, and JC may have borrowed some details from Enrique Clerici's *Thirteen Stories* of 1900. It seems that both the revolt in Sulaco and the central events of the novel occur about 1884 and that Viola-Culiolo is about seventy years old.

2804 Mursia, Ugo. "Storia e geografia della Costaguana" (History and Geography of Costaguana), *Conrad, Romanzi Occidentali* (Conrad, Novels of the West), (Milan: Mursia, 1972), pp. 1073–82; rpt. in part as "The Fictional State of Costaguana," *L'Époque Conradienne*, No. 5 (May 1979), pp. 85–107.

JC did extensive research on the subject of the fictional country of Costaguana, the setting of *Nostromo*. Especially useful to him were R. B. Cunninghame Graham and Perez Triana, both of whom had written on subjects which helped afford background details. The important contemporary historical event was the secession of Panama from Colombia in 1903, the very year in which JC began to write his novel. Costaguana is located in South America, being part of the area of what was once Gran Colombia, created by Simon Bolívar, including what is now Colombia, Venezuela, Ecuador, and Panama. The Golfo Placido lies on the Pacific Ocean. It seems likely that Edward Whymper's book, *Travels Among the Great Andes of the Equator* (1892), is a minor source of *Nostromo*. But one must remember that however close to geography JC remained, Costaguana is an imaginary state put together by the author. The composite background of the novel appears to extend from the beginning of the Wars of Independence against the Spanish rule in 1811 through 1903, the date of the secession of Panama from Colombia. This account of the geography and history of Costaguana helps in seeing how the author's mind operates in the process of creating a major work.

2805 Na, Yong-gyun. "The Original Sin Motif in 'Heart of Darkness,'" *Studies in English Literature* (English Literary Society of Japan), English number (1972), pp. 97–107.

Seen as a modern parable of "Original Sin," "Heart of Darkness" has as central theme the quest for knowledge of self through a journey into the heart of darkness. Not knowing himself at first, the protagonist, Marlow, through a "provisional descent into the primitive and unconscious sources of Kurtz," emerges a mature man at the end, capable of manhood and moral survival. JC's story contains many parallels to that of Adam and Eve in the Bible, and the repetitive "harking back" to the earliest age of the world purposefully reminds us of the "age of Adam." The story of the Fall has a claim to universal validity, a validity which justifies Marlow's attitude toward Kurtz. Marlow's "choice of nightmares," a deliberate choice of Kurtz, is "right" because Kurtz finally discovers himself and becomes fully human. His last cry is an insight into the potentialities of all men.

2806 Najder, Zdzislaw. "Conrad romansowy" (Romantic Conrad), *Tw*, XXVIII, No. 7 (1972), pp. 59–77.

In 1895, JC met Emilie Briquel at Champel, near Geneva, and a correspondence followed later. [Letters and commentary are given.] [See also Joseph Conrad, *Listy* (Letters), ed. by Zdzislaw Najder (Warsaw: Panstwowy Instytut Wydawniczy, 1968), pp. 75, 80.] [In Polish.]

2807 Najder, Zdzislaw (ed.). "Wstep" (Introduction), *J. Conrad Wybor Opowiadan* (J. Conrad, Collected Tales), (Wroclaw and Krakow: Ossolineum, 1972), pp. iii–lxxviii.

Polish Romantic literature and French realistic prose influenced JC's art. The Polish literary tradition rarely occurs as direct borrowings, but as general categories of thought and imagination. The French influences are concerned with the craft of writing, especially in JC's earlier works. Later, he created his own type of narrative, and still other influences became apparent (Henry James, Anatole France, Dostoevski). Polish readers, accustomed to courtly traditions of love, accept his heroines and their admirers as old acquaintances. JC likes to describe himself as "a gentleman"; hence his preoccupation with knightly and military virtues: honor, loyalty, courage, and the cult of friendship. These come from the heritage of the Polish gentry, unusual in English literature. According to this tradition, women are either guardians of the highest values and worshiped, or sexual animals. JC's women are variations of the first type. The idea of "gentry" is linked with contempt for earning a living and manual labor. But JC, on the contrary, had a cult for work, and treats those who avoid it with sarcasm. Of course, for the greater part of his life, JC had no contact with the gentry, but he inherited their ideals from Polish literary traditions.

To define JC as a psychological writer leads to mistaken interpretations of his work. His psychological attitude toward fiction is reminiscent of the nineteenth-century Polish novel rather than of English or French bourgeois novels. His heroes are types, and JC is more concerned with moral and social circumstances and with what links his characters with a community. [In Polish.]

2808 Nelson, Carl. "The Ironic Allusive Texture of *Lord Jim*: Coleridge, Crane, Milton, and Melville," *CON*, IV, No. 2 (1972), pp. 47–59.

JC "mediates" the story of the misadventures of the protagonist of *Lord Jim* by a system of ironical allusions, thereby establishing a consistent perspective on Jim and the motives for his actions. This process evokes the debilitating effects of Jim's fantasies and exposes the fallacious logic of Marlow's sympathetic narrative. Allusions to Coleridge's "The Ancient Mariner" establish the type of both the romantic voyage and the dissociated realms of visionary fantasy which is its goal. JC's description of the voyage inverts and parodies the redemptive journey of Coleridge's mariner and mediates the ironic inability of either Jim or Marlow to confront the meaning of existence. JC also merges allusions to "The Ancient Mariner" with imagery from "Kubla Khan" to develop strikingly the contrast between the wishful dream and the contingent world. Allusions to Crane's *The Red Badge of Courage* enable JC further to burlesque romantic self-deception within a naturalistic frame. In the last part of the novel, JC introduces a devastating reduction of the romantic circle of fantasy and its promised salvation from reality with allusions to the Miltonic and Christian myth of the early paradise and fall. And failure of a series of incarnations of aged wisdom culminating in Marlow is strikingly depicted through allusions to Melville's *The Confidence-Man*. JC's complex system of allusions provides an ironic perspective to temper his tale of Jim's and Marlow's effort to escape from contingent reality.

2809 Nettels, Elsa. "James and Conrad on the Art of Fiction," *TSLL*, XIV (Fall 1972), pp. 529–43.

Both Henry James's and JC's writings on the art of fiction set them apart from their fellow contemporary English writers. Sharing many views, both stressed that their novels were the result of a "system" or "method." Both viewed form and substance as a single, indivisible entity, and rejected "sharp distinctions between moral and aesthetic values in fiction." Furthermore, both writers denied being a part of any particular school of fiction and believed that such labels as realism and naturalism were dangerous because they restricted a writer's freedom. Though alike in many ways, James and

JC do not always share the same views on the creative process. Whereas James saw his task as "pressing" the artistic work out of the subject itself, for intance, JC described the writer's task as "squeez[ing] out" of himself the work of art. Also, JC did not describe his or his characters' relationship to each other in James's terms of "intimacy." Instead, he stressed the hopelessness of understanding another person or of getting into another's consciousness. These two writers did, though, stand alone together in their dedication to the craft of fiction.

2810 Newell, Kenneth B. "Science Fiction and the Merging of Romance and Realism," *Extrapolation: A Journal of Science Fiction and Fantasy,* XIV (December 1972), pp. 6–12.

A trend toward the merging of romance and realism produced a relatively new type of fiction, since called symbolic fiction; and the best illustrations of merging, outside of science fiction, are the works of Hardy, Woolf, Joyce, Graham Greene, and JC. In *Within the Tides,* JC states the need for "romance subject matter" to be treated realistically in order to "make unfamiliar things credible." One step further is H. G. Wells, with interest in the "extraordinary." The main stream of modern fiction flows not from Wells but from Hardy and JC. Wells, however, has led to the work of Arthur C. Clarke and Harlan Ellison.

2811 Pagetti, Carlo. "Joseph Conrad: Avventure metafisiche per mare" (Joseph Conrad: Metaphysical Adventures on the Sea), *Umanita'* (14 April 1972), p. 10.

The attraction of *The Shadow-Line* lies in the tone of nostalgia which runs through it—in its quality of emblematic memory, decisive for an entire lifetime. The autobiographical elements were stressed by JC himself, but these are sublimated in a cosmic vision of reality; the captain reaches his destination, and yet in the victory there is no cause for triumph. On the contrary, if anything, there is a farewell to youth and joy. [In Italian.]

2812 Pappas, John J. "Victorian Literature of the Divided Mind: A Study of the Self in Relation to Nature," *DAI,* XXX (1972), 693A–94A. Unpublished dissertation, Columbia University, 1968.

2813 Payne, John R. *Modern British Fiction: An Exhibit of Books, Paintings and Manuscripts, November–December 1972,* intro. by Alan Friedman (Austin: Humanities Research Center, 1972).

[Contains Walter Tittle's portrait of JC, accompanied by a brief description of the holograph, the typescript, the carbon typescript, and the first and second issues of the first edition of *Chance*.]

2814 Pinsker, Sanford. "Language, Silence and the Existential Whisper: Once Again at the 'Heart of Darkness,'" *Modern Language Studies*, II, No. 2 (1972), pp. 53–57.

Like Marlow, the framing narrator of "Heart of Darkness" is a "mix" of sensibilities and separate languages, and, too, JC juxtaposes these conflicting sensibilities and languages in ways that make paradoxically clear his ironic point about the impossibility of communication. The Marlow of the *Nellie* orders experience in a rational manner even though he realizes that such experiences are always irrational. In his speech about early England and the ancient Romans, he reveals more about himself than about the conditions of Roman commanders in a savage England. By insisting on some measure of difference between the exploiting Romans and his companions, Marlow, in effect, becomes an apologist for the very kind of Victorian values he had aroused in the framing narrator. If language becomes synonymous with absurdity, Marlow's initiation into what he calls the "primeval mud" stands in sharp contrast to the pathetic attempts of man to control the uncontrollable. Marlow's major weapon in face of the jungle's existential silence is his anticipated conversations with Kurtz; he is making a journey, as it were, into the heart of language. After his return to the Intended, Marlow's particular anguish is a compulsion to tell what, in a very deep sense, he knows cannot be told. He thus resembles the Ancient Mariner, damned to retell his story as an act of expiation. Only in the process of art may the figure in the carpet emerge; this is the illusion at the "Heart of Darkness." Any other alternative would be entirely too dark.

2815 Platzner, Robert L. "The Metaphysical Novel in England: The Romantic Phase," *DAI*, XXXIII (1972), 2390A. Unpublished dissertation, University of Rochester, 1972.

2816 Pomian, John (ed.). *Joseph Retinger: Memoirs of an Eminence Grise* (Sussex: University Press, 1972), pp. 16–27, 31, 36–38, 42–43.

By the end of 1911, at a time when Poland and the Poles scarcely appeared in any newspaper or publication, Joseph Retinger succeeded in opening the Polish Bureau in London, and by 1914 he was collecting much information about them. During World War I, Retinger, who as a Pole was opposed to the Russians, the Austrians, and the Germans, found himself in a very "delicate" situation. In his efforts to meet people and to make friends with anyone who was potentially important, he met JC, who was then living in Kent. Although nearly twenty years older than Retinger, JC came to like the young man, and they soon became close friends. In the summer of 1914, Retinger and his wife went back to Poland with JC, where they were stranded for a while. Then, during Retinger's attempt to obtain some tangible support for the Allied cause among the Poles in the U.S., Retinger had the assistance of JC, even if his help was impractical. In 1916, JC was sympathetic with Retinger's work for the cause, the "resurrection" of Poland. Even if JC rarely invited Americans to his home, one important exception was "Miss A," or Jane Anderson, a beautiful woman who "turned the heads of many . . . famous men both in Europe and in his own country." She became "part heroine" in JC's *The Arrow of Gold*, and she apparently caused "a certain estrangement" between JC and Retinger; she may have been the cause of the subsequent break between Retinger and his wife. By 1918, JC heard for the last time from his friend.

2817 Prorok, Leszek. "Wachta z Conradem" (A Watch With Conrad), *Szkice Bałtyckie* (Baltic Sketches), (Wroclaw: Ossolineum, 1972), pp. 143–78.

Interest in JC's works in Poland before World War II was greatest among university students, Sea Scouts, and the like, and it contributed to the formation of the Polish opposition movement during the War, with ideals of loyalty even in hopeless situations. In this respect, JC was independent of religious or political motives, but he provided support when a heroic deed had its own intrinsic value or was not necessarily relevant to systems of value. JC's works contain elements of the existentialist attitude found in Pascal through Sartre and Camus. But Kott's essay (1946) accused him of serving capitalism, and he became suspect; he was no longer written about and the influence of his prose decreased, as did spiritual contact with the new generations, as witness a questionnaire (1957) in which the difficulties of his style were pointed out and his cult of heroism deemed anachronistic. The new phase of interest in him in Poland is now partly due to the increase of JC studies and English generally and a decline of American neo-naturalism. [In Polish.]

2818 Purdy, Dwight H. "Joseph Conrad and the Truth of Fiction," *DAI*, XXXIII (1972), 324A. Unpublished dissertation, University of Texas at Austin, 1972.

2819 Rachman, Shalom. "Personal Moral Sensibility in Conrad's *Under Western Eyes*," *Studies in the Twentieth Century*, IX (Spring 1972), pp. 59–75.

In his Author's Note to *Under Western Eyes*, JC's claim of impartiality is inaccurate. Instead of impartiality, there is subtly woven in the novel a "discordant note" in JC's attitude towards his characters. The result of this discordance is that he puts aside political and social morality and concentrates instead on individual integrity, and from time to time sympathizes with the revolutionaries. The juxtaposition of characters best illustrates this point. Though the main character is Razumov, he is overshadowed at times by Victor Haldin, the Russian revolutionary. The question, however, of whether Haldin's assassination of Mr. de P– is morally a crime is examined only from Razumov's point of view, and JC at times in part sympathizes with Razumov's condemnation. But JC, in spite of the murder, portrays Haldin as a sympathetic character. His antithesis is Nikita, who is a betrayer and who is thus like Razumov, who betrays Haldin. But Razumov is portrayed unsympathetically at times; his significance should not, therefore, be underestimated. The novel is clearly Razumov's story: he is situated between Haldin, whose ideals he admires but cannot follow, and Nikita, whose tactics he imitates but whose existence he cannot accept because of basic differences. Between the two men and what they represent, Razumov at the end of the novel finds his moral salvation.

2820 Rapin, René. "Reality and Imagination in the Works of Joseph Conrad (Part I)," *CON*, IV, No. 3 (1972), pp. 22–33.

Few novelists other than JC seem to be more impregnated with experienced reality, and yet his work, which remains independent of the real, comes from two main sources of his inspiration: his memory and his imagination, both of which were exceptional. *Almayer's Folly*, for example, represents a whole group of novels and short stories inspired by the reality lived by the author. Surprising in this novel is the unity and the intensity of atmosphere; surprising also is the fact that Almayer, or Olmayer, whom JC met in Borneo in 1887 and who seemed to be forgotten for a while, fiercely haunted JC's imagination from 1889 to 1894. At last, JC's imagination created an Almayer more real than this real one. JC's short stay in the East inspired fifteen novels and short stories, one-third of his works. Unlike as these stories are, they are similar in their Equatorial atmosphere, in the same Malaysian villages perched on piles above the silt of the river, the same sea and blue sky troubled occasionally by a tropical storm, the same swarm of people, the same Oriental plots and passions seen in *Folly*. The center of interest, too, lies in the struggle of a man who is weak, like Almayer, strong like Captain MacWhirr, a weak man who thinks he is strong, like Lord Jim or Heyst. This man finds himself "tragically" isolated, facing a hostile nature or unfriendly men and isolated also to meditate upon the somber side of things. JC is able to portray such feelings because he himself has felt them. [Continued in *Conradiana*, V, No. 3 (1973), pp. 46–57.]

2821 "The Richard Curle Conrad Collection," *Bookman's Journal*, Third Series, XV (1972), pp. 109–10, 113.

[Reports on the sale of Richard Curle's collection of JC first editions and manuscripts, and reprints bibliographical descriptions of the rarest works from the Curle sale catalogue.]

2822 Ridd, Carl. "Saving the Appearances in Conrad's 'Heart of Darkness,'" *Studies in Religion: A Canadian Journal*, II (Fall 1972), pp. 93–113.

In "Heart of Darkness," Kurtz dies before Marlow can get him out of Africa. A product of Europe, he has become, in the wilderness, incapable of either Africa or Europe. When Marlow tries to save him by bringing him out, it precipitates the crisis of his perception and final death—he comes alive enough to die. It also precipitates Marlow's own crisis, for in the remarkable agent Mr. Kurtz he comes to see himself. The shock of it sends him back to civilization, no longer innocent, to preach to other rivers and other hearts of darkness the "scandalous truth" of human beings; that "it is nothing, and when it is, it is not." The old metaphysical expression, "to save the appearance," meant to reconcile the evidences given one through the senses with the evidence one already knew through inherited world view. Since consciousness changes, these are always in some kind of tension. "Heart of Darkness" is the story of the appalling collision between what Marlow knows as western man and what he must know because . . . well, because it appears to have happened. The story is the story of the recession of solid, "foursquare European reality, and of the astonishing encounter with reality that comes only then." JC is not a cheerful optimist: he is perpetually negating his affirmations. But the affirmations are there, in the very heart of the negatives. Marlow learns to enter into the "imprecision and 'hypocrisy'" which, from the European perspective, all facts seem to have; the light he finds is "*the* 'kind' light": it shows the opposites in their "kindred relation." Marlow thus becomes a psychologist.

2823 Ryf, Robert S. "*The Secret Agent* on Stage," *Modern Drama*, XV (March 1972), pp. 54–67.

The modestly successful stage production of his *Victory* encouraged JC to begin in November, 1919, a dramatization of *The Secret Agent*. Although beset by doubts of his ability as a dramatist and by difficulties in getting the play produced, the initial performance was held on November 2, 1922, with the condemnation of the critics the next day. The play closed November 11, a failure. It contains too much exposition, an unbelievable situation, and unnecessary contrivance. JC felt deeply the wound of the play's failure, even if he later claimed that it did not affect him at all. But he did not consider writing another play.

2824 Sacks, Sheldon. "*Clarissa* and the Tragic Traditions in Eighteenth Century Culture," *Irrationalism in the Eighteenth Century* (Cleveland and London: The Press of Case Western Reserve University, 1972) [Studies in Eighteenth Century Culture, Vol. 2], pp. 195–221.

It is ironic that in spite of his stated plan and conscious intention to write a book of the "tragical" kind in *Clarissa*, Richardson failed to accomplish his intention, at least according to one kind of twentieth century criticism which insists that Clarissa asserts her own personal triumph as well as the triumph of all the values her creator wants to emphasize. In this respect, Richardson is among interesting company: a modern critic, Murray Krieger, deplores the ending of JC's *Victory* as a "culpable" deviation from the desirable starkness of a "tragic vision," which he thinks of as being the most desirable modern relationship of the ethical to the tragic, although almost the opposite of poetic justice. The ending of JC's novel, we are told, is "a retreat from the tragic to the sentimentally ethical" that demands blind faith in life and love. Here JC has run a risk: unwilling to abide with the tragic vision and able only to withdraw before it because he cannot go beyond, he has still dared to try high tragedy. The complex demands that must be satisfied in creating a moving tragedy account for many of JC's "brilliant" narrative experiments in *Lord Jim*. The initial narrator so fully reveals the internal consciousness of the "callow, romantic boy" that, given the conditions on the *Patna*, we must regard Jim's leap both as a "psychological inevitability" and as an "act that ensures his still undefined but immediate doom."

2825 Sampson, George. *The Concise Cambridge History of English Literature* (Cambridge: At the University Press, 1972), pp. 867–69.

The Pole, JC, has a claim to be considered "the greatest English novelist of the period between James and Lawrence" and also is "perhaps the most remarkable figure in the whole history of English literature." We should stress, as he did, "the profound influence of the French masters," as well as the Russian novelist Turgenev. His third novel, *The Nigger of the Narcissus*, gave him his first "indisputable claim to classic rank." He is "rightly regarded" as "the best writer about the sea and seamen who has ever lived." His "most ambitious" novel, *Nostromo*, is highly organized in the manner of Henry James;

The Secret Agent is a "Dickensian study" of an anarchist plot in London; *Under Western Eyes* takes place in Russia and in "that refuge for revolutionaries, Switzerland." JC's last works are not, on the whole, "so impressive as his earlier ones." His "incidental weaknesses" are obvious: his perception of human nature degenerates almost into melodrama, and sometimes his wisdom is perfunctory. Another fine novelist, E. M. Forster, speaks of his "noble obscurity": "The secret casket of his genius contains a vapour rather than a jewel"—a criticism, "it must in justice be added," which has "sometimes been applied to the critic's own work." [Seems to be an accurate assessment of JC's achievement, one which still leaves him in the vanguard of major writers of the world, especially in fiction.]

2826 Sanchez, Ricardo. "Two Years Ago," *CON*, IV, No. 1 (1972), p. 33.

[Verse. Compares the poet's "neo conradism" in his "ode to a sick society" to the "hectic passage" of the *Narcissus* and to "spastic Lord Jim."]

2827 Saveson, John E. "Conrad's Acis and Galatea: A Note on *Victory*," *Modern Language Studies*, II, No. 2 (1972), pp. 59–61.

Near the climax of *Victory*, Jones, observing Lena and Ricardo in Heyst's bungalow, draws a comparison with Acis kissing the sandals of the nymph, Galatea. Other details also suggest this analogue: the eastern setting recalling Sicily, home of the Cyclops; Heyst's resemblance to Polyphemus and Lena's "goddess' stance"; and the similarity between the deaths of Acis and Ricardo. The parallel supports a twentieth-century allegorical interpretation of the novel in which Heyst (Polyphemus) stands for sexual inadequacy. In its use of the Cyclops myth and its attack on asceticism, *Victory* is "anti-Schopenhauerian and pro-Nietzschean." [Included in *Conrad, The Later Moralist* (1974).]

2828 Saveson, John E. "Conrad West," *Novel*, V (Spring 1972), pp. 266–68.

Norman Sherry, in *Conrad's Western World* (1971), suggests that Jessie Conrad inspired JC's portrait of Winnie Verloc in *The Secret Agent*. This idea is, however, out of keeping with the "reverberating ironies" of the novel. What is wrong is that Winnie is not a natural but an unnatural instinct because Stevie is not her son but her brother, and the novel gives her passion "an erotic tinge." Winnie, unlike Jessie Conrad, is not an exemplary mother.

2829 Saveson, John E. *Joseph Conrad: The Making of a Moralist* (Amsterdam: Rodopi NV, 1972).

Psychological "literacy" in JC is an assumption readily arrived at from the fact of his intimacy with H. G. Wells when both writers were in the formative period of their careers. It seems that Wells assisted JC in several ways; it is likely that in certain "matters of intellect" Wells was JC's mentor. Through Wells, JC "would have gained" ready access to the scientific literature of the time and to the thinking of the leading English psychologists. Wells's basically Spencerian and Utilitarian beliefs were modified or changed by his attention to the German Pessimists, and through him JC evolved as a moralist according to a similar pattern.

JC's assumptions in *Almayer's Folly* were "scientific" in that they are Spencerian. For *Lord Jim*, JC used both Sir James Brooke (heretofore recognized as a source) and post-Spencerian concepts like those of W. E. H. Lecky, St. George Mivart, and Alfred Russel Wallace. In addition, JC found Edouard von Hartmann's philosophy of the Unconscious useful, making *Jim* appear against the background of Kant, Bain, Brooke, T. H. Green, and Hartmann, by way of Schopenhauer. JC's earliest mature work is predominantly Utilitarian and Spencerian, as in *The Nigger of the Narcissus*; in developing the main character in *The Secret Agent*, JC adheres to the criminal psychology of Lombroso, whose theories were well known to Wells. [Five chapters of this book appeared previously as articles in periodicals.]

2830 Saveson, John E. "The Moral Discovery of *Under Western Eyes*," *Criticism*, XIV (Winter 1972), pp. 32–48.

JC's development as a thinker has great consistency. His early works react against idealism and pessimism from the bias of a modified Utilitarianism; his last works accept Nietzschean realism and seek to reconcile or modify "altruism" with Nietzschean "egoism." Razumov in *Under Western Eyes* has an extreme, even malign, hatred of individuals; he revives, in fact, the demonic JC's twentieth-century novel, a view which is essentially Nietzsche's doctrine of the demonic as expressed in *Beyond Good and Evil*. In *Eyes*, JC applies Nietzsche's terms "cynicism" and "mysticism" naturally to the Russian people. Razumov becomes "evil" in the sense meant by Nietzsche; also, Peter Ivanovitch and his coterie reflect the psychology of those who submit by violence and by a "transvaluation of values." The Nietzschean quality of *Eyes* allows the reader to assess the novel's morality by recognizing the presence of "Nietzschean analysis": Razumov's character largely determines the meaning of fate in the book. JC reveals his attitude toward autocracy, and the author also reveals his earlier view of altruism as modified by Nietzschean concepts. Although the modified Spencerian and Utilitarian morality in JC's fiction dating at least from "Heart of

Darkness" survives in this novel, it is not its complete morality. The "moral discovery" is discovery of those "moral phenomena indigenous to a master-slave society, surviving in modern Russia." [Included in *Conrad, The Later Moralist* (1974).]

2831 Saveson, John E. "[A Review of] *Conrad's Western World*, by Norman Sherry," *N&Q*, XIX (February 1972), pp. 76–77.

After completing *Lord Jim*, JC writes in his letters of his fear of having dried up as a writer. These letters further indicate that whereas JC previously wrote from his own experiences, he now had to turn to second-hand and, in some instances, third-hand sources. He wrote *Nostromo* because he could tap Cunninghame Graham as a reliable source of information about South America. When writing *The Secret Agent*, he likewise turned to Ford Madox Ford, who knew anarchists. This desperate effort to discover new sources for novels ended in "an achievement of the greatest magnitude."

2832 Saveson, John E. "Sources of *Nostromo*," *N&Q*, XIX (September 1972), pp. 331–34.

In writing *Nostromo*, JC filled in the rich detail, drawing upon historical works on South America supplied by Cunninghame Graham. Although neither Graham nor JC identified the works, Graham's *A Vanished Arcadia* provides clues to these sources, and Graham refers to three additional works which appear to have been influential: G. F. Masterman's *Seven Eventful Years in Paraguay* (London, 1869), Charles A. Washburn's *History of Paraguay* (Boston, 1871), and J. P. and W. P. Robertson's *Letters on Paraguay* (London, 1839). Although each book has its own relevance to JC's work, Masterman's is the most useful for comparison.

2833 Schultheiss, Thomas. "Conrad Bibliography: A Continuing Checklist," *CON*, IV, No. 1 (1972), pp. 77–82.

[A continuation of Schultheiss's valuable bibliography.]

2834 Schultheiss, Thomas. "Conrad Bibliography: A Continuing Checklist," *CON*, IV, No. 2 (1972), pp. 75–79.

[A continuation of Schultheiss's valuable bibliography.]

2835 Schwarz, Daniel R. "The Journey to Patusan: The Education of Jim and Marlow in Conrad's *Lord Jim*," *SNNTS*, IV (Fall 1972), pp. 442–58.

Fiction is a linear form; consequently, one cannot completely understand a novel by discussing it "in its moment of stability" immediately upon completion. If we are to do justice to the complexity of a novel, we must "'report' on the crucial process between reader and novel during which tentative patterns of meaning are proposed, tested, transformed, and/or discarded." At the beginning, *Lord Jim* explores the response to the objective world through Jim and Marlow; then the novel dramatizes the gradual shift of Jim toward Marlow's position and Marlow's toward Jim's. Marlow's quest culminates "with the blurring of the distinction between objective and subjective experience" and with his realizations of the world outside oneself. In Patusan, Jim's "dreams and fantasies" take shape according to values earlier represented by Marlow. Jim's vision seems to be fulfilled when Gentleman Brown's appearance demonstrates the futility of permanently escaping his past. Once again, Jim's "intrinsic character" is demonstrated by external circumstances over which he has no control.

2836 Sherry, Norman. *Conrad and His World* (London: Thames and Hudson, 1972).

[A general but accurate life of JC, extremely well illustrated. Many photographs are accompanied by appropriate quotations from JC's works.]

2837 Sherry, Norman. ["Introduction to *Nostromo*"], *Nostromo* (London: Dent [Collected Edition of the Works of Joseph Conrad], 1972), pp. v–xi.

JC was able to create such a comprehensive tale as *Nostromo* by careful research in books. Frederick Benton Williams' book, *On Many Seas: The Life and Exploits of a Yankee Sailor*, relates the story of a theft of a lighter filled with silver. The background for the torture of Dr. Monygham, the rule of Guzman Bento, and the fate of Don Jose Avellanos originates in *Seven Eventful Years in Paraguay* by George Frederick Masterman. JC also consulted *Venezuela* by Edward B. Eastwick for the historical and geographical details, and he referred to Garibaldi's autobiography for Giorgio Viola's character and Senor Hirsch's torture. In the respect that it was based primarily on reading and not personal experience, *Nostromo* is remarkable and entirely different from JC's preceding work. The greatest strength of the novel comes from the author's ability to present the story in the variety and fullness of its history. This quality, though, involved him in the disunified method of construction which literally stuns the reader. Still, his method of roving freely through time enabled him to present fully the complexity of history and its relationship to humanity. The fate of the major characters is transient: JC's concept of history destroys their sense of importance. In this light, *Nostromo* is JC's comment on the fate of all mankind.

2838 Spiers, James G. "The Background of the Political Philosophy of Conrad and Lawrence," *DAI*, XXXII (1972), 7007A. Unpublished dissertation, University of Toronto, 1970.

2839 Stallman, Robert Wooster. *Stephen Crane: A Critical Bibliography* (Ames: The Iowa State University Press, 1972), pp. 69, 294, 296, 303, 304, 305, 308, 310, 312, 314, 316, 320, 323, 324, 325, 327, 328, 348, 372, 380, 443, 448, 468, 483, 590, 598, 606, 610, 613.

In October, 1897, Stephen Crane first met JC and began a friendship which lasted until the year of his death, 1900. JC's writings about Crane, about thirty in number, range through a quotation from *A Personal Record*, his "Stephen Crane: A Note Without Dates" (1919), his introduction to Thomas Beer's *Stephen Crane: A Study of American Letters* (1922), Edwin Pugh's attempt to undercut JC's friendship with Crane (1924), and JC's preface to *The Red Badge of Courage* (1925). Crane's novel influenced *The Nigger of the Narcissus*, since both Crane and JC were interested in impressionism at the time. Henry James and Crane subscribed, "in effect," to the credo JC expressed in his preface to *Nigger*. [Stallman is especially helpful with the Crane-JC relationship. Among many things, he has proved JC wrong in his declaration about Crane in a letter of 1912 to Peter F. Somerville: "Believe me dear Sir no paper, no review, would look at anything that I or anybody else would write about Crane." Stallman also provides evidence of the scope of JC's reputation today by noting the many publications on him not only by English speaking scholars but also by those in countries such as France, Germany, Russia, Sweden, Italy, Japan, Holland, Brazil, and Argentina.]

2840 Stegmaier, E. "The 'Would-Scene' in Joseph Conrad's *Lord Jim* and *Nostromo*," *Modern Language Review*, LXVII (July 1972), pp. 517–23.

The first scene in *Nostromo*, that in which Linda and Giselle crouch on either side of their mother, employs "would" in "would be provoked" and "she would retort" to permit the reader to survey an unspecified number of similar events; he is therefore both inside and outside the scene. This "would-scene" occurs more frequently in *Nostromo* than in *Lord Jim* because it is the most appropriate means of suggesting the vastness of Costaguana and the endless number of events and details behind the glimpses that actually appear and because it is also a fictional concretion of the theme of repetitiveness and of stagnation or even the sameness of events. This kind of scene in *Jim* reminds the reader that he is not following directly the events in the story. With both Mitchell and Marlow of the two works, this kind of scene implies a view of the fictional present which mirrors and is the expression of the continuing sameness of an already hopeless situation and the impossibility of change. Dickens is JC's forerunner in the use of this "would-scene."

2841 Stein, Marian L. "John Conrad at Home," *CON*, IV, No. 2 (1972), pp. 67–71.

John Conrad's father's friends were also his friends, such people as Edward Garnett; Cunninghame Graham; Richard Curle, JC's "closest friend"; Arthur Marwood; and Hueffer [Ford Madox Ford]. JC had "a tremendous sense of humor and a great way of ticking people off without them realizing it until they came to think it over." Most of JC's drawings are doodles "in the sense that he didn't sit down to make the drawings." JC was very fond of Kent. And "he was one of the most modest persons" John Conrad ever came across. [This information is taken from statements by John Conrad, JC's second son, now a retired architect, in a tape-recorded interview for *Conradiana*, made by Marian L. Stein during a visit to Mr. and Mrs. Conrad at their home, Riversdale, 6 August 1971.]

2842 Steiner, Joan E. "Joseph Conrad and the Tradition of the Gothic Romance," *DAI*, XXXII (1972), 6456A–57A. Unpublished dissertation, University of Michigan, 1971.

2843 Strojan, Richard Franklin. "Conrad's Marlow Stories," *DAI*, XXXIII (1972), 4433A–34A. Unpublished dissertation, University of Pittsburgh, 1972.

2844 Sullivan, Walter. "The Dark Beyond the Sunrise: Conrad and the Politics of Despair," *Southern Review*, VIII (July 1972), pp. 507–19.

In *Under Western Eyes*, which caused JC much difficulty in the writing, the author probes some of his old themes. Razumov knows that his life has become, after his betrayal of Haldin, the "toy of fate," that things for him can never be the same again. But this knowledge does not relieve him from the obligation to choose, nor does it make the choice easier. So, in turn, Razumov embraces both his alternatives: first, he attempts to arrange Haldin's flight and then he reports Haldin to the police. His guilt is modified by innocence; his innocence is tainted with guilt. JC knew exactly what he was doing in *The Secret Agent*, but in *Eyes* he perpetrated a major flaw: Razumov, because of his isolation, has no larger source, such as society, from which to receive guidance, nor does the novel leave any significant ground for a meaningful and sustained public action. The existence of "a proper politics, a proper social fabric" in *Agent* is lacking in *Eyes*. This last of JC's political novels is prophetic of the decay of public institutions and public morality that was to become one of the significant influences on the fiction of our time. *Eyes*, with no moral center to anchor it, generates little affirmation and less hope.

2845 Tartella, Vincent P. "Symbolism in Four Scenes in *Nostromo*," *CON*, IV, No. 1 (1972), pp. 63–70.

JC once wrote that all great literary creations "have been symbolic." His judgment is borne out by the symbolism in four scenes in *Nostromo*. First, the end of Part I, in which the girl Morenita cuts the silver buttons from Nostromo's coat, identifies the Capataz with the silver that Gould chooses, in vain, to build his life and a nation upon. Symbolically, silver having the value of the moon, changeable and changing, and the human organization built on it, moves as a vain cycle of positive and negative phases in which the perishing of the present good is always impending. Second, in the scene in Part I in which Charles Gould meets Emilia in a funereal room in the Italian mansion, there is an elaborately carved but now cracked marble vase which represents the ruin his father has suffered because of the silver mine; and Gould now stands for the "fatally fallen world of his primal ancestors." Third, as Decoud sits alone writing an account of the havoc of the day, a locomotive thunders by, headlights blazing, with a Negro on the last car swinging a torch in an endless circle, the circle of light in the darkness suggesting to Decoud that for him there will be a point in which *all* (the revolutionary activity) becomes *nothing*. And four, Hirsch's irrational death dramatizes JC's "impressionist philosophy" that, in seeking to find the truth of any objective reality, man runs the risk of proving himself radically absurd. There seems to be nothing in *Nostromo* to offset the "grim nihilism" dramatized in these four symbolic scenes.

2846 Trigona, Prospero. "Il dramma del colonialismo nei primi romanzi di Joseph Conrad" (The Drama of Colonialism in Joseph Conrad's Early Novels), *Trimestre* (Pescara, I–II (1972), pp. 127–48.

The fundamental problem which JC confronted throughout his work, beginning with *Almayer's Folly*, was the moral attrition of the individual and his conditioning by moral values. These affect also the indigenous characters when they come into contact with European civilization. Colonialism, in all its forms of economic pressure, competition, and corruption, is the essence of "Heart of Darkness." *An Outcast of the Islands* is rich in questions capable of later development and, despite many defects, it depicts the continued conflict between the reality of the age of imperialism and the falsity, ignorance, and vanity which it generates. "An Outpost of Progress" also depicts a world of oppression and colonial exploitation in which not only the natives but also the traders are victims. [In Italian.]

2847 Trilling, Lionel. *Sincerity and Authenticity* (Cambridge, Massachusetts: Harvard University Press, 1972), pp. 106–11, 133.

JC's "Heart of Darkness" is the "paradigmatic literary expression of the modern concern with authenticity," in which Kurtz is part of "one of the most brazen political insincerities ever perpetrated": Leopold II, having sovereignty over the Congo Free State, ruled as a tyrant, while he convinced the world of his benevolent intentions to civilize the native.

2848 van Ingen, Ferdinand. "Des Dichters Bildnis: Zu Bobrowskis lyrischen Porträts" (The Portrait of the Poet: On Bobrowski's Lyrical Portraits), *Dichter und Leser: Studien zur Litteratur* (Poet and Reader: Studies in Literature), ed. by Ferdinand van Ingen, Elrud Kunne-Ibsch, Hans de Leeuwe, and Frank C. Maatje (Groningen: Wolters-Noordhoff, 1972), pp. 234–60.

Johannes Bobrowski wrote on poets; among his poems is "Joseph Conrad," published in *Sarmatische Zeit*, 1961. The East European setting of this poem is characteristic of Bobrowski's poetry. [Cf. Brigitte Bischoff, "Der polnische Zimmermann: Zu dem Gedicht 'Joseph Conrad' von Johannes Bobrowski," *Neophilologus*, 59 (1975), pp. 579–91.] [In German.]

2849 Vidan, Ivo. "*The Red Badge of Courage*: A Study in Bad Faith," *Studia Romanica et Anglica Zagrebiensia*, Nos. 33–36 (1972–73), pp. 93–112.

Stephen Crane was scarcely aware of the originality of his book, *The Red Badge of Courage*. His technique, usually called impressionism, seems to have been so named first by JC, who obviously did not associate Crane with a school of painting. He commented on Crane's novel about the author's seeing "the outside of many things and the inside of some." He was soon profoundly hurt by W. L. Courtney's review of his *The Nigger of the Narcissus*. In both works, the action consists of episodes which follow a linear manner without implying a tight casual connection beyond the gradually accumulating experience, with a "rhythmical sequence of stress and lull." JC's perspective is largely, unlike Crane's, from above, with a patronizing attitude toward the crew—a far cry from the impersonal objectivity of the best omniscient narrators, like his own in *Nostromo*. Crane's achievement was seminal in his novel's impact not on *Nigger* but on his twentieth-century novel of extreme situation, *Lord Jim.*

2850 Walt, James. "Conrad and Katherine Mansfield," *CON*, IV, No. 1 (1972), pp. 41–52.

Katherine Mansfield's "adventures" as a literary critic began in the spring of 1919 and ended in the fall of 1920, during which time she reviewed scores of ephemeral books for the *Athenaeum*, of which her husband John Middleton Murray was editor. In her review of JC's *The Arrow of Gold* (1919), she made it clear that JC was a master of contemporary literature but left some doubts as to whether his new book should be considered as a disappointment or a disaster. She made no observations on her own about the idealistic hero, but she described the heroine with irony. For her, JC attempted to hide the vagueness of his thoughts "beneath a storm of rhetoric"; the reality she demanded had eluded him in *Arrow*. The about-face she made in her review of *The Rescue* (1920) is somewhat curious, but Tom Lingard might have seemed to her an idealized version of Sir Harold Beauchamp, her father; and in her eyes the masculine traits of JC's work offered a pleasing contrast to the usual tone of the other fiction she reviewed. When she praised the "rich action" of the novel, she was clearly consulting her personal taste rather than literary standards. And it is doubtful that *Rescue* introduces a "romantic vision of the hearts of men," as she says it does. She failed, also, to note the two Lingards in the two halves of the book. She did, however, point out JC's ability to "focus an intense light upon a few scattered moments as if they were the concentrated stuff of a whole life," and she wisely emphasized the freshness of his material and the depths of his insights rather than his technical achievements.

2851 Walt, James. "Conrad in Poland—1970," *CON*, IV, No. 3 (1972), pp. 48–51.

Polish interest in JC intensified so greatly in the 1960s that the Poles, who established a Society of Friends of the Marine Museum in Gdansk, became interested in the fate of the *Otago*, the only seagoing vessel JC commanded. Gradually, this interest increased to include plans for a gallery devoted to a collection of artifacts and documents related to JC and also plans for much-needed new translations of the Anglo-Pole's works. both plans are now under way.

2852 Williams, Pieter D. "The Captain of *Nostromo*," *North American Mentor*, X, No. 4 (1972), pp. 35–40.

The caption of *Nostromo*, "so foul a sky clears not/ without a storm" (*King John*, II, ii, 108), identified by JC only as "Shakespeare," supplies similarities and parallels to JC's novel which deal with "political maneuvering, divided loyalties, innocence and experience, guilt and remorse." The "aerial" imagery of the caption indicates to some degree the texture and the structure of the novel. Conceptually, the caption implies an approach to art and a method of presentation common to the time-oriented art forms, such as drama, poetry, music, and narrative—and as in *Nostromo* in the fog on the Golfo Placido. The sense of isolation on the Gulf indicates a "foul" sky. A Conradian irony might account for the caption: its apparent lack of relevance, its "vignette-like" quality, its "flashback" nature suggest Sulaco [consistently misspelled "Sulace"] cause us to wonder about its significance and to realize new truths about both Sulaco and the human situation.

2853 Young, Gloria L. "The Sea As Symbol in the Work of Herman Melville and Joseph Conrad," *DAI*, XXXII (1972), 6463A. Unpublished dissertation, Kent State University, 1971.

2854 Zak, William F. "Conrad, F. R. Leavis, and Whitehead: 'Heart of Darkness' and Organic Holism," *CON*, IV, No. 1 (1972), pp. 5–24.

In 1948, F. R. Leavis disparaged JC's apparent straining for a significance in "Heart of Darkness" which is merely emotional and rejected the novelist's notion of mystery and paradox. In theory at least, JC endorsed a primary emphasis on language as meaningful which subsumes paradox and ambiguity and a thorough-going organic holism in artistic epistemology. For both Whitehead and JC, the "prehensive" (unified, relational) character of space-time is fundamental; for both, too, reality is process, potential; it is meaningful, valuable. This bifurcated vision suggests why the structure of "Heart of Darkness" is dialectical as Marlow moves from one provisional formulation to another and, more importantly, suggests the meaning of Marlow's relationship to Kurtz and its subsequent effects. Kurtz's "prehensive" aspiration makes him powerful, and his recognition of limitation, his verbal formulation at his death, makes him valuable to Marlow, who learned from him the value of self-knowledge, the recognition of limitation, and separation from the primeval, all symbolized in his last cry. From his experience in the jungle, Marlow discovers that he can assert on the formless powers of the jungle a legitimate civilized reality, that of work. And the power of the primeval is powerless to defeat either Kurtz or Marlow: the former finally chooses not to attend the midnight rites and achieves in his dying words a victory over the darkness; the latter, refuting Leavis's argument, fully accepts his responsibility for and final transcendence of Kurtz. Marlow's adherence to the values of civilization allows him to overcome irrationality and later to perpetuate civilization with the gift of a lie to the Intended.

2855 Zellar, Leonard. "Conrad and Dostoevsky," *The English Novel in the Nineteenth Century: Essays on the Literary Mediation of Human Values*, ed. by George Goodin (Urbana, Chicago, London: University of Illinois Press, [Illinois Studies in Language and Literature 63], 1972), pp. 214–23.

Despite JC's clear and intense dislike for Dostoevski, there are "remarkable and significant" similarities in their fiction. Likenesses exist between Razumov and Raskolnikov, both of whom have separated themselves from their fellow men in keeping with a belief in their superiority based on a morality of intellect. Also, these two authors share a sense of the existential quality of life, a belief in the ultimate efficacy of a simple, earned value, and a sacramental vision of life. But the two differ in that JC's vision is finally humanistically oriented; Dostoevski's is theistically. The leap of faith separates them. The "germs" that Raskolnikov dreams of at the end of *Crime and Punishment* are the disease of modern, western secular civilization. This "plague out of Europe" appears frequently, as with Raskolnikov, Stavrogin, and Ivan Karamazov, as a "fever" that either purifies or kills, and similarly in JC, it appears as a physical condition of "rot or sterility." For both authors, the "larger justice" inheres in a sacramental view of life: life is a whole which must be accepted and loved for its totality; life is existential in that it is immediate, here and now. Ivan and Decoud "murder life" by abstracting it; Charles Gould and Nostromo also murder life by giving themselves to abstraction.

1973

2856 Amoruso, Vito. "Joseph Conrad grande borghese" (Joseph Conrad Grand Bourgeois), *L'Unità* (22 August 1973), p. 3.

Oliva and Portelli consider the bourgeois artist to be inevitably destined to an apologetic relationship towards his own class of origin, to a defeat both of his own critical awareness and also of his role of opposition. There is also a fully evident but not paradoxical contradiction, i.e., the explicitly objective summon to complicity of the artist who has consciously obscured the actual processes of history. JC does not contain doubledealing, and Oliva and Portelli's criticism goes beyond the text in its contradictory tension, and this is interpreted in the light of an intention on the part of the author outside the text, judged moralistically and not historically. [Review of R. Oliva and A. Portelli, *Conrad: L'Imperialismo Imperfetto* (Torino: Rinaudi, 1973).] [In Italian.]

2857 Anderson, James A. "Conrad and Baroja: Two Spiritual Exiles," *KN*, XX, No. 4 (1973), pp. 363–71.

"As a spiritual exile, Joseph Conrad as a man was not unlike the characters of Baroja's novels who wandered the world, on sea or land." JC's work has a Spanish Baroque quality.

2858 Baird, Newton D. "The Mystery in Conrad's *Lord Jim*," *Individualist*, IV, No. 2 (1973), pp. 9–14.

Lord Jim is about a hero's search for self-esteem and an ideal. Its theme consists of the imperfect and tragic nature of man. Some elements, especially those of time and point of view, can be used to solve the mystery of the novel, which is: What is the destructive element, and what is the meaning of the novel? The major clue is Stein's butterfly, for this specimen is what JC uses to stress man's imperfection. Through this concept, it is clear that Jim cannot see or understand the inexplicable. [Consists of tedious retelling of the story, rehashes existing criticism, and offers no original insight into the novel.]

2859 Baldi, Sergio. "Fortuna di Conrad" (Conrad's Fortune), *L'Approdo Letterario*, 61, No. 5 (1973), pp. 123–25.

The first volume of the Mursia edition of JC's complete works in Italian was introduced by Elio Chinol, who stressed JC's pessimism on man's fate; the second volume was also introduced by Chinol, who indicated the centrality of *Lord Jim*, a psychological and moral drama. The third volume has instead an introduction with a Marxist bias, by Franco Marenco, which has intrinsic advantages and limitations; since more or less all these novels deal with social and political problems, aesthetic considerations are therefore relegated to the background, in favor of a sociopolitical appraisal on the part of the critic. [Review of *Romanzi occidentali* (Milan: Mursia, 1972).] [In Italian.]

2860 Bazin, Nancy Topping. *Virginia Woolf and the Androgynous Vision* (New Brunswick, New Jersey: Rutgers University, 1973), pp. 22, 25, 27.

Virginia Woolf, believing that "life itself" can be seized only in a "moment of vision," recognized the fact that JC likewise used the phrase "moment of vision" and noted in 1923 after reading his works that a novelist by the use of a few well-chosen details can "light up a whole character in a flash." In 1923, too, Woolf learned how to adopt and, of course, modify for her own purposes JC's technique of representing in different characters the selves of which a total self might be composed. For example, just as Lord Jim is Marlow's "shadow-self," Septimus Smith in *Mrs. Dalloway* is Clarissa's shadow-self.

2861 Bergonzi, Bernard. *The Turn of a Century: Essays on Victorian and Modern English Literature* (London: Macmillan; New York: Barnes & Noble, 1973), pp. 7, 74, 88, 95–98, 139, 141, 142, 145, 172, 173.

After 1907, the friendship between H. G. Wells and JC apparently waned. At this time, Wells was reacting sharply against the "novel of aesthetic concentration," of which he thought James and JC to be the most eminent practitioners. He refers disparagingly to JC in *Boon* (1915). The "quap" episode of *Tono-Bungay* has a definite "Conradian air"; the most significant link between Wells and JC is found in the capture of the *Maud Mary*. And Wells, in *Experiment in Autobiography*, caricatures JC in his depiction of the captain of the *Maud Mary*.

2862 Birdseye, Lewis E. "'Chaos Cosmos': A Study of Conrad's Major Short Fiction," *DAI*, XXXIII (1973), 5714A. Unpublished dissertation, Columbia University, 1970.

2863 Bitterli, Urs. *Conrad—Malraux—Greene—Weiss: Shriftsteller und Kolonialismus* (Conrad, Malraux, Greene, Weiss: Writers and Colonialism), (Zurich: Benziger, 1973), pp. 27–60.

Even if there is an echo of imperialistic illusions and dreams in JC's novels, his characters are outsiders and outlaws of the society and certainly not the active and successful imperialists and jingos of the "Second Empire." [In German.]

2864 Bonney, William Wesley. "Semantic and Structural Indeterminacy in *The Nigger of the Narcissus*: An Experiment in Reading," *ELH*, XL (Winter 1973), pp. 564–83.

The Nigger of the Narcissus demonstrates particularly apt examples of semantic indeterminacy and discontinuity. The narrator tells in retrospect a tale that involves futurity, and the reader learns from one who already has certain knowledge and yet seems to be learning himself even as he tells his tale. Wait's influence discomposes the narrator, and the major structural principle of the novel involves the disintegration of the narrator's initial complementary response to Wait. Wait's conduct radically alters the narrator's rhetorical values. The narrator's interpretational struggle reaches a climax in the description of the rescue of Wait from his cabin. Wait's cowardly passivity affects the narrator, who begins to grasp the weak and merely mortal essence of the miserable man. As the narrator describes the rescue, Wait appears shockingly mortal, and the narrator combines death images with equally prominent suggestions of a trying childbirth. Wait's metaphoric birth both from himself and the sea is important: no longer is he primeval and frightening to the narrator, but he becomes "immaterial like an apparition," and the burial allows Wait's body to be engulfed by the sea. That the dominant character of *Nigger* should manifest a high degree of discontinuity which causes structural indeterminacy reveals a paradox in JC's art: JC believes that human consciousness cannot begin to conceive of the phenomenal world; he merely sustains his own epistemological assumptions within the novel and insists that a measure of indeterminacy limit subtly even the aesthetic convention of omniscience.

2865 Bradbury, Malcolm. *Possibilities: Essays on the State of the Novel* (London, Oxford, New York: Oxford University, 1973), pp. 5, 7, 84–86, 92, 120, 133–34, 141, 162, 176.

Modernism in the novel "considerably pre-dates" the 1920s, and the main changes in aesthetic assumption occurred somewhat earlier, when a "symbolist mode, a fresh tactical logicality," entered the novel in the middle career of Henry James, in the early writings of JC, and in the "new novel" of D. H. Lawrence. The modernists who, in the 1910s and 1920s, established a new modern form of the novel (Joyce, Lawrence, and Woolf) included JC. *Lord Jim*, along with *A Passage to India, Women in Love*, and *Ulysses*, is one of the "classic" novels of the twentieth century. Ford Madox Ford as a novelist is closest to JC. Irony has become a central strand in the evaluation of modernism; it is seen well in *The Secret Agent*, a novel with "no hero, no plot, no real location to which value can be attached, and which moves within the circular, raw, grotesque world of its own anarchy."

2866 Brady, Frank, John Palmer, and Martin Price (eds.). *Literary Theory and Structure: Essays in Honor of William K. Wimsatt* (New Haven and London: Yale University, 1973), pp. 154, 167.

The detective story is more game than novel: its character may be rudimentary and its plot more ingenious than plausible. If its function were not precisely to tease and test us, we should scarcely tolerate this mode of narration, although we accept something close to it in Henry James and JC—but for a different kind of reward. Some novelists have a tendency to surround their heroes with mystery and to make them "loom larger in the mists of surmise"; accompanied by a somewhat primitive setting, as in JC's use of Patusan in *Lord Jim*, it may have the effect of "mythicizing" the central character as the "Jim-myth" generalizes and makes Jim a representative man and his situation a universal predicament.

2867 Bruss, Paul S[amuel]. "Marlow's Interview with Stein: The Implications of the Metaphor," *SNNTS*, V (Winter 1973), pp. 491–503.

Near the center of *Lord Jim*, Marlow introduces Stein as a man who has withdrawn from active life, from the community of man, into the "catacombs" of his insect collection; at the end, he explains how greatly Stein ages after his encounter with the embittered Jewel. Both passages indicate that Stein, since his retreat from Celebes, fails to enjoy intimate involvement with people and life. Now in the prime of his life, he has become the butterfly pinned in his collection. Only when Stein responds to Marlow's plea for help does this philosopher fully reveal the problems inherent in his withdrawal; then, in a series of subtle metaphors he states a rigid philosophy of balance and contingency and emptiness that is basic in JC's early fiction. And he also provides the wonderful lines about submitting oneself to the destructive element, envisioning the balance: the swimmer will neither attempt to climb out into the air (as the romantic Jim does) nor suicidally resign himself to sinking into the depths (as the disillusioned Brierly does) but will try to balance himself by submitting himself to the sea and swimming there (as Marlow does). Ultimately, however, the metaphor of immersion avoids the rigidity of Stein's other metaphors: the swimmer has the almost limitless surface of the sea to prompt him in change and development. But Stein remains solitary and loses much of Marlow's respect.

2868 Bruss, Paul S[amuel]. "'Typhoon': The Initiation of Jukes, *CON*, V, No. 2 (1973), pp. 46–55.

In "Typhoon," the tension between the imaginative Jukes's awakening and Captain MacWhirr's narrowness of perspective is of major importance because it reveals the fact that Jukes, not MacWhirr, matures during the typhoon. Jukes moves toward a larger "perspective of reality" through his exposure to three physical and psychic "typhoons." The first of these, MacWhirr's verbal absurdity, a psychic typhoon, undermines the mate's confidence in himself. The storm itself causes Jukes to begin to discover the necessity and the validity of action which merely keeps him alive; in this ordeal he comes to respect the office of captain even in the dull MacWhirr. Jukes encounters his third typhoon in the bunker with the fighting coolies, where he proves himself a leader and finds a "cosmic peace" as his reward for having reached maturity. JC thus opposes Jukes's maturation to MacWhirr's reliance on the familiar habits of routine.

2869 Butler, Lord. "The Prevalence of Indirect Biography," *Transactions of the Royal Society of Literature of the United Kingdom, Essays by Divers Hands,* XXXVII (1973), pp. 17–30.

Many examples of indirect biography exist, instances or writing in which an author has almost undisguisedly written about his own life in a work published in the form of a novel or an alleged fiction of one sort or another. Among these are Somerset Maugham's *Of Human Bondage,* D. H. Lawrence's *Sons and Lovers,* Tolstoy's portrayal of Levin in *Anna Karenina,* Charlotte Bronte in *Villette,* and JC in *The Shadow-Line,* written as if to illustrate his own "coming through to survival out of some neurotic disorder." JC produced a great deal of indirect autobiography, as seen in "Youth"; *The Nigger of the Narcissus,* since no one but an eyewitness could describe the storm in the Indian Ocean; and *Lord Jim* because Jim's conflict has some parallel in JC's life. Other writers of indirect biography include Smollett, Walter Scott, Dickens, Meredith, George Eliot, Mrs. Gaskell, Katherine Mansfield, Samuel Butler, Disraeli, Ernest Hemingway, and Scott Fitzgerald. But JC makes the theme of inner conflict so prevalent in his works that one must be careful not to include every work of this nature.

2870 Capone, Giovanna. "Joseph Conrad: La commedia bassa e il suo luogo" (Joseph Conrad: The Low Comedy and Its Place), *Spazi Della Scena Comica Nella Narrativa Inglese (Spaces of the Comic Scene in English Fiction),* (Pisa: Goliardica, 1973), pp. 159–81.

A ship, an island, or an exotic setting accentuates the sense of isolation in JC's works. Tragic and comic scenes are both present, and in his ironic pessimism JC points in the direction of the Absurd. Jim is able only to see the scene of low comedy. It is a scene of low comedy in which the crew of the *Patna* grotesquely strive around the life boats: they are unable to perceive the beauty of Jim's passivity and inanition. Jim in turn is the victim of their practical joke, an absurd and irrational trap that forces him to jump. This central scene, in which the irrational triumphs over the rational, better corresponds to JC's most genuine aspiration. To the same series of scenes belong the absurd struggle of the Chinamen for a few dollars in "Typhoon," the inane strife of the crew in *The Shadow-Line,* or the contrast between Heyst and the deadly trio in *Victory.* The theme of comedy is most evident in *Chance,* where sentences like "the comic when it is human becomes quickly painful" sound Dickensian, while Flora's life, seen "as a tragi-comical adventure" evidently reflects the lesson of Meredith. In "The Secret Sharer," the double is the shadow that, leaving the man to whom it belongs, provokes in him an existential fracture. [In Italian.]

2871 Conrad, Joseph. *The Mirror of the Sea and a Personal Record* (London: Dent [Everyman's Library], 1973).

[Contains no introduction or notes, but offers a one-paragraph biographical sketch, a list of JC's major writings, and a highly selective bibliography of criticism.]

2872 Cox, C. B. "Joseph Conrad and the Question of Suicide," *Bulletin of the John Rylands University Library of Manchester*, LV (Spring 1973), pp. 285–99; rpt. *Joseph Conrad: The Modern Imagination* (London: Dent; Totowa, N.J.: Rowman & Littlefield, 1974).

In 1878, JC half-heartedly attempted suicide, an act that was a cry for help. He suffered for the rest of his life from fits of depression and nervous breakdowns. In his fiction, suicide and thoughts of suicide occur. Basic causes for his depressions are the conditions of his childhood, his self-imposed exile, and his "conscious" philosophy, his nihilism derived from reading and from the climate of thought of the late nineteenth century. He believed in a divorce between man and the inadequacy of our thought processes to comprehend our experience; for him, even the finest products of art have developed from undifferentiated matter. He struggled with a serious paradox: the artist must be engaged in making shapes to prove that shapes cannot be made, in giving form to the formless. According to JC, the proper response to the suicidal claims of moral nihilism is a stoical recognition of the "precarious status of mind": the artist builds in language an "acknowledgment of our incomprehension, a form of poised irresolution." JC's best work casts doubt on the validity even of the order and work ethic imposed on the crew of a ship. The suicide of Brierly in *Lord Jim* is a good example of JC's method: since no real reason can be given for his suicide, the novel offers no resolution, even about Jim's final act, and the work therefore "never rests finally in any decisive posture." JC's response to pessimism is an art that accepts the impossibility of clear values and positive commitment.

2873 Cox, C. B. "Joseph Conrad's *The Secret Agent*: The Irresponsible Piano," *Critical Quarterly*, XV (Autumn 1973), pp. 197–212.

The piano of JC's *The Secret Agent*, which entertains customers in the famous Silenus Restaurant, seems, like several other objects, to exist in complete freedom from the control or understanding of the people in the novel. The linear development of the plot is rendered absurd by the existence of another kind of discovery: Verloc, Mrs. Verloc, and Ossipon experience a moment of understanding themselves which plunges them into despair. What is difficult to assess is the total ironic tone of the book, the comic exuberance in the tone of the writing as JC creates his extraordinary world of fat human beings and lively pianos. The irony, though, creates its own values and, pushing away the characters to a distance, protects itself from involvement. The house, 1 Chesham Square, fits in well with the wayward behavior of inanimate objects, and things are apparently more permanent than people. The city of London, the outdoor world, seems to be suffering from a slow process of decomposition, and whereas man-made objects dissolve into primary elements, only men themselves possess the freedom to kill and to die. In drawing circles, Stevie is the one true anarchist, attempting on blank paper (a parody of JC's own fiction) to create an art to emcompass chaos and eternity. But Stevie's efforts to interfere with the "muddles and tragedies" of life result only in "grotesque misfortune." His mangled remains represent the condition to which society is moving; interference by the artist can only hasten the process. The truth seen by the narrator is that human forms of identity are self-created illusions; he escapes by his ironic detachment from the tragic spectacle.

2874 Cox, C. B. "The Metamorphoses of *Lord Jim*," *Critical Quarterly*, XV (Spring 1973), pp. 9–31; rpt. *Joseph Conrad: The Modern Imagination* (London: Dent; Totowa, N.J.: Rowman & Littlefield, 1974).

In *Lord Jim*, JC has Marlow describe characters as if they were undergoing a series of transformations; e.g., the German captain of the *Patna* is first a "trained baby elephant walking on hindlegs," next, a "sixteen-hundredweight sugar-hogshead wrapped in striped flannelette," and then a "green-and-orange beetle." After this protean description, the character mysteriously vanishes from sight. This description of the captain is typical and not at all unique in the novel. JC's characters in *Jim* commonly undergo transformation and vanish at times only to reappear at another time. The author's search throughout the book assumes, moreover, that like Jim's search for heroic action and for an acceptable place in the community, there is "virtue" in the quest, even though it must end in failure.

2875 Davidson, Arnold E. "Recent Books on Modern Fiction: British," *MFS*, XIX (1973–74), pp. 631–35.

When questioned about Lord Jim, "Did he deserve a better end or did he not?" JC replied, "I did my best for him. He was one of us."

2876 Davis, John Roderick. "Joseph Conrad's *Under Western Eyes*: A Genetic, Textual, and Critical Study," *DA*, XXXVII (1973), 3639. Unpublished dissertation, Columbia University, 1973.

2877 Davis, Kenneth W., and Donald W. Rude. "The Transmission of the Text of *The Nigger of the Narcissus*," *CON*, V, No. 2 (1973), pp. 20–45.

The preparation of a critical edition of JC's *The Nigger of the Narcissus* begins with the collation of the holograph manuscript with the editions of the work printed during the author's lifetime. The text of the novel exists, in addition to the holograph, written in ink, in seven distinct states, which contain approximately 2000 variant readings. JC's manuscript indicates that the novelist made changes largely to achieve a sharper focus in descriptions, to effect a more carefully delineated characterization, to reposition sentences to heighten their dramatic effectiveness, to heighten connotative qualities, or to revise the punctuation. Apparently, an intermediate draft of the novel is now lost. Moreover, numerous variant readings distinguish the serial edition of the novel in the *New Review* from both the first American and the British edition of *Nigger*, some of which probably resulted from editorial intervention. Further complications arise from several additional changes and from a number of revisions by JC. These many changes and revisions reveal JC'c concern with the craft of his fiction. [Contains four valuable tables, one of which shows diagrammatically the transmission of the text of the novel. An invaluable revelation of JC's methods of working and reworking his writings.]

2878 Ellman, Richard. *Golden Codgers: Biographical Speculations* (New York and London: Oxford University, 1973), pp. 17–19, 114, 121, 123–24, 126, 129, 113–31.

Much of the narrative of "Heart of Darkness" has an immediate parallel in JC's own experience, but the story is quite different from "The Congo Diary" and from the letters of the time. The motive power of the story is, apparently, JC's attempted suicide: the qualities prized by the young Marlow in "Heart of Darkness" are the exact opposites displayed by the young JC. His calling his villain Kurtz (German for "short") was to memorialize this part of his life when he was not yet JC but still Konrad Korzeniowski—a name likely to be shortened to Korz. If JC virtually died when he confirmed his navigational skill and executive capacity in 1875, 1886 was the year of his virtual resurrection because he then qualified as first mate, became a British subject, and began to write. Writing was a way of avenging his suicide attempt, which was extrapolated as the self-abandonment and moral cowardice of the European Kurtz; and the confrontation with Marlow, captain of English ships and master of English prose, was symbolically rehabilitative. In *Nostromo*, silver is the central motif. The meaning of the hero's name, Nostromo, becomes as ambiguous as silver; a lifetime of virtue is placed against an ineradicable moral fault, and Nostromo dies—an example of JC's fallen man, partially at least saved by misery and death.

2879 Epstein, Harry S. "*Lord Jim* as a Tragic Action," *SNNTS*, V (Summer 1973), pp. 229–47.

JC's artistry can be seen as his response to his task of rendering Jim as tragic in an ambiguous moral universe with skeptical assumptions about order in that universe and materialistic assumptions about the human psyche. The novel thus reflects modern man's dilemma: in order to function successfully, the community must consider individuals responsible for their acts, and the individual at the same time can be coerced into actions he does not approve of by pressures beyond his control. Ambiguity is a part of JC's material: because Jim's failure is evidence of man's potential failure, Jim's position arouses terror, and because he feels anguish as he recognizes his failure, he arouses pity. JC uses structure to develop tragedy; the action of the novel falls into three sections: (1) the short chronicle of Jim's experience on the training ship, told from the omniscient point of view; (2) Jim's jump from the *Patna*, his subsequent wanderings, and his successful adventures in Patusan, told in the author's best impressionistic manner; and (3) the Gentleman Brown episode, in which Jim and all his achievements in Patusan are destroyed. In the second section, Jim becomes a fully developed tragic figure, but not in the predicament of the conventional tragic protagonist. In Patusan, Jim's extreme good fortune places him in a position for a tragic fall, which follows when he has a choice, chooses poorly, and is destroyed by the unknown— the secret channel known only to Cornelius. But JC the artist preserves Jim's tragic significance and creates a new and important kind of tragic power.

2880 Erzgräber, Willi. "Joseph Conrad: *Lord Jim*," *Der Englische Roman im 19. Jahrhundert: Interpretationen* (The English Novel in the 19th Century: Interpretation), ed. by Paul Goetsch, Heinz Kosok, and Kurt Otten (Berlin: Erich Schmidt, 1973), pp. 288–306.

Lord Jim is an instance of "the crisis of the hero" in the modern novel. The absurd world of the novel anticipates Samuel Beckett's plays and novels, especially *Endgame*. *Jim* is influenced by Schopenhauer's philosophy. [An excellent interpretation of *Jim*.] [In German.]

2881 Farkas, Paul D. "The Aesthetics of Darkness: Joseph Conrad and the Aesthetics of the Symbolists," *DAI*, XXXIII (1973), 4411A. Unpublished dissertation, Louisiana State University, 1972.

2882 Fisher, Philip. "The Failure of Habit," *Uses of Literature*, ed. by Monroe Engel (Cambridge, Massachusetts: Harvard University [Harvard English Studies 4], 1973), pp. 3–18.

The defense of habit indicates equally efficiency and anxiety. Underneath work lies the "habit structure" that efficiently simplifies both acts and awareness, but in the moral life habit betrays an anxiety in the face of the unexpected, the future, the emergency in which panic and haste will distort reasoning. In addition, it is the anxiety about the sudden revelation of the true self. The French captain in *Lord Jim* credits to habit, necessity, and the eyes of others his standing for twelve hours on the deck of a ship that might at any moment sink under him, and, unlike Jim, he did not leap or give way to panic. Walter Pater identifies habit as the basis of our erosion of life. It is difficult to call JC's captain a hero because his act omits the consciousness which, for Jim, makes both heroism and its double, cowardice, possible. Unlike Jim and Pater, the captain has no "experience": he seems absent during the hours he stands, inattentive to the dangers of death. He owes his triumph to habit, which extends control into moments of extinguished or, as in Jim's case, dangerous consciousness.

2883 Fries, Maureen. "Feminism—Antifeminism in *Under Western Eyes*," *CON*, V, No. 2 (1973), pp. 56–65.

Peter Ivanovich is the "great antifeminist" of *Under Western Eyes*, and JC, in spite of his well known attitude toward women, approaches much closer to feminism in this novel than in any other work. A definition of feminism, given by Bakunin's anarchist disciple, Nechaev, in his *Catechism of Revolution*, on whom JC modeled Peter Ivanovich, has women constitute the sixth and "most important" category of society. In *Eyes*, JC both displays "great sensitivity" to the perversion of the doctrine of feminism by the Russian anarchists and gives, in the female characters whom Peter Ivanovich uses or attempts to use, examples of each of the three subclasses of women: (1) Tekla, of the first subclass, those of no account, is shamelessly exploited; (2) Sophia Antonovna, a member of the *Catechism's* third class, the adepts, is the most attractive and least exploited woman in the book, and (3) Nathalie Haldin, of the second subclass, is one of the enthusiasts who are revolutionaries in words only. JC, who usually feared and "looked down upon" women, supplies evidence in *Eyes*, in his sympathetic characterization of Nathalie and Sophia, of women as "the industrial, mental, political, social and sexual equals of men," thereby indicating that he was capable of "entertaining more than one view of woman's place."

2884 "Front Matter: Conrad Manuscripts Given to the Berg Collection," *Bulletin of the New York Public Library*, LXXVII (Autumn 1973), p. 7.

In April 1973, the Library's already important JC collection was augmented by a gift from Doubleday & Company of a large file of manuscripts, letters, and other materials relating to the long and productive relationship of JC and that firm. Included are the original typescripts of *Victory* and *The Rescue*; correspondence about publication rights and plans for publication after JC's death, and related interoffice memoranda; a typescript of the preface to *The Shorter Tales of Joseph Conrad*; photographs; and five pen-and-ink sketches by JC of stage settings for the dramatization of *The Secret Agent.*

2885 Glassman, Peter [Joel]. "Language and Being: Joseph Conrad and the Literature of Personality," *DAI*, XXXIII (1973), 2723A. Unpublished dissertation, Columbia University, 1972.

2886 Goffredo, Michele. "Un giudizio imperfetto su Conrad" (An Imperfect Judgment on Conrad), *Rinascita*, XL (7 December 1973), p. 20.

Through a peculiar use of symbols in "Heart of Darkness" and an artful juxtaposition of ideology, politics, and economics in *Nostromo*, JC (according to Oliva and Portelli) neutralizes the intrinsically polemic charge of his themes. But a serious ideological misunderstanding lies beneath this kind of interpretation. JC is not a reactionary; indeed, he is acutely aware of the contradictions of his own times. In the death of the intellectual Martin Decoud, for example, he portrays the self-conscious knowledge of the end of a role, of the impossibility to give a rational answer to the crisis of the bourgeois world. [Review of Oliva and Portelli, *Conrad: L'Imperialismo Imperfetto* (Torino: Einaudi, 1973).] [In Italian.]

2887 Greiff, Louis K., and Shirley A. Greiff. "Sulaco and Panama: A Geographical Source in Conrad's *Nostromo*," *JML*, III (February 1973), pp. 102–104.

Although there is some early evidence that the Sulaco of *Nostromo* is based on Panama, a close comparison of E. M. W. Tillyard's map of Sulaco's Pacific coast (in *The Epic Strain in the English Novel*, 1958), (C, I, No. 1508) and a reliable map of the Panamanian Pacific coast shows that, while the imaginary place is much smaller, the physical configuration of the two is nearly identical. Although some significant discrepancies between the two areas exist, JC also borrowed for his novel certain place-names from Panama.

2888 Gurko, Leo. "*Of Mice and Men*: Steinbeck as Manichean," *University of Windsor Review*, VIII (Spring 1973), pp. 11–23.

In Manicheism, there is the dark belief that God not only can be beaten but also has been beaten. The greatest and the most influential of Manichean writers is JC, whose early masterpieces, *The Nigger of the Narcissus* and "Heart of Darkness," have left their direct influence, through Hemingway, on John Steinbeck, especially in *Of Mice and Men*. In *Nigger*, the dark powers are embodied in Donkin and Wait; the forces of light in Captain Allistoun. In "Heart of Darkness," Kurtz is the "Primal Man" in Manichean mythology, "captured" by the darkness, and Marlow is an "agent of light." JC does not morally weigh one against the other; the world, though morally neutral, is psychologically intense, with "an intensity rooted in the perpetual clash of conflicting principles" which JC sees reflected in the divisions within human nature itself. [Deals mainly with *Of Mice and Men*.]

2889 Hamill, Paul. "Conrad, Wells, and the Two Voices," *PMLA*, LXXXIX (May 1973), pp. 581–82.

In "Conrad, Wells, and the Two Voices," (*PMLA*, LXXXVIII [October 1973], pp. 1049–65), Frederick R. Karl writes about JC's rejection of science, his seeking within individual isolation and loneliness for some code of behavior or rule of morality that would, at least temporarily, give order to chaos and cover over anarchy. JC was arriving at a rarefied view of art while Wells was ready to commit himself to social criticism. But JC had not arrived at a "rarefied" view; he had, instead, achieved a "wisdom inherently personal." Humanism—books—provided his instruments but no more claimed proprietary interest than the scientist claims territorial rights over reason. JC was "scientifically better" than Wells.

2890 Havely, Cicely. *The Nineteenth Century Novel and Its Legacy: Unit 27, "Heart of Darkness,"* (Walton Hall, Milton Keynes: The Open University, 1973; New York: Harper and Row, 1976).

[Cicely Havely's instructional guide to Conrad's "Heart of Darkness" is cast in the form of a Socratic dialogue which poses essential questions relating JC's story to earlier Victorian novels and leading to the discovery of its key themes. Havely provides no new interpretations, chooses rather to synthesize accepted analyses of the text and to provide also a close reading of the novel. This guide should be useful to anyone who wants to study the text outside the formal classroom situation.]

2891 Hay, Eloise Knapp. "Conrad Between Sartre and Socrates,"
Modern Language Quarterly, XXXIV (March 1973), pp. 85–97.

Three authors of recent boks on JC, Bruce Johnson, *Conrad's
Models of Mind* (1971), Royal Roussel, *The Metaphysics of Darkness:
A Study in the Unity and Development of Conrad's Fiction* (1971), and
Leon F. Seltzer, *The Vision of Melville and Conrad: A Comparative
Study* (1970), conclude that JC thought matter and consciousness
antagonistic by nature, but JC qualifies such statements in his
works by saying either that he is pretending to be "severely
scientific" or else saying that "reason" tells man he is alien and
victimized within physical nature. All three of the new books
disregard the emphasis that JC places on the power of the
imagination, "heart," and "faith" to restore "dismemberments" that
reason effects (in the preface to *The Nigger of the Narcissus* and
elsewhere). The order reflected by the whole, the *entire*, mind is not
for JC finally absurd or aimless, as it is for Sartre. JC incessantly
explores "models of mind" in which certain faculties predominate,
but he is at no time ignoring as inhuman animal passions such
things as sexuality and hunger. He sums up his position in speaking
of life as a warfare between two opposing armies, neither of which
ever annihilates the other, as a nihilist would hold. The two forces,
"passions" good and bad, and "gods," ideational ambitions which
may be either good or bad, are not completely divided; instead the
"gods" hold a higher place in JC's view of the struggle. Marlow's
standard of truth is noted by the expression, "one of us," which
signals the human condition in which bonds connect trustworthy
men: he follows Socrates, Montaigne, Pascal, and Turgenev.

2892 Hay, Eloise Knapp, and Cedric Watts. "To Conrad from
Cunninghame Graham: Reflections on Two Letters," *CON*, V, No. 2
(1973), pp. 5–19.

Only two letters from Robert Cunninghame Graham to JC
survive. Dated 3 December 1923 and 7 December 1923, and both
rapid jottings, they touch some of the deepest concerns of the two
men. They remind us of Cunninghame Graham's lifelong attachment
to France; they point out the similarity between the Polish merchant
marine officer turned English novelist and the Scottish aristocrat
turned revolutionary socialist. Other parallels include the
significance of the horse for Cunninghame Graham and of the sailing
vessel for JC, the becoming of South America and north Africa for the
Scotsman and of the sea for the Pole as places of escape from
despair, an interest in violent activity and the love of mortal danger
as "rescue work" for both personal and political codes in their
careers, JC's reliance on Cunninghame Graham in writing *The
Inheritors* and *Nostromo*, the common defense of "eclipsed" nations,

and their common devotion to the "theme" of lost causes, failed heroes, and "rescue work." [The two letters, first published here, are in the Beinecke Library at Yale University.]

2893 Henig, Suzanne. "The Second and Third International Conferences of Conrad Scholars," *ELT*, XVI, No. 1 (1973), pp. 7–9.
[Report of Conferences on JC in London and Warsaw and on the planned publication of papers presented.]

2894 Higdon, David Leon. "Pascal's *Pensée* 347 in *Under Western Eyes*," *CON*, V, No. 2 (1973), pp. 81–83.

The unusual allusiveness of *Under Western Eyes* sets this novel apart from many other works by JC, who clearly alludes to such figures at Dostoevski, Tolstoy, Rousseau, Hoffmann, and Borel. Pascal, too, appears plainly in a passage which is either a free translation of a partly remembered quotation from *Pensée* 347, about man as a thinking reed. Razumov, in defending his right to be a thinking man, has recognized the irrational forces surrounding him without having accepted Pascal's arguments about the severe limitations of human reason. The thought expressed in Razumov's comment and alluded to in two earlier letters by JC is definitely JC's, but the imagery, the epigrammatic quality, and in the novel, even the syntax are Pascal's.

2895 Hoffmann, Gerhard. "Joseph Conrad: 'The Secret Sharer,'" *Die Englische Kurzgeschichte* (The English Short Story), ed. by Karl Heinz Göller and Gerhard Hoffmann (Düsseldorf: Bagel, 1973), pp. 47–59, 355–57.

JC's story, "The Secret Sharer," emphasizes the writer's artful use of "space" and "time," the problem of identity, JC's morals, and the initiation elements of the story. The work is ambiguous, full of associations and echo structures; it is an "open" story, with "open" symbols and an "open" hero. [In German.]

2896 Jacobson, Sibyl C., and Todd K. Bender. "Computer Assisted Editorial Work on Conrad," *CON*, V, No. 3 (1973), pp. 37–45.

Under the general direction of Todd K. Bender at the University of Wisconsin, JC's complete works are being prepared for computer analysis of a larger program including several authors. The purpose of this project is to "build up" a substantial library of complex literary texts in computer readable form and to explore ways to deal with problems in editorial and bibliographic theory and practice. The editorial and bibliographic work on JC will focus on the production of concordances, indices, word frequency tables, and similar sets of data, and on the production of eclectic texts through collation of sets of variant versions of a single work. To deal with JC's interesting style, a new conception of the format for the concordance is needed, the "key-word-in-context" format (KWIC). Several bothersome problems arise, but with the works of JC, where no definitive edition exists, the citing of pagination to a number of editions enables the concordance to create its promised text; the field of reference for a concordance with a "key-word-out-of-context" (KWOC) format is the raw material for subsequent editorial work assisted by the frequency tables and index to other contexts. The complete collation can save the textual editor much labor. In effect, the computer programmer's collation is based on a desire to determine as nearly as possible the author's final intent and to print that as the definitive text.

2897 Jacobson, Sybil C., Robert J. Dilligan, and Todd K. Bender. *A Concordance to "Heart of Darkness"* (Carbondale: Southern Illinois University, 1973).

[The concordance consists of two microfilms, the first card containing two prefaces to "Heart of Darkness" and the text, the second card containing the word list and various tables and charts. The scholarship is impressive, but the fact that the concordance is available only on microfiche provides many troublesome disadvantages: for example, the concordance is restricted to university library use, and one cannot look at both the word list and the text at the same time. Moreover, the word list fails to supply the context of the words themselves, which sometimes necessitates awkward and time consuming shifts from one card to the next.] [On microfiche only. Useful but annoying.]

2898 Johnson, J. J. "Joseph Conrad and André Gide—Further Correspondence—An Article Note," *CON*, V, No. 3 (1973), pp. 77–78.

Gabrijela and Ivo Vidan have collected and annotated ten previously unpublished letters in "Further Correspondence Between Joseph Conrad and André Gide," *Studia Romanica et Anglica Zagraebiensia*, 29–32 (1970–71), pp. 523–36, with dates ranging from 1912 to 1922. Five letters of 1919 concern the translation of *The Arrow of Gold* into French; others deal with the relationship between Gide and JC.

2899 Johnson, J. J. "Saint-John Perse to Joseph Conrad—A Letter—An Article Note," *CON*, V, No. 3 (1973), p. 76.

A previously unpublished letter dated February 26, 1921, from Saint-John Perse to JC (published in *Le Figaro Litteraire*, November

18, 1972) is mainly a response by Perse to JC's stated curiosity about China. Perse specifically remembers one evening when JC expressed his admiration for the work of Edward Lear and admitted that Zola and Molière were the two French authors he knew best. JC denied wanting to write sea tales. Perse, considering JC to be the "most humane man of letters he has ever met," expresses his belief that both JC and he are "constantly revivified from the past by their spiritual alliance with the sea." Perse then considers the great land mass of China as having paradoxical similarities with the sea which both he and JC understood well.

2900 Kane, Thomas S. "The Dark Ideal: A Note on 'The Secret Sharer,'" *CEA*, XXXVI (November 1973), pp. 28–30.

Comparing Leggatt and the unnamed narrator of "The Secret Sharer" reveals Leggatt as "a character in his own right." His courageous actions aboard the *Sephora* preview the narrator's "future possibilities." But Leggatt's less courageous action similarly suggests another possible response by the narrator to a threatening challenge. Leggatt does not recognize the wrong in his strangling the mutinous seaman, nor does the narrator find anything wrong in Leggatt's actions. Subsequent developments in the story point out, however, that there is a difference between the two men: the narrator in a manner gives Leggatt his life when he hides him and lies to the captain of the *Sephora*, whereas Leggatt denies life when he murders the sailor.

2901 Kaplan, Morton, and Robert Kloss. "Fantasy of Immortality: Conrad's *The Nigger of the Narcissus*," *The Unspoken Motive: A Guide to Psychoanalytic Literary Criticism* (New York: Free, 1973), pp. 5, 6, 13, 18, 37, 47–62, 136.

The key to understanding why the crew in *The Nigger of the Narcissus* identifies with James Wait is found in his own defenses against his approaching death, which are unconsciously taken up by the crew. His defenses are outright denial, a pretense that his illness is a deliberately chosen sham, and a denial of his own fears, all of which result in his playing the role of a malingerer whose shamming achieves other defensive purposes: Wait can actively associate himself with death rather than passively be its victim. His exercising choice allays the fear of death. His defenses are never successful because they contradict one another, making his assertions and actions irrational. By alternatively asserting and denying that he is dying, he keeps the men in endless doubt so that eventually they seek an extraordinary defense against fear. A "miserable gang of immortals" they are because they accept consciously the misery of servitude to Wait in order to share the unconscious fantasy of being immortal. Theirs is a society founded on a shared delusion which cannot last. The entire journey symbolizes death and cannot be completed until death is consummated.

2902 Karl, Frederick R. "Conrad, Wells, and the Two Voices," *PMLA*, LXXXVIII (October 1973), pp. 1049–65.

The two voices we all hear are those of logic and poetry; these voices have divided individuals as certainly as they have divided cultural history since Plato and Aristotle. The unpublished JC-Wells correspondence housed in the University of Illinois library enables us to see the development of the relationship between these two writers during the formative years of the 1890s. The eventual lapse of intimacy occurs as JC listens increasingly to the voice of art and Wells to the voice of science. The line was drawn in 1903, when JC was working on *Nostromo*.

2903 Karl, Frederick R. "The Letters of Joseph Conrad: Textual and Editing Problems," *CON*, V, No. 3 (1973), pp. 28–36.

Since there are so many variables in JC's approximately 3500 letters written in Polish, French, and English, the editor must avoid most generalities and rely on the individual letter. Textual problems arise because: (1) the originals of numerous Polish letters have been lost; (2) the problem of reconstruction, especially with the French correspondence, is great, and (3) the 3000 letters in English, even with some of the originals undiscovered, are comparatively easy to work with. The principles of editing include transcribing JC's letters exactly as they appear in the original holograph or typescript, providing a text representing what JC wrote—what his recipients read—letting his errors in punctuation, grammar, spelling, and idioms stand as they are, and printing every JC letter, telegram, postcard, note, and brief message available. The value of the edition as a whole will be the "charting" of JC's journey "from Poland to France, the sea, England, authorship, international acclaim." All letters will be dated as exactly as possible, and the ten-volume collection will be as complete as possible. [Karl and Zdzislaw Najder of Poland are preparing this much-needed collected edition of JC's letters.]

2904 Karrer, Wolfgang, and Eberhard Kreutzer. *Daten der Englischen und Amerikanischen Literatur von 1890 bis zur Gegenwart* (Dates of English and American Literature from 1890 to the Present Day), (Munich: Deutscher Taschenbuchverlag, 1973), pp. 13, 14, 16, 18, 19, 73–74, 76, 77–78, 83, 87–88, 91–92, 98–99, 102, 105–106, 130, 134, 148, 248.

JC's novels deal with main in extreme situations. [Summaries of *The Nigger of the Narcissus*, "Heart of Darkness," *Lord Jim, Typhoon and Other Stories, Nostromo, The Secret Agent, Under Western Eyes, Chance,* and *Victory.* [In German.]

2905 Kenner, Hugh. "The Urban Apocalypse," *Eliot in His Time: Essays on the Occasion of the Fiftieth Anniversary of the Waste Land,* ed. by A. Walton Litz (Princeton, New Jersey: Princeton University, 1973), pp. 23–49; rpt. *Literary Criticism: Idea and Act (The English Institute, 1939-1972: Selected Essays),* ed. by W. K. Wimsatt (Berkeley, Los Angeles, London: University of California, 1974), pp. 616–35.

In *The Waste Land,* T. S. Eliot's ex-sailor who has fought in some analogue of the First Punic War indicates that the present is inferior to its own "best potential" insofar as it suggests resemblance to the past. The JC epigraph later proposed by Eliot ("Did he live his life again in every detail of desire, temptation and surrender during that supreme moment of complete knowledge?") enforces this theme of paralyzing reenactment. Eliot's decision to entitle the poem *The Waste Land* seems to have come late; its only occurrence in the manuscripts is on a title-page with the JC epigraph, typed on the machine on which "The Fire Sermon" was transcribed. These facts help somewhat in reconstructing the poem's composition.

2906 Kittrell, Ethel Jean. "The Audacious Philosophy of Joseph Conrad," *DAI,* XXXIV (1973), 5976A. Unpublished dissertation, Southern Illinois University, 1973.

2907 Kleiner, Elaine L. "Joseph Conrad's Forgotten Role in the Emergence of Science Fiction," *Extrapolation: A Journal of Science Fiction and Fantasy,* XV (December 1973), pp. 25–34.

The Inheritors (1901) by JC and Ford Madox Ford may be seen as an effort to create a "new novel," an early attempt, however flawed it may be, to write in a genre which is still in the process of being formulated. No doubt influenced by H. G. Wells, the collaborators chose to set their novel in the immediate future, following up JC's interest in the x-ray machine. They imagined the future somewhat like a kernel contained within the seed of the present, coexisting with the present as an alternative universe on a different plane in time, its inhabitants gradually attaining dominance over present forms of life. Evolution was conceived as a process of "weeding out" and exterminating the unfit to make way for existing stronger forms, such as the "new Man," the *Übermensch* of the future. The plot of the novel reveals this pattern in its fable of three "Dimensionista," a politician, a "yellow journalist," and a woman-of-fortune, all members of a race of superseders who will "inherit the earth." The method of storytelling was intended to reflect a symptom of confusion and helplessness, a condition which could prevail during the future decline of a world power and entrance into a future where the value of the individual would give way to mass value. *Inheritors*, a forgotten novel, is perhaps better than Orwell's *1984*. [A valiant attempt to make both science fiction and *Inheritors* "respectable."]

2908 Knowles, Owen. "Commentary as Rhetoric: An Aspect of Conrad's Technique," *CON*, V, No. 3 (1973), pp. 5–27.

Subtle reasons for JC's manipulation of the commentator's role in several works are: (1) the largeness and diversity of vision this role allows, which mediates between local and general values, the single dilemma and man's condition as a whole; (2) the commentary containing a usually unnoticed flexibility made up of many tones which coexist with the dramatized voices of the characters; and (3) JC's voice always active, in direct and oblique ways, in order to extend the limits of the novel from the inner world of fiction to the values of the outer world. Typical of JC's practice are, first, his omniscient assessment of individuals in which he analyzes and evaluates single characters, the delayed disclosure of characters, extended comment, the combination of commentary with more dramatic and oblique methods of character-reading, an enlargement by authorial commentary, and the interweaving of the dramatic and fully informed views of the author in suggesting the typical Conradian irony. A second major device is the philosophic bias of JC's commentary, by which much of his fiction gives a sense of two highly important statements running side by side and being interlocked, one a dramatic situation and the other a supporting commentary which mediates between the local and the universal. Still another characteristic of JC's commentary is his appeal to "universal experience"; a very unattractive or exotic character may be linked by means of commentary to our own situation. [This major contribution to understanding JC's achievement deserves much fuller commentary.]

2909 Kowalska, Aniela. "Conrad (1896–1900): Strategia wrazen i refleksji w narracjach Marlova" (Conrad [1896–1900]: Strategy of Impressions and Reflections in Marlow's Narratives), *Prace Wydzialu I Lodzkiego Towardzystwa Naukowego* (Publications of the First Section of the Lodz Scientific Society), (Lodz, 1973), No. 73, pp. 1–132.

The independent attitude and idealism of R. Cunninghame Graham helped JC determine the concepts and themes in Marlow's narratives in "Youth," "Heart of Darkness," and *Lord Jim*. JC admired the article on Rimbaud by Charles Whibley, "A Vagabond Poet," published in *Blackwood's* (February 1899, pp. 402–15; rpt. here, pp. 120–26), which may be a source for Kurtz. JC also admired *Une Saison en Enfer* and used "infernal" imagery in the letters of 1896–1900. [English summary, pp. 127–28.] [In Polish.]

2910 Kowalska, Aneila. "Niedoceniona—czy zapomiana napoleonska opowesc Conrada (Uwagi ma marginesie 'Duszy wojownika'" (Underrated–or Forgotten–Comments on Conrad's Napoleonic Tale, "The Warrior's Soul"), *Prace Polonistyczne* (Lódz, 1973), XXXIX, pp. 213–26.

[Close analysis of the tale, "The Warrior's Soul," with its metaphorical title, shows it to be autobiographical and deeply humanistic. It provides an argument against the generally held view that after "The Secret Sharer," JC's powers began to decline.] [In Polish.]

2911 Laine, Michael. "Conrad's *The Rover*: The Rejection of Despair," *Queen's Quarterly*, LXXX (Summer 1973), pp. 246–55.

JC's last completed novel, *The Rover*, succeeds in its attempt to provide an answer to questions posed by life and reaches an affirmative view which denies despair and supports the possibility of finding an organized and dignified answer to the problem of "how to be." Peyrol, the novel's central character, is a kind of Odysseus, a sailor who returns to a country which appeals to him because it seems to remain the same, but he exists outside any of the relationships that are set up in the novel, outside the triangle of the other three major characters. Great change has come to the country but not to Peyrol the exile, just as JC's own politics have changed very little since 1905 when he published "Autocracy and War." Peyrol's last act is a rejection of ease and of the despair that must come to such a man through idleness or rustication. His death is moving, and the epitaph provided by the book's final paragraph supplies in poetic and almost tragic terms the last words of affirmation.

2912 Langbaum, Robert. "Thoughts of Our Time: Three Novels on Anarchism," *American Scholar*, XLII (Spring 1973), pp. 227–50.

Terrorism is the center of interest in the two conservative novels, Henry James's *The Princess Casamassima* (1886) and JC's *The Secret Agent* (1907) as well as in Dostoevski's *The Possessed* (1871–72), "the greatest political novel of them all." In *Agent*, JC, like James, breaks through politics at the end to reconstruct the old nonpolitical values. He wants to show the absurdity of "a few broken-down old revolutionaries trying to change the world when they cannot agree

among themselves on what they want." Their political professions
are matched against their personal characters and motives. Verloc
represents an entire society made up of naturally supporting vested
interests. His corpulence is a sign of his moral nihilism, the nihilism
which infects the whole society. JC uses the word "nihilism" to mean
the rejection of all values. Whereas pity and the other values which
help make an idealistic political movement are negated, the
"reconstitution" starts when Vladimir is able to stir Verloc out of his
indolence.

These novels that suggest revolutionary political values in favor
of traditional moral values show that societies fall from the top and
that revolutions are initiated from the top also by middle- and upper-
class intellectuals.

2913 Lauterbach, Edward S., and W. Eugene Davis. *The Transitional
Age: British Literature, 1880–1920* (Troy, New York: Whitston
Publishing Co., 1973), pp. 11–13, 16, 18, 20, 118–22, 188, 261, 279.

JC's main concern in several of his major novels is that there are
"terrible dangers" to man's freedom and individuality in serving
material interests. [Contains a short sketch of JC's life and a
bibliography of his fiction, his autobiography, his letters, his
collected works, bibliographical works about him, and biographical
and critical books. Evaluates JC's achievement: "No man of the
period made a more significant contribution to the art of the novel
than Conrad."]

2914 Lentz, Vern B. "Ford's Good Narrator," *SNNTS*, V (Winter 1973),
pp. 483–90.

John Dowell, in *The Good Soldier*, becomes the spokesman for
the working principles which Ford Madox Ford derived from his
collaboration with JC. Repeated references to the imaginary fireside
scene consisting of Dowell speaking with a sympathetic friend
constitute a narrative framework within which Dowell's story is set.
By addressing his account to a specific listener, Dowell creates a
narrative framework for the central action of the novel. This frame
gives Dowell-the-narrator a "concrete narrative presence," much like
that of JC's Marlow. In this role, Dowell both utters Ford's critical
views and is himself the ideal narrator.

2915 Lombardo, Agostino. "Romanzi occidentali" (Western Novels),
Il Mondo (28 June 1973), p. 21.

[A general survey of JC's reception in Italy and a perceptive
review of *Romanzi Occidentali* (Milan: Mursia, 1972) and of Oliva and
Portelli, *Conrad: L'Imperialismo Imperfetto* (Turin: Einaudi, 1973).]
[In Italian.]

2916 Lynd, Robert. "Review," *Daily News* (London, 15 January 1914), p. 4; rpt. *CCH*, pp. 271–73.

If JC had introduced his characters in *Chance* in the ordinary way, he could have cut his book in half, but he is mainly occupied not with the story, but with "creating an atmosphere of stranger motives." He is more of a poet than Henry James, but less of a craftsman. His interest in people is not their "complete humanity," but their "curious and occasional aspects."

2917 Maack, Annegret, and Hans Otto Thieme. "Literatur zum englischen Roman des 19. Jahrhunderts: Eine ausgewählte Bibliographie" (Literature on the English Novel of the 19th Century: A Selected Bibliography), *Der Englische Roman im 19. Jahrhundert: Interpretationen* (The English Novel in the 19th Century: Interpretations), ed. by Paul Goetsch, Heinz Kosok, and Kurt Otten (Berlin: Erich Schmidt, 1973), pp. 318–31.

[A well-chosen bibliography; lists bibliographies, periodicals, surveys, studies of several types of novels (e.g., industrial novel, social novel, maritime novel, pastoral novel), analyses of individual aspects. Useful to the JC scholar.] [In German.]

2918 MacKenzie, Norman, and Jeanne MacKenzie. *H. G. Wells: A Biography* (New York: Simon and Schuster: 1973), pp. 103, 114, 122, 137–38, 140–46, 154, 167, 177, 241, 242, 276, 277, 291, 306.

It was the support of H. G. Wells that kept JC going in the years before his books began to yield a living income. Wells reviewed enthusiastically JC's first two novels. The friendship which developed was long, intimate, and mutually rewarding. Gradually, though, the trials of the JC family came to irritate Wells. He wanted JC "to deal with more passionate issues" of politics instead of trying to refine his style and technique. For all their differences, there was something in common among Wells, Ford, and JC: in various ways all were outsiders—as writers as well as in their backgrounds, no one of them received a fraction of the sales that were reached by popular authors of the time, and all of them worked to make a living at the edge of the literary world.

In 1901, Wells helped JC place some articles with a publisher. By the time JC dedicated *The Secret Agent* to Wells, he no longer had the same hopes for him as artist that had been aroused by his earlier work. In the years when Wells was close to Ford, James, and JC, he valued their good opinion, but even then he was rejecting their criticisms. In 1912, Wells further widened the gulf that had opened between him and his old literary friends: he refused to join the Academic Committee of the Royal Society of Literature because, as he said, he objected to such academies. But Wells was so socially involved with his friends that he was to need another such following in the near future.

2919 Martin, Joseph J. "Edward Garnett and Conrad's Plunge into the 'Destructive Element,'" *TSLL*, XV (Fall 1973), pp. 517–36.

The most fundamental single turn in JC's development as an artist, his shift in 1896 from subjective to objective realism, was largely the result of the continuing critical pressure of Edward Garnett, the publisher's reader who recommended JC's first book for publication and then served as his private literary critic during the first four years of his literary life ashore. Garnett, who preferred the objective method to the subjective, criticized JC's writing from *An Outcast of the Islands* in 1895 to the editor's response to "The Return" in 1897 and disapproved mainly of passages in which JC employed the subjective method to analyze and present his characters' state of mind. JC's most obvious fault was his ironic editorializing on human illusions, but a more fundamental weakness was his very shaky handling of point of view. In *The Nigger of the Narcissus*, Garnett was largely concerned with JC's remaining objective, with seeing that his descriptive writing was "crisply realistic," and with making sure that JC was dramatizing his ideas. Not long after "The Return," JC, first in "Youth" and "Heart of Darkness" and then in *Lord Jim*, was to use successfully the first-person narrator, centripetal analysis through a large cast of characters as commentators, and the Conradian time shift. Garnett may therefore be considered as JC's "literary father."

2920 Martin, W. R. "Beginnings and Endings in Conrad," *CON*, V, No. 1 (1973), pp. 43–51.

The design of JC's most successful works is that of allowing or encouraging the reader to adopt an attitude based on presented "facts" or "action," and then surprising him by disclosing the truth that underlies them. This method finds its first and perhaps fullest expression in "Heart of Darkness," in which the reader must not merely modify his first impressions, as he must do in *The Nigger of the Narcissus*, but must abandon them. In his mature period, JC employs a narrator like Marlow or "reflectors" like Decoud and Mitchell in *Nostromo*, and in this way achieves a similar ironic effect. *The Secret Agent*, being a special instance in which irony is pervasive, contains no principal character, except perhaps the Assistant Commissioner, who turns out to be what one expects. This method seems to be absent from JC's short stories, as it is from his early and later novels. *Lord Jim* lacks this kind of irony and so suffers from a "stasis"; Jim therefore fails a second time at the end of the novel. *The Shadow-Line* is the last work in which this ironic device is prominent.

2921 McLauchlan, Juliet. "Conrad's 'Famous Telegram'—An Article Note," *CON*, V, No. 2 (1973), pp. 85–86.

In his article, "Conrad's 'Famous Cablegram' in support of a Polish Loan," *Polish Review*, XVII (Spring 1972), pp. 69-77, Alexander Janta's inclusion of the printed text of the cable reveals the fact that most but not all of JC's rejected words in the cable are shown here. [For the details about JC's cablegram, see Janta's article.]

2922 McLaurin, Allen. *Virginia Woolf: The Echoes Enslaved* (Cambridge: Cambridge University, 1973), pp. 34–37, 49, 106.

While Roger Fry and Virginia Woolf were investigating, in their different ways, methods of representation, of special importance were JC's investigations. In his work, there are interesting parallels with certain aspects of Woolf's *Night and Day*; and that "moment of vision" which was near to Fry's aesthetic contemplation is also close to the heightened "moments" which Woolf praised in JC's novels, those times when he, like Fry's ascriptions to Cezanne's paintings, brought his figures into perfect relation with their background. Ralph, of *Night and Day*, like Heyst in *Victory*, looks past character and ideals to see the emptiness "at the heart of life" which is Woolf's most consistent vision. Woolf reinforces, as does JC, and symbolizes her vision of the insubstantial nature of our world and life by a visual impression, without hard outlines, and with the nature of reality depending on the point of view or the quality of the light. In *The Revival of Aesthetics*, published by Leonard and Virginia Woolf by the Hogarth Press, Hubert Waley describes "moments of vision" similar to those in Woolf's novels and to what she saw in JC's works.

2923 Meyers, Jeffrey. "Conrad and Roger Casement," *CON*, V, No. 3 (1973), pp. 64–69.

In June, 1890, at Matadi, Roger Casement first met JC and there spent some time with him. Casement was perhaps the only person in the Congo whom JC liked and respected. Their later meetings from time to time, until 1911, were pleasant, and Casement's ideas about the Congo were similar to JC's as he expressed them in "Heart of Darkness." In 1903, however, JC referred to Cunninghame Graham Casement's request for support for his reform movement in Africa; and Casement followed up this request with two visits to JC. In 1910, Casement was knighted for his work in Africa and the Amazon. In 1911, he met JC by chance, and for the last time, in the Strand. In 1916, Casement was convicted of treason and hanged because of his activities in Ireland. JC's description of Casement's emotional and temperamental nationalism is close to his unfavorable attitude toward Casement in 1916. This reversal on JC's part was caused by his entertaining the overzealous nationalism of a foreigner who adopted an alien country as his own; also, JC was uneasy about and revolted by the homosexuality revealed in Casement's frank diaries, which were discovered by Scotland Yard and used to discredit his character.

2924 Meyers, Jeffrey. "Joseph Conrad: The Meaning of Civilization," *Fiction and the Colonial Experience* (Ipswich: Boydale; Totowa, New Jersey: Rowman & Littlefield, 1973), pp. 55–78.

Kipling and JC were the only great authors who wrote about imperialism during the height of its power and influence. JC displays his view of civilization in "Heart of Darkness" and *Nostromo*, which contain some similarities. The setting of each, for example, is characterized by a "gloomy and brooding darkness" that symbolizes moral blindness and the evil hidden in man; both places, the Congo and Costaguana, are the sources of great wealth for the white men and are inhabited by savages less ferocious and corrupt than the white men who rule the country; the settings are violently hostile to men and express the immense difference of things that swallow up Kurtz and Decoud; and the conclusions of both works reflect JC's most vital style. As for the meaning of civilization, the imperialistic manifestation of the remote European civilization, a "crass material progress without any corresponding value," is totally destructive and fails totally in both locations. JC believes that civilization can flourish only when it is carefully guarded and protected by a few select men who remain faithful to their code of honor. This civilization cannot be transplanted and cannot survive in remote places where great temptation and danger exist. Both novels show how the evil and corrupt part of man betrays his civilized ideals.

2925 Meyers, Jeffrey. "Readers' Queries," *N&Q*, N.S. XX (February 1973), p. 58.

[Information is requested on the whereabouts of JC's unpublished essay on Kipling, "Concerning a Certain Criticism," which was sent to *Outlook* in 1898 but not printed. JC mentions it in three letters of January–February 1898, as does Jocelyn Baines in his biography, p. 183.]

2926 Meyers, Jeffrey. "To Die for Ireland: The Character and Career of Sir Roger Casement," *London Magazine*, XIII (April–May 1973), pp. 23–50.

Sir Roger Casement's efforts on behalf of the rubber workers in the Congo and his complex character and career illuminate a particular phase of Irish history, the independence movement of 1916. His work for the rubber workers brought him fame and a knighthood; his attempt to aid Ireland led him to the gallows. Born in Ireland in 1864, he first met JC on the Lower Congo. Both men wrote about the releasing of white men's basest and cruelist instincts under conditions of absolute power in the wilderness. Like his friend JC, Casement was one of the first men to question the then dominant idea of progress. [A detailed account of Casement's life which supplies good background material for a knowledge of his relationship with JC.]

2927 Milosz, Czeslaw. "Apollo N. Korzeniowski: Joseph Conrad's Father," *Mosaic*, VI, No. 4 (1973), pp. 121–40. Trans. by Reuel K. Wilson.

Since JC's father was a writer and together they constitute a "dynasty," there is a continuity of emotional tone in their lives and works. JC's grandfather, Theodore Korzeniowski, served with Napoleon's Polish army in 1812; later he participated in the 1830 Uprising, and he was also a *pater familias* and a landowner in the Ukraine. His second son, Apollo, who married Evelina Bobrowska in 1856, spent most of his life in the Ukraine. He translated several literary works from French and English into Polish. Primarily a poet, however, his derivative writing represents the "second wave" of the Romantic movement. Unlike Apollo, his brother-in-law, Tadeusz Bobrowski, who became JC's guardian, had nothing of the revolutionary about him. Apollo's political activities caused his exile in northern Russia in 1862. According to Korzeniowski, the fear of Russia was a motivating force behind European politics in the nineteenth century. JC remained faithful in his way to his father's concept of "an idea without a tomorrow." Like his father, he was untouched by nineteenth-century optimism. Both father and son measured the greedy bourgeois by the same standards of decency and honesty which binds together a ship's crew in its fight with "the dark element." For Apollo, the crew was "the Nation or Europe, the dark element—Russia." For JC, the crew signified "humanity in its struggle with destiny."

2928 Naremore, James. *The World Without a Self: Virginia Woolf and the Novel* (New Haven and London: Yale University, 1973), pp. 5, 45, 84, 121.

When Virginia Woolf, in *The Voyage Out*, has the party of people from Santa Marina make the voyage inland upriver, the rhythm of her style suggests JC's insistence on mood, and her images seem vaguely reminiscent of his story in "Heart of Darkness." Beautifully-mannered and poetic prose styles are "legitimate" when they seem to be accompanied by some special intensity of vision as in Faulkner, Joyce, Woolf, and JC. Woolf, unlike James, Joyce, Faulkner, and JC, frequently relies on an imperceptible shift from one character's view to that of another, a kind of "multipersonal subjectivity."

2929 Nersevova, M. A. "Dzhozef Konrad" (Joseph Conrad), *Bol'shaia Sovetskaia Entsiklopediia,* third ed., XIII (Moscow: Sovetskaia entsiklopediia, 1973), pp. 36–37.

The center of *Lord Jim* is the coming to moral maturity of a young man. "Heart of Darkness" depicts the activities of Imperialist colonizers. JC's heroes are outcasts from the bourgeois world, manfully encountering the blows of fate. JC did not believe in the success of social revolution, as seen in *Nostromo,* and *Under Western Eyes* bears evidence of the influence of Dostoevski. [In Russian.] [English translation in *Great Soviet Encyclopedia* (New York: Macmillan, 1976).]

2930 Nettels, Elsa. "'Heart of Darkness' and the Creative Process," *CON,* V, No. 2 (1973), pp. 66–73.

"Heart of Darkness" portrays the initiation and self-discovery of Marlow, analyzes the evils of European imperialism, and very importantly symbolizes the creative process as JC saw it. Marlow's narrative is comparable to that of the artist in that both Marlow and the artist seek to penetrate the darkness of their inner beings: in both there is the consciousness of physical strain, of danger, of constant struggle against obstacles, and a terrible feeling of utter solitude. The most severe test of the seeker is the absence of rules and restraints imposed by society: Kurtz succumbs to the temptations of man's baser impulses; Marlow accepts the claims of his fellow men to be saved. Kurtz, the eloquent man, who, like the artist, has the power to touch the source of a person's emotions and to move him deeply, is "seduced" by his own words. JC has an ambivalent attitude toward the power of rhetoric: he both extolls the power of words and betrays a deep mistrust of this power. He considers the artist's sacrifice of his self-possession—an abhorrent act to JC—and his yielding completely to mysterious forces. These conflicting attitudes represent inseparable sides of JC's own nature, and both Kurtz and Marlow are rescuers of their creator, who (1) dramatizes through Kurtz the soul-destroying power of eloquence and (2) celebrates through Marlow a victory over that destructive power by one who, in narrating his ordeal, seeks words to touch the "secret spring of responsive emotion" in his listeners. The powers of intellect and feeling which save Marlow from Kurtz's fate are basically those which safeguard the artist in his inner world of solitude.

2931 Ohno, Mitsuhiko. "Reason and Fanaticism: On Joseph Conrad's *Under Western Eyes*," *Hiroshima Studies in English Language and Literature*, XIX, No. 2 (1973), pp. 64–81.

JC describes fanatics of both the left and the right as mean and little in *Under Western Eyes*, whose background is Czarist Russia on the eve of the Revolution. Victor Haldin, a student revolutionist who believes in "the power of the people's will and embraces it as his 'religion,'" is delineated as "this sanguine fanatic" or "that fanatical idiot." But this novel not only reveals what JC thought to be the true character of fanatics, who are ruled by unreasonableness, but also discloses what he regarded as the real character of persons who are under the control of reason. Such men of reason are represented by Razumov, a student whose name is derived from a Russian word which means "reason" in English. And JC characterizes this young man as a "weak, unreliable, and irresolute person." JC thinks that reason denies any absolute value or authority and that too much emphasis on reason destroys one's "inner standpoint" and makes him a "mental rover" in the world—the world where there can be no relief either through unreasonableness or through reason itself. [Based on an abstract in English by the author.] [In Japanese.]

2932 Oliva, Renato. "Dalla commedia della luce alla tragedia della tenebra, ovvero l'ambigua redenzione di Kurtz" (From the Comedy of Light to the Tragedy of Darkness, or The Ambiguous Redemption of Kurtz), Renato Oliva and Alessandro Portelli, *Conrad: L'Imperialismo Imperfetto* (Conrad: The Imperfect Imperialism), (Turin: Einaudi, 1973), pp. 7–70.

JC's colonialism has some serious limitations: what is under accusation is simply individuals and not the imperial idea nor the institutions of British colonialism. At the time of the Boer War, JC did not condemn the war itself; he was not a pacifist. In "Heart of Darkness," one is not justified to favor the symbolic level as against the historical and political levels. What is worse is that the symbolic darkness which covers London is meant to tranquilize the reader, who is moralistically satisfied that "a symbol as well as useless judgment has been passed on sharp practice and speculation." The two levels, which should be complementary, are only partially and contradictorily developed by JC, and this fact impairs the issue of the story. JC believed in the redeeming idea, in the possibilities of civilizing action, but he offered no precise formulae, no alternative proposals; he accepted the forms of British colonialism because it was more sophisticated than the rude Belgian colonialism he attacked in order to divert the reader's attention from the other target. JC tried to move the focus of his tale from the "comedy of light" (social and political) of colonialism to the tragedy of darkness (natural and individual) of Kurtz, promoting him from conqueror to colonist. [In Italian.]

2933 Oliva, Renato, and Alessandro Portelli. *Conrad: L'Imperialismo Imperfetto* (Conrad: The Imperfect Imperialism), (Turin: Einaudi, 1973).

[Contents, abstracted under year of first publication: Renato Oliva, "Dalla commedia della luce alla tragedia della tenebra, ovvero l'ambigua redenzione di Kurtz" (From the Comedy of Light to the Tragedy of Darkness, or The Ambiguous Redemption of Kurtz), pp. 7–70; Allessandro Portelli, "Relazione sui recenti avvenimenti politici verificatisi nella repubblica di Costaguana (basata sulle informazioni fornite dal signor Joseph Conrad nel suo libro *Nostromo*), (Report on Recent Political Happenings in the Republic of Costaguana, Based on Information Supplied by Mr. Joseph Conrad in his Book *Nostromo*), pp. 71–123; and a postface by Giorgio Melchiori, pp. 129–32. (Turin: Einaudi, 1973.)] [In Italian.]

2934 Otten, Kurt. "Strukturen und Wandlungen des Englischen Romans im 19. Jahrhundert" (Structures and Changes of the English Novel in the 19th Century), *Der Englische Roman im 19. Jahrhundert: Interpretationen*, ed. by Paul Goetsch, Heinz Kosok, and Kurt Otten (Berlin: Erich Schmidt, 1973), pp. 11–21.

JC is a writer of "mythical" novels. In his works, "truth" and "empiric facts" are no longer the same. His novels describe man's dignity in a state of loneliness. [In German.]

2935 Page, Norman. "Dickensian Elements in *Victory*," *CON*, V, No. 1 (1973), pp. 37–42.

Hard Times seems to be the closest Dickensian influence in the early chapters of *Victory*, but certain stylistic features from *Our Mutual Friend* also pervade JC's novel. More central to the main situation of the book, though, is the imagery used in connection with the three villains, who seem most closely related to *Dombey and Son* by means of animal imagery for the delineation of these grotesque characters and, specifically, the resemblance between Dickens's Carker and JC's Ricardo. The three villains have in common the fact that none is fully human, and at this point their relation to Heyst (and to a lesser degree to Lena) becomes clear: Heyst, unlike the villains, represents the fully human. JC dramatically opposes the man who is too good for "the wide world" with a trio who are too bad for it. And in giving embodiment, within the framework of a realistic novel, to this somewhat abstract moral plan, JC owes Dickens, and particularly *Dombey and Son*, a considerable debt.

2936 Palmer, Helen H. and Anne Jane Dyson. *English Novel Explication: Criticisms to 1972* (Hamden, Connecticut: Shoe String, 1973), pp. 41–63.

[A bibliography of critical materials on JC's novels from 1958 to 1972 which have appeared in books and periodicals, in English and foreign languages. Follows the checklist, Inglis F. Bell and Donald Baird, *The English Novel* (1959), (C, I, No. 1524).]

2937 Pasqualato, Roberto. "Le ragione storiche e retoriche de *Nigger of the Narcissus*" (Historical and Rhetorical Laws of *The Nigger of the Narcissus*), *Annali della Facolta di Lingue e Letterature Straniere di Ca'Foscari* (Venice), XII, No. 4 (1973), pp. 149–269.

[Examines bibliographical sources, date of composition, relationship to *The Rescue* (quoting the British Library [Ashley] manuscript), and JC's debt to Maupassant and Flaubert in studying *The Nigger of the Narcissus.*] [In Italian.]

2938 Paterson, John. "Joseph Conrad: To Make You See," *The Novel as Faith: The Gospel According to James, Hardy, Conrad, Joyce, Lawrence, and Virginia Woolf* (Boston: Gambit, 1973), pp. x–xi, 69–106, 108, 115, 132, 142, 143, 146, 163, 184, 195, 230, 232–34, 251–52, 261, 268, 273, 275, 280, 286.

Reality for JC was entirely empirical and secular, "immanental, not transcendental"; the universe was inherent in the particular. The novelist was not a systematic philosopher; his task was to record not *a* reality but *the* reality; he was basically the man who observed. The novel was distinguished by its "particularity, its specificity, its saturation in data and detail." Since the novel's proper subject was the ordinary and the commonplace, the novelist made characters instead of contriving plots. Because the essential was not distinguishable from the existential, the aesthetic of the novel was necessarily one of ambiguity and even one of obscurity; the world, in its phenomenal character, remained enigmatic and inscrutable. JC found both form and style necessary to his work. Character and psychology had priority over plot and action; what a character thought and felt was JC's concern. To represent the world was to reveal its inner meaning, and the novel expressed the part of the individual which united him with other men and things. For James, Joyce, Lawrence, Woolf, and JC, life was neither tragic nor comic, but a mysterious mixture of the two. For JC, the novelist was an artist because he was neither a poet-philosopher nor an empirical scientist: he was a being who included and reconciled them.

2939 Perosa, Sergio. "Romanzi che son quasi profezie" (Novels That are Almost Prophecies), *Corriere della Sera* (4 February 1973), p. 11.

[Review of Joseph Conrad, *Romanzi occidentali* (Milan: Mursia, 1972).] [In Italian.]

2940 Pinsker, Sanford. "Desire Under the Conradian Elms: A Note on *An Outcast of the Islands*," *CON*, V, No. 3 (1973), pp. 60–63.

To some degree, JC was, in his first two novels, in the process of creating an audience rather than writing for one already established. The major portion of *An Outcast of the Islands* pits Willems against the forces of annihilating nature and an equally threatening woman, Aissa, and the "fecund vegetation" of the jungle. JC opposes the "language of love" against the "immense silence" of the jungle so that both heroic gesture and authentic tragedy are impossible. Heterosexual desire was usually deadly for JC's works, and when it occurred "under the elms fashioned by Conradese" (JC's word for his melodrama or symbolic description), "*rigor mortis* had a nasty habit of setting in early."

2941 Portelli, Alessandro. "Relazione sui recenti avvenimenti politici verificatisi nella repubblica di Costaguana (basta aulla informazioni fornite dal signor Joseph Conrad nel suo libro *Nostromo*), (Report on Recent Political Happenings in the Republic of Costaguana, Based on Information Supplied by Mr. Joseph Conrad in his Book *Nostromo*), Renato Oliva and Alessandro Portelli, *Conrad: L'Imperialismo Imperfetto* (Conrad: The Imperfect Imperialism), (Torino: Einaudi, 1973), pp. 71–123.

Whereas in *Nostromo* JC denounces a series of facts which seem absurd in his eyes and in those of his characters, he is not aware of a major absurdity: that a party which has reached power with a parliamentarian and liberal program should almost immediately suspend the constitution and set up another dictatorship. This is possible only in the logic of colonial powers and "strong governments" founded on the belief that the populace is inferior, especially if in underdeveloped countries. JC does not fully analyze the racial and social situation of Costaguana: he leaves historical, political, and economic data in the background, focusing his attention on the personal histories of some characters whom he considers emblematic, stressing the morbid link between Gould and the mine, which he tries to explain through symbolic, emotional, sentimental, and family reasons, independently of the fact that through the mine Gould becomes immensely rich. The mixing of economic matters and ideology, structure and superstructure, is commonly employed by bourgeois writers to cover an operation in which material interests are not the corrupting elements of noble ethics, but its very end. [In Italian.]

2942 Price, Antony. *"Chronological Looping" in Nostromo* (Kuala Lumpur: University of Malaya Library, 1973).

The difficulties presented by *Nostromo* because of the uncertain and self-contradictory time scheme have been recognized often enough, but not entirely solved. They can be resolved only by the "existence of an otherwise unrecorded day in the middle of the three-day sequence," a day which can be only May third. More important, the difficulties result in a blurring of the effects JC wanted to achieve since much of the reported action is misplaced far too early in the novel. The jumbling counteracts the very effects JC was trying to achieve. [A valuable fifteen-page essay.]

2943 Pulc, I. P. [pseud. of Irmina Pulc Plaszkiewcz]. "Reviews: Andrzej Braun's Visit to Atjeh—An Article Note," *CON*, V, No. 2 (1973), pp. 86–94.

Andrzej Braun has located, and visited, the settings of JC's Eastern stories and novels, most notably that of *Lord Jim's* Patusan. In "Indonezja Conradowska" (Conradian Indonesia), he provides a valuable supplement to the earlier and more extensive studies of John Dozier Gordan (C, I, No. 1096) and Norman Sherry (C, I, No. 1967) and also supplies important evidence that the actual locale of Patusan is Teunom, on the west coast of Atjeh, in northwestern Sumatra. [An important survey of what is known about this subject.]

2944 Rapin, René. "André Gide et sa traduction du *Typhoon* de Joseph Conrad (avec trois lettres inédites)," *La Revue des Lettres Modernes*, 374–79 (1973), pp. 187–201.

[Rapin notes a number of errors in André Gide's translation into French in 1923 and published by *La Nouvelle Revue Française*, of "Typhoon"—errors of negligence, omission, and of more serious substance—and writes to Gide. On 8 and 17 June, Gide writes to Rapin to thank him, and again on 24 June 1927 to assure him that the corrections have been incorporated in a new edition of the translation. Gide alleges that the errors were in part caused by his reworking a bad translation by Isabelle Rivière, but Rapin reveals that from evidence in Gide's *Journal* his translation, published first in *La Revue de Paris* and then in a limited edition in 1918, and subsequently in 1923, was undertaken out of love of JC's work and not to save Rivière's reputation, although this was the motive for Gide's working on Rivière's translation of *Victory*.] [In French.]

2945 Rapin, René. "Reality and Imagination in the Works of Joseph Conrad (Part II)," *CON*, V, No. 3 (1973), pp. 46–59.

Written a number of years after the events which inspired them, *The Nigger of the Narcissus*, "Youth," "Heart of Darkness," and *The Shadow-Line* show by their lyricism JC's personal emotion. The interest of *Nigger* lies in the struggle of a few men against the "hostility of things" and in progressive discovery that the nigger is sick, desperately alone, and lost in the face of death. In the other three stories, in which JC actually writes about himself, a miracle happens: the main character of each demonstrates the triumph of JC's art and imagination, his "true" victory over the past and over distance, and his triumph over the temptation of cynicism and forgetfulness.

Three other novels, which depend least on JC's personal experience, demonstrate his imagination as being more active than reality. The essential part of *Nostromo* is that played by the silver mine in the destiny of all the characters, the basic element of *The Secret Agent* is the profoundly human drama, and the fundamental matter in *Under Western Eyes* is the fatalistic and unavoidably tragic character given by JC's imagination to the action of the novel. It is clear that JC's novels and stories "remain essentially the work of his imagination"; they transcend and transmute the reality of his own experience. [A continuation of Rapin's article of the same title (Part 1), in *Conradiana*, IV, No. 3 (1972), pp. 22–33.]

2946 Rawson, C. J. *Gulliver and the Gentle Reader: Studies in Swift and Our Time* (London and Boston: Routledge & Kegan Paul, 1973), pp. 55, 67–68, 143, 146–47, 152, 164, 182, 183.

In "Heart of Darkness," dreams have a force which is more than that of the merely real. JC was not given to sentimental evasion, nor was he ignorant of "the Africa within." He openly explores the "civilized" man's response to its call and registers the doubts and the conflicts of loyalty. Not he, but Marlow, draws back from the abyss. He clearly respects Marlow's drawing back, and distances himself behind two narrators. The novel is a tribute to "the call of the wild" and its powers, but it remains outside the domain of polarizing commitments, whether of abandonment of the self to the lure or of total suppression from within. The only character who takes an absolute step in either direction is Kurtz, and in spite of his great symbolic importance, he is a shadowy figure in the story and is seen relatively little. In both Jonathan Swift and Norman Mailer, we are far away from the oscillations of a "liberal" novelist like JC in "Heart of Darkness," excepting the choices between a traditional "European" morality and the teasing atavistic appeal of savagery.

2947 Renato, Oliva. "Dalla commedia della luce alla tragedia della tenebre, ovvero l'ambigua redenzione di Kurtz" (From the Comedy of Light to the Tragedy of Darkness, or The Ambiguous Redemption of Kurtz), *Conrad: L'Imperialismo Imperfetto* (Conrad: The Imperfect Imperialism), (Turin: Einaudi, 1973), pp. 9–70.

"Heart of Darkness" asks questions which demand an answer, and the allusions, to both classical materials and to Dante, cannot be ignored, despite the "arts of the magazine writer" with its artificial intensity (F. R. Leavis). In the tale, nature and story are closely integrated and should be fully realized in Kurtz, but the ambiguity of Kurtz reveals ideological uncertainty. The ambiguity of Conrad-Marlow and Kurtz becomes apparent: why does JC continue to make us see Kurtz through the eyes of stupid and brutal persons, and why is he "hollow at the core"? JC's constant polemic with "material interests" is often expressed symbolically by the river-sea antithesis, with the river symbolic of commerce with its negative connotations and the sea as fraternity and freedom from economic interests. [In Italian.]

2948 Roberts, Cecil. "Beerbohm Remembered," *Books and Bookmen*, XVIII, No. 8 (1973), pp. 40–45.

Beerbohm "envied" Cecil Roberts his "contacts with Joseph Conrad, whom he met once, and whom he had admiringly parodied in *A Christmas Garland*."

2949 Roberts, Mark. "Joseph Conrad and the Springs of Action: A Study of *Victory*," *The Tradition of Romantic Morality* (London: Macmillan, New York: Barnes & Noble, 1973), pp. 259–87.

Victory often verges on the allegorical, with specific characters predominantly good, like Heyst, and others bad, like Jones. Lena is obviously allegorical: her name means the strength or vigor which enables one to persevere through trials and difficulties. She differs from Heyst in that the source of her strength lies in the instinctual side of her nature whereas Heyst's instinctual life has largely atrophied from lack of use. In a way, Ricardo is the antithesis of Heyst: his contempt for the world does not lead him to pessimism. For Heyst, the world is contemptible because of its ultimate pointlessness; Ricardo's contempt is an aspect of his own power and strength, and his contempt attaches him to the world. Self-control and hypocrisy are closely related, if not ultimately identical; in Ricardo, JC takes a close look at the Romantic morality. But even if Ricardo is in a sense a "bad" character, he is bad rather because he has the fierceness of a wild animal than because of the corruption of his character. Heyst's sudden *volte-face* near the end occurs because he finally finds, in his relationship with Lena, the greatest reality he has ever known, and he risks in that relationship his physical existence. This is the price of his rediscovery of the "life" within him. It is now *this* life that he learns to trust, not the external and material conditions of life. Although JC is not a "Romantic moralist," in *Victory* he carefully examines what seems to him the fundamental truth in what Romantic moralists were saying.

2950 Rubino, Carl A. "Le clin d'oeil échangé avec un chat," *Modern Language Notes*, LXXXVIII (December 1973), pp. 1238–61.

"Heart of Darkness" dramatizes a four-fold concept of imperialism—the ideas of dominating oneself, of dominating another culture, of dominating other individuals, and of dominating nature—in an attempt to deny the otherness of the other. Kurtz is the representative European who discovers that his domination of his otherness and of others does not succeed with nature, and he is ultimately made to realize his own emptiness and the savageness of all Europe. [In French.]

2951 Ruotolo, Lucio P. *Six Existential Heroes: The Politics of Faith* (Cambridge, Massachusetts: Harvard University Press, 1973), p. 6.

Such "demoniac existentialists" as Raskolnikov in *Crime and Punishment* can never be free, short of self-destruction, of the external world they choose to abrogate. Similarly, the Professor in JC's *The Secret Agent*, drinking "to the destruction of what is," lives in counterpoint to those he victimizes. As JC finally describes his being: "he had no future." For such figures, reality remains an abstract extension of their own static death wish.

2952 Saunders, William S. "The Unity of *Nostromo*," *CON*, V, No. 1 (1973), pp. 27–36.

Although we cannot neatly integrate all the subjects in *Nostromo* into a world view, nor sympathize wholly with any one character, nor feel a strong authorial conviction emerging, the novel is unified by a "determined consistency of attitude" toward all its many subjects, an attitude of "detached critical intelligence" which, because of its detachment, is capable of a "multiple focus," a moving from character, to scene, to historical development. We can find no single theme to unify the novel. Although JC is sometimes "trivially laborious" in attempting to make everything plausible, one benefit he gains is freedom to deal with characters on a variety of levels. As for JC's relationships to his characters, his own voice is not similar to any one of them; his critically detached style creates a feeling of spaciousness; and his control conveys the sureness and smoothness of his work as an artifact. In this novel, JC expresses a unique sense of what reality is: "everything going on in a certain area during a certain length of time." The historical forces, the sociological conditions, and the human drama all fit into this total scene.

2953 Saveson, John E. "Conrad as Moralist in *Victory*," *Costerus: Essays in English and American Language and Literature*, VIII (1973), pp. 177–92.

Two psychological influences lie back of *Victory*: (1) the associational-Utilitarian psychology of the period as found in, for example, Théodule Ribot and Henry Maudsley, and (2) a Nietzschean psychology harmonized with the first. The novel, about a deteriorating love relationship, uses symbolism indicating that the cause of the deterioration is the temperament of the middle-aged Heyst; Ricardo the tiger, Nietzsche's "beast of prey," is a follower; Jones is what Nietzsche sees in modern man, the blonde beast that is "beginning to pollute present-day Europe." All three bandits are, indeed, "aspects" or "potentialities" of Heyst's temperament. The alienation of Jones and Ricardo because of the latter's attraction to Lena conveys a sense of psychic change and a dangerous fragmentation of mind, a "disequilibrium" between higher moral faculties and basic instincts and desires. To relieve that pain and to get rid of "disgust," Heyst or Jones, aiming at Ricardo, shoots Lena, thus killing the cause, and in due time he will kill the effect. The title of the novel is therefore ironic: no one gains a victory. To what is basically a Nietzschean ethic JC gives a transcendental coloring, a mark of nineteenth-century optimism. Thus the finished quality of *Victory* is seen in considerable detail, and judged in this way it is JC's greatest novel.

2954 Saveson, John E. "*Nostromo* and the London *Times*," *RES*, XXIV (February 1973), pp. 52–58.

JC's knowledge of politics in Chile, which seems to be useful to him in departing from ordinary chronology and the use of narrators in *Nostromo*, came largely, no doubt, from Maurice Hervey's lengthy summaries in the London *Times* of 28 April and 19 May, 1891, of events in the civil war in Chile. Many details in the novel are similar in some way to those in Hervey's dispatches: Charles Gould must be modeled on Augustin Edwards, a Chilean of English descent; Montero, though somewhat different from the Chilean President, resembles him in important ways; and the clearest journalistic account of the fighting in Chile is Hervey's letter in the *Times* of 28 April. JC, it appears, drew upon analyses of political alignments and general summaries of the progress of the war, but most useful to him were the detailed actions in the North. Frequently, though, JC modified the accounts in the *Times* to clarify visual images and to achieve a more concentrated narration. [Incorporated in *Conrad, The Later Moralist* (1974).]

2955 Schenck, Mary-Low. "Seamanship in Conrad's 'The Secret Sharer,'" *Criticism*, XV (Winter 1973), pp. 1–15.

The captain in "The Secret Sharer" is completely in control of both ship and crew as he approaches Koh-ring, and it is only in the final inshore tacking maneuver that he temporarily loses his grasp of his situation, and that for perfectly valid psychological reasons. Leggatt is not particularly the "dark" or "violent" side of the captain; he is a legate or envoy who brings to the captain nothing less than the authority of command. Leggatt's example and his actual presence "educate" the captain, first, by forcing him to stand apart from his crew and, second, by welding the ship and the "underlings" into a perfect tool with which the captain may accomplish whatever he chooses. After Leggatt has forced the captain to share his command only with him, he then insists on being put ashore. In performing this task, the captain must assemble all the skills that JC is suggesting are required of a sailing master. The tacking movement is essential to the captain's plan to put Leggatt off the ship without detection by the crew. Responsible for Leggatt's life, the captain must create an "artificial" emergency in order to get every man on deck while Leggatt is escaping undetected. His maneuver is, in fact, dangerous only to Leggatt. The parting is, though, almost traumatic to the captain. When he falters at the end, because his "model" has left, the model unwittingly but importantly provides a final "saving mark," a kind of crown which Leggatt symbolically passes to the captain. A man's life is more important than the worst that might have happened to the ship, a minor wreck.

2956 [Schultheiss, Thomas.] "Conrad Bibliography: A Continuing Checklist," *CON*, V, No. 3 (1973), pp. 79–83.

[A continuation of Schultheiss's valuable checklist.]

2957 Sertoli, Giuseppe. "Una negazione testuale (Frammento di lettura da *The Nigger of the Narcissus* di Joseph Conrad)," (A Textual Negation [Fragment of a Reading from Joseph Conrad's *The Nigger of the Narcissus*]), *Nuova Corrente*, 61–62 (1973), pp. 383–412; enlgd. as "Conrad o dello scambio fra la vita e la morte: Interpretazione di *The Nigger of the Narcissus* (Conrad, or Of the Reversal Between Life and Death: Interpretation of *The Nigger of the Narcissus*), *Annali della Facolta' di Lettere e Filosofia della Universita' Degli Studi di Perugia*, XI (1973–74), pp. 1–179.

The story of *The Nigger of the Narcissus* takes place on two levels: on the one hand, at the surface level of the author's mind, the declared intentions and those put into practice, the plot, and, on the other hand, at the deep level of the subconscious which belies the author's intentions and tells another story. In short, it presents what the author did not want to present, what, on the contrary, he denies and, vice versa, denying what he had stated, it brings about an inversion: it violates the author's order and sets up another order, or better, the disorder of that order. On the surface level, the story sets out to be the story of the decline of civilization (the ship) and, at the same time, to reassert the "ideal values" of this civilization, at the very time when he shows them to be going through a crisis. JC brings to life the "idea" of the English lower middle class, still faithful to little England. But beneath this level, another story is being told; here the values of man are "un-values" while nature and life are the real values. After Jimmy's death, the ethos of the ship is reestablished, and the *Narcissus* sails safely homeward to the "fatherland." [In Italian.]

2958 Seymour-Smith, Martin. *Guide to Modern World Literature* (London: Wolfe Publishing, 1973), pp. 195–96; *Funk and Wagnalls Guide to Modern World Literature* (New York: Funk & Wagnalls, 1973), pp. 195–96.

JC deals with evil and its moral opposite, with human solitude and human relationships, and he demonstrates "a skepticism about the validity of human attitudes." Some readers dislike JC's "ponderousness" of style, which may be due to his difficulty with the English language. He was "the Polish 'master of English prose,' but of his stature, his subtlety, his seriousness, there can be no doubt."

2959 Sherry, Norman (ed.). *Conrad: The Critical Heritage* (London and Boston: Routledge and Kegan Paul [The Critical Heritage Series], 1973).

Criticism by JC's contemporaries and near-contemporaries is arranged in chronological order under each of JC's works included, linked in places by commentaries by the editor. Contents, abstracted under year of first publication [all periodicals are British unless otherwise indicated, and bibliographical information appears as Sherry lists it]: Norman Sherry, "Introduction," pp. 1–44 (1973); Norman Sherry, "Note on the Text," p. 45 [not abstracted].
Criticism, mostly reviews, of *Almayer's Folly*: "Unsigned Notice," *Daily News* (25 April 1895), 6; "Unsigned Review," *Scotsman* (29 April 1895), 3; "Unsigned Review," *Daily Chronicle* (11 May 1895), 3; Arthur Waugh, "Notice," *Critic* (11 May 1895), xxxvi, 349; "Unsigned Review," *World* (15 May 1895), 31; "Unsigned Review," *Athenaeum* (25 May 1895), 3526, 671 [C, I, No. 1]; H. G. Wells, "Unsigned Review," *Saturday Review* (15 June 1895), 797; James Ashcroft Noble, "Review,"

Academy (15 June 1895), 1206, 52 [C, I, No. 2]; "Unsigned Review,"
Speaker (29 June 1895), 722–23; "Unsigned Review," *Guardian* (3 July
1895), 1001; "Unsigned Review," *Bookman* (September 1895), 176;
"Unsigned Review," *Literary News* (September 1895), xvi, 268–69;
"Unsigned Review," *Nation* (New York: 17 October 1895), lxi, 278;
"Unsigned Review," *Spectator* (19 October 1895), 530.

Criticism of *An Outcast of the Islands*: "Conrad on the Literary
Profession," [not abstracted]; "Unsigned Review," *Daily Chronicle* (16
March 1896), 3; "Extracts from Notices in Two Scottish Papers,"
Scotsman (16 March 1896) and *Glasgow Herald* (19 March 1896);
James Payn, "Review," *Illustrated London News* (4 April 1896), 418;
"Unsigned Review," *Daily News* (4 April 1896), 6; "Unsigned Review,"
National Observer (18 April 1896), 680; "Unsigned Review," *Sketch* (6
May 1896), 62; "Unsigned Article," *Bookman* (May 1896), 41; H. G.
Wells, "Unsigned Review," *Saturday Review* (16 May 1896), 509–10;
"Unsigned Review," *Manchester Guardian* (19 May 1896), 5; "Unsigned
Review," *Spectator* (30 May 1896), 778; "Unsigned Review,"
Athenaeum (18 July 1896), 3586, 91 [C, I, No. 6]; "Unsigned Review,"
Nation (New York, 15 April 1897), 287.

Criticism of *The Nigger of the Narcissus*: "Arnold Bennett on
Conrad and Kipling," [from a letter of 8 December 1897 to H. G. Wells
(*Letters of Arnold Bennett*, ed. by James Hepburn, 1968), II, 94];
"Unsigned Notice," *Daily Mail* (7 December 1897), 3; W. L. Courtney,
"Review," *Daily Telegraph* (8 December 1897), 4; "Unsigned Review,"
Spectator (25 December 1897), 940 [C, I, No. 8]; I. Zangwill, "Unsigned
Review," *Academy* (1 January 1898), 1–2; "Arthur Symons on Kipling
and Conrad," *Saturday Review* (29 January 1898), 145–46; Harold
Frederic, "Unsigned Review," *Saturday Review* (12 February 1898),
211.

Criticism of *Tales of Unrest*: "Unsigned Review," *Daily Telegraph*
(9 April 1898), 8; "Unsigned Review," *Daily Mail* (12 April 1898), 3;
Edward Garnett, "Unsigned Article," *Academy* (15 October 1898), 82–
83 [C, I, No. 15]; "Unsigned Article," *Academy* (14 January 1899), 65–
67 [C, I, No. 33].

Criticism of *Lord Jim*: "Unsigned Review," *Manchester Guardian*
(29 October 1900), 6; W. L. Courtney, "Review," *Daily Telegraph* (7
November 1900), 11; "Unsigned Review," *Academy* (10 November
1900), 443 [C, I, No. 38]; "Unsigned Sketch," *Sketch* (14 November
1900), 142; "Unsigned Review," *Spectator* (24 November 1900), 753;
"Unsigned Review," *Speaker* (24 November 1900), 215–16; "Unsigned
Review," *Pall Mall Gazette* (5 December 1900), 4; "Unsigned Review,"
Daily News (14 December 1900), 6; "Unsigned Review," *Bookman*
(February 1901), 161 [rpt. unchanged in *Bookman* (New York), April
1901]; "Unsigned Review," *Critic* (New York: May 1901), 437–38.

Criticism of *Youth: A Narrative and Two Other Stories*: "Conrad on 'Heart of Darkness,'" [not abstracted]; Edward Garnett, "Unsigned Review," *Academy and Literature* (6 December 1902), 606 [C, I, No. 48]; "Unsigned Review," *Manchester Guardian* (10 December 1902), 3; "Unsigned Review," *Times Literary Supplement* (12 December 1902), 372 [C, I, No. 53]; "Unsigned Review," *Athenaeum* (20 December 1902), 3921, 824 [C, I, No. 52]; "George Gissing on Conrad," [letter to Miss Collet: 12 December 1902 (*Letters of George Gissing to Members of His Family*, ed. by A. and E. Gissing, 1927), 391]; John Masefield, "Review," *Speaker* (31 January 1903), 442 [C, I, No. 58].

Criticism of *Typhoon, and Other Stories*: "Unsigned Review," *Morning Post* (22 April 1903), 3; "Unsigned Review," *Daily Mail* (22 April 1903), 4; "Unsigned Review," *Glasgow Evening News* (30 April 1903), 2; "Unsigned Notice," *Academy* (25 April 1903), [quotes the American (New York)]; "Unsigned Review," *Academy* (9 May 1903), 463–64 [C, I, No. 59]; A. T. Quiller-Couch, "Review," *Bookman* (June 1903), 108–109 [C, I, No. 61]; "Unsigned Review," *Speaker* (6 June 1903), 238–39.

Criticism of *Nostromo*: "Conrad on Writing Nostromo," [not abstracted]; "Arnold Bennett on *Nostromo*," (22 November 1912), (*Letters of Arnold Bennett*, ed. by James Hepburn, 1968), II, 143; "Conrad as a Personality in Modern Literature," *Academy* (20 February 1904) [C, I, No. 77]; "Unsigned Review," *Times Literary Supplement* (21 October 1904), 320; "Unsigned Notice," *Review of Reviews* (1 November 1904), 539; "Unsigned Notice," *Black and White* (5 November 1904), 668; "Unsigned Review," *Daily Telegraph* (9 November 1904), 4; C. D. O. Barrie, "Review," *British Weekly* (10 November 1904), 129; "Unsigned Review," *Manchester Guardian* (2 November 1904), 5; Edward Garnett, "Review," *Speaker* (12 November 1904), 138–39; John Buchan, "Unsigned Review," *Spectator* (19 November 1904), 800–01 [C, I, No. 68]; "Unsigned Notice," *Illustrated London News* (26 November 1904), 774.

Criticism of *The Secret Agent*: A. N. Monkhouse, "Review," *Manchester Guardian* (12 September 1907); "Unsigned Review," *Times Literary Supplement* (20 September 1907), 285 [C, I, No. 103]; "Unsigned Review," *Country Life* (21 September 1907), 403–05; "Arnold Bennett on *The Secret Agent*," [extract from Bennett's journal (*The Journals of Arnold Bennett*, ed. by Newman Flower, 1932), I, 256–57]; Edward Garnett, "Unsigned Review," *Nation* (28 September 1907); "Unsigned Notice," *Truth* (2 October 1907), 817; "Unsigned Review," *Glasgow News* (3 October 1907), 5; "Conrad's Reply to the Garnet [sic] Review," [not abstracted]; "Unsigned Notice," *Star* (5 October 1907), 1; Stewart Edward White, "Review," *Bookman* (New York: January 1908), 531–32 [C, I, No. 119]; "Unsigned Article,"

Edinburgh Review (April 1908); "John Galsworthy on Conrad," *Fortnightly Review* (April 1908), 89, 627–33.
    Criticism of *A Set of Six*: Robert Lynd, "Review," *Daily News* (10 August 1908), 3; W. L. Courtney, "Review," *Daily Telegraph* (12 August 1908), 4; "Unsigned Review," *Country Life* (15 August 1908), 234–35; "Conrad's Response to the Reviews," [not abstracted]; Edward Garnett, "Unsigned Review," *Nation* (22 August 1908), 746, 748; "Conrad on Garnett's Review in *Nation*," [not abstracted]; Edward Thomas, "Review," *Bookman* (October 1908), 39.
    Criticism of *Under Western Eyes*: "Unsigned Review," *Pall Mall Gazette* (11 October 1911), 5; Richard Curle, "Review," *Manchester Guardian* (11 October 1911), 5; "Unsigned Review," *Morning Post* (12 October 1911), 3; "Unsigned Review," *Westminster Gazette* (14 October 1911), 12; "Conrad's Defense of *Under Western Eyes*," [not abstracted]; Edward Garnett, "Unsigned Review," *Nation* (21 October 1911), 140–42; Ford Madox Hueffer, "Signed Article," *English Review* (December 1911–March 1912), 69–83 [C, I, No. 127, in part only].
    Criticism of *'Twixt Land and Sea*: Robert Lynd, "Review," *Daily News* (14 October 1912), 8; John Masefield, "Review," *Manchester Guardian* (16 October 1912), 7; "Unsigned Review," *Standard* (25 October 1912), 7; "Extract from *Spectator*" (16 November 1912), 815.
    Criticism of *Chance*: "Conrad, Letter to J. B. Pinker," [not abstracted]; "Conrad on Selling His Work in America," [letter to Alfred A. Knopf, not abstracted]; "Henry James's Criticism," [from "The New Novel" in *Notes on Novelists* (1914), 271–80], [C, I, No. 189]; Robert Lynd, "Review," *Daily News* (15 January 1914), 4; C. E. Montague, "Review," *Manchester Guardian* (15 January 1914), 6; "Arnold Bennett's Opinion," [extracts from *The Journal of Arnold Bennett*, ed. by Newman Flower, 1932 (18 January 1914, II, 79) and (24 January 1914), II, 80]; Edward Garnett, "Unsigned Review," *Nation* (24 January 1914), 720–22; "Some Opinions of *Chance*" (January 1914), [short comments from six reviews, all praising the novel]; "Unsigned Review," *Glasgow News* (5 February 1914, 10.
    Criticism of *Victory*: Robert Lynd, "Review," *Daily News* (24 September 1915), 6; "Unsigned Review," *Scotsman* (27 September 1915), 2; Walter de la Mare, "Unsigned Review," *Times Literary Supplement* (30 September 1915), 330 [C, I, No. 208]; Walter de la Mare, "Review," *Westminster Gazette* (2 October 1915); "Unsigned Review," *Nation* (2 October 1915), 25–26; "Unsigned Review," *Atlantic Monthly* (October 1915), 511 [C, I, No. 224]; Gerald Gould, "Review," *New Statesman* (2 October 1915), 622–23; "William Lyon Phelps on *Victory*," [extract from *The Advance of the English Novel* (1917), 217].
    Criticism of *The Shadow-Line*: "Unsigned Review," *Nation* (24 March 1917); "Extract from Unsigned Review," *Morning Post* (26 March 1917), 4; "Extract from Review," *Bookman* (June 1917), 98 [C, I,

No. 264]; Gerald Gould, "Review," *New Statesman* (31 March 1917), 618.

Criticism of *The Arrow of Gold*: "Extract from Review," *New Republic* (10 May 1919), 56 [C, I, No. 302]; "Unsigned Review," *Morning Post* (6 August 1919), 3; Walter de la Mare, "Unsigned Review," *Times Literary Supplement* (7 August 1919), 422 [C, I, No. 308]; "Unsigned Review," *New Statesman* (16 August 1919), 497; "W. L. Courtney on Conrad's Admirers and Detractors," *Daily Telegraph* (29 August 1919), 4; "Unsigned Review," *Nation* (6 September 1919), 680–82.

Criticism of *The Rescue*: "Conrad on Completing *The Rescue*," [not abstracted]; "Unsigned Review," *Morning Post* (25 June 1920), 4; Virginia Woolf, "Unsigned Review," *Times Literary Supplement* (1 July 1920), 419 [C, I, No. 324]; "Unsigned Review," *Punch* (14 July 1920), 39; "Unsigned Review," *Nation* (17 July 1920), 503–04; W. Douglas Newton, "Review," *Sketch* (21 July 1920), 428; "Unsigned Review," *London Mercury* (August 1920), 497–98; "E. M. Forster's Criticism of Conrad," [extracted from "Joseph Conrad: A Note" (1920), in *Abinger Harvest* (1942)].

Criticism of *The Rover*: "Unsigned Review," *Manchester Guardian* (3 December 1923), 5; Frederic F. Van de Water, "Review," *New York Tribune* (4 December 1923), 16; "Unsigned Review," *Times Literary Supplement* (6 December 1923), 849 [C, I, No. 435]; "Unsigned Review," *Glasgow Evening News* (6 December 1923), 2; Raymond Mortimer, "Review," *New Statesman* (15 December 1923), 306 [C, I, No. 437]; "Conrad, Letter to John Galsworthy" (22 February 1924), [not abstracted]; "Desmond MacCarthy on the Quality of *The Rover*," [extracted from MacCarthy, *Portraits* (1931), [C, I, No. 931].

Criticism of *Suspense, A Napoleonic Novel*: "Conrad on the Reception of *The Rover* and *Suspense*," [not abstracted]; "J. C. Squire on the Death of Conrad," *London Mercury* (September 1924), 449–50 [C, I, No. 491]; P. C. Kennedy, "Review," *New Statesman* (26 September 1925), 666 [C, I, No. 627]; Leonard Woolf, "Review," *Nation and Athenaeum* (3 October 1925), 18 [C, I, No. 667]; "Garnett's Answer to Kennedy's Review," *Weekly Westminster* (10 October 1925); "Unsigned Review," *Spectator* (10 October 1925), 613–14; Milton Waldman, "Review," *London Mercury* (November 1925), 97–98 [C, I, No. 664]; "W. Somerset Maugham on Conrad's Bornean Novels" (1933), [the fictional discussion in Maugham's story "Neil MacAdam" between MacAdam and his wife Darya represents Maugham's own point of view].

[An invaluable collection of criticism of JC's works now very difficult to find.]

2960 Sherry, Norman. "Introduction," *CCH* (1973), pp. 1–44.

On the whole, JC fared "extremely well" at the hands of contemporary reviewers, but from the beginning the critics recognized the characteristics which would prevent him from becoming a "popular" writer. Initially, reviewers were puzzled as to how to "place" him and how to compare him with contemporary writers. An interesting aspect of his reputation is his reaction to the criticism, his constant attempts, increasing in later years, to assist in moulding it. He was deeply concerned about the reputation of his works; he wanted his "art" to be properly understood and he also wanted to make money out of it. His basic need being the earning of a living, he had some problems with publishers. The first two novels were considered as the works of "a writer of genius"; *The Nigger of the Narcissus* added to his fame; and *Lord Jim*, "Youth," and *Typhoon* made him especially well known to the critics. *Nostromo*, *The Secret Agent*, and *Under Western Eyes* met a somewhat unsympathetic public; but his later works, including *Chance* and those that followed, led the critics from evaluation to adoration. *The Arrow of Gold* made him "the grand old man of letters," even if a decline is seen in his last works. [Sherry provides an excellent survey of the contemporary criticism of JC and also includes the major critical works since 1930.]

2961 Siciliano, Enzo. "Cittadino del romanzo" (Citizen of the World of the Novel), *IL Mondo*, XXV, 34–35 (30 August 1973), p. 20. rpt. in part as the introduction to *Con gli occhi dell'occidente* (Under Western Eyes), ed. by Enzo Siciliano (Milan: Garzanti, 1973), [pp. xv-xix].

The strength of *Under Western Eyes* lies in the deciphering with an intuitive sense, the making of a Fascist avant-lettre. Razumov is a Fascist; the son of a nobleman, he has no roots; his only hope of social advancement frustrates his projects and destroys his whole life. [In Italian.]

2962 Singh, Ramchander. "Nostromo: The Betrayed Self," *Literary Criterion* (University of Mysore), X (Summer 1973), pp. 61–66.

In *Nostromo*, JC tries to show the impact of a kind of social organization on the self. The incorruptible Nostromo is nothing but what his society reflects back to him, but it becomes so much a part of his thinking and of his psyche that any change in this idea is suggestive of a change in the world. This change begins when a shipment of silver from the Gould mine is endangered by the Monterist revolution. Nostromo's mission to save the silver proves suicidal for him, for his "self-idea" is undermined by Teresa Viola, wife of old Giorgio, who curses him because he refuses to bring a priest for her when she is dying. After he has been compelled to renounce his public splendor and considered now as an ordinary man, he begins his conversion to material things. After his return with General Barrios's army, he is totally devoid of social status. The only flaw in his honesty is the suspicion that he is suspected, but he now wanders, isolated from others in the act of serving. His very identity has been lost. The disgusting consequence of his loss of moral identity in the public and his feelings of guilt entrap him and lead him to his death.

2963 Slade, Joseph W. "The World's Greatest Fiction Writer: An American Poet on Joseph Conrad," *CON*, V, No. 1 (1973), pp. 5–11.

Edwin Markham, the best known American poet of the first decade of the twentieth century, knew JC's work well and published several comments on it. He also wrote to JC, who answered at least twice. His major statement about the Anglo-Polish writer was, "The World's Greatest Fiction Writer: Why This Honor Goes to Joseph Conrad, Born a Pole—A Stranger to the English Language for Seventeen Years." He recognized in JC the reconciliation of the two opposing aspects of his own literary consciousness which he could not attain, romanticism and realism. [Reprints two of JC's letters to Markham, a "thank you" note dated July 10, 1912, and a partially handwritten and partially dictated and typed letter of June 30, 1920.]

2964 Spiegel, Alan. "Flaubert to Joyce: Evolution of a Cinematographic Form," *Novel*, VI (Spring 1973), pp. 229–43.

In a substantial body of the fiction produced in the last hundred years, including the reified art of Flaubert and such modern "reificationists" as JC, Joyce, Faulkner, Nabokov, and Robbe-Grillet, the action of the works is often understood in terms of what is seen, that is, transmitted in words that evoke expressive visual images. This form "presents and portrays rather than comments and explains—in terms of an action that is *seen*." JC seems to have utilized this "film space" throughout his literary career. "Heart of Darkness," for example, contains a somewhat exaggerated and "aggressive display" of "camera vision" and also has the remnants of Flaubert's legacy of an entire literary era "permeated by the results of analytic, objectivistic, and Positivistic thinking." And like Henry James, JC literally "decomposes his field" into an arrangement of successive views, but he does not make one view flow logically into the next, but rather orders the visual fragments into a relatively discontinuous sequence. He uses this "cinematic razzle dazzle" in order to create a visual field and a manner of apprehension that is commensurate with a context of mystery, physical adventure, and moral enigma. What JC sees and what he knows about what he sees often represent two different levels of cognition that do not easily

mix. JC is thus a major part of the modern novel from Flaubert to
Robbe-Grillet.

2965 St. Aubyn, F. C. "The Secret Sharers: Conrad and Schehadé,"
Revue de Littérature Comparée, XLVII (July–September 1973),
pp. 456–64.

JC's "The Secret Sharer" is comparable to the Lebanese Georges
Schehadé's play, *Le Voyage,* in many ways, although the two works
are quite different in spirit. Both works dramatize stories of the
nineteenth-century British merchant marine, both take place in
exotic locales, both are concerned with self-identification, both deal
with pardoxes of innocence and guilt, both satirize British
tradesmen, both play on the meanings of proper names, both have
major characters who figuratively lose their heads, and both end with
an act of generosity.

2966 Strojan, Richard F. "Conrad's Marlow Stories," *DAI,* XXXIII
(1973), 4433A. Unpublished dissertation, University of
Pittsburgh, 1972.

2967 Sullivan, Walter. "Irony and Disorder: *The Secret Agent,"
Sewanee Review,* LXXXI (Winter 1973), pp. 124–31.

JC's ironic view of human behavior is most clearly drawn in *The
Secret Agent.* Every character's thoughts and actions are directed
towards satisfying his own interests. Because selfishness, not the
ideals of society, or a group, motivates the characters of the novel,
men stand alone. Quite pointedly in this respect, the novel, through
its series of characters, demonstrates that men cannot successfully
solve their own problems independently or survive by merely
depending on their individual intellectual capabilities. For instance,
Verloc, beginning with the intention of serving as a revolutionary, is
easily swayed from this course of action by his own need for comfort
to satisfy his slothful nature. Unwilling either to live a life of austerity
or to work, he becomes a counteragent, informing on his fellow
revolutionaries. Mrs. Verloc, too, violates the ideals of society, for she
marries Verloc not for love but for security. Likewise, the
revolutionaries, like Mr. Vladimir, do not live for a common cause or
ideal. Inspector Heat, no better than the representative of the
repressive society of Russia, exploits it for his own interest. *Agent* is
timely, for it clearly reflects our own age.

2968 Thornton, Weldon. "An Episode from Anglo-Irish History in
Conrad's *The Secret Agent,"* *English Language Notes,* X (June
1973), pp. 286–89.

JC's brief account of Michaelis's imprisonment in *The Secret Agent* refers directly to an event in Manchester, England in September, 1867, which remained an important point of Anglo-Irish contention on into the twentieth century: the trial and hanging of three Fenians, called the "Manchester murders." JC's use of this incident confirms his interest in anarchistic activities and offers another source for the character of Michaelis.

2969 Turnbull, Andrew (ed.). *The Letters of F. Scott Fitzgerald* (New York: Charles Scribner's, 1973), pp. 97, 102, 151, 169, 182, 187, 211, 300–01, 309, 342, 362–63, 480, 482, 510–11, 543.

Many writers, JC for instance, have been aided by being brought up in surroundings utterly unrelated to literature. The first people who "risked" JC certainly did not support him as a commercial venture. He has been [in 1928] "the healthy influence on the technique of the novel." The theory in his preface to *The Nigger of the Narcissus* is that "the purpose of a work of fiction is to appeal to the lingering after-effects in the reader's mind as differing from, say, the purpose of oratory or philosophy which respectively leave people in a fighting or thoughtful mood." Both Ernest Hemingway and Fitzgerald "got the germ" of the idea that "the dying fall was preferable to the dramatic ending under certain conditions" from JC. Eugene O'Neill in *The Emperor Jones*, Joseph Hergesheimer in *Java Head*, Fitzgerald in *The Great Gatsby*, and Somerset Maugham in *The Moon and Sixpence* imitated JC. In reading *Manila Galleon*, Fitzgerald was reminded of *Victory*, just as I suppose Conrad was reminded of something when he wrote *Victory*. "I loved it." [Random comments on JC from Fitzgerald's letters.]

2970 Vigini, Giuliano. "Romanzi occidentali" (Western Novels), *Letture* (Milan), XXVIII, 5 (1973), pp. 426–27.

[Short review, mainly descriptive of contents, of the Italian edition (*Romanzi occidentali*, Milan: Mursia, 1972), of *Nostromo, The Secret Agent, Under Western Eyes, Chance*.] [In Italian.]

2971 Walsh, Dennis M. "Christian Allusion in the Fiction of Joseph Conrad," *DAI*, XXXIV (1973), 2660A. Unpublished dissertation, University of Notre Dame, 1973.

2972 Ward, David. *T. S. Eliot Between Two Worlds* (London and Boston: Routledge and Kegan Paul, 1973), pp. 47, 71–73, 79, 110–11, 116–17, 253–54, 281.

When T. S. Eliot was young, he and other scholars were interested in the development of anthropology in order to learn what they could about the genesis and development of European civilization as a means of coming to terms with the present. For this was an age when European man came to feel less and less secure in the pride of his civilization and to realize how deeply it was rooted in patterns of inherited primitive thought and feelings. The realization of this veneer of civilization was probably most strongly expressed in JC's "Heart of Darkness" (1902). Eliot's first choice of an epigraph for *The Waste Land,* from "Heart of Darkness" (later replaced by one from Petronius) is in some ways a more fitting preparation for the poem: Kurtz, unlike the Sibyl, is prophetic only in the sense that he is finally brought to the point where the entire structure of action and belief collapses upon itself and leaves only emptiness, hopelessness, and horror, which seem to depict the universe. The opening of the Thames-daughters passage in Eliot's poem seems to be unlike JC's description of the scene when Marlow stops talking. In some important ways, though, Eliot's journey in *The Waste Land* resembles Marlow's in "Heart of Darkness."

2973 Watt, Ian. "Composition of *The Secret Agent,*" *CSAC* (1973), pp. 13–25.

[An account of JC's development of *The Secret Agent* from a short story, "Verloc," to the completed novel, with emphasis on the "Author's Note" by JC, written in 1920 and with several quotations from JC's letters which most clearly reveal the stages of the composition of the novel.]

2974 Watt, Ian (ed.). *Conrad, The Secret Agent: A Casebook* (London: Macmillan, 1973).

Part One, "Critical Survey," Ian Watt: "Composition of *The Secret Agent,*" "Contemporary Reviews," "Later Criticism During Conrad's Lifetime," "Modern Criticism: General Trends," "Some Other Critical Issues," "The Versions of *The Secret Agent*" (1973).

Part Two, "Critical Essays": John Galsworthy, "Joseph Conrad: A Disquisition," *Fortnightly Review* (1 April 1908), (C, I, No. 108); Thomas Mann, "Joseph Conrad's *The Secret Agent,*" from *Past Masters, and Other Papers* (1933); Hugh Walpole, "From A *Conrad Memorial Library: The Collection of George T. Keating* (1929), (C, I, No. 899); F. R. Leavis, "From *The Great Tradition: George Eliot, Henry James, Joseph Conrad*" (1948); V. S. Pritchett, "An Emigré," from *Books in General* (1953), (C, I, No. 1288); Irving Howe, "Conrad: Order and Anarchy," from *Politics and the Novel* (1957); Albert J. Guerard, "A Version of Anarchy," from *Conrad the Novelist* (1958), (C, I, No. 1477); Robert D. Spector, "Irony as Theme: Conrad's *The Secret Agent,*" from *Nineteenth-Century Fiction,* XIII (1958), (C, I, No. 1503); Avrom Fleishman, "The Symbolic World of *The Secret Agent,*" from

English Literary History, XXXII (1965), (C, I, No. 1866); J. Hillis Miller, "From *Poets of Reality: Six Twentieth-Century Writers* (1965), (C, I, No. 1897); Norman Sherry, "The Greenwich Bomb Outrage and *The Secret Agent*," from *Review of English Studies*, ns. XVIII (1967); Ian Watt, "The Political and Social Background of *The Secret Agent*" (1973). [A "Select Bibliography" lists other major commentaries on *The Secret Agent*. "Notes on Contributors" briefly identifies each contributor chosen for this volume. The range of critical essays is excellent, as are the contributions of the editor.]

2975 Watt, Ian. "Contemporary Reviews," *CSAC* (1973), pp. 26–58.

Not long after the publication of *The Secret Agent* in 1907 in both London and New York, JC considered it an "honourable failure" as to reviews and sales. The critics gave him a certain deference because he was an important established author; but never forgetting that he was a Slav, they tended to treat him mainly as a curiosity. Furthermore, they concentrated on the things in the novel which were most likely to cause the ordinary reader to turn away from it. [The "mixed reception" of *Agent* is told largely in selections from letters and contemporary reviews.]

2976 Watt, Ian. "Later Criticism During Conrad's Lifetime," *CSAC* , ed. by Ian Watt (London: Macmillan) (1973), pp. 59–65.

From John Galsworthy's perception of the irony in *The Secret Agent* in his essay of 1908 until after the end of World War I, the amount of writing about JC increased rapidly, especially after Richard Curle's book of 1914; but most of it was journalistic. Since the main emphasis lay on the tales of the sea, *Agent* was relatively neglected.

2977 Watt, Ian. "Modern Criticism: General Trends," *CSAC* (1973), pp. 66–76.

JC's death in 1924 brought about a flood of tributes, of which Ford Madox Ford's *Joseph Conrad: A Personal Remembrance* (1924) is most important. In the 1920s, the two most significant treatments of *The Secret Agent* were probably by Hugh Walpole and Thomas Mann. In the 1930s, JC's "pessimistic conservatism" was out of accord with the prevailingly radical ideology; the "most interesting" study of this decade was Edward Crankshaw's book of 1936 in that, among other things, he recognized the importance of narrative point of view and believed *Agent* to be JC's greatest technical achievement. After World War II, the great boom in JC studies began. Important are the works of F. R. Leavis, Irving Howe, John Hagan, Jr., and E. M. W. Tillyard. The symbolic approach is well represented by Robert W. Stallman and Avrom Fleishman, the phenomenological attitude by J.

Hillis Miller, and the psychological analysis by Albert Guerard. Some lack of enthusiasm for *Agent* is noticeable. Bernard Meyer's recent biography raises a basic problem: we do not have enough evidence to reconstruct adequately JC's inner life. The many critical stances remain, though, far from exhausting the critical issues raised by *Agent.* [A good survey of criticism of JC in general.]

2978 Watt, Ian. "The Political and Social Background of *The Secret Agent,*" *CSAC* (1973), pp. 229–51.

Although Norman Sherry gives (in "The Greenwich Bomb Outrage and *The Secret Agent,*" *Review of English Studies,* ns. XVIII [November 1967], pp. 412–28) a careful account of the main historical source of *The Secret Agent,* the Greenwich Park explosion of 14 February 1894, JC also received material or suggestions from various writings of Ford Madox Ford, even if they are not historically accurate, and from the example of a former Russian Minister of Police, General Seliverskov. JC increases the distance between fact and fiction by creating a tighter domestic drama and by adding Vladimir. Although *Agent* is neither an historical nor a Naturalistic novel, "its distance from reality, though varying, is never very great." JC includes a wide spectrum of persons and motives in his anarchists, but he spares the English, perhaps because some of his friends had been associated with anarchism and also because his own "notion of decorum made him adverse to any direct political criticism of his adopted country."

2979 Watt, Ian. "Some Other Critical Issues," *CSAC* (1973), pp. 77–80.

One important question about *The Secret Agent* remains unanswered in the body of critical writing: how so depressing a tale should be, for some readers at least, tonic rather than depressive in its final effect. The elements of the comic style in the novel need to be defined, for this style invites us to join in JC's process of looking closely and darkly at modern urban civilization without being overwhelmed.

2980 Watt, Ian. "The Versions of *The Secret Agent,*" *CSAC* (1973), pp. 81–85.

The Secret Agent may be said to exist in six versions: JC's complete manuscript, the serial version, the book forms, JC's two dramatizations of the novel, and a film version named *Sabotage* in England and *A Woman Alone* in the United States.

2981 Webb, Michael. "Conrad's Use of the Motto *'Usque ad Finem'* in *Lord Jim* and a Letter to Bertrand Russell," *CON*, V, No. 2 (1973), pp. 74–80.

The Latin motto, "*usque ad finem*" (unto the end), which appears in Stein's reflections on Jim's "case" in chapter 20 of *Lord Jim* (1900), appears also in a letter of Tadeusz Bobrowski of 9 November 1891 to JC, and it turns up again in a letter of 22 December 1913 from JC to Bertrand Russell. Bobrowski's use of the motto probably came from the Book of Job: for JC's uncle, duty meant obedience and resignation to one's situation in life. It seems likely that JC was impressed by the ideas in his uncle's letter, received soon after his return from the Congo. According to Bobrowski, there were two strains in JC's temperament, the stoic and determined, which he approved of, and the idealistic and visionary, the unfortunate strain from his father's family. JC's use of sources from his past experiences must have been largely conscious. In the passage in *Jim*, he has adapted his uncle's view of his own "romantic" character and, by way of Stein, attributed it to Jim. Stein's statement makes the Latin tag more ambiguous than Bobrowski's meaning of the phrase. From one point of view, Jim's death is a victory, from another, his only possible escape. It may be that JC's irony constitutes the feeling of the contingency of human ideals; his extremes of disdain and depravity are balanced by his basic, though simple, loyalties. His detachment is best seen in *Jim*, "Heart of Darkness," *Nostromo*, and *Victory*.

2982 Weiss, Alan Z. "Free Trade, Parasitism, Protection: Studies in the Fiction of English Imperialism, 1886–1910," *DAI*, XXXIII (1973), 4438A. Unpublished dissertation, SUNY-Buffalo, 1972.

2983 Weston, John Howard. "The Vision of Joseph Conrad, 1885–1900," *DAI*, XXXVII (1973), 3656. Unpublished dissertation, Columbia University, 1973.

2984 Wiley, Paul L. (comp.). *The British Novel: Conrad to the Present* (Northbrook, Illinois: AHM Publishing Corporation [Goldentree Bibliographies in Language and Literature], 1973), pp. 24–32.

[This lengthy bibliography, with very few annotations, includes items classified as "Texts," "Bibliographies," "Critical and Bibliographical Books," and "Critical Essays." The items included are reasonably good for the space allotted to JC.]

2985 Wilhemus, Thomas Alan. "Grotesque Irony and Popular Entertainment, A Public and Private Motif in Joseph Conrad's

Fiction," *DAI*, XXXIII (1973), 5755A. Unpublished dissertation, University of Notre Dame, 1973.

2986 Wyatt, Robert D. "Joseph Conrad's 'The Secret Sharer': Point of View and Mistaken Identities," *CON*, V, No. 1 (1973), pp. 12–26.

JC's problem in "The Secret Sharer" was, in a work rendered by a first person narrator, to remain personally indifferent and yet provide a basis for a judgment from the dramatic whole. This he achieved by the devices of the narrator's consistency, repetition of key words and phrases, and foil characters. Early in the story, the reader begins to doubt the narrator's reliability; and he soon notes the "split consciousness" of the captain, who accepts Leggatt's tale too readily and projects onto Archbold several doubts which are more appropriate to his own relationship with Leggatt. The ending of the story also shows the narrator's behavior to be "less than laudable": the captain, having completely lost control of his ship, is able by the mere chance of the appearance of the hat on the water, to save his vessel. JC, then, reveals a character who attributes meanings to events which are not justified by the events themselves. His behavior displays "impulse, oversight and obsession and is proportional to that immense insecurity which generates his need for illusion." Critical disagreement about this story has come from overlooking such formal problems as point of view and mistaken identities.

1974

2987 Adams, Barbara Block. "Sisters Under Their Skins: The Women in the Lives of Raskolnikov and Razumov," *CON*, VI, No. 2 (1974), 113–24.

Both Dosteovski and JC use female characters to manipulate their male protagonists and to propel the action of the stories. In *Crime and Punishment*, the women are responsible for both the fall and the subsequent rise of Raskolnikov; in *Under Western Eyes*, Razumov is driven to his dilemma not by any particular woman but by the symbolic woman, Mother Russia, who betrays and rejects him. He does not receive active redemption through the women in the novel as does Raskolnikov, but he receives at least "just" punishment and exposure so that he is no longer alone in his "moral abyss." JC's women "mirror" Dostoevski's: their relationships to Razumov and Raskolnikov reveal the true nature of these alienated men who want to be left alone, yet fear loneliness. Dostoevski's man was trying to enter the "godless twentieth century" but did not go all the way; his women helped him remain in the familiar Christian nineteenth century. JC's man is the "modern, guilt-ridden existential exile, facing moral dilemma without the crutch of religion" ; his women help him to come in from the cold of moral isolation into "the imperfect world of men where answers are temporary and relative." Thus the roles of the women, the same in both centuries, remain "eternal figures" in what is still a man's world.

2988 Andersen, Steen. "Aksel Sandemose og Joseph Conrad" (Aksel Sandemose and Joseph Conrad), *Om Sandemose: En Rapport Fra Janta,* ed. by Johnnes Vaeth (Nykobing, Mors: Attika, 1974), pp. 141–54.

[Mainly on Sandemose.] The allegations that Sandemose was influenced by JC were contemptuously denied by the former, and with some justification. Yet parallels exist in the works of both of these writers of sea-novels, particularly in their recurring themes of flight and isolation. [In Norwegian.]

2989 Belden, Daniel M. "The Hero as Failure in an Age of Hero Worship: Five Victorian Writers," *DAI,* XXXV (1974), 393A. Unpublished dissertation, University of Michigan, 1973.

2990 Bennett, Arnold. "Some Personal Memories of Conrad: 'Cad' as a New Word: His 'Twilight,'" *The 'Evening Standard' Years: 'Books and Persons' 1926–1931,* ed. with an introduction by Andrew Mylett (London: Chatto & Windus, 1974), pp. 96–98.

Bennett first met JC in 1899 at the home of H. G. Wells. It was evident even then that for him his writing was more of a war than a literary pursuit. His working days were terrible, and he gained his victories only at great cost. At that time, his English was not perfect, and he did not fully understand English literature. He was, though, reading all he could. He once learned from Bennett the word "cad." He also gloomily complained of feeling trapped in a groove because of his relations with his publisher. Later, in Bennett's copy of *The Rover,* JC wrote: "Twilight lies already on these pages."

2991 Bennett, Ernest. "Where to Start with Conrad," *JCSN,* [I], No. 3 (February 1974), p. 7.

It is difficult to suggest a starting place for the new readers of JC; possibilities are *Nostromo, Lord Jim, The Rover, A Set of Six,* or the gun-running episode of *The Mirror of the Sea.* Perhaps one should follow his own predilections and enthusiasm.

2992 Brandi, Cesare. "Conrad nei ricordi del figlio" (Conrad in His Son's Souvenirs), *Libertá* (15 October 1974), p. 3; rpt. "Joseph Conrad fu per me soprattutto un padre appassionato di letteratura" (For Me Joseph Conrad Was Above All a Father Fond of Literature), *Corriere del Ticino* (30 October 1974), p. 3; rpt. "Conrad," *La Provincia* (7 February 1975), p. 3.

[A report on the Canterbury JC Conference of 1974 and an interview with Borys Conrad, whose words, however, are all to be found also in the Italian edition of his reminiscences. Repeats three times the absurd claim that JC spent long decades of his life on the *Otago.*] [In Italian.]

2993 Brebach, Raymond T. "The Making of *Romance*, Part Fifth," *CON*, VI, No. 3 (1974), pp. 171–81.

The extant fragments of manuscripts and typescripts of *Romance* make it possible to chart stages in the novel's complex development and to speculate with "a fair degree of accuracy" about the working relationship between Ford Madox Ford and JC. Material for Part Fifth of *Romance* can be traced back to its origin in an early unpublished novel which Ford wrote independently in the 1890s, and the corrected proofs for this section, especially for JC's revisions of the last three pages, give a "clear and unambiguous" picture of the way Ford and JC worked as collaborators. In "Seraphina," Ford's first version of the work (completed by November, 1898), the author failed to exploit possibilities for building suspense and he left the plot too loose. After agreeing to collaborate on the story, Ford and JC proposed a kind of working outline which indicates the degree and quality of the difference between Ford's story and the novel projected by the two men. It appears that Ford learned a great deal about writing and revising fiction from JC and that he was able to apply his knowledge to working on the proofs of *Romance*. But Ford was definitely the apprentice to JC, the master craftsman, in constructing a plot, providing suitable introductions and motivations for characters, and keeping the facts of previous events in a story before the eyes of a reader without seeming to let them intrude.

2994 Bruss, Paul S[amuel]. "Conrad's 'Youth': Problems of Interpretation," *College Literature*, I (Fall 1974), pp. 218–219.

The question as to whether the young Marlow in "Youth" matures on his way to the East is complicated by the confusion surrounding the older Marlow's narrative irony, by the second mate's enthusiasm for romance, and by the conclusion that the young Marlow's supposed development during the voyage on the *Judea* is rather sudden. The logical conclusion is that the young Marlow develops from the six-month delay at Falmouth to his eventual realization that he can accept both the romance and the tedium of the journey; that is, he is reconciled to the ill-fate of the hapless *Judea* and the leisurely satisfaction of his desire for adventure, thus becoming a part of the navigator's tradition which includes both tedium and romance. In this way the young Marlow matures in a natural manner and is therefore immune to the self-deprecatory constructions the sentimental and ironic elder Marlow places on his behavior twenty-two years earlier.

2995 Bruss, Paul S[amuel]. "*Lord Jim* and the Metaphor of Awakening," *Studies in the Twentieth Century*, No. 14 (Fall 1974), pp. 69–89.

The resolution of the problem as to whether or not Jim, in *Lord Jim*, is triumphant in Patusan is difficult: the reader must, if he is to interpret Jim's final action as being redeeming or foolhardy, or whatever, first of all not be prejudiced by Marlow's early narrative of Jim before he enters Patusan. And then later, when Marlow is no longer in direct contact with Jim in Patusan and consequently has muted his judgments of Jim, the reader must still maintain a proper distance from Marlow, this time in order to "locate the subtle metaphoric patterns in which [Marlow] has disguised his judgment." In Marlow's Patusan narrative, there are two distinct narratives, one clearly a surface narrative and the other metaphoric. The surface story, dominated by Jim, usually persuades the casual reader into thinking that Jim is finally mature and successful, e.g., in his triumph over Sherif Ali and his men. The subtlety of the metaphoric level, however, clearly suggests the contrary. At strategic points in the Patusan narrative, Marlow describes Jim as awakening from a passive state, as when Jim is inside the stockade and when "he comes to himself" in the mudbank and both times fights seemingly like a hero for his life. The metaphor of awakening from passivity is, however, ironic. Instead of being motivated by a mature view of courage, Jim is again influenced by the dream world of his egotism that contributed to his dismal failure aboard the *Patna*. [An extension of Elliott B. Gose, Jr., "Pure Exercise of Imagination: Archetypal Symbolism in *Lord Jim*," (C, I, No. 1790).]

2996 Buczkowski, Yvonne. "Female Characters in Conrad's Novels and Short Stories: A Bibliographical Note," *Modernist Studies*, I, No. 3 (1974–1975), pp. 51–57.

To date there has been no agreement about the nature of JC's attitude towards women. Some authors maintain that JC had little knowledge of feminine psychology, some stress the variety of types he created, others differ as to whether his heroines are modeled on any literary tradition or whether they follow conventional "character" patterns, and still others ask to what extent his treatment of women may be judged as superficial. The attached bibliography consists of presently available material in which JC's presentation of female characters is discussed at some length. Original and Russian studies not yet translated into English have been abstracted. [Seven Polish and Russian items and twelve in English are abstracted.]

2997 Chapple, J. A. V. "Conrad," *The English Novel: Select Bibliographical Guides*, ed. by A. E. Dyson (London: Oxford University Press, 1974), pp. 300–13.

[Consists of discussions and lists of JC's texts; critical studies and commentaries, emphasizing the major works; biographies and letters; bibliographies; background reading; and an additional list of "References," with comments. Unfortunately, textual problems are slighted.]

2998 Chung, Hae-Ja Kim. "Point of View as a Mode of Thematic Definition in Conrad and Faulkner," *DAI*, XXXV (1974), 442A–43A. Unpublished dissertation, University of Michigan, 1973.

2999 Cianci, Giovanni. "'Heart of Darkness': Il compromesso con l'ippopotamo" ("Heart of Darkness": The Compromise with the Hippopotamus), *Studi Inglesi*, 1 (1974), pp. 167–201.

The various stages that take Marlow to the heart of the Congo constitute the several moments of the moral definition of Kurtz's tragic greatness. The narration of the long, mysterious journey through the hostile solitude of nature, with partial anticipations and long digressions, represents the historical dimension in which Kurtz's macabre choice has matured. Marlow is able to relate his experience in the wider context of colonialism, even though episodically, because he has only a very short glance at reality, half waking, between fits of fever and hallucinations. But he does not go beyond the final threshold; he does not live his experience to the full. And consequently, Kurtz's final cry can merely suggest the picture of his own moral degradation: this compromise in the quest for truth is the indispensable condition to make the narrative possible. It is, on a symbolic level, the compromise between the slight scent of the chief accountant and the disgusting smell of the rotting hippopotamus in the steady buzz of flies, in the insoluble mystery of the forest. If Marlow is to survive, he cannot help breathing, if only for a second, that appalling atmosphere. [In Italian.]

3000 Citati, Piero. "Fantasma dal nulla" (A Phantom out of Nothingness), *Corriere della Sera* (12 May 1974), p. 12.

[Review of *Cuore di tenebra* (Heart of Darkness), (Turin: Einaudi, 1974).] [In Italian.]

3001 Clareson, Thomas D. "Robert Silverberg: The Compleat Writer," *Magazine of Fantasy and Science Fiction*, XXV (April 1974), p. 76.

[Robert Silverberg finds reinforcement for his novel *Downward to the Earth* by evoking the image of Kurtz in "Heart of Darkness."]

3002 Collins, Patrick R. "Existentialist Qualities of the Protagonist in Selected Stories and Novels by Joseph Conrad," *DAI*, XXXIV (1974), 7185A. Unpublished dissertation, Bowling Green State University, 1973.

3003 Conrad, Borys. *Coach Tour of Joseph Conrad's Homes in Kent* (Farnham, Surrey: Farnham Printing Company, 1974).

Contents, abstracted under year of first publication: "Pent Farm, Postling, Nr. Hythe, 1898–1907" ; "Capel House, Orlestone, Nr. Ashford, June 1910–March 1919"; "Spring Grove, Wye, Nr. Ashford, March–September 1919" ; "'Oswalds,' Bishopsbourne, Nr. Canterbury, September 1919–August 1924." [Gives unpaged pamphlet, c. fifteen pages.]

3004 Conrad, Borys. "Joseph Conrad's Homes in Kent: 1. Pent Farm, Postling, Nr. Hythe, 1898–1907," *Joseph Conrad Society Newsletter* (U.K), [I], No. 4 (June 1974), p. 12; rpt. *Coach Tour of Joseph Conrad's Homes in Kent* (Farnham, Surrey: Farnham Printing Company, 1974), unpaged.

Pent Farm, and old farmhouse, was the second home occupied by JC and his family after his marriage. JC took over the tenancy from Ford Madox Hueffer. Works associated with the Pent are "Youth," "Heart of Darkness," *Lord Jim, Tales of Unrest, Nostromo,* "Typhoon," *The Secret Agent, Chance, The Mirror of the Sea,* and "The End of the Tether." Such people as the following visited JC at the Pent: John Galsworthy, H. G. Wells, William Rothenstein, Stephen Crane, R. B. Cunninghame Graham, Fountain Hope, Henry James, W. H. Hudson, Sir Hugh Clifford, Roger Casement, and Major A. J. Dawson and his brother Ernest, who aroused in JC an interest in motor cars. Mrs. Conrad's increasing incapacity and the advent of Borys's small brother necessitated the move to a larger house.

3005 Conrad, Borys. "The Joseph Conrad Homes in Kent: 2. Capel House, Orlestone, Nr. Ashford, June 1910–March 1919," *JCSN*, [I], No. 5 (October 1974), pp. 7–8; rpt. *Coach Tour of Joseph Conrad's*

Homes in Kent (Farnham, Surrey: Farnham Printing Company, 1974), unpaged.

Capel House was undoubtedly the happiest of the JC homes. Reginald Perceval Gibbon became a friend of Borys's and helped induce him to buy a "secondhand 12-horse-power Cadillac," which both of JC's parents learned to drive. In addition to the friends from the Pent, other people visited JC: Arthur Marwood, Hugh Walpole, Jean-Aubry, Norman Douglas, and Richard Curle. Here, too, the Conrads made the acquaintance of Warrington Dawson, and André Gide and Valery Larbaud came to visit the Conrads there. Joseph Retinger and his wife came in 1912, and then they accompanied the JC family to Poland in 1914.

3006 Conrad, Borys. "'Oswalds,' Bishopsbourne, Nr. Canterbury, September 1919–August 3, 1924," *Coach Tour of Joseph Conrad's Homes in Kent* (Farnham, Surrey: Farnham Printing Company, 1974), unpaged.

On the whole, JC was happy at "Oswalds." He published *The Arrow of Gold* the same month in which he moved to this home. In 1920, the Conrads were joined in Corsica by J. B. Pinker and his wife. After their return home, the number of visitors seemed to increase. One of them, John Powell, the American pianist, played Chopin on the baby grand piano for JC by the hour. It was there that JC died, with Borys and his younger brother present. [The last of four brief articles by Borys Conrad.]

3007 Conrad, Borys. "Spring Grove, Wye, Nr. Ashford, March 1919–September 1919," *Coach Tour of Joseph Conrad's Homes in Kent* (Farnham, Surrey: Farnham Printing Company, 1974), unpaged; rpt. "Joseph Conrad's Homes in Kent: 3, Spring Grove, Wye, Canterbury, March–September 1919," *JCSN*, [I], No. 6 (March 1975), p. 12.

To Spring Grove came the vast circle of friends who had been visiting JC in the past, including Pinker, JC's agent, Jean-Aubry, who was to be his biographer, in addition to two American ladies, Mrs. Grace Willard and her daughter Catherine, who seemed to have no connection to literature. Catherine tried to obtain a part in *Victory*, which was then being dramatized by Macdonald Hastings. Here, the Conrads acquired their first "really high performance" car, a Cadillac. The brief stay at Spring Grove was a happy time for the JC family.

3008 Conrad, Jessie, and Borys Conrad. *Joseph Conrad: L'Uomo. Testimonianza a Due Voci,* ed. by Mario Curreli (Milan: Mursia,

1974), (editor's note, p. 78), (appendix, "Three Unpublished Letters by Jessie Conrad" by Ugo Mursia, pp. 237–43.)

[Italian translation of Jessie Conrad, *Joseph Conrad as I Knew Him* (1926) and of Borys Conrad, *My Father: Joseph Conrad* (1970).] [In Italian.]

3009 Cox, C. B. "Introduction," *Youth, Heart of Darkness, The End of the Tether* (London: Dent [Collected Editions of the Works of Joseph Conrad]; [Everyman's Library], 1974), pp. vii–xxii.

In the *Youth* volume, JC revealed two aspects of his personality. One, as seen in the story "Youth," is energetic and steadfast: the story is accordingly a lively account of a journey to the East. The other aspect of his personality, as illustrated in "The End of the Tether," is moody, neurotic, and despairing. In "Heart of Darkness," these two aspects are combined and enter into open conflict. Marlow's voyage in "Youth" is one toward self-discovery. Through attainment of a sense of will, fortitude, and vitality, the protagonist is able to assert his manhood. When he looks back on his experience, he feels much diminished in comparison with his youthful experiences. Hence the conclusion is vague, for Marlow recognizes that he has lost his romance and illusions. The journey in "Heart of Darkness" has been interpreted in several different ways, but there is no one central meaning which readers can extract from it, for in it there is a great number of possible meanings. Unlike Marlow in these works, Captain Whalley in "The End of the Tether" is a different type of man, because he has a distinct tragic dignity. He is a man who once revealed an unquenchable vitality. Yet he finds that he is not ideal, that he can be corrupted. Through the contrast of Whalley's old and new natures, JC implies that the debased materialism of the present has corrupted the hero's behavior of the past. [Includes a select bibliography and a brief biographical sketch.]

3010 Cox, C. B. *Joseph Conrad: The Modern Imagination* (London: Dent; Totowa, New Jersey: Rowman & Littlefield, 1974).

JC's "stoical recognition of the precarious status of mind" of modern man is a basic element in the modern imagination. In his major novels, JC reveals his full concept of this imagination, with *Lord Jim* containing all the central problems. This novel dramatizes the claims of both a complete moral nihilism and a commitment to the ideals of service to the community, but it does not finally rest on any decisive conclusion. Jim's adventures are the modernist's search for a new kind of fiction, but the last word about Jim can never be said. "Heart of Darkness" is a "powerful fable" of the divided consciousness, of the various values of passion and restraint, represented in part by Kurtz's savage woman and his sterile

Intended. *Nostromo* presents two irreconcilable points of view: a profound skepticism and the human and moral claims best represented by Emilia Gould. *The Secret Agent* seems to be JC's most pessimistic novel. In Razumov's confession of his guilt in *Under Western Eyes*, JC seems to be developing towards the ideals of fellowship and community at the heart of such later novels as *Chance*, *Victory*, *The Arrow of Gold*, and *The Rover*. JC's best fictions often seem to be moving towards some satisfying resolution of a moral dilemma, but then deliberately frustrate the reader's expectations. His maintaining the validity of irreconcilable points of view suits his purpose of reflecting the precarious quality of human apprehensions of society.

3011 Crompton, John. "*Chance*," *JJCS*, I, No. 4 (June 1974), p. 8.

[A little epistolary exchange between Neil Montgomery and John Crompton reveals some strengths of *Chance*: the prose style is excellent, Flora is JC's most successful female portrait, and "little Fyne" is a successful comic character.]

3012 Crompton, John. "Teaching and Examining Conrad Texts, Part 1," *JJCS*, I, No. 4 (June 1974), pp. 9–11.

In recent years, works used at the "Ordinary Level" for teaching JC are usually the more demanding "sea-action" stories. The pattern is using these lighter works in the fourth or fifth year of secondary school, then moving on to JC's "masterworks" on the upper, or "A" level. In general, JC is considered difficult for both "O" and "A" levels. [Followed by Crompton, "Teaching and Examining Conrad, Part 2," *Journal of the Joseph Conrad Society* (U.K.), I, No. 5 (October 1974), pp. 9–11.]

3013 Crompton, John. "Teaching and Examining Conrad, Part 2," *JJCS*, I, No. 5 (October 1974), pp. 9–11.

Since it seems that JC, in spite of his complex prose style, should be taught in schools, different kinds of students may be introduced to his works in various ways, such as reading a story to them, letting them read a story for themselves, using discussion appropriate to the level of the class, using the critics to a restricted degree, and requiring only a limited amount of analysis. [Provides an impressive list of principles to guide the teacher in employing JC's works in schools. Preceded by Crompton, "Teaching and Examining Conrad Texts, Part 1," *Journal of the Joseph Conrad Society* (U.K.), I, No. 4 (June 1974), pp. 9–11.]

3014 Culbertson, Diana. "'The Informer' as Conrad's Little Joke," *SSF*, XI (Fall 1974), pp. 69–90.

JC devised an intricate tale within a tale with meanings on several levels, one of which is a joke on the readers of *Harper's*, for which "The Informer" was written. In the story, Mr. X, who is in part JC's voice, describes "an idle and selfish class [that] loves to see mischief being made, even if it is at its own expense." Dropping hints and clues, and making outright statements, JC mocks his readers and slyly parodies himself, enjoying it all very much.

3015 Cuthbertson, Gilbert M. "Freedom, Absurdity, and Destruction: The Political Theory of Conrad's *A Set of Six*," *CON*, VI, No. 1 (1974), pp. 46–52.

The unifying theme of *A Set of Six*, freedom, absurdity, and destruction, are avant-garde in JC. In "Gaspar Ruiz," the suffering of the masses is absurd, freedom and destruction are linked in the absurd situation, and absurdity of character supplements situational and conceptual absurdity. Severin, of "The Informer," who informs on a group of anarchists and thereby foils their plot, is an "anarchist of anarchists," in a story with a "fine interplay of absurd character and situation." "An Anarchist" is "a fine political satire." The principal absurdity in "The Duel" lies in the affair's being "a duel over a duel." And in "The Brute," the *Apse Family*, an inanimate object, absurdly struggles for freedom from its owners. The linkage of these stories is undoubtedly unintentional on JC's part, but the collection provides an effective medium for political philosophy.

3016 Dabrowska, Maria. "Conradiana: wybor i opracowanie Tadeusz Bobrowski" (Conradiana: Selection and Notes by Tadeusz Bobrowski), *Literatura na Swiecie* (Warsaw), 2 (1974), pp. 108–31.

JC was not only a literary problem for Dabrowska. Her husband Marian had the first Polish interview with JC (1914), and her second husband, Stanislaw Stempkowski, had a Ukrainian background like JC's and shared his intellectual and moral views. She also knew Aniela Zagorska and J. Ujejski well. [Extracts from Dabrowska's published diaries follow: 1926–1938, 1943–1950, and 1958–1965.] [In Polish.]

3017 Daleski, H. M. "Hanging On and Letting Go: Conrad's *The Nigger of the Narcissus*," *Hebrew University Studies in Literature*, II, No. 2 (Autumn 1974), pp. 171–96; rpt. and expanded in *Joseph Conrad: The Way of Dispossession* (1976).

The metaphysical emptiness that is asserted in *The Nigger of the Narcissus* is also, ultimately, the basis of the individual nullity pervading whole societies which would preoccupy JC years later in *Nostromo*, *The Secret Agent*, and *Under Western Eyes*. In *Nigger*, the pilgrimage enacts the journey of life in a mechanical and godless

universe. The structural principle of the novel is contrast: the central
epiphany of the work is what both the storm and the calm do to the
ship. When the ship is lying on its side, Jimmy's experience is
analogously subject to drift—the drift toward death. The novel is
concerned with two kinds of drift which are related, the drift of
meaninglessness and the drift toward death. In a world without god,
attitudes toward the two kinds of drift are related, and the author is
largely concerned with the "hazardous enterprise of living." On the
ship, panic is depicted by Jimmy's being trapped in the sick-bay
when the ship turns on its side and by the crew's almost general
panic, a desire to "cut loose" and let go. Singleton exemplifies the
alternative of hanging on. But Captain Allistoun takes pity on Jimmy
and deserts his crew when he refuses to reverse his order. JC seems
to grasp the fact that the paradoxical condition of full possession
may, where necessary, be a readiness to let go. What is emphasized
in *Nigger* is the need to hang on. Grace appears in the Conradian
universe when Jimmy's body finally moves into the sea and a breeze
releases the ship from its becalming.

3018 Davis, Kenneth W., Lynn F. Henry, and Donald W. Rude.
"Conrad's Trashing/Thrashing Sails: Orthography and a Crux in
The Nigger of the Narcissus," *CON*, VI, No. 2 (1974), pp. 130–33.

The sentence in *The Nigger of the Narcissus*, in which JC wrote
about the sails that "trashed" in the holograph and sails that
"thrashed" in the Heinemann-Doubleday edition, demands that the
editors of a textual edition choose between the two words without
any external evidence to guide them. JC's curious orthography gives
evidence for the second reading, as does his confusion in spelling
words with "th" sounds. [A pendant to Kenneth W. Davis and Donald
W. Rude, "The Translation of the Text of *The Nigger of the Narcissus*,"
Conradiana, V, No. 2 (1973), pp. 20–45.]

3019 Davis, Roderick. "Under Eastern Eyes: Conrad and Russian
Reviewers," *CON*, VI, No. 2 (1974), pp. 126–30.

Although *Under Western Eyes* failed with the public in England,
JC learned that it received a very favorable reception in Russia. The
reasons for the novel's success there may be found in two Russian
reviews of 1912 and of one Russian translation of the work and in two
other reviews of 1925 of another translation. These reviews indicate
that JC was recognized in Russia for the accuracy of his depiction of
political Russia, his knowledge of the subject, the merit of the work
as something like fictionalized history and also as a convincing
psychological drama, his psychological perceptivity and
sophisticated artistry, and the fact that praise for the book appeared
under both Tsarist and Communist regimes. [The four reviews are:

[no title], *Russkoye Bogatstvo*, IX (1912), p. 221; M. N., [no title], *Novyi Zhurnal Dlya Vsekh*, VIII (1912), p. 123; I. Fried, [no title], *Novy Mir*, VIII (1925), pp. 154–55; and M. Leitelzen, [no title], *Pechat I Revolutsia*, IV (1925), pp. 285–86.]

3020 Digaetani, John Louis. "Wagnerian Patterns in the Fiction of Joseph Conrad, D. H. Lawrence, Virginia Woolf and James Joyce," *DAI*, XXXIV (1974), 7745A. Unpublished dissertation, University of Wisconsin, 1973.

3021 Dunn, Albert A. "Time, Character, and Narration in the Victorian Novel," *English Symposium Papers*, IV (Fredonia: Department of English, State University of New York College at Fredonia, 1974), pp. 1–40.

A logical extension of a character's subjective sense of time is the dislodging of character by intense experience from the objective world which disorients his sense of time. JC uses such distortion in describing Nostromo's after his fourteen hours' sleep: Nostromo's subjective feeling is presented through metaphor which implies that there is actually no break in time. With JC, one can readily locate the crystallizing moments of consciousness. Lord Jim's interview with Gentleman Brown or Charles Gould's acceptance of the justice of the comparison of himself and the bandit Hernandez could represent all those moments which allow a glimpse of the hidden truth. JC first impresses the reader with his narrative forms in order to manipulate them. This manipulation allows him to move freely back and forth along the social continuum to present both personal and social histories from a multiplicity of temporal perspectives. These temporal displacements serve to distance the action and treat it as legend, tale, or fiction. As he moves into the past and closer to the action, he brings the reader to the truth, the reality which undermines the legend. In *Lord Jim*, Marlow discloses his impression of his own moment of vision: the story is the product of the truth disclosed in a moment of illusion just as a character's spiritual identity is. The truthful use of illusion which is the novelist's art preserves the truth against time's passage which allows perceived truth to be distrusted and to recede into the past as public

3022 Duval, Joanne G. "Conrad's *The Shadow-Line*: A Critical Edition," *DAI*, XXXV (1974), 1652A. Unpublished dissertation, Fordham University, 1974.

3023 Feldman, Rose T. "From Short Story to Novel: A Critical Study of Selected Fiction by Joseph Conrad," *DAI*, XXXV (1974), 2265A. Unpublished dissertation, University of Pittsburgh, 1974.

3024 Freeman, Anne P. "Joseph Conrad and the Absurd," *DAI*, XXXV (1974), 448A. Unpublished dissertation, University of Texas, Austin, 1974.

3025 French, Warren. "Face to Face: Film Confronts Story," *English Symposium Essays*, IV (Fredonia: Department of English, State University of New York College at Fredonia, 1974), pp. 43–74.

Huntington Hartford's Face to Face of 1953, an "omnibus presentation" pairing film versions of Stephen Crane's "The Bride Comes to Yellow Sky" and JC's "The Secret Sharer," remains relatively unknown. Director John Brahm's "The Secret Sharer" is one of the most faithful reproductions ever to reach the screen by the "externals" of a famous source, yet changes in the dialogue result in the film's emphasizing incidents' social, rather than psychological, significance. The controlling voice provides a predominantly social commentary on the British class system. Early in the film, emphasis is placed on the question of whether the man who has advanced rapidly because of a superior education actually has the "know-how" to be placed in command over those who have earned their positions through long and painful experience. At the end, Leggatt functions to initiate the captain fully into his position. The film version of JC's story reshapes, what had been in the source, a story of internal transformation. The title and the pretext for bringing the two works together is, however, inadequate, and neither film measures up to the vision of the original work. This situation includes the larger question as to whether a visual medium can handle material from other media that deals primarily with the inner struggles of individuals without shifting emphasis to the primary social aspects of those conflicts.

3026 Friedman, Alan Warren. "Conrad's Picaresque Narrator: Marlow's Journey from "Youth" through *Chance*," *JCTWF* (1974), pp. 17–39.

A very distinctive feature of twentieth-century fiction is its self-conscious pluralism, especially in the form of the multivolume novel, of which JC's four works which contain Marlow may be read as a unit—" Youth," "Heart of Darkness," *Lord Jim*, and *Chance*. Marlow serves as the intrusive "interpreting consciousness" and becomes the "moving center" of a larger episodic fiction. He both frames the tales he narrates and ages from one tale to another. Although the four fictions supply different characters with the force and validity of protagonists in their own right, taken together the four shape stages in Marlow's personal, moral, and aesthetic journeying from youth to maturity. But there is also a disturbing inconsistency beneath Marlow's evolving, a serious inadequacy that his immediate human appeal seeks to mask—racism, sexism, an utter inability to reconcile words and deeds. His many grand pronouncements he subsequently contradicts, usually without realizing that he is doing so. Ultimately, Marlow causes us to doubt our instincts: he embodies the multiple claims our deepest experiences make upon us, not the answers but the quest that life's central questions imply. [A major article which deserves close attention.]

3027 Galvano, Eugenio. "Nella zuppa di pesce, Conrad ritrovava il sapora del suo passato" (In His Fish Soup Conrad Found Again the Savor of His Own Past), *Gazzetta del Mezzogiorno* (28 July 1974), p. 4.

[A report on the 1974 JC International Conference at Canterbury: mostly anecdotal.] [In Italian.]

3028 Geddes, Gary. "*The Rescue*: Conrad and the Rhetoric of Diplomacy," *Mosaic*, VII (Spring 1974), pp. 107–25.

In *The Rescue*, there are several linguistic elements that are structurally important, some of which have the word "diplomacy" as the key word in a peculiar "community" of words. This word reminds us that in the novel there is a clear division between the diplomats and those whose dealings are "direct and above board." There is also some distinction in the work among the kinds of diplomacy; even Lingard is drawn into the realm of diplomacy. Irony, too, appears in JC's uses of the word "diplomacy." JC attempts to establish Lingard as a figure from a simpler, more heroic age and Edith Travers as the true female counterpart to him. In this novel, JC explores the relation between speech and sentiment, between statement and meaning. In the world of his book, speech is the "miracle" that bridges the separateness of men; therefore JC gives close attention to the psychology of speech and communication. For him here, speech is many-faceted and functions both on the real and the symbolic levels. Thus even d'Alcacer is one of JC's "fine consciences." When JC eventually completed *Rescue*, by examining closely the medium of language, he had found a style.

3029 Giddey, Ernest. "Homage to René Rapin (1889–1973)," *CON*, VI, No. 3 (1974), pp. 153-54.

[An appreciation of the late René Rapin, whose major work was a critical edition of the correspondence exchanged between JC and Marguerite Poradowska from 1890 to 1920.]

3030 Gillon, Adam. "Conrad in Poland," *Pol R*, XIX, No. 34 (1974), pp. 3–28.

Most early Polish critics of JC regarded him as a Polish writer only. Stefan Zablerowski's *Conrad in Poland* (1971) is, however, a systematic analysis of the critical reception of JC's work from 1896 to 1967, showing how the early misconceptions in Poland were replaced by more balanced judgments of the novelist's achievement. Today's Polish Conradists discern two aspects of JC's personality, the Romantic and the Positivist. JC's Polish personality naturally captured critics and readers in Poland. The early simplistic view of the writer's youth gave way, in due time, to the Positivist emphasis on social and economic elements instead of the more obvious Romantic qualities. Critics differed on JC's reasons for leaving Poland; the best explanation is Wit Tarnawski's idea that he was attracted by the English language itself, which enabled him to say effectually what he had in mind. Several Polish critics stressed JC's loneliness; only Zdzislaw Najder differed. JC's complex, contradictory nature baffles Polish critics who cannot separate JC the Pole from JC the English novelist. JC's successful career in Poland can be attributed to his Polish origin and the appeal of the work itself, its "moral-philosophical" no less than its artistic merit. [Includes remarks on several specific comparative critiques of JC's accomplishments; an excellent survey of Polish criticism.]

3031 Gillon, Adam. "Joseph Conrad: Polish Cosmopolitan," *JCTWF*, VII, Nos. 23–25 (1974), pp. 41–69.

Not a Polish novelist, JC has both a personal and literary cosmopolitanism which "stems from the psychological awareness of being an *émigré* even after he had established himself as an Englishman. He may be called a "Polish cosmopolitan," because of his heritage from his father of a feeling of intense nationalism, a hatred of Russia, and a love of French Romanticism and Shakespeare. JC's nationalism was somewhat ambivalent: women often appear as a national group with "distinct deficiencies," and the Germans fare worse. JC habitually sees people in terms of nationality, perhaps because of his own inner conviction of being a foreigner. If any of the characters in *Nostromo* may be identified with the author, it is Decoud. *Under Western Eyes* illustrates JC's response to Dostoevski's *Crime and Punishment* and the influence of Russian literature on the novelist. For JC, England was the "fatherland of choice or adoption" ; France, his "fatherland of sensibility" ; and Poland, that of his soul. His world is both Eastern and Western. Perhaps the true meaning of his cosmopolitanism lies in his "unique conception of the world that transcends . . . national boundaries," with a tragic and ironic vision of life that is both modern and humanistic.

3032 Glasgow, Joanne. "Conrad's *The Shadow-Line*: A Critical Edition," *DAI*, XXXV (1974), 1652A. Unpublished dissertation, Fordham University, 1974.

3033 Greene, Graham. "Lord Jim," *TLS* (6 December 1974), p. 1389.

It is well known that for *Lord Jim* JC drew on the history of the pilgrim-ship *Jeddah* and that Augustus Podmore Williams, the mate of that ship, may have been the original for Lord Jim. But perhaps "a young man" of "good conduct" but of unknown name, the captain's nephew, may also have contributed something to JC's portrait of Jim. This possibility arises from an essay written for the *Fortnightly Review* in 1881 and included in Wilfrid Scawen Blunt's *The Future of Islam* of 1882.

3034 Grieff, Louis K., and Shirley A. "Sulaco and Panama: A Geographical Source in Conrad's *Nostromo*," *JML*, III (February 1974), pp. 102–04.

A comparison of Tillyard's map of the Occidental province of *Nostromo* (*The Epic Strain in the English Novel*, 1958) and a reliable map of the Pacific coastal area of Panama reveals that whereas the imaginary place is much smaller, the physical configuration of the two is nearly identical. In addition to physical features, JC also borrowed certain Panamanian place-names such as Azuera and Punta Mala. Two discrepancies in the correspondence between Sulaco's geography and Panama's exist: JC's imaginary coastline runs from north to south instead of from east to west, and unlike the narrow isthmus of Panama, Sulaco is an integral part of the main continent of South America.

3035 Guerard, Albert J. "Notes on the Rhetoric of Anti-Realist Fiction," *Triquarterly*, No. 30 (Spring 1974), pp. 3–50.

Among the current anti-realist novelists, there is a great distrust of the inherited novel form. JC who, in fact, renewed the novel in many ways, was in his time somewhat like these novelists: he saw the novelist as "condemned to *rabâcher* the old formula until the new man came along," who did come along in the person of James Joyce. The "culminating work" of "Conradian impressionism" is Faulkner's *Absalom, Absalom!*: it depends on unprovable conjecture as an ultimate avenue to "truth," which is "no other than collaborative myth."

3036 Hamill, Paul. "Conrad, Wells, and the Two Voices," *PMLA*, LXXXIX (May 1974), pp. 581–82.

[Response to F. R. Karl's "Conrad, Wells, and the Two Voices,"
PMLA, LXXXVIII (1973), pp. 1049–65. Hamill's emphasis is on a
comparison between H. G. Wells and C. P. Snow, with only passing
reference to JC.]

3037 Hammer, Kenneth W., Jr. "Melville, Dana, and Ames: Sources
for Conrad's *The Nigger of the Narcissus*," *Pol R*, XIX, No. 34
(1974), pp. 29–33.

Some significant parallels exist between JC's *The Nigger of the
Narcissus* and Melville's *White Jacket*, especially in the descriptions
of the events brought about by the rough weather around the capes.
There is also some evidence that Melville and JC may have used a
common source for some of their material: Melville's *Redburn* has a
cook who is similar in some ways to Podmore in *Nigger*. But it
appears that both Melville and JC are indebted to Richard Henry
Dana's *Two Years Before the Mast* for the cook. And Dana's book
could have led JC to read another nautical book that contains
material similar to some in *Nigger*—Nathaniel Ames's *A Mariner's
Sketches* of 1830.

3038 Harkness, Bruce. "Conrad, Graham Greene, and Film," *JCTWF*,
VII, Nos. 23–25 (January 1974), pp. 71–87.

JC's novels are very individualistic, as *Lord Jim*, the classic
example, makes clear. The reader's response and its resolution
concern not the end of action but the essence of character. Also,
"Conradian necessities" require Jim to relate himself to the total
society: an individual problem becomes one of the relationship to
the total community. From this fact comes the "solidarity" of JC
criticism and of his own theory. The "progression," seen well in
Razumov, is apparent in many of his novels. Ultimately, individual
man depends upon community for self-definition. Movies are unable
to follow this progression, and since films made of JC's fiction must
work on both levels successfully, they have consequently failed.
Because this problem does not exist in Graham Greene, his novels
have been made into excellent films. Although Greene learned from
JC the techniques of the narrator and that of the time shift, in a
paradoxical sense Greene rejects the outer society which JC
ultimately accepted.

3039 Harris, Wilson. "Fossil and Psyche," *Occasional Publications
of the African and Afro-American Research Institute*, No. 7
(Austin: University of Texas, 1974), pp. 1–12.

JC's "Heart of Darkness" and Patrick White's *Voss* are similar in
that a certain "malaise of identity" appears in both Kurtz and Voss.
Marlow brings back to Kurtz's Intended only an ability to fall back

upon a "fetish of truth" in the form of a compassionate lie. [Contrasts Laura and Rose Portion in *Voss* with Kurtz's Intended, and also White's Judd with JC's Marlow.]

3040 Hecker Filho, Paulo. "Conrad," *Minas Gerais, Suplemento Literario,* XXI (September 1974), p. 2.

Victory, an extraordinarily well-structured novel, is a work of art, a poem, a grand, tragic, breathtaking spectacle. JC is reminiscent of Shakespeare and Dostoevski, the two supreme dramatists of stage and novel. A marriage of the work of these two supreme predecessors of JC would suggest *Victory.* A stoic, JC lacks the snobbery of Shakespeare and the religious sadomasochism of Dostoevski, for he can find virtue in the common man, and he focuses on this life rather than on the next.

Still, JC is reactionary. Stoicism is a heroic intertia which fails to perceive the movement of society and human life which is in history. JC sometimes fails to see this. Yet he is also the finished product of liberalism, shrewder than Kipling. He never strays from his concern with the human heart to sing the glories of empire. We intellectuals of a later time are the direct heirs of liberal culture. This is basic to the problem confronting modern literature. We must go beyond JC. But JC with his stoic heroism will always remain the highest example in narrative art of the liberal spirit and thus of the secret image in our own hearts. [In Portugese.]

3041 Higdon, David Leon. "The Conrad-Ford Collaboration," *CON,* VI, No. 3 (1974), pp. 155–56.

The periodical *Conradiana* sponsored a seminar at the 1973 convention of the Modern Language Association of America to consider the "puzzling and provocative" relationship between JC and Ford Madox Ford. This relationship has three significant "dimensions," textual, psychological, and aesthetic. [*Conradiana* reprints in this issue four of the five papers prepared on this subject for the meeting: John A. Meixner, "Ford and Conrad"; Raymond T. Brebach, "The Making of *Romance*: Part Fifth"; Charles Rose, "*Romance* and the Maiden Archetype"; and P[aul] L. Wiley, "Two Tales of Passion."]

3042 Hollahan, Eugene. "Beguiled into Action: Silence and Sound in *Victory,*" *TSLL,* XVI (Summer 1974), pp. 349–62.

A motif that informs JC's *Victory* is "a pair of polarized terms: *silence* and *sound.*" Both words and forms of these words are repeated throughout the novel. JC apparently perceives that "existence . . . alternates between silence and sound, extremes which in human life are modes of inaction and action, . . . detachment and involvement." The characters of the novel range from one extreme to another. Silence is associated with "introversion, mystery, fear, deep joy, withdrawal, domination, submission." And sound is orchestrated throughout as "voices, thuds, footsteps, pants, splashes, . . . howls, grunts, whistles, yells [and] are linked with fundamental attitudes, temperament, philosophy of life, and personal morality, all of which are shown in crucial decisions and consequential actions." The characters that are generally silent are Old Heyst, Wang, Jones, and Lena; the silence is broken by the actions of the "noisy characters," Zangiacomo, Pedro, Schomberg, and Ricardo. Axel Heyst is suspended in a tension between the two extremes of silence-detachment and sound-involvement. He prefers detachment, but becomes involved with Morrison and Lena. When finally confronted with Lena, however, he does not openly express his love for her and thus in silence chooses detachment and retreats from life.

3043 Hutcheon, Philip Loring. "Affirming the Void: Futilitarianism in the Fiction of Conrad and Faulkner," *DAI*, XXXV (1974), 2271A. Unpublished dissertation, Rice University, 1974.

3044 Jones, Michael Pusey. "All the Past Was Gone: Four Heroic Tales of Joseph Conrad," *DAI*, XXXV (1974), 1104A–05A. Unpublished dissertation, Boston College, 1974.

3045 Joy, Neill R. "'Would it bore you very much reading a MS in a handwriting like mine?': Catalogue of a Memorial Exhibition of the MSS., Letters, Editions and Memorabilia of Joseph Conrad in the Everett Needham Case Library," *Philobiblon: The Journal of the Friends of the Colgate University Library*, No. 10 (Summer 1974), pp. 1–25.

[Describes 41 items exhibited at Colgate University on the occasion of the fiftieth anniversary of JC's death.]

3046 Keech, James M. "The Survival of the Gothic Response," *SNNTS*, VI (Summer 1974), pp. 130–44.

The response to the Gothic novel is fear, universally inherent in man's nature, and also developed by the frightening supremacy of power over weakness. This effect is found also in later works of the Brontës, Dickens, Faulkner, and JC. "Heart of Darkness" is a Gothic novel, not traditional, with Gothic trappings, but embodying what is basically Gothic: "apprehensive fear, ominous atmosphere, the sense of frightening power inherent in evil." To JC, fear was in "integral" element in the nature of man.

3047 Kehler, Joel R. "The Centrality of the Narrator in Conrad's 'Falk,'" *CON*, VI, No. 1 (1974), pp. 19–30.

In "Falk: A Reminiscence," the heavier stress is on the latter part of the title, not on Falk himself. The narrator of the story detaches himself as a defense mechanism; there are actually two narrative consciousnesses at work in the telling of the story. One is trying to recreate from memory a world that had had a special meaning and attraction for its youth; the other is supplying, unconsciously and against its will, the insights of age. The narrator is constantly looking ahead to the part of his story that will undermine the beliefs of his younger self, and from his suppression of his later insights results quite a bit of grotesquely ironic humor. Like the triad in "The Secret Sharer," the narrator speaks of "me, my enemy Falk, and my friend Hermann," the last of which is a "super-ego" figure. The young captain is dumbfounded by Falk's attempt to steal the *Diana*, and he shrinks from relying upon Falk's towing facilities. Gradually, however, the young captain moves away from the initial influence of Hermann and into the influence of Schomberg, then into Falk's. His experiences establish at least one connection between Falk and everyone else in the port: if Falk is a "beast," he is at least a beast undisguised whereas the other people in the port hide their animal natures behind a facade of convention and morality. When, then, the narrator's final insights as to Falk's significance provide him a means for ordering the chaos of impressions that have pressed him from the beginning, he experiences a momentary vision of the "universal mechanism" which reduces all human pretensions to a "uniform, animal level, governed by impersonal law." The narrator is, for a time, an existential man. Falk is the enemy of man: he represents a truth destructive to the illusions of man.

3048 Kennard, Jean E. "Emerson and Dickens: A Note on Conrad's *Victory*," *CON*, VI, No. 3 (1974), pp. 215–19.

Verbal echoes in the first paragraph of JC's *Victory* associate the world of the novel with Emerson and Dickens and thereby add density to its texture. They also "underscore" the major theme of JC's novel, the relationship between coal and diamond, "the practical and the mystical." Emerson and Dickens may be seen as representing two aspects of nineteenth-century thought, the idealistic and the realistic, which "create the major conflict of that century." Possibly *Victory* demonstrates by way of Dickens the inadequacies of Emerson.

3049 Kimble, Terry L. "Conrad's *Nostromo* and the Imagery of Despair," *DAI*, XXXV (1974), 1105A–1106A. Unpublished dissertation, University of the Pacific, 1974.

3050 Kittrell, Ethel Jean. "The Audacious Philosophy of Joseph Conrad," *DAI*, XXXIV (1974), 5976A. Unpublished dissertation, Southern Illinois University, 1973.

3051 Kocówna, Barbara. "Bohater conradowski: w 50-lecie smierci" (The Conradian Hero: on the Fiftieth Anniversary of His Death), *Polonistyka* (Warsaw), XXVIII, No. 6 (1974), pp. 3–8.

JC's heroes are generally average individuals who begin to express themselves only when an unusual incident affects their existence, as with Almayer, Jim, and MacWhirr. They have potential sources of energy which incline them to the unusual, though most often they cannot liberate themselves, being absorbed in everyday routine. [In Polish.]

3052 Komar, Michael. "O Conradzie" (On Conrad), *Miesiecznik Literacki* (Warsaw), IX, No. 12 (1974), pp. 76–92.

To JC, Poland was not a literary theme but a basic, vital problem. His country provided him with a special framework, especially regarding the question of Fate. This is evident from his early years (death of father and mother in 1865 and 1869) and his upbringing in a patriotic and revolutionary atmosphere, with the ideal of a noble death for a "Cause," which had no chance of success. T. Bobrowski was a decided opponent of anti-Tsarist activities directed towards the liberation of Poland. Thus the psychological approach to JC's work should be replaced by political and historical approaches. JC's generation was brought up between a belief in Nemesis and cold common sense, and so was under pressure from two different ideologies, between practising loyalty towards the Russian authorities together with a hidden hatred for them and attachment to traditions and ritual. [In Polish.]

3053 Korn, Frederick Benjamin. "'Condemned to Consequences': A Study of Tragic Processes in Three Works by Joseph Conrad and Graham Greene," *DAI*, XXXIV (1974), 5977A. Unpublished dissertation, University of Illinois at Urbana-Champaign, 1973.

3054 Korzeniewska, Eva. "Wstep" (Introduction), *Szkice Conradzie*, ed. by Maria Dabrowska (Warsaw: Czytelnik, 1974), second ed., pp. 5–34.

Lord Jim, JC's first work published in Polish (1904), was intended for the intellectual elite, but it was poorly translated. Knowledge of JC in Poland remained slight until the 1920s, when critical articles appeared in literary magazines and *The Nigger of the Narcissus* was serialized. JC authorized Aniela Zagórska to publish her translation of *Almayer's Folly* (1920), and Stefan Zeromski, the novelist, urged the publication of JC's complete works in Polish and contributed a preface to the project. Maria Dabrowska, an admirer of both Zeromski and JC, regarded it her duty to popularize JC's work, with special references to his moral attitudes and art. Her work in the Ministry of Public Education in Poland in the thirties caused JC's publications to be recommended for Polish high schools. In the thirties, however, the "cult" of JC was attacked for political reasons. During World War II and after, Dabrowska replied to new attacks on JC by Jan Kott. During the time of the "cult of the individual" (1948– 54) in Poland, JC was neither published nor discussed. In 1957, though, Dabrowska was invited to contribute an article in relation to the centenary and, as in 1923, she decided to continue her work of popularizing JC's works and to encourage further study of his movements. Up to 1961, Dabrowska's interests in JC's writings were threefold: popularization, her own concern with the intent and purpose of creative writing, and the question of JC's "Polishness." She had no access to contemporary critical studies of JC in English or French. [In Polish.]

3055 Krzeckowski, Henryk. "Slowo wstepne" (Introductory Note), *Conrad w Oczach Krytyki Swiatowej* (Conrad Seen by World Criticism), sel Zdzislaw Najder (Warsaw: Panstwowy Instytut Wyudawniczy, 1974), pp. 5–7.

[In this collection of essays, the Polish reader will notice the marked attention of foreign critics to the subject of JC's origins. This problem, which is obvious and not controversial at all for Poles, seems to be an open question for foreigners, especially for the English, who are disturbed by the clearly non-English accents in JC's works. Only a few of them seem to understand that the question is not merely one of JC's Polish origins but primarily the fact that despite becoming an English writer, JC remained a Pole. Thanks to this fact, he brought to English literature a note which no native or adopted writers had hitherto attained.] [In Polish.]

3056 Larsen, Michael Joseph. "The Concept of the 'Double' in the Works of Joseph Conrad," *DA*, XXXVII (1974), 2861. Unpublished dissertation, University of Toronto, 1974.

3057 Lee, Sang-ok. "Experience into Fiction: An Aspect of Joseph Conrad's Idea of the Novel," *English Language and Literature*, No. 49 (Spring 1974), pp. 63–84.

Experience was an indispensable element in nourishing JC's artistic imagination. JC had to solve certain major problems while engaged in serious creative work. One is the problem of what might

be called fidelity to fact: it seems that his creative imagination
worked most brisky when it was upheld by a solidly apprehended
sense of reality, by the kind of fact he thought he knew best through
direct experience. Also, credibility of fact was first in his convictions.
He believed that life and art are two correlative terms. Second, an
autobiographical novel for JC was more than anything else a product
of the author's "necessity of self-disguise," and it also proposed to
exploit such experiences as may have contributed to the
development of the writer's own personality. Third, some
modification of facts is necessary, so that JC did not write "strict
autobiography"; he used many historical facts in addition to the
elements of personal experience. Most recurrent in his tales is the
theme of initiation, the initiation of the heroes into the world of self-
discovery or self-knowledge, as in "Heart of Darkness," "The Secret
Sharer," and *The Shadow-Line*. JC thus felt "rather free" in using
facts in whatever transposed form he wanted.

3058 "Letter from Perceval Gibbon to Conrad," *JJCS*, I, No. 5
(October 1974), pp. 6–7.

[Reprints a letter from Perceval Gibbon to JC, dated February 27,
1917, which is probably the only letter in existence from Gibbon to
JC.]

3059 Lippincott, H. F. "Sense of Place in Conrad's *The Rover*," *CON*,
VI, No. 2 (1974), pp. 106–12.

The Rover, marred in some ways, has as a principal virtue an
acute sense of place, with the French island of Porquerolles, off the
French Côte de Provence near Toulon, as a fixed point of reference
for the action. This "inner" roadstead is contrasted with the
nonspecific "outer" world from with Peyrol has come, even if he may
have been born on the island. JC effectively narrows our view from
the Eastern oceans and the forty-four years of Peyrol's past to an
isolated spot in time and place, the attic of the Escampobar
farmhouse and the present time of the novel. It seems that Peyrol has
come home again, but even so, he is "the prototypical modern hero,
rootless and faced with problems of personal identity." The precise
geographical description orients the reader for the sea action of the
final chapter. Peyrol serves more than one purpose: he outwits the
English ship because he is perfectly familiar with the surroundings;
he avoids visiting Porquerolles, a symbol of personal limitations, a
place not to be visited; and he metaphorically fuses JC's "practical
(seafaring) and creative (novelistic) imaginations in decline."
[Contains a map of the area.]

3060 Loe, Thomas Benjamin. "The Gothic Strain in the Victorian Novel: Four Studies," *DAI*, XXXV (1974), 2231A. Unpublished dissertation, University of Iowa, 1974.

3061 Lombrassa, Francesco. "Conrad marinaio e artista" (Conrad the Sailor and the Artist), *Le Prealpina* (10 October 1974), p. 8.

JC's greatness is not to be found in *Lord Jim* and *The Secret Agent*, which gave him fame and wealth, but in the tales. [Offers no new information.] [In Italian.]

3062 Maillot, Jean. "André Gide Traducteur de Conrad," *Babel: An International Journal of Translation*, XX (1974), pp. 63–71.

André Gide's 1923 translation of "Typhoon," first in a series of JC's works under the direction of Gide and G. Jean-Aubry, is very mediocre, particularly in its failure to be faithful to the original. JC's style is not respected. Gide eliminates passages while adding others pleonastically. He does not observe JC's changes in levels of usage, he translates idiomatic expressions literally, he renders with the same French word an English term whose definition changes through the text, and on the other hand he changes by French variants many terms whose sense remains the same throughout the text. [In French.]

3063 Marin, Clive. "*Blackwood's*," *Midwest Quarterly*, XV (Summer 1974), pp. 417–28.

The *Blackwood* "attitude of friendly openness was critical in the development of writers such as Conrad and Eliot." JC said, "If *Blackwood's* take me, I want no better luck."

3064 Martin, David M. "The Function of the Intended in Conrad's 'Heart of Darkness,'" *SSF*, XL (Winter 1974), pp. 27–33.

In "Heart of Darkness," two journeys are antithetical to each other, Marlow's journey through the jungle toward the significance of Kurtz and his counter-journey through the city toward the significance of the Intended. Marlow comes to recognize the affirmation in Kurtz's last cry only through his encounter with the Intended. His journey to her contains many parallels to his previous journey to Kurtz, and several parallels with Kurtz establish her as a great spokesman of truth as Kurtz in his own way is. Like Kurtz, she is a "voice," and both voices speak "from beyond the threshold of an eternal darkness." But the Intended's cry is one of horror also, a horror that she has survived the man she loved. Her greatest regret is that, in her despair, she has not acted. Kurtz's last word as offered by Marlow is consistent with Kurtz's final affirmation: if his affirmation recognized as real a subjectively human standard, then Marlow is true to that affirmation, for both "superimpose an intentional reality upon experiential reality"; and if Kurtz embodied experiential reality, then the Intended as clearly embodies intentional reality, thus complementing Kurtz's reality even if her truth is not entirely Marlow's. The two voices ultimately define the parameters of human consciousness in Marlow himself. By integrating the stark objectivity of the universe of Kurtz's vision with the subjectivity of the human personality, the Intended's illusion, Marlow's consciousness achieves the mid-point of stasis which holds the ends together in a viable balance, and the stasis is maintained by the retelling of the story.

3065 Martin, David M. "The Paradox of Perspectivism in Conrad's The Lagoon,'" *SSF*, XI (Summer 1974), pp. 306–307.

Since the white man in "The Lagoon" is a spokesman for the world outside Arsat's illusion and a figure calling Arsat back to that world, his statement that "There is nothing" suggests that as Arsat becomes aware that he has created his own world-view and begins to move out of it, a concurrent awareness emerges that we can see reality only in world-views. Arsat himself seems to sense the relativism of the white man's comment as, at the end of the story, he looks "beyond the great light of a cloudless day into the darkness of a world of illusions." This is a perception of the real world perceived; Arsat perceives that in its meaning the world is the darkness of his own illusions. The story implies, though, that Arsat will pursue action beyond this point, presumably by returning to the land of his enemies to avenge his brother's death.

3066 Martin, Joseph J. "Edward Garnett and Conrad's Reshaping of Time," *CON*, VI, No. 2 (1974), pp. 89–105.

JC's radically unorthodox treatment of time in some of his major works came not from Ford Madox Ford, who claimed to be the originator of Impressionism in fiction, but from the criticism of Edward Garnett, his publisher's reader and his private literary critic, during the years 1896–99. In "Karain," JC first greatly increased his technical skill by following Garnett's advice, which must have included making a careful study of Turgenev's story, "A Lear of the Steppes." And "Karain" is clearly a "dry run" for *Lord Jim*, which far surpasses the short story. JC learned to use two main formal devices, the "*in medias res* portrait" of the hero and the long-withheld flashback, which helped him to maintain an objective focus while penetrating to the depths. Later, in *Nostromo* and *Chance* especially, JC, by means of these technical devices, built fictional structures in which the central moral experience shaped the plot and reflected the writer's tragic concept of fatality or inevitability which are integral to his vision. [Martin, in "Edward Garnett and Conrad's Plunge Into the 'Destructive Element,'" *Texas Studies in Language and Literature*, XV (Fall 1973), pp. 317–36, provides a detailed account of Garnett's decisive role in urging JC toward the objective approach in his works.]

3067 Martin, W. R. "Compassionate Realism in Conrad and *Under Western Eyes*," *English Studies in Africa*, XVII (1974), pp. 89–100.

The Russian setting of *Under Western Eyes* is analogous to the marine settings of other novels by JC in that the author thought he could best investigate human nature by portraying human beings under extreme pressure. Those of JC's heroes who stand up to the pressure of their environment do so with either intense cynicism of "compassionate realism." The cynic understands the horror in himself and in his neighbors; the compassionate realist understands the horror of evil in man, but he is willing to live according to man's admittedly illusory ethical values. JC marks the tension between the cynics and the compassionate realists in *Eyes* with imagery of motion and stasis. Cynics Mrs. Haldin, General T—, and Madame de S— are disturbingly inanimate; compassionate realists Tekla and Nathalie are always in motion. Razumov sinks into stasis when he betrays Haldin; he regains animation when he confesses to Nathalie. The greatest contrast of stasis and motion in the novel is between the Eastern and the Western settings. The placidity of Geneva reflects the placidity of Western man's unconscious confidence in his political illusions; the turmoil of Russia reflects the turmoil of the Russians' constant introspection. Even though the Russian autocracy is a horrible political system, it does have a salutary effect on those of its citizens who are strong enough to respond positively to its horror.

3068 Mathews, James W. "Ironic Symbolism in Conrad's 'Youth,'" *SSF*, XI (Spring 1974), pp. 117–23.

In the older Marlow's telling of his youthful adventure in "Youth," he is still a romantic for whom age is an excuse, and because of their strong attachment to illusion neither the young nor the old Marlow can be called heroic. Young Marlow is a victim of youthful egocentricity; the older Marlow is captive of a deeper "malaise"—a romantic cynicism which obfuscates the meaning of the tale he relates. In twenty-two years, Marlow has not changed, fundamentally. He is oblivious to the deeper irony of the story which JC articulates through the pattern of symbols. Since all the metaphorical images involve characters and formulas which have long held positive spiritual meaning for Western man but which have been transformed by the author into cryptic signs of negation, JC is advancing a veiled but significant opinion about the inefficacy of the Christian religion in developing man's knowledge of himself and his acceptance of the blackness of the universe. Bangkok, the East, suggests the human desire to return to the source of life, as it also symbolizes the attraction of the origin of the great religions of the world. The Marlow who looks back knows only the poignancy of the abortive hope of the East, not the reason for the brevity of its promise. JC indicates the reality of which Marlow is oblivious by such devices as the use of the inversion of names which normally connote hope and salvation (*Judea*, "Do or die"), and by the use of Captain Beard's travesty of the Last Supper. Although Marlow expresses truth, he does not accept it, thereby revealing his condition as a worse death and burial than that of the energy and hope of youth.

3069 Mayoux, Jean-Jacques. "Zachód w dziele Conrada" (The West in Conrad's Works), *Literatura na Świecie* (Warsaw), No. 7 (1974), pp. 88–107.

Nostromo is proof of JC's preoccupation, perhaps unconsciously, with the great basic principles of the West, the criminal usurpation of land and nature by the White races, and genocide, with elements of love and truth, represented by Dr. Monygham, the broken victim of dictatorship. [In Polish.]

3070 McDonald, Walter. "On Conrad's Secret Agent," *CON*, VI, No. 2 (1974), p. 125.

[A poem relating *The Secret Agent* to other works by JC.]

3071 Meixner, John A. "Ford and Conrad," *CON*, VI, No. 3 (1974), pp. 157–69.

Although the 1950s were a "breeding time" of many changes in an understanding of the relationship between Ford Madox Ford and JC and even if much remains to be learned, the available evidence indicates that the time of Ford in JC's life was the time of JC's greatness. There were, for example, many practical ways in which the younger man was useful to JC and his work: neither *The Mirror of the Sea* nor *A Personal Record* would have been written without Ford's "enterprise"; JC took from Ford the basic situation of his story, "Amy Foster"; Ford supplied the central situation of *The Secret Agent*; and Ford actively helped JC on several occasions with his writing. Furthermore, Ford supplied JC with money as well as with other kinds of assistance. In the collaborations, the conceptions began in Ford's mind. Ford also provided much artistic, moral, and spiritual support for JC. Ford's relationship with Violet Hunt caused a general ostracizing among his literary peers. For JC, the break which followed was disastrous. But whatever the reasons for the break, the year of mid-1909 to mid-1910 marks a decisive turning point in his career. After this time, "the heroic psychological probings and vital interior tensions that are the constituent powers of his best fiction" have largely vanished, to be replaced by conventional values of storytelling.

3072 Messenger, William E. "Conrad and His 'Sea Stuff,'" *CON*, VI, No. 1 (1974), pp. 3–18.

When JC turned to writing sea fiction, first with Part One of *The Rescue* and then with *The Nigger of the Narcissus*, he was facing the choice between writing for popular success and writing according to the dictates of his artistic conscience. In various letters of the time, he displays both his serious ambition and his casual aristocratic attitude. In 1896, when he followed Edward Garnett's advice to take up the sea story, JC felt a strong contempt for the reading public and also strongly desired popularity; he thus courted the very public he scorned. Abandoning *The Sisters*, he wrote all he could of *Rescue*; then *Nigger* became, no doubt, a substitute with which he could appeal to the public. But his inability to give up his old mode made this work "indubitably Conradian" but also a flawed masterpiece. This last real training exercise gave him, though, full command of his powers and enabled him to move on to his greater works. Because he may have felt that he was "selling his artistic soul to the commercial devil," his later, and now famous, preface to *Nigger* reveals the true victor.

3073 M[iccinesi], M[ario]. "Nel cinquantenario della morte di Conrad l'editore Mursia inaugura une collana nel nome di 'Cuore di tenebre'" (On the Fiftieth Anniversary of Conrad's Death Messrs. Mursia Inaugurate a Series in the Name of the Prestigious Author of "Heart of Darkness"), *Uomini e Libri*, X, 51 (November–December 1974), p. 44.

[Review of Baines's biography and Jessie and Borys Conrad's reminiscences.] [In Italian.]

3074 Michael, Marion C. "James Wait as Pivot: Narrative Structure in *The Nigger of the Narcissus*," *JCTWF*, VII, Nos. 23–25 (January 1974), pp. 89–102.

Important to the theme of *The Nigger of the Narcissus* is JC's conception of James Wait as both within and exploiter of a real illusion. Fearing death, Wait convinces himself that his illness is nothing more than pretense, by which he can escape his duties on the ship. Thus Wait ironically and paradoxically makes his imminent death an accomplice in what becomes a complex art of self-deception, in terms of which the reader reaches an understanding of the way in which Wait becomes the "centre of the ship's collective psychology and the pivot of the action." The feelings of the crew about Wait shift from time to time; the men's failure to understand the truth of Wait's dilemma leads to the mutiny, only after which do they realize that he is dying. The evidence of authorial revisions reveals that the alternations between the crewman narrator, with his limited knowledge, and the omniscient author, with his entire knowledge, provide the aesthetic distance from which the reader views events and ironically interprets them. JC strove deliberately to authenticate his narrative simultaneously on two levels of meaning.

3075 Mikellatos, J. E. "Treasure, Power and Death—Part One of a Study of Themes in Conrad," *JCSN*, [I], No. 3 (February 1974), pp. 7–8.

The interrelated themes of treasure, power, and death appear clearly in some six of JC's works. In certain books, the image of the river winding far into the unknown and dangerous interior is used. In *An Outcast of the Islands*, Willems acts out the story in its simplest form: "discovery, corruption by greed, treachery and consequent destruction." The hero of *Lord Jim*, when faced with the need to recognize that heroism is not entirely pure, fails and thereby brings destruction on all those involved with him. The irony leads, in "Heart of Darkness," the men inland to the beginning of the world, to the innermost heart or primitive and unconscious depth of every human being, to the treasure, ivory, which is power. Ironically, men of vision like Jim and Kurtz, are cursed with the ability to dream, an ability which makes them "hollow at the core" as they come to believe themselves to be supermen. But Marlow is capable of feeling the pull of power and of resisting it, taking from it only minor injury. [Followed by Mikellatos, "Treasure, Power and Death—Part Two," *Joseph Conrad Society (U.K.) Newsletter*, [I], No. 4 (June 1974), pp. 4–5.]

3076 Mikellatos, J. E. "Treasure, Power and Death—Part Two," *JCSN*, [I], No. 4 (June 1974), pp. 4–5.

The treasure, silver, exerts its fatal power in *Nostromo*. Sotillo fails to help Pedrito Montero and loses the opportunity of a lifetime. The rebels are defeated, but the treasure still imposes its power: Sulaco is established under a benevolent oligarchy, but all is not well there. Charles Gould, who tries to establish the riches for the general good, has enough integrity to save his soul, but he loses his personal life with its human warmth and affection. Nostromo is finally transformed by the power of the treasure into a greedy, worthless "lay-about" and meets an ignominious death.

Peyrol in *The Rover*, immune from the "siren song" of power given by the treasure, performs a consummate feat of seamanship which is both a personal triumph to him and an important act in defense of his country. But still the theme is not optimistic.

JC implies that the pattern is inescapable, a part of human destiny. But men like Marlow and Peyrol receive little harm because they, unlike Jim and Kurtz, do not have hollow cores that wait to be filled with visions of power and glory.

3077 Montgomery, Neil. "*The Arrow of Gold*," *JJCS*, I, No. 5 (October 1974), pp. 3–6.

The clue to the mysteries about the characters in *The Arrow of Gold* and their absurd Carlist intrigues lies in the enigmatic personality of Doña Rita, one of the rarest women on earth. She is not merely a woman; she haunts everything which is connected with her, and she gives meaning to everything. She creates values. The bond between her and M. George is their common youth, transient with him, eternal with her. Her instinctive knowledge has been inherited from the ancient tradition of the Basque peasant. But her inherited strength can have no adequate defense against Señor Ortega who, too, comes from the old Basque tradition. As for her leaving her lover at the end of the book, she must not permit the woman in her to outweigh the goddess. It is strange that JC, who scarcely believes in God, is able to create a goddess. [Rpt. from *Purpose*, 1932, pp. 165–69, according to end note.]

3078 Montgomery, Neil. "Conrad in the 1920s," *JCSN*, [I], No. 3 (February 1974), pp. 3–4.

Some early readers of JC thought that psychology was the key to an understanding of his works but later decided that not psychology but "that curious association of the Conradian magic with an *object*," like the San Tomé silver or the ivory in "Heart of Darkness," is the key to his genius.

3079 Moore, Harry T. *The Priest of Love: A Life of D. H. Lawrence* (New York: Farrar, Straus and Giroux, 1974), pp. 170, 199.

In 1912, D. H. Lawrence found that *Under Western Eyes* "bored" him; he could not forgive JC "for being so sad and for giving in." In 1913, Lawrence found fault with the contemporary writers, Bennett, Galsworthy, and JC; he was casting off the traditionalists and preparing to assess the Futurists, who were right, he thought, in trying to destroy the ancient forms and beliefs and sentimentalities.

3080 Moser, Thomas C. "Conrad, Marwood, and Ford: Biographical Speculations on the Genesis of *The Good Soldier*," *Mosaic*, VIII (October 1974), pp. 217–27; rpt. *JC* (1976), pp. 174–82.

In *The Good Soldier*, Ford Madox Ford created his "sole masterpiece," no doubt out of agony which came from drastically altered relations with the people he loved: his first wife, Elsie Martindale; Violet Hunt, the "other woman"; his and Elsie's mutual friend, Arthur Pearson Marwood; his wife Caroline; and his next best friend, JC. By 1913, Ford realized that the two English gentlemen whom he loved best in the world could no longer bear him, and by that time he had also to deal with the appearance of JC's *Chance*. It is clear that connections between Ford's novel and his friends are implicit throughout the work. Beyond Ford himself, Marwood was the chief model for Edward Ashburnham, and the model for John Dowell is JC, an impressionistic personal narrator somewhat like Marlow. Dowell's main purpose in telling his story is to get it out of his mind. Ford thus wrote *The Good Soldier* "out of personal, agonized involvement" and thereby created his masterpiece. And like Dowell, Ford concluded unwisely, that Marwood was himself.

3081 Moser, Thomas C. "From Olive Garnett's Diary: Impressions of Ford Madox Ford and His Friends, 1890–1906," *TSLL*, XVI (Fall 1974), pp. 511–33.

On 15 November 1901, Olive Garnett wrote in her diary about visiting the Conrads at the Pent, where JC spoke "very despondingly" of his work and said he often wished to return to the sea. JC was "most hospitable, most simple in a good mood." On 31 March, Olive wrote of her second visit with JC, at Hythe, a pleasant experience also. And on 13 February, 1964, Olive went at last to one of Ford's literary parties: she had a "crush" on Henry James.

3082 Mroczkowski, Przemyslaw. "Joseph Conrad's International World of Men," *KN*, XXI, No. 2 (1974), pp. 171–91.

JC's fiction contains a world in which many materials conflict with each other. The English characters consist of a range of figures objectively drawn, officers as well as simple men, merchants, a few professional people, and other kinds of people, and Marlow, in some ways JC's alter ego. An obvious juxtaposition of English and Polish appears in "Amy Foster," in which Yanko Goorall fails completely in "interhuman communication." Among JC's North American characters are Captain Blunt and Mr. Holroyd. There are several Dutchmen and Scandinavians, including Almayer, Cornelius, and Axel Heyst. Among the several Germans are Stein, the Hermanns, Schomberg, and Kurtz. Razumov represents the Russian element. The Latins include *Citoyen* Peyrol, Martin Decoud, and the Spanish in *Nostromo*, which provides a significant British–Spanish contrast, as does *Romance* also. *Nostromo*, too, includes a Jew and some outstanding Italians. JC's early novels treat Malays and their relationships with the whites. Arabs, Chinese, and Negroes also appear in JC's works. Yet, it appears that all the national features, linguistic and otherwise, remain on the surface; JC's concern with people lies at a much deeper level, with "problems of duty, of personal loyalty or devotion, or the heights of human nobility and self-sacrifice, or the depths of depravation, of fault and atonement." As for women, they are for JC "a mystery in their own right"; therefore, they follow the men of their choice.

3083 Mursia, Ugo. "Il mistero del luogo di nascita di Joseph Conrad" (The Mystery Concerning the Birthplace of Joseph Conrad), [appendix in] Jocelyn Baines, *Joseph Conrad: Biografia Critica* (Milan: Mursia, 1974), pp. 543–51; rpt. in part as "The True Birthplace of Joseph Conrad," in *JC*, pp. 199–205.

To date, the three major biographers of JC have named different places as JC's birthplace, choosing Berdicev, Terechovaja, and Derebynska. But additional evidence appears to establish the actual place as Ivankovcy. [Frederick R. Karl, in *Joseph Conrad: The Three Lives* (1979), gives JC's birthplace as being "near Berdichev."]

3084 Naipaul, V. S. "Conrad's Darkness," *New York Review of Books*, XXI (17 October 1974), pp. 16–21.

There is in "The Lagoon" much of JC's passion. Expressing his sense of the abyss, the solitude, and the futility of man's illusions, it is probably the purest thing he ever wrote. *Lord Jim*, like "Karain," is influenced by an unwillingness to let the story say all it should; hence this novel reveals a hesitation to express all its mystery. Because the situation in it is left so vague, and because it is not expressed in a straightforward manner, *Jim* succumbs to mystification. *The Secret Agent* is simply a police thriller. It ends as soon as it begins, and it has about it a shadow of Arnold Bennett and H. G. Wells. The theme of *Under Western Eyes* is one of betrayal. Originally, this novel had the hope of being similar to the work of Dostoevski, but it ultimately dissipated into nothing more than analysis. *Victory* is too "set up," and *Nostromo* is hindered by a confusion of characters and themes. "An Outpost of Progress" is the finest piece JC ever wrote. But it has the common pattern of a white man going mad in the tropics, the same pattern which appears in "Heart of Darkness." "The Return," written at the same time as "Karain," is only an imaginative essay. To understand JC, a reader must discard all ideas of what a novel is supposed to do. Especially, one must rid himself of the corruptions of the genre. There is about

JC's work something unexercised; his imagination is flawed. [The bulk of this article is given to Naipaul's own personal responses to JC's writings.]

3085 Najder, Zdzislaw. "Conrad and the Idea of Honor," *JCTWF*, VII, Nos. 23–25 (January 1974), pp. 103–14.

The idea of honor was very important for JC, a moral writer. This ideal requires that one remain faithful to his principles and defend them at all times, but it also determines largely the kind of principles one ought to endorse. Honor has its public face, reputation, and its private face, consciousness. This essential duality has been present in the ideal since its very beginnings, which go back at least to Homeric Greece. This concept of honor, basically a secular ideal, sees man as an individual person who has higher and lower elements in him, so that he must be carefully educated. Within the ethic of honor, a morally relevant act has, in principle, irreversible consequences. What matters most is fidelity to a principle. Poland, JC's mother country, in its struggle for national identity, was concerned with honor because of its ancient tradition of literature steeped in the idea of honor. The view of life associated with honor is essentially tragic. JC does not idealize work, but he does idealize duty. What the ethic of honor is finally about is saying "No" to death.

3086 Najder, Zdzislaw. "Conrad's Casement Letters," *Polish Perspectives*, XVII, No. 12 (December 1974), pp. 25–30.

In 1903, Roger Casement was working on his famous report on the condition in the Congo, which was issued 15 April 1904. [Three hitherto unknown letters from JC to Casement from this period are published here, with some comment on Casement and JC's own explanation for his refusing to sign an appeal for a reprieve for Casement when he was convicted for his activities in the cause of Irish independence.]

3087 Najder, Zdzislaw (ed.). "Listy Conrada do J. B. Pinkera: wybór i opracowanie" (Conrad's Letters to J. B. Pinker: A Selection and Notes), *Literatura na Swiecie* (Warsaw), 2 (1974), pp. 67–81.

[Extracts (1899–1919) from the 1300 letters JC wrote to J. B. Pinker once a week on the average, now in the New York Public Library, Gordan bequest.] [In Polish.]

3088 Najder, Zdzislaw. "Listy Conrada do Rogera D. Casementa" (Conrad's Letters to Roger D. Casement), *Tw*, XXX, 8 (1974), pp. 31–35.

JC wrote on 1 December 1903 and on 17 December 1903 thanking Roger D. Casement for a copy of Morel's pamphlet on commercial policies and administrative methods in the Belgian Congo. Morel's views were correct. On 21 December 1903, JC wrote to Casement that the Belgians in the Congo were worse than the seven plagues of Egypt. [In Polish.]

3089 Najder, Zdzislaw. "Próby, poszukiwania, rozterki" (Trials, Searches, Distractions), *Literatura na Swiecie* (Warsaw), 2 (1974), pp. 4–65.

[Biographical account of the years 1895–1898, based largely on JC correspondence with E. Garnett and others.] [In Polish.]

3090 Natanson, Wojciech. "Nieznany list Saint-John Perse'a do Josepha Conrada" (Unknown Letter from Saint-John Perse to Joseph Conrad), *Literatura na Swiecie* (Warsaw), 2 (1974), pp. 82–85.

[First published in French in *Le Figaro* 18 November 1972 and dated from Peking, 28 February 1921.] [In Polish.]

3091 Nettels, Elsa. "The Grotesque in Conrad's Fiction," *NCF*, XXIX (September 1974), pp. 144–63.

The grotesque is of essential importance in JC's treatment of his "central subject" in several works: the experience of the protagonist who loses those illusions of self and the world in which he once found security. To the protagonist, the grotesque usually manifests itself in the appearance and actions of characters who contribute to the destruction of his illusions and in the sinister or dreamlike quality in which he sees the world after his sense of security has been destroyed. *Almayer's Folly* depicts a protagonist whose inflated view of himself is seen as grotesque when it is symbolized by the shadow which exaggerates his sleeping figure. *Lord Jim* presents Marlow's vision of the skipper of the *Patna* as intensifying the horror of the scene on the disabled ship, and *Victory* shows how Heyst, in watching Mr. Jones who has destroyed the safety of the island refuge, discovers that he himself has been betrayed. Like Dickens and Hoffmann, JC works within a tradition well established in the nineteenth century. The bond between JC's protagonists and their grotesque counterparts indicates that JC shared Victor Hugo's belief that portraying the grotesque is necessary for a complete picture of life. Among JC's novels, *The Secret Agent* is unique in its depiction of characters who are at the mercy of a chain of events initiated by human acts seemingly beyond human control, but *Under Western Eyes* gives the fullest and most sustained picture of grotesque realities as they are reflected by a tormented consciousness.

3092 Niccoli, Roberto. "Dopo mezzo secolo si torna a Conrad" (Return to Conrad Fifty Years Later), *Cultura di Destra*, I, 2 (December 1974), pp. 21–25.

Even if the Left has tried to appropriate JC, he is one of the most remarkable writers belonging, culturally and politically, to the Right. He was an antidemocrat, and his letters to Cunninghame Graham clearly show his disgust with democracy. The suicide of his characters demonstrates the dramatic conflict among the sacred values of honor, friendship, duty, faith, and deceiving and enigmatic reality. [A rather rambling splutter of no interest whatsoever.] [In Italian.]

3093 Paris, Bernard. "The Dramatization of Interpretation: *Lord Jim*," *A Psychological Approach to Fiction: Studies in Thackeray, Stendhal, George Eliot, Dostoevsky, and Conrad* (Bloomington and London: Indiana University Press, 1974), pp. 215–74.

JC avoids many of the pitfalls of the realism of the nineteenth century by making the problematic nature of experience—in *Lord Jim*, the meaning of Jim's character and fate—into the novel's central theme. This he achieves by means of a narrative technique which dramatizes interpretation: he surrounds the issues which he explores with a variety of perspectives, each belonging to the character in the work and in keeping with his psychology. The novel as a whole entertains all of these perspectives, but offers none of them as adequate or final; each one is seen as being valid, but limited. There are, therefore, many truths, but there is no "Truth." The novel does not achieve thematic coherence because the two perspectives of the omniscient narrator of the first four chapters and the relativistic perspective which dominates when Marlow becomes narrator cannot be reconciled. Despite its flaw, however, *Jim* achieves greatness in its rendering of the uncertainty of human knowledge and the relativity of human judgments. Jim is "wedded forever" to his idealized image. But Marlow, too, suffers; he suffers from a combination of high standards and low self-esteem. [Needs much more explanation of Paris's interpretation of Jim.]

3094 Pearce, Richard. "Enter the Frame," *Triquarterly*, XXX (Spring 1974), pp. 71–82.

In the transition from fiction to "surfiction," in which the narrator is no longer situated between the subject and the reader, JC supplies an important step. In Henry James's *The Turn of the Screw*, only the interpretation of the story remains beyond our final grasp so that the story itself is not unclear but ambiguous. JC's "Heart of Darkness," like James's story, is also structured on the principle of a frame within a frame, but the dynamics are different. The largest frame is provided by an unnamed narrator; within his frame sits Marlow, in the Lotus Posture, who tells the main story. But the subject of "Heart of Darkness" is not a series of events contained within a frame but Marlow's story as story, a dynamic process in which style, description, characters, symbols, actions are constantly evolving, and in which these elements are brought into the same field of imaginative perception and meaning. The resulting picture is not clear because JC's focus is not on the "enveloping" and developing "tale." In William Faulkner's *Absalom, Absalom!*, the legend of Sutpen is beyond our perception because of the psychological and historical limitations of the four characters from whose vantage the center of the story is approached. And Samuel Beckett, in breaking from traditional fiction in his trilogy, creates a new subject, the conflict between his narrator and the narrative voice, or between his main character and the limits of his medium. JC thus provides a major impetus in the development of surfiction in which Beckett is followed by Robbe-Grillet, Pinget, Calvino, Cortázar, Borges, and Barth.

3095 Porter, Kathleen Zamloch. "The Epistemological Novels of Joseph Conrad and Henry James," *DAI*, XXXIV (1974), 6654A. Unpublished dissertation, Syracuse University, 1973.

3096 Powell, Anthony. "Conrad and Proust," *TLS* (27 September 1974), p. 1042.

The malapropisms of the master of the brigantine that took Lord Jim to Patusan strangely resemble those of the manager of the Grand Hotel at Balbec in Proust's *Remembrance of Things Past*. These may be "chance, unconscious memory, or a perfectly legitimate representation of a similar eccentric use of language in a different setting."

3097 Powers, Lyall H. "Point of View as a Mode of Thematic Definition in Conrad and Faulkner," *DAI*, XXXV (1974), 442A. Unpublished dissertation, University of Michigan, 1973.

3098 Prorok, Leszek. "Drogi fascynacji: w 50 rocznice zgonu Conrada" (Ways of Fascination: on the 50th Anniversary of Conrad's Death), *Wiez* (Warsaw), 7–8 (1974), pp. 141–53.

[Biographical notes on W. Tarnawski, S. Zabierowski, Jozef Milobedzki, G. Morf, E. A. Bojarski, and J. Kagarlitskii.] [In Polish.]

3099 Pulc, I. P. [pseud. of Irmina Pulc Plaszkiewicz]. "The Imprint of Polish on Conrad's Prose," *JCTWF*, VII, Nos. 23–25 (1974), pp. 117–39.

JC's prose, which sounds somewhat strange to English readers, sounds familiar to Polish ears. Traces of Polish appear in JC's diction: he reveals his native language in idiomatic phrases and single words which retain their foreign flavor when rendered literally into English, in similar borrowings that fit well into their new surroundings, and in Polish proverbs that have no exact equivalents in English. JC's "exoticism" as a stylist stems largely, however, from rhetorical features that were much more current in the Polish than in the English of his time. His descriptive style, in particular, displays a fondness for such figures as the asyndeton, the anaphora, and triple parallelism, which are common in Polish writers of the nineteenth and twentieth centuries but unusual in British novelists of the same period. And occasionally these patterns reveal what is probably JC's most "exotic" trait as a stylist—his affinity for falling rhythm, the major rhythm of his native language. [Contains several valuable analyses of JC's prose rhythms.]

3100 Pulc, I. P. [pseud. of Irmina Pulc Plaszkiewicz]. "Pulc on Braun," *CON,* VI, No. 1 91974), pp. 63–67.

It appears that JC's flamboyant descriptions of tropical nature in some parts of the Southeast Asian archipelago are authentic. It also seems that the "dingy, fat Rajah" visiting on board the *Vidar* and laughing loudly at the mention of Almayer's name was a real Rajah Patololo, whose name JC transferred to the "Borneo world" and whose person he drew upon in creating Karain. [Rev. of Andrzej Braun's *Karain's Domain and the Rajah Patololo—An Article Note* (1970).]

3101 Pulc, I. P. [pseud. of Irmina Pulc Plaszkiewicz]. "Slady polskie w prozie Conrada" (Polish Traces in Conrad's Prose), *Literatura na Swiecie* (Warsaw), 2 (1974), pp. 237–50.

The Polish tone in JC's prose is less the result of transferring Polish idioms into English than the consequence of the interaction of Polish rhetorical habits (literary and colloquial), of which he did not entirely rid himself. They recur in syntax and characteristic prose rhythms. JC used borrowings, e.g., colloquial similes and metaphors appropriate to his new environment; literary translations of idiomatic phrases and words; and Polish proverbs and sayings for which there is no precise English equivalent. [In Polish.]

3102 Renner, Stanley. "Affirmation of Faith in *Victory* and *Murder in the Cathedral,*" *Christian Scholar's Review,* IV, No. 2 (1974), pp. 110–19.

JC's "Heart of Darkness" still stands as one of the darkest visions of fatal pessimism in all of literature" [a statement which may be questioned], and T. S. Eliot's *The Waste Land* describes "a spiritual landscape of utter sterility" which has become "a definitive symbol of twentieth-century despair." Both authors of these portraits of "the dark night of the human spirit" move on in later works to affirm the meaning of life despite the "disillusionments" of the modern world. JC never overcame his "deep agnosticism," yet in his fiction human values such as love, compassion, solidarity, and devotion to duty transcend the "paralyzing recognition of human perversity in a universe devoid of moral order." One of the clearest affirmations of faith in human life appears in *Victory*, whereas Eliot, in *Murder in the Cathedral*, strikes the note of Christian affirmation which is heard through his later works. The important difference in their affirmations is that JC's is wholly secular and Eliot's is Christian.

3103 Renner, Stanley. "A Note on Joseph Conrad and the Objective Correlative," *CON*, VI, No. 1 (1974), pp. 53–56.

About the time 1919 to 1920 both T. S. Eliot and JC used some of the same words to describe a similar method of writing. It appears that around 1920 Eliot had perceived in JC's early work ("Heart of Darkness" and related writings of the same period) something which did not become generally apparent until well into our time; at the very least, he recognized that both JC's method and his vision were somehow interrelated with his own. Both authors mention JC's early fiction in the language of Eliot's objective correlative. Perhaps Eliot saw in JC a mind "constantly amalgamating disparate experience" into "new wholes," perhaps there is something of Marlow in the shadowy persona of *The Waste Land*. In "Heart of Darkness" and Eliot's poem, there is a similar loss of faith in God and man, a similar longing for spiritual sustenance, a similar mood of despair, a similar inconclusiveness. JC may have been making a "formula of expression" for the contents of his works while Eliot may, somehow, have been following JC's lead.

3104 Rose, Charles. "*Romance* and the Maiden Archetype," *CON*, VI, No. 3 (1974), pp. 183–88.

Romance fails because the heroine, Seraphina, is primarily a sublimation of the dynamics of the relationship between Ford Madox Ford and JC. Her role in Kemp's adoration is an anima which ignores the dark side of the archetype, yet this side sometimes appears in Kemp's seizures of doubt and despair and in his childish sense of passivity when he considers his own unworthiness. But he is eventually saved because he keeps her image inviolate. Apparently what was intended as an adventure story turned into a fantasy of hope. It appears that Seraphina was necessary for the author's relationship to continue, precisely because she is not a decisive anima for either Ford or JC. The source of her sublimation lay in their unwillingness, at this time, to come to terms with the anima. Seraphina was Ford's own conception, which he insisted on keeping. His part in the deception was to neutralize the anima, to "draw out its paralyzing sting." JC's was to lend it divinity through the rubric of incantation."

3105 Ross, Duncan Michael. "The Indispendable Invalid: Joseph Conrad's Treatment by the Freudian Critics," *DAI*, XXXV (1974), 471A. Unpublished dissertation, University of Michigan, 1973.

3106 Ross, Stephen M. "Conrad's Influence on Faulkner's *Absalom, Absalom!*" *Studies in American Fiction*, V (Autumn 1974), pp. 199–209.

Having read JC from the fourth grade on, William Faulkner acquired much from his practices: he learned to use several "techniques of Impressionism" and shared certain of the epistemological assumptions underlying these techniques. More specifically, *Absalom, Absalom!* echoes *Lord Jim* and "Heart of Darkness" in rhetorical pattern, in its tone of narration, and sometimes in imagery. Both Marlow and Mr. Compson acknowledge the impossibility of ever reaching final truth. Faulkner's authoritative manner also comes from the rhetorical procedures he learned from JC—and improved upon. Although Faulkner does not alter JC's techniques in any drastic way, he does enlarge the role played by subjective impressions in determining the impact of the novel. Marlow and Quentin Compson talk alike because they tell about similar confrontations with the human capacity for evil; both meditate on and relive symbolic journeys into darkness.

3107 Rude, Donald W. "Conrad as Editor: The Preparation of *The Shorter Tales of Joseph Conrad*," *JCTWF*, VII, Nos. 23–25 (January 1974), pp. 189–96.

The posthumous anthology, *The Shorter Tales of Joseph Conrad* (Garden City, New York: Doubleday, Page, 1924), is of much importance because JC himself was seriously involved in its preparation; because a group of six letters to his American publisher, F. N. Doubleday (only two of which have been published), cast new light on JC's views of his short fiction; and because the letters provide new insight into his working relationship with the Doubleday firm. [The unpublished letters are in the Princeton University Doubleday Collection.]

3108 Said, Edward W. "Conrad: The Presentation of Narrative,"
Novel, VII (Winter 1974), pp. 116–32.

In both his fiction and his autobiographical works, JC was trying
to achieve something that his experience as a writer revealed to be
impossible: his major "mode," although he was a *writer,* is seen as
oral, and he desired mainly to move towards the visual, toward
situations employing yarns, tales, and "utterances" for their
depiction. For him, the text was the "never-ending product of a
continuing process," a process in which he found loneliness,
darkness, and the necessity of writing; hearing and telling were the
most stable sensory activity, whereas *seeing* was a "precarious
achievement" and a much less stable matter. For JC, the meaning
produced by writing was a kind of "*visual outline*" to which language
can approach "only from the outside." His letters perpetually portray
him struggling with language, which is for him a "*passive,*
retrospective transcription of action." Within himself, JC had the
dubious privilege of witnessing the change from storytelling as
"useful, communal art" to "novel-writing as existentialized, solitary
art." This change entailed stronger emphasis on the medium of
delivery, variation of words and tone, dramatization of the listener,
and conceiving narrative as "utterance" rather than as useful
information. *Lord Jim* is one of JC's first extended narratives to make
knowledge, intelligibility, and vision into functions of utterance. Both
words and objects are memorable in JC's fiction; much of the action
is organized around such substances as Lingard's gold, Kurtz's ivory,
and Gould's silver. In attempting to negate his writing *as writing,* JC
permits himself such things as the use of English, the use of
experiences from the past, and the use of events about which no
explanation is satisfactory; he uses substance instead of words.

3109 Sams, Henry W. "Malinowski and the Novel: or, Cultural
Anthropology versus Mere Fiction," *Journal of General
Education,* XXVI (1974), pp. 125–38.

Bruno Malinowski saw his anthropological work in New Guinea
(1914–1918) as fulfilling a high idealistic purpose, but he was
invariably tormented with guilt when he indulged himself with
fiction, in flights of fancy which removed him from his
responsibilities of research. His guilty sense of wasting time with
fiction was brought on by his habit of identifying emotionally with
fictional characters and fictional situations which constantly
reminded him of his personal and professional failings.

Malinowski was able to accept the works of Rudyard Kipling and
JC. He accepted them as his own equals, but each in a different way.
He frequently used Kipling's novels as sources of information on
their settings. He found Kipling to be informative, but he recognized

his artistic inferiority to JC. JC was Malinowski's "author" because his novels reflected almost perfectly Malinowski's experiences in the jungles of New Guinea. His sense of experiential kinship with JC had a direct bearing on the development of his thesis that the study of social sciences should be approached through the determination of "laws" which governed the behavior of men in groups. JC's attempts to examine the relationship of language and action in such novels as *Lord Jim* indicate a similarity in outlook with Malinowski's sense that language, a product of collective psychology, is a mode of action in society. His sense of the connection between life and art has not been challenged.

3110 Sanders, Scott. *D. H. Lawrence: The World of the Five Major Novels* (New York: Viking, 1974), pp. 208, 211.

The earlier Victorian novelists presented both community and individual as knowable, either by the narrator, as in Scott, or by a central observer, as in Jane Austen; and the same novelists treated the social order, imperfect as they may have seen it, as the product of human reason and desire. After 1848, the fictional world appears progressively less rational and intelligible, particularly in the later works of Dickens, Eliot, and Hardy, and in Gissing and JC. D. H. Lawrence reproduces this evolution of a century within the space of his own career—from *Sons and Lovers* through *Lady Chatterley's Lover*. The nature of community and character did not, however, become suddenly problematic in Lawrence's mature fiction; the pressure of these concerns was increasing throughout the latter half of the century, conspicuously in the works of Hardy and JC. [JC is seen here as at least partially a Victorian.]

3111 Sarbu, Aladar. *Joseph Conrad Világa* (The World of Joseph Conrad), (Budapest: Európa konyviado, 1974), p. 255.

JC's works were not translated into Hungarian during his lifetime. Only *Victory* (1970), *Lord Jim* (1972), and *Nostromo* (1973) have appeared in Hungarian. The essential features of JC's art are seen in *Almayer's Folly*: the dreamer incapable of action, solitude, the exotic background, and the faults such as the mixture of realism and romanticism in depicting character and events due to lack of auctorial distance. Many ideas in *The Nigger of the Narcissus* reappear in later novels. An important source for *Nostromo* was JC's attitude to and recollections of Poland. *Under Western Eyes* may be compared to Dostoevski's *Crime and Punishment*. JC's greatest weakness is his unjustifiably stressing the character of Russian society at the end of the nineteenth century. [In Hungarian.]

3112 Saveson, John E. "Conrad, *Blackwood's*, and Lombroso," *CON*, VI, No. 1 (1974), pp. 57–63.

A logical source in an attempt to understand JC's opinions of anarchists is *Blackwood's Magazine* where, between 1899 and the publication of *The Secret Agent* in 1907, the periodical printed four "useful long editorial articles" upon Lombroso's classification of anarchists as criminal degenerates. Although it is not known that JC necessarily took his opinions from *Blackwood's*, both he and the magazine are in accord with each other and with Lombroso also. Stevie of *Agent* agrees with such description, as well as with that of Henry Maudsley, the leading English criminal psychologist of the time. Descriptive phrases in *Blackwood's* also suggest such characters in the novel as the Professor, Ossipon, Karl Yundt, and Michaelis. Revolutionaries for JC are "superficial, cruel, vain, indolent." It appears, then, that the thematic quality of *Agent* is "not highly original," but it is clear that for JC the anarchist is "despicable." [Refutes a position taken by Robert G. Jacobs, "Comrade Ossipon's Favorite Saint: Lombroso and Conrad," *Nineteenth-Century Fiction* (June 1968). Incorporated in *Conrad, The Later Moralist* (1974).]

3113 Saveson, John E. *Conrad, The Later Moralist* (Amsterdam: Rodopi NV, 1974).

Four years after completing *Lord Jim*, JC published what he was to consider his best novel, *Nostromo*. The derivative nature of his later fiction is illustrated by his reliance on newspaper reports like those in the London *Times* about the revolution in Chile, which provided details for *Nostromo*. The dependency of this work on his reading is followed by that of *The Secret Agent* and *Under Western Eyes*. A second characteristic of his later novels is that they are about subjects of contemporary interest, as seen in *Nostromo*, *Eyes*, and *Agent*. The agitations of well-known feminists like Mrs. Pankhurst resemble those of Mrs. Fyne in *Chance*, and financial schemes and disasters like de Barral's in *Chance* and Morrison's in *Victory* were very common. JC wrote strictly according to the principle of his "chief" master, Turgenev, who did not point out morals but in subtler ways drew out definite attitudes in his readers. JC invested contemporary subjects with ironies and complexities which are often difficult to identify. A third aspect of JC's later fiction is a qualification of the topical nature of his subjects. In the last three important novels, *Eyes*, *Chance*, and *Victory*, in an increasing degree, the topical is displaced in favor of a more abstract and philosophical subject. JC thus moved gradually into final maturity as a moralist. Just as his earlier novels embody Kantian and Schopenhauerian themes which late nineteenth-century intellectuals found absorbing, so his last three novels embody Nietzschean themes found absorbing to early twentieth-century thinkers.

3114 Schultheiss, Thomas. "Conrad's Stein: Sidelight on a Source," *Pol R*, XIX, No. 34 (1974), pp. 35–37.

The probable source for Stein's idea about "Nature—the balance of colossal forces" is an exchange between JC and Tadeusz Bobrowski in a letter of late 1891. The expression used by Chester in *Lord Jim* to describe Jim's certificate as that "bit of ass's skin" appears also in one of Bobrowski's letters to JC in June, 1880. Another parallel passage in one of Bobrowski's letters of 1879 to Stefan Buszcynski is remarkably similar to the last paragraph of *Jim*. It seems, then, that JC wrote about Stein with his uncle closely in mind and that in his art he reverted to a portion of a letter received nearly twenty years before he started to write *Jim*.

3115 Seltzer, Alvin J. "The Rescued Fragment: Elusiveness of Truth in Conrad's *Lord Jim*," *Chaos in the Novel: The Novel in Chaos* (New York: Schocken Books, 1974), pp. 80–91.

JC uses the novel to "excavate the core of reality buried beneath a familiar surface of people and events," but because the author has no means of cracking that core the result is a novel which contemplates experience instead of penetrating it. Contemplation becomes, then, both subject and method of JC's novels, and he turns life's mystery into his main theme. In "Heart of Darkness" and *Lord Jim*, for example, he accepts the unknowable as the most fundamental part of his knowledge. For him, the chief characteristic of truth is its elusiveness, but even if it can never be grasped, it can sometimes be apprehended, felt, sensed. The author's task is to present its ambience so clearly and vividly that the truth will emerge "as submerged within the texture of the moment," the "moment of vision," which brings meaning to action. *Jim* is a work focused on chaos so consistently that it finally becomes the central subject of the novel. JC fails in attempting to elucidate Jim's character by taking the reader inside him; then he turns his narrative over to Marlow and to various observers, but he fails to solidify the reader's nebulous impression of the man. Since no one can confront fully the ability to know another man, Jim becomes "one of us," a fellow searcher for knowledge. Ultimately, the philosophical consequences of Jim's action are finally the denial of man's ability to penetrate life's mystery. Man must not, however, cease in his efforts: he must do as Marlow does—offer a weak light against the forces of darkness and disorder.

3116 Sertoli, Giuseppe. "Nota introduttiva" (Introductory Note), *Cuore de Tenebra* (Heart of Darkness), (Turin: Einaudi, 1974), pp. v–xliii; enlgd. as "Conoscenza e potere: Su 'Heart of Darkness' di Joseph Conrad" (Knowledge and Power: On Joseph Conrad's "Heart of Darkness"), *Altri Termini*, 4–5 (January 1974), pp. 115–99.

There are three levels in "Heart of Darkness": (1) realistic-political, (2) psychological-ethical-cognitive, and (3) linguistic-metanarrative, whose objects are (a) the economic and political reality of imperialism, (b) the ethics and the cognition of the white man, and (c) the language of civilized man and his *Kultur*. Civilization, a blank, produces an inhabited, dark, evil devastation; progress is irrational: its object is brutal exploitation. Beneath the Victorian ideology of economic and political power lurks sexuality. Marlow, unlike Kurtz, answers the charm of the wilderness with restraint, with the sublimation of the values of his civilization, work and duty, but these are mere tricks, beliefs, screens, against nature. Knowledge is power: the cognitive act obeys the rules of power; its law is the same that governs power: knowledge is appropriation. Imperialism is cultural prevarication. There is an imperialism of cognition; knowlege is imperialistic. Rejection of power must be rejection of knowledge, respect of the "other." Marlow knows himself, and self-knowledge is self-criticism. Since Marlow has discovered that darkness belongs to civilization, he must go back to the place where darkness is bred. Kurtz is the rhetoric of ideology: his eloquence hides the brutal reality of exploitation. Words are the noble facade of civilization; they hide its sordid reality. [In Italian.]

3117 Sherry, Norman. "The Essential Conrad," *Essays and Studies*, XXVII (1974), pp. 98–113.

JC defies chronology in his autobiography, *A Personal Record*, in order to focus on his psychological responses to the two central moments in his life: his first sea voyage and his first novel. By narrating the details of these two moments in a seemingly haphazard manner, he is able to recapture his sense of his experiences. His narrative strategy is to present an event or theme by demonstrating ways in which people respond to these important matters. The reader learns by piecing together the multitude of responses and interpretations present in the narrative; he enters the process of the narrative. As he becomes part of the narrative's search for truth, the reader understands the impossibility of reaching a moral "verdict." JC builds *Lord Jim*, for example, around numerous interpretations of Jim's actions and motivations. The irony of the novel is that Marlow, Stein, et al., are incapable of leaving their individual illusions in order to understand Jim. In "Heart of

Darkness," JC presents, from various standpoints, the process of colonization. By demonstrating the unchanging nature of man's desire for conquest, the narrative transcends time to attack the notion of progress. By underlining the ironic distance between the characters' aspirations and their achievements, *The Secret Agent* shows the reader that the preservation of society depends upon the delicate balance of contradictory elements within the society. JC's ability to involve his reader in his narrative removes the possibility of superficial answers to the moral questions raised by the novels. His fiction is truly "open-ended."

3118 Sherry, Norman. "Introduction," Joseph Conrad, *The Nigger of the Narcissus, "Typhoon," "Amy Foster," "Falk," "To-morrow"* (London: Dent [*Collected Edition of the Works of Joseph Conrad*], 1974), pp. v–xvii.

JC wrote *The Nigger of the Narcissus* because he wanted to give an accurate representation of life at sea, he wanted to provide a testimonial to his fellow seamen, and he hoped to create a group of men who derive some kind of meaning out of their lives when they face certain problems. JC's historical and personal purpose accounts for the many factual details in the novel, but his basic interest is the crew. How the sailors, individually and as a group, react to Jimmy Wait, a man "living with death," is of the greatest importance. Whereas Jimmy "moves" men on a personal and individual plane, Donkin "moves" them on a communal level, serving as the "true example" of anarchism. Over and above the conflicts among the crew are the forces of the warring elements: man—the crew—is set against the universe, which dwarfs him despite his endurance and courage. The whole voyage of the ship presents a "microcosmographical" portrayal of human society, and yet JC avoids detracting from the quality of the life described. "Typhoon," like *Nigger*, "celebrates" man's stand against the sea, but is a slighter story. "Falk" demonstrates a man's determination to survive, and "To-morrow" presents the restlessness that prevents a man from settling down. Both "Falk" and "Amy Foster" display JC's perception of the effects of the bizarre and the grotesque on the normal or settled community. [Contains a brief bibliography and some notes on nautical terms.]

3119 Sherry, Norman. "Introduction," *Lord Jim* (London: Dent [Everyman's Library], 1974), pp. vii–xix.

Lord Jim is a relatively straightforward adventure story with a typical romantic hero who is repeatedly tested for courage and initiative. JC, however, gives the tale a complicated surface and transforms the convention through his use of multiple narrators and a complex time-scheme. *Jim* becomes a novel of inquiry, but there is no simple solution at the end. The inquiry, as a result of the novel's complexity, reveals parallels and inconsistencies of character and circumstances which are true enough to the human condition to make the story a touchstone for human nature. The various narrative points of view and the compression effected through the complex time-scheme make, for example, Brierly's career parallel with Jim's: a situation in which each character illuminates the other although there is no allowance for a general conclusion. Jim, when tested, consistently fails because the "dichotomy between his dreams and his ability to realize them leaves him unprepared." He suffers from an excess of imagination which not only permits him to deny reality, but also carries him beyond the adventure story to the realm of the terrifying possibilities which paralyze him. He fails Brown's test, because Brown's claim of kinship paralyzes him. Jim commits suicide; he, like Brierly before him, meets his destiny on his own terms, but it is left to the reader to complete the story. [This edition includes "Notes," which explain the four major sources of *Jim* (personal experience, observation, the experience of others, and reading), and a glossary.]

3120 Sherry, Norman. "Introduction," *The Secret Agent* (London: Dent [*Collected Edition of the Works of Joseph Conrad*]; [Everyman's Library], 1974), pp. vii–xx.

JC's interest in *The Secret Agent* lies largely in the circumstances surrounding the basic story and the light it casts upon human nature. The novelist finds the so-called civilized life of the city as dangerous as that of the jungle he had portrayed in "Heart of Darkness"; he displays Stevie, Verloc, and his wife, Winnie, with a terrifying sequence of events that leads to their deaths, events made more terrifying by the madness and despair which can exist in the urban, domestic, and apparently safe world of the Verloc household. The most important level of existence is that of the inner spiritual and psychological realm which ultimately erupts into violent expression because it is least apparent; the surface of the novel is undisturbed. The story, presented through a series of confrontations between various characters, contains interior scenes which often, in turn, contain some form of mad and ironic activity beneath the surface. Outside the interiors in which discussions are carried on and important decisions are made is a primitive and threatening environment of "murk and gloom," a world which suggests a "topography of hell." The novel further dramatizes the way in which a stable and secure society avoids an active use of imaginative sympathy in order to avoid suffering. Too scrupulous an examination of such people as the anarchists produces only horror at their lack of imagination. Their blindness to other kinds of pain results in a physical grotesqueness and a bizarre imagery of violence, impotence, and cannibalism.

3121 Sherry, Norman. "Introduction," *Nostromo* (London: Dent [Everyman's Library], 1974), pp. v–xi.

In his earlier works, JC is chiefly concerned with man in a state of isolation; in *Nostromo*, he turns to political and social themes. After 1911, except for *Victory* and *The Shadow-Line*, there is a falling-off in his work. *Nostromo* thus stands between, or "straddles," the two most fruitful periods of JC's writing life. The basic origins of *Nostromo* JC found in his reading, especially in a book called *On Many Seas: The Life and Exploits of a Yankee Sailor*, by Frederick Benton Williams. But most of his novel is derived from his readings about South America; little evolves from his personal experience. JC often tests his characters in various ways, but not men but silver can be seen as the "pivot" of events, and many of the individual fates are seen in a direct relationship to it. It is JC's ability to perceive and to present as "the fundamental" of his story the solid presence of Costaguana in all its variety and its significance in terms of man's history that is at once his greatest strength and perhaps his greatest weakness. A large part of the inherent irony of the novel comes from a sense of history that is constantly being "formed and re-formed" by mankind, whose actions will inevitably become not only a part of the present but also a part of the past and are constantly working for the "erosion" of what has been achieved. Thus the fate of the main characters can be only ephemeral, thereby making the novel a commentary upon the fate of mankind as JC saw it.

3122 Sierz, Krystyna. "Learning the English Language—A Love-Hate Relationship?" *JJCS*, I, No. 4 (June 1974), pp. 5–6.

Because of such problems as a large vocabulary in English, pronunciation, the illogical nature of the language, and auxiliary verbs, English is a very difficult language for foreigners to learn. It is, then, small wonder that JC had difficulty in mastering it.

3123 Sierz, Krystyna. "Lord Jim in Polish Disguise?" *JCSN*, [I], No. 3 (Fall 1974), pp. 5–6.

According to Wit Tarnawski (in *Conrad Żywy* [*The Living Conrad*], 1957), JC was haunted all his life by a "treason complex." The first literary voice to reach him from Poland was that of a novelist of some standing, Orzeszkowa, who attacked him in *Kraj* (published in Petersburg) in 1899; she was wrong in her accusations, but JC took her words seriously. How obsessed he was by the "treason idea" is seen by the number of stories in which it is used: *Lord Jim, The*

Outcast of the Islands, "Karain," "Falk," *Nostromo*, and *Under Western Eyes*.

3124 Slade, Joseph W. *Thomas Pynchon* (New York: Warner Paperback Library [Writers for the Seventies], 1974), pp. 16, 20–21, 23, 24–25, 153.

Thomas Pynchon has assimilated some of JC's ideas for his stories and novels. In the story, "Mortality and Mercy in Vienna," Pynchon evokes "Heart of Darkness" in treating Washington as a "jungle" like the one in JC's tale: Cleanth Siegel suffers from an inner void as does Kurtz. And in *The Crying of Lot 49*, Pynchon may be following JC as he underlines his vision of modern reality.

3125 Smitten, Jeffrey R. "Flaubert and the Structure of *The Secret Agent*: A Study in Spatial Form," *JCTWF*, VII, Nos. 23–25 (January 1974), pp. 151–66.

The concept of spatial form in the novel is explained in Joseph Frank's essay, "Spatial Form in Modern Literature" (1945), where the author takes as example the agricultural fair scene in *Madame Bovary*. Here, Frank finds two general structural techniques which are applicable to JC's *The Secret Agent*, fragmentation of the narrative sequence and juxtaposition of these fragments, and unification of the fragments in the reader's mind as he perceives the analogy and contrast among them. In *Agent*, JC combines the time-shift technique and suppression of transitions to fragment his narrative into parts which the reader must juxtapose, thereby noting JC's ironic effects. Thus the unity of the novel as a whole depends upon the reader's apprehension of a configuration of causes and effects as well as of multiple analogies and contrasts within that configuration. [A close examination of the text of *Agent* within the concept of spatial form clarifies several of JC's achievements in this novel.]

3126 Solinas, Stenio. "Un gentiluomo polacco di nome Joseph Conrand [sic]," (A Polish Gentleman Named Joseph Conrand), *L'Italiano*, XV (16 November 1974), pp. 763–64.

[Platitudes of no critical interest.] [In Italian.]

3127 S[pina], G[iorgio]. "L'uomo Joseph Conrad" (Joseph Conrad the Man), *Il Lavoro* (11 December 1974), p. 3.

[Review of Jessie and Borys Conrad, *Conrad L'Uomo: Testimonianza a Due Voci* (Milan: Mursia, 1974).] This book has nothing to do with literary criticism; still it is an exceptional document in that it presents through a myriad of incidents and details the picture of JC the man. [In Italian.]

3128 Stade, George (ed.). "Introduction," *Six Modern British Novelists* (New York and London: Columbia University Press, 1974), pp. vii–xv.

The great English literature of the modernist era, from about the nineties until World War II, was written by Irishmen, Americans, a Welshman, and a Pole—JC. The most common characteristic of the modernist writers was an adversary or alienated relationship to their own culture. The techniques used to represent the world of "dissolving appearances and discontinuous selves," of crumbling institutions and discredited authorities, are also the techniques that bind one part to another and the part to the whole with an "unprecedented force." For esemplasticity the modern classics are unequalled. The English modernists looked around them at new occasions demanding new practices. English writers like Ford Madox Ford, Virginia Woolf, E. M. Forster, and Evelyn Waugh, finding national character problematic, something to be discovered and defined, again and again posed their national types against a background of others, as JC did with his Jim, his Gould, his Lingard. [Clearly places JC among Arnold Bennett, Evelyn Waugh, Ford Madox Ford, Virginia Woolf, and E. M. Forster, the authors written about in this book. Reprints Robert S. Ryf, *Joseph Conrad* (1970).]

3129 Stallman, R[obert] W[ooster]. "Checklist of Some Studies of Conrad's *The Secret Agent* Since 1960," *CON*, VI, No. 1 (1974), pp. 31–45.

[This checklist was distributed by Professor Stallman at the First International Conrad Conference, held in 1972 at the University of London. Consisting of 73 items, several of which are annotated, the list is an invaluable source of recent information about *The Secret Agent*. The annotations are especially helpful—and often frank in Stallman's inimitable manner, as in "What nonsense!," "I disagree," "a dead book." Items annotated in Teets and Gerber, *Joseph Conrad: An Annotated Bibliography of Writings About Him* (1971), are so identified.]

3130 Stark, Bruce R. "Kurtz's Intended: The Heart of 'Heart of Darkness,'" *TSLL*, XVI (Fall 1974), pp. 535–55.

The concluding scene of JC's "Heart of Darkness," although seemingly "tacked on and anticlimactic," is crucial to the form and meaning of the novel. Marlow's interview with Kurtz's Intended "locks in" all of the preceding narrative and "makes of that story something quite on another plane than an anecdote of a man who went mad in the centre of Africa." The "Sepulchral City," not the inner station, is the center of Hell, or "Europe in general and this city in particular" are the source of the darkness, not the jungle. Thus, implicit in the structure is the "ironic reversal" that makes "Whites . . . spiritually black" and "Blacks . . . spiritually white." The source of this darkness is clearly the Intended's house: metaphorically it is associated with a cemetery, a mausoleum, a tombstone, and a sarcophagus—all of the trappings of death and darkness. Furthermore, the house is thematically and semantically associated with and is the source of Kurtz's station. Also, if the sepulchral city is the source of the darkness that invades the jungle, the Intended's house is at the center of the innermost circle and the Intended is its chief representative. It is Marlow's lie to the Intended that suggests his "moral defeat," his acceptance of the deadly illusion that she represents, whereas it is Kurtz's understanding of the illusion that his Intended represents that "wins for [Kurtz] the 'moral victory' that transforms him into the deeply ironic tragic hero of the tale." [Perceptive or ingenious?]

3131 Steinmann, Theo. "Lord Jim's Progression Through Homology," *Ariel*, V (January 1974), pp. 81–93.

Although JC appears to leave the telling of *Lord Jim* to his narrator Marlow, he employs other male protagonists as examples of a Jim that might have been. He uses the device of juxtaposition in such a way as to present to the reader and to Jim, if he were not flawed by moral dyslexia, characters who are projections of different facets of Jim's personality: the third engineer, Brierly, the French officer, Captain Robinson, Stein, and Gentleman Brown function, through JC's treatment, as Jim's potential personae.

3132 Steinmann, Theo. "The Perverted Pattern of *Billy Budd* in *The Nigger of the Narcissus*," *English Studies*, LV (June 1974), pp. 239–46.

Basically, *Billy Budd* and *The Nigger of the Narcissus* have the same structure, a comparable moral conflict, and analogous sets of characters, but in *Nigger* all these elements are vitiated in one way or another although both Melville and JC seem to believe in ethical values. The crew of the *Narcissus* feels bound to James Wait by a sense of "love-hatred," an unsound fascination with his slow struggle against death. He is the negative replica of Billy Budd, the "Handsome Sailor." As for the moral conflict, Melville portrays the archetypal conflict between good and evil in the encounter of the two men, Claggart and Billy Budd, who are fated to destroy each other because of their opposite temperaments, and JC dramatizes the same archetypal situation, opposing the naive, morally sound crew to two men, Jimmy Wait (who personifies Claggart's deceitfulness) and Donkin (his compulsive urge to hurt and destroy). Both captains know at all times what is best to do. JC's Captain Allistoun is practically identical to Captain Vere, but Vere's emotional involvement becomes a separate entity, deformed into Belfast's unilateral, undignified servitude. Billy dies, unlike the usual hanged man, without the least spasm, but Jimmy's very body seems to cling to the ship. With Billy Budd and Claggart, innocence and guilt changed places, but with Jimmy and the sailors, Jimmy initially shammed his sickness and the men eventually had to admit that what they thought to be dissimulation was the truth. The complexity of Melville's protagonists disintegrates into one-dimensional types; his themes dissolve into uncertain speculations. To Melville's religious ethics corresponds JC's dogma of the good sailor and the corrupt landsman.

3133 Tarnawski, Wit. "Conrad, the Man, the Writer, the Pole," *JJCS*, I, No. 3 (February 1974), p. 5.

Two main ideas seem to have dominated JC's life and writing: the relationship to his country of origin and the charge of desertion placed against him there, and the passionate critique of Western materialist civilization which inspired "Heart of Darkness" and *Nostromo*. [Published in Polish as *Conrad Czlowiek—Pisarz—Polak* (London: Polish Cultural Foundation, 1972), pp. 308, ill. 22, 23.]

3134 Tarnawski, Wit. "From Achievement to Decline," *JCSN*, [I], No. 4 (June 1974), pp. 2–3.

Whereas there is no exact dividing line between JC's earlier and his later work, the change seems to come about somewhere between the period which ends with the completion of *Under Western Eyes* in 1910 and the initial work done on *Chance*. JC's falling off in power can be sufficiently explained as the onset of premature old age. As a writer, JC apparently crossed his own "shadow-line" in his early fifties, an early time for aging to influence both his mental and physical "framework." When, at age forty, he took to writing as a profession, he had to adapt himself to a new way of life that would affect his health adversely. Under the circumstances, it was amazing that he could produce in the last years of his life the small masterpiece, *The Rover*. In his later works, notable are the hardening of moral principles, the abandonment of passionate probing into the riddle of human life and character, a general tendency of the imagination toward romantic dreaming and a withdrawal into the region of past memories and reminiscence, and symptoms of "creeping artistic decline." But JC escaped mental decline until the very end of his life.

3135 Thornton, Lawrence Allen. "Beyond *Le mot juste*: Flaubertian Aesthetics in Joseph Conrad and Ford Madox Ford," *DAI*, XXXV (1974), 482A–83A. Unpublished dissertation, University of California, Santa Barbara, 1973.

3136 Tolliver, Harold. *Animate Illusions: Explorations of Narrative Structure* (Lincoln: University of Nebraska Press, 1974), pp. 5, 6, 15, 16, 40, 115, 117–19, 256–47, 251, 266.

For JC, the roles of fiction and history were almost interchangeable—except that writers of fiction are likely to be more accurate in some respects than those who find their material largely in documents. The modern modes closest to traditional myth, romance, sacred parable, and religious epics, in that modern romance tends to replace the expanded vista of the tradition with a sense not of transcendent being but of non-being, are antiromances like those of Hawthorne, Kafka, Barth, and JC. The "interfering power" in a modern work of this type is not likely to be either a nameable divine force of Malory's type or a definable force of realism like those found in Hemingway, Wright Morris, Edith Wharton, William Styron, or Norman Mailer. A notable modern example of the most radical narrative form is "Heart of Darkness," in which the central intelligence, Marlow, discovers not a "grail fellowship" but a demonic equivalent. Like the voyages of Malory's knights away from the logic of the Arthurian kingdom and its chivalric order, Marlow's journey takes him beyond the accustomed order of "modern bureaus" and the capitalist empire in Africa. His way stations lead downward to the darkness. Since the heart is total darkness, any "view" that Marlow might have of it is contradictory. He therefore plunges through stages of illusory vision to an "unspeakable anguish, an epistemological negation." But unlike Galahad, Marlow comes back to the living, where he tells the story in all its contradictions once as a lie to Kurtz's Intended and again to his fellow seamen as an exposure of the lie.

3137 Tolomei, Ugo. "Ricordi di Conrad" (Conradian Memories), *Il Giornale Nuovo* (20 November 1974), p. 3.

[Review of Jessie and Borys Conrad's reminiscences in Italian.] [In Italian.]

3138 Umavijani, Montri. "Artist of the Perceived World: A Study of the Making of Joseph Conrad," *DAI*, XXXIV (1974), 6001A. Unpublished dissertation, Northwestern University, 1973.

3139 Urbanowski, Bohdan. "Navigare necesse est," *Miesiecznik Literacki* (Warsaw), IX, 11 (1974), pp. 72–79.

JC's work is full of surprisingly clumsy blunders. Time is complicated; indeed, it does not exist. A character's story can begin anywhere, including the moment of death, as with Brown in *Lord Jim*. The beginning and the end often have to be reconstructed by fitting in fragments of time, and the order is relative. Jim's story is all Marlow's hypotheses. Then, out of the chaos of events, a chain of cause and effect suddenly emerges, ending in tragedy. The secret of JC's heroines is isolation, which is the cause of the failure of dialogues and blunders in composition. It paralyzes human lives and renders cooperation impossible. Three attitudes towards isolation may be seen: obtuseness without honor, passivity and contempt, or the heroism of a soldier who fights despite all and without counting on victory. [In Polish.]

3140 Urbisz, Krystyna. "The Theme of Isolation in Joseph Conrad," *Zeszyty Naukowe Uniwersytetu Jagiellonskiego* (Cracow), 29 (1974), pp. 291–305.

JC frequently states that isolation is a dangerous and tragic situation; he considers community with a group as the source of moral and ethical strength which enables the individual to live with the idea of honor and prevents the disintegration of personality. JC's view of the world is one in which almost every individual experiences some kind of isolation. This condition is caused by egoism, daydreaming, idealism, and skepticism. JC did not believe in any radical cure for isolation: indeed, he saw it as unavoidable. The meaning of life lies in striving for the unattainable, which is the lot of every individual. [In English, with a summary in Polish.]

3141 Ure, Peter. "Character and Imagination in Conrad," *Yeats and Anglo-Irish Literature, Critical Essays by Peter Ure*, ed. by C. J. Rawson (New York: Barnes & Noble, 1974), pp. 227–42.

JC's reluctance and equivocations in face of his self-imposed imaginative task affords some help in explaining the nature of his heroes. These heroes, partly fashioned in JC's own image, are sometimes highly imaginative men and yet men who can be punished by a "degeneration" of the imaginative faculty, or their imagination in a state of decay becomes the symbol of their loss of selfhood. In "Typhoon" and *The Shadow-Line*, JC's theme is that of a mere, blank resistance to those "potencies" in and outside a man which threaten to destroy his capacity for service. *The Nigger of the Narcissus* is complementary to *The Shadow-Line* in that it further explicates the answer Captain Giles could not get: an entire crew become the victims of disorder of heart and mind. *Almayer's Folly* and *An Outcast of the Islands* may be read as preparations for the greater *Lord Jim*. In the last, should Jim have "resisted"? JC's reply is ambiguous. In *Nostromo*, the terrible failure of the Capataz and the terrible success of Charles Gould are tragedies of men who are "self-betrayed by the ambiguity of their most expressive and valuable impulses." This novel "plumbs the depth" of JC's pessimism. In *Victory*, though, JC shows how far he can go. Heyst's greatest achievement is in making possible the conditions for Lena's victory. The struggle in the book is between "love and inhuman evil incarnate" in Ricardo and his gang. From Lord Jim, "that lofty and solitary existence," to the "creative and interacting duality, Heyst-Lena," lies JC's progress from the epic to the drama.

3142 Vidan, Ivo. "Conrad's Legacy: The Concern with Authenticity in Modern Fiction," *JCTWF*, VII, Nos. 23–25 (1974), pp. 167–86.

JC, the only major novelist who was also master of a craft outside the liberal professions and who embodied, in one way or another, his relationship to that craft in his works, created characters who are constantly confronted with their "original project" (Sartre), and seamanship is appropriate as a metaphor for it. The tradition in the novel established by JC is notable for the manner in which the awareness of vocation causes men to define themselves through the various codes of ethics they assume. The authenticity of the "Conradian personality" is tested in terms of its adequacy to its fundamental choice. This manner is unique to JC but in the Puritan inheritance of Henry James and in the Protestant conscience of George Eliot's heroines. In one sense, Stephen Crane anticipated the problem of *Lord Jim*. Several later authors have undoubtedly felt the impact of JC's handling of this theme: Fitzgerald in *Tender is the Night*, Hemingway, Malraux, Saint-Exupéry, Graham Greene, William Faulkner, Robert Penn Warren, and Malcolm Lowry in *Under the Volcano*. The problem of authenticity as it reappears in Bellow, Ellison, and Mailer is unrelated to JC's genuine concern with authenticity in such works as *The Nigger of the Narcissus, The Shadow-Line, Jim, Under Western Eyes, The Secret Agent*, "Heart of Darkness," and *Nostromo*.

3143 Viswanathan, Jacqueline. "Point of View and Unreliability in Brontë's *Wuthering Heights*, Conrad's *Under Western Eyes*, and Mann's *Doktor Faustus*," *Orbis Litterarum*, XXIX (1974), pp. 42–60.

In Emily Brontë's *Wuthering Heights*, JC's *Under Western Eyes*, and Thomas Mann's *Doktor Faustus*, the narrators interfere in the course of their stories with extensive comments of a type common to omniscient narrators—they express their opinions about the moral significance of the story; they pass judgment on the moral values of the characters. In comparable scenes in the three novels, the narrators relinquish the enlarged perspective they use in most parts of the narrative (the knowledge of the whole story before starting the account) for the limited perspective which was theirs when they witnessed the events; hence the revelation of their mistakes. These mistakes arise from their refusal to recognize the uncommon nature of characters and of their conflicts as well as from their reluctance to accept the occurrence of extremely tragic episodes. In *Eyes*, for instance, the narrator's perspective is abandoned temporarily for a "dive" into Natalia Haldin's heart. The dominant effect of the double perspectives is that the standards used by the narrators in their comments do not apply to a deeper, darker region of the characters' personality, the region which is expressed in the characters' symbolic imagery. This practice reveals nothing more of the characters' "essential mystery," and the full reliability of the narration is undermined without the substitution of any other truth. In all three novels, the heroes' lives are shaped like destinies; i.e., their entire existence is a preparation for their ending. Each novel sounds a warning against the comfortable security which the conventional views of the narrators have fostered, and the narrators create a world torn between forces of order and irrationality.

3144 Voytovich, Edward R. "The Problems of Identity for Conrad's Women," *Essays in Literature: A Journal of Graduate Scholarship*, II (March 1974), pp. 51–68.

The women in JC's works confront a number of problems. Some of them, such as Kurtz's Intended, Jewel, Emilia Gould, and Winnie Verloc, need a sense of self-definition and of self-actualization. Several are dependent on men: Joanna and Aissa in *An Outcast of the Islands*, like Nina and Almayer's wife in *Almayer's Folly*, and Flora in *Chance*. JC frequently reaffirms the idea that women are made for love and men for adventure, as noted in Winnie Verloc. Even the strongest women rarely find themselves utterly alone in the world: Edith Travers, Lena, Sophia Antonovna, and Winnie Verloc illustrate this situation. Some of JC's women are, to a certain extent, self-actualizing, like Mrs. Schomberg, Tekla in *Under Western Eyes*, and Axel Heyst's Lena. Emilia Gould is one of JC's women whose strongest character is self-control; Teresa Viola and her daughters, Linda and Giselle, are essentially flat characters. And whereas few of JC's characters have mothers, few of them become mothers, either.

3145 Voznesenskaia, I. A. "Dzhozef Konrad i naturalisticheskii roman v Anglii" (Joseph Conrad and the Naturalistic Novel in England), *Voprosy Filologii* (Leningrad), IV (1974), pp. 176–85.

The work of the English Naturalists was significant to JC only inasmuch as he opposed the didactic nature of the Victorian novel at the end of the nineteenth century. But his search for the truth to reality and his impersonal narration—as opposed to the Naturalists—corresponded to the artist's right to the use of imagination, the use of material drawn from life, and the subjective evaluation of the author. [In Russian.]

3146 Walsh, Dennis M. "Conrad's 'Typhoon' and the Book of Genesis," *SSF*, XI (Winter 1974), pp. 99–101.

In JC's "Typhoon," Jukes, the first mate, not MacWhirr, experiences a fall. The storm in the story is overtly like the choas before the creation, and "the order and light that comes [sic] into this demonic world" are created by the effort of men. The captain's "solidarity with mankind" is symbolized by his embrace of Jukes. Jukes completes his journey into the depths of the ship, where the confusion and torment are a direct reflection of the disorder outside the ship. In the engine room, Jukes finds a scene of comparative peace—light and order. The first step of biblical creation is the creation of light. For man to create light in the universe is demonic (vide Prometheus). MacWhirr and his crew, without divine sanction, create order and light on the *Nan-Shan*. After the storm, nature provides a symbolic background for humanly created light and order.

3147 Walt, James. "Conrad and James Huneker," *CON*, VI, No. 2 (1974), pp. 75–88.

JC's reputation in America came largely from Stephen Crane through James Huneker to H. L. Mencken. Huneker, drawn to JC by the "masculine vision" and the "sweeping conflicts" that distinguish his works from the "delicate fiction of the tea-table novelists" of the time, wrote largely impressionistic and intuitive criticism of JC's publications, but he wrote with freshness and excitement which still make his writings about the Anglo-Pole worthwhile. His correspondence with JC, begun in 1909 and continued for twelve years, brought Huneker to spend a few hours in 1912 at JC's farmhouse in Kent. There Huneker found his host's "chameleon-like personality," and the friendship grew stronger after the interview. In his article, "The Genius of Joseph Conrad" of 1914, Huneker included independent views along with old-fashioned eulogy. In his autobiography, *Steeplejack* (1920), he furnished a "misty and poetic" description of the Slavic element in JC and found his irony injurious to his reputation in England. He reserved his strongest praise for the romantic side of JC's genius. Huneker also wrote about JC in several periodicals; his contribution to *Puck*, for example, found the Anglo-Pole to be "a rare literary artist, but . . . a profounder moralist." Even if

Huneker was unable to give JC's individual works their due, and although he was unable to enunciate principles like those of Henry James, a history of JC's reputation in the United States will have to show this half-forgotten journalist's relationship to JC as "a human document well worth studying."

3148 Wasserman, Jerry. "Narrative Presence: The Illusion of Language in 'Heart of Darkness,'" *SNNTS*, VI (Fall 1974), pp. 327–38.

A recognition of Marlow's concern with language is a necessity for an understanding of "Heart of Darkness": Marlow's problem, like JC's, is to make his audience "see" the actuality of his experience in the Congo. But in the Congo, he has learned that words can both falsify and illuminate, can conceal truth as well as reveal it; so he, as a storyteller, must use ambiguous language as his major means of communicating with his audience. On one level, language is a metaphor or a function of civilization, an important psychological element of the imperialist conquest; but at the same time, Marlow's narrative includes a commentary on his seemingly futile attempt to reconstruct in words the experiences he and Kurtz have undergone. Finally, in order to make both his and Marlow's audiences see, JC reverts to the strategy of using Marlow as both the physical and the visual embodiment, the objective correlative indeed, of his own tale. His audience must read him as the reader reads JC's words on the page. The final result if that the style of the novel, as far as it includes Marlow's narration, is the theme.

3149 Watt, Ian. "*Almayer's Folly*: Memories and Models," *Mosaic*, VIII (Fall 1974), pp. 165–82.

In his first novel, *Almayer's Folly*, JC kept the facts very close to their origin. He is "characteristically uncommunicative" as to how his memories of Olmeijer urged him to write a novel and as to why he made only slight changes in minor details. One may surmise that for JC writing fiction tests his own conviction of the real existence of his fellow men, since people seem to have more faith in their own beliefs once someone else has agreed with them. Also, perhaps JC began to write fiction partly because it strengthened his conviction of his own reality. JC included in *Folly* some characteristics of both the popular romance and the adventure story, but he could not accept uncritically the fantasies and illusions which are the main target of his critical irony in the central character of the novel. His early conception of serious fiction was based primarily on the works of Daudet, Maupassant, and especially Flaubert. Both Emma Bovary and Almayer are petty-bourgeois versions of romantic aspirations. But even though JC fully absorbed Flaubert's *mystique* of the novelist, he was also trying to write for a different audience, thereby composing a more loosely focused work than anything done by Flaubert. Retrospective writing appears in *Folly* in a new way, the narrative point of view feeds our curiosity at the cost of starving our understanding, and direct access to Almayer's inner life is made difficult. Later, JC achieved more freedom, mainly through the use of intermediate narrators. [A seminal study of JC's development of character in his works.]

3150 Watt, Ian. "Conrad's Preface to *The Nigger of the Narcissus*," *Novel*, VII (Winter 1974), pp. 101–15.

In any rigorous sense of the word, JC had no theory of fiction; but in his own way he was from the beginning aware of his position among the critical traditions of his century. His preface to *The Nigger of the Narcissus* is centered on three large Romantic issues: (1) literature embodies kinds of "humanly necessary truths or values" unattainable elsewhere; (2) it has a higher kind of utility than the material or the quantitative; and (3) it is produced by and communicated to the imagination or the sensibility, constituents of the human personality unavailable to scientific psychological study. JC represents the same central tradition of Romanticism of which Wordsworth is probably the most representative figure. His use of the word "temperament" is unfortunate: he used the word in its original English meaning, which it retains in French only. Since JC's writing in the preface is somewhat less than exact, only a careful reading reveals how JC is either closer to modes of thought later than those of the Romantic poets or is largely original. Some of his positions seem especially important: his treatment of the means of expression, of visual impressions, of time, and of solidarity. His language, much more "elevated" than that of usual literary criticism, serves his purpose in the preface of setting "his own personal feelings about writing within the general context of other human activities in the ordinary world." [A rewarding analysis of JC's "critical bearings."]

3151 Watts, C. T. "Nordau and Kurtz: A Footnote to 'Heart of Darkness,'" *N&Q*, XXI (June 1974), pp. 226–27.

From Max Nordau's *Degeneration* (1896) may have come the initial idea of Kurtz's psychology. If so, in exploiting that basis JC criticized the moralistic confidence implicit in Nordau's punditry, partly by emphasizing Faustian aspects of Kurtz's career, partly by dramatizing the paradox of the virtue of evil, and largely by the tale's insistence that a "quality or irrationality" inheres in what the Nordaus of this world would consider as civilized normality.

3152 Wegelin, Christof. "'Endure' and 'Prevail': Faulkner's Modification of Conrad," *N&Q,* XXI (October 1974), pp. 375–76.

William Faulkner's Nobel Prize speech of 1950 obviously echoes JC's essay on Henry James (1905), but with a difference. Whereas Faulkner expressed an essentially hopeful view, JC was at best dubious about man's end. JC's artist may bolster the endurance man has learned in the school of "misery and pain"; Faulkner's poet achieves much more: his "voice need not merely be the record of man, it can be one of the props, the pillars to help him endure and prevail." Four years after Faulkner's Nobel Prize speech, his affirmation of man's immortality appears in *A Fable,* but he radically modifies his Stockholm speech by giving man's "immortality" not a moral foundation but a technological one. If "space" remained an alien domain to JC, so did the "extraterrestrial cosmos" of the spirit. He thought that our ethical norms have only a "purely spectacular" value, an "absurdist" view which Faulkner declined to accept.

3153 Weinstein, Arnold L. *Vision and Response in Modern Fiction* (Ithaca and London: Cornell University Press, 1974), pp. 50–57, 215.

Unlike Balzac and Dickens, Ford Madox Ford, Henry James, and JC "dramatize the act of the imagination . . . and tend to make it the subject of their fiction." *Lord Jim* and "Heart of Darkness," for example, can be seen as unceasing scrutinies of motive. Omniscient-author narrators yield to unreliable author narrators, like Marlow, and vision is increasingly restricted as the fictional work itself becomes more open-ended. What matters most is sensitivity, the "quality" of the vision, not the "value" of the action. JC's major works deal with the precise conflict between "the image of the self" and "the patterns of conduct" which men must enact. This clash usually appears as a betrayal of trust, with the only reconciliation the acknowledgment of both parts of the self. The basic problem, an epistemological impasse, is: how does one learn of others? *Jim* focuses more on Jim's impact on others than on his opinion of himself; the variety of responses to Jim (Brierly, Chester, Brown, Marlow, the reader) asserts the tentative, arbitrary nature of judgment of JC's interest in perception as theme. For JC, "the truth is a void" and we live out "the procedural drama" of fighting against masks. JC's most authentic note is that, even if the masks do not fit, they are all we have. Codes are, therefore, precious to us. JC's solution is to overwhelm us with the reality of the search for the nonexistent self in the hope that we will also accept "the illusion of the vision," as Mrs. Verloc finds in her suspicion that "life doesn't bear much looking into"—it leads to her death.

3154 Weston, John Howard. "'Youth': Conrad's Irony and Time's Darkness," *SSF*, XI (Fall 1974), pp. 399–407.

"Youth" is a complex work in which JC explores depths which, "epistemologically if not morally," are as deep as those of "Heart of Darkness." Time is structurally important in the story: for Marlow, the older narrator who imagines himself to be tested, both the world and time exist to serve him because he turns them into images of himself; objective reality—the physical world and chronological time—become "pure subjective experience" for the young, imaginative sailor. But to the older Marlow, the reality of the physical world is purposeful and cruel; for him, time and physical reality are as hostile as they are encouraging to his younger self. The symbols created by both Marlows are projections of their own inner lives upon the outer world. The younger Marlow, arrived in the East, maintains his romantic vision of reality; the older Marlow, equally sure in his vision, minimizes the importance of the early moment which is, to young Marlow, all-important. Thus early romantic idealism and later skepticism are illusions. The older Marlow's image of existence is more enduring than that of his younger self because the various frames of the central, static "picture," the burning of the *Judea*, reveal a movement from dynamism to stasis, so that Marlow's final victory is tragic: he exchanges an image of great beauty for one of less, but never sees the *facts* of existence in themselves.

3155 Widmer, Kingsley. "Conrad's Pyrrhonistic Conservatism: Ideological Melodrama Around 'Simple Ideas,'" *Novel*, VII (Winter 1974), pp. 133–42.

Much of the effect of "modernist culture," including the major literature between mid-nineteenth century and World War II, rests on its nihilism. JC's place in this modernism is perplexing. His skepticism is the very manner of his art, yet his simple conservative moral claims for art often make the morality pyrrhic; simple goodness of character is the only defense against the "moral chaos." JC's emphasis on "Fidelity" in his "A Familiar Preface" to *A Personal Record* is too indefinite in that it lacks an object—fidelity *to* something. JC's faith, then, is "almost entirely negative." The simplicities arising from desperate skepticism and its aesthetics are not the same as those from stupid, authoritative simpleness, or what JC calls "saving dullness." Episodes from three of his most important novels illustrate the issue posed by an art that attempts to be intellectually simple-minded and nihilistic. In *Lord Jim*, the suicide of Captain Brierly demonstrates a melodramatic instance of the precariousness of conventional standards and simple faith which need protection from "deep-delving" ideas, and Jim's "self-sacrificial death" follows the somewhat uncertain parallel of

The Secret Agent contains the apparently righteous passion of Stevie, brought on by his simple fidelity to Verloc, which leads to his death. *Nostromo*, though, contains the man of action, Decoud, who dies from isolation, not skepticism, though JC tells us otherwise. The unresolvable difficulties of JC's conservative dilemma and his powerful skepticism should, however, be respected.

3156 Wiley, P[aul] L. "Two Tales of Passion," *CON*, VI, No. 3 (1974), pp. 189–95.

Several of JC's best known works are labeled "tales." A revival of the British tale in the nineteenth century brought to prominence such writers as Hardy, Stevenson, Kipling—and JC. In this milieu, JC wrote *The Nigger of the Narcissus* in 1897. The characteristics of the folk tale of India seem to correspond to essentials of the tale almost anywhere: oral narration, primacy of story with interest in the surprising, and assumption of some kind of communal audience. Some so-called flaws in *Nigger* have met with objection because the work is a tale, not a novel. The narrator, for example, associated with such alternatives as "I," "we," and "they," reveals not instability but a necessity to persuade his audience that his narrative omits nothing important but not necessarily that he knew anything at first hand. *Nigger* is also an experience of passion: at the end, men are brothers through "a fundamental capacity for suffering," an effect of passion achieved by the narrator's turning from a "they" to a "we" association with the ship's company. In his "they" role, the narrator is usually objective but also gives, in places, praise of the traditional and ideal; but as "we," the narrator becomes "personal, excited, and self-tormenting." Another tale of passion, Ford Madox Ford's *The Good Soldier*, has a narrator who is more vital to the tale than is JC's. These two masterpieces were written in a time of transvaluation in both literary and social values; in them, the adaptations from the oral tale resulted in highly sophisticated forms.

3157 Williams, Ioan. *The Realist Novel in England: A Study in Development* (London and Basingstoke: Macmillan Publishing, 1974), p. 186.

George Meredith did not, in his realistic novels, ask the questions of the younger artists of the period who have since come to seem truly modern. His questions reduce to one basic question: how to preserve a belief that life is meaningful in circumstances which seem to deny it? This was what preoccupied Thackeray, Clough, George Eliot, and Arnold, but not Henry James, Yeats, James Joyce—nor JC; they were conscious of new forces at work in contemporary society, of which Meredith was aware but to which he responded in a different manner. The accompanying sense of freedom, however, lost the more recent novelists a solid yet flexible framework, into which they could assimilate themes, patterns, and situations from science, social studies, and other forms of literature, but which gave them a means of presenting what it was like to live in his period, and of commenting on, analyzing, and explaining the meaning of life as a whole.

3158 Winter, Geoffrey L. "The Last of the *Otago*," *JJCS*, I, No. 5 (October 1974), p. 12.

[A history of the barque *Otago*, JC's only command. The hulk is now rotting on the eastern bank of the Derwent, seven miles above Hobart, where many JC fans go to visit her.]

3159 Zabierowski, Stefan. "Conrad's Polish Career, 1896–1968," *CON*, VI, No. 3 (1974), pp. 197–213.

Both JC's literary output and his biography almost always met, in Poland, his homeland, "with considerable good will" and a very high estimate on the part of the Polish journalists, literary critics, and historians. Interest in his life began in 1896, a year after the publication of *Almayer's Folly*. Contemporary critics perceive in JC a fascinating personality, a remarkable writer, and a profound thinker. The Polish attitude toward his creative output divides itself into two distinct phases, with the years 1932 to 1934 providing the boundary line. The first period emphasized the moral-philosophical aspect of his work: as a writer he was most esteemed for those qualities which could be genetically derived from either romanticism or realism. Critics valued especially, in his books, voluntarism, irrationalism, intuitionism, and the sense of the mystery of human existence. In the years after 1932 to 1934, biographic concerns declined in interest for attention to JC's literary work, which did not, at first, fit in well with contemporary Polish literature. Only after 1956, with the work of Zdzislaw Najder, Roza Jablkowska, Andrzej Busza, and Barbara Kocowna, did interest in JC as a creator of a new novelistic mode and a new vision of the world develop. In the 1960s, much space was given to explaining the riddles of JC's biography, while several studies showed how much he owed to Polish culture and literature. Studies by Wit Tarnawski, Kazimierz, Roza Jablkowska, and Andrzej Busza placed JC's life and his literary output "in a Polish cultural ambience." [Translated by I. P. Pulc.] [In Polish.]

3160 Zabierowski, Stefan. "Piec interpretacji *Lorda Jima*" (Five Interpretations of *Lord Jim*), *Przeglad Humanistyczny* (Warsaw), No. 12 (1974), pp. 1–24.

Lord Jim has been interpreted as (1) the mirror of personal realities, situations, and topography, (2) a symbolic account of JC's guilt complex towards Poland, (3) a work dealing with crime,

punishment, and rehabilitation, (4) a work of literary art, and (5) a
work to be considered in its cultural, philosophical, and literary
context of the period when it was written, with elements of
innovation. [In Polish.]

3161 Zabierowski, Stefan. "Polskie spory o Conrada w latach 1945–
1049" (Polish Disputes on Conrad in the Years 1945–1949),
Rocznik Komisji Historyczno-Literacki (Cracow), XII (1974), pp.
177–203.

During World War II, JC enjoyed particular moral authority in
Poland, an authority which increased after 1945, when readers could
express their opinions openly. But in spite of public demand, JC's
works were not printed in Poland until 1948, beginning with *The
Arrow of Gold*, intended as the first volume of Collected Works, which
was not completed. Shorter works in translation, biographical, and
critical essays, were published in journals, mostly Catholic. Certain
left-wing and Marxist critics, however (Kott and others), adopted a
negative, even hostile attitude towards JC's philosophy. Counter-
attacks in support of JC were also printed (Chalasinski, Dabrowska,
Golubiew), questioning the validity of Marxist methodology in
analyzing JC's works, although they sometimes went too far and
drew analogies with fashionable existentialism. *Lord Jim* and *The
Mirror of the Sea* (1949) were the last works printed in "the past
period," though this was the result of "administrative decisions" by
the State publishing house, not of the polemics. [In Polish.]

3162 Zyla, Wolodymyr T., and Wendell M Aycock (eds.). *Joseph
Conrad: Theory and World Fiction* (Lubbock, Texas: Texas Tech
University Press [Proceedings of the Comparative Literature
Symposium, Vol VII, January 23, 24, and 25, 1974], 1974).

Contents, abstracted under date of first publication [all under
1974]: Wolodymyr T. Zyla and Wendell M. Aycock, "Preface"; David
Leon Higdon, "'The Precious Yesterday': Commemorative Remarks
for the Joseph Conrad Symposium"; Alan Warren Friedman,
"Conrad's Picaresque Narrator: Marlow's Journey from 'Youth'
through *Chance*"; Adam Gillon, "Joseph Conrad: Polish
Cosmopolitan"; Bruce Harkness, "Conrad, Graham Greene, and
Film"; Marion C. Michael, "James Wait as Pivot: Narrative Structure in
The Nigger of the Narcissus"; Zdzislaw Najder, "Conrad and the Idea
of Honor"; I. P. Pulc, "The Imprint of Polish on Conrad's Prose";
Norman Sherry, "The Essential Conrad"; Jeffrey R. Smitten, "Flaubert
and the Structure of *The Secret Agent*: A Study in Spatial Form"; Ivo
Vidan, "Conrad's Legacy: The Concern with Authenticity in Modern
Fiction"; and Donald W. Rude, "Conrad as Editor: The Preparation of
The Shorter Tales."

1975

3163 Achebe, Chinua. *The Chancellor's Lecture Series 1974–1975* (Amherst: University of Massachusetts, ca. 1975), pp. 31–43.

JC's "Heart of Darkness" displays extremely well the desire and the need in Western psychology to set Africa up as a foil to Europe, a place of negations both remote and vaguely familiar in comparison with which Europe's own state of spiritual grace will be manifest. JC's story projects the image of Africa as "the other world," the antithesis of Europe and therefore of civilization. The evocation of the African atmosphere is only a steady, ponderous, "fake-ritualistic" statement about the silence and the frenzy of the continent. After portraying Africa in the mass, JC chooses a specific example of a native who remains in his proper place. His portrait of an African woman in her place fulfills a structural requirement of the story: a savage counterpart to the refined Intended of Kurtz. JC speaks through Marlow, who is thoroughly reliable as a representative of the English liberal tradition. JC was, in fact, "a bloody racist," a fact glossed over in criticisms of his work. Africa is unusually employed as setting or backdrop which eliminates the African as a human factor. "Heart of Darkness," which dehumanizes, which depersonalizes a portion of the human race, cannot be called a work of art. The author certainly "had a problem with niggers." His depiction of the people of the Congo is grossly inadequate. He did not, however, originate this image of Africa: he merely followed the stereotype image which already existed. [Achebe is a writer whose opinion here may merit serious consideration.]

3164 Alter, Robert. *Partial Magic: The Novel as a Self-Conscious Genre* (Berkeley, Los Angeles, and London: University of California Press, 1975), pp. xiii, 23, 137.

A "self-conscious" novel is not at all identical with an elaborately artful novel, in which the artifice may be prominent. The first-person narrative, for example, of JC's *Lord Jim* and Ford Madox Ford's *The Good Soldier* in some ways reveal their artifice, but in both these works the artifice exists for the sake of a moral and psychological realism. JC and Ford reveal the world through a "labyrinthine" narrative because that seems to them the most faithful way of representing a labyrinthine world. Also, the "self-conscious" novelist makes use of the double with a "conscious quality of intellectual playfulness," contrasted sharply to writers like Poe, Dostoevski, and JC, who attempt to give the double its "full mythic resonance," as an embodiment of the "dark Other side" of the self. Melville's ambivalent sense of his vocation, combining much excitement at the idea of the novel might do with an increasing vexation over the truths it will not yield, is "profoundly modern." His "true heirs" in imagination are JC, who reflects in fiction on the "illusion-masked abyss of emptiness" over which everything human is built, including the fiction; Kafka, hopelessly committed to writing even as he ordered his books to be burned for their lack of truth; and Beckett, who produces literature about the end of literature, stubbornly attempting with words to reach a reality beyond language.

3165 Anderegg, Michael A. "Conrad and Hitchcock: *The Secret Agent* Inspires *Sabotage*," *Literature/Film Quarterly*, III (Summer 1975), pp. 215–25.

In his film *Sabotage*, Alfred Hitchcock derived much from JC's *The Secret Agent* but exhibits little "respect" for his source: the plot is truncated, most of the characters are altered beyond recognition, and the motivations are considerably changed. And at least one very important character, Ted, has been added. The milieu of JC's lower and middle-class London is a world that Hitchcock makes his own. Whereas JC's denouement is inevitably catastrophic, Hitchcock's is the conventional "happy ending." Oddly, though, Hitchcock's ending supports one of JC's major themes: the idea that the terrorist and the policeman are much the same. In spite of differences of tone, plot, and incidents, JC and Hitchcock make nearly parallel statements: both novel and film create a milieu where what seems to be tawdriness, laziness, and stupidity are in fact the external manifestations of genuine evil. Hitchcock demonstrates how an intelligent and "creative" director may ignore such matters as plot, character, and even theme, and find in his source various kinds of inspiration that will influence his own creation in unexpected and extremely fruitful ways.

3166 Astaldi, Maria Luisa. "Il complice di Conrad" (Conrad's Accomplice), *Avanti*, (5 October 1975), p. 6.

[Review of Giacobelli's Italian edition of *The Secret Sharer* (1975). A biographical survey which offers no new information and makes some absurd claims: after he had been robbed by a prostitute, JC attempted suicide in Marseilles; then his uncle took him to London where he attended a training school for officers of the merchant service.] [In Italian.]

3167 Azzali, Ferrante. "Conrad segreto" (Secret Conrad), *La Nazione*, 19 February 1975, p. 4; rpt. in part in *Il Resto Del Carlino* (11 March 1975).

[Review of Jessie and Borys Conrad, *Conrad L'Uomo: Testimonianza a Due Voci* (Milan: Mursia, 1974.] [In Italian.]

3168 Baccolo, Luigi. "Lo scrittore odiava il mare" (The Writer Hated the Sea), *La Fiera Letteraria*, LI, 18 (4 May 1975), p. 12.

[An appreciative and perceptive review of the Italian editions of Baines's critical biography of JC and Jessie and Borys Conrad's reminiscences.] [This review was employed by "D. C.," "Visse la sua vita come se fosse un romanzo" (He Lived his Life as Though if Were a Novel), *Secolo D'Italia* (21 August 1977), p. 3.] [In Italian.]

3169 Baird, Newton. "Conrad's Probe to Absolute Zero," *Armchair Detective*, IX (1975), pp. 43–49.

The Secret Agent, of 1907, JC's conceptualization of a "pattern of anarchy" at the end of the nineteenth century, is the first serious work in the form of an "offshoot" of detective fiction, the secret agent or spy story. It is related to the spy genre in plot, but even more so in atmosphere. The theme, an abstract projection of the "metaphysical nature of man in an irrational state of moral unconsciousness," is integrated in character, setting, and plot. Much of the philosophical meaning of the novel resides in the characterization, which reveals "only a slim structure of volition and good in man." The book is, however, in the mainstream of the literature of detection in its objective logical and highly innovative plotting. The absence of a hero or a unifying central character is offset by the scornful search for truth, and unity is achieved in the duality between characters, as seen in Stevie and the Professor, the latter of whom in "the satan of Conrad's anarchia," the "representation of absolute zero." Winnie Verloc represents a form of evasive idealism; her husband is an abstraction from Dante's lowest circle of evil: treachery. Vladimir and the Professor, both of whom lust for power, are doubles. But in its intricate structure and levels of meaning, *Agent* is far removed from the later spy thriller.

3170 Bantock, G. H. "Joseph Conrad: Reality and Illusion," *Sewanee Review*, LXXXIII (July–September 1975), pp. 502–10.

In his attempt to present truth, JC uses truth as the subject of his works, but truth at a level which offers opportunities of universalization through its appeal to the senses transmitted in a mood of the greatest sincerity. For JC, the duality of man's nature implies the fundamental conflict of good and evil which informs the human situation. Reality is defined as those characteristics of the surface—work and environment—which protect a man from the conflicts of his own dualism or provide a way of escaping their consequences; but it also, in other contexts, subsumes and faces the dualism. JC at his greatest is concerned with the "cores" of men in a world which provides no transcendental support or social sanction other than the integrity and the essence of the finer sensibilities. His use of illusion provides the rhetoric appropriate to a metaphysical world and a corrupt or inadequate social order. In this way he is part romantic. In this facing of reality and its definition in terms of the duality of man and the opportunities for integrity and fidelity afforded men with "finer" consciences lies the experience of life as JC sought to transmit it through his fiction, especially in *Nostromo* and *The Secret Agent.* Thus JC is not "modern" and "nihilistic;" he is committed to reality wherever it leads. His concern with the human condition allows him to illuminate some permanent problems of civilized life.

3171 Baum, Joan. "The 'Real' 'Heart of Darkness,'" *Con,* VII, No. 2, (1975), pp. 183–187.

In spite of all its meanings as symbol and myth, "Heart of Darkness" is "essentially" a tale about the real adventure of history in the Congo in the 1880s and 1890s. It may not be so much a conscious "design of ambiguity" as an honest but confused attempt to reconcile the author's sympathy and social position about the "carving" of the Congo. Neither Marlow nor JC ever assigns responsibility where it ultimately belongs—beyond Kurtz and Antoine Klein, the agent at Stanley Falls in 1899—to the governments of Portugal, the Netherlands, Belgium, France, and Great Britain. JC must have realized the hypocritical role played in this matter by his adopted country, but he must also have recognized his own uncertain position as a critic in a land where he was a newly naturalized citizen. His confusion of sympathies may help explain some inconsistencies in the tale. He surely knew something about the two men who were probably most responsible for making the policies that would be carried out by such men as Kurtz—H. M. Stanley and Cecil Rhodes, whose exploits were widely known and well publicized. Seen against the real policies of exploitation, the "vicious" statements of fiction may take on a clearer meaning than that hitherto noted in "Heart of Darkness."

3172 Beeton, Ridley. "Joseph Conrad and George Eliot: An Introduction of the Possibilities," *Pol R,* XX, Nos. 2–3 (1975), pp. 78–86; rpt. *JCCE* (1975), pp. 78–86.

Although there seems to be no direct influence of George Eliot on JC, certain elements in common suggest a better understanding of both writers and point toward a further extension of such an investigation. Specific passages in *Nostromo* by JC and *Romola* by Eliot indicate an "affinity" of style or parallels in the tradition of a great moral subject, and passages about *Lord Jim* also resemble some of Eliot's remarks. Also, a series of intimations from *Middlemarch* can be referred forward to statements on morality, combined with the shrewd assessment of character found in *Nostromo* and *Lord Jim.* In addition, "Heart of Darkness" and *Silas Marner,* two parables, contain contrasting journeys—JC's story into darkness, Eliot's into light. Both *Nostromo* and *Silas Marner* are unified structurally by silver and gold respectively, and both Marner's gold and the silver of the San Tomé mine are continually changing their color and their real qualities. [Contains some tantalizing possibilities for further study, but supplies little more than suggestions.]

3173 Beidler, Peter G. "Conrad's 'Amy Foster' and Chaucer's Prioress," *NCF,* XXX (June 1975), 111–15.

One source for "Amy Foster" seems to be the description of the Prioress and her tale in Chaucer's General Prologue to *The Canterbury Tales.* Amy and the Prioress are alike in possessing a mixture of pity and cruelty, sympathy and antipathy; JC's characterization of Amy is similar to Chaucer's description of the Prioress; and Chaucer's phrasing may have suggested to JC a pattern of "animal-in-trap" images. There are also parallels between Chaucer's "litel clergeoun" and JC's Yanko Goorall. And in both stories we are shown innocence destroyed, but not corrupted, by a morally inferior society, the theme of the lack of Christianity in Christians.

3174 Bender, Todd K. "Computer Analysis of Conrad," *Pol R* (1975), pp. 123–32; rpt. *JCCE* (1975), pp. 123–32.

The complete works of JC are in the process of preparation for computer analysis at the University of Wisconsin–Madison. The main application of the computer lies in the comparison and indexing of features of a text for the production of tables of information such as concordances of collations of versions of the work. It will be possible, by this means, to do many things, such as indexing the vocabulary of an early novel and comparing it with another, and studying the collocations of words much as psychologists practice word association tests. These possibilities will enable scholars to study more effectively the author's process of creation; the variations of spelling, punctuation, and style to suit shifting audiences; and preserve and investigate ambiguities of textual transmissions more efficiently than working with the limitations of printed paper. [For further information about this work, see Bender, "Computer Assisted Editorial Work on Conrad," *Conradiana,* V, No. 3 (Fall 1973), 37–45.]

3175 Bergeron, Alvin Wilhelm, Jr. "A Dictionary to Joseph Conrad's Novels: *Almayer's Folly* to *Lord Jim*," *DAI*, XXXV (1975), Unpublished dissertation, University of Georgia, 1974.

3176 Berman, Jeffrey. "Writing as Rescue: Conrad's Escape from the Heart of Darkness," *Literature and Psychology*, XXV, No. 2 (1975), pp. 65–78; rpt. *Joseph Conrad: Writing as Rescue* (1977).

Until recently, JC's attempted suicide at age twenty was unknown to scholars, but his letters written before and after this event to his uncle Thaddeus Bobrowski were often morbid. What remained constant with JC was writing as rescue. Few novelists, if any, found the process of artistic creation more "torturous" than did JC. His view of such creation was incurably romantic; the mysteriousness of creation involved the necessity of surrendering completely to the "demon" within him. Writing was for him a dangerous journey into the unknown, similar to his expedition into the Belgian Congo in 1890. His early fiction emphasizes the precariousness of the descent for the explorer and the artist alike. The Wordsworthian theory of emotion recollected in tranquillity gave way to the Conradian theory of "adventure relived in turbulence." Writing also exerted excruciating strains upon his physical and mental health, strains heard in his letters as in Jessie Conrad's two biographies. A fear of failure often appears; one situation frightened JC more than the ordeal of writing—the inability to write. Like Hemingway, JC felt a strong preoccupation with self-destruction. The twentieth century has witnessed an astonishing number of "haunted" artists whose writings seem driven to the form of confession, punishment, and psychic release. But unlike many of the artists who followed him, JC was able to exploit a private vulnerability into enduring artistic success.

3177 [Il Bibliotecario], (The Librarian). "Jessie e Borys Conrad, *Joseph Conrad, L'Uomo*" (Jessie and Borys Conrad, *Joseph Conrad, The Man*), *Il Borghese*, 9 February 1975, p. 458.

[A review of the Italian edition of Jessie's and Borys's reminiscences, in a right-wing journal, which tends to make JC look like a Facist; of no critical or ideological interest.] [In Italian.]

3178 Bienkowska, Ewa. "Literatura i los: *Zwyciestwo* Josepha Conrada i filozofia F. W. Nietzschego" (Literature and Fate: Joseph Conrad's *Victory* and the Philosophy of F. W. Nietzsche), *ZNAK* (Cracow), XXVII, No. 6 (1975), pp. 1025–1030.

Paradoxically, the extreme philosphy of Nietzsche attacking the entire manner of thought and world-view represented by philosophy in general brings to mind Heyst in JC's *Victory*, one of his most profound works. Heyst's disillusionment is so deep that it permeates any kind of participation in life or association with human beings. The skeptical and pessimistic philosophy of Heyst's father is somewhat in the manner of Schopenhauer, who was Nietzsche's teacher. In solitude, Heyst reverts to his father's philosophy, but JC puts him to yet another test: by chance, he is obliged to assist a young girl; i.e., he has become responsible for another person and has to undertake a struggle which is hateful to him. But his last attempt to form an alliance with life is defeated. In giving this novel its title, JC refers to the drama of human conversion and a return to active participation in vital values, with the full awareness that he will have to pay the price for his choice. This process is the "victory" of that which is most valuable in an individual. To Nietzsche, the original sin of philosophy is a flight into the abstract and a rejection of the human condition. [In Polish.]

3179 Biles, Jack I. "'It's Proper Title': Some Observations on *The Nigger* of the Narcissus," *Pol R*, XX, Nos. 2–3 (1975), pp. 181–88; rpt. *JCCE* (1975), pp. 180–87.

The title, *The Nigger of the Narcissus*, contains some important metaphoric implications. "Nigger," for example, derives from the Latin *niger*, with such meanings as "night," "black," and "pertaining to death." This "nigger" is set in opposition to "narcissus," a white, or pale yellow, flower, with significations the reverse of those of "nigger." Upon this contrast rests such antagonisms as "black/white," "land/sea," "dark/light," "death/life," and "evil/good." James Wait, the "nigger" of the *Narcissus*, has two partial sources in actual life, a Barbados Negro named George White (pronounced, no doubt, by JC as "wite") and another Negro seaman, Joseph Barron, who was on the actual *Narcissus* with JC in 1884 and died at sea. The opposition of the black "Niger" and the white "Narcissus" in the title suggests the customary dichotomy between good and evil and also implies that James Wait is the Black Man, Satan. In addition, the *Narcissus* exists as a microcosm which suggests self-love, and the Greek youth and the flower into which he was metamorphosed supply the basis for the ship as a "reflection" symbol. Wait reminds the members of the crew that they are all human and must therefore die; thus after Wait's death, the fear of death remains among the crew. What Wait is, each man of the crew is.

3180 Birdseye, Lewis. "*Chance*: Conrad's Modern Novel," *Studies in the Twentieth Century*, No. 15 (Spring 1975), pp. 77–94.

Chance is JC's one modern novel in that it functions effectively as a portrait of the artist, Marlow; it seems remarkably modern in a tradition carried on today by Samuel Beckett and Alain Robbe-Grillet in the pattern set by James Joyce. In such early works as "Youth," "Heart of Darkness," and *Lord Jim*, the author is interested primarily in unlooked-for disasters and the human response they evoke; in these works, *Chance* is subordinate to its result, the test. Flora in *Chance* is not to be held accountable, as Jim is, for her actions; she has no function to perform and remains passive throughout. Her major discovery is not an inner weakness but learning that others are filled with evil. JC no longer sees his characters as part of the world of evil and darkness; he sees them as figures of purity attacked by an external evil. Although "Chance" is the title of the book, the workings of chance do not constitute its theme; the title and the epigraph from Sir Thomas Browne's *Religio Medici* suggest that the workings of chance be taken ironically. JC elevates chance to an unusual position of prominence in this novel because Marlow is the artist who recognizes and "almost incessantly" calls our attention to its workings. Marlow's new role is thus like that of an omniscient author: in using his imagination to fabricate scenes he has not experienced, he is remarkably like an artist. All the "involuted convolutions" of the book exist for Marlow's sake; it is he who must piece together a meaningful whole, a work of art, from the scattered pieces given to him by the characters.

3181 Bischoff, Brigitte. "Der polnische Zimmermann: Zu dem Gedicht 'Joseph Conrad' von Johannes Bobrowski" (The Polish Carpenter: On Johannes Bobrowski's Poem, "Joseph Conrad"), *Neophilologus*, 59 (1975), pp. 579–91.

[An interpretation of Johannes Bobrowski's poem "Joseph Conrad." Asks who the carpenter in Bobrowski's poem is and suggests several answers: the Polish people; Mickiewicz; Towianski, or Apollo Koszeniowski; JC himself; JC's uncle Tadeusz Bobrowski. A brilliant poem and an excellent interpretation.] [In German.]

3182 Bojarski, Edmund A. "Mama Knew Conrad," *JJCS*, II, No. 2 (December 1975), p. 13.

The Cracow magazine, *Przekroj* (Cross-section), No. 1548, December 8, 1974, carried a letter from a lady named H. Rostafinska-Choynowska, of Warsaw, which gives an interesting glimpse of JC as a boy. [The letter is reprinted here.]

3183 Bonney, William Wesley. "Narrative Perspective in *Victory*: The Thematic Relevance," *Journal of Narrative Technique*, V (January 1975), pp. 24–39.

In the Author's Note to *Victory*, JC directly expresses his views on "detachment and involvement," favoring the former while mocking the latter, and in the novel, he contrives to "mislead" those readers who naively believe that "getting involved" or committing oneself to a code "is inherently valuable and praiseworthy, even if ultimately disastrous." For JC, the tragedy of the human condition is that there is no single code for all men. In *Victory*, which favors a code of detachment, JC places his characters in a "continuum with reference to their proximity to the detached attitudes of Old Heyst." The anonymous narrator "remains a static, detached, ironic voice" and "seems to use the subject matter of his narrative as a buffer between himself and his world." JC uses an onmiscient narrative point of view in the latter part of the novel because only by doing so can he report the internal conflicts and misgivings of Lena and Axel. Like JC in the Author's Note and the first-person narrator, the omniscient narrator preserves detachment through irony. Still another narrator, Davidson reports the final view of the events of the work, and in keeping with the theme and contributing to the unity, he too is detached. But unlike the other narrators, his aloofness is the result of his "superficial intellect." Davidson, as a character in the novel, represents the two extremes of the "continuum," ranging from the detachment of Old Heyst to the fatal involvement of Jones and Axel Heyst.

3184 Boulton, Marjorie. *The Anatomy of the Novel* (London and Boston: Routledge and Kegan Paul, 1975), pp. 5, 14, 22, 27–28, 43–44, 63, 68–70, 71, 78, 86–87, 100–101, 102, 122–24, 137, 139, 141, 144, 146, 147, 159, 160, 172 [index incorrect].

[Contains mainly passing references to JC; dwells mostly on *The Secret Agent*, but merely relates it to the topics of different chapters, such as "Verisimilitude," "Point of View," and "Plot."]

3185 Bradbook, Muriel. "Narrative Form in Conrad and Lowry," *The Proceedings and Papers of the Sixteenth Congress of the Australian Universities Language and Literature Association held August 1974 at the University of Adelaide, South Australia,* ed. by H. Bevan, M. King, and A. Stephens (no publisher given, ca. 1975), pp. 20–34.

Man and his myth have become part of the novels of both Malcolm Lowry and JC; both worked and reworked "their own past," so that the novels and stories, while not rooted in history, would "transform it from particular to general, and appeal to the unusual emotions." *October Ferry to Gabriola*, "Through the Panama," and "The Forest Path to the Spring" offer a "configuration" relating to *Victory*. Life ordeals in the writing were apt to become imaginatively enlarged: JC's attempt at suicide became, for example, a duel, and his first command a more melodramatic story than history can confirm.

JC's works invite a varied response from each reader, and the element of "performance" is suggested by various devices, of which the simplest is the seaman's tale. Lowry's early *Ultramarine* is a minor variation of *Lord Jim*. JC radically changed the character of the tales he told: "Typhoon," for example, grew out of a tale of Chinese coolies shipped in a heavy sea, but MacWhirr grew out of twenty years' experience of the sea. "The Secret Sharer" contains characters radically altered, and JC emphasized the element of the supernatural in *The Shadow-Line*. JC believed in rendering the truth, but as novelist he introduces the dislocations of time, the elaborate shifts and breaks in narration which give depth to the action and set up a rival sequence. He constantly remade his own life for himself. The plot of *Victory* is reshaped from JC's own story, "Because of the Dollars." [A major article on JC.]

3186 Bross, Addison C. "*A Set of Six*: Variations on a Theme," *CON*, VII, No. 1 (1975), pp. 27–44.

The question raised in JC's greatest works always concerns the nature of belief, and this theme also appears "quite saliently" in *A Set of Six*. "The Brute," in which a ship epitomizes the physical universe, displays the truth that the meaning of the phenomenal world is elusive. "Gaspar Ruiz" raises the doubtful question "whether a cynical and audacious egoism or a spurious idealism . . . is the more honorable;" it represents a noble but futile idealism. In "An Anarchist," the failure of anarchism to serve as a worthy idealism is epitomized in personal relationships. "The Informer" shows that human beings are incapable of being influenced by the ideals they possess. Latent in "The Duel" is the situation of the innocent man forced into an inappropriate role by "the gratuitous, simplistic beliefs" of his fellowmen, but this potential remains forgotten. And "Il Conde" examines the psychic phenomena of "our over-refined idealism and insidious egoism" and reveals how a man may live and die "entirely by the occult force of his imagination." Although these six tales abound with disturbing insights into the nature of belief, the process of believing seems to be obscure and unpredictable in its workings; the stories supply no easy answer to the question of the moral value of man's will to believe.

3187 Brown, Ruth Christiani. "'Plung'd in that Abortive Gulf': Milton in *Nostromo*," *Pol R*, XX, Nos. 2–3 (1975), pp. 31–57; rpt. *JCCE* (1975), pp. 31–57.

JC wove into the intricate fabric of his "modern epic," *Nostromo*, many echoes of Milton's epic, *Paradise Lost*. The setting of JC's novel in which the shining heights of Higuerota, the dark gulf, and the Isabels offer a sense of *déjà vu*, supplies a feeling of familiarity if not of strangeness. JC's opening chapter seems to reflect in several ways the setting of Milton's epic of the fall of man; his echoes of Milton intensify our response to the tragedy that is overtaking Costaguana. Costaguana can be rather clearly linked to the present Colombia *before* the loss of its westernmost province, which became the republic of Panama. Many verbal echoes from Milton appear in *Nostromo*, JC's Placid Gulf is similar in several ways to Milton's Chaos, and sometimes JC refers to scenes in which air and water appear to be confounded, as with Decoud when the journey across the gulf begins. Also, Decoud, like Satan, functions as a tempter in Paradise. [Accompanied by diagrams which show visually several parallels between the two works.]

3188 Bufkin, E. C. "Conrad, Grand Opera, and *Nostromo*," *NCF*, XXX (September 1795), pp. 206–14.

Opera, especially grand opera, can provide a new approach to *Nostromo*. JC was well acquainted with works by Bizet, Verdi, Wagner, and Meyerbeer, and references to music appear occasionally in his fiction. Opera must have been for him a general kind of influence or source. In *Nostromo*, two favorite themes of grand opera, religion and the supernatural, appear importantly. Gould, the aristocrat, belongs to the tragic world; Nostromo, the man of the people, belongs to the melodramatic world. The end of the novel does not suffer a falling-off; instead, JC's change of style is here appropriate to the melodramatic decline and death of the "operatically colorful" Nostromo.

3189 Burjorjee, Dinshaw M. "Comic Elements in Conrad's 'The Secret Sharer,'" *CON*, VII, No. 1 (1975), pp. 51–61.

In addition to a number of serious themes, "The Secret Sharer" contains also a "current of humour" as a "vital element" in this work. There are, of course, the more obvious devices of the use of disguises and doubles, but the action of the tale also is humorous when it is compared with the genesis of the story, the *Cutty Sark* affair of 1880. The characterization is consistent with the comic element in the action, as seen in the young captain, the ship's officers, and the captain of the *Sephora*. Much of the diction of the story, too, especially in the dialogues, is "indisputably comic." The comic counterpoint brings into sharper relief the psychological effects of the Doppleganger in the story and at the same time alleviates the "Dostoevskian bitterness of its moral thrust."

3190 Burnstein, Janet Handler. "Journey Beyond Myth: The Progress of the Intellect in Victorian Mythography and Three

Nineteenth-Century Novels," *DAI*, XXXVI (1975), 2838A.
Unpublished dissertation, Drew University, 1975.

3191 Cady, Louise Lamar. "On Conrad's Compositional Effects in
Razumov's Decision to Betray Haldin," *West Virginia University
Philological Papers*, XXII, No. 5 (1975), pp. 59–62.

At the end of *Under Western Eyes*, although Razumov is
physically ruined, he has achieved a personal dignity, bought by an
awful expiation for his youthful betrayal of Haldin to the authorities.
At the time of his enormous mistake in judgment, Razumov's ego has
not yet developed beyond an overdependence on intellection and
authoritarian structures. In an early passage, JC fashions an
intricate rendering of this unbalanced consciousness in moral
conflict: between the time Razumov beats Ziemanitch and the time
he rushes to Prince K- in order to turn Haldin in and seek moral
support for himself, the protagonist's movements, thoughts, and
emotional tides are finely orchestrated by his creator. Although JC
presents a sympathetic view of Razumov's moral dilemma, he uses
his customary irony. Various interludes resolve into the theme of
overpowering loneliness. The varying tempo of the narrative works in
conjunction with Razumov's mental vacillations. Eventually,
Razumov, in submerging his ego and identifying with the traditional
order, chooses to betray not only the revolutionary Haldin but also
himself.

3192 Caramello, Charles. [Rev. of Edward Murray, *The Cinematic
Imagination: Writers and the Motion Pictures* (1972)], *Style*, IX
(Fall 1975), pp. 543–48.

[Flaubert, Hardy, and JC "anticipated film grammar," and *Lord
Jim* has been used to support the claim that the film is no match for
the novel in style. Slight.]

3193 Castiglione, Luigi. "Goethe e Conrad" (Goethe and Conrad),
L'Informatore Librario, V, 2 (February 1975), 3; enlarged in
L'Osservatore Romano, 12 May 1975.

[Review of the critical biographies of Goethe and Conrad by
Friedenthal and Baines.] [In Italian.]

3194 Clades, Urio. "Vitalità di Conrad" (Conrad's Vitality), *Gazzetta
di Parma* (24 June 1975), p. 3; rpt. *Giornale di Brescia* (25 June
1975), p. 3; rvd. "Recenti studi conradiani" (Recent Conradian
Studies), *Nuova Antologia* (January 1976), pp. 105–107.

[A collection from the news and notes section of the *Newsletter of
the Joseph Conrad Society (Italy)* and from Mario Curreli,

introductory note to *Joseph Conrad: L'Uomo* (Milan: Mursia, 1974).] [In Italian.]

3195 Coustillas, Pierre. "Conrad and Gissing: A Biographical Note," *SJC* (1975), pp. 37–52.

By late 1896, JC's work must have had a meaning for George Gissing, since he first met H. G. Wells in November of that year. Wells had recently made JC's acquaintance. However unlike Gissing and JC may have been, they were alike in that their eventful lives offer some striking resemblances: both were born in 1857, their childhoods had been darkened by family disasters, both were voracious readers from childhood on, both held a melancholy outlook on life, and they had a common restlessness which perpetually unsettled their existences. Both young men had a love affair, JC rashly went out to sea and Gissing rashly determined to make a living by his pen, both had high-strung temperaments, by 1901 both had solid reputations as writers. After 1901, Gissing became a "regular propagandist" of JC's merits. Both Gissing and JC had a deep distrust of Germany and, in a certain sense of the word, they feared democracy. Gissing admired especially the outstanding linguistic feat JC had achieved. At once solitary and sociable, both writers were and remained essentially exiles. [Contains an unpublished JC letter to Gissing, dated 21 December 1902.]

3196 Crompton, John. "News from Brighton," *JJCS*, I, No. 6 (March 1975), p. 7.

Cedric Watts pointed out in a letter to John Crompton that the narrative techniques of *Nostromo* (especially the time-shifts) are a "perfect therapy for moral myopia," because they force the reader to interrelate past, present, and future, the particular and the general, in ways that most of the characters fail to do. So the whole book is "like the paradox of the Cretan who said that all Cretans are liars!"

3197 Crosland, Andrew. "*The Great Gatsby* and *The Secret Agent*," *Fitzgerald/Hemingway Annual* (1975), pp. 75–81.

F. Scott Fitzgerald's *The Great Gatsby* and JC's *The Secret Agent* exhibit distinct similarities. *The Secret Agent* may well have been one of the sources for Fitzgerald's novel. The name Michaelis, for example, appears in both works as do the names Tom and Vladimir. The characters Gatsby and Stevie parallel each other in their idealism and suffering, and Daisy and Winnie are similar in their strong desires for security and their preferences for the superficial. In addition, the titles of both novels are ironic. Possibly, then, Fitzgerald intentionally employed various elements of JC's work in *The Great Gatsby*.

3198 Curle, Adam. *The Last of Conrad* (Farnham, Surrey: Farnham Printing Co. [Joseph Conrad Society (U.K.)], 1975).

[Richard Curle's account, in an eighteen-page pamphlet, of JC's last days, prefaced by a brief memoir of Curle by his son, Adam Curle, and followed by a "Postscript" by Juliet McLauchlan. Although similar material was used in the chapter, "Conrad's Last Day" in Richard Curle's *The Last Twelve Years of Joseph Conrad* (1928), (C, I, No. 794), there are substantial differences.]

3199 Curle, Adam. "Richard Curle," *JJCS*, I, No. 6 (March 1975), pp. 12–14.

Richard Curle's relationship with Sir Ralph Wedgwood and, "pre-eminently," JC, were closer than that with his son Adam. Although JC died almost half a century before Curle did, he was constantly in Curle's thoughts. The two men shared a "profound sense of the inwardness of things, of mystery, of the strange hidden behind the banal," and both travelled widely and were fascinated by the use of words to describe "nuances of feeling and atmosphere." To Curle, JC was like a "strong and understanding brother." Curle appreciated his friend's talents and greatly enjoyed his company. But Curle's admiration was almost entirely uncritical. [A sketch of Richard Curle's entire life.]

3200 Currell, Mario, and Cedric Watts. "Conrad and Zangwill: A Note on *The Premier and the Painter*," *KN*, XXII (February 1975), pp. 240–42.

Possible connections between Israel Zangwill's *The Premier and the Painter* (1888) and some of JC's works are the use of the *Doppelganger* theme; the idea of the secret seizure of political power by an alien figure who, unrecognized, subverts a political party from within, as in JC's collaboration with Ford Madox Hueffer, *The Inheritors*; and the "remarkable anticipations" ·in Zangwill's novel of JC's elliptical and evasive narrative technique. And the conception of political history as ironic farce may have pressed JC towards the manner of presentation of *The Secret Agent*.

3201 Daleski, H. M. "'The Secret Sharer': Questions of Command," *Critical Quarterly*, XVII (Autumn 1975), pp. 268–79.

JC's art insists that "true self-possession" is based on a "capacity for abandon," as is seen in "The Secret Sharer." Since JC's concern in this story is with "the coexistence in the individual psyche of radically opposed qualities," his conceiving a character in a certain moral scheme and making him consistent is impossible. The young captain-narrator, in his response to Leggatt's story of a holding on that is also a letting go (Leggatt at the throat of an unruly member of the crew) helps to clarify the implications of an actual holding on that is also a letting go. But such a paradox is not easily accommodated by a conventional narrator. Leggatt's arrogance allows him to arrogate to himself the right to fix the price not only for his insolence but also for his death.

The fact that the young captain has a secret sharer before Leggatt appears on the scene is clear. The main test demanded of the captain is responsibility. Just as Leggatt is most notably characterized by the image of him at the sailor's throat, so the quality of the young captain is epitomized in the picture JC gives of his handling of the ship when he helps Leggatt to escape. And finally the captain sees himself as having fully taken possession of his ship just as he has also ceased to be "somewhat of a stranger" to himself.

3202 Dalgarno, Emily K. "The Textual History of Conrad's 'The Partner,'" *Library: A Quarterly Review of Bibliography and Library Lore*, XXX (1975), pp. 41–44.

Informed criticism of JC's fiction is dependent on the establishment for each work of a copy-text from the available manuscript and typescripts. The reconstruction of "The Partner" from the manuscript, partial typescript, serial proofs, and related correspondence with Pinker illustrates the particular problems of choosing a copy-text for JC's works. [The details of this procedure for "The Partner" are given.]

3203 Darras, [Jacques]. "Chains of Dissidence," *LC*, No. 1 (March 1975), pp. 1–4.

The role played by Kurtz in "Heart of Darkness" is, with a few similarities and differences between the two characters, that played by Grabot in Malraux's *Voie Royale*. Kurtz is a riddle revealed only indirectly; Grabot, a monster who is revealed at once. JC's story is built on a parody of the Royal Road, in which Grabot, Perhen, and Claude are dissidents who are united by a spirit of adventure which is also a search for absolute liberty. The Royal Road, a forest into which Grabot, Perken, and Claude, like Marlow, walk, is like a threat to life, with dissidence as the common denominator. Yet, at the end of the book, standing beside Perken's corpse, Claude, the archaeologist, is ready to complete his master's work. Marlow, unlike Claude, will not go beyond the crucial scene when he rescues Kurtz; the chain of dissidence is seen between Marlow the actor and Marlow the narrator, between the gigantic and yet banal quality of Kurtz's life. In most of JC's works, the infinitely extensible space of *Voie Royale* is narrowed down to small points on the map where, though, disasters due to man are concentrated. JC's space is neither human nor superhuman; it is a lie. Deprived of the ground of fiction, the tale is "bound to recede towards the horizon of its own reproduction." [Trans. from Darras's article "Voix Royales et Voies du Silence."] [In French.]

3204 Debenedetti, Antonio. "La moglie di Conrad" (Conrad's Wife), *Il Mondo*, XXVII, 4 (23 January 1975), p. 21.

[A review of Jessie and Borys Conrad's reminiscences and a general discussion of JC's personality.] [In Italian.]

3205 Deurbergue, Jean. "The Opening of *Victory*," *SJC* (1975), pp. 239–70.

The subtitle of *Victory*, "An Island Tale," leads us to expect something more or less foreign to a straightforward narrative, and the epigraph from Milton's *Comus* suggests insubstantial powers. *Victory*, then, tells of a journey through deceptive appearances and illusions. From the first sentence, the reader is warned that he must perceive the very close moral and metaphysical relation between two seemingly remote forms of negation, embodied in Baron Heyst Senior and "plain Mr. Jones." Jones serves as a *Doppelganger* to Axel Heyst, and Lena as an avatar of the "Phallic Woman, a Goddess of Death"—or, metaphorically, of castration. These inferences come from the opposition of coal and diamonds. Also, the era of science, industry, and finance is equated with "a garish, unrestful hotel"—with a suggestion of wilderness surrounding it. The second paragraph initiates a devious process of answering the several questions pressed on the reader's mind in the first paragraph. Various differences which become more important later in the story appear: the deceptiveness of oppositions diffuses ambivalence, which is itself a mode of deceptiveness in appearances. The text of this opening of a story has a threefold content: (1) the objective level, a matter of silence, a solitary meditation, and alternating light and shade; (2) the symbolic level of "sub-systems," that of space; and (3) the darker, demonic area where divided selves are born. In the beginning of the novel, the end is suggested. The entire book, though, does not sustain the high level of its opening.

3206 D'Hangest, Germain. "Sense of Life and Narrative Technique in Conrad's *Lord Jim*," *SJC* (1975), pp. 129–60

In *Lord Jim*, JC's world is one of which the central truth cannot be ascertained. His imagery, of which the cloud that enwraps Jim is only a part, reveals his basic concept that truth forever escapes us. Marlow, the central witness and narrator, always feels baffled or doubtful of his interpretation of the main character. JC's obsessive sense of the universal mystery, of the elusive, inaccessible nature of truth, has a no less obsessive sense of solitude for an obvious corollary—no truth will finally be known about Jim. JC's narrative method is a direct consequence of his deep-set, ineradicable notion of truth as something inacessible and unascertainable. Because he believed his art was to mirror in a truthful way his experience and his sense of life, it must refrain from providing the reader with a total, omniscient vision. Marlow is thus a central device in JC's narrative technique. Within the world of the book, however, Marlow's stepping forward and taking over the narrative function from the author appears artificial. The delayed introduction of Marlow as narrator contrasts powerfully with two worlds, that of Jim's story, which Marlow is telling, and that in which Marlow speaks and in which his friends listen to him, ultimately leaving a sense of ambiguity because of the superimposition of two time sequences. As a consequence of the time-scheme, dramatic irony becomes possible, arising from the fact that whereas Marlow cannot know of Jim's tragic end, JC naturally knows all about it. JC's presence is felt behind that of the narrator and is also distinct from it. Marlow thus emphasizes the poetic quality of JC's narrative technique.

3207 Dobinsky, Joseph. "The Son and Lover Theme in *Lord Jim,*" *SJC* (1975), pp. 161–66.

JC's development from an early orphan to a tortured man and a tragic novelist as seen in Bernard C. Meyer, *Joseph Conrad: A Psychoanalytic Biography* (1967), invites further exploration. In *Lord Jim*, the consistent singularity of Jim's episodic connections with his "female partners" should be stressed in support of it. In Doramin's wife, the hero's "genetrix," conspicuously absent from this "bowdlerized novel of education," finds a natural and partly explicit substitute. After Jim's escape from the Rajah's stockade, the chieftain's wife takes care of him. And Jewel's attitude to her lover is always protective. This "tutelar girl-friend" is repeatedly compared to, or associated with, her dead mother, and Jewel herself is constantly depicted as a wraith. Jewel is thus a typical Conradian heroine. JC's "self-mystifying rhetoric" suggests a psychobiographical reading of *Jim*, one of his "most emotionally charged novels."

3208 Eddleman, Floyd Eugene, David Leon Higdon, and Robert W. Hobson, "The First Editions of Joseph Conrad's *Almayer's Folly,*" *Proof 4: The Yearbook of American Bibliographical and Textual Studies*, ed. by Joseph Katz (Columbia, SC: J. Faust, 1975), pp. 83–108.

[A history of the English and American first editions of *Almayer's Folly* and a discussion of the substantive variants and emendations.]

3209 Eiland, Howard A. "Double Vision in Conrad, Woolf, and Mann," *DAI*, XXXV (1975), 7300A. Unpublished dissertation, Yale University, 1974.

3210 Emmett, V. J., Jr. "Carlyle, Conrad, and the Poetics of Charisma: Another Perspective on 'Heart of Darkness,'" *CON*, VII, No. 2 (1975), pp. 145–53.

Internal evidence suggests that JC had in mind, while writing "Heart of Darkness," Carlyle's *On Heroes, Hero-Worship and the Heroic in History* (1840). This evidence is of different kinds: (1) there are stylistic similarities between the two works, (2) JC uses Carlyle's concepts of the unconscious racial memory and of the empty or hollow man, and (3) JC gives Kurtz some of the characteristics of the six kinds of hero discussed by Carlyle. But the basic resemblance between the two works involves ironic inversion (the divine in *On Heroes* becomes diabolic in "Heart of Darkness") and shows the influence to be largely negative: Kurtz's diabolism is JC's derisive comment on the enthusiasm of Carlyle's hero worship; primitive man is, for JC, an "altogether more Hobbesian creature" than Carlyle could imagine. When Marlow is given the choice between the "nightmare manager" and the "nightmare madman," Kurtz, his choice is natural: the question is, which is worse, "that a Kurtz (or a Hitler) should exist, or that people should fail to perceive his evil?" JC warns us against both the charismatic villain and those who fail to recognize villainy when they see it. JC's explanation of charisma contradicts Carlyle, and goes beyond Max Weber, who wrote in the 1920s.

3211 Evans, Frank B. "The Nautical Metaphor in 'The Secret Sharer,'" *CON*, VII, No. 1 (1975), pp. 3–16.

In "The Secret Sharer," JC uses nautical maneuvers to form an elaborate metaphor through which the narrator "formulates and expresses" the meaning of his story. The exterior nautical events become an objective correlative of the narrator's interior psychological journey. The captain's impulsive acceptance of Leggatt has trapped him into a serious dilemma: Leggatt has failed as a ship's officer, and the captain too will fail unless he manages to keep faith both with Leggatt and his own "secret self," and also with his own need to be a "responsible commander." He thus needs to change course with respect to Leggatt, and the mate's willingness to go his way as an outcast provides a way out of the dilemma which will not require betrayal. The ship's slow approach to Koh-ring parallels the captain's slow development of his plan to maroon Leggatt. The captain hopes Leggatt will understand that he both sympathizes with and repudiates Leggatt's behavior on board the *Sephora*. The dangerous nautical maneuver is therefore only symbolically dangerous. The hat on the water saves both the ship and the captain: the narrator's pity for Leggatt saves him as a man capable of sympathy for a fellow human being, but it is also Leggatt's disappearance from the ship and from the captain's spirit which now permits him to complete his deliverance and to emerge from his private world into the public one of his crew as his ship completes its maneuver.

3212 Finzi, Gilberto. "Testimonianza a due voci" (Testimony by two voices), *Giorno*, 29 January 1975, p. 10.

[Review of Jessie and Borys Conrad's reminiscences.] [In Italian.]

3213 Fletcher, John. *Claude Simon and Fiction Now* (Critical Appraisals Series), (London: Calder and Boyars, 1975), pp. 34, 43–46, 51, 69, 70, 137, 214, 319, 226.

From JC, Claude Simon learned a basic matter: "how to construct a fiction." He shares JC's emphasis "on visualization, on making palpable, on creating a sensuously experienced world, rather than conveying a message." Examples of such novels are Simon's *The Flanders Road*, *The Palace*, and *The Wind*. Simon, like JC, in *Under Western Eyes*, includes a narrator who acquires his knowledge of the story only gradually. In *The Grass*, Simon transcends and absorbs this fruitful influence: he no longer employs an omniscient narrator like the one who tells about Decoud's death in *Nostromo*. But Simon probably owes more to Faulkner than to JC. He follows closely the great moderns: Dostoevski, Proust, Joyce, Faulkner, and JC; but he is in a more radical tradition than any of these. He begins where Virginia Woolf and Faulkner leave off.

3214 Fontanesi, Carla. "Il ritorno di Conrad" (Conrad's Return), *L'Osservatore (Politico Letterario)*, (April 1975), pp. 73–78.

[A second hand uninformed review of the Italian edition of Baines's critical biography, mostly taken from introductory notes to JC's works published in Italy.] [In Italian.]

3215 Ford, Jane M. "The Father/Daughter/Suitor Triangle in Shakespeare, Dickens, James, Conrad, and Ford," *DAI*, XXXVI (1975), 4507A. Unpublished dissertation, SUNY, Buffalo, 1975.

3216 Fortunati, Vita. "La collaborazione con Conrad" (The Collaboration with Conrad), *Ford Madox Ford: Teoria e Tecnica Narrativa* (Ford Madox Ford: theory and narrative technique), (Bologna: Patron, 1975), pp. 23–32.

[Retraces the collaboration of Ford and JC, quoting from letters and contemporary sources. JC is frequently quoted elsewhere in this perceptive study.] [In Italian.]

3217 Franco, Jean. "The Limits of the Liberal Imagination: *One Hundred Years of Solitude* and *Nostromo*," *Punto de Contacto*, I, No. 1 (1975), pp. 4–16.

Nostromo is a penetrating study of European manipulation of the politics of a dependent country. Because the drama focuses on Europeans whose activities transform the society of Sulaco, the novel presents the reverse side of Macondo in Gabriel Garcia Marquez's *One Hundred Years of Solitude*, a place whose inhabitants never project their desires into durable institutions. The tragedy of Sulaco is presented in terms of the Europeans who become corrupted because their ambitions are acted out in an independent nation; in opposition to this situation, the tragedy of Macondo is that of a dependent population who can no longer maintain an inviolate imagination. In *Nostromo*, JC's main interest is in ideology: he is concerned with the way that certain national ideals promote the "neo-colonist venture" while concealing its true nature from the participants. The symbolic agents in the transformation of Sulaco to an era of financial and industrial dependency are the railway and the Ocean Navigation Company (the silver, usually seen as the symbol of all the catastrophes in the novel, is useless without the British-owned railroad and steamship line).

3218 Friedman, Alan Warren (ed.). *Forms of Modern British Fiction*, (Austin and London: University of Texas Press [Symposia in the Arts and the Humanities, No. 2], 1975), pp. 3, 9, 20–21, 94, 133, 159, 204, 205.

Hardy's *Tess of the D'Urbervilles* anticipates the "tag and technique" of impressionism associated with such early moderns as Ford and JC. In 1898, JC wrote ironically to John Galsworthy that his *Jocelyn* is faithful only to the surface of life, but that this is not being shallow; and JC was right in his judgment. D. H. Lawrence's most vital characters must, as Stein advises in JC's *Lord Jim*, immerse themselves in the "destructive element." JC's "Heart of Darkness" is evoked in the final scene of the Olivers' reunion in Virginia Woolf's *Between the Acts* to describe their "fate of love and conflict." [Passing comments by Alan Warren Friedman, James Gindin, James C. Cowen, and Avrom Fleishman.]

3219 Fuentes Bobo, Julio B. "Joseph Conrad: Hacia una nueva valoracion de su obra maritima" (Joseph Conrad: Toward a New

Evaluation of His Maritime Work), *Filología Moderna*, (Madrid), XV (1975), pp. 313–38.

In "Typhoon," the storm is raised to the level of protagonist opposed to MacWhirr. Of all JC's seamen, he has received most attention from critics, some of whom doubt whether he actually merits the designation of hero, alleging his lack of imagination, his stupidity, and his obstinacy. Such opinions should be qualified by his reputation, by the shipowner's care in choosing him, and by the fact that a mariner must inevitably seem unimaginative to men of letters. An analysis of "Typhoon" from a nautical point of view should throw light on the problem. Another seaman deserving attention in this respect is Singleton of *The Nigger of the Narcissus*, a realistic depiction of an old "sea wolf" and a personification of humanity in its primitive state. Singleton is a kind of noble savage. MacWhirr seems to act against all wisdom, including that of his officers. In spite of his virtues, he seems in the highest degree stubborn to such a reader, and it seems only by chance that he survives. [Detailed analysis of MacWhirr.] [In Spanish.]

3220 Fwastadi, Wabeno. "'Heart of Darkness': Le Voyage de Marlow vers l'interieur" ("Heart of Darkness": Marlow's voyage toward the interior), *Cahiers de Litterature et de Linguistic Applique*, VII–VIII (1975), pp. 85–92.

In "Heart of Darkness," JC employs a commonly used traditional artistic method to sound certain facets and potentialities of the self—the voyage, which serves at once as form and symbol. The traveler undertakes a voyage toward his own self even as he comes to know the different facets of the condition surrounding him—represented by the intrigue and the symbolism of the work. It is thus that observation and revelation acquire a social, a psychological, and even a philosophical dimension. By design, JC transports his readers far from civilized society in order to show his personages in situations which they must confront with no interference from conventions, manners, or traditions, like Marlow in "Heart of Darkness," who goes on a spiritual voyage of self-discovery. The problem which occupies him is to know whether, being given such circumstances, a man can face the darkness he meets. Seen in this manner, the tale consists of a series of moments of revelation experienced by Marlow while expressing the mystery of the most secret potentialities of man. Eventually, Marlow finds a major revelation as he sees into the secret self of the ivory trader whom he has formerly admired. In the middle of the African continent, Marlow finds the shadows which each man is forced sooner or later to confront. Since Marlow remains faithful to Kurtz, his voyage is a progressive development of the conscience of the narrator, and it explores and reveals the phenomenon of idealism incited by the thirst for power. Since Kurtz's and Marlow's experiences are complementary, they are the two halves of the same person, who comes to comprehend the ultimate evil. [In French.]

3221 Gaston, Paul L. "The Gospel of Work According to Joseph Conrad," *Pol R*, XX, Nos. 2–3 (1975), pp. 203–10; rpt. *JCCE* (1975), pp. 202–9.

JC's "Heart of Darkness" is the "most thorough and forceful analysis in the nineteenth century of the popular faith in the value of work." Later novels by JC, such as *Nostromo*, *The Secret Agent*, and *Under Western Eyes*, also develop dramatic paradoxes in the "Gospel of Work," as do earlier novels and stories. JC's first novel, *Almayer's Folly*, introduces Almayer, in whom work represents an unproductive past effort to be forgotten, but Almayer's inconsistent attitudes about work explain his downfall. In *An Outcast of the Islands*, Willems again believes in another illusion, the hope of instantaneous wealth, but like Almayer, he loses both money and power, thus demonstrating the dangers of idleness implicit in the traditional regard for work. *The Nigger of the Narcissus* continues to refine the ideas of work suggested in the earlier novels. The microcosm of the ship at sea demonstrates that for civilization to exist, men must know their work and do it. And all three of JC's collected tales in 1898, *Tales of Unrest*, are, in effect, stories of relationships which disintegrate when customary expectations are frustrated, communication is broken, and the ordinary enterprises of life cannot continue. [To be developed through JC's other works.]

3222 Giacobelli, Francesco. "Nota del curatore" (Editor's Note), *Il Compagno Segreto* (The Secret Sharer), (Milan: Rizzoli, 1975), pp. 25–40.

[Brief description of theme, structure, and archetypes of this tale written at the end of the collaboration with JC's impulsive secret sharer, Ford.] [In Italian.]

3223 Gillie, Christopher. *Movements in English Literature, 1900–1940* (Cambridge: University Press, 1975), pp. 38–46, 51, 141, 142, 158, 185–86.

JC considered his art as a work of lonely dedication without popular appreciation, he maintained a "cosmopolitan awareness," and he left the impression of possessing an unremitting watchfulness. What distinguishes his works is his constant preoccupation with moral ordeal, as seen in *The Nigger of the Narcissus*. Donkin, the base and destructive man who "cannot rise to the meanest level of moral disinterest," becomes a "familiar style" of character in JC's works. So does Singleton, the man who is so "simple-minded and simple-hearted" that his integrity is unshakeable. The third of the three main "styles" of character in JC is the man of imagination; he is the protagonist in *Lord Jim*, "Heart of Darkness," *The Secret Agent*, *Under Western Eyes*, "The Secret Sharer," *Victory*, and *The Shadow-Line*. *Nostromo* is JC's greatest work. With the exception of Thomas Hardy, JC is the most pessimistic of English novelists.

3224 Gillon, Adam. "Joseph Conrad and Shakespeare, Part Four: A New Reading of *Victory*," *CON*, VII, No. 3 (1975), pp. 263–81.

JC's use of Shakespearean archetypes in *Lord Jim*, *The Shadow-Line*, *Under Western Eyes*, *Nostromo*, and other works reaches a culminating point in *Victory*. Several elements of this novel are drawn from *The Tempest*, including the problems of failure to understand, to communicate, to develop faith in humanity and in one's self. The use of light signals and light symbolism, associating light with life and darkness with death, suggests Shakespearean imagery in *Othello*, *Macbeth*, and other plays. JC, who was eager to have *Victory* dramatized, sees in the novel the incongruities of life as a kind of show or play, sometimes comic, sometimes tragic, or at times a combination of both. Since JC's view of man and his world is invariably that of Shakespeare in his tragedies, his fiction is "positively flooded" with the pervasive word "darkness" and its derivatives. Some very ominous Shakespearean echoes link *Victory* and its major themes to *King Lear* and *Hamlet*. The philosophical affinity between *Lear* and JC's novel is made clear by the basic themes of the two works. In *Victory*, "nothing" is used to create the effect of dramatic irony in a scene reminiscent of Lear's request to his daughters, except that the roles here are reversed. Also, the name *Victory* and the concept affect many things in the novel.

3225 Gillon, Adam. "Joseph Conrad and Shakespeare: Part Five: *King Lear* and 'Heart of Darkness,'" *Pol R*, XX, Nos. 2–3 (1975), pp. 13–30; rpt. *JCCE* (1975), pp. 13–30.

JC's "Heart of Darkness" contains many Shakespearean motifs from *King Lear*, the most profound affinity being perhaps a paradoxical view of man, with evil and goodness as two necessary aspects of human nature. JC's short novel parallels the "linguistic and the philosophical revelations" of Shakespeare's tragedy. Lear and Gloucester in the one and Marlow and Kurtz in the other discover the gap between expression of emotion and idealism. Language itself becomes an index of truth. Both Kurtz, entrusted with making a report for the future guidance of the International Society for the Suppression of Savage Customs, and Lear, wishing to entrust his kingdom to his three daughters for the sake of peace in the land, fail miserably and ironically. The twin image of "heart-of-darkness" acquires a broad application: heart is love, idealism, fidelity, the "essence and kernel of things"; darkness represents physical and moral decay, death, corruption, and the "general monstrosity of human nature." Marlow and Kurtz, like Lear and Gloucester, must travel through a moral desert of which they themselves are a part, and all of them must have their choices of nightmares before they can ascend to the upper region of enlightenment. The purpose of these journeys is the same in both works, to learn the true meaning of love, of truth, and of justice. And as the beginning of each work contains the welding of the two images, darkness and love, so does the ending of each work again demonstrate their stylistic affinity.

3226 Gillon, Adam. "Preface," *Pol R*, XX, Nos. 2–3 (1975), p. 7; rpt. *JCCE* (1975), p. 7.

[An explanation of the selections published in the proceedings of the International Conference of Conrad Scholars, 1974.]

3227 Gillon, Adam. "Reviews," *CON*, VII, No. 1 (1975), pp. 87–93.

[Rev. of Stefan Zabierowski, *Conrad w Polsce: Wybrane Problemy Recepeji Krytycznej w Latach 1896–1969* (Conrad in Poland: Selected Problems of Critical Reception in the Years 1896–1969), (Gdansk: Wydawnictwo Morskie, 1971).]

Stefan Zabierowski's *Conrad in Poland* is a much needed systematic analysis of the critical reception of JC's work during the period 1896–1969, showing how the early misconceptions in Poland gave way to more accurate judgments of the novelist's achievement. The author has chosen what he considers the most valuable and significant critical opinions of Conradists during the past sixty years.

Zabierowski first deals with the criticism pertaining to JC's creative personality and the various interpretive schools. Then he tries to rescue JC's attitudes towards Polish and other literary traditions, such as romanticism, realism, and naturalism. Next, he summarizes the conclusions of these findings, bringing the sources up to 1969. The book is concluded with a bibliography of selected studies about JC by Polish authors or those of Polish descent. [Zabierowski's book, a major contribution to the study of Conrad's place in Poland, should be carefully used.]

3228 Gillon, Adam (ed.). *Joseph Conrad Today: The Newsletter of the Joseph Conrad Society of America*, I (October 1975).

[This eight-page, well printed first issue of the JC newsletter contains a remarkable amount of information about various activities related to JC and his works. Included are a list of the current officers of the Joseph Conrad Society of America: report on and announcements of MLA seminars and special conferences on JC; information about other newsletters in the United Kingdom, France, and Italy; a record of recent publications on JC; a book review; a poem inspired by the death of a lover of JC's works; a short article on JC's influence on Thomas Pynchon; a short history of the Polish Conrad Club; and additional items of interest to Conradians.]

3229 Gillon, Adam, and Ludwik Krzyzanowski (eds.). "Joseph Conrad: Commemorative Essays (The Selected Proceedings of the International Conference of Conrad Scholars, University of California, San Diego, August 28–September 5, 1974)," *Pol R*, XX, Nos. 2–3 (1975), pp. 1–222; rpt. *JCCE* (1975), pp. 1–222.

[Contents, abstracted under year 1975: Antoni Slonimski, "Conrad"; Adam Gillon, "Preface"; Suzanne Henig, "Introductory Address"; Jonas Salk, "In Tribute to Jacob Bronowski and Joseph Conrad"; Adam Gillon, "Joseph Conrad and Shakespeare: Part Five: *King Lear* and "Heart of Darkness"; Ruth C. Brown, "'Plung'd in that Abortive Gulf': Milton in *Nostromo*"; Suzanne Henig and Florence Talamantes, "Conrad and Balzac: A Trio of Balzacian Interrelationships"; Glenn Sandstrom, "The Roots of Anguish in Conrad and Dostoevsky"; D. Ridley Beeton, "Joseph Conrad and George Eliot: An Indication of the Possibilities"; Przemyslaw Mroczkowski, "Joseph Conrad the European"; David Leon Higdon, "The Text and Context of Conrad's First Critical Essay"; Donald W. Rude, "Conrad's Revision of the First American Edition of *The Arrow of Gold*"; Todd K. Bender, "Computer Analysis of Conrad"; Bruce E. Teets, "Realism and Romance in Conrad Criticism"; Harry T. Moore, "Leitmotif Symbolism in *The Secret Agent*"; Leon Guilhamet, "Conrad's *The Secret Agent* as the Imitation of an Action"; Peter Sloat Hoff, "*The Secret Agent*: A Typical Conrad Novel?"; Owen Knowles, "'To Make You Hear . . .': Some Aspects of Conrad's Dialogue"; Jack I. Biles, "'Its Proper Title': Some Observations on *The Nigger of the Narcissus*"; Juliet McLauchlan, "Conrad's 'Three Ages of Man': The 'Youth' Volume"; Paul Gaston, "The Gospel of Work According to Joseph Conrad"; Gustav Morf, "*The Rescue* as an Expression of Conrad's Dual Personality"; and John S. Lewis, "Conrad in 1914."]

3230 Goldpaugh, Thomas. "Conrad's Influence on Thomas Pynchon," *JCT*, I (October 1975), p. 7.

From his first short story, "Mortality and Mercy in Vienna," to *Gravity's Rainbow*, Pynchon's works have reflected JC's "Heart of Darkness" in various ways: in the form of direct references to JC's novel, in stylistic affinities with JC, and in a concern with certain themes which are handled in a Conradian manner. Pynchon has also given a denunciation of colonialism which is possibly more vehement than JC's. And all of Pynchon's work reveals traces of the darkness of JC, of the hollowness and the blackness in men.

3231 Guggenbuhl, Rolf. "Wandel im Seeroman des 19. Jahrhunderts: Marryat—Melville—Conrad" (Changes in the Maritime Novel of the Nineteenth Century: Marryat, Melville, Conrad). Unpublished dissertation, University of Zurich, 1975. [In German.]

3232 Guilhamet, Leon. "Conrad's *The Secret Agent* as the Imitation of an Action," *Pol R*, XX, Nos. 2–3 (1975), pp. 145–53; rpt. *JCCE* (1975), pp. 144–52.

As a result of his classical education and of his reading French literature, JC was probably somewhat of an Aristotelian, and *The Secret Agent* might be read from an Aristotelian perspective: all the characters participate in a unified action, which is finally an attempt to "grasp the inconceivable" based on the assumption that the concept of *praxis* is the movement of the mind towards the good. In general, the characters share a delusive sense of well-being because they only "dabble" in revolutionary schemes. The common pattern of behavior in *Agent* begins with anger caused by injustice, which leads to an act of violence. The next possible step is contemplation of death as reality, then fear, and then the final insight: life is what matters. Only Winnie Verloc is heroic enough to complete the pattern and recognize the falsity of her initial assumptions.

3233 Hagen, William Morice. "Realism and Creative Fable in *Nostromo* and *Under the Volcano*: An Approach to Technique and Structure," *DAI*, XXXV (1975), 4522A. Unpublished dissertation, University of Iowa, 1974.

3234 Hardy, Barbara. *Tellers and Listeners: The Narrative Imagination* (London: University of London, The Athlone, 1975), pp. xii, 29, 42–45, 48–49, 55, 84, 154–66, 226, 267.

Jim, of *Lord Jim*, may be defined as a will to retrieve the dream after losing it "in the most shattering and shameful way, as romantics do, by dithering and doddering romantically instead of acting." His final action, however, is romantic in its ideal of moral being but is unlike the two earlier failures in will, activity, and success. Jim's fate shows the possibility of staying romantically ambitious. Marlow is the true artist, whose form is created by his feeling. In "Heart of Darkness," Marlow believes that he has lived through Kurtz's extremity and can remember it better than his own.

He cannot, however, always make a report of that experience truthfully. Marlow recognizes his own condition in Jim, as he does in Kurtz. This sympathy reflects the involvement of the artist which is as dangerous and as essential as his detachment. Since it seems reasonable to give a concluding prominence to fatigue, age, and the preparation for death, the last words are Stein's. But the last image leaves the question open: is Jim like the butterfly, his feet in the dirt, his flight depending on the sacrifice of Jewel, or is he unlike the butterfly, "choosing only shadows"? Marlow's questions indicate the author's sense that the imagination cannot solve but must try to appreciate the difficulties of being human. Marlow stands at an oblique angle to the action of the story, where he is a mirror for JC.

3235 Harkness, Bruce. "Conrad Computerized and Concordanced," *Costerus*, IV (1975), pp. 123–36.

The concordance to "Heart of Darkness" (Sibyl C. Jacobson, with Robert J. Dilligan and Todd K. Bender. *Concordance to Joseph Conrad's "Heart of Darkness"* [Carbondale: Southern Illinois University Press, 1973]) is to be commended "very highly indeed." Not perfect, it is "available, cheap, relatively usable." It will not greatly advance the "revolutionary wave" of microfiche, but it should be judged on its own rights without reference to the electronic data bank for which it may be "the tip of the iceberg rising out of the waves." We should be "glad and grateful to have it."

3236 Harm, Roger Lee. "The Literature of Imperialism: Kipling, Conrad, and Forster," *DAI*, XXXVI (1975), 2845A–46A. Unpublished dissertation, Stanford, 1975.

3237 Hay, Eloise Knapp. "Book Reviews," *Journal of English and Germanic Philology*, LXXIV (October 1975), pp. 592–98.

Three recent books on JC may be read together as a debate on JC's position in modern fiction: *Conrad: The Critical Heritage*, edited by Norman Sherry (1973); *Joseph Conrad: The Modern Imagination*, by C. B. Cox (1974); and *Conrad's Romanticism*, by David Thorburn (1974). Cox and Thorburn take opposite sides; Sherry serves as moderator. Thorburn is interested in the "romantic" and the "heroic" in JC's vision; Cox focuses on the "brutally realistic" and the "morbid." In the end, JC seems to be a part of three traditions: the "old lost chivalries of Nicholas Bobrowski and Don Quixote," the "weatherworn gospel of work and merit" advocated by Victorian shipmasters, and the mid-twentieth century's code of "total transvaluation" in the face of disintegrating trust and global wars. But all three critics would agree with one character in Somerset Maugham's story, "Neil MacAdam," "I don't think it's a mean achievement to have created a country, a dark, sinister, romantic and heroic country of the soul."

3238 Hay, Eloise Knapp. "Conrad's Self-Portraiture," *JCCP* (1975), pp. 57–71.

Although JC is one of the most autobiographical of novelists, he seems to be equally the most evasive of novelists. Some readers consider his self-portraiture most direct and revealing in works like *Lord Jim,* "Heart of Darkness," *Nostromo, Under Western Eyes,* and *Victory* where he claimed especially that he had worked principally from sources other than memory. In these books, marginal criminals like Jim, Kurtz, and Razumov, or despairing suicides like Decoud and Heyst, are considered as more truly confessional figures than the ones JC himself labeled as self-portraits, either in fictionalized memories like "Prince Roman" and *The Shadow-Line* or in straightforward narratives. But in his own memories, *The Mirror of the Sea* and *A Personal Record,* he disclosed practically the same self. Central forces in *Mirror* appear to be on the world of ships and national heroes. *Record* is a more perfectly controlled and finished self-portrait, with "respice ad finem" as a major theme. Both volumes interfuse actual memories with fictional and allegorical figures that have dominated the artist's imagination. Except for the suicide attempt, nothing of great importance was omitted from JC's memoirs as far as we know. The whole of his self-portraiture, in its unity and artistry, reflects JC the child, the seaman, the artist, the man.

3239 Hay, Eloise Knapp. "Joseph Conrad and Impressionism," *Journal of Aesthetics and Art Criticism,* XXXIV (Winter 1975), pp. 137–44.

Brunetière was the first writer to apply the principles of impressionist painting to literature: his comments are similar in important ways to JC's preface to *The Nigger of the Narcissus,* written about twenty years later. JC's writings about impressionism reveal three "fairly distinct" phases: his disgust with a collection of impressionist paintings in 1891, his qualified praise of Stephen Crane's art in 1897, and his curious reversal of opinion at the end of his life. He moved on from a phase of despising impressionism to one in which he sees it as an appealing but superficial way of creating art. Like Cezanne, he seeks structure beneath the surfaces, however rich they may be in themselves. He emphasizes his own power of analysis, a quality which he admires in Proust. And both JC and Proust consider "temperament" an important aspect of impressionism. JC's last brief phase of interest reveals his revised opinion of Crane's work, which he now praises highly; and he also states that he did not want to go to the depth of things. Perhaps he had come to believe it better not to look too deeply into things as they are. [A very important contribution to the understanding of literary impressionism. Hay is wrong, though, in stating that JC's name became associated with impressionism after his death: the word "impressionism" was used frequently for his work at least from 1898 on.]

3240 Heimer, Jackson W. "Betrayal in *The Secret Agent*," *CON*, VII, No. 3 (1975), pp. 245–51.

In *The Secret Agent*, betrayal is prevalent, but painted on a much smaller scale than in *Lord Jim* or *Nostromo*. In *Jim* and *Nostromo*, acts of betrayal are grandiose and lofty; those in *Agent* are "petty and grubby." And JC's "ironic method" used in treating them reduces them still further. The betrayers of the novel are Verloc and his wife Winnie, the former guilty of political and domestic betrayal, the latter, mainly of domestic betrayal. They move through two closely related patterns, the major, or basic, pattern—act, confession, attempted redemption, and punishment—and the minor pattern—isolation, involvement, and isolation. Verloc's act of betrayal is marked by his failure as a protector of the home; Winnie's failure results from her refusal to pry, with any depth, beneath the surface. Whereas Jim and Nostromo may tend to emerge as tragic characters, Verloc and Winnie fail to do so: Verloc's conduct appears no better or worse than his environment, and Winnie emerges as a comic character because she is "a fool and a flunkey."

3241 Helder, Jack. "Fool Convention and Conrad's Hollow Harlequin," *SSF*, XII (1975), pp. 361–68.

The harlequin in "Heart of Darkness," drawn from a common theatre tradition, represents many of the fundamental ontological assumptions inherent throughout time in the essence of fools. JC's Russian harlequin is a more "sophisticated" version of the commedia dell'arte tradition. His clothing serves as an image of the conflicting forces at work in the story. The aspects of both moral disorder and the possibility of order symbolized in the fool's motley are dramatized in Kurtz's fall and final recognition of sin. The fool's face reveals Kurtz's shifting moods which correspond to the ruling images of darkness and light which constantly alternate in the tale, thus demonstrating the harlequin's confusion and moral ignorance. His gabbing reveals his ignorance of the moral dimension of human affairs. A part of his deformity displays the essential moral and spiritual poverty apparent in nearly all that Marlow sees in "Heart of Darkness." And Marlow judges Kurtz by the way he judges the harlequin, even in his change of attitude toward the efforts made by colonization. The harlequin has contributed to Kurtz's "victorious corruption" by his failure to represent any moral standard. Altogether he portrays "an uncomprehending moral vacuum." Although Marlow's mind is enlarged through his acquaintance with Kurtz, the Russian remains a fool, and a sinister one. But his character is an appropriate foil to Marlow's developed moral consciousness.

3242 Henig, Suzanne. "Dr. Jacob Bronowski," *Pol R, XX*, Nos. 2–3 (1975), pp. 8–10; rpt. *JCCE* (1975), pp. 8–10.

[A tribute to JC and Dr. Jacob Bronowski, a lover of JC, to the memory of whom the International Conference of Conrad Scholars, University of California, San Diego, 1974, was dedicated.]

3243 Henig, Suzanne. "(From) River of Prague," *JCT*, I, No. 1 (October 1975), p. 6.

[A poem inspired by the death of Dr. Vera Beck, a lover of JC's works.]

3244 Henig, Suzanne, and Florence W. Talamantes. "Conrad and Balzac: A Trio of Balzacian Interrelationships," *Pol R, XX*, Nos. 2–3 (1975), pp. 58–70; rpt. *JCCE* (1975), pp. 58–70.

Balzac was the first novelist to discover and use the literary device of having the same characters, at different stages of their lives, appear in various novels and stories, thereby forming a "subtle liason" of connection. In using this device, JC had Doña Rita first appear in his fiction as a child in his unfinished work, *The Sisters*, started in 1896; she was still in his mind when he wrote "The Tremolino" for *The Mirror of the Sea* (1903–1904); and she appears in *The Arrow of Gold*, worked on 1917–1918. Strangely, no one has observed this device of recurrent characters, and no one has pointed out JC's reliance on Balzac's *Histoire de Treize* as a major source for the three works which include Rita. Also, Dominic Cervoni of Corsica appears in both "The Tremolino" and *The Arrow of Gold*, where he is an embodiment of the Latin Code of Honor, a form of old hereditary feud which appears also in Balzac's *La Fille des Yeux D'Or*.

3245 Hewitt, Douglas. *Conrad: A Reassessment* (London: Bowes and Bowes, 1975), third ed.

[This republication of Hewitt's 1952 and 1969 book is substantially the same, but it contains a "Preface to the Third Edition" and a new chapter, "Conclusion (1975)." Hewitt finds it somewhat "comic and disconcerting" to be labelled as one of the founders of the "Achievement-and-Decline" theory of JC criticism, and he is not seriously interested in JC's decline. But he takes issue with the general misconception that JC is a "systematic metaphysical thinker."]

The books between "Youth" and *The Secret Agent* share an "individual vision," and JC's concern is with a powerful sense of potential weakness and betrayal lying under an apparent confidence in an established code of behavior and waiting for the right circumstances of stress to emerge, often with devastating power. JC is not, though, a systematic metaphysical thinker; at the heart of his work is not metaphysics, but politics—politics understood in the widest sense. His interest lies in the interplay of groups, the conflict between personal feelings and professional duties. The pessimism of his sea stories is modified by his positive values, such as a belief in doing one's work properly and in accepting blows stoically. His political view is one of gloomy skepticism and even despairing, and his skepticism is more "corrosive" than one may think. This view of politics appears most strongly in *Nostromo*.

3246 Higdon, David Leon. "The Text and Context of Conrad's First Critical Essay," *Pol R*, XX, Nos. 2–3 (1975), pp. 78–86; rpt. *JCCE* (1975), pp. 78–86.

JC's first critical essay, the long-suppressed "Author's Note" to *Almayer's Folly*, was written late in 1894 and was not published until 1920, when it appeared in the Doubleday Sun-Dial Edition. This essay was a response to "Decivilizes" by Alice Meynell, first published in the *National Observer* in 1891 and reprinted in Meynell's collection, *The Rhythm of Life*, in 1893. JC's essay emphasizes, in opposition of Meynell's claim, the idea that the "savage surroundings" of his novel have only the function of throwing into sharp relief the basic similarities of man. No reason is known why JC's first critical work was not published as the preface to *Folly*. It is important, though, because it supplies the first clear view of the "critical, theoretical, and literary" JC, it establishes the critical assumptions with which JC began writing, and it startlingly anticipates his later and better known statements.

3247 Hilson, J. C., and D. Timms. "Conrad's 'An Outpost of Progress' or, The Evil Spirit of Civilization," *SJC* (1975), pp. 113–28.

In both "An Outpost of Progress" and "Heart of Darkness," JC is far more interested in what happened to the whites in the Congo than in what happened to the blacks. The first story victimizes Kayerts and Carlier, not the heart of darkness; JC's main purpose in this story is social comment. The tale is a somewhat bitter attack on what the author called "masquerading philanthropy." White men and black are alike in many ways: both are unhappy, both are manipulated by men who serve the same ends and the same means.

Makola's actions point to the conclusion that the methods of civilization and those of savagery are the same. Kayerts kills himself because he may participate in the hypocrisy of "progress" or he may confess that he killed Carlier and return to civilization to face the consequences. But by so bringing things into the open, he will become liable to the "justice" of "civilization." His suicide is a choice of nightmares similar to that which faces first Kurtz, then Marlow, in "Heart of Darkness," an attempt to free himself from the victimization of "progress." "An Outpost of Progress" is thus a lesser "Heart of Darkness," inferior in lacking the symbolic suggestiveness of the later work.

3248 Hoff, Peter Sloat. "*The Secret Agent*: A Typical Conrad Novel?" *Pol R, XX*, Nos. 2–3 (1975), pp. 154–63; rpt. *JCCE* (1975), pp. 153–62.

In spite of many surface differences, the essential substance of *The Secret Agent* is very much like the substance of JC's other great works. Thematically, the novel contains at least four crucial concepts which appear importantly in some of JC's other writings. The ideal conception of the self and the question as to whether a man can be true to it, which forms a *raison d'etre* for every character in *Agent*, is vital in *Lord Jim* and *Nostromo*. The theme of betrayal, which defines *Jim* and *Under Western Eyes* and figures prominently in *Nostromo*, binds together a diverse set of characters in *Agent*. The doubling of characters, which develops *Agent* "in kaleidoscopic fashion," is both a technique and a theme in "The Secret Sharer," *Jim*, and *Nostromo*. And rendering a vision of "the Horror at the Heart of Darkness" is common in JC's works.

3249 Ho Lung, Richard R. "'Life's Womb': A Jungian Archetypal Study of Five Novels by Joseph Conrad," *DAI, XXXV* (1975), 7256A. Unpublished dissertation, Syracuse University, 1974.

3250 Hoogenakker, J. L. "Joseph Conrad as Precursor of the Absurdist Vision," *DAI, XXXVI* (1975), 4476A. Unpublished dissertation, University of Kansas, 1975.

3251 Hruska, T. J. "The Influence of Joseph Conrad's Attitude Toward Race on the Dramatic and Thematic Structure of His Fiction," *DAI, XXXVI* (1975), 3689A. Unpublished dissertation, Michigan State University, 1975.

3252 Hughes, Douglas A. "Conrad's 'Il Conde': 'Deucedly Queer Story,'" *CON, VII*, No. 1 (1975), pp. 17–25.

The Count's relation of his "adventure" in "Il Conde" may be "an elaborate fabrication" to preserve his reputation, and several suggestive details and the discrediting of the narrator's judgment provide evidence that the old man may be lying. There is good reason to believe that the Count is "a lonely, vulnerable pederast" who becomes involved in the "pathetic tale" of the subtitle of the story. JC here uses his familiar device of two narrators, with one narrator, in this instance, seeming to be questionable, just as there are many reasons to doubt the truth of Il Conde's version of his "adventure."

3253 Jablkowska, Roza. "Foreword," *JCCP* (1975), pp. 7–8.

[The sessions of the Joseph Conrad colloquy emphasized JC's Polish heritage, his art of impressionism, and a review of recent trends in JC scholarship. The first international conference on JC held in Poland in 1957 was "on a very modest scale."]

3254 Jablkowska, Roza (ed.). *Joseph Conrad Colloquy in Poland, 5–12 September 1972: Contributions* (Wroclaw, Warszwa, Krakow, Gdansk: Polish Academy of Sciences, Neophilological Committee, 1975).

Contents, abstracted in alphabetical order by author, 1975: Roza Jablkowska, "Foreword"; Eloise Knapp Hay, "Conrad's Self-Portraiture"; Julian Krzyzanowski, "The Inaugural Address"; Gustav Morf, "Polish Proverbial Sayings in Conrad's Works"; Thomas Moser, "Conrad, Ford and the Sources of *Chance*"; Ugo Mursia, "The Italian Source of Nostromo"; René Rapin, "André Gide's Translation of Joseph Conrad's 'Typhoon'"; Ian Watt, "Pink Toads and Yellow Curs: An Impressionistic Device in *Lord Jim*." [A selection from the papers read during the 1972 Joseph Conrad Colloquy held in Warsaw, Krakow, Zakopane, and Gdansk, 5 to 12 September 1972. Contains the program of the colloquy and a complete list of the contributions.]

3255 "Joseph Conrad: An Unpublished Letter to Carlo Placci," *JCCS*, II, No. 2 (December 1975), pp. 5–6.

JC's constant aspiration in writing was, by means of stylistics, the external world around us, the emotions of man, the sensations of the soul, and the ineffable secret of mysterious nature, to make his reader *see*. In doing so, he "reproposes" to the reader what he felt when experiencing the impact of a natural phenomenon; he awakens problems in the reader through the magic of his means of expression, by attempting to lift linguistic expression to the level of symbol. He was always concerned with the ideal value of things, facts, people: the details, humorous, pathetic, passionate, sentimental, follow by themselves. In October, 1911, he wrote a letter from London to the musicologist Carlo Placci in Florence, which demonstrates better than any critical analysis his task as a writer. JC made every effort to make the word more than alive. [Author's name not given. Translated by John Crompton and M. Walters. The letter is quoted only in part. Originally appeared in complete form in *Paragone*, VIII, No. 88 (1957).]

3256 Kam, Rose Sallberg. "Silverberg and Conrad: Explorers of Inner Darkness," *Extrapolation*, XVII (December 1975), pp. 18–28.

Echoes of "Heart of Darkness" appear in several works of science fiction, but closest of all in demonstrating at length the influence of such work is Robert Silverberg's *Downward to the Earth*. Silverberg names a major character Kurtz and translates to an alien planet the insights JC gleaned from an "alien continent." But he does not copy JC: he develops more fully the biblical archetype of man and serpent; and on the pattern of the quest on which "Heart of Darkness" is also based, Silverberg "weaves his own tapestry of light and darkness." Common to the two books are the brooding jungle toward which each protagonist is drawn, but the personal odysseys of Marlow and Gundersen differ greatly. The difference between the themes of the two stories seems more a matter of degree than of kind: JC's Marlow brings back to his people only a murky sort of light whereas Silverberg's Gundersen comes to terms with the powers against which Kurtz rages and emerges with what he sees as the greatest boon for "all souled beings," a union of minds and immortality. [No explanation of the value of JC's influence on science fiction is offered.]

3257 Karl, Frederick R. "Introduction," *JCCC* (1975), pp. 1–12.

[Gives a sketch of JC's life and justifies the choice of critical essays in Karl's collection.]

3258 Karl, Frederick R. "Selected Bibliography," *JCCC* (1975), pp. 147–52.

[This selected bibliography of writings by and about JC contains materials on "Novels and Short Stories," "Essays and Reminiscences," "Dramatic Works," "Letters," "Collected Editions," and "Selected Writings about Conrad," making a very useful reference for important works.]

3259 Karl, Frederick R. (ed.). *Joseph Conrad: A Collection of Criticism* (NY: McGraw-Hill [Contemporary Studies in Literature], 1975).

Contents, abstracted under year of first publication: Frederick R. Karl, "Introduction," (1975); Bernard Meyer, ["The Secret Sharer,"] from *Joseph Conrad: A Psychoanalytic Biography* (1967); Frederick R. Karl, "'Heart of Darkness': Introduction to the *Danse Macabre*," from *A Reader's Guide to Joseph Conrad* (1969); Dorothy Van Ghent, "*Nostromo*," from Joseph Conrad, *Nostromo: A Tale of the Seaboard* (1961), (C, I, No. 1655); Robert Wooster Stallman, "Time and *The Secret Agent*," from *The Houses that James Built* (1961), (C, I, No. 1561); Albert Guerard, "Two Versions of Anarchy: *Under Western Eyes*," from *Conrad the Novelist* (1958), (C, I, No. 1470); R. W. B. Lewis, "The Current of Conrad's *Victory*," from *Twelve Original Essays on Great English Novels*, ed. by Charles Shapiro (1960), (C, I, No. 1599); Eloise Knapp Hay, "'The Artist of the Whole Matter,'" from *The Political Novels of Joseph Conrad* (1963), (C, I, No. 1724); John A. Palmer, "'Achievement and Decline': A Bibliographical Note," from *Joseph Conrad's Fiction: A Study in Literary Growth* (1968); Frederick R. Karl, "Selected Bibliography," (1975), [not abstracted].

3260 Kehler, Joel R. "A Note on the Epigraph to Conrad's *The Rescue*," *English Language Notes*, XII (March 1975), pp. 184–87.

The quotation from Chaucer's *Franklin's Tale* used as the epigraph of *The Rescue* is appropriate because Edith Travers is forced to admit her enslavement to convention. JC's choice of the tale itself is appropriate also because chivalric idealism and *amour courtois* are central to both works. And on a deeper level, Chaucer's Dorigen and Edith Travers, both captives of illusion, have the illusion dispelled and then return to their husbands. Whereas Dorigen is an unwilling captive who returns happily to her husband, Edith, a willing captive, returns to her husband with a sense of loss. The similarities of plot and characater extend also to the husbands. The two works, then, parallel each other in a number of ways. JC demonstrates in this novel, as in many others, that "knightly" can be the gorgeous facade of "benighted."

3261 Kertzer, J. M. "Conrad's Personal Record," *University of Toronto Quarterly*, XLIV (Summer 1975), pp. 290–303.

JC's *A Personal Record* is "not profoundly personal and none too accurate a record," and his "Familiar Preface" is not familiar. The information given is often inadequate, and this book may be considered more profitably as an extension of JC's novel writing. Like *Lord Jim, Nostromo*, or *Under Western Eyes*, *Record* explores moments of decision in a person's life, the attempt to come to terms with past actions, the desire to live up to traditional standards of excellence. It provides the clearest example of one of JC's major themes: the efforts of the individual to establish a moral pattern in his life. The individual, JC himself, offers, as in his novels, an "elaborate, public, literary performance." He is always the craftsman, organizing and interpreting, remaining aloof in order to be sufficiently detached. Beginning as reminiscence and reverie, the book gradually turns into a "carefully controlled confession" in which the author seeks justification for his own life. He wants to find out how his two major decisions, to go to sea and to write a novel, figure in the moral structure of his life. Since only through the probing of memory can he find meaning in the flow of his life, his book progresses through digressions, making the "time-shift" technique basic to his self-analysis. Key scenes, from which the account digresses and to which it periodically returns, supply coherence to the whole. The first focal point is Rouen, where JC is at work in his two professions of author and sailor. The second "current of memory" is the voyage: he traces the journeys on which he carried the manuscript of *Almayer's Folly*. His uncle's home in the Ukraine, the center of the third current of memory, considers his origins. The fourth current examines the circumstances that prompted his second choice of life; several digressions make this part unusually rambling. The last current, centered in London and Marseilles, is a recapitulation. Throughout the book, JC insists on the temporal coherence of tradition, which explains his complementary and distasteful references to revolution. He discovers that the acuteness of perception which enables him to explore his past proves to be a basic force behind all his writing, that his two professions have much in common. He celebrates the common values—fidelity, courage, endurance, dignity—which figure in his novels. Thus JC turns his life, with a "formal beauty," into a moral romance based not on "anguished self-justification" but on "recollection in tranquillity."

3262 King, Russell S. "Conrad's *Almayer's Folly* and Lenormand's *Le Simoun*: Some Aspects of Characterization," *Revue de Litterature Comparee*, XLIV (April–June 1975), pp. 302–11.

Henri-René Lenormand and JC, who met in Ajaccio in 1921, observed certain similarities and certain fundamental differences in their two works, JC's *Almayer's Folly* of 1899 and Lenormand's play, *Le Simoun*, of 1920. The two works bear close resemblances to each other, especially in their choice of characters and plots. JC, who "presents" Almayer rather than explaining, judging, or analyzing him, has his narrator remain detached from his subject and appeals strongly to the senses, particularly to sight. JC's use of narrator-judge in places and free indirect speech suggests, through irony, a complex personality. The hero's powerful visual imagination finally destroys his sanity. Since the key to Almayer's character is his weakness of will, his character is not of psychological interest per se;

the focus is on the effects of his weakness rather than on the cause and nature of it. Whereas "*see*" dictates narrative technique in *Folly*, the key word in *Le Simoun* is "*comprendre*"; therefore, the comparison of the two works is valuable for the two writers' divergent views in their presentation of character: JC avoids the extremes of the psychological novel whereas Lenormand uses the play's exoticism to symbolize the mysterious and the inexplicable. The meeting of JC and Lenormand is significant because Lenormand relates the only known judgment JC explicity passed on Freud and his potential contribution to the creative artist.

3263 Knowles, Owen. "Conrad's Anatomy of Women: Some Notes on *Victory*," *JCCS*, II (August 1975), pp. 3–6.

Of all of JC's works, *Victory* is the most ambitious and interesting venture into "prickly" sexual matters and female psychology. In this book, the figure of Arthur Schopenhauer is a pervasive influence. JC wrestles with Schopenhauerian misogyny and sexual disgust. The philosopher considered the female as a creature of "ulterior will." As a guardian of human kind, she lives more for the species than the individual and hence acts as a vehicle through which the Will attains its purpose. In his description of the female as archetypal temptress yet unconscious priestess of nature's intention, Schopenhauer anticipates JC's Lena. *Victory* gains much of its interest and stature from its relationship with Schopenhauer's fixed imperatives in man–woman relations. Especially at the end of the novel, Lena becomes the "grand simplifying example" of the "burning will-for-life" confronting all danger and menace on the earth. After Lena's death-scene, JC's final chapter returns to the Schopenhauerian world of "male awkwardness, purposeless violence, suicide," and finally reaches its climax in the last word of the novel, "Nothing," which word also concludes Schopenhauer's *The World as Will and Idea*.

3264 Knowles, Owen. "'To Make You Hear . . .': Some Aspects of Conrad's Dialogue," *Pol R*, XX, Nos. 2–3, pp. 164–80; rpt. *JCCE* (1975), pp. 163–79.

Generally, JC has only average success with finely shaded and continuous dialogue, and he tends to be less successful with the intricate spoken word of "high passion" between men and women. Most characteristically, he makes us "hear" the spoken word by making it subject to the selective and ordering devices of his impressionism and by exploiting broken and interrupted speech, short bursts of conversation, and indeterminate passages of Edwardian stage language. JC's ability makes us "hear" (1) by means of the materials and methods of character individualization so that each speaker tends to be a very distinct "voice," a "speech-burst" "poised between monologue and conversation, report and mimicry," as in MacWhirr's commands during the typhoon; (2) by the dramatization of the more subtle motives, inner tensions, and tangled communications, as with Jim, who cannot explain himself either to Marlow or to himself; and (3) by the role of the conversation piece between the young captain and Archbold in "The Secret Sharer." JC realized the necessity of dramatizing speech if he wanted to get at the whole truth about people.

3265 Kowalska, Aniela. "Conrad i jego 'polskie co do kobiet zludzenia' (Wokol tajemnicy marsylskiej Conrada)," (Conrad and his "Polish Illusions as to Women"), *Prace Polonistyczne* (Lodz), XXXI (1975), pp. 117–28.

The Golden Arrow was inspired not so much by the wish to defend the good name of a "woman of all times," as the need to create a beautiful fairy-tale about JC's own youthful desires. It is thus an act of revenge for the hard and cruel fate of youth. "The Warrior's Tale" is another example, in which JC depicts Tomassowa and her mother—products of drawing-room refinement and depravity—through the eyes of a young man. [In Polish.]

3266 Kramer, Dale. *Thomas Hardy: The Forms of Tragedy* (Detroit: Wayne State University Press, 1975), pp. 19, 113, 126.

Hardy's novels as a whole suggest an environment compatible with the momentousness of tragedy. In this way, they differ sharply from those of Faulkner and JC, both of whom have attempted, and in varying degrees succeeded in composing, "tragic fictions." *Tess of the D'Urbervilles* emphasizes the subjectivity of experience and judgment, a concept which was strongly brought to Western consciousness by Rousseau, continued in Keats's odes and Wordsworth's *The Prelude*. Such later works as Faulkner's and JC's novels are good examples of the capacity of the mind to make its own "self-signifying" world. Also in *Tess*, although Angel cannot be blamed rationally for Alec's death, Alec dies because Angel—like JC's Lord Jim—is incapable of action in an unanticipated situation.

3267 Krzyzanowski, Julian. "The Inaugural Address," *JCCP* (1975), pp. 9–10.

[The welcoming address given to the international colloquy on JC in Poland.]

3268 Lafferty, William. "Conrad's 'A Smile of Fortune': The Moral Threat of Commerce," *CON*, VII, No. 1 (1975), pp. 63–74.

The central problem for the young captain in JC's "A Smile of Fortune" is discovery of his moral identity, since he has not committed himself completely to the "commercial" life nor come to understand all it includes. He has a tendency to vacillate between two moral spheres, business and noncommercial activity. By the end of the story, he is still unable to choose between the two worlds. When the captain becomes too deeply involved with Jacobus for his common ideas of decency, he must reject the commercial ritual; then his sympathies with the Jacobuses begin to wane. If he had not been close to his involvement with Alice, he might have recognized the elements of Jacobus's commercial method; but he is eventually caught in the middle of Jacobus's plot. The turning point of the story is the narrator's seeing the contrast between his commercial self (the purchase of a ship and the bags) and his noncommercial self (kissing Alice); and he, now realizing that his moral identity rather than his sexual prowess is at stake, reverts at once to his commercial self and agrees to take the potatoes. The captain's moral identity thus remains uncertain, even though he has achieved a limited moral victory.

3269 Lee, Sangok. "Conrad's Artistic Manifestoes: Five Essays," *DAI,* XXXVI (1975), 2849A. Unpublished dissertation, SUNY-Stony Brook, 1975.

3270 Lemon, Lee. "Readers, Teachers, and Critics and the Nature of Literature," *Publications of the Arkansas Philological Association,* I, No. 2 (1975), pp. 2–13.

[Lemon uses "Heart of Darkness" to show that, for an understanding of a literary work, his students, as nonprofessional readers, do not need comprehension of "every metaphor, every situation, every nuance, every what-have-you." Rather, they need help in making certain that they have identified all the significant patterns in the work and understand how these patterns "interrelate."]

3271 Lewis, John S. "Conrad in 1914," *Pol R,* XX, Nos. 2–3 (1975), pp. 217–22; rpt. *JCCE* (1975), pp. 216–21.

The year 1914 "cuts a shadow-line" across JC's literary career: after finally achieving success with *Chance,* JC was working to finish *Victory.* In the spring, probably in May, a young and unknown pianist, Arthur Rubinstein, visited JC at Capel House. Rubinstein later remembered JC as being "stiff and formal." JC had not been in Poland since 1893; in 1914, he and his family were there to visit relatives and friends. The beginning of World War I kept them virtually prisoners in Poland for more than two months, during which time JC met young Rubinstein and had time to consider Poland's future with him and others. His enforced sojourn in Poland finally convinced him that an autonomous, perhaps an independent, Poland was possible. At any rate, this visit was to mark a definite change in JC's attitude toward his native land. Thus a few remarks by a young, unknown pianist to a man thirty years older may have led JC "across his own shadow-line," an emotional and intellectual return to Poland.

3272 Lincoln, Kenneth R. "Conrad's Mythic Humor," *TSLL*, XVII (Fall 1975), pp. 635–51.

JC's humor, "mostly dark and disguised," runs underground. An artist needs distance and self-awareness, the essentials of humorous vision, to face "the horror" at the core of Western civilization, perhaps at the heart of human nature, in order to tell his stories. A firm agnostic, JC often satirizes Christian evangelism, as seen in Podmore in *The Nigger of the Narcissus*, in the "pilgrims" crusading in "Heart of Darkness," and in the American capitalist in *Nostromo*. The "impossible standards" of Christian idealism provide the backdrop for Jim's anguish in *Lord Jim*. JC pities Jim while he rejects the nineteenth-century models that Jim acts out, including his death from an obese chieftain who takes the part of Pontius Pilate. JC appeals to the laughter of the mind when he juggles classical and Christian parodies in "Falk." Here, JC sports with Darwinian theory, his satire of mercantilism, his disdain for bourgeois pettiness, and his parodies of classical myth and Christian ritual. In *The Secret Agent*, JC offers his own mock variants on Nietzsche's posing of Dionysus against Christ-Apollo, on classicism and primitivism as warring complements in Western civilization—Apollonian order and reason subverted by Dionysian disorder and irrationality. Ossipon and the Professor symbolize JC's mock variants and this opposition. JC's mythic humor counsels the reader to resist suffering for the world's blunders. In print, the artist weeps secretly, but he manages an ironic smile.

3273 Lindsay, Clarence Binnes, Jr. "Character and Morality in Conrad's Fiction," *DAI*, XXXV (1975), 7912A. Unpublished dissertation, University of Minnesota, 1974.

3274 Lombard, François. "Conrad and Buddhism," *SJC* (1975), pp. 103–12.

Two images are central to the Buddhist creed: the Circle, and the Wheel of becoming or Karma. The circle is a major Conradian image. Existence, conditioned by the circular ego of man, is to JC, as to Buddha, the very prison of life. The image of the Wheel is an image of "fatality," a kind of fatality linked with the "mathematical recurrence of evil, as long as it has not been redeemed." We are, like Jim and Heyst, prisoners to that "wheel of Becoming." According to Buddhism, men are condemned to such a Wheel of Being as long as they believe in appearances. Jim seems to follow the Buddhistic itinerary: thwarting the determinism of the Wheel through taking his destiny into his own hands, to destroy himself consciously and willingly, in a "supreme act of negative will." Jim acts intuitively, and intuition is the basis of Buddhism. It is such individual intuition that MacWhirr chooses to be guided by when faced with the typhoon; symbolically he chooses the "Middle-Way." In his works, JC shows that the sea is, first and foremost, a retreat in which man can find the true meaning of his existence. The "union of man's self with the selves of others (and ultimately with the self of the universe, perhaps)" is found in most of JC's books, especially in *Lord Jim.* His "Buddhistic strain" is perhaps best illustrated by Marlow's character and his role. He is, at the center of JC's works, "Buddha exorcising Conrad's creatures of darkness out of their Karma—exorcising Conrad, perhaps? It is hoped, then, that he was successful." [Perhaps a bit far-fetched.]

3275 Lombard, François. "Conrad's Catholicism," *LC,* No. 1 (March 1975), pp. 27–39.

JC's attitude toward religion is ambiguous, but for him the universe could not have existed without a "Commanding Officer." The love of ritual was one mark of his Catholicism; what he rejected was the textual interpretation of the Scripture. When lost in attempts of expression, he knew that word could never come up to expectations or reveal half the mystery he felt—thus his ambiguity. His stories progress mostly as rituals in which "the characters are but the priests performing rites of Eternity in the perspective of Time." Jim's rite of re-creation is, for example, typically Conradian: Jim *will* perform the ritual of his dream up to the final holocaust. Heyst, in *Victory,* also culminates in a holocaust after he "jumps" from the "Father's world" and comes to life in his own. The same pattern is found in "The Planter of Malata" and "Typhoon." The belief in evil spirits and instances of possession are also other points which associate JC with Catholicism, as seen in *The Shadow-Line* and *An Outcast of the Islands.* The removal of a curse can also be conceived in terms of confession, as in *Nostromo.* Renunciation appears in *Lord Jim, Victory, The Rover,* "The Secret Sharer," *The Secret Agent, Chance,* and *Under Western Eyes.* There is, though, no promise of eternal life in JC's works. But JC did not renounce his religion; readers were misled because JC strongly rejected two major poles of Catholicism: the Lord of Hosts, Jehovah, and heaven.

3276 Lombard, François. "Joseph Conrad and Henry James: The Cosmic Pattern," *LC*, No. 1 (March 1975), pp. 21–26.

One of the most basic resemblances between Henry James and JC is their leaving home for the world of adventure and both probably discovering that any world of any kind could be such a world. In *The Ambassadors*, a study in the cosmic forces that shape man's destiny, Maria Gostrey represents a cosmic force that drives man, very often in spite of himself, into the path that is meant for him. In this novel by James, as in most of JC's works, the same cosmic pattern appears: the Father (Waymarsh, JC's "great autocrat," who resembles both Jehovah and Jove), the Son (Strether, who will partake of the imperfection of the world in a kind of incarnation also found in JC's novels, as with Jim, who jumps, or falls, into the abyss of animality), and "Woman who is opposed to the Virgin" (Maria Gostrey who, like Miss Moorsom of "The Planter of Malata," is the catalyst of man's capacity for perfection who will soon find herself confronted with "Woman," the source of imperfection "as a producer of flesh and all the more so in the person of young Chad's mistress"). Very much as the Son is a half-human image of the Father, the Virgin is another image of the "female pendant of the Father." There are reminders here of both Christianity and pagan mythology. Strether, like Nostromo, belongs to no class; he has come "down" to a world of types, the same as with such persons in JC's work, "to rescue man" from his split into a variety of types, to help these types regain their "fundamental, original unity." The gift of vision which both James and JC have may be their metaphysical interpretation of art—to make the reader see, to "recompose the artistic picture of the world in the light of the universe."

3277 Lombard, François. "Shakespeare, Conrad and Humanism," *LC*, No. 1 (March 1975), pp. 14–20.

The three main concepts of "humanism" of Renaissance England, found in varying degrees in both Shakespeare and JC, are: the Wheel of Fortune, which symbolized the circle in which man finds himself a prisoner, similar to what we call Fate; the "Chain of Beings," the hierarchy going up from Satan to God, with men precariously placed at the center of these two extremes; and Redemption, the help of God as it was revealed through Christ's life. Shakespeare used the concept of the Great Chain of Being, especially in his tragedies, where frail man is seen to be in danger of failing—a pessimistic attitude toward life. Both the Wheel of Fortune and Fate play a greater part in Shakespeare than does the grace of God, and they are also found in JC's works. There is a difference, though, between the concept of the general predestination of man in Shakespeare and in JC. The conclusions of *Hamlet* and *Lord Jim*, for example, are somewhat different: whereas Hamlet makes his final decision as an impulse, Jim knows perfectly well what he is doing. When Jim realizes the meaninglessness of life, he takes the courageous decision not to act and thus "jams" the Wheel of Fate and then takes the greatest risk possible to man—annihilation. But through his feeling of communion with the people of Patusan and of leadership, Jim has redeemed his "sin." He is not, though, a triumphant hero, because JC leaves everything in the "artistic and metaphysic veil of uncertainty." Both Shakespeare and JC see man as poised between the forces of evil and the forces of light, with Fate in the middle to tip the balance one way or the other. But in both writers there is a frail power to triumph with Henry V and MacWhirr, or, more often to fall, like Othello and Jim. In both instances, we have humanistic pictures of men.

3278 Loretelli, Rosamaria. "La citta in *The Secret Agent* di Conrad" (The Town in Conrad's *The Secret Agent*), *Studi Inglesi*, 2 (1975), pp. 211–31.

Recent critics have denied the centrality of the anarchist theme in *The Secret Agent*, moving the focus from the political to the social sphere, and assuming the city to be the unifying element of the novel. These critics do not seem, however, to perceive the monstrosity of the town, which causes alienation. Avrom Fleishman stresses the centrality of the theme of the social fragmentation of the city, but uses a series of images that have little to do with the city itself.

London, enormous, mysterious and dark as an unexplored continent, has the same function as Africa or South America in other novels, isolating characters and putting them in an atmosphere of incomprehensible horror. Squalor, moral degradation, monotony, dinginess, all these negative connotations are transferred from the town to anarchism. [In Italian.]

3279 Martin, David M. "The Diabolic Kurtz: The Dual Nature of His Satanism in 'Heart of Darkness,'" *CON*, VII, No. 2 (1975), pp. 175–77.

In "Heart of Darkness," JC associates Kurtz with two antithetical images of Satan: one, the orthodox image of Satan as "Princeps Mundi," identified with the materialism of "this" world and man's "lower" nature; the other, the romantic image of Satan as "Lucifer," identified with the rebellious assertion of self against cosmic tyranny and seen in Kurtz's cry of horror. In due time, Marlow understands Kurtz's cry as both a revolt and an affirmation.

3280 Martin, Jacky. "J. Conrad's *The Shadow-Line* ou les intermittances du texte" (J. Conrad's *The Shadow-Line* or the Irregularities of the Text), *SJC* (1975), pp. 271–92.

The plurality of the text of *The Shadow-Line* is illustrated by the very spacing and plurisignation of the words on the title page, one of whose meanings, around with others revolve, is that the shadow is an obstacle and a boundary which divides life into two parts—youth and what follows it. Still another ambiguity is contained in "Confession," implying either a statement of truth or of self-accusation. Structurally the divisions of the tale do not come at the points of logical interruption of the action but rather at crucial points in the evolution of the hero whose progress is illuminated by the juxtaposition of secondary plots. The hero's initiation alludes to similar cultural codes outside the text—the Odyssey, the Phantom Ship, the Ancient Mariner—which are made to parody the romantic conception of the hero to emphasize the theme that evil is not outside the self but in the individual's self-absorption. The symbolism of the tale is articulated between the extremes of enjoyment and trading values. The narration of the tale hides beneath its reassuring conventions of the bourgeois novel the secret of despair, but this narration of despair, recalling the original series of events, is a protection, an intercession, against a spiritual death and assures its survival. [In French.]

3281 Mayoux, Jean-Jacques. "L'Absurde et le grotesque dans l'oeuvre de Joseph Conrad" (The Absurd and the Grotesque in Joseph Conrad's Work), *SJC* (1975), pp. 53–82.

JC tried to solve the problem of the absurdity of life through his characters, but always had to return to it in his own life. Existential absurdity appears in many of his works. The confused chronology and the suicide of Decoud in *Nostromo* represents a vain attempt by the author to exorcise his feelings of absurdity. In *Under Western Eyes*, Razumov finds his promising future becoming an extension of the nothingness of his past by the presence of Haldin. Although the objective reality of life is still the same, the relation between the hero's conception of life and its reality of insignificance has changed: the insignificance of life becomes absurd when personal and objective reality no longer correspond. In *Victory*, although Heyst already is aware of life's absurdity, his claim to defy the fates on Samburan makes the reader more aware, by dramatic irony, of the cruel absurdity of life. Again in *Under Western Eyes*, Razumov's very identity is taken from him by others who create a new identity for him, as Heyst discovers has also happened to him in listening to Lena. Lena and Heyst become victims of Heyst's reluctance to combat this absurd world. Often joined to JC's rendering of the absurd is his expressionistic vision of the grotesque derived from the incongruity between a serious act and its undignified manifestation, as in the description of the hanged man in "An Outpost of Progress." Perhaps the best example of such a reduction is found in the treatment of the satanic trio in *Victory*. [In French.]

3282 McIntyre, Allen J. "Psychology and Symbol: Correspondence Between 'Heart of Darkness' and *Death in Venice*," *Hartford Studies in Literature*, VII (1975), pp. 216–35.

Thomas Mann and JC shared a "fundamental agreement in outlook" which makes *Death in Venice* a "spiritual German cousin" to "Heart of Darkness." A structural device which acts as an organizing principle in both novellas is the journey, a journey that provides a basis for the threads of psychology and symbol which make the "single fabric" of moral and physical reality and is at the same time a descent in which both protagonists go down to "southern climes" where the isolated and inflated ego acquires a taste for chaos and is at last absorbed into infinity, lost in the void. Mann's hero, Gustav von Aschenbach, literally falls to pieces without any overt action in the external world; JC, however, puts himself at several removes from events. Of the two, Mann can more easily be explicit; JC tends toward the implicit because his events occur in the contemporary, external world, in which Victorian prohibition suppresses frankness. Both Aschenbach, the artist, and Kurtz, the entrepreneur, are unable to resist the fatal temptation in beauty and power. In Aschenbach, degeneracy expresses itself in irresistible infatuation with a fourteen-year-old boy; in Kurtz, the desire for power is "seduced" by the jungle, becoming a wasting fever. From the beginning, sickness and death await the victims civilization has subtly undermined. Since death is the unconscious goal of these travelers, death appears to them in appropriate forms along their ways. To be gifted, then, to be highly civilized, is to be decadent and prey to a ferocious attack from which there is no escape. Both Mann and JC insist on the inevitability of moral sickness in civilization; both artists are, then, "deeply pessimistic."

3283 McLauchlan, Juliet. "Conrad's 'Three Ages of Man': The *Youth* Volume," *Pol R*, XX, Nos. 2–3 (1975), pp. 189–202; rpt. *JCCE* (1975), pp. 188–201.

JC's *Youth* volume, originally intended to contain the sketch, "Lord Jim," is actually a group of related stories in which the Marlow of "Youth" and "Heart of Darkness" are two entirely different persons. The unity of the "trio" is thematic, and all three stories rank among JC's "most profound and disturbing work." The essential preoccupation is with the pattern of youth, middle age, and old age.

In "Youth," the young Marlow makes his first voyage as an officer and views the illusory "East" while keeping all of life before him as "beautiful, varied, new." An older Marlow makes his two-way voyage in "Heart of Darkness." And Captain Whalley's voyage in "The End of the Tether," his last voyage, is in every way a journey into darkness. Each tale involves the presence of darkness, but in each there is a different metaphorical significance: in "Youth," there is neither Kurtz's degradation nor Whalley's partial corruption; in the third story, all the concerns of the first two come together. "Youth" contains the genuine qualities of the young Marlow as a seaman. In "Heart of Darkness," the human is embodied primarily in Marlow in his fully human responses to the wilderness and in his active humanity. Whalley, in the last story, undergoes a shattering of all the major illusions by which humanity lives. But the "final flame" in the *Youth* volume is invisible, "the pure inner flame of a sacrificial love."

3284 McLauchlan, Juliet. "Love and Metaphor in Conrad," *JJCS*, II (August 1975), pp. 6–8.

The usual assumption that love and women formed for JC the "uncongenial subject" is offset by the "demonstrable fact" that each woman functions in precise ways within a tight metaphysical structure to which she is essential, as in "The Planter of Malata," "Freya of the Seven Isles," and "Amy Foster," all of which illustrate how metaphor extends to become universal. *Almayer's Folly*, too, is a sustained metaphor. Throughout the book, the contrast between Almayer's illusory vision and Nina's realistic dream demonstrates that even though it may be impossible to live by an illusion, it is even more impossible to live without it. A basic life-death antithesis involves the two dreams: only Dain can offer life to Nina, and Almayer, absorbed in his own folly, or madness, effectively ceases to exist. JC's imagery reinforces the major theme of the novel, which continues to the end.

3285 Miller, Eugene Louis, Jr. "Tragicomic Vision in *The Nigger of the Narcissus*," *DAI*, XXXVI (1975), 4478A. Unpublished dissertation, University of Toledo, 1975.

3286 Mole, John. "Joseph Conrad on TV," *TLS* (14 March 1975), p. 276.

[A poem about an actor portraying JC on "Omnibus."]

3287 Monteiro, George. "Addenda to the Bibliographies of Conrad, Cooke, Damon, Ford, Glasgow, Holmes, Jewett, Lewis, Mumford, Robinson, and Scott," *Papers of the Bibliographical Society of America*, LXIX (1975), pp. 273–75.

[Lists four items to be added to *A Bibliography of Joseph Conrad*, compiled by Theodore G. Ehrsam (1969) and to *Joseph Conrad: An Annotated Bibliography of Writings About Him*, edited by Bruce E. Teets and Helmut E. Gerber (1971).]

3288 Moore, Harry T. "Leitmotif Symbolism in *The Secret Agent*," *Pol R*, XX, Nos. 2–3 (1975), pp. 141–44; rpt. *JCCE* (1975), pp. 140–43.

As the circles which Stevie draws in chapter III of JC's *The Secret Agent* appear throughout the novel, developing suggestions of rondure, they cross and intertwine with others that flash with fire, thereby connoting "cosmic chaos" and the "mad art attempting the inconceivable" which reflects JC's attitude toward the anarchists. This "leitmotif symbolism" includes Stevie at fourteen setting off fireworks, and also the parlor with two burning gas jets and a "glowing grate" where the anarchists meet, which represent symbolically Stevie's death by the red-hot explosion. The fire-and-light images also include Winnie Verloc's statement to her husband in chapter IX that Stevie "would go through fire for you," the "red glow" of the eating-house seen by Winnie soon after she has killed Verloc, the Professor's round india-rubber ball which he carries as a detonator, and the Greenwich Observatory itself. Nowhere else does JC use recurring symbol-themes so consistently as in *Agent*.

3289 Morf, Gustav. "Polish Proverbial Sayings in Conrad's Works," *JCCP* (1975), pp. 89–92.

JC uses proverbial sayings several times in his works (in such stories and novels as "Gaspar Ruiz," *Victory, Nostromo*, "The Duel," *The Rescue*, and *Under Western Eyes*). Occasionally he refers to a Polish proverb, which may have come from Mickiewicz, as being Russian. Being firmly convinced that any association with Poland could only dim his prospects as a writer, JC chose Russian because Russian literature had become very popular in England.

3290 Morf, Gustav. "*The Rescue* as an Expression of Conrad's Dual Personality," *Pol R*, XX, Nos. 2–3 (1975), pp. 211–16; rpt. *JCCE* (1975), pp. 210–15.

JC began *The Rescue* in 1896, but did not write much beyond its first part until he returned to it nineteen years later and finished it in 1919, at the time when Poland was reborn as an independent country. The novel begins with praise of the Malayan "freedom fighters" and strong Polish undertones which would naturally lead to action and deeds of heroism, but JC's inability to maintain this early level a "very Nalecz Korzeniowski trait" as well as a trait common to many Polish leaders of the time. After the yacht *Hermit* arrives, Lingard no longer knows his own mind, and JC was unable to continue writing shortly after Lingard decided to sacrifice Hassim and Immada and all they represent. This blocking of inspiration arises from an inner conflict within the artist himself: as a Pole, he highly admired the Malay freedom fighters and held the greatest contempt for the imperialistic powers who took both the land and the people, but as an English writer who wanted to be successful, he could not allow any harm to come to the English people cruising for their pleasure. His great concession to the reading public, who wanted a love story, caused him to lose the power to continue writing.

3291 Moriarty, Bonnie R. "Onlookers at a Game: A Study of the Narrator-Device in Joseph Conrad's *Lord Jim, Under Western Eyes,* and *Chance,*" *DAI,* XXXVI (1975), 6087A. Unpublished dissertation, Lehigh University, 1975.

3292 Morina, Gerardo. "The Freedom from the Absolute: "The Secret Sharer," *LC,* No. 1 (March 1975), pp. 5–7.

JC intends in "The Secret Sharer" to prolong the young captain's meeting with Leggatt from a certain moment on, not relating him with time but with discovery and the "continuous renewal of existence as experience." When the captain finds himself alone with his ship, loneliness, supported by strangeness, appears. The young man is at a crossroad: the tendency to "non-experience" would lead him blindly. The world of the absolute (rationality) is represented by the crew of the ship; the world of the relative (experience), by the real alternative the captain is offered. Leggatt comes in to "turn up the clods" of the captain's existence. JC's main interest is in the "disintegrity" or self-dissolution which, paradoxically, makes one free to be a presence in the world, a meaning. The conversation between the captain and Leggatt soon becomes an intra-personal one, and the captain's strangeness to the "Self" is eliminated by his communication with Leggatt. Since ethical creeds are subjective, man must learn how to act "now." His is a philosophical choice.

3293 Moser, Thomas C. "Conrad, Ford, and the Sources of *Chance,*" *JCCP* (1975), pp. 33–56; rpt. *CON,* VII, No. 3 (1975), pp. 207–24.

Chief public sources of JC's *Chance* are the Victorian Pre-Raphaelite past of the Garnetts and the Hueffers and the Edwardian present of Ford and JC. Also, the theme of the novel, an endlessly unconsummated love affair, recurs in most of Ford's novels, before and after *Chance.* Reciprocally, Ford's masterpiece, *The Good Soldier,* owes more to *Chance* than to any novel JC wrote except *Lord Jim.* In *Chance,* Roderick Anthony and his father resemble Milnes Patmore and his son, Coventry Patmore, the poet. The public sources of Flora and her father were probably inspired by Therese and

Frederic Humbert, whose case was widely discussed in Paris and London papers in 1902 and 1903, and Whitaker Wright, notorious swindler whose well known deeds of 1897 to 1904 coincided with the most intense period of JC's creativity and his friendship with Ford. Post-1907 material used in *Chance* is, very likely, Ford's disastrous financial mismanagement of *The English Review* in 1909, and JC's mixed feelings about Ford in 1911 may have informed his attitudes toward both the villain, de Barral, and the hero. [Supported by copious evidence and logical speculation.]

3294 Mroczkowski, Przemyslaw. "Conrad the European," *Pol R*, XX, Nos. 2–3 (1975), pp. 87–96; rpt. *JCCE* (1975), pp. 87–96.

JC's fiction reveals that for him the crucial point or value of his time is the human person, conceived both individually and socially. To some of the ideologies of the last three decades of the nineteenth century must be added humanitarianism and pacifism, with emphasis on averting pain and war. Generally, JC centers his attention on the individual. He also utilizes the theme of man's solitude, which he inherited from the Romantics, or he portrays an individual solving the problems of his relationship to his human surroundings in another sense, like James Wait on board the *Narcissus*. The basic content of much of JC's fiction may be said to deal with the integrity of a human being, or with the ways in which it may be jeopardized. And JC seems to declare or imply his adherence to an "organicist" program of society. JC's essays and letters also illuminate his place as a European. For him, human dignity, freedom, and knowledge are essential to human existence. Nations of the Continent and England should live as members of "a higher unity." The opposites denounced in "Autocracy and War" which help the reader to grasp the positive context are largely three: greed, war, and despotism. But JC, being the artist he is, should not be taken seriously as a guide to political or other philosophy.

3295 Mroczkowski, Przemyslaw. "Miedzynarodowy swiat Conrada" (Conrad's International World), *Polonistyka* (Warsaw), XXVIII, No. 2 (1975), pp. 12–21.

JC's British characters are described objectively (officers, seamen), or subjectively (Marlow, upon whom is concentrated much of the "Englishness" which JC had acquired). Of Polish characters, Yanko is an example of the total lack of understanding between human beings, and "Prince Roman" is a traditionally sad portrait of a castaway who has experienced a national tragedy. Portraits of Americans are infrequent, and not detailed. Of the relatively large number of Dutch and Scandinavians, many are merely background figures, though some (Almayer, Willems) are striking as studies in human failure or sin. Germans vary from the noble Stein with his German syntax; others are repulsive (Schomberg, Kurtz). Russians are depicted as basically "different" from the Western world. French (Peyrol), Spanish, and Italians also appear. JC's women are also conditioned in some way or another by their nationality. JC was well aware of the distance separating individuals, the basis of which includes differing national traditions. [In Polish.]

3296 Najder, Zdzislaw. "Conrad to 1898," *SJC*, No. 2 (1975), pp. 19–36.

JC's first attempt to express his mature views on human nature and on man's place in the universe are not a methodical exposition of his theories, but the basic ideas remained the same. The scientific picture of the world provides no grounds for regarding any values or ideals as better than others. There is a "chasm" between nature and man: nature is totally indifferent to humanity. And men are hopelessly weak. The fact that man's consciousness makes him different from other creatures is the source of the tragedy of his fate. Human nature cannot be reformed. JC was not a nihilist and never questioned the validity of all moral ideals. He wanted to remain faithful to "faith, honour, and fidelity to truth."

Upon leaving Poland, JC found himself in "an international sociocultural vacuum." The British merchant marine was for him a school of life, but it was a one-sided and insufficient education for a writer and an intellectual. He wanted to belong to England and English literature, but he did not want to become fully immersed in the English society. He recognized his own "dissimilarity and strangeness," and yet he wanted the comforting sense of belonging. And thanks to Marlow's duality, a model English gentleman and an ex-officer of the merchant marine, JC could feel "solidarity with, and a sense of belonging to England by proxy." [Two fragments from a forthcoming biography.]

3297 Najder, Zdzislaw. "*Lord Jim*: A Controversial Masterpiece," *JJCS*, II (August 1975), pp. 8–10.

Lord Jim is often misinterpreted because two aspects of the novel have not been sufficiently explained. First, in considering the narrative point of view, we must go beyond Marlow. We must check constantly to see whether his is to be taken as a final view or as a stepping-stone to another. Second, we must separate psychology from ethics; moral problems are not internal though moral experience is. Jim finds shame more important than guilt: he feels ashamed, but not guilty. [A "version" of Najder's comments at a lecture.]

3298 Nettels, Elsa. "Vision and Knowledge in *The Ambassadors* and *Lord Jim*," *ELT*, XVIII, No. 3 (1975), pp. 181–93.

The Ambassadors and *Lord Jim* reveal as clearly as any examples the likenesses and differences between the "dramas of consciousness" of Henry James and JC. Among the resemblances are the portrayal in both novels of the bond between a man of middle age and a young man just starting his career, the seeking advice of a friend by both Strether and Marlow whose knowledge or wisdom they believe to surpass their own, the noting in each novel of the older man's awareness that his nature is basically different from that of the young man, and the preoccupation in both novels with the means of revealing truth. Fundamental differences include the various views of the two novelists of the extent to which one person can know another, the essentially different kinds of action and mental experience, and the divergence of the kinds of bonds which join the characters in the books. Both James and JC may be called skeptics and agnostics, but James portrays characters in the process of discovering that which can be known, whereas JC exhibits glimpses of that which cannot be fully revealed or understood. The capacity of characters like Strether and Marlow to feel and suffer and care for a standard of conduct provides both of their stories the values which are appropriate to both novelists.

3299 Nnolim, E. C. "Pejorism as the Organizational Principle in Joseph Conrad's 'Heart of Darkness,'" *DAI*, XXXVI (1975), 1531A. Unpublished dissertation, Catholic University of America, 1975.

3300 Oates, Joyce Carol. "'The Immense Indifference of Things': The Tragedy of Conrad's *Nostromo*," *Novel*, IX (Fall 1975), pp. 5–22.

In JC's major works, the author admires, in a way, his idealists (Jim, Kurtz, Charles Gould), even if he cannot take them seriously, but if his idealists are greatly limited in vision, his skeptics (Marlow, Stein, Dr. Monygham, Nostromo) offer very little. Both bring death to the human community. *Nostromo* is not a human work; its subject is time, the "inexorable process" of time, which can neither be stopped nor fixed into an aesthetic structure. The riddle in JC's art may well be how tragedy is to be avoided, when one's "*living, breathing self, defined in and by action, is also inferior to one's ideal, Platonic essence.*" For JC, man does not much matter in the "immense indifference of things." *Nostromo* is too big, too broad; it seethes with too much life. Martin Decoud, with whose appearance the book becomes alive, is an egoist whose egoism is largely a matter of JC's rhetoric, not his dramatization. The "tragedy" of the novel reduces human beings to mere units in the "*farce macabre* of history." Decoud's death leaves no center of consciousness for the work. JC

uses civil war in Costaguana to dramatize such kinds of division as
that between the poor and the exploiters; his work painfully
prophesies the state of the mid-twentieth century. The silver is the
true subject of the book in a symbolic sense; the motif of civil war is
its dominating theme. The tragedy is the fear of union; there can be
no synthesis of the ideal and the real. Perhaps JC felt how the novel
destroys, instead of affirming, any human values whatsoever.

3301 O'Connor, Peter D. "The Function of Nina in *Almayer's Folly*,"
CON, VII, No. 3 (1975), 225–32.

In *Almayer's Folly*, there is a pattern of imagery which sets Nina
apart from her father, Almayer, and establishes her as a moral and
psychological norm. Light in the darkness is a key image because it
contrasts sharply with the disembodied glitter of Almayer's dream
visions. In contrast, Nina is consistently characterized by a mixture
of light and dark imagery; whereas Almayer turns away from the
darkness of nature, she is constantly depicted as staring into it, filled
with expectations for the future. Her search for the light is a powerful
reaching through nature for the sake of love, as demonstrated in the
two scenes of union between her and Dain. Thus the development of
the image patterns in *Folly* takes the form of two intersecting lines:
while Almayer moves from light to darkness, Nina moves from
darkenss to light. Through Nina, we discover that the darkness of
nature has within it the potentiality for the light of life; through
Almayer, we learn that artificial and irrelevant visions of light, like
his, are only "thrusts in the darkness of a trance that is worse than
death."

3302 Oliva, Renato. "Nota introduttiva" (Introductory Note),
Racconti di Mare e di Costa (*'Twixt Land and Sea*), (Turin:
Einaudi, 1975), pp. v–xxv.

Despite the optimism of the conclusion, "The Secret Sharer"
remains intimately disquieting: the ship of the mind is constantly on
the verge of shipwreck and could, from one moment to the next, turn
into disaster. The fragility of the psyche, the malice of fate, which in a
moment can turn a man into a murderer, are traps which are always
ready to snap shut. At every decisive step, our secret companion may
reappear, asking for our sympathy and complicity. "Freya of the
Seven Isles" forms a kind of dyptich with "A Smile of Fortune." If
"Freya of the Seven Isles" portrays profane, sensual, earthly love, "A
Smile of Fortune" portrays the ideal "marine" love, made for a pure
life of travel, swept by salty winds, on a white brig. [In Italian.]

3303 Pagetti, Carlo. "Biografie e reminiscenze conradienne" (Conradian Biographies and Reminiscences), *Letture* XXX, (Milan), 11 (1975), pp. 741–44.

[A closely reasoned and insightful review of the Italian editions of Jocelyn Baines's biography and of Jessie's and Borys's reminiscences (Milan: Mursia, 1974).] Baines is a scrupulous and impartial gatherer of documents, but he does not succeed in molding biography, social and cultural background, and aesthetic values; he is not able to handle critical instruments, and his critical vision goes back to the first decades of this century and, partly, to Leavis. He denies the existence of deeper meanings, of symbolic levels and narrative structures. The best aspects of his biography will be found in his accurate documentation, compact presentation of information, and absolute lack of rhetorics. Jessie's and Borys's reminiscences are not wholly sincere, but rather edifying and celebrative. JC's torments hardly crop up in his wife's and son's records: their devotion allows only insignificant idiosyncracies to come to the surface. These reminiscences, with their passionate tone, perfectly integrate Baines's objective account. [In Italian.]

3304 Pagetti, Carlo. "'Cuore di tenebra': Viaggio al centro della terra" ("Heart of Darkness": Journey to the Center of the Earth), *Letture* (Milan), XXX, 4 (1975), pp. 281–84.

[Perceptive review of "Cuore di tenebra" (Introduction by Giuseppe Sertoli, Turin: Einaudi, 1974); R. Oliva and A. Portelli, *Conrad: L'Imperialismo Imperfetto* (Turin: Einaudi, 1974P; G. Cianci, "'Heart of Darkness': il compromesso con l'ippopotamo," *Studi Inglesi,* I (1974). These interpretations have a markedly ideological bias, and therefore constitute a restrictive interpretation of JC's art. In Oliva's essay, Marlow's contradictions are transferred to the writer himself to show the mystifying and ambiguous qualities of JC's operation; whereas, according to Sertoli, JC has lucidly denounced the evils of imperialism through the character of Kurtz, who represents the "rhetorics of ideology." Cianci has rightly observed that Kurtz, stepping beyond the threshold of "Truth," pays for this with his life and is able to pass his judgment on the conditions in which he has operated his research.] [In Italian.]

3305 Paruolo, Elena. "Una passione chiamata Conrad" (A Passion Called Conrad), *Paese Sera* (11 April 1975), p. 8.

[Review of the Italian edition of Baines's critical biography of Conrad (Milan: Mursia, 1974).] [In Italian.]

3306 Pearce, Richard. "Enter the Frame," *Surfiction: Fiction Now . . . And Tomorrow*, ed. by Raymond Federman (Chicago: Swallow Press, 1975), pp. 47–57.

A new kind of fiction, called "surfiction," derives from "a radical change in narrative dynamics": both the narrator and the reader are drastically affected. Henry James's *The Turn of the Screw* goes as far as traditional fiction can go in the use of story frames. In JC's "Heart of Darkness," with its unnamed narrator as the largest frame and Marlow within this frame, the subject of the story is not a series of events but Marlow's "story as story," a dynamic process which is constantly evolving so that the resulting picture is unclear enough to make this tale an "ideal transitional" work between fiction and surfiction. Faulkner's *Absalom, Absalom!* has as subject a montage of four storytellers so that the resulting picture or view loses its traditional clarity. Samuel Beckett's trilogy completes the transition from fiction to surfiction. [JC is seen in a new way as being a transitional figure.]

3307 Perez Firmat, Gustavo. "*Don Quixote* in 'Heart of Darkness': Two Notes," *Comparative Literature Studies* XII (University of Illinois), (December 1975), pp. 374–83.

Although the extent of JC's acquaintance with Spanish letters is difficult to determine, the most fundamental of the different texts that comprise "Heart of Darkness," Kurtz's Report for the International Society for the Suppression of Savage Customs, seems to have been inspired by Hamete Benengali's notebooks, Cervantes' transcription of which putatively constitutes *Don Quixote*. The ultimate purpose of the parallels between the Report and the plot of "Heart of Darkness" is to reproduce, on the reader's level, Marlow's experiences. Since the reader is faced not with a jungle but with an agglomeration of texts, their features resemble the principal events in the novel (the journey, the encounter with Kurtz, and the interview with the Intended). With *Don Quixote* as an example, JC here uses more subtly one of Cervantes' tricks. Like the notebooks, Kurtz's manuscript becomes a novel, with the difference that instead of recording the fortunes of a fictive protagonist, it reveals those of a real enough though innocent one: the reader. Kurtz's paradoxical madness closely resembles that of Don Quixote. Both men distinguish themselves as orators, both stand in direct conflict with their peers, and both have in common the practice of various professions. And like Dulcinea, the Intended represents love and illusion.

3308 Petroni, Mario. "L'occhio di Conrad" (Conrad's Eye), *Servizio Informazioni Ed. Avio* VII–VIII (Roma: Armando), (1975), pp. 168–70.

In JC's persuasion to make one see, there is no ideological prevarication: the author makes the landscape undergo an impressionistic manipulation. [In Italian.]

3309 Phillips, Steven R. "The Monomyth and Literary Criticism," *College Literature*, II (Winter 1975), pp. 1–16.

"The Secret Sharer" is a psychological study of a young captain's confrontation with his other self, and most of the action in the story concerns the captain and how he hides his other self from his crew. In terms of the monomyth, the captain stands at the brink of adventure, for he experiences an archetypal rite of passage. The first stage in the process of his transformation is his escape from society. The first page of the story suggests this separation stage of the myth. Leggatt functions as the guardian or helper to the captain as he enters the testing stage of the monomyth. Once Leggatt assists the captain into his test and the captain no longer needs him, Leggatt leaves. The captain then meets "the climax of the monomyth" alone, and as soon as the climax is over, the last stage of the monomyth is complete. In the whole process, the captain has been able to discover himself.

3310 Pomian, John (ed.). *Under Polish Eyes: As Seen by Joseph Retinger* (Farnham, Surrey: Farnham Printing Co. [Joseph Conrad Society (UK)], 1975).

[A series of extracts from J. H. Retinger, *Conrad and His Contemporaries* (1943), (C, I, No. 1109). Contains a brief memoir of Retinger by Pomian and matter of some bibliographical interest from a source not readily accessible.]

3311 Porzio, Domenico. "Conrad il polacco scrisse in inglese la solidarieta" (Conrad the Pole Wrote in English About Solidarity), *Famiglia Mese* (May 1975), pp. 20–21.

[Review of the Italian edition of Baines and of Jessie and Borys Conrad's reminiscences.] [In Italian.]

3312 Praz, Mario. "Conrad l'oscuro" (Conrad the Obscure), *Il Giornale Nuovo* (23 March 1975), p. 3.

JC did not succeed in creating characters like those of Balzac, Tolstoy, Dostoevski, and George Eliot; he admired Hugo's unreadable *Travailleurs de la Mer* and used emphatic and vague adjectives which are far from *le mot juste*. He has many defects, but in the end, as with Byron, he wins the game. [In Italian.]

3313 Prisco, Michele. "Testimonianze su Joseph Conrad" (Conradian Reminiscences), *Corriere Della Sera* (10 February 1975), p. 3; rpt. with title "Conrad intimo" (Intimate Conrad), *Il Mattino* (18 June 1975), p. 3.

JC's life-long agonies do not crop up in his wife and son's reminiscences, while a sort of resentment against Ford is not hidden. [Review of the Italian edition of Jessie and Borys's reminiscences, *Conrad L'Uomo: Testimonianza a Due Voce* (Milan: Mursia, 1974).] [In Italian.]

3314 Raimondi, Giuseppe. "Il capitano ha visioni" (The Captain has Visions), *Il Giorno* (27 February 1975), p. 3.

[The publication of the Italian edition of Baines's biography of JC recalls to the minds of the writers of Raimondi's generation the period in which they discovered JC, who taught them the morality of art.] [In Italian.]

3315 Rapin, René. "André Gide's Translation of Joseph Conrad's Typhoon,'" *JCCP* (1975), pp. 73–88.

In July, 1911, André Gide became personally acquainted with JC, and by 1917 he had become responsible for the publication of a complete French edition of JC's works. His translation of "Typhoon" (the 1912 story of that title), the fourth volume in this edition, was a "labor of love." René Rapin made a close comparison of his own translation of "Typhoon" with Gide's—to find that, however felicitous on the whole Gide's translation was, it contained a number of small, and "sometimes not so small," inaccuracies, omissions, and confused and even meaningless phrases. At Gide's request, Rapin sent to the translator his own record of the inaccuracies (most of which Gide later accepted), and Gide explained that he had been persuaded to revise the translation of the book by the inexperienced Isabelle Rivière, wife of his friend Jacques Rivière, then editor of the *Nouvelle Revue Française*. Subsequent information reveals, however, that JC must have confused the two translations on which he had been working in 1917, "Typhoon" and a revision of Isabelle Rivière's translation of *Victory*.

3316 Renner, Stanley. "The Garden of Civilization: Conrad, Huxley, and the Ethics of Evolution," *CON*, VII, No. 2 (1975), pp. 109–20.

In several of JC's works, both early and late, there are strong reflections of a line of evolutionary thought characteristic of the time and most clearly stated by Thomas Henry Huxley in his "Prolegomena" to *Evolution and Ethics* (1894). Briefly put, Huxley builds his argument around the analogy of civilization and a garden:

as a garden creates a "state of Art" out of the "state of nature," so man creates civilization out of "uncivilization" by cultivating qualities which promote civilization and weeding out those which oppose it. There is also a struggle in the garden for the existence of living creatures against the cosmic process which can never cease. *Almayer's Folly* is largely a parable of the foolish gardener (Almayer) who fails the test of self-assertion. As if dramatizing Huxley's argument, JC contrives in *The Nigger of the Narcissus* to bring the civilization of the ship to the combined test of the cosmos and of the self-assertion in human nature, with Captain Allistoun, the careful gardener, preserving his ship. In "Heart of Darkness," JC, like Huxley, uses the analogy of colonization to reach similar ethical conclusions about cultivating a garden of civilization from the state of nature. In *Victory*, JC dramatizes Huxley's warning against excluding self-assertion too thoroughly from the garden of civilization. Neither Heyst nor Lena has a victory: only Wang has a victory, and that by default. This analogy with Huxley's thinking clearly indicates that JC did not move away from his Victorian background and enables us to see his work as a whole.

3317 Renucci, Antoine. "Jim's Last Song of Innocence," *LC*, No. 1 (March 1975), pp. 8–13.

In chapter II (in the fourth paragraph, near the beginning of *Lord Jim*), we can see Jim in his last moments as an innocent man, at a time when he can, for the last time, be alone with his dream which, to him, is the only reality that contains any meaning. Chapters I and II of the novel indicate clearly that Jim is not prepared for his ordeal on the *Patna* and that when the shock of initiation into experience and reality comes, it is bound to be unmerciful. But in his moments of peace before the disaster, everything around him—the sea and the quiet of the ship—seems to conspire to help him dream. And the sensual quality of JC's prose in this passage makes the reader hear, feel, and see. JC's stories contain two "races" of men, those with power to resist flesh and fate and those without such a power. Jim, the imaginative man, is a victim of fate from his very birth. Men like Jim and Hamlet are poised in a perilous equilibrium between action and taking the risk of falling, and their tendency not to act. After Jim falls, he takes the only possible action to escape his fate: he jumps out of the circle of trying to redeem himself and, unable to escape his fate, he has to try something else. Through the feeling of communion with the people in Patusan, Jim redeems his sin and becomes again "Lord Jim," "the primate." But even so, he is not a hero: JC leaves all decision "in the artistic and metaphysic veil of uncertainty." JC's is a very humanistic picture of man.

3318 Rice, Thomas J. "'Typhoon': Conrad's Christmas Story," *Cithara* (St. Bonaventure University), XIV, No. 2 (1975), pp. 19–35.

Inevitably, JC's Catholic upbringing fundamentally influenced his world view and even the very "substance" of his work, as "Typhoon" reveals. The symbolism here makes the work a coherent and symbolic novel. The symbolism is "firmly grounded" in the Christian tradition: the story is both "an allegory of the Christian Incarnation, a surface action occurring on Christmas eve and morning," and a "demonstration of the Incarnation's revolutionary effect on mankind in general" through the transformation of one "very ordinary man," Captain MacWhirr. JC overcame the problem of depicting the inner workings of Captain MacWhirr, a person whose mind is purportedly empty, by having the Captain's character alter, beginning shortly after the storm breaks, and by the end of the story, we are aware that he "has done something rather clever." The second problem, that of JC's passing over the second half of the hurricane, should be seen as being deliberate and of special symbolic significance. In the beginning, MacWhirr is figuratively a "new born," a complete innocent, who will, when confronted by JC's familiar test, mature throughout the course of the work. The Captain faces his own imminent death and therefore comes to a realization of "his own identity and individuality," being literally reborn in the hurricane. After the storm, the Chinese passengers of the *Nan-Shan* become human beings to MacWhirr, and the second mate represents an evil force that must be subdued. Seemingly slight details provide the "felt-life" realism of the novel, and most of JC's detail is given to depicting MacWhirr as a "fool" for Christ, a "saintly fool."

3319 Riley, William Patrick. "Encounter Criticism: Identity Development Through Prose Fiction," *DAI*, XXXVI (1975), 2202A. Unpublished dissertation, Middle Tennessee State, 1975.

3320 Rogers, William N., II. "The Game of Dominoes in 'Heart of Darkness,'" *English Language Notes*, XIII (September 1975), pp. 42–45.

The opening scene of "Heart of Darkness" is more than a convenient lead-in; it is carefully designed to establish imagery and tonality for the remainder of the work. The dominoes provide a subtle image of black and white, which alludes to the civilized and the uncivilized and to the present and the past. The game of dominoes, ruled by chance, is like the more serious game Marlow is playing, when, on several occasions, luck is needed for his survival.

3321 Rude, Donald W. "Conrad's Revision of the First American Edition of *The Arrow of Gold*," *Pol R*, XX, Nos. 2–3 (1975), pp. 106–22; rpt. JCCE (1975), pp. 106–22.

The two distinct issues of the first American edition of *The Arrow of Gold*, published in 1919, are set apart by nearly 50 variants, resulting from JC's having made a final revision of the edition after Doubleday, Page and Company had printed it. Among the many revisions are three types of changes which appear in the text: changes involving accidentals, changes which reflect the author's concern with rhetoric and idiom, and numerous instances of revision in which JC's alterations of diction or syntax, his cancellations and his additions, produce a heightened stylistic effect or introduce a subtle nuance. Throughout the novel, JC attempted to make Dona Rita an enigmatic figure, and frequently his revisions heighten our awareness of her paradoxical nature. [Contains a table of variants in the first and second issues of the first American edition of *Arrow*.]

3322 Rude, Donald W., and David Leon Higdon. "Conrad Bibliography: A Continuing Checklist," *CON*, VII, No. 3 (1975), pp. 283–92.

[A continuation of *Conradiana*'s indispensable JC bibliography.]

3323 Said, Edward W. *Beginnings: Invention and Method* (New York: Basic Books, 1975), pp. 9, 10, 11, 24, 84–85, 100–107, 144, 151, 161, 229–30, 232, 233–34, 237, 240, 261, 262, 263, 287–88.

One of the chief characteristics shared by Joyce, Yeats, Freud, Mann, Nietzsche, and JC, along with others, is a necessity "*at the beginning*" for them to see their work, first, with reference to other works, but also to the reader and reality, "by adjacency, not sequentially or dynastically." Marlow and JC "so beautifully" catch the predicament of the writer, who declares his ambition to make the reader see, but Jim and Kurtz are no clearer objects of vision than are the meanings of the words used to describe them. The lack of starting points in JC's stories is caused by the lack of a clear starting point in his own life; he therefore has an ambiguous conception of character. At the end of the nineteenth century and the beginning of the twentieth, novels increasingly take the form of retrospective, puzzling adventure. *Nostromo* is a major novel of this period. The large cast of characters in the book is held together by two "inner affinities": every person of the novel has an unnecessary interest in the fortunes of Costaguana, and nearly everyone seems extremely eager about keeping and leaving a personal "record" of his thoughts and actions. While composing this novel, JC found himself to be a "*homo duplex*": while suffering the agonies of writing, he was concerned with his real struggles and also with his public image, each of which was making acute claims on him. The task of the novelist is to represent the actuality, to record it as by an individual, and to portray the individual himself in the act of being an author as he mediates between the actuality and the record. In *Nostromo*, each character is portrayed as the author of a record which conflicts with several other records. The reconciliation between action and record is achieved only by Emilia Gould, the one character in the novel "with really accurate vision." *Nostromo* is a novel about political history, the most immediate fact of which is Costaguana. Charles Gould's world as ruler becomes Emilia's also, until she eventually outshines her husband's faded story. Three energetic characters, Decoud, Nostromo, and Dr. Monygham, like Charles, also undergo a death of the soul. The real action of the book is psychological. [Should be studied as a whole.]

3324 Said, Edward W. "The Text, The Word, The Critic," *Bulletin of the Midwest Modern Language Association*, VIII, No. 2 (1975), pp. 1–23.

JC's narratives generally dramatize, motivate, and "circumstance" the occasion of their telling. They instance the "chain of humanity": the transmission of actual speech (and thereby existence) from one human being to another; therefore, they are still presentations in the making. [Said uses the example of JC's works to illustrate his partial thesis that literary texts exist as language "in the world" and, therefore, "impose constraints and limits on their interpretation." He does not cite any particular work.]

3325 "Saint-John Perse to Joseph Conrad," *JJCS*, II, No. 2 (December 1975), pp. 7–9.

Saint-John Perse, the poet who worked in a kind of "complicity with the cosmos" and indicated the necessity of the irrational, wrote a letter from China to JC, dated February 26, 1921, in which he lauds JC for being "the most humane of the men I have met in literary life" and recognizes the East and the sea as having affected his own writings. [The letter, translated by John Crompton, is reprinted from *Le Litteraire*, November, 1972.]

3326 Salk, Jonas. "In Tribute to Jacob Bronowski and Joseph Conrad," *Pol R*, XX, Nos. 2–3 (1975), pp. 11–12; rpt. *JCCE* (1975), pp. 11–12.

[Salk comments on the appropriateness of dedicating the International Conference of Conrad Scholars, University of California, San Diego, 1974, to both JC and the late Dr. Jacob Bronowski and notes similarities of the two men, both of whom were born in Poland.]

3327 Sandstrom, Glenn. "The Roots of Anguish in Dostoevski and Conrad," *Pol R*, XX, Nos. 2–3 (1975), pp. 71–77; rpt. *JCCE* (1975), pp. 71–77.

Even if JC consistently expressed his detestation of Dostoevski, "The Secret Sharer" closely parallels the Russian novelist in his *The Double*, and *Under Western Eyes* directly challenges *Crime and Punishment*. Examining Dostoevski's total concept of man and then reading some of JC's major works from that point of view provides a move toward a coherent "Conradian view of man's moral anatomy." In *Lord Jim*, Jim's "analog" among Dostoevski's heroes is Dmitri Karamazov: both men must endure humiliation, trial, and exile, and must wait for another chance. But whereas Dmitri learns a value beyond honor, the true criterion, a selflessness that dictates service to others even when such service gives no grandeur to one's self-image, does not appear to give Jim a basis for authentic action. Jim's death is morally ambiguous. Kurtz, in "Heart of Darkness," has a Dostoevskian analog in Nikolai Stavrogin of *The Devils*. At the center of each man is, or was at one time, a desire to do good, but evil in both men is a perversion of the will to do good. In *Victory*, Heyst's Dostoevskian analog is Prince Myshkin in *The Idiot* in his mild and kindly instincts, and also much of the intellectual conviction of Ivan Karamazov. These three men of JC's are seen more clearly in the light of Dostoevski's vision.

3328 Saracino, Doriano. "Jocelyn Baines: Tutto su Conrad" (Jocelyn Baines: All about Conrad), *Momento Sera* (26 March 1975), p. 10.

[Review of the Italian edition of Baines's critical biography of JC (Milan: Mursia, 1974), and of Jessie and Borys Conrad's reminiscences (Milan: Mursia, 1974).] [In Italian.]

3329 Schneider, Daniel J. "The Dream and the Knitting Machine: Joseph Conrad's Symbolism," *Symbolism: The Manichean Vision, A Study in the Art of James, Conrad, Woolf, and Stevens* (Lincoln: University of Nebraska Press, 1975), pp. 40–61.

Men cannot endure JC's concept of a machine that knits, that "knits us in and . . . knits us out," knitting time, space, pain, death, corruption, despair, and all the illusions. But his spirit embroiders endlessly its design in beautiful colors, "the beautiful fictions of truth, beauty, and virtue." His fiction dramatizes the great tension in man's existence and thereby acquires its "remarkable vitality." In *The Nigger of the Narcissus*, JC first achieves an "astonishing exfoliation" of symbolism, a vision which is still Manichean, but he has virtually created a new style. He now sees that every detail in his image of life has symbolic significance; he has created a totally symbolic world. In *Lord Jim*, the central conflict is between dream and reality. The novel works extensively with the paradox that the real is unreal and dead, whereas the unreal alone is real and alive. Four "enormous families" of contrasting symbols are generated from the first paragraph of the novel: symbols of heights and depressions, of animality and spirituality, of color, and of straightness and crookedness or malformation. In *Nostromo*, *The Secret Agent*, and *Under Western Eyes*, there exists an abundance of symbolism of disorder, drunkenness, farce, and absurdity. Irony deepens. Now JC's intent shifts from the interest in the psychology and the irrational to a concentration on the political and social implications of irrationality. Now, too, all the apparently civilized beings are revealed as beasts; the Manichean vision is compounded of paradox and contradiction; nothing is what it seems.

3330 Schwarz, Daniel R. "'A Lonely Figure Walking Purposefully': The Significance of Captain Whalley in Conrad's 'The End of the Tether,'" *CON*, VII, No. 2 (1975), pp. 165–73.

"The End of the Tether" is JC's "Mutability Canto," his tale of the complex problem of aging. Captain Whalley's faith is carried on from an earlier age; it is what JC believed to be the illusion of religious faith, just as Whalley lives in another age, becoming an anachronism through no fault of his own. His hubris is paradoxically in his faith, in his belief that he considers himself part of a universal history, directed by God, from the creation to "the fulfillment of the Covenant." He finds that like all men, he must reach the end, and he then instinctively reverts to an older tradition of ending his life nobly. The traditional metaphor of a voyage through time replaces the typological perspective of a contemporary man as a patriarch. His faith demonstrates that a human life is not significant in a pattern of history informed by God.

3331 Shilinia, B. "Funktsiia prirody i mira veshchei v romane Dzh. Konrada *Kapriz Olmeiera*" (The Function of Nature and the World of Things in J. Conrad's Novel *Allmayer's Folly*), *Uchenye Zapiski* (Riga: Latvian University, 1975), CCIX, pp. 176–83.

Whereas things provide Almayer with his background in *Almayer's Folly*, the background for Nina and Dain is nature or, on a compositional level, the narrative proceeds as a conflict between the civilized world and that of nature. Almayer is surrounded by worn out, decayed objects, including his house, which reflects his psychology. He contemplates nature, i.e., the river, without seeing it, or things are illuminated in a closed circle by the moon. In contrast, the world of nature—river, moon, storm—provides the idea of vital, natural, and harmonious forces of life which surround Nina and Dain and give a symbolic background to their love. It does not guarantee happiness, however, and on some occasions constitutes a symbolic and metaphorical picture of life as dangerous and threatening. [In Russian.]

3332 Shilinia, B. "Nekotorye osobennosti kompositsii romana Dzhozefa Konrada *Pobeda*" (Some Features of the Composition of Joseph Conrad's Novel *Victory*), *Uchenye Zapiski* CCIX, (Riga: Latvian University, 1975), pp. 159–75.

Like all of JC's novels, *Victory* is based on conflicts in the sphere of morality. This characteristic of JC's work is associated with trends in literature at the end of the nineteenth century when conflicts between the individual and hostile society were frequent and led to dissatisfaction and a tendency to Neo-romantic transformations of reality. Heyst, who has characteristics of a traditional, romantic individualist, is in conflict with society. By using different points of view, JC contrasts systems for evaluating his protagonist: romantically and also socially, historically, and critically.

The inner subject line of *Victory* is the relation and conflict between good and evil on a social and ethical level. Heyst and Jones, though, have in common something neither obvious nor commented on by JC—a philosophical and symbolic relationship between the two extreme contrasts. Both men are products of the same process of "alienation," though these relationships may be interpreted in various ways. In parts 3 and 4 of the novel, goodness and active evil collide in situations and dialogues which reveal that genuine good is neither abstract nor passive. The entire structure of *Victory* is based on shifts in narrative point of view, all of which JC uses to reach the objective truth. [In Russian.]

3333 Slade, Mark. "The New Metamorphoses," *Mosaic*, VIII (1975), pp. 131–39.

In "Heart of Darkness," JC creates an image of man living and finding his meaning "in a flicker." Yet so many different flickers follow each other that finding a meaning is very difficult. The setting of the story is in the "savage crotch" at the Inner Station where Kurtz exists; here he succumbs to the savage forces of JC's jungle. Freud, JC's contemporary, also delves into a type of Inner Station, the unconscious, to conclude that the unconscious contrasts with the conscious. Kurtz's problem is that he reverses the normal order of these two parts of the mind so that the reality of the unconscious dominates. JC perceives the tension existing between the Inner and Outer mental Stations. If a man leaves the secure Outer Station to plumb the depths of the Inner, as Kurtz does, he must have more profound personal strength than Kurtz has. He, a fool, has no resistance to the flood of sensory inputs and eventually comes to question which civilization is the more savage—his or the natives'.

Man in the twentieth century has found many ways of drawing himself into the same confrontation that Kurtz does, and in order to resist the same consequences he must organize a system of primitive moving images originating in primordial myths. The main characteristic of these myths is metamorphosis, which is an irrational process of change. Civilization and humanization are, therefore, not the same. Man must accept the fact that the primitive mind can help civilized man understand his own Inner Station. [The essay's vitality is impressive, but there is a lack of clarity in the style and of logical development so that the ideas sometimes become incomprehensible.]

3334 Slonimski, Antoni. "Conrad," *Pol R*, XX, Nos. 2–3 (1975), pp. 5–6; rpt. *JCCE* (1975), pp. 5–6.

[A poem about JC's death.]

3335 Smee, Gillian. "The Creation of Suspense," *JJCS*, I, No. 6 (March 1975), pp. 3–7.

JC's genius for holding the attention of his audience is best seen in his use of occasional hints, suggesting an inevitable doom, which intensify the reader's emotional involvement and leave him torn between "desperate hope" and the knowledge of ultimate disaster. This method is seen clearly in the early stages of *Lord Jim* and also later in the work, during Jim's period as a water clerk. A similar effect is found early in "Freya of the Seven Isles." But much more is added to this expectation of ultimate catastrophe by a skillful use of imagery and symbolism, and by a close identification with the inner feelings of the characters. And, too, the reader senses tragedy not only in the threatening atmosphere but also in the beauty which is threatened, as with the brig in "Freya of the Seven Isles." No method of creating suspense is more effective, however, than the personification of evil in certain characters: in Cornelius and Brown in *Jim*, in Heemskirk in "Freya of the Seven Isles," and in the steward and the chief mate in "The Secret Sharer."

3336 Solomon, Barbara H. "Conrad's Narrative Material in 'The Inn of the Two Witches,'" *CON*, VII, No. 1 (1975), pp. 75–82.

A comparison of JC's "The Inn of the Two Witches" and Wilkie Collins's "A Terribly Strange Bed," in *After Dark* (1856), reveals three traits that are characteristic of JC's fiction: his interest in depicting a strained mental state caused by a terrifying incident rather than in depicting the event itself, his preference for using the framing narrator to provide a convenient way of changing the distance of the reader from the story, and his successful employment of the narrator for his ironic or detached voice which undercuts the statements or reactions of the character who participates in the experience.

3337 Steinman, Theo. "Il Conde's Uncensored Story," *CON*, VII, No. 1 (1975), pp. 83–86.

The uncommon moral effect of the Count's reactions to a banal incident in "Il Conde" is revealed in some slips of the tongue and a few veiled contradictions. JC apparently tells only part of the truth or relates a distorted version of the facts. We cannot know whether the Count's homosexuality was latent and unacknowledged by himself or if he intentionally hid several facts from his interlocutor. But his account is "filtered through his delicacy of taste and expression" which would not allow him to make any gross allusion to "the facts of life." The Count knows that the robber has discovered his basic inclination and could blackmail him, being therefore traumatized by the sudden confrontation with one aspect of his nature which he may have avoided recognizing before. Since neither JC nor the society of his time was prepared to face directly certain embarrassing aspects of human life, JC chose ambiguity and indirection in order to be read by "the discerning and by the indiscriminate public alike."

3338 Sugg, Richard P. "The Triadic Structure of 'Heart of Darkness,'" *CON*, VII, No. 2 (1975), pp. 179–82.

"Heart of Darkness" is best understood as a record of the artist's efforts to develop beyond and thereby liberate himself from the dualistic Victorian mentality. Its triadic structure, based on the relationship of reason, passion, and imagination, is indicated by the three numbered parts of the novel, numbered not by Marlow but by the writer "I." In the first part, Marlow shares in some degree the faith in the "idea" which, presumably, took the colonists to Africa. In the second section, Marlow explores the powers and limitations of the body and the passions, and also realizes his brotherhood with the cannibals and with the jungle. In the last part, Marlow learns from Kurtz the importance of individuation through vocal affirmation and the fact that the passions affirm life. Back in Europe, Marlow is supplanted by the original "I" of the story, who makes a final comment on it. Through the creation of forms revealing his own life, the artist is capable of rendering his own intuitive truths. Through art, the imagination brings about that "Fidelity" which JC praised and which Marlow desires and affirms. From Marlow's attempt, the "I" has learned to tell a self-contained story. Kurtz taught Marlow the importance of speech, and Marlow in turn taught "I" the necessity of shaping and framing its speech.

3339 Syer, Geoffrey. "*Lord Jim*," *TLS* (3 January 1975), p. 14.

It is known that JC's description of the *Patna* in *Lord Jim* is based on the history of the *Jeddah* and that JC may have drawn upon Wilfrid Scawen Blunt's *The Future of Islam*. A notable coincidence—and probably no more than that—is that Blunt himself was wrecked on a similar pilgrim ship, the *Chibine*, in March, 1900, the same month in which JC's chapters appeared in *Blackwood's*. Although the captain does not desert the ship, he earns Blunt's disapproval for his incompetence. The account appears in *My Diaries*, Part One (1919), pp. 434–48. [This letter to the editor is a reply to Graham Greene's letter, "*Lord Jim*," *Times Literary Supplement* (London), 6 December 1974.]

3340 Szczepanski, Jan Josef. "In Lord Jim's Boots," *Polish Perspectives*, XVIII (January 1975), pp. 31–44.

[Relates the meaning of *Lord Jim* to a younger generation which lived after the domination of puritanical moral standards when Jim seemed to be "one of us." A God exists between the covers of JC's books; he exists as a law, unnamed but very stern and allowing no free interpretation. This writer's generation did not identify JC's "Lawmaker"; what they most needed were rules of behavior. European civilization appeared to JC at its most perfect in its English version, in a "merchant civilization." Hence the mythologized figure of the shipowner, a "remote providence" equipped with the power to reward and to punish. In his "proud despair," JC, unlike the "Great Shipowner," tried to write "in mercy"; but with Jim he failed. He gave Jim the second chance of Patusan only to kill him in "a morally more convenient but thoroughly fictitious situation." And yet he was for the writer "a prophet of hope."]

3341 Tarnawski, Wit. "Conrad," *JJCS*, I, No. 6 (March 1975), p. 2.

[A poem translated from the Polish by Andrzej Busza.]

3342 Tarnawski, Wit. "'The Secret Sharer,'" *JJCS*, I, No. 6 (March 1975), pp. 8, 11.

"The Secret Sharer" seems to be an illuminating pendant to *Under Western Eyes*, containing several similarities to the longer novel and showing a totally different reaction on the part of the hero to the almost identical situation in the scene between Razumov and Haldin, after which Razumov betrays Haldin to the police. In "The Secret Sharer," JC shows how he thought a decent man would behave in such circumstances. Although in "The Secret Sharer" the fugitive's act is much less admirable than Haldin's and the comradely bond between the two men is much less close, in this work the situation itself tightens the human tie so that it needs no explanation. The story is a tribute to comradeship and also a condemnation of Razumov, because chance guides the swimmer to the ship whereas Haldin had deliberately put himself in Razumov's power. This interpretation, however, need not exclude the common one about the duality of the human personality indicated by the title.

3343 Teets, Bruce E. "Literary Impressionism: Conrad and Ford," *Literary Impressionism in Ford Madox Ford, Joseph Conrad and Related Writers*, ed. by Todd K. Bender (Madison: Text Development Program, 1975), pp. 35–42.

Critical commentary on the works of JC has included "impressionism" and closely related terms at least since 1898. JC thought of the artist as having no special wisdom; like everyone else, he has only what he perceives by means of his senses, and his one moral imperative is to be true to his "own sensations." The forms of his novels are therefore intentionally obscure because he allows them to evolve from his vision of things, not from theories. *Lord Jim* seems to be considered, generally, as representative of JC's impressionistic work. Although there are many differences between the French impressionist painters and the impressionist writers, in JC and Ford many similarities exist: the consideration of capturing the fleeting moment of time as a kind of realization, the relying on the personal, subjective attitudes and moods of the artist, and thinking "rendering" of more importance than mere "reporting." Both painters and writers carried their practices so far that such a weakness as a lack of structure or inability to reach any reality led them either to new techniques or to a kind of tiredness and decline of intensity, as in the later works of JC and Ford. The collaboration and experimentation of the two men produced, though, at one time or another, such major impressionistic works as JC's *Jim* and *Nostromo* and Ford's *The Good Soldier* and *Parade's End.*

3344 Teets, Bruce E. "Realism and Romance in Conrad Criticism," *Pol R,* XX, Nos. 2–3 (1975), pp. 133–39; rpt. *JCCE* (1975), pp. 133–39.

From 1895, the date of publication of JC's first novel, that his writing is realistic or romantic has been persistently debated as shown by a study of more than 3,000 items. JC's early reviewers frequently labeled his work impressionistic, but made no particular distinction between this characteristic and realism. Eventually, in 1922, Ruth M. Stauffer in *Joseph Conrad: His Romantic Realism,* found an almost equal balance between realism and romanticism, and succeeded in arousing a further interest in this matter. From 1939 to 1958, JC criticism expanded in volume, in complexity, and in ingenuity, but the realism-romanticism debate was not resolved. In recent years, during which time further characteristics have been studied, critical emphasis seems to lean toward JC as a romantic.

3345 Temple, Frédéric-Jacques. "Joseph Conrad à Montpelier," *SJC* (1975), pp. 13–18.

[An account of the stay of JC, his wife, and his son Borys in Montpellier, where they went for the convalescence of Jessie in 1906 and again in 1907, this time with a second son. JC worked there as usual, this time writing "Karain." There he saw "une jeune femme timide et effrayée," who would later become Lena of *Victory*. Montpellier especially attracted this writer, who loved to lose himself in local places.] [In French.]

3346 Thomas, Claude. "Foreword," *SJC*, No. 2 (1975), pp. 9–12.

[Recognizes JC's interest in Montpelier, where he first saw, in one of his sojourns there, the original of Lena in *Victory*.]

3347 Thomas, Claude. "Structure and Narrative Technique of *Under Western Eyes*," *SJC*, No. 1 (1975), pp. 205–21.

Under Western Eyes is JC's most convincing portrayal of two "illegalities," autocracy and revolution. In this story of a double agent engaged in double dealings, everything is naturally double: the action takes place in two different settings, in the macrocosm of Russia and in the microcosm of Geneva; from the beginning, Razumov is faced with the choice of either becoming the unwilling accomplice of Haldin or of betraying him; and Razumov is ground down between the two "stones" of "Absolutisme et Revolution," even if he is not the only victim. The novel is made up of four parts: (1) an introduction and three numbered sections, in which the chief motives of the action are revealed and interspersed with digressions on the Russian temper; (2) a moving of the scene from Saint Petersburg University to Switzerland. In time, the second part is anterior to the first, and the double steps in and becomes an actor. The basic theme of the novel is that all political activity finally mutilates everybody, corrupting rulers and the ruled over. Irony in this novel denatures Razumov's tragedy and makes of it a pitiful comedy. This book should be valued because Razumov is Lord Jim's brother and because the narrative technique, though not so complex as that of *Lord Jim*, serves "magnificently the psychological analysis and the political message." [An unusually astute analysis of *Eyes*.]

3348 Thomas, Claude (ed.). *Studies in Joseph Conrad* (Montpelier: Université Paul-Valréy [Cahiers d'Etudes et de Recherches Victoriennes et Edouardiennes, No. 2], 1975).

Contents, abstracted in order of appearance in the book: Claude Thomas, "Foreword," pp. 9–12; Frédéric-Jacques Temple, "Joseph Conrad a Montepellier," pp. 13–18; Zdzislaw Najder, "Conrad in 1898," pp. 19–36; Pierre Coustillas, "Conrad and Gissing: A Biographical Note," pp. 37–52; Jean-Jacques Mayoux, "L'Absurde et le Grotesque dans L'Oeuvre de Joseph Conrad," pp. 53–82; Pierre Vitoux, "Marlow: The Changing Narrator of Conrad's Fiction," pp. 83–102; François Lombard, "Conrad and Buddhism," pp. 103–12; J. C. Hilson and D. Timms, "Conrad's 'An Outpost of Progress' or, The Evil Spirit of Civilization," pp. 113–28; Germain D'Hangest, "Sense of Life and Narrative Technique in Conrad's *Lord Jim*," pp. 129–60; Joseph Dobrinsky, "The Son and Lover Theme in *Lord Jim*," pp. 161–66; Ivo Vidan, "'Heart of Darkness' in French Literature," pp. 167–204; Claude Thomas, "Structure and Narrative Technique of *Under Western Eyes*," pp. 205–22; David Thorburn, "Evasion and Candor in *A Personal Record*," pp. 223–38; Jean Deurbergue, "The Opening of *Victory*," pp. 239–70; Jacky Martin, "J. Conrad: *The Shadow-Line* ou Les Intermittences du Texte," pp. 271–92; and "Notes on Contributors," pp. 293–94 [not abstracted].

3349 Thorburn, David. "Evasion and Candour in *A Personal Record*," *SJC* (1975), pp. 223–38.

JC's *A Personal Record* of 1912 is one of the author's most subtle and most deliberately constructed books. Nothing in all of his works is "more effectively complex" in its management of chronology than part IV of this volume. But the chief cause of the "record's" grace and distinction is JC's narrative strategy, his decision to tell his story in slightly literary but nonetheless conversational accents, and to tell it in his "characteristically evasive, dodging manner." He avoids melodrama while still achieving the truly dramatic. A "semi-whimsical tone" rings true and undercuts the visible temptations of oversolemnity. The transition from one tone to another is the result of "high art" only. The "genius" of the work is to expose and to clarify "those ambiguities not in its manifest content but in the subtle, immensely revealing drama of its form": the evasiveness of the style, JC's fidelity to his impressionistic method, and a digression that refuses to digress. The "seminal intuition" of the scene between Jacques and JC in the latter's cabin is that our precarious relationships with others occur unexpectedly and cannot endure, but that we are nevertheless driven to make them and to find them.

3350 Thurley, Geoffrey. *The Psychology of Hardy's Novels: The Nervous and the Statuesque* (Queensland: University of Queensland Press; Atlantic Highlands, New Jersey: Humanities Press, 1975), pp. 56, 225–27.

A passage of Thomas Hardy about the stars and astronomy in *Two on a Tower* has an air of "indubitably ungrasped horror," unlike JC's "Inscrutables" and "Ineffables"; whereas JC half-relishes the "frisson," Hardy genuinely fears the insight which retains the integrity of his words. Then, too, JC refers "scathingly" to Hardy's poem, "The Convergence of the Twain," because he, "the old sea-dog," was naturally furious and contemptuous of the brash floating palace which was the *Titanic*, but Hardy actually expresses the awe caused by the collision of the two "great things," the most that man can conceive and "Nature's tremendous answer." JC's invective blurs the real issue of the poem.

3351 Todorov, Tzvetan. "Connaissance du vide," *Nouvelle Revue de Psychoanalyze*, XI (1975), pp. 145–54.

JC's "Heart of Darkness" superficially resembles an adventure story, but the danger comes only from the interior; the adventures spring from the spirit of the explorer, Marlow, not from the situations he meets. Marlow seeks not to conquer but to understand; the story is a tale of understanding in which several emblematic episodes indicate that it is one in which an art of interpretation predominates. JC uses obscurity to symbolize darkness, danger, and despair. His title refers to all kinds of darkness that are suggested in the work. Kurtz is the center of the tale, the heart of darkness itself—but this center is empty: we hear in Kurtz's dying words an absolute horror for which we know no object. That the art of this darkness is impossible to know, that JC's voyage goes to the very depths of being, which is nonexistent, means that art, too, is nonexistent. Marlow is only a voice; he is only the definition of an artist, a writer. Kurtz is only a voice for Marlow. Every reader wants to know the object of a story as Marlow desires to understand Kurtz, but Kurtz, in Marlow's tale is as impossible to know as it is impossible to understand things by words only. The heart of the story is empty, void; words can transmit words only. Ultimate truth exists nowhere because there is no interior and the heart is void; there is only the return, circular and however necessary, from one surface to another, from words to words. [In French.]

3352 Urnov, Dmitri. "A Russian in Search of Conrad," *JJCS*, II, No. 2 (December 1975), pp. 9–13.

[In December 1970, Borys Conrad received a letter from Dmitri Urnov of Moscow, expressing an interest in JC. In June, 1973, Urnov wrote again, informing Borys Conrad of an article on JC which he had published in Russia. In June, 1974, Urnov again wrote to Borys Conrad. The "greater part" of this letter is reprinted here. Extracts from Urnov's article, "Joseph Conrad Keeps Watch," especially those parts which shed light on the Russian view of JC and those which evoke the places of JC's childhood are reprinted here. The English translation, supplied by John Simmons and "amended, corrected and supplemented by Stewart Hancock," is from "Vokrug Sveta" (Around the World), 1973.]

3353 Vidan, Ivo. "'Heart of Darkness' in French Literature," *SJC* (1975), pp. 167–204.

André Gide organized and controlled all translation of JC's works into French. Some of his own works (*Voyage au Congo* [1927] and *Le Retour du Tchad* [1928]) show himself as a searcher for truth, this time concerned with the way in which social relationships function. Stuart Gilbert's translation of André Malraux's *La Voie Royale* (1935) is much closer to JC's story in the translation than in the original. In both this book and *Les Conquerants*, Malraux seems to follow JC's pattern of "Heart of Darkness" and *Lord Jim*, that of gradually establishing the mutual closeness of two men. Louis-Ferdinand Celine shares JC's vision of African society because it has relevance to an image of modern chaos that goes beyond JC's. One episode of *Voyage au Bout de la Nuit* takes place in Africa and contains several parallels to "Heart of Darkness": the decision to go to Africa, the boat trip to Africa, disembarkation in an important port, the journey to a military station closer to the jungle, and the journey from that place to a distant trading post in order to meet the collector of the precious merchandise, ivory or rubber. And a work like Jean Genet's *Les Nègres* suggests a thematic kinship with "Heart of Darkness": both authors would agree about the natural authenticity of the black existence. JC's famous story has been an incitement to authors of great range and stature.

3354 Vitoux, Pierre. "Marlow: The Changing Narrator of Conrad's Fiction," *SJC*, No. 2 (1975), pp. 83–102.

Since Marlow in JC's early tale "Youth" (1898) has an audience with a common bond—all began life in the merchant service—he is able to assume a certain complexity with his fictitious hearers. The story of his first voyage as a second mate on the *Judea* is both a tale of apprenticeship and the paradigm of man's growing into maturity. Marlow uses his status as unopposed narrator to establish his vision of youth on the basis of a necessary consensus on the meaning of human existence, in terms of the ever-present conflict between romance and duty. In "Heart of Darkness" (1899), JC expresses throughout the limitation of speech and the impossibility of enclosing some well-defined and readily accessible meaning in the "rounded shell of a tale." The elaborate structure of *Lord Jim* (1900) reflects the fact that Marlow reexamines the standards that prevail in "Youth." He holds firmly his position as a unifying center of consciousness: his is the voice and the vision. But Marlow as narrator can lead his reader only to an open ending. As narrator in *Chance* (1913), Marlow displays mainly his reflective tendencies and his faculty for imaginative sympathy and understanding. But there is still too much of Marlow left: the treatment of the story as a whole is out of proportion with the human elements that are finally explored. The feeling that there is more at the heart of his subject than he can cope with makes *Chance* a minor work of fiction.

3355 Watt, Ian. "Pink Toads and Yellow Curs: An Impressionistic Narrative Device in *Lord Jim,*" *JCCP* (1975), pp. 11–31.

The chronological problem of how to combine a forward movement with adequate explanation of events and characters, a dominant preoccupation for modern novelists, was always a "particularly difficult" problem for JC, in his life as well as in his narrative technique. His solving the difficulty of simultaneously describing an event and making the reader understand it was an intensive adaptation of Impressionist technique to painting, to "delayed decoding," a narrative technique. Delayed decoding, a means of weaving necessary anterior information into the main narrative texture, served JC in several novels and stories, including *Lord Jim*. In this work, JC uses delayed decoding on three separate occasions, the third of which, by far the most important, is that of Marlow's noting the "yellow-cur thing." In this incident, Jim does, among other things, make a fool of himself.

The use of delayed decoding seems to be peculiar to JC, and to him in his early works. His use of this device looks forward to the nouveau roman. After 1900, JC concentrated more on such large scale narrative techniques as the use of multiple narrators and the time shift.

3356 Watts, C. T. "'Heart of Darkness': The Covert Murder-Plot and the Darwinian Theme," *CON*, VII, No. 2 (1975), pp. 137–43.

The plot of the manager of the company's central station in Africa, in JC's "Heart of Darkness," to delay relief from moving on its way to Kurtz is essentially a plot to eliminate Kurtz. In his *Origin of Species*, Darwin attempted in his conclusion to leave an impression of optimistic teleology to evolutionary theory; but Darwin's own findings had shown that the very force that had brought man into existence might operate, in some future time, to eliminate him. JC's tale enforces Darwin's pessimistic conclusion by its constant descriptive emphasis on the great might of the natural environment. And his manager, however base, prevails because he is physically fitter to survive than is Kurtz. This local struggle may be applied as a "critical paradigm" to benevolent and moralistic interpretations of evolutionary theory. Whether or not JC had Darwin's ending of the *Origin of Species* especially in mind, his tale displays human beings competing with the natural environment, and competing also for survival and promotion. His elliptical presentation of the manager's plot against Kurtz emphasizes subliminally that the evolutionary continuity between the savages and the Europeans may indicate that often "civilized" conduct is a "hypocritical and perverse sophistication of savagery."

3357 Watts, Cedric. "Women in Conrad's Fiction," *JJCS*, II, No. 1 (August 1975), pp. 2–3.

On "women's lib," JC prophesies that although women have long been bullied and exploited, the movement for feminine emancipation is likely to be just as "bullying, possessive and egoistic" as the "female chauvinists" they oppose. This prophecy is implicit in *Chance*. Sexual relationships seem paradoxically to emasculate the man. This pessimistic pattern extends from *Almayer's Folly* to late works like *Victory* and *The Rescue*. In *The Rescue*, JC indicates that Helen of Troy is a more attractive guide than Freud. *Victory*, too, contains parodic echoes of the legend of the abduction of Helen, and one of the heroine's names, Lena, may invoke ironic memories of Helena, the abducted Helen of Troy. Several of his heroines, unlike Hermione in Shakespeare's *The Winter Tale*, appear to be flesh and blood but actually belong to the condition of statuary and are always striving to return to their natural condition, like Kurtz's Intended, Felicia Moorsom, and Hermann's niece in "Falk." These statuesque heroines stand in extreme contrast to the passionate native girls like Nina and Aissa in the Malayan novels. Some of JC's women, such as Mrs. Gould and Antonia Avellanos in *Nostromo* and Nathalie Haldin and Tekla in *Under Western Eyes*, are credible and sympathetic for the reader. [A series of brief notes.]

3358 Weder, Alex. "Joseph Conrad: A Christian Writer?: An Analysis of the Christian and Catholic Ideas in Conrad's Works." Inaugural—Dissertation zur Erlangun des Grades eines Doktors der Philosophie der Philosophischen Fakultat der Universitat Freiburg, 1975.

JC's life reveals a picture of him as he forms his convictions of pessimism and still retains a vein of hope found in his Catholic youth. His world was, though, one of order, as seen in the struggle of Sulaco in *Nostromo*. His works deal with a contest for order, peace, and progress, and order is essentially centralized and autocratic, dictated from above. Only spiritual values, as demonstrated by Dr. Monygham, can bring about peace. Individuals who need order are represented by Heyst; those who do not want order are represented by Kurtz. JC's concept of order in the universe is basically Thomistic.

3359 Welsh, Alexander. "Realism as a Practical and Cosmic Joke," *Novel,* IX (Fall 1975), pp. 23–39.

By the end of the nineteenth century, the conditions of existence were commonly regarded as a "bad joke," as instanced by JC in *Lord Jim* (1900), who made the situation of Jim on the *Patna* a "bad joke," worse than the source of his story. Writers like Hardy and JC were forced to contemplate a universe without conscious purpose.

3360 Weston, Michael. *Morality and the Self* (New York: New York University Press, 1975), pp. 16–19, 30–38, 47–66, 76–82.

In *Lord Jim,* Jim attempts to prepare himself for the achievement of a worthwhile life of heroic adventure by imaginary dangers and his courage in facing them. When, at the end of the novel, he goes to the headman to receive his sentence, his act "matters little to him, neither as means, nor goal, nor in terms of his relation to a goal, nor even under the rubric 'This is morally good.'" Since Jim knew that he was going to his death, the relationship within which the act was performed provided Jim a way of making sense of his death. Only if he had not gone to the headman would there have been betrayal of the relationship. The act of dying occurs within the context of the relationship which called it forth. When Jim realizes that he is unworthy in his new role, he calls in question the old one; when Nostromo, however, discovers the unworthiness of others, not of himself, he retains his old role and determines upon revenge.

3361 Whitehead, Lee M. "The Active Voice and the Passive Eye: 'Heart of Darkness' and Nietzsche's *The Birth of Tragedy*," CON, VII, No. 2 (1975), pp. 121–35.

JC's vision of life as presented in the major works of his middle period is very much like Nietzsche's in *The Birth of Tragedy,* and in "Heart of Darkness" Marlow's function is similar to the tragic chorus. His character is a union of the antithetical qualities embodied in the satyr chorus: "the active voice and the passive eye as it were." Marlow accepts his kinship with the savages, but he also recognizes his difference from them: Kurtz's cry, "the horror!" expresses his own nauseating insight into the truth of himself and the world. His "mirror-image," Marlow, shares the insight and gives it voice. The Russian harlequin and Marlow are similar enought to be in some sense projections of JC himself. Between them, they share the roles played, according to Nietzsche, by the satyr of the tragic chorus. In "Heart of Darkness," the final confrontation between Marlow and Kurtz's Intended demonstrates that the vision of love in its ambiguity is compounded of the vision of youth (the harlequin) and the vision of tragedy (Marlow). The "necessary lie" is not a lie; it is Marlow's expression of a deeper truth and a gleam of light in his act of mercy. The activity of the voice creates the experience of the tragic vision. [Whitehead considers JC's works and Nietzsche in an earlier article, "Conrad's 'Pessimism' Re-examined," *CON*, II, No. 3 (1969–70).]

3362 Yarrison, Betsy C. "The Symbolism of Literary Allusion in 'Heart of Darkness,'" *CON*, VII, No. 2 (1975), pp. 155–64.

The many literary allusions in "Heart of Darkness," rather than duplicating or contradicting one another, unearth the elements which certain religious and literary traditions share with the story and, by implication, with each other. JC's explicit textual reference to four earlier epics may have been deliberate: JC, too, tells the tale of a heroic pilgrimage and its effect upon the man who undertakes it. Marlow's typical voyage to hell and back represents the pilgrimage of modern man into the "core of the self." JC's judicious use of materials familiar in earlier literature forces the literate reader to juxtapose the familiar items with the new context to create a new effect, among others, to convict the reader of complicity in colonial exploitation. A certain validity accrues around a symbol or pattern repeated over a long period of literary history. Each reader constructs patterns of meaning for "Heart of Darkness" which are conclusive for each individual; suggestiveness, then, not literal interpretation of the story, is a "key" characteristic of JC's symbolism. The meaning of a story by JC can thus be seen to exist largely in the mind of the reader. Literary allusion as JC uses it unites precision of reference with "infinite suggestiveness of meaning," thereby making possible a modern epic even though the epic has ceased to exist vitally in Western literature.

3363 Young, Gloria L. "Chance and the Absurd in Conrad's 'The End of the Tether' and 'Freya of the Seven Isles,'" *CON*, VII, No. 3 (1975), pp. 253–61.

JC recognized his writings as "rescue work" which revealed "struggling forms" endowed with permanence; his characters "structure" experience in "orientations" or "cockleshells" in which, more or less seaworthy, they pursue their "voyage." The cockleshells of Captain Whalley and Jasper, based on a false view of the sea, provide ironic counterpart to the actual reality of the sea. The theme of "The End of the Tether" and "Freya of the Seven Isles" is that because man's mythologies have no relevance to reality, they betray him. Long before his physical blindness affects him, Whalley is blind to reality, and the sea of the absurd, of meaningless chance, draws him down. "Freya of the Seven Isles" dramatizes the theme that mythological ways of ordering the universe, however noble, are also "cockleshells on the sea of life." The beautiful sea is indifferent to the destinies of the characters. JC uses mythological allusions to create a fable of existential absurdity. Read in this way, these two stories may reveal much about JC's view of life in his later works, in which he turned more and more to psychological explorations of how, and how not, to live.

3364 Zanzotto, Andrea. "Nota introduttiva" (Introductory Note), *Il compagno segreto* (*The Secret Sharer*), (Milan: Rizzoli, 1975), pp. 15–23.

[A brief discussion of the theme of the double.] [In Italian.]

3365 Zapatka, Francis E. "On the Meaning of *Nan-Chan* in Conrad's Typhoon,'" *American Notes and Queries*, XIII (May 1975), pp. 152–53.

Geographically, Nan-Shan is the name of a mountain range in western China. In "Typhoon," there are several images directly and indirectly related to mountains or hills. But "South," the primary sense of "nan," is used frequently. JC's decision to change the name of the S.S. *John P. Best*, the historical ship associated with "Typhoon," to the *Nan-Shan* was, in view of the mountain images in huge, stormy southern seas, an appropriate choice.

INDEX

AUTHORS

Included here are authors of articles and books on Conrad, editors and compilers of works in which criticism on Conrad appears. Editors and translators are identified parenthetically: (ed), (trans). Numbers after each name refer to the item(s) in the bibliography where the name occurs.

Tittle, Walter 661.1
Titus, Edward E., Jr. 448.1
Tobin, A. I. 938.1
Todorov, Tzvetan 3351
Tolley, A. T. 1970.1
Tolliver, Harold E. (ed): 2733,
    3136
Tolomei, Ugo 3137
Torchiana, Donald T. 2076
Towlinson, T. B. 2707
Tredrey, F. D. 1307.1
Trigona, Prospero 2846
Trilling, Lionel 1918.1, 2077,
    2847
Tucker, Martin 2255
Turnbull, Andrew (ed): 2969

Ujejski, Jozef 1027.1, 1027.2,
    1045.1
Umavijani, Montri 3138
Urbanowski, Bohdan 3139
Urbisz, Krystyna 3140
Ure, Peter 3141
Urnov, Dmitri 3352
Urnov, M.V. 2256, 2580, 2588
Ursell, Geoffrey 2251, 2581

Van de Water, Frederick F. 449.1
Van Domelen, John E. 2582,
    2583, 2584
Van Ingen, Ferdinand (ed): 2848
Van Marle, A. 2078, 2258
Verschoor, Edith E.N. 2585
Vidan, Gabrijela 2586
Vidan, Ivo 2079, 2080, 2450,
    2586, 2587, 2588, 2589,
    2849, 3142, 3353
V[igini], G[iuliano] 2081, 2259,
    2322, 2970
Villiers, Alan John 1072.1, 2260
Vines, Sherard 778.1
Viswanathan, Jacqueline 3143
Vitoux, Pierre 3354
Volpe, Edmond L. (ed): 1472.1,
    (ed): 2082

Voytovich, Edward R. 3144
Voznesenkaia, I.A. 3145

Wagar, W. Warren 1656.1, 2451
Wagner, Geoffrey 2590
Walbridge, Earle 1027.3
Walch, Günter 2591
Walcutt, Charles Child 1974.1,
    (ed): 2261
Walker, Franklin 2453 (ed):
    2454, 2552
Walker, Warren S. 2592
Walpole, Hugh 986.1
Walsh, Dennis M. 2971, 3146
Walt, James 2455, 2456, 2457,
    2593, 2710, 2850, 2851, 3147
Walton, James [H.] 2083, 2084,
    2085, 2086, 2458
Walz, Lawrence Arnold 2594
Ward, A[lfred] C[harles] 939.1,
    1840.1
Ward, David 2972
Ward, Herbert 2459
Warner, John M. 2595
Warner, Oliver 1840.2
Wasserman, Jerry 3148
Wasserstrom, William (ed):
    1919.1
Watson, Wallace S. 2087
Watt, Ian 2262, 2263, 2596,
    2973, (ed): 2974, 2975, 2976,
    2977, 2978, 2979, 2980,
    3149, 3150, 3355
Watts, C[edric] [T.] 1976.1, 2088,
    (ed): 2406, 2892, 3157, (ed):
    3200, 3356, 3357
Waugh, Arthur 2.6
Wayman, Leonard 2526
Webb, Michael 2981
Webster, H.T. 1208.1
Weder, Alex 3358
Weeks, Edward 966.1
Wegelin, Christof 3152
Weinstein, Arnold L. 3154
Weinstock, Donald 2264

INDEX

TITLES OF SECONDARY WORKS

Titles of articles in periodicals and chapters in books are in quotation marks; book titles are in italics; translations of article titles originally appearing in a foreign language are in parentheses. Numbers after each title refer to the item in the bibliography where the title appears.

(Conrad As Realist) 322.1
"Conrad a tradyoja literacka" 1708.1
"Conrad at the Crossroads: From Navigator to Novelist with Some New Biographical Mysteries": 2110
"Conrad, Between Fact and Fiction": 2765
"Conrad Between Sartre and Socrates" 2891
"Conrad Bibliography: A continuing Checklist"" 2423, 2424, 2425, 2443, 2564, 2694, 2695, 2696, 2833, 2834, 2956, 3322
"Conrad, *Blackwood's*, and Lombroso": 3112
"Conrad Centenary": 1412.2
"Conrad, Chronicler of the Sea": 1005.1
"Conrad Collected": 1163.1
"Conrad Collection": 763.2
"Conrad Computerized": 3235
"The Conrad-Ford Collaboration": 3041
"Conrad Dark and Hollow": 2754
"Conrad, Dickens, and the Detective Novel": 2458
"Conrad en Constaguana": 2686
"Conrad Explains. His Debt to Garnett: The Collected Prefaces": 1051.1
"A Conrad Family Heirloom at Harvard": 1591
"Conrad, Ford, and the Novel": 2356
"Conrad, Ford, and the Sources of *Chance*": 3293
"Conrad for the Magazines": 2587
"Conrad for the Seventies": 2759
"Conrad, F. R. Leavis, and Whitehead: 'Heart of Darkness' and Organic Holism": 2854
"Conrad—Galsworthy: A Record of Their Friendship in Letters": 2162
"Conrad, Graham Greene, and Film" 3038
"Conrad, Grand Opera, and *Nostromo*" 3188
Conradian Commentaries 2539
"Conradiana: wybor i opracowanie Tadeusz Drewnowski" 3016
"The Conradian Hero and the Death of Language: A Note on *Nostromo* 2215
"Conrad i Bobrowski" 1351.2
"Conrad i Dostoevski" 1745.1
"Conrad i jego 'polskie co do kobiet zludzenia' (Wokól tajmenkcy marsylakiej Conrada)" 3265
"Conrad i kryzys powiesci psychologiezenj" 1011.1
"Conrad il palacco scrisse in inglese la solidarieta" 3311
"Conrad Incident" 1246.1
"Conrad in Extract" 414.1
"Conrad in Fashion 2489
"Conrad in His Historical Perspective" 2679

"'Oswalds,' Bishopsbourne, Nr. Canterbury, September 1919-August
    3, 1920" 3006
(The *Otago*) 993.3
"The *Otago*" 2669
"O tragedii na Samburanie" 990.1
"O tragieznej decyzji krakowskiej Konrada Korzeniowskiego: pare,
    uwag w zwiazk z ksiazha professora Ujejskiego O *Konradzye
    Korzeniowskim*" 1032.1
"Our Awards for 1897: The 'Conrad' Books" 19.2
(*An Outcast of the Islands*) 6.1, 6.2, 6.3, 6.4
"*An Outcast of the Islands*: A New Reading" 2323
"Outer and Inner Perspectives in the Impressionist Novels of Crane,
    Conrad and Ford" 2344

*Paradise of Snakes: An Archetypal Narrative of Conrad's Political
    Novels* 2060
"The Paradox of Perspectivism in Conrad's 'The Lagoon'" 3065
Partial Magic: The Novel as a Self-Conscious Genre 3164
"Particularity and Polarization: Realism in the Fiction of Hardy and
    Conrad" 2388
"Pascal's *Pensées* in *Under Western Eyes*" 2894
"Passion and the Tradition: A Critical Appraisal of Ford Madox Ford"
    1321.2
"The Pathos of 'Il Conde'" 1876.1
Paths of Loneliness: The Individual Isolated in Modern Society
    1293.1
"A Pattern of Parallel and Double: The Function of Myrtle in *The
    Great Gatsby*" 2294
"Patterns of Betrayal in the Novels of Joseph Conrad" 2026
"Patusan" 2112
"The Patusan Crisis: A Revaluation of Jim and Marlow" 2223
"Pejorism as the Organizational Principle in Joseph Conrad's 'Heart
    of Darkness'" 3299
Pen and Brush: The Author as Artist 2437
Periscopio 2727
"The Personal and the Political in *Under Western Eyes*" 2503
"Personal Moral Sensibility in Conrad's *Under Western Eyes*" 2819
"A Personal Tribute to the Late Percival Gibbon and Edward Thomas:
    903.1
"Per un racconto di Conrad" 1212.1
"Per un secondo tempo di Conrad" 1259.3
"The Perverted Pattern of *Billy Budd* in *The Nigger of the Narcissus*"
    3132
"The Phantasmagoria of the East" 39.3
(The Philosophical Romance) 39.4

INDEX

PERIODICALS AND NEWSPAPERS

Included here are periodicals and newspapers for which entries occur in the bibliography. Numbers after each title refer to the number(s) of the item in the bibliography where the title appears.

Crux (Pretoria) 2391, 2407
Cuadernos Hispano-Americanos (Madrid) 2686
Cultura di Destra 3092
Current Literature 94.4
Czas (Warsaw) 757.1
Daily Chronicle (London) 2.9, 6.6, 7.6, 189.3
Daily Inter-Ocean (Chicago) 13.2
Daily Mail (London) 7.1, 32.2, 62.1
Daily News (London) 2.1, 2.10, 28.1, 38.1, 111.1, 145.1, 221.1, 2916
Daily Telegraph (London) 6.12, 30.3, 37.1, 77.3, 105.1, 179.1, 292.1
Daily World 8.3
Dalhousie Review 2008, 2418, 2641
Dartmouth College Library Bulletin 1795.1
Descant 2692
Detroit Free Press 6.10, 8.18
Dial 233.1
Dialog (Warsaw) 1496.1
Die Neuren Sprache 2209, 2634
Diliman Review 1746.1, 1822.1, 1903.2, 2510
Discourse 2327
Dissertation Abstracts 1321.2, 1370.2, 1382.1, 1985, 1994, 1998,
    2061, 2070, 2083, 2087, 2092, 2113, 2116, 2152, 2173, 2180, 2186,
    2192, 2237, 2254, 2270, 2276, 2282, 2299, 2319, 2321, 2344, 2365,
    2376, 2388, 2415, 2444, 2469, 2505, 2537, 2568, 2876, 3056
Dissertation Abstracts International 2330, 2351, 2385, 2394, 2406,
    2428, 2439, 2480, 2527, 2530, 2542, 2546, 2547, 2556, 2576, 2594,
    2605, 2607, 2609, 2615, 2623, 2631, 2640, 2681, 2682, 2688, 2689,
    2712, 2735, 2738, 2741, 2744, 2747, 2755, 2756, 2766, 2778, 2784,
    2794, 2795, 2796, 2812, 2815, 2818, 2838, 2842, 2843, 2853, 2862,
    2881, 2885, 2906, 2966, 2971, 2982, 2983, 2985, 2989, 2998, 3002,
    3020, 3022, 3023, 3024, 3032, 3043, 3044, 3049, 3050, 3053, 3060,
    3095, 3097, 3105, 3135, 3138, 3175, 3190, 3209, 3215, 3233, 3236,
    3249, 3250, 3257, 3269, 3273, 3285, 3291, 3299, 3319
Dissertations in English and American Literature 2421
Double Dealer 496.1
Duke University Library Notes 2760
Edinburgh Review 107.1
Elegie (Warsaw) 838.2
Emerson Society Quarterly 1929.4
Encounter 2765
English 2495
English Journal 2007, 2023, 2051, 2416, 2591
English Language and Literature 3057
English Language Notes 2672, 2968, 3260, 3320
English Life 465.2, 529.1

INDEX

FOREIGN LANGUAGES

Included here are the languages in which articles and books listed in the bibliography originally appeared. Numbers under each language refer to items in the bibliography where the foreign-language title is given. English-language titles are not listed.

INDEX

PRIMARY TITLES

Included here are all titles by Conrad which occur in titles of articles or books or in the abstracts. Numbers after each title refer to the item in the bibliography where the title appears.

Almayer's Folly 0.9, 1.1, 1.2, 1.3, 1.4, 2.1, 2.2, 2.3, 2.4. 2.5, 2.6, 2.7, 2.8, 2.9. 2.11, 5.1, 6.7, 6.10, 8.3, 9.2, 398.1, 437.1, 445.4, 451.1, 454.1, 482.2, 529.1, 615.1, 838.1, 914.1, 938.1, 966.1, 1056.1, 1339.2, 1352.1, 1423.2, 1734.1, 1747.1, 1892.1, 1893.1, 1936.5, 1960.1, 2031, 2090, 2110, 2114, 2212, 2225, 2243, 2244, 2302, 2323, 2364, 2382, 2408, 2420, 2463, 2482, 2611, 2632, 2678, 2788, 2789, 2820, 2829, 2846, 2959, 3054, 3091, 3111, 3141, 3144, 3149, 3159, 3175, 3208, 3221, 3246, 3261, 3262, 3284, 3301, 3316, 3331, 3357

"Amy Foster" 61.1., 62.1, 64.1, 171.1, 482.2, 1208.1, 1225.1, 1815.1, 1815.3, 2003, 2359, 3071, 3082, 3118, 3173, 3284

"An Anarchist" 451.1, 1815.1, 2127, 2698, 3015, 3186

The Arrow of Gold 287.1, 292.1, 293.1, 300.2, 300.3, 763.1, 935.1, 1163.1, 1238.2, 1352.1, 1815.2, 1960,1, 2057, 2205, 2302, 2446, 2449, 2478, 2506, 2509, 2525, 2586, 2601, 2638, 2688, 2816, 2850, 2898, 2959, 2960, 3006, 3010, 3077, 3161, 3229, 3244, 3265, 3321

"Autocracy and War" 1897.3, 2005, 2599, 2911

"Because of the Dollars" 1075.1, 2225, 2582, 3185

"Books" 2632

"The Brute" 105.1, 111.1, 2103, 2127, 3015, 3186

Chance 171.2, 175.1, 176.1, 176.2, 177.1, 179.1, 185.1, 189.1, 189.3, 190.1, 191.1, 197.1, 197.2, 221.1, 231.1, 372.1, 375.1, 379.1, 387.1, 451.1, 493.1, 799.1, 1148.2, 1189.1, 1192.1, 1234.1, 1289.1, 1320.1, 1330.2. 1354.1, 1611.1, 1629.1, 1639.2, 1661.1, 1786.1, 1815.2, 1815.4, 1822.1, 1940.2, 1948.1, 1960.1, 1992, 2026, 2045, 2054, 2123, 2124, 2159, 2164, 2169, 2183, 2214, 2218, 2219, 2238, 2257, 2262, 2273, 2302, 2308, 2322, 2382, 2438, 2449, 2455, 2506, 2507, 2509, 2519, 2540, 2649, 2663, 2697, 2714, 2792, 2813, 2870, 2904,

2714, 2774, 2782, 2870, 2895, 2900, 2910, 2955, 2965, 2986, 3025, 3046, 3057, 3166, 3185, 3189, 3201, 3211, 3223, 3248, 3259, 3264, 3275, 3292, 3302, 3309, 3327, 3335, 3342, 3364

A Set of Six 71.11, 108.1, 111.1, 117.1, 118.1, 354.1, 378.1, 379.1, 1784.1, 1787.1, 1822.2, 1978, 2127, 2959, 2991, 3015, 3186

The Shadow-Line 255.1, 256.1, 265.1, 312.1, 695.2, 916.2, 1024.1, 1162.1, 1205.3, 1212.1, 1339.2, 1635.2, 1638.1, 1748.2, 1786.1, 1830.1, 1901.2, 1919.1, 1924.2, 1929.2, 2014, 2035, 2053, 2061, 2096, 2128, 2158, 2169, 2212, 2254, 2303, 2328, 2374, 2387, 2455, 2540, 2560, 2582, 2592, 2629, 2641, 2649, 2657, 2690, 2714, 2717, 2811, 2869, 2870, 2920, 2945, 2959, 3022, 3032, 3057, 3121, 3141, 3142, 3185, 3223, 3224, 3238, 3275, 3280, 3348

"The Silence of the Sea" (Uncollected; first published in the DAILY MAIL, 18 Sept 1909; rptd by Paul Kirschner, NOTES & QUERIES, XV (Aug 1968), pp. 292-94) 2168, 2284

The Sisters 1050.2, 1848.1, 2044, 2205, 2280, 2281, 2318, 2446, 2471, 2489, 2525, 2566, 2635, 3072, 3244

"A Smile of Fortune" 137.1, 145.1, 158.1, 1830.1, 2244, 2513, 2554, 2611, 3268, 3302

Some Reminiscences (Also as *A Personal Record*) 582.3

Suspense 579.1, 596.1, 614.1, 635.1, 635.2, 656.1, 657.1, 1205.3, 1667.1, 1669.3, 1815.2, 1815.3, 2626, 2781, 2959

"The Tale" 1999, 2269

Tales of Unrest 8.17, 8.18, 8.19, 9.1, 12.1, 13.3, 13.5, 13.6 17.4, 17.5, 17.6, 19.1, 27.8, 27.9, 27.10, 29.4, 30.1, 30.2, 30.3, 916.1, 994.1, 1353.1, 1747.1, 2143, 2657, 2959, 3004, 3221

"To-morrow" 171.1, 986.1, 1208.1, 1496.1, 2436, 3118

Twixt Land and Sea 137.1, 137.2, 138.1, 145.1, 145.2, 158.1, 451.1, 799.1, 1152.1, 1978, 2618, 2959, 3302

"Typhoon" 17.1, 300.1, 440.1, 482.2, 487.1, 538.1, 935.1, 939.1, 1150.2, 1208.1, 1259.1, 1265.1, 1293.1, 1330.1, 1341.1, 1450.2, 1635.2, 1748.2, 1786.1, 1897.1, 1901.2, 1937.1, 1977, 2103, 2125, 2212, 2306, 2357, 2363, 2371, 2455, 2540, 2553, 2584, 2592, 2647, 2668,